HU ANGLAIS *Littérature*

AN INTRODUCTION TO ENGLISH LITERATURE

From Philip Sidney to Graham Swift

Françoise Grellet,
professeur de Première supérieure, Lycée Henri IV
Marie-Hélène Valentin,
inspectrice générale de l'Éducation nationale

HACHETTE
Supérieur

To Denis Girard

We are grateful to Ross Hutchison,
who read the manuscript and made valuable suggestions,
and to Shelley Ochanine,
for her constant help and encouragement.

ISBN 2.01.020862.5

45, bd de Grenelle, F 75905 Paris Cedex 15

Foreword

The purpose of this book is to introduce English literature to students in their first years at university. Rather than offering a wide range of texts, ***we have chosen to select fewer writers but give the students real help in the fields of literary terminology, cross-reference and critical as well as contextual documents.***

The book is divided into two parts:

A short introduction to critical vocabulary. *This section provides students with the literary terms and concepts they are most likely to need to understand and use. These have been grouped under eleven headings (e.g. Narrative Technique; Wit, Humour, Satire and Irony) representing the most common areas with which students have difficulty. The definitions of terms and the explanations are usually followed by a few exercises for illustration and practice. References to relevant sections in this part will be found after most of the excerpts given in the book.*

An anthology, *arranged chronologically. For the sake of clarity, we have distinguished seven periods characterized by a specific spirit:*

- *The Elizabethan Age,*
- *From the Metaphysical poets to the Commonwealth,*
- *The Restoration and the Age of Pope,*
- *The Rise of the Novel,*
- *Romanticism,*
- *The Victorian Age,*
- *The Modern Age.*

At the beginning of each of these sections, ***a few pages set out the social, philosophical or artistic background*** *which influenced the literature of the period. Rather than commenting on this background, we chose to present it, whenever possible, through the writings of historians (e.g. Trevelyan), philosophers (e.g. Bacon or Locke) or critics (e.g. Ruskin). The student is thus given key-texts and invited to find out how the movements of ideas they illustrate were important for literature.*

The texts that follow appear chronologically, by genre (poetry, then prose and drama).

A similar pattern can be found in the treatment of each author:

- *a chronology of his life and works;*
- *a few introductory lines explaining the situation of the writer in his age, his main themes and his originality;*
- *a passage from his works;*

(A minimum of footnotes appear, to avoid over-loading the text. As a rule, we have tried to gloss the text when it contained obscure allusions, archaic words or unusual structures the student would have difficulty understanding. Words that are simply difficult or uncommon have not been glossed if they appear in standard dictionaries.)

- *a number of texts and documents that throw light on the passage. These include:*

– the writer's comments on his own work and art. Such texts are obviously particularly helpful and appear whenever possible, provided they are relevant to the excerpt selected. In a way, this book is therefore also an anthology of literary manifestos (e.g. passages from Wordsworth and Coleridge's Lyrical Ballads *or T.S. Eliot's* Sacred Wood*, James on the art of fiction, Hopkins on Sprung Rhythm, etc.);*

– short critical passages about important aspects of the text. These are generally taken from well-known critics (e.g. Frye or Leavis) and open up new directions of study or suggest possible interpretations. In a few cases, however, the critical text chosen is an actual commentary on the passage given (e.g. Ian Watts's commentary on the passage from Moll Flanders*). This, we have found, can provide the students with interesting examples of the ways a text can be analyzed;*
– parallel or contrasting passages, for comparison. One of the best ways of assessing the merit of a text is to compare it with texts related by form or content. This use of "counterpoints" could also provide examples for those students preparing for exams that include such comparative analysis of literary texts;
– documents (e.g. paintings) relating the passage to its social or artistic background. We have tried, as often as we could, to show the correspondences between literature and the arts. The works chosen rarely aim at merely illustrating the texts, but try to show how some currents of ideas can be reflected, for instance, in both literature and painting.
The aim of these various documents is obviously not *to give the students a ready-made analysis of the passages we propose, but rather to restore some of the context or suggest a few possible directions of study.*

This conception of the book accounts for the relatively limited number of authors selected, but we believe that it is preferable to offer students a substantial amount of help rather than aiming at breadth of coverage for its own sake.
Though we have tried to include lesser-known texts, it has often been difficult to avoid famous passages, unmatched in the author's works, which it is essential that a student of English should be familiar with.
We hope this book will be enjoyable and lead to genuine appreciation of literature, but most of all that it will provide incitement to further reading.

THE AUTHORS

Table of Contents

An Approach to Critical Vocabulary

verse form and poetic genres

Here are some common types of poems in English:

Type	Characteristics/Theme	Form
Ballad	A poem, originally meant to be sung, which tells a story. It was transmitted orally, with variants. **Broadside ballads:** ballads printed on broadside (piece of paper), usually about a current problem, and sung to a popular tune. **Literary ballads:** poems by well-known poets, imitating the form of traditional ballads.	— Several ballad stanzas (quatrains) 4 stresses 3 stresses ← rhyme 4 stresses 3 stresses ← — Use of refrains, very often.
Ode	Long lyric poem with — serious, dignified subject: usually the praise of sb. or sthg., — high, passionate tone, — complex structure.	**Pindaric Ode :** 3 stanzas, the first two being similar. But many poets have long since adapted it, giving each stanza a different pattern. **Horatian Ode:** All the stanzas have a similar form. The tone is quieter and more restrained. In either type, the stanzas have no distinctive form.
Sonnet	Short lyric poem.	Rhyme : **Petrarchan sonnet** a → b → b → a a → b → b → a c → d → e c → d → e **Shakespearean sonnet** a → b → a → b c → d → c → d e → f → e f → g → g
Epigram	Very short poem, about any subject, which is very condensed and incisive. Often concludes with a witty thought.	
Epic	**Heroic poem:** — Long narrative poem. — Serious subject. — Elevated tone. — Focused on a heroic figure who is often of national importance. The future of a race or nation depends on his actions. — Vast setting which can even be the whole world, or cosmic. — Superhuman deeds. Supervised by the gods. A **mock-heroic poem** (or **mock-epic**) makes fun of the style and form of heroic poetry, treating an unimportant event or a low subject in a grandiose way. e.g. Pope's *The Rape of the Lock.*	— The narrator of the epic always starts by explaining his argument. — The narrator begins *in medias res* (right in the middle of the action).

Type	Characteristics/Theme	Form
Pastoral	Poem which, through the description of the idyllic life of shepherds, expresses the poet's yearning for peace, a simple life and nature.	No given form.
Occasional poetry	Poems written for a special occasion (e.g. a death, a victory, etc.).	
Elegy	Poem of lament for sb's death, or sometimes only a poem of meditation about death or the passing of things.	
Dirge	Same as elegy but shorter, more solemn, and often meant to be sung.	
Epithalamion	Poem written in honour of a marriage.	
Light verse	— Informal tone. — The subject (which can be light or serious) is treated gaily, humourously or satirically.	

How would you define the following poems?
(A ■ means that only an excerpt from the poem is given.)
The titles are not given since many actually tell what the kind of poem is. But you will find them at the bottom of page 6.

a

Earth has not anything to show more fair:
Dull would he be of soul who could pass by
A sight so touching in its majesty;
This City now doth, like a garment, wear

The beauty of the morning ; silent, bare,
Ships, towers, domes, theatres, and temples lie
Open unto the fields, and to the sky;
All bright and glittering in the smokeless air

Never did sun more beautifully steep
In his first splendour, valley, rock, or hill;
Ne'er saw I, never felt, a calm so deep!

The river glideth at his own sweet will ;
Dear God! the very houses seem asleep;
And all that mighty heart is lying still!

W. Wordsworth

b ■

ARIEL *sings.*

Full fathom five thy father lies;
  Of his bones are coral made;
Those are pearls that were his eyes:
  Nothing of him that doth fade,
But doth suffer a sea-change
Into something rich and strange.
Sea-nymphs hourly ring his knell. *Burthen: Ding-dong*

W. Shakespeare

c ■

Weep no more, woeful shepherds, weep no more,
For Lycidas, your sorrow, is not dead,
Sunk though he be beneath the watery floor;
So sinks the day-star in the ocean bed,
And yet anon repairs his drooping head,
And tricks his beams, and with new-spangled ore
Flames in the forehead of the morning sky:
So Lycidas sunk low, but mounted high,
Through the dear might of Him that walked the waves,
Where, other groves and other streams along,
With nectar pure his oozy locks he laves,
And hears the unexpressive nuptial song,
In the blest kingdoms meek of joy and love.

J. Milton

d ■

Like the vain Curlings of the Watry maze,
Which in smooth streams a sinking Weight does raise;
So Man, declining alwayes, disappears
In the weak Circles of increasing Years;
And his short Tumults of themselves Compose,
While flowing Time above his Head does close.
  Cromwell alone with greater Vigour runs,
(Sun-like) the Stages of succeeding Suns:
And still the Day which he doth next restore,
Is the just Wonder of the Day before.
Cromwell alone doth with new Lustre spring,
And shines the Jewel of the yearly Ring.

A. Marvell

e ■

Here men walk alone
For most of their lives,
What with hydrants for dogs,
And windows for wives.

O. Nash

f ■

The Rum Tum Tugger is a Curious Cat:
If you offer him pheasant he would rather have grouse.
If you put him in a house he would much prefer a flat,
If you put him in a flat then he'd rather have a house.
If you set him on a mouse then he only wants a rat,
If you set him on a rat then he'd rather chase a mouse.
Yes the Rum Tum Tugger is a Curious Cat –
  And there isn't any call for me to shout it:

For he will do
As he do do
And there's no doing anything about it!

T. S. Eliot

g ■

Mean while the Adversary of God and Man,
Satan with thoughts inflam'd of highest design,
Puts on swift wings, and toward the Gates of Hell
Explores his solitary flight; som times
He scours the right hand coast, som times the left,
Now shaves with level wing the Deep, then soares
Up to the fiery concave touring high.

J. Milton

h ■

Calm was the day, and through the trembling air,
Sweet breathing Zephyrus did softly play
A gentle spirit, that lightly did delay
Hot Titan's beams, which then did glister fair:
When I whom sullen care,
Through discontent of my long fruitless stay
In Prince's Court, and expectation vain
Of idle hopes, which still do fly away,
Like empty shadows, did afflict my brain,
Walk'd forth to ease my pain
Along the shore of silver streaming Thames,
Whose rutty Bank, the which his River hems,
Was painted all with variable flowers,
And all the meads adorn'd with dainty gems,
Fit to deck maidens' bowers,
And crown their Paramours,
Against the Bridal day, which is not long:
Sweet Thames run softly, till I end my Song.

E. Spenser

i

Season of mists and mellow fruitfulness,
Close bosom-friend of the maturing sun,
Conspiring with him how to load and bless
With fruit the vines that round the thatch-eaves run;
To bend with apples the mossed cottage-trees,
And fill all fruit with ripeness to the core;
To swell the gourd, and plump the hazel shells
With a sweet kernel; to set budding more,
And still more, later flowers for the bees,
Until they think warm days will never cease,
For summer has o'er-brimmed their clammy cells.

Who hath not seen thee oft amid thy store?
Sometimes whoever seeks abroad may find
Thee sitting careless on a granary floor,
Thy hair soft-lifted by the winnowing wind;
Or on a half-reaped furrow sound asleep,
Drowsed with the fume of poppies, while thy hook
Spares the next swath and all its twined flowers;
And sometimes like a gleaner thou dost keep
Steady thy laden head across a brook;
Or by a cider-press, with patient look,
Thou watchest the last oozings hours by hours.

Where are the songs of spring? Aye, where are they?

Think not of them, thou hast thy music too –
While barred clouds bloom the soft-dying day,
And touch the stubble-plains with rosy hue;
Then in a wailful choir the small gnats mourn
Among the river sallows, borne aloft
Or sinking as the light wind lives or dies;
And full-grown lambs loud bleat from hilly bourn;
Hedge-crickets sing; and now with treble soft
The redbreast whistles from a garden-croft;
And gathering swallows twitter in the skies.

J. Keats

j
The fair breeze blew, the white foam flew,
The furrow followed free;
We were the first that ever burst
Into that silent sea.

Down dropt the breeze, the sails dropt down,
'Twas sad as sad could be;
And we did speak only to break
The silence of the sea!

S. T. Coleridge

a Wordsworth, *Composed Upon Westminster Bridge* **b** W. Shakespeare, *The Tempest* **c** J. Milton, *Lycidas* **d** A. Marvell, *The First Anniversary of the Government under O. C.* **e** Ogden Nash, *The City* **f** T. S. Eliot, *The Rum Tum Tugger* **g** J. Milton, *Paradise Lost* **h** E. Spenser, *Prothalamion* **i** J. Keats, *To Autumn* **j** S. T. Coleridge *The Rime of the Ancient Mariner.*

versification

Rhythm and accentuation

English poetry is based on **rhythm** rather than on the number of syllables in a line (as often in French verse) or on quantity (that is to say the alternance of long and short syllables, as in ancient Greek and Roman poetry.)
Rhythm consists in the succession of stressed and unstressed syllables.
Each line can be divided into a number of **feet** or **beats**, each foot being made up of a number of syllables (usually 2 or 3) which contain at least one stressed syllable.
Here are the most common types of metrical feet:

The iamb Weak (= unstressed) syllable + strong (= stressed) syllable: [∪ —]

∪ — ∪ — ∪ — ∪ — ∪ —
I grant/indeed/that fields/and flocks/have charms. G. Crabbe

The trochee Strong syllable + weak syllable: [— ∪] (the reverse of the iambic foot)
It is often found at the beginning of a line, to convey strength.

— ∪ ∪ — ∪ — ∪ — ∪ —
Flutters/in blood/and pant/ing beats/the ground. A. Pope

The anapest Two weak syllables + one strong syllable: [∪∪—]
The effect produced is rapidity.

∪ ∪ — ∪ — ∪ — ∪ —
And the good/south wind/still blew/behind. S. T. Coleridge

The dactyl One strong syllable + two weak syllables: [—∪∪]

— ∪ ∪ — ∪ —
Wind of the/western/sea. Lord Tennyson

The spondee Two strong syllables: [— —]
It is rare, except at the beginning of lines.

— —
Speak, spirit!... P. B. Shelley

Remarks

- When the foot ends with a strong syllable, one speaks of a **rising rhythm** (iambs, anapests), as opposed to a **falling rhythm** (trochees, dactyls).
- In regular lines of verse, the same kind of metrical foot is repeated:

∪ ∪ — ∪ ∪ — ∪ ∪ —
I perceive/a young bird/in this bush! /
= **anapaestic trimeter** (anapests - 3 feet) or

∪ — ∪ — ∪ — ∪ — ∪ —
Who gave/the ball/or paid/the vi/sit last? A. Pope
= **iambic pentameter** (iambs - five feet)

This verse pattern (also called **blank verse**) is usually considered as the basic English one, though its regularity would soon make it very monotonous, and a number of variations (e.g. a trochee at the beginning of a line) can usually be found.
One speaks of **monometers** (lines of 1 foot), **dimeters** (2), **trimeters** (3), **tetrameters** (4), **pentameters** (5), **hexameters** (6), **heptameters** (7) and **octameters** (8).-

- Here is how a few lines can be scanned:

∪ ∪ — ∪ — ∪ —
How the chim/ney swee/per's cry
— ∪ — ∪ — ∪ —
Every/black'ning/church ap/pals
∪ ∪ — ∪ — ∪ —
And the hap/less sol/dier's sigh
— ∪ — ∪ — ∪ —
Runs in/blood down/palace/walls. W. Blake

Note the similarity of rhythm between lines 1 and 3 (both start with an anapest) and lines 2 and 4 (heavy trochaic rhythm).

- Endings

In iambic rhythm it is common to find an extra unstressed syllable at the end of the line. This is called a **feminine ending** as opposed to a **masculine ending** when the line ends with a strong syllable.
e. g. Lines 2 and 3 have a feminine ending in the following passage from *Prometheus Unbound*:

Disdain! Ah no! I pity thee. What ruin
Will hunt the undefended through wide Heaven!
How will thy soul, cloven to its depth with terror,
Gape like a hell within! P. B. Shelley

Feminine endings are often less heavy and tend to open up the line.

- When the pause falls at the end of a line, the line is said to be **end-stopped**:

The grey gaunt days dividing us in twain
Seemed hopeless hills my strength must faint to climb. T. Hardy

The following two lines, on the contrary, are **run-on lines** (one also speaks of **enjambments**):

And I have loved thee, Ocean! and my joy
Of youthful sports was on thy breast to be
Borne, like thy bubbles, onward... Lord Byron

- Other kinds of English verse

Sprung rhythm, which can be found in the poems of G. M. Hopkins (cf. p. 211). It is a strong-stressed rhythm based on clusters of several stressed syllables, often followed by successions of weak syllables. The effect conveyed is strength and a panting, stammering rhythm, with sudden powerful bursts, that is reminiscent of speech or music.

— ∪ — ∪ ∪ ∪ — — — ∪ — ∪ —
Woe, world-sorrow; on an age-old anvil wince and sing... G. M. Hopkins

Free verse is verse which follows no regular pattern as far as stress, rhyme, or the form of the poem are concerned.One can already find instances of free verse in some of Shakespeare's last plays, but it prevails among a number of 20th century writers such as T.S. Eliot.

What kind of verse-patterns do the following lines exemplify?

Marks of weakness, marks of woe. W. Blake

Merrily, merrily, shall I live now. W. Shakespeare

With eyes severe and beard of formal cut. W. Shakespeare

When they said, "Is it small? "
He replied, "Not at all." E. Lear

Like a pillow of thorns for thy slumberless head. P. B. Shelley

Scan the following lines. Can you find any regular iambic pentameters? Find instances of iambs, trochees, anapests and dactyls. How do they contribute to break the rhythm and underline the ideas expressed?

To-morrow, and to-morrow, and to-morrow,
Creeps in this petty pace from day to day,
To the last syllable of recorded time;
And all our yesterdays have lighted fools
The way to dusty death. Out, out, brief candle!
Life's but a walking shadow; a poor player,
That struts and frets his hour upon the stage,
And then is heard no more: it is a tale
Told by an idiot, full of sound and fury,
Signifying nothing. Shakespeare

Rhyme and alliteration

• Rhyme

One can distinguish:

End-rhyme (at the end of lines)

Gus is the cat at the Theatre Door.
His name, as I ought to have told you before,
Is really Asparagus. That's such a fuss
To pronounce, that we usually call him just Gus. T. S. Eliot

Internal rhyme, inside a line

The body of my brother's son
Stood by *me*, knee to *knee*. S. T. Coleridge

Sight rhyme (or **Eye rhyme**)
The words look alike but are pronounced differently.

"There was an Old Man who said "Hush!"
I Perceive a young bird in this bush!" E. Lear

Slant rhyme
Imperfect rhyme (often used by 20th century poets as a reaction against the constraints of regular rhyme):

Pale flakes with fingering stealth come feeling for our faces,
We cringe in holes, back on forgotten dreams and stare, snow-dazed,
Deep into grassier ditches. So we drowse, sun-dozed,
Littered with blossoms trickling where the blackbird fusses. W. Owen

Masculine rhyme
Single stressed syllables:

Macavity's a Mystery Cat: he's called the Hidden Paw –
For he's the master criminal who can defy the law. T. S. Eliot

Feminine rhyme
Stressed syllables followed by unstressed syllables:

Macavity, Macavity, there's no one like Macavity,
He's broken every human law, he breaks the law of gravity. T. S. Eliot

NOTE: When iambic pentameters rhyme in pairs (**aa**, **bb**, **cc**...), they are called "heroic couplets":

> Youth, beauty, graceful action seldom fail;
> But common interest always will prevail,
> And pity never ceases to be shown
> To him who makes the people's wrongs his own. J. Dryden

• Alliteration

Alliteration:
The repetition of initial consonants:

> *F*ull *f*athom *f*ive thy *f*ather lies... Shakespeare

It was a common feature of Old English verse, in which alliteration was almost compulsory.

> Wyth *ch*ynne and *ch*eke full swete... Sir Gawain and the Green Knight

Consonance
The repetition of consonants:

> A*l*one, a*l*one, a*ll*, a*ll* a*l*one... S. T. Coleridge

Assonance
The repetition of vowel sounds within a line:

> Of power, of honour, of omnipotence... C. Marlowe

Study the rhyme and alliteration patterns of the poems on pages 89, 171, 207 and 257.

novel and prose types

Match the following passages and the different kinds of "genre" mentioned below:
1 Detective story.
2 Gothic/Horror story.
3 Realistic novel.
4 Psychological novel.
5 Guidebook.
6 Scientific treatise.

a Sophia walked alone, with tired limbs, up the damaged oak stairs to the flat. (...) The stairs, which smelt of damp even in summer, disgusted Sophia. She thought of the flat with horror and longed for green places and luxury.

b Edward opened the door of the drawing-room and cast a glance round the hall. He stood for a moment, his hand on the doorknob, listening. Then he seemed to make up his mind and Brenda saw him cross the hall and go up the stairs quickly and noiselessly.

c Turn right when leaving the dining-room and you will find yourself back in the hall. Before going upstairs to visit the bedrooms, pause for a moment to admire the graceful lines of the spiral staircase which is original mahogany. It is a masterpiece of craftsmanship and elegance. Go up the stairs and turn left on the first floor landing.

d She began to go slowly upstairs, with her hand on the banisters, as if she had left a party, where now this friend now that had flashed back her face, her voice.... Like a nun withdrawing, or a child exploring a tower, she went upstairs, paused at the window, came to the bathroom.

e ... hastily closing the door, she took her lamp, and passed up the staircase. Trembling came upon her as she ascended through the gloom. To her melancholy fancy this seemed to be a place of death, and the chilling silence that reigned confirmed its character.

f The first thing that a man does when he ascends by steps is to free the leg which he wishes to raise from the weight of the trunk which is resting upon this leg, and at the same time he loads the other leg with his entire weight including that of the raised leg. Then he raises the leg and places the foot on the step where he wishes to mount.....

a... **b...** **c...** **d...** **e...** **f...**

a Arnold Bennett, *The Old Wives' Tale.*
d Virgina Woolf, *Mrs Dalloway.*
e Ann Radcliffe, *The Mysteries of Udolpho.*
f Leonardo da Vinci, from the *Notebooks.*

characters and characterization

- Characters can be described as:

Humours (or **Characters of Humour**)
They are characters conspicuous for one prevailing feature, or humour, such as greed, cowardice, boastfulness (cf. *Comedy of Humours*, p. 24). Here is how Congreve defined Humour:

> I take it to be a singular and unavoidable manner of doing, or saying anything, Peculiar and Natural to one Man only; by which his Speech and Actions are distinguish'd from those of other Men... A Man may change his Opinion, but I believe he will find it a Difficulty, to part with his Humour...
>
> W. Congreve, *A Letter to John Dennis Concerning Humour in Comedy*, 1695.

Round or **flat**
According to the distinction made by E. M. Forster in *Aspects of the Novel* (cf. p. 13):

> We may divide characters into flat and round.
> Flat characters were called "humours" in the seventeenth century, and are sometimes called types, and sometimes caricatures. In their purest form, they are constructed round a single idea or quality: when there is more than one factor in them, we get the beginning of the curve towards the round. The really flat character can be expressed in one sentence such as "I will never desert Mr Micawber". There is Mrs Micawber – she says she won't desert Mr Micawber; she doesn't, and there she is. (...) One great advantage of flat characters is that they are easily recognized whenever they come in. (...) A second advantage is that they are easily remembered by the reader afterwards. (...) The test of a round character is whether it is capable of surprising in a convincing way. If it never surprises, it is flat.

Consistent or **inconsistent**
A character's behaviour is consistent if it is in keeping with his usual temperament. It is inconsistent if it changes in a random and haphazard way.

Static or **dynamic**
Some characters remain the same throughout a work; others are less predictable and change and develop.

Reliable or **unreliable**
A character/narrator is reliable when the reader can "trust" him, when his vision of himself or the world is not contradicted in the rest of the book. He is unreliable when his vision of things is distorted, when (often unconsciously), he relays to us facts and ideas that are different from those of the implied author and that are often corrected by another character.

Stock characters
They are recurring, conventional character types in a given genre: e. g. the buffoon in a comedy.

- Character presentation:

Telling. The author tells us about the characters, their ideas, their motivations, etc.

Showing: We see the characters behaving and talking, and draw our own conclusions from this.
Cf. Narrative Technique, p. 15.

Now read the passages mentioned below and decide how you would describe the characters and their presentation:

	Characters	**Characterization**
The History of Clarissa, p. 139		
Joseph Andrews, p. 144		
Pride and Prejudice, p. 188		
Portrait of a Lady, p. 228		

Further reading:

We may divide characters into flat and round.

Flat characters were called "humours" in the seventeenth century, and are sometimes called types and sometimes caricatures. In their purest form, they are constructed round a single idea or quality: when there is more than one factor in them, we get the beginning of the curve towards the round. The really flat character can be expressed in one sentence such as "I never will desert Mr Micawber". There is Mrs Micawber – she says she won't desert Mr Micawber; she doesn't, and there she is. Or: "I must conceal, even by subterfuges the poverty of my master's house". (...)

One great advantage of flat characters is that they are easily recognized whenever they come in – recognized by the reader's emotional eye, not by the visual eye which merely notes the recurrence of a proper name. In Russian novels, where they so seldom occur, they would be a decided help. It is a convenience for an author when he can strike with his full force at once, and flat characters are very useful to him, since they never need reintroducing, never run away, have not to be watched for development, and provide their own atmosphere – little luminous disks of a pre-arranged size, pushed hither and thither like counters across the void or between the stars; most satisfactory.

A second advantage is that they are easily remembered by the reader afterwards. They remain in his mind as unalterable for the reason that they were not changed by circumstances; they moved through circumstances, which gives them in retrospect a comforting quality, and preserves them when the book that produced them may decay. The Countess in *Evan Harrington* furnishes a good example here. Let us compare our memories of her with our memories of Becky Sharp. We do not remember what the Countess did or what she passed through. What is clear is her figure and the formula that surrounds it, namely, "Proud as we are of dear papa, we must conceal his memory". All her rich humour proceeds from this. She is a flat character. Becky is round. She, too, is on the make, but she cannot be summed up in a single phrase, and we remember her in connexion with the great scenes through which she passed and as modified by those scenes – that is to say, we do not remember her so easily because she waxes and wanes and has facets like a human being. All of us, even the sophisticated, yearn for permanence, and to the unsophisticated permanence is the chief excuse for a work of art. We all want books to endure, to be refuges, and their inhabitants to be always the same, and flat characters tend to justify themselves on this account. (...)

As for the round characters proper, they have already been defined by implication and no more need be said. All I need do is to give some examples of people in books who seem to me round so that the definition can be tested afterwards:

All the principal characters in *War and Peace*, all the Dostoyevsky characters, and some of the Proust – for example, the old family servant, the Duchess of Guermantes, M. de Charlus, and Saint Loup; Madame Bovary – who, like Moll Flanders, has her book to herself, and can expand and secrete unchecked; some people in Thackeray – for instance, Becky and Beatrix; some in Fielding – Parson Adams, Tom Jones; and some in Charlotte Brontë, most particularly Lucy Snowe. (And many more – this is not a catalogue.) The test of a round character is whether it is capable of surprising in a convincing way. If it never surprises, it is flat. If it does not convince, it is a flat pretending to be round. It has the incalculability of life about it – life within the pages of a book. And by using it sometimes alone, more often in combination with the other kind, the novelist achieves his task of acclimatization, and harmonizes the human race with the other aspects of his work.

E. M. Forster, *Aspects of the Novel,* Edward Arnold Publishers Ltd.,

narrative technique

Point of view

- The following table, presented in 1943 by Cleanth Brooks and Robert Penn Warren, is helpful to distinguish different points of view in narration:

	Internal analysis of events	**Outside observation of events**
Narrator as a character in the story	1 Main character tells his story.	2 Minor character tells main character's story.
Narrator not a character in the story	4 Analytic or omniscient author tells story.	3 Author tells story as observer.

- Another useful classification is that proposed by G. Genette in *Figures III* (1980, *Narrative Discourse)*, where he considers a three-term typology:

> The first term corresponds to what English-language criticism calls the narrative with omniscient narrator and Pouillon calls "vision from behind"., and which Todorov symbolizes by the formula *Narrator > Character* (where the narrator knows more than the character, or more exactly *says* more than any of the characters knows). In the second term, *Narrator = Character* (the narrator says only what a given character knows); this is the narrative with "point of view" after Lubbock, or with "restricted field" after Blin; Pouillon calls it "vision with". In the third term, *Narrator < Character* (the narrator says less than the character knows); this is the "objective" or "behaviorist" narrative, what Pouillon calls "vision from without".
>
> © 1980 Cornell University.

e.g.
1 Most of the novels by Dickens, G. Eliot.
2 James's *Portrait of a Lady;* Richardson's *Clarissa,* with multiple points of view.
3 Hemingway, *A Clean and Well-lit Place.*

Telling v. showing

Telling

The narrator himself relates what happens through description, summary or commentary of the characters' words, attitudes or actions.

> Punctually on the appointed day but not a minute too soon, for he did not believe in sacrificing time he was not paid for, Leadbitter drew up at the door of Lady Franklin's house. It was a good house, he could tell that by the gloss on the front door...
>
> L.P. Hartley, *The Hireling.*

Showing

The narrator only presents the words and gestures of the characters without explaining their motives and thoughts. The reader draws his own conclusions.

> The door of Henry's lunch-room opened and two men came in. They sat down at the counter.

> "What's yours?" George asked them.
> "I don't know", one of the men said. "What do you want to eat, Al?"
> "I don't know," said Al. "I don't know what I want to eat." Outside it was getting dark. The street-light came on outside the window. The two men at the counter read the menu. From the other end of the counter Nick Adams watched them. He had been talking to George when they came in.
>
> E. Hemingway, *The Killers.*

Cf. Percy Lubbock's *Picture and Drama* (p. 19).

Self-conscious narrators

They are conscious that they are story-tellers and mention their difficulties as they go along. We are therefore reminded not only of the presence of the narrator but also of the process which led to the composition of the work.

> But I must remember on what subject I am writing, and not trespass too far on the patience of a good-natured critic. Here, therefore, I put an end to the chapter.
>
> Fielding, *Tom Jones.*

Degrees of distance[1]

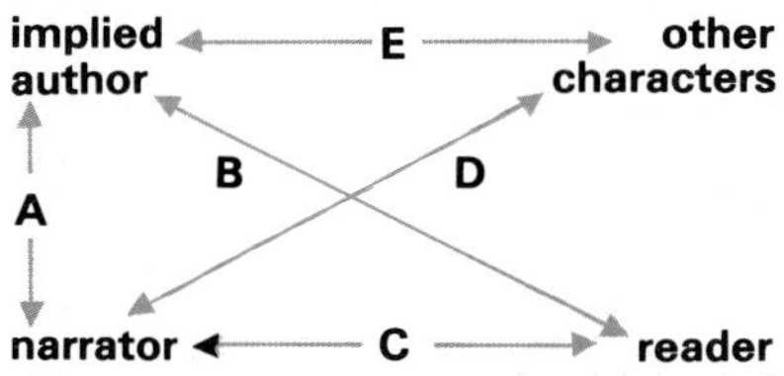

A Distance between the narrator and the implied author
Moral distance, e.g. Defoe — Moll.
Intellectual distance, e.g. Salinger — Holden

B Distance between the implied author and the reader
The reader cannot always espouse the implicit ideas of the book.
Moral distance, e.g. Sade.

C Distance between the narrator and the reader
e.g. Anthony Burgess — Alex in *A Clockwork Orange.*

D Distance between the narrator and the other characters
e.g. The distance between the narrator and the little boy he used to be in Hartley's *The Go Between.*

E Distance between the implied author and the characters
Some implied authors never judge their characters. Others, like Jane Austen, usually do.

1 See W.C. Booth, *The Rhetoric of Fiction*, The University of Chicago Press, 1961.

Read the following passages and study the perspective chosen by the author in each of them.

	Point of view	Telling or showing?	Self-conscious narrator?
a Mr Crawley had declared to Mr Robarts, that he would summon no legal aid to his assistance at the coming trial. The reader may, perhaps, remember the impetuosity with which he rejected the advice on this subject which was conveyed to him by Mr Robarts with all the authority of Archdeacon Grantly's name. "Tell the archdeacon," he had said, "that I will have none of his advice". And then Mr Robarts had left him, fully convinced that any further interference on his part could be of no avail. Nevertheless, the words which had then been spoken were not without effect. This coming trial was ever present to Mr Crawley's mind, and though, when driven to discuss the subject, he would speak of it with high spirit, as he had done both to the bishop and to Mr Robarts, yet in his long hours of privacy, or when alone with his wife, his spirit was anything but high. "It will kill me," he would say to her. "I shall get salvation thus."			
b "Is this a house or a hutch? It is meant, I suppose, for human habitation", said Blanche's father, walking about his new home. "It is well that I shall soon be gone and leave you alone in it. For it is better for one than for two as I cannot but see." "Come, Father, pluck up heart. You are an able-bodied man and not a crippled woman. I must not be given any more to bear. You must remember your poor invalid, though I never remind you that I am that." "If that was not a reminder, I need not take it as one. I grant that that fall made a poor thing of you, but you want a chair to sit upon, all the more. And I don't see where we are to put one, on a first sight." "There are plenty of chairs, Father. Let us sit down in two of them. Come, I think they have done their best. It only needed a little best for such a little home, but such as it had to be, I think it is done. And we must be as grateful as they will expect us to be." Blanche's sister put back her head and went into mirth. "This room is quite a pretty little place. So we must try to feel at home in it. We are not people to fail in courage." Matilda Seaton was two years older than Blanche, of the same height as her sister, but of the suppler, stronger build of her niece, Justine. She had hair less grey than her sister's, a darker skin less lined,			

	Point of view	Telling or showing ?	Self-conscious narrator ?
and the same narrow, dark eyes looking out with a sharper, deeper gaze. A fall from a horse had rendered her an invalid, or rather obliged her to walk with a stick, but her energy seemed to accumulate, and to work itself out at the cost of some havoc within her.			
c As soon as I got to Borstal they made me a long-distance cross-country runner. I suppose they thought I was just the build for it because I was long and skinny for my age (and still am) and in any case I didn't mind it much, to tell you the truth, because running had always been made much of in our family, especially running away from the police. I've always been a good runner, quick and with a big stride as well, the only trouble being that no matter how fast I run, and I did a very fair lick even though I do say so myself, it didn't stop me getting caught by the cops after that bakery job.			
d Yes because he never did a thing like that before as ask to get his breakfast in bed with a couple of eggs since the *City Arms* hotel when he used to be pretending to be laid up with a sick voice doing his highness to make himself interesting to that old faggot Mrs Riordan that he thought he had a great leg of and she never left us a farthing all for masses for herself and her soul greatest miser ever was actually afraid to lay out 4d for her methylated spirit telling me all her ailments she had too much old chat in her about politics and earth-quakes and the end of the world let us have a bit of fun first God help the world if all the women were her sort down on bathingsuits and lownecks of course nobody wanted her to wear I suppose she was pious because no man would look at her twice I hope I'll never be like her.			
e And now, having brought this fiction to a thoroughly traditional ending, I had better explain that although all I have described in the last two chapters happened, it did not happen quite in the way you may have been led to believe. I said earlier that we are all poets, though not many of us write poetry; and so are we all novelists, that is, we have a habit of writing fictional futures for ourselves, although perhaps today we incline more to put ourselves into a film. We screen in our minds hypotheses about how we might behave, about what might hap-			

	Point of view	**Telling or showing ?**	**Self-conscious narrator ?**
pen to us; and these novelistic or cinematic hypotheses often have very much more effect on how we actually do behave, when the real future becomes the present, than we generally allow. Charles was no exception; and the last few pages you have read are not what happened, but what he spent the hours between London and Exeter imagining might happen.			

Further reading:

Picture and drama – this is an antithesis which continually appears in a novel, and I shall have much to say of it.

(...) In one case the reader faces towards the story-teller and listens to him, in the other he turns towards the story and watches it. (...)

It is the method of picture-making that enables the novelist to cover his great spaces of life and quantities of experience, so much greater than any that can be brought within the acts of a play. As for intensity of life, that is another matter; there, as we have seen, the novelist has recourse to his other arm, the one that corresponds with the single arm of the dramatist. Inevitably, as the plot thickens and the climax approaches – inevitably, wherever an impression is to be emphasized and driven home – narration gives place to enactment, the train of events to the particular episode, the broad picture to the dramatic scene. But the limitation of drama is as obvious as its peculiar power. It is clear that if we wish to see an abundance and multitude of life we shall find it more readily and more summarily by looking for an hour into a memory, a consciousness, than by merely watching the present events of an hour, however crowded. Much may happen in that time, but in extent it will be nothing to the regions thrown open by the other method. A novelist, with a large and discursive subject before him, could not hope to show it all dramatically; much of it, perhaps the greater part, must be so marshalled that it may be swept by a travelling glance. (...)

Most novelists, I think, seem to betray, like Thackeray, a preference for one method or the other, for picture or for drama; one sees in a moment how Fielding, Balzac, George Eliot, incline to the first, in their diverse manners, and Tolstoy (certainly Tolstoy, in spite of his big range) or Dostoevsky to the second, the scenic way.

Percy Lubbock, *The Craft of Fiction,* 1921, Jonathan Cape.

a A. Trollope *The Last Chronicle of Barset.*
b I. Compton-Burnett, *A Family & a Fortune.* © 1939 by I. Compton Burnett and Curtis Brown.
c A. Sillitoe, *The Loneliness of the Long-Distance Runner.* © 1959 by A. Sillitoe and A. Knopf. *Tessa Sayle Literary Agents.*
d J. Joyce, *Ulysses.*
e J. Fowles, *The French Lieutenant's Woman.* © 1969 by John Fowles and Little Brown & Co. *Wallace and Shell Agency Inc.*

presenting the characters' words and thoughts

Compare these 6 sentences:

1 "It is over!" she said.
2 "It is over!"
3 She said it was over.
4 She said "it was over".
5 It was over.
6 She was relieved when she found herself alone again.

1 Direct speech
The character's words or thoughts are introduced by a clause
("he said/ answered/ reported", etc.)
and quotation marks.

2 Free direct speech
The character's words or thoughts are given directly,
without any introductory sentence.
It is as if the narrator stood aside.

3 Indirect speech
The character's words are no longer quoted but reported.
The words remain the same but some changes take place (pronouns, verb tense, place/ time reference, etc.)

4 Semi-indirect speech
Similar to indirect speech,
but the quotation marks are kept.

5 Free indirect speech
Same form as indirect speech,
but the introductory clause is omitted.

6 Narrative
The words or thoughts are reported,
but they are summed up or reworded by the narrator.

What kinds of speech/thought presentation are exemplified in the following sentences? (There may be several in each excerpt quoted.)

	Speech type
a He then called to Joseph, asking him, "if he had not seen the light." H. Fielding	
b "If I do it you won't ever worry? – I won't worry about that because it's perfectly simple. – Then I'll do it. Because I don't care about me. – What do you mean? – I don't care about me. – Well, I care about you." E. Hemingway.	

	Speech type
c She found herself accosted by Captain Wentworth, in a reserved yet hurried sort of farewell. He must wish her good night. He was going – he should get home as fast as he could. J. Austen	
d "Boy", said the gentleman in the high chair, "listen to me. You know you're an orphan, I suppose?" "What's that, sir?" inquired poor Oliver. Ch. Dickens	
e The clock struck the half-hour and Mrs Thompson said that she'd better attend to the chicken. J. Braine	
f Squiff, who always talked with a good deal of hesitation, started to explain about the accident but Lubbock, furiously stubbing out one cigarette and in another second lighting another, shouted that he didn't want to hear a lot of crap like that. H. E. Bates	

- Now consider the 6 types of presentation defined on the preceding page and classify them according to the degree of narrator involvement they imply.

Narrator's presence felt. + ...
...
...
...
...
...
Narrator's presence not noticeable. –

- What is the main effect created by each type of presentation?

the elizabethan stage v. the picture stage

The Elizabethan stage
Seen from above:

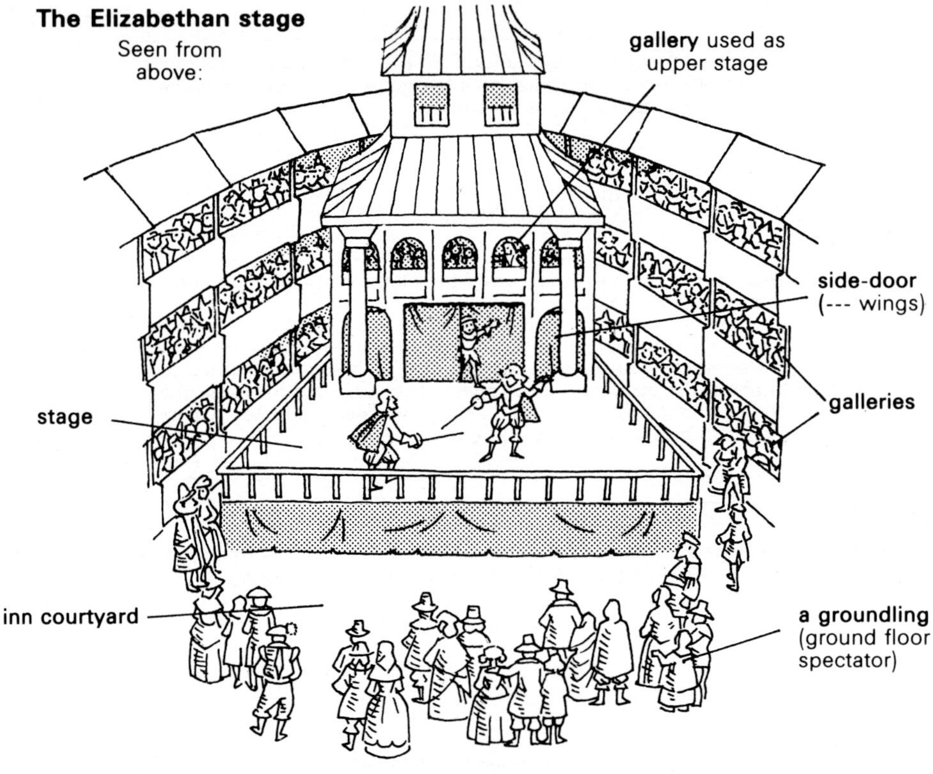

The Picture stage
Seen from above:

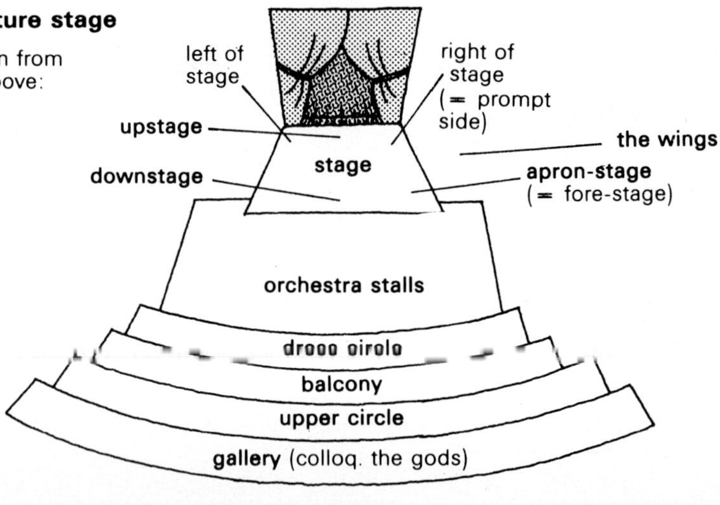

tragedy

Some well-known forms of English tragedy

Miracle or Morality plays

They were religious plays in medieval England, the first forms of drama in English. **Miracle plays** were based on the lives of the Saints and Apostles: **Mystery plays** on the Bible in a more general way.

As for **Morality plays** they aimed at moral teaching. They showed a hero representing the average man (e.g. *Everyman)* and characters who embodied vices and virtues. In the Old Vice, one of the stock characters of such plays, we find the origin of both the villains and the buffoons of Elizabethan drama.

Senecan tragedies

An imitation of the plays of Seneca, they were meant to be recited, not staged, and were characterized by violence, brutality and an atmosphere of horror meant to arouse the emotions of the listeners. The best-known of these tragedies is *Gorboduc* (1562) by Norton and Sackville.

The revenge tragedy

A type of play which flourished during the Elizabethan age and which directly derived from the Senecan type of plays. It dealt with the theme of retribution in a manner that was often bloody and gruesome, involving murders, suicides and supernatural phenomena. Kyd's plays (e.g. *The Spanish Tragedy,* 1585-9) and many of Marlowe's, Chapman's, Webster's and Shakespeare's plays belong to this category.

Heroic drama

A form of drama characteristic of the Restoration and imitating French classical tragedy. Such plays respected the three unities, were written in rhyming couplets, and dealt with the themes of love, honour and duty to one's country. The best-known example of a heroic tragedy is probably Dryden's *Conquest of Granada* (1670-1).

The atmosphere and effect of tragedy: a few key words

Catharsis

A term defined by Aristotle in his *Poetics,* applies to the effect on the audience of tragedy, which arouses pity and fear and therefore leaves the spectators purified.

Pathetic, dramatic or tragic

– A play or a scene is **pathetic** if it presents an affecting or mournful situation that arouses pity in the audience.
– It is **dramatic** if the audience witnesses the struggles and conflicts of the heroes.
– Finally, it is **tragic** if the final catastrophe that engulfs the hero is brought about by his *own* actions (Macbeth and Faustus, for instance, are perfect examples of tragic heroes.)
However useful these distinctions are, the three terms often tend, in fact, to be loosely used.

The word **Pathos** can qualify scenes of high sentimentality, exciting pity and tenderness. (e.g. Farewell and death scenes.)

Dramatic irony

It is created when the audience knows something that one of the characters is not aware of. The character's behaviour is therefore incongruous or inappropriate in the situation as we understand it. Cf. p. 28.

Comic relief

The atmosphere of a tragedy can be alleviated by the use of **comic-relief,** that is to say the presence of lighter scenes and comic characters. (e.g. *Hamlet's* grave diggers scene)

comedy

- The following types of comedy may be distinguished:

Comedy of humours
The term best applies to the kind of comedies written by Ben Jonson, in which each character embodies the exaggerated development of one humour (passion or tendency). The main types of disposition were:
– sanguine (too much blood); vigorous, active but violent;
– choleric (too much choler = bile): lean, sensitive, but impulsive and jealous;
– melancholic (too much melancholy = black bile): thin, reserved, dreamy, sometimes mad;
– phlegmatic (too much phlegm): fat, calm, but wavering and spiritless.

Comedy of manners
It presents the way of life of an aristocratic and sophisticated society with very little respect for decency and morality. The comedy usually results from a very clever and witty dialogue. The Restoration theatre gives an excellent example of this type of comedy.

Romantic comedy
It presents a love story which, after all the obstacles have been overcome and errors found out, will end happily.

High and low comedy
The terms were defined by G. Meredith in *The Idea of Comedy* (1877).
High comedy appeals to the intellect and usually implies laughter at the sight of human foibles and stupidity.
Low comedy is more akin to farce and is based on puns, jokes and funny situations.

Farce
A type of comedy based on improbable and ridiculous situations. Here is how Dryden defined it:

> ... Comedy consists, though of low-persons, yet of natural actions and characters; I mean such humours, adventures, and designs as are to be found and met with in the world. Farce, on the other side, consists of forced humours and unnatural events. Comedy presents us with the imperfections of human nature. Farce entertains us with what is monstrous and chimerical: the one causes laughter in those who can judge of men and manners, by the lively representation of their folly or corruption; the other produces the same effect in those who can judge of neither, and that only by its extravagances. The first works on the judgement and fancy; the latter on the fancy only: there is more of satisfaction in the former kind of laughter, and in the latter more of scorn.
>
> J. Dryden, *Preface to An Evening's Love* 1671.

Tragi-comedy
A play in which characters both of the upper classes and of the lower classes are to be found. It ends happily although it contains elements of tragedy.

● What types of comedy do you think the following excerpts exemplify?

a

MRS. FORD: What shall I do? – There is a gentleman, my dear friend; and I fear not mine own shame so much as his peril: I had rather than a thousand pound he were out of the house.
MRS. PAGE: For shame! never stand "you had rather" and "you had rather:" your husband's here at hand; bethink you of some conveyance: in the house you cannot hide him. O, how have you deceived me! Look, here is a basket: if he be of any reasonable stature, he may creep in here; and throw foul linen upon him, as if it were going to bucking: or – it is whiting-time – send him by your two men to Datchet-mead.
MRS. FORD: He's too big to go in there. What shall I do?
FALSTAFF: *(Coming forward)* Let me see't, let me see't, O, let me see't! I'll in, I'll in. Follow your friend's counsel. I'll in.
MRS. PAGE: What, Sir John Falstaff! Are these your letters, knight?
FALSTAFF: I love thee, and none but thee; help me away: let me creep in here. I'll never
– He gets into the basket; they cover him with foul linen.
MRS. PAGE: Help to cover your master, boy. Call your men, Mistress Ford. You dissembling knight!

---

b

ORLANDO: Then love me, Rosalind.
ROSALIND: Yes, faith will I, Fridays and Saturdays and all.
ORLANDO: And wilt thou have me?
ROSALIND: Ay, and twenty such.
ORLANDO: What sayest thou?
ROSALIND: Are you not good?
ORLANDO: I hope so.
ROSALIND: Why then, can one desire too much of a good thing? – Come, sister, you shall be the priest and marry us. – Give me your hand, Orlando. What do you say, sister?
ORLANDO: Pray thee, marry us.
CELIA: I cannot say the words.
ROSALIND: You must begin, – "Will you, Orlando."
CELIA: Go to. – Will you, Orlando, have to wife this Rosalind?
ORLANDO: I will.
ROSALIND: Ay, but when?
ORLANDO: Why now; as fast as she can marry us.
ROSALIND: Then you must say, "I take thee, Rosalind, for wife."
ORLANDO: I take thee, Rosalind, for wife.
ROSALIND: I might ask you for your commission; but, I do take thee, Orlando, for my husband: there's a girl goes before the priest; and, certainly, a woman's thought runs before her actions.

---

c

TANNER: I had no intention of suggesting anything discreditable. In fact, I am a bit of a Socialist myself.
STRAKER: *(Drily.)* Most rich men are, I notice.
MENDOZA: Quite so. It has reached us, I admit. It is in the air of the century.
STRAKER: Socialism must be lookin up a bit if your chaps are taking to it.
MENDOZA: That is true, sir. A movement which is confined to philosophers and honest men can never exercise any real political influence: there are too few of them. Until a movement shews itself capable of spreading among brigands, it can never hope for a political majority.

---

d

SIR JOHN BRUTE: If women were to have their wills, the world would be finely governed!
LADY BRUTE: What reason have I given you to use me as you do of late? It once was otherwise; you married me for love.
SIR JOHN BRUTE: And you me for money; so you have your reward, and I have mine.
LADY BRUTE: What is it that disturbs you?
SIR JOHN BRUTE: A parson.
LADY BRUTE: Why, what has he done to you?
SIR JOHN BRUTE: He has married me. *(Exit* SIR JOHN BRUTE)
LADY BRUTE: *(Sola)*. The devil's in the fellow, I think! – I was told before I married him that thus 'twould be. But I thought I had charms enough to govern him, and that where there was an estate a woman must needs be happy; so my vanity has deceived me, and my ambition has made me uneasy. But some comfort still; if one would be revenged of him, these are good times; a woman may have a gallant and a separate maintenance too. –

In these passages, or in other excerpts from plays in the book, can you find instances of

pun?
paradox?
banter?
repartee?
pantomine?
slapstick humour?
horseplay?
wit?
burlesque?

(cf. Wit, humour and irony, p. 27)

a W. Shakespeare, *The Merry Wives of Windsor*, III, III.
b W. Shakespeare, *As You Like It, IV, I.*
c G.B. Shaw, *Man and Superman, III.*
d J. Vanbrugh, *The Provok'd Wife, I, I.*

wit, humour, satire and irony

Wit and humour

- **Wit**

Brilliant style, concise and often paradoxical aiming at surprise and amusement.

> **Politics: The conduct of public affairs for private advantage.** A. Bierce

Wit can be harmless or aggressive.

Repartee [repa:'ti:]

Applies to a situation in which two characters try to vie in wit with each other.

> MRS ALLONBY: *(Goes over to Lord Illingworth.)* **There is a beautiful moon tonight.**
> LORD ILLINGWORTH: **Let us go and look at it. To look at anything that is inconstant is charming nowadays.**
> MRS ALLONBY: **You have your looking-glass.**
> LORD ILLINGWORTH: **It is unkind. It merely shows me my wrinkles.**
> MRS ALLONBY: **Mine is better behaved. It never tells me the truth.**
> LORD ILLINGWORTH: **Then it is in love with you.**
>
> O. Wilde

- **Humour**

Applies to any situation that is comic; but the smile or laughter it provokes is kind and sympathetic, never derisive and critical. Whereas wit is only conveyed through words, a situation, a gesture, etc., can also be humourous.

> **An old lady to another old lady (after decimalization was introduced in Great Britain): "I think they should have waited until all the old people had died."**

Satire and burlesque

- **Satire**

Making a person, a thing, an idea... ridiculous. Laughter is this time used against something, often to mock folly and evil.

> **While pensive poets painful vigils keep**
> **Sleepless themselves to give their readers sleep.**
>
> A. Pope

- **Burlesque**

One form of satire. The satire is aimed at a given literary genre or work and is achieved through a ridiculous imitation of it.
Here are two common forms of burlesque:

Parody

Imitating the serious and elevated tone of a work and applying it to a low and trivial subject.

Dear Mamma,

O what news, since I writ my last! the young Squire hath been here, and as sure as a Gun he hath taken a Fancy to me: *Pamela*, says he, (for so I am called here) you was a great Favourite of your late Mistress's; yes, an't please your Honour, says I; and I believe you deserved it, says he; thank your Honour for your good Opinion, says I; and then he took me by the Hand, and I pretented to be shy: Laud, says I, Sir, I hope you don't intend to be rude; no, says he, my Dear, and then he kissed me, 'till he took away my Breath – and I pretended to be Angry, and to get away, and then he kissed

me again, and breathed very short, and looked very silly; and by Ill-Luck Mrs, *Jervis* came in, and had like to have spoiled Sport. – *How troublesome is such Interruption!* You shall hear now soon, for I shall not come away yet, so I rest,

Your affectionate Daughter,

H. Fielding, *Shamela.*

Travesty

Dealing with the serious and dignified subject of a given work in a low manner.
e.g. The first scene of John Gay's *The Beggar's Opera* (Act 1, scene 1) which aims at ridiculing the Italian Opera popular at the time:

Scene, PEACHUM'S *House*
PEACHUM *(Sitting at a table, with a large book of accounts before him):*
Air 1: "An old woman, clothed in grey".

"Through all the employments of life,
  Each neighbour abuses his brother;
Whore and rogue, they call husband and wife:
  All professions be-rogue one another.
The priest calls the lawyer a cheat:
  The lawyer be-knaves the divine:
And the statesman, because he's so great,
  Thinks his trade as honest as mine."

A lawyer is an honest employment, so is mine. Like me too, he acts in a double capacity, both against rogues, and for 'em; for'tis but fitting that we should protect and encourage cheats, since we live by them.

Irony

Saying something very different from what one means in order to make one's point.

What did you learn in school today, dear little boy of mine?
What did you learn in school today, dear little boy of mine?
I learned that Washington never told a lie,
I learned that soldiers seldom die,
I learned that everybody's free,
And that's what the teacher said to me,
And that's what I learned in school today. A song by Tom Paxton

Here are two common forms of irony:

Sarcasm

Exaggerated praise meant as a criticism.
e.g. Calling somebody "clever" when he's made a mistake.

Dramatic irony

Applies to a situation in which both the narrator/author and the reader know something that one of the characters does not know.

(Duncan admires Macbeth's castle:)

This castle hath a pleasant seat, the air
Nimbly and sweetly recommends itself
Unto our gentle senses. *Macbeth* I, VI

but the reader knows that Duncan will be killed in that very castle.

a H.L. Mencken; **b** J. Swift; **c** O. Wilde; **d** J. Dryden; **e** J.K. Jerome; **f** R.B. Sheridan; **g** S. Leacock.

How would you classify the following excerpts?

		Type
a	*The Declaration of Independence in American* When things get so balled up that the people of a country got to cut loose from some other country, and go it on their own hook, without asking no permission from nobody, excepting maybe God Almighty, then they ought to let everybody know why they done it, so that everybody can see they are not trying to put nothing over on nobody.	
b	He that can, with Epicurus, content his ideas with the films and images that fly off upon his senses from the superficies of things; such a man, truly wise, creams off nature... This is the sublime and refined point of felicity, called the possession of being well-deceived, the serene peaceful state of being a fool among knaves.	
c	LADY BRACKNELL: Do you smoke? JACK: Yes, I must admit I smoke. LADY BRACKNELL: I am glad to hear it. A man should always have an occupation of some kind.	
d	A man so various that he seemed to be Not one, but all mankind's epitome. Stiff in opinions, always in the wrong; Was everything by starts and nothing long: But, in the course of one revolving moon, Was chemist, fiddler, statesman, and buffoon.	
e	Have you ever been in a house where there are a couple courting? It is most trying. You think you will go and sit in the drawing-room, and you march off there. As you open the door, you hear a noise as if somebody had suddenly recollected something, and, when you get in, Emily is over by the window, full of interest in the opposite side of the road, and your friend, John Edward. is at the other end of the room with his whole soul held in thrall by photographs of other people's relatives.	
f	SIR PETER: No, no, madam, you shall throw away no more sums on such unmeaning luxury. 'Slife! to spend as much to furnish your dressing-room with flowers in winter as would suffice to turn the Pantheon into a greenhouse, and give a *fête champêtre* at Christmas. LADY TEAZLE: Lord, Sir Peter, am I to blame, because flowers are dear in cold weather? You should find fault with the climate, and not with me. For my part, I'm sure, I wish it was spring all the year round, and that roses grew under one's feet! SIR PETER: Oons! madam – if you had been born to this, I shouldn't wonder at your talking thus; but you forget what your situation was when I married you. LADY TEAZLE: No, no, I don't; 'twas a very disagreeable one, or I should never have married you.	
g	The Great Detective sat in his office. He wore a long green gown and half a dozen secret badges pinned to the outside of it. Three or four pairs of false whiskers hung on a whisker-stand beside him. Goggles, blue spectacles, and motor glasses lay within easy reach. He could completely disguise himself at a second's notice.	

Further reading:

You may estimate your capacity for Comic perception by being able to detect the ridicule of them you love, without loving them less: and more by being able to see yourself somewhat ridiculous in dear eyes, and accepting the correction their image of you proposes(...)

If you detect the ridicule, and your kindliness is chilled by it, you are slipping into the grasp of Satire.

If instead of falling foul of the ridiculous person with a satiric rod, to make him writhe and shriek aloud, you prefer to sting him under a semi-caress, by which he shall in his anguish be rendered dubious whether indeed anything has hurt him, you are an engine of Irony.

If you laugh all round him, tumble him, roll him about, deal him a smack, and drop a tear on him, own his likeness to you and yours to your neighbour, spare him as little as you shun, pity him as much as you expose, it is a spirit of Humour that is moving you.

The Comic, which is the perceptive, is the governing spirit, awakening and giving aim to these powers of laughter, but it is not to be counfounded with them: it enfolds a thinner form of them, differing from satire, in not sharply driving into the quivering sensibilities, and from humour, in not comforting them and tucking them up, or indicating a broader than the range of this bustling world to them.

G. Meredith, *The Idea of Comedy and the Uses of the Comic Spirit,* 1897.

figurative language

Imagery ['imidʒəʀi]
The set of metaphors and similes one can find in a given text or work. It refers to the whole of the figurative language used by the author.

Simile ['simili]
Comparison introduced by "like" or "as".

> **When she I loved looked every day**
> **Fresh as a rose in June...** W. Wordsworth

Metaphor
Giving something a name that does not usually apply to it.

> **... All the world's a stage**
> **And all the men and women merely players.** W. Shakespeare

world's = **tenor** (subject, thing being characterized)

stage = **vehicle** (metaphoric word)

Mixed metaphor
Several metaphoric vehicles are mixed.

> **... Was the hope drunk**
> **Where in you dress'd yourself?** W. Shakespeare

hope
drunk
dress

hope → drunk
hope → dress

Subdued metaphor
One which runs implicitly through a series of images.

> **... he stood upon the ramparts of his soul, before the lost land of himself; heard inland murmurs of lost seas...** T. Wolfe

---

Dead metaphor
A metaphor that has become so common that it has lost its strength. e.g.: "the horns of a dilemma".

Implicit metaphor
The tenor is not mentioned, only implied.

> **A wild angel had appeared to him, the angel of mortal youth and beauty...** J. Joyce

Here, the angel obviously refers to a girl.

Here are well-known types of "implicit metaphors":

Metonymy
Instead of using the word for a thing, one uses the word for one of the attributes of the thing, or a closely related term. e.g. "a hand" instead of "a worker".

Synecdoche [si'nekdəki]
One form of metonymy: the part stands for the whole. e.g. "the printed word" instead of "the book".

Personification or Prosopopeia [prɔsoupə'pi:ə]
Endowing an object or concept with human characteristics:

> **Season of mists and mellow fruitfulness,**
> **Close bosom-friend of the maturing sun...** J. Keats *To Autumn*

Cf pathetic fallacy, p. 00.

Synesthesia [sinis'θi:ziə]
Describing a sensation in terms of another sensation.

> **Upon the bank she stood**
> **In the cool**
> **Of spent emotions.**
> **She felt, among the leaves,**
> **The dew**
> **Of old devotions.** W. Stevens

Kenning
"An oblique description which calls the body the bone-house and the sea the whale-road." N. Frye

Often found in Old English poetry.

● **Conceit** [kən'si:t]
Far-fetched parallelism, comparison made between two very different things whose common points are not immediately obvious.
Conceits can mainly be found
– in the exaggerated comparisons used by Petrarch to describe the cold mistress and the languishing lover,
– in the unexpected comparisons Donne and many 17th Century metaphysical poets made use of.

> **Motion as in a Mill**
> **Is busie standing still.** W. Cartwright

● **Hyperbole** [hai'pə:bəli]
Exaggeration or overstatement used for rhetorical effect.

> **..... my hand will rather**
> **The multitudinous seas incarnadine,**
> **Making the green one red.** W. Shakespeare

Contrary = <u>understatement.</u>

● **Symbol** A word which suggests something particular which has a further significance in a given culture or for the author. e.g. "Wings" are often a symbol of imagination, thought and spirituality.

Each of the quotations that follow contains at least one example of the following figures of speech:
simile – metaphor – dead metaphor – mixed metaphor – metonymy – personification – synesthesia – conceit – hyperbole.
Find out which figure(s) of speech are contained in each passage.

		Figures of speech
a	A soft liquid joy like the noise of many waters flowed over his memory. — J. Joyce	
b	And this same flower that smiles to-day, To-morrow will be dying. — R. Herrick	
c	I closed my lids, and kept them close, And the balls like pulses beat... — S.T. Coleridge	
d	My vegetable love should grow Vaster than empires, and more slow; An hundred years should go to praise Thine eyes, and on thy forehead gaze ; Two hundred to adore each breast; But thirty thousand to the rest. — A. Marvell	
e	If they be two, they are two so As stiffe twin compasses are two, Thy soule to fixt foot, makes no show To move, but doth, if the'other doe. — J. Donne	
f	As I walked out one evening, Walking down Bristol Street, The crowds upon the pavement Were fields of harvest wheat. — W.H. Auden	
g	I'll have this crown of mine cut from my shoulders... — W. Shakespeare	
h	As from thy presence showers a rain of melody. — P.B. Shelley	
i	Then, quick as lightning, the back of his hand struck her. — D.H. Lawrence	

1. The Elizabethan Age

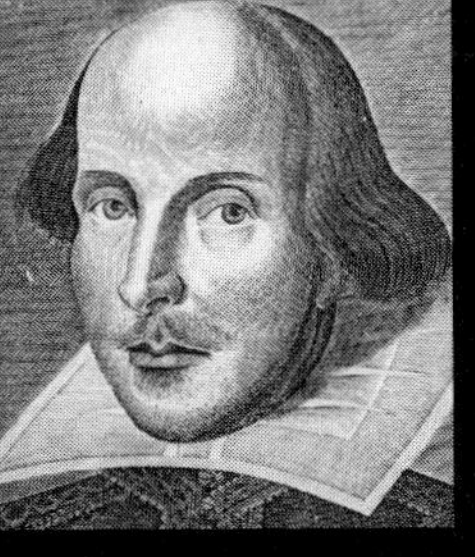

the social order

For the idea of Order see Shakespeare, Troilus and Cressida *I, 3.*

For Disorder and Chaos, see Shakespeare, Macbeth, *II, 4.*

... though the general medieval picture of the world survived in outline into the Elizabethan age, its existence was by then precarious. There had been Machiavelli, to whom the idea of a universe divinely ordered throughout was repugnant, and in the seventeenth century men began to understand and heed and not merely to travesty and abuse him. Recent research has shown that the educated Elizabethan had plenty of text-books in the vernacular instructing him in the Copernican astronomy, yet he was loth to upset the old order by applying his knowledge.

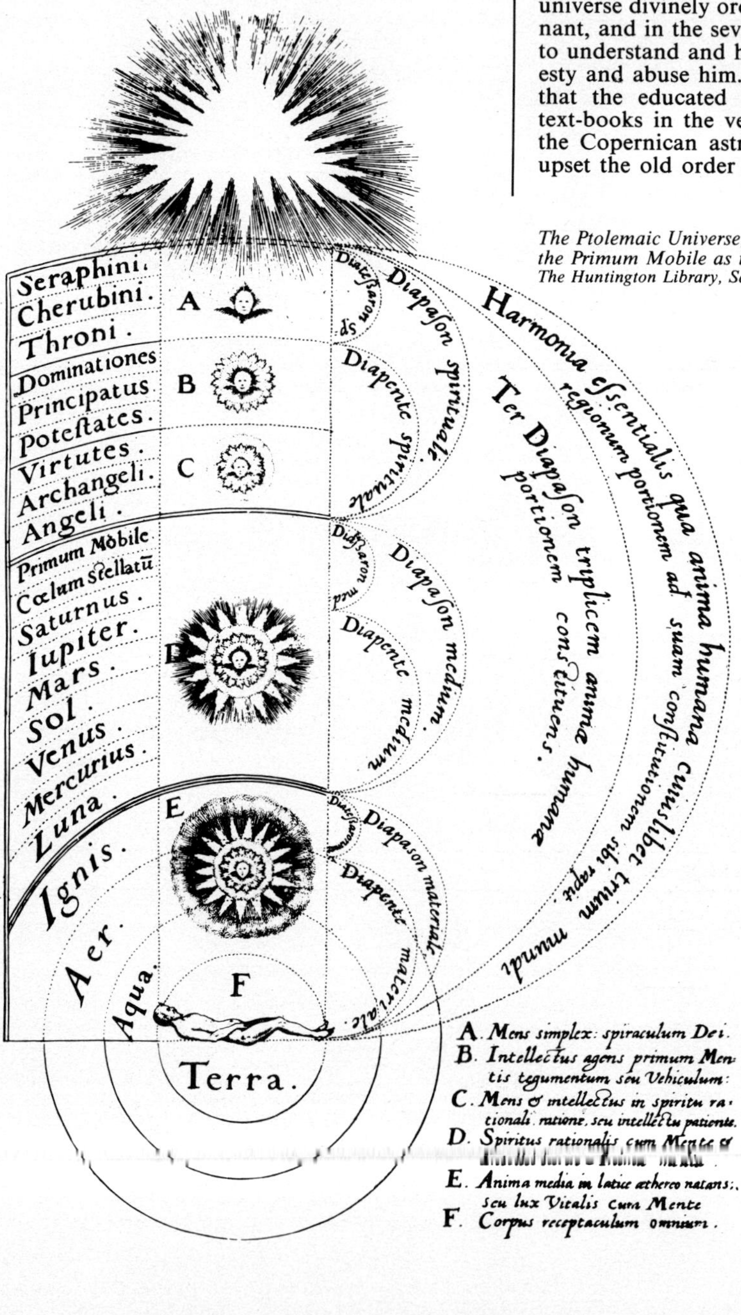

The Ptolemaic Universe, with the earth at the centre and the Primum Mobile as the last sphere.
The Huntington Library, San Marino, Cal.

	Politics and Society	**Literature and the Arts**
1558	The French take Calais. Accession of Queen Elizabeth I.	
1559	Peace between England and France. Acts of Supremacy and Uniformity (definition of the Church of England as a middle way between Catholicism and Lutheran Protestantism).	
1560	Reformation in Scotland (J. Knox).	
1564		Birth of Marlowe and Shakespeare.
1570	Queen Elizabeth excommunicated.	
1576		First playhouse (the Theatre) built in London.
1578		LYLY: *Euphues.*
1579		SPENSER: *The Shepherd's Calendar.*
1580	Drake's return from his first voyage round the world.	
1581		SIDNEY: *Astrophel and Stella.*
1587	Mary Queen of Scots executed for treason.	KYD: *The Spanish Tragedy.* MARLOWE: *Tamburlaine,* I-II. HOLINSHED: *Chronicles* (2nd edition).
1588	Defeat of the Spanish Armada.	MARLOWE: *Doctor Faustus* (or later?).
1590		SIDNEY: *The Arcadia.* SPENSER: *The Faerie Queene* (I-III). SHAKESPEARE: first plays (*Henry VI,* 1, 2 & 3 – see p. 56 for a complete chronology).
1592		MARLOWE: *Edward II.*
1593	Plague in London.	
1595		SPENSER: *Amoretti, Epithalamion.*
1597		BACON: *Essays* (first edition).
1598		JONSON: *Every Man in his Humour.*
1599		Opening of the Globe Theatre. JONSON: *Every Man out of his Humour.*
1601	Revolt and execution of Essex.	
1603	Accession of James I (James VI of Scotland).	
1604	Peace between England & Spain.	
1605	Gunpowder Plot.	
1606		JONSON: *Volpone.* TOURNEUR: *The Revenger's Tragedy.*
1609		SHAKESPEARE: *Sonnets.*
1610		CHAPMAN: *The Revenge of Bussy d'Ambois.* JONSON: *The Alchemist.*
1611		Authorized version of the Bible. WEBSTER: *The White Devil.*
1612		DONNE: *The Second Anniversary.* WEBSTER: *The Duchess of Malfi.* Shakespeare's last plays (Henry VIII).
1616		Death of Shakespeare.

The new commercialism was hostile to medieval stability. The greatness of the Elizabethan age was that it contained so much of new without bursting the noble form of the old order. It is here that the Queen herself comes in. Somehow the Tudors had inserted themselves into the constitution of the medieval universe. They were part of the pattern and they made themselves indispensable. If they were to be preserved, it had to be as part of this pattern. It was a serious matter not a mere fancy if an Elizabethan writer compared Elizabeth to the "primum mobile", the master-sphere of the physical universe, and every activity within the realm to the varied motions of the other spheres governed to the last fraction by the influence of their container. (...)

One of the clearest expositions of order (and close to Shakespeare's though a good deal earlier in date) is Elyot's in the first chapter of the *Governor*. (...)

"Hath not God set degrees and estates in all his glorious works? First in his heavenly ministers, whom he hath constituted in divers degrees called hierarchies. Behold the four elements, whereof the body of man is compact, how they be set in their places called spheres, higher or lower according to the sovereignty of their natures. Behold also the order that God hath put generally in all his creatures, beginning at the most inferior or base and ascending upward. He made not only herbs to garnish the earth but also trees of a more eminent stature than herbs. Semblably in birds beasts and fishes some be good for the sustenance of man, some bear things profitable to sundry uses, other be apt to occupation and labour. Every kind of trees herbs birds beasts and fishes have a peculiar disposition appropered unto them by God their creator; so that in everything is order, and without order may be nothing stable or permanent. And it may not be called order except it do contain in it degrees, high and base, according to the merit or estimation of the thing that is ordered." (...)

But the negative implication was even more frequent and emphatic. If the Elizabethans believed in an ideal order animating earthly order, they were terrified lest it should be upset, and appalled by the visible tokens of disorder that suggested its upsetting. They were obsessed by the fear of chaos and the fact of mutability; and the obsession was powerful in proportions as their faith in the cosmic order was strong. To us "chaos" means hardly more than confusion on a large scale; to an Elizabethan it meant the cosmic anarchy before creation and the wholesale dissolution that would result if the pressure of Providence relaxed and allowed the law of nature to cease functioning.

E.M.W. Tillyard,
The Elizabethan World Picture,
E.M.W. Tillyard's Literary Estate and Chatto & Windus. 1952.

literature and philosophy

Francis Bacon (1561-1626) was one of the major thinkers of the English Renaissance. A member of Parliament and an adviser of Queen Elizabeth, he received patronage from Essex for whose conviction he was, however, partly responsible. His political career ended in 1621 when he was found guilty of corruption and neglect.

In his philosophical works (1605: The Advancement of Learning; *1623:* De Augmentis Scientiarum*) he advocated the "advancement of learning". He believed that science could give men limitless powers. But the search for knowledge should be methodical and experimental, starting from the study of events and things. (Hume was later to develop this inductive method.) The same principles ought to be applied to the study of human nature and of political science.*

In politics, Bacon saw the necessity of a strong, wealthy and well-armed government. For him (as for the Tudors), absolutism was the only solution. The following excerpt is from his Essays *(first edition 1597, final edition 1625). See how it relates to the "Elizabethan World Order" (cf p. 36).*

Concerning the Materialls of Seditions. It is a Thing well to be considered: For the surest way to prevent Seditions (if the Times doe beare it), is to take away the Matter of them. For if there be Fuell prepared, it is hard to tell whence the Spark shall come that shall set it on Fire. The Matter of Seditions is of two kindes; Much Poverty and Much Discontentment. It is certaine, so many Overthrowne Estates, so many Votes for Troubles. Lucan noteth well the State of Rome before the Civill Warre:

"Hinc Usura vorax, rapidumque in tempore Fœnus,
Hinc concussa Fides, et multis utile Bellum".

This same "Multis utile Bellum" is an assured and infallible Signe of a State disposed to Seditions and Troubles. And if this Poverty and Broken Estate, in the better Sort, be ioyned with a Want and Necessity in the meane People, the danger is imminent and great. For the Rebellions of the Belly are the worst. As for Discontentments, they are in the Politique Body like to Humours in the Naturall, which are apt to gather a preternaturall Heat and to Enflame.

And let no Prince measure the Danger of them by this, whether they be Iust, or Uniust? For that were to imagine People to be too reasonable, who doe often spurne at their owne Good; Nor yet by this, whether the Griefes, wherupon they rise, be in fact great or small; For they are the most dangerous Discontentments, where the Feate is greater then the Feeling. "Dolendi Modus, Timendi non item". Besides, in great Oppressions, the same Things that provoke the Patience doe withall mate the Courage; But in Feares it is not so. Neither let any Prince or State be secure concerning Discontentments, because they have been often, or have been long, and yet no Perill hath ensued; For as it is true that every Vapor or Fume doth not turne into a Storme, So it is, neverthelesse, true that Stormes, though they blow over divers times, yet may fall at last; And as the Spanish proverb noteth well ; "The cord breaketh at the last by the weakest pull".

The Causes and Motives of Seditions are, – Innovation in Religion; Taxes; Alteration of Lawes and Customes; Breaking of Priviledges; Generall Oppression; Advencement of unworthy persons; Strangers; Dearths ; Disbanded Souldiers; Factions growne desperate; And whatsoever in offending People ioyneth and knitteth them in a Common Cause.

For the Remedies: There may be some generall Preservatives, whereof we will speake; As for the iust Cure, it must answer to the Particular Disease; And so be left to Counsell rather then Rule.

F. Bacon, *Essays XV. Of Seditions and Troubles.*

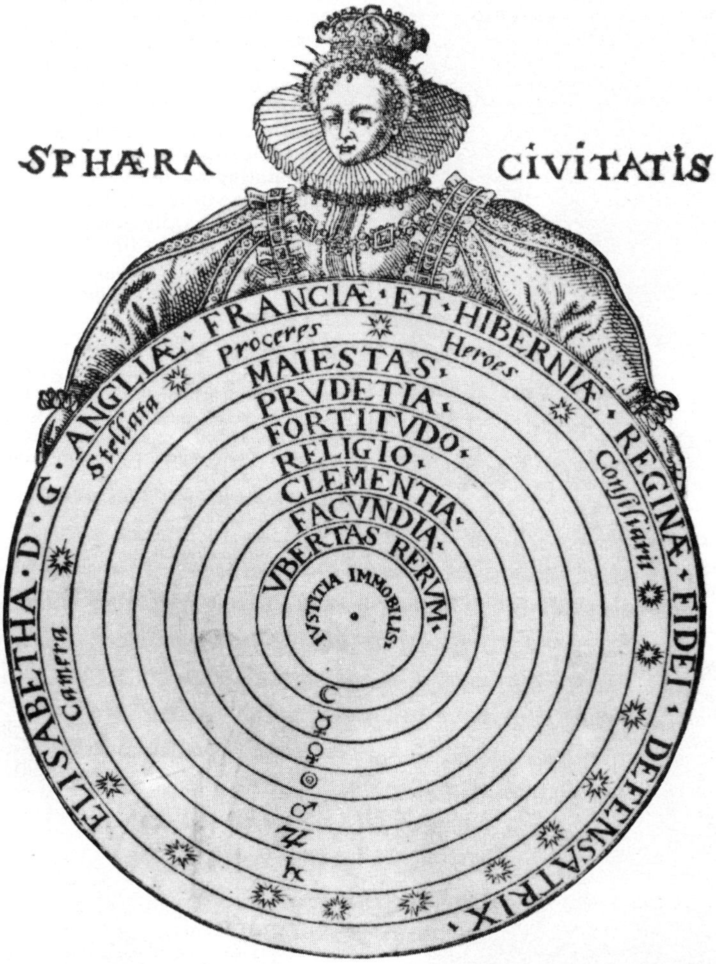

This figure by John Case (from Sphaera Civitatis *– 1588?) shows Queen Elizabeth as the prime mover in the ninth sphere. All the other spheres show correspondences between planets and virtues of government*

In H. Shire, A Preface to Spenser, *Longman.*

Nicholas Hilliard: Elizabeth I, *c. 1580.*
Private collection. Ph. © Zoltan Wegner.

literature and the arts

Painting: the art of miniature

... (one) point is fundamental to a consideration of Elizabethan painting – that, as at no time later, the art of miniature (called 'limning' at this time) far surpasses in quality and contemporary esteem all other forms of painting. Alone of painters in Elizabeth's time, Nicholas Hilliard and his pupil and rival, Isaac Oliver, are worthy to be named as contributors to the age of Shakespeare. It was these miniaturists whose practice and aesthetic were valid for this age, and the historian of painting in Britain must accord them a degree of attention which the art of miniature does not require in later centuries. It would seem that both Hilliard and Oliver did sometimes (but not often) also practise painting on the scale of life. But what is a superlative virtue in the private and intimate art of miniature hardly admits of being transplanted onto the scale of life.

E. Waterhouse, *Painting in Britain, 1530 to 1790, The Pelican History of Art, Penguin Books Ltd.*

Cf. Some call her Pandora: some Gloria some Cynthia: some Belphoebe: some Astrala; all by several names to express several loves: Yet all those names make but one celestial body, as all those loves meet to create but one soul. I am of her own country, and we adore her by the name of Eliza.

Thomas Dekker, *Old Fortunatus.*

Self-portrait, *c. 1577.*
Victoria and Albert Museum.

Unknown lady, *c. 1590.*
Victoria and Albert Museum.

The three main themes of these miniatures are:
- *Portraits of Elizabeth I, usually painted in full regalia, and surrounded with a complex pattern of symbols (e.g. the sieve or the eglantine for chastity, the olive for peace, the sword of justice, the pillar of constancy or fortitude, etc.).*
- *Chivalry (cf. the poems of Sidney and Spenser).*
- *Melancholy (cf. the division into humours – p. 70) which was supposed to be the mood of lovers.*

See yonder melancholy gentleman,
Which hood-wink'd with his hat, alone doth sit!
Thinke what he thinks, and tell me if you can,
What great affaires troubles his little wit.
He thinks not of the warre twixt France and Spaine,
But he doth seriously bethinke him whether
Of the Gull'd people he be most esteem'd
For his long cloake or for his great black feather,
By which each gull is now a gallant deem'd,
Or of a journey he deliberates,
To Paris-garden, Cock-pit or the Play:
Or how to steale a dog he meditates,
Or what he shall unto his mistress say.

Sir John Davies.

Isaac Oliver: Young Man Leaning against a Tree, *c. 1590-1595*

Elizabethan and Jacobean architecture

Why so large cost, having so short a lease,
Dost thou upon thy fading mansion spend ?

Shakespeare, *Sonnet* CXLVI.

Hatfield House, Hertfordshire, *1607-1612.*
In D. Yarwood, Outline of English Architecture, Batsford Ltd.

Little Moreton Hall, Cheshire, *1559-80, ibid.*

In this period architecture in England is unique and quite different from contemporary Continental development. Italian Renaissance influence had been cut off earlier in the century by Henry VIII's break with Rome and the geographical barrier of the Channel was sufficient to curtail the infiltration of French and Italian designs, though a number of Continental craftsmen worked here. Renaissance forms and ideas did percolate through, however, and these were chiefly from Flemish and German sources so that English architecture of the era before Inigo Jones was a mixture of styles. The Perpendicular Gothic form had not died out nor had the taste for picturesque, asymmetrical manor houses, with courtyards and Tudor chimneys over romantic rooflines. The design and pattern books from Flanders, France and Germany inspired English masons and carpenters with Renaissance forms but it was "Mannerist" Renaissance design, with emphasis on strapwork, masks, curved gables and cresting. (...)

The Elizabethan and Jacobean age was a time of great domestic building activity. Few churches were erected, there was little public or university building; the wealth of the era went, architecturally, into the great houses. These were owned, and often partly designed, by the aristocracy who vied with one another to create palaces suitable for the monarch, accompanied by the court retinue, to visit on the summer tours. (...)

In areas where stone was less plentiful many brick houses were built and also, especially for smaller homes, half-timber work was common. Such designs were most decorative, and characteristically English with their overhanging first storeys and charming porches. A very famous example is Little Moreton Hall, with its carved barge-boards and corner-posts.

D. Yarwood, *Outline of English Architecture. ibid.*

Music

The Elizabethan age was the golden age of English music. Among the varied production of that time, one should note.

THE WILLOW SONG

The poor soul sat sighing by a sycamore tree;
Sing willow, willow, willow;
With his hand in his bosom, and his head upon his knee;
O willow, willow, willow,
O willow, willow, willow, willow shall be my garland.
Sing all a green willow, willow, willow, willow!
Ay me, the green willow must be my garland.
He sighed in his singing and made a great moan,
I am dead to all pleasure, my true love she is gone.
Come all you forsaken, and mourn you with me;
Who speaks of a false love, mine's falser than she.
Take this for my farewell and latest adieu;
Write this on my tomb, that in love I was true.

Othello, IV, 3.

FULL FATHOM FIVE

Full Fathom five thy father lies;
Of his bones are coral made;
Those are pearls that were his eyes:
Nothing of him that doth fade,
But doth suffer a sea-change
Into something rich and strange.
Sea nymphs hourly ring his knell.
Hark! Now I hear them.
Ding dong bell.

The Tempest, I, 2.

THE WIND AND THE RAIN

When that I was and a little tiny boy,
With hey, ho, the wind and the rain,
A foolish thing was but a toy.
For the rain it raineth every day.

But when I came to man's estate,
With hey, ho, the wind and the rain,
'Gainst knaves and thieves men shut their gate
For the rain it raineth every day.

But when alas I came to wife,
By swaggering could I never thrive,

But when I came unto my bed,
With toss-pots still had drunken head,

A great while ago the world began,
With hey, ho, the wind and the rain,
But that's all one, our play is done
And we'll strive to please you every day.

Twelfth Night, V, 1.

Church music

... though it was gradually changing direction in Anglican England. The name most commonly associated with sacred music during the Renaissance is that of William BYRD, *who composed Masses and a book of* Cantiones Sacrae *(1575).*

Instrumental music

... at the time, however, often considered as secondary: mainly pieces for the virginal, the organ, the lute or the viol. e.g. The Mulliner Book 5 *(1585),* Consort Lessons (MORLEY, *1599*), The Fitzwilliam Virginal Book *(Collective work, 1612).*

Songs

... which were very popular and gave Elizabethan music its fame and originality. Music was closely linked to poetry and the theatre, partly under the influence of the court, the sovereign and the aristocracy who gave patronage to both poets and composers. Shakespeare's plays, for instance, contain numerous songs whose function is not merely "decorative", but which create an atmosphere or, reflect on the characters who sing them or on the situation.

Main forms:

- madrigals *(William* BYRD, *Orlando* GIBBONS, *Thomas* MORLEY, *Thomas* WEELKES, *John* WILBYE*);*
- ayres *(John* DOWLAND, *Thomas* CAMPION*). Ayres gave prominence to the voice and thus ensured that the text was understood. Hence the common use of texts borrowed from well-known poets. The usual accompaniment was the lute or the "broken consort": viol, viola da gamba, flute, lute, cittern and pandora.*

The music of the Elizabethan madrigal and the lyric poetry to which it was wedded expressed the reasonable joy in life of a people freed from medieval and not yet oppressed by Puritan complexes and fears; rejoicing in nature and the countryside in whose lap they had the felicity to live; moving forward to a healthy agricultural and mercantile prosperity, and not yet overwhelmed by the weight of industrial materialism.

G.M. Trevelyan

Unknown: Portrait of Sir Henry Unton, *c. 1596 (detail).* One can see a treble violin, a flute, a cittern, a pandora, a lute, a drum, a basa viola. *National Portrait Gallery.*

Sir Philip SIDNEY 1554-1586

1554 *Born to a noble family.*
A student at Shrewsbury then Oxford.
1572-75 *Grand tour on the Continent.*
1575 *Through the influence of the Earl of Leicester, his uncle, he was admitted to court.*
1576-1585 *Sent on different missions to Ireland, Germany, France, Italy and the Netherlands.*
1579 *Close acquaintance with Spenser. Became a patron of letters.*
1580 Arcadia *(pub. 1590).*
1581 Astrophel and Stella *(pub. 1591).*
The Defence of Poesy *(or* An Apology for Poetry) *(pub. 1595).*
1583 *Married to Frances Walsingham.*
1586 *Death in the Netherlands where he had been appointed Governor of Flushing.*

The perfect humanist, courtier and diplomat, Sir Philip Sidney marked his age by his personality as much as by his works. The first of these, Arcadia, *is a pastoral tale using the traditional themes & devices of romance (chivalry, shipwrecks, imprisonments, rescues, etc.) and dealing through dialogues with the themes of love, the duties of princes and a number of metaphysical questions.*

His Defence of Poesy *was written in reply to Gosson's* The School of Abuse – *a Puritan warning against the dangers of art. In clear and simple prose, Sidney shows how the poet's power of invention and creation places him far above the philosopher and historian.*

But the work which most influenced following generations was Astrophel and Stella, *a collection of sonnets in the tradition of Petrarch, expressing his love for Penelope Devereux, the daughter of the Earl of Essex. Considering the preciosity and conventions of the time, the main originality of these poems is their sincerity and directness.*

The light graceful melody of some songs is perfectly in keeping with the general trend of Elizabethan lyrics, while the more masculine and rugged verse of some sonnets, the colloquial language, the vivacity of some dialogues and dramatic monologues, the elaboration of some conceits are so many signs of a powerful personality.

M. Poirier.

Astrophel and Stella (1591)

Having this day my horse

Having this day my horse[1], my hand, my lance
Guided so well that I obtained the prize,
Both by the judgment of the English eyes
And of some sent from that sweet enemy France;
Horsemen my skill in horsemanship advance[2]
Townfolks my strength; a daintier judge applies
His praise to sleight which from good use doth rise;
Some lucky wits impute it but to chance;
Others, because of both sides I do take
My blood from them who did excel in this,
Think Nature me a man-at-arms did make.
How far they shot awry ![3] The true cause is,
Stella looked on, and from her heavenly face
Sent forth the beams which made so fair my race.

1. In 1581, Sidney took part in a tournament held in honour of the French embassy which came to discuss the possible marriage of Queen Elizabeth with the Duc d'Alençon. The tournament may have inspired this poem. – 2. *advance:* greatly praise – 3. *awry:* wrong (ly).

Sidney on his art:

But truly, many of such writings as come under the banner of unresistible love, if I were a mistress would never persuade me they were in love; so coldly they apply fiery speeches, as men that had rather read lovers' writings (and so caught up certain swelling phrases, which hang together like a man which once told me the wind was at north-west and by south, because he would be sure to name winds enough) than that in truth they feel those passions; which easily, as I think, may be bewrayed by that same forcibleness, or *energeia* (as the Greeks call it) of the writer. But let this be a sufficient, though short note, that we miss the right use of the material point of poesy.

Now for the outside of it, which is words, or (as I may term it) diction, it is even well worse; so is that honey-flowing matron, Eloquence, apparelled, or rather disguised, in a courtesan-like painted affection: one time with so far-fetched words, they may seem monsters, but must seem strangers, to any poor Englishman; another time with coursing of a letter, as if they were bound to follow the method of a dictionary; another time with figures and flowers extremely winter-starved.

Sir Philip Sidney, *The Defence of Poesy,* 1595.

A critic on Sidney :

(He) is direct, concise, exact. There is an efficiency in his language and syntax which reveals an active intelligence and an unusual sense of reality, qualities which remind us that Sidney was more than a poet: the man of affairs, and of the greatest affairs, the aristocrat who cultivated his mind for action, the courtier who could write as he did to Queen Elizabeth on her proposed marriage to the Duc d'Alençon, formed habits of expression which did not fail to affect his verse. (...)

Throughout *Astrophel and Stella* we feel the pressure, direct or indirect, of complex actual circumstances, of a day-to-day life in which the poet and his love are enmeshed. If there is a touch of play-acting about the young courtier going through the motions of the tournament, it is an added grace, rather than a false note. The court was like this, and no one should underestimate the importance of its apparent trivialities. There is the core of fact, and within that a core of truth. Sidney's horsemanship, his noble blood, his standing with all sorts of people, his discreet but firm ostentation of himself and his gifts: all these are conveyed. And at the heart of his poem, as of his life, Sidney puts a secret passion which gives it the indispensable further dimension.

F.T. Prince, *The Sonnet from Wyatt to Shakespeare in Elizabethan Poetry,* Stratford Upon Avon Studies, II, 1960.
By permission of Edward Arnold Publisher Ltd.

Isaac Oliver: Edward Herbert, 1st Baron Herbert of Cherbury, *c. 1610-15. The Earl of Powis.*

Sidney and the Elizabethan sonnet:

The great outburst of Elizabethan sonneteering was almost confined to the 1590s. *Astrophel and Stella,* printed in 1591, and the signal setting many of the minor poets to work, of course belongs to the earlier 1580s; Shakespeare's *Sonnets,* the greatest poetry produced by the whole *furore,* though not printed until 1609, have been felt to belong for the most part to the preceding decade. The concentration of most of the Elizabethan sonnet-writing into a space of ten years gave it something of the air of a poetical debauch, and may have contributed to the disfavour into which the form soon fell.

ibid.

Compare the poet's attitude towards the world and his mistress or friend in Sidney's poem and in the following two sonnets (cf. Verse form and poetic genres, p. 2.):

SONNET XXIX

When, in disgrace with fortune and men's eyes,
I all alone beweep my outcast state,
And trouble deaf heaven with my bootless cries,
And look upon myself, and curse my fate,
Wishing me like to one more rich in hope,
Featured like him, like him with friends possess'd,
Desiring this man's art and that man's scope,
With what I most enjoy contented least;
Yet in these thoughts myself almost despising,
Haply I think on thee, and then my state,
Like to the lark at break of day arising
From sullen earth, sings hyms at heaven's gate;
For thy sweet love remember'd such wealth brings
That then I scorn to change my state with kings.

W. Shakespeare, *Sonnets.*

LII

So oft as homeward I from her depart,
I go like one that having lost the field,
Is prisoner led away with heavy heart,
Despoiled of warlike arms and knowen shield.
So do I now myself a prisoner yield
To sorrow and to solitary pain;
From presence of my dearest dear exiled,
Long-while alone in languor to remain.
There let no thought of joy, or pleasure vain,
Dare to approach, that may my solace breed;
But sudden dumps, and dreary sad disdain
Of all world's gladness, more my torment feed.
So I her absence will my penance make,
That of her presence I my meed may take.

E. Spenser, *Amoretti.*

Edmund SPENSER c. 1552-1599

1552 *Born in London.*
1569 *Entered Pembroke Hall in Cambridge as a sizar (a poor student).*
1578 *Met Sidney, whose uncle, the Earl of Leicester, gave Spenser a secretarial postion in 1579. Belonged to the Areopagus, a group of poets which included Greville and Sidney.*
1579 *Publication of* The Shepherd's Calendar.
1580 *Became secretary to the Lord Deputy of Ireland. For the rest of his life, Spenser settled in Ireland where he held several official positions.*
1590 *Pub. of* The Faerie Queene *(Books I-III).*
1591 *Pub. of* Mother Hubberds Tale.

Spenser's translations of Petrarch and du Bellay when he was very young marked all his works which keep to the forms and themes of the Petrarchan tradition. He loved the English language and greatly contributed to a national poetry by trying to revive Chaucerian English, which Sidney called "old rustic English".

The Shepherd's Calendar *is a collection of pastoral poems (one for each month) about various subjects — Moral, Recreative and Plaintive (love, the praise of the sovereign, the lack of respect for poetry...) The* Amoretti *(see above) are love sonnets describing first the despair of the lover, then his happiness when his mistress accepts his vows. They were inspired by Spenser's love for Elizabeth Boyle and it is rare in Elizabethan poetry to find*

1595 *Pub. of* Amoretti and Epithalamion.
Colin Clouts Come Home Againe.
1596 *Pub. of* The Faerie Queene *(Books IV-VI).*
Prothalamion.
1598 *Pub. of* View of the Present State of Ireland.
Tyrone's rebellion in Ireland.
1599 *Death in London.*

such a peaceful description of love. The same purity and quiet joy characterize Spenser's two marriage poems: the Epithalamion *(written for his own wedding) and the* Prothalamion.

As for the Faerie Queene, *on which Spenser worked most of his life, it is both an allegory and a heroic poem which presents different knights embodying the main virtues defined by Aristotle: the Red Cross knight is Saint George and holiness, Sir Guyon is temperance, Artegall is justice, etc. The narrative is a romance of chivalry, full of ideals, noble feats and patriotism taking place in a sort of fairy-land of forests and enchantments. The allegory can be read on different levels: political (it celebrates the power of the nation and praises its policies), religious or moral and is addressed to Elizabeth I who appears in the poem as Gloriana – the sum of all virtues.*

The Faerie Queene (1590)

The end of Canto XI tells how the Red Cross Knight kills the dragon.

The joyous day' gan early to appear:
And fair Aurora from the dewy bed
Of aged Tithone[1] 'gan herself to rear
With rosy cheeks, for shame as blushing red:
Her golden locks, for haste, were loosely shed
About her ears, when Una[2] her did mark
Climb to her charet[3], all with flowers spread,
From heaven high to chase the cheerless dark;
With merry note her loud salutes the mountain lark.

Then freshly up arose the doughty[4] knight,
All healed of his hurts and woundes wide,
And did himself to battle ready dight[5];
Whose early foe awaiting him beside
To have devour'd, so soon as day he spied,
When now he saw himself so freshly rear,
As if late fight had nought him damnified,[6]
He woxe[7] dismay'd, and 'gan his fate to fear;
Nathless[8] with wonted rage he him advanced near;

And in his first encounter, gaping wide,
He thought at once him to have swallow'd quite,
And rush'd upon him with outrageous pride;
Who him rencount'ring fierce, as hawk in flight,
Perforce rebutted back[9]: the weapon bright,
Taking advantage of his open jaw,
Ran through his mouth with so importune[10] might,
That deep empierced his darksome hollow maw[11],
And, back retired, his life-blood forth withal did draw.

So down he fell, and forth his life did breathe,
That vanish'd into smoke and cloudes swift;
So down he fell, that th' earth him underneath
Did groan, as[12] feeble so great load to lift;
So down he fell, as an huge rocky clift[13],

Whose false foundation waves have wash'd away,
With dreadful poise[14] is from the mainland rift,
And rolling down, great Neptune doth dismay:
So down he fell, and like an heaped mountain lay.

The knight himself ev'n trembled at his fall,
So huge and horrible a mass it seem'd;
And his dear lady, that beheld it all,
Durst not approach for dread which she misdeem'd[15],
But yet at last, whenas the direful fiend
She saw not stir, off-shaking vain affright
She nigher drew, and saw that joyous end:
Then God she praised, and thank'd her faithful knight,
That had achieved so great a conquest by his might.

Book I, Canto XI.

1. *Tithone:* Aurora had married Tithonus – 2. *Una:* the embodiment of truth – 3. *charet:* chariot – 4. *doughty:* brave – 5. *dight:* bedight, ceremoniously dress for battle – 6. *damnified:* harmed – 7. *woxe:* waxed (became) – 8. *nathless:* nevertheless – 9. *rebutted back:* drove back – 10. *importune:* violent – 11. *maw:* stomach – 12. *as:* as if – 13. *clift:* cliff – 14. *poyse:* strength – 15. *which she misdeemed:* in which she was mistaken.

Spenser's intention in The Faerie Queene*:*

The generall end therefore of all the booke is to fashion a gentleman or noble person in vertuous and gentle discipline: Which for that I conceiued shoulde be most plausible and pleasing, being coloured with an historicall fiction, the which the most part of men delight to read, rather for variety of matter, then for profite of the ensample: I chose the historye of king Arthure, as most fitte for the excellency of his person, being made famous by many mens former workes, and also furthest from the daunger of envy, and suspition of present time. (...)

I labour to pourtraict in Arthure, before he was king, the image of a braue knight, perfected in the twelve private morall vertues, as Aristotle hath deuised, the which is the purpose of these first twelve bookes: which if I finde to be well accepted, I may be perhaps encoraged, to frame the other part of polliticke vertues in his person, after that hee came to be king. To some I know this Methode will seeme displeasaunt, which had rather haue good discipline deliuered plainly in way of precepts, or sermoned at large, as they use, then thus clowdily enwrapped in Allegoricall deuises. But such, me seeme, should be satisfide with the use of these dayes, seeing all things accounted by their showes, and nothing esteemed of, that is not delighfull and pleasing to commune sence. (...)

In that Faery Queene I meane glory in my generall intention, but in my particular I conceive the most excellent and glorious person of our soueraine the Queene, and her kingdome in Faery land. (...)

So in the person of Prince Arthure I sette forth magnificence in particular, which vertue, for that (according to Aristotle and the rest) it is the perfection of all the rest, and conteineth in it them all, therefore in the whole course I mention the deedes of Arthure applyable to that vertue, which I write of in that booke. But of the xii other vertues, I make xii other knights the patrones, for the more variety of the history:

Letter to Sir Walter Raleigh, 23 January 1589.

Spenser's rhythm:

Spenser concentrates the reader's attention on to the movement of his stanza, by the use of archaic words and constructions, so that one is at a safe distance from the exercise of an immediate judgment, by the steady untroubled flow of similar lines, by making no rapid change of sense or feeling, by sustained alliteration, parallel adjectives, and full statement of the accessories of a thought, and by the dreamy repetition of the great stanza perpetually pausing at its close. *Ababbcbcc* is a unit which may be broken up into a variety of metrical forms, and the ways in which it is successively broken up are fitted into enormous patterns. The first quatrain usually gratifies the ear directly and without surprise, and the stanzas may then be classified by the grammatical connections of the crucial fifth line, which must give a soft bump to the dying fall of the first quatrain, keep it in the air, and prevent it from falling apart from the rest of the stanza.

It may complete the sense of the quatrain, for instance, with a couplet, and the stanza will then begin with a larger, more narrative unit, *ababb,* and wander garrulously down a perspective to the alexandrine. Or it may add to the quatrain as by an afterthought, as if with a childish earnestness it made sure of its point without regard to the metre, and one is relieved to find that the metre recovers itself after all.

William Empson, *Seven Types of Ambiguity*,
Chatto and Windus.

Cf. Versification, p. 7.

William Blake: The Faerie Queene.
National Trust, Petworth.
Ph. G. H. Roberton/The Bridgeman Art Library, London/Ziolo.

Blake painted in watercolour 'The Characters of *The Faerie Queene*' showing them as a procession or cavalcade. Blake was alone in his time to appreciate Spenser as an 'astronomicall poet', to feel the planetary forces at work in the design and matter of Spenser's romance.

Blake's 'visionary conception' of *The Faerie Queene* was of a progress led by the main figures of Book I, followed by key characters from the ensuing Books in order. They are moving forward is a cosmic landscape that shows in the heavens powers raining influence on those below them and regions there above that are significant of stages in the progress of the cavalcade – and of mankind.

Helena Shire.

Lewis Carroll's Jabberwocky *(cf. p. 265) can be read as a parody of the slaying of the dragon in medieval and Elizabethan literature:*

There was a book lying near Alice on the table, and while she sat watching the White King (for she was still a little anxious about him, and had the ink all ready to throw over him, in case he fainted again), she turned over the leaves, to find some part that she could read, "– for it's all in some language I don't know," she said to herself.

It was like this.

JABBERWOCKY

'Twas brillig, and the slithy toves
Did gyre and gimble in the wabe:
All mimsy were the borogoves,
And the mome raths outgrabe.

She puzzled over this for some time, but at last a bright thought struck her. "Why, it's a Looking-glass book, of course! And, if I hold it up to a glass, the words will all go the right way again."

This was the poem that Alice read.

JABBERWOCKY

'Twas brillig, and the slithy toves
  Did gyre and gimble in the wabe:
All mimsy were the borogoves,
  And the mome raths outgrabe.

"Beware the Jabberwock, my son!
  The jaws that bite, the claws that catch!
Beware the Jubjub bird, and shun
  The frumious Bandersnatch!"

He took his vorpal sword in hand:
  Long time the manxome foe he sought –
So rested he by the Tumtum tree,
  And stood awhile in thought.

And, as in uffish thought he stood,
  The Jabberwock, with eyes of flame,
Came whiffling through the tulgey wood,
  And burbled as it came!

One, two! One, two! And through and through
  The vorpal blade went snicker-snack!
He left it dead and with its head
  He went galumphing back.

"And hast thou slain the Jabberwock?
  Come to my arms, my beamish boy!
O frabjous day! Callooh! Callay!"
  He chortled in his joy.

'Twas brillig, and the slithy toves
  Did gyre and gimble in the wabe;
All mimsy were the borogoves,
  And the mome raths outgrabe.

Lewis Carroll, *Through the Looking-Glass.*

The English Bible

The Bible, which was to have such an influence on English thought and literature, was first translated into English at the end of the 7th century (by Caedmon) but it was John Wycliffe, in the late 14th century, who first undertook a complete translation of the Bible, probably because he saw how a widespread use of the Bible could propagate a popular movement that would put moral power in the hands of the people and thus endanger the authority of the church establishment. He was imprisoned but the Lollards were to inherit his ideas.

During the two centuries that followed, several versions of the Bible appeared. The best-known are:

- Tyndale's Bible *(1534) which is striking by the simplicity of its vocabulary and the strength of its syntax. A very similar version, by Coverdale, appeared in 1535. Matthew's Bible, made from the works of Tyndale and Coverdale, was the first Bible to be printed in England in 1537.*
- The Great Bible, *commissioned by the king in 1539, became the first official Bible.*
- The Geneva Bible *(1560) was translated by English Protestants in exile during the reign of Queen Mary and was printed in England when Queen Elizabeth I acceded to the throne. It is a very accurate text, in simple English, and the tone is generally more passionate than in the preceding translations. It was revised between 1561 and 1568 and the resulting Bishops' Bible became the official Bible under Queen Elizabeth.*
- The Douai-Rheims Bible *was published in 1609-10 by Catholic priests in exile. It aimed at correcting the mistakes and corruptions of the Protestant versions and became the Bible of the Catholics for over a century.*
- The Authorized Version *(1611) was commissioned by King James I. The scholars who worked on it consulted preceding translations as well as the original texts in order to obtain as faithful a version as possible. King James's Bible is still the most widely read version nowadays.*

Compare the following versions of Psalm XXIII:

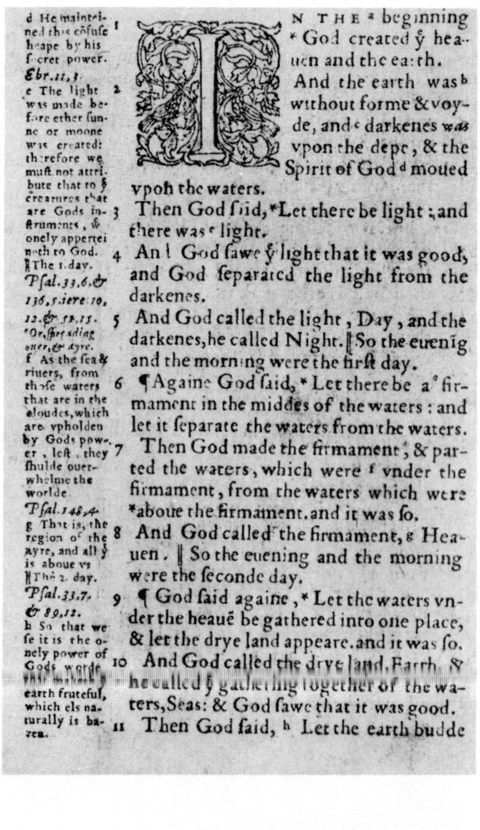

1 IN THE a beginning
* God created ẏ hea-
uen and the earth.
2 And the earth was b
without forme & voy-
de, and c darkenes *was*
vpon the depe, & the
Spirit of God d moued
vpoñ the waters.
3 Then God said, *Let there be light: and
there was e light.
4 And God sawe ẏ light that it was good,
and God separated the light from the
darkenes.
5 And God called the light, Day, and the
darkenes, he called Night. ‖ So the euenĩg
and the morning were the first day.
6 ¶ Againe God said, * Let there be a ° fir-
mament in the middes of the waters: and
let it separate the waters from the waters.
7 Then God made the firmament, & par-
ted the waters, which were f vnder the
firmament, from the waters which were
*aboue the firmament. and it was so.
8 And God called the firmament, g Hea-
uen. ‖ So the euening and the morning
were the seconde day.
9 ¶ God said againe, * Let the waters vn-
der the heauẽ be gathered into one place,
& let the drye land appeare. and it was so.
10 And God called the drye land, Earth, &
he called ẏ gathering together of the wa-
ters, Seas: & God sawe that it was good.
11 Then God said, h Let the earth budde

d He mainteined this cõfuse heape by his secret power.
Ebr. 11, 3.
e The light was made before ether sunne or moone was created: therefore we must not attribute that to ẏ creatures that are Gods instruments, ẇ onely apperteineth to God.
‖ The 1. day.
Psal. 33, 6. & 136, 5. iere. 10, 12. & 51, 15.
° *Or, spreading ouer, & ayre.*
f As the sea & riuers, from those waters that are in the cloudes, which are vpholden by Gods power, lest they shulde ouerwhelme the worlde.
Psal. 148, 4.
g That is, the region of the ayre, and all ẏ is aboue vs
‖ The 2. day.
Psal. 33, 7. & 89, 12.
h So that we se it is the onely power of Gods worde that maketh ẏ earth fruteful, which els naturally is barren.

From the first edition of the Geneva Bible.
British Museum. Ph. Hachette/Landin.

Matthew's Bible, 1537

PSALM XXIII, PSALM OF DAVID

The Lord is my shepherd I can want nothing.
He feedeth me in a green pasture and leadeth me to a fresh water.
He quickeneth my soul and bringeth me forth in the way of righteousness for his names sake.
Though I should walk now in the valley of the shadow of death yet I fear no evil for thou art with me: thy staff and thy sheephook comfort me.
Thou preparest a table before me against mine enemies: thou anointest my head with oil, and fillest my cup full.
Oh let thy loving kindness and mercy follow me all the days of my life, that I may dwell in ye house of the Lord for ever.

The Great Bible, 1539

PSALM XXIII, PSALM OF DAVID

The Lord is my shepherd: therefore can I lack nothing. He shall feed me in a green pasture, and lead me forth beside the waters of comfort. He shall convert my soul, and bring me forth in the paths of righteousness for his names sake. Yea, though I walk through the valley of the shadow of death: I will fear no evil, for thou art with me: thy rod and thy staff comfort me. Thou shalt prepare a table before me against them that trouble me: thou hast anointed my head with oil, and my cup shall be full. But (thy) loving kindness and mercy shall follow me all the days of my life, and I will dwell in the house of the Lord for ever.

The Authorized version, 1611

PSALM XXIII, A PSALM OF DAVID.

The Lord is my shepherd; I shall not want.
2 He maketh me to lie down in green pastures: he leadeth me beside the still waters.
3 He restoreth my soul: he leadeth me in the paths of righteousness for his name's sake.
4 Yea, though I walk through the valley of the shadow of death, I will fear no evil: for thou *art* with me ; thy rod and thy staff they comfort me.
5 Thou preparest a table before me in the presence of mine enemies: thou anointest my head with oil; my cup runneth over.
6 Surely goodness and mercy shall follow me all the days of my life: and I will dwell in the house of the LORD for ever.

The metaphysical poet George Herbert (1593-1633) also wrote a version of Psalm XXIII:

The God of love my Shepherd is,
And he that doth me feed;
While he is mine and I am his,
What can I want or need?

He leads me to the tender grass,
Where I both feed and rest;
Then to the streams that gently pass:
In both I have the best.

Or if I stray, he doth convert,
And bring my mind in frame,
And all this not for my desert
But for his holy name.

Yea, in death's shady black abode
Well may I walk, not fear;
For thou art with me, and thy rod
To guide, thy staff to bear.

Nay, Thou dost make me sit and dine
Ev'n in my enemies' sight;
My head with oil, my cup with wine,
Runs over day and night.

Surely thy sweet and wondrous love
Shall measure all my days;
And, as it never shall remove,
So neither shall my praise.

The Temple, 1633.

Christopher MARLOWE 1564-1593

1564 *Born at Canterbury; his father was a shoemaker.*
1580-1587 *Corpus Christi College, Cambridge. Probably started to work for the government as a spy.*
1587 Tamburlaine *performed (pub. 1590). Settled in London where he met Nashe, Kyd, Chapman. Knew the London criminal fraternity well and kept working as a secret agent.*
1592 The Tragical History of Doctor Faustus *published.*
1593 *Stabbed to death during a quarrel. Many later accused him of treason and blasphemy.*
1594 *Publication of* Edward II *and* Dido Queen of Carthage *(the latter prepared for publication by Nashe).*
1598 *Publication of* Hero and Leander.
1633 The Jew of Malta *published.*

Often considered as cruel and intemperate, as a rebel against society and an atheist, Marlowe was one of the first professional playwrights. He belonged to the group of the "University Wits", young men (like Peele, Lodge and Nashe) who, at the Universities of Oxford and Cambridge, had started writing drama in order to make a living. Kyd, Shakespeare and Ben Jonson later joined their circle.

The themes of ambition and the rise to power, recurrent in the plays of Marlowe, are typical of the Renaissance, of the discovery of the new fields, material and intellectual, open to man. Marlowe's heroes always yield to temptation, they are always lured away to destruction by Satan: Tamburlaine, the conqueror, rises to domination through violence and egoism; in Faustus, *the hero's passion is forbidden knowledge; Barabas, in* The Jew of Malta *craves for wealth.*

Marlowe's plays are striking for the passion and energy of their characters, for the emotional power of many of the scenes, especially the soliloquies. This is underlined by rich imagery and free and vigorous use of blank verse – Marlowe's "mighty line".

The Tragical History of Doctor Faustus (1592)

In accordance with the terms of his compact with Satan, Faustus has had all he wanted for twenty-four years. They have elapsed and the time has now come for him to surrender his soul to the Devil.

(The clock strikes eleven.) Ah, Faustus,
Now hast thou but one bare hour to live,
And then thou must be damned perpetually!
Stand still, you ever-moving spheres of heaven,
That time may cease, and midnight never come:
Fair Nature's eye, rise, rise again, and make
Perpetual day; or let this hour be but
A year, a month, a week, a natural day[1]
That Faustus may repent and save his soul!
O lente, lente, currite, noctis equi![2]
The stars move still, time runs, the clock will strike,
The devil will come, and Faustus must be damn'd.
O I'll leap up to my God! – Who pulls me down? –
See, see, where Christ's blood streams in the firmament!
One drop would save my soul, half a drop: Ah! my Christ! –
Ah, rend not my heart for naming of my Christ!
Yet will I call on him: O spare me, Lucifer! –
Where is it now? 'tis gone: and see, where God
Stretcheth out his arm, and bends his ireful brows!
Mountains and hills, come, come, and fall on me,
And hide me from the heavy wrath of God!
No, no!

Then will I headlong run into the earth:
Earth, gape! O, no, it will not harbour me!
You stars that reigned at my nativity,
Whose influence hath allotted death and hell,
Now draw up Faustus, like a foggy mist,
Into the entrails of yon labouring clouds
That when you vomit forth into the air,
My limbs may issue from your smoky mouths,
So my soul may but ascend to heaven! *(The clock strikes.)*
Ah! half the hour is past! 'twill all be past anon.
O God,
If Thou wilt not have mercy on my soul,
Yet for Christ's sake, whose blood hath ransom'd me,
Impose some end to my incessant pain;
Let Faustus live in hell a thousand years,
A hundred thousand, and at last be sav'd!
O no end is limited to damned souls!
Why wert thou not a creature wanting soul?
Or why is this immortal that thou hast?
Ah, Pythagoras' metempsychosis[3], were that true,
This soul should fly from me, and I be chang'd
Into some brutish beast! All beasts are happy,
For, when they die,
Their souls are soon dissolv'd in elements;
But mine must live still to be plagu'd in hell.
Curs'd be the parents that engender'd me!
No, Faustus, curse thyself, curse Lucifer
That hath depriv'd thee of the joys of Heaven. *(The clock strikes twelve.)*
O it strikes, it strikes! Now, body, turn to air,
Or Lucifer will bear thee quick[4] to hell! *(Thunder and lightning.)*
O soul, be chang'd into little water-drops,
And fall into the ocean, ne'er to be found! *(Enter devils.)*
My God, my God, look not so fierce on me!
Adders and serpents, let me breathe a while!
Ugly hell, gape not! Come not, Lucifer!
I'll burn my books! – Ah, Mephistopheles! *(Exeunt devils with Faustus.)*

Scene 17.

1. *a natural day*: a day of ordinary length – 2. *O lente, lente, currite noctis equi*: O run slowly, slowly, horses of the night (Ovid, *Amores*, I, XII, 40.) – 3. *Pythagoras' metempsychosis*: according to Pythagoras, the soul was transferred to another creature after death – 4. *quick*: alive.

The Faustian legend also inspired Byron in his dramatic poem Manfred *(1817).*
Compare Faustus's soliloquy with the last scene of Manfred. *(Manfred has tried to forget a mysterious past crime but cannot find oblivion. When the demons come to fetch him, he defies them.)*

SPIRIT. Mortal! thine hour is come – Away! I say.
MANFRED. I knew, and know my hour is come, but not
To render up my soul to such as thee:
Away! I'll die as I have lived – alone.
SPIRIT. Then I must summon up my brethren. – Rise!
(Other Spirits rise up)
ABBOT. Avaunt! ye evil ones! – Avaunt! I say, –
Ye have no power where piety hath power,
And I do charge ye in the name –
SPIRIT. Old man!
We know ourselves, our mission, and thine order;
Waste not thy holy words on idle uses,
It were in vain: this man is forfeited.
Once more I summon him – Away! away!
MANFRED. I do defy ye, – though I feel my soul
Is ebbing from me, yet I do defy ye;
Nor will I hence, while I have earthly breath

To breathe my scorn upon ye – earthly strength
To wrestle, though with spirits; what ye take
Shall be ta'en limb by limb.
SPIRIT. Reluctant mortal!
Is this the Magian who would so pervade
The world invisible, and make himself
Almost our equal? – Can it be that thou
Art thus in love with life? the very life
Which made thee wretched!
MANFRED. Thou false fiend, thou liest!
My life is in its last hour, – *that* I know,
Nor would redeem a moment of that hour.
I do not combat against death, but thee
And thy surrounding angels; my past power
Was purchased by no compact with thy crew,
But by superior science – penance – daring –
And length of watching – strength of mind – and skill
In knowledge of our fathers – when the earth
Saw men and spirits walking side by side
And gave ye no supremacy: I stand
Upon my strength – I do defy – deny –
Spurn back, and scorn ye! –
SPIRIT. But thy many crimes
Have made thee –
MANFRED. What are they to such as thee?
Must crimes be punished but by other crimes,
And greater criminals? – Back to thy hell!
Thou hast no power upon me, *that* I feel;
Thou never shalt possess me, *that* I know:
What I have done is done; I bear within
A torture which could nothing gain from thine:
The mind which is immortal makes itself
Requital for its good or evil thoughts,
Is its own origin of ill and end,
And its own place and time – its innate sense,
When stripp'd of this mortality, derives
No colour from the fleeting things without,
But is absorbed in sufferance or in joy,
Born from the knowledge of its own desert.
Thou didst not tempt me, and thou couldst not tempt me;
I have not been thy dupe nor am thy prey –
But was my own destroyer, and will be
My own hereafter – Back, ye baffled fiends!
The hand of death is on me – but not yours!
(The Demons disappear.)
ABBOT. Alas! how pale thou art – thy lips are white –
And thy breast heaves – and in thy gasping throat
The accents rattle. Give thy prayers to Heaven –
Pray – albeit but in thought, – but die not thus.
MANFRED. 'Tis over – my dull eyes can fix thee not;
But all things swim around me, and the earth
Heaves as it were beneath me. Fare thee well –
Give me thy hand.
ABBOT. Cold – cold – even to the heart –
But yet one prayer – Alas! how fares it with thee?
MANFRED. Old man! 'tis not so difficult to die.
(MANFRED *expires.*)
ABBOT. He's gone – his soul hath ta'en its earthless flight –
Whither? I dread to think – but he is gone.

Marlowe's Dr Faustus: a woodcut, *1636.*
Mansell Collection.

John Martin: Manfred on the Jungfrau, *1837,*
Birmingham Museums and Art Gallery, Birmingham.

John Martin (1789-1854) specialized in paintings of doom and holocaust and in romantic illustrations of the Bible, Milton and fairy tales. His best paintings show grandiose, awe-inspiring or supernatural landscapes emphasizing the loneliness and quest of man.

Cf. Versification p. 7; Tragedy, p. 23; The Elizabethan stage v. the Picture stage, p. 22.

William SHAKESPEARE 1564-1616

1564 *Born at Stratford-upon-Avon.*
1582 *Married Anne Hathaway.*
1583-1585 *Birth of his three children.*
1591-1592* Henry VI *(1,2,3);* The Comedy of Errors, Richard III; The Sonnets*(?).*
1593-1594 *Joined in creating the Lord Chamberlain's Company of actors.* Venus and Adonis; The Rape of Lucrece; Titus Andronicus; The Taming of the Shrew; The Two Gentlemen of Verona; Love's Labour's Lost; Romeo and Juliet.
1595 Richard II; A Midsummer Night's Dream.
1596 King John; The Merchant of Venice.
1597 *Bought New Place in Stratford.* Henry IV *(1,2).*
1598 *Acted in Ben Jonson's* Every Man in his Humour. Much Ado About Nothing.
1599-1600 *Opening of the Globe Theatre.* Henry V; As You Like It; Julius Caesar; Twelfth Night.
1601 Richard II *performed just before the rebellion of Essex.* The Merry Wives of Windsor; Hamlet, Troilus and Cressida.
1603 *Shakespeare's Company became the King's Men.* All's Well that Ends Well.
1604 Measure for Measure; Othello.
1605 King Lear; Macbeth.
1607 Antony and Cleopatra.
1608 *The Blackfriars Theatre acquired by the King's Men.* Coriolanus; Timon of Athens; Pericles.
1609 Cymbeline.
1610 *Retired to Stratford.* The Winter's Tale.
1611 The Tempest.
1612 Henry VIII.
1613 *Globe Theatre burnt down.*
1616 *Died in Stratford.*
1623 *First Folio edition of Shakespeare's plays.*

* *The dates of the plays are those proposed by Sir E. Chambers in his* William Shakespeare: A Study of Facts and Problems, *1930.*

Though the classification is often arbitrary, it is common to divide Shakespeare's works into several groups:

The Comedies

Most of Shakespeare's romantic comedies were written early in his life. They are light plays, dealing with the theme of love, and making use of such devices as mistaken identities (e.g. in The Comedy of Errors*) and disguise (e.g. in* The Two Gentlemen of Verona*) – often a woman dressed as a man – enhanced at the time by the fact that women's parts were acted by men. The comic effects are based on practical jokes and farcical scenes (as in* The Taming of the Shrew*) as well as on wit and puns. The plots are often intricate.*

But a change of tone can be felt in Shakespeare's later comedies, written after 1598 (e.g. Much Ado about Nothing, As You Like It, Twelfth Night*). Even though some boisterousness remains (Falstaff in* The Merry Wives of Windsor *or Sir Toby Belch and Sir Andrew Aguecheek in* Twelfth Night*), they are characterized by the intrusion of fancy and romance, of meditation and melancholy. The themes of fickle love, of illusion and self-deception appear, announcing the tragedies to come. This is reflected in the character of the clown (Touchstone in* As You Like It, *Feste in* Twelfth Night*) with his distant, disillusioned and humorous look at life.*

As often with Shakespeare, the plays show a blend of realism with a fanciful or fairy-like atmosphere, such as the moonlight madness and the fairies of A Midsummer Night's Dream, *or the enchanted scenes of Illyria and the Forest of Arden.*

Some of Shakespeare's comedies remain apart, however. The Merchant of Venice *has a more complex plot and deals with traditional antisemitism, greed, and a love story. The more serious theme of justice and mercy in* Measure for Measure *is typical of Shakespeare's last comedies.*

The Histories

Though Shakespeare's first and last plays were history plays (Henry VI, Henry VIII)*, most of his histories were written in the middle of his career, between 1595 and 1600. Such plays were not new. Their theme was indeed topical at a time when fear of rebellion prevailed in England (the revolt of Essex took place in 1601) and the Elizabethan playwrights were usually on the side of order and authority.*

Shakespeare's main history plays (Richard III, Richard II, Henry IV, Henry V*) tell the story of the rise and fall of the kings who preceded the Tudor dynasty. "The royal office is assumed to be divinely instituted, the necessary guarantee of order in a state [illegible] and [illegible] conceived, the political thought expressed in these plays combines the fervent nationalism of the day, fostered for practical ends by the ruling dynasty, with sacramental notions of monarchy..." (D.*

Traversi). Their aim is to show the danger of division inside the kingdom, since it leads to rebellion and usurpation; and the disastrous consequences of weak governments and lack of authority. After the weak king, Richard II, Richard III, a cruel usurper and the inheritor of Machiavelli, the cycle ends when authority and legitimacy combine in the person of Henry V.

In Henry IV, *the comic character of Falstaff, a braggart and a coward only interested in women and drink, overshadows the rest of the play.*

Though they do not really belong to this category, most of the so-called "Roman plays" (e.g. Julius Caesar*) stress the same need for order.*

The Tragedies

Shakespeare's great tragedies (Hamlet, Othello, King Lear, Macbeth, Timon of Athens) *were written between 1601 and 1608, during his period of maturity. They are sombre plays that reflect disillusion and often bitterness. In his* Shakespearean Tragedy, *A.C. Bradley defines Shakespeare's tragic heroes as "conspicuous persons", "of high degree", led to death by suffering and calamity. But "the calamities and catastrophe follow inevitably from the deeds of men and (...) the main source of these deeds is character". These heroes are always endowed with an overwhelming passion (jealousy in the case of Othello, ambition in that of Macbeth) which, after moral conflicts, is always fatal to them: "poetic justice" is the rule and moral order is finally restored on all levels. For the deeds of the characters always reverberate on a cosmic plane. Killing goes against nature and the whole universe reacts against it. Hence the upheaval and chaos (the storm in* King Lear, *the strange and unheard of events in* Macbeth*) that accompany tragic deeds and find their counterparts in man himself who ends up distorted and abnormal (e.g. Lear's madness, Lady Macbeth's sleepwalking).*

Most of all, "we should regard each play as a visionary whole, close-knit in personification, atmospheric suggestion, and direct poetic-symbolism" (W. Knight), which is best achieved through a rich pattern of symbolic imagery.

Even the darkest plays contain moments of humour and comedy, comic relief which enhances the tragedy to come or lessens the tension (e.g. the old nurse in Romeo and Juliet, *the gravediggers in* Hamlet, *or the fools).*

The Last Plays

Written after 1608, around the time when Shakespeare retired to Stratford, Pericles, Cymbeline, The Winter's Tale *and* The Tempest *form a coherent group. They are romances, far more lyrical and serene than the earlier plays. Behind the theme of faithfulness in* Cymbeline, *behind the pastoral freshness of* The Winter's Tale, *the magic of Prospero and the opposition between the spiritual (Ariel) and the savage (Caliban) in* The Tempest, *lies a common pattern. These plays all deal with reconciliation and the righting of wrongs. Their starting point is always evil, division, a lack of harmony, usually embodied by the loss of a child, Marina in* Pericles, *Perdita in* The Winter's Tale. *But torment and remorse lead to reunion and forgiveness. The plays oppose the corruption of civilisation to generosity and love. Their setting is pastoral and a sense of unreality pervades them, partly due to the use of supernatural elements and improbable events.*

The Poems

Both Venus and Adonis *and* The Rape of Lucrece *are long narrative poems. The former, Shakespeare's first work, follows the erotic fashion of the time and describes with piquancy the wooing of Adonis. As for* The Rape of Lucrece, *it is a fairly heavy rhetorical poem, relating the conflict between lust and conscience in Tarquin's mind and the despair of Lucrece.*

The Sonnets, *addressed partly to a fair young man, partly to a dark lady, deal with the themes of friendship, love, time and morality. They show more originality and depth than most of the sonnets in vogue at the time and even include a satire of Petrarchism (cf p. 44).*

Richard II (1595)

Under the government of Richard II, England has fallen into a "shameful" condition, so that authority and allegiance have lost their meaning. When John of Gaunt dies, Richard seizes the estates that rightly belong to Gaunt's son, Bolingbroke, now in exile, and therefore violates his legitimate right of succession. Bolingbroke comes back to claim his land and leads a rebellion, with the help of Northumberland, making Richard prisoner in Flint Castle. The following scene takes place in the garden of the Duke of York (Richard's uncle).

(Enter a Gardener and two Servants).
GARDENER. Go, bind thou up yon dangling apricocks,
Which, like unruly children, make their sire
Stoop with oppression of their prodigal weight:
Give some supportance to the bending twigs,
Go thou, and like an executioner,

Cut off the heads of too fast growing sprays,
That look too lofty in our commonwealth:
All must be even in our government.
You thus employ'd, I will go root away
The noisome weeds, that without profit suck
The soil's fertility from wholesome flowers.
FIRST SERVANT. Why should we in the compass of a pale[1]
Keep law and form and due proportion,
Showing, as in a model, our firm estate,
When our sea-walled garden, the whole land,
Is full of weeds, her fairest flowers chok'd up,
Her fruit-trees all unprun'd, her hedges ruin'd,
Her knots[2] disorder'd, and her wholesome herbs
Swarming with caterpillars?
GARD. Hold thy peace:
He that hath suffer'd[3] this disorder'd spring
Hath now himself met with the fall of leaf;
The weeds that his broad-spreading leaves did shelter,
That seem'd in eating him[4] to hold him up,
Are pluck'd up root and all by Bolingbroke:
I mean the Earl of Wiltshire, Bushy, Green[5].
FIRST SERVANT. What! are they dead?
GARD. They are; and Bolingbroke
Hath seiz'd the wasteful king. O! what pity is it
That he hath not so trimm'd and dress'd his land
As we this garden. We at time of year[6]
Do wound the bark, the skin of our fruit-trees,
Lest, being over-proud[7] with sap and blood,
With too much riches it confound itself:
Had he done so to great and growing men,
They might have liv'd to bear and he to taste
Their fruits of duty: surperfluous branches
We lop away that bearing[8] boughs may live:
Had he done so, himself had borne the crown,
Which waste of idle hours hath quite thrown down.
FIRST SERVANT. What! think you then the king shall be depos'd?
GARD. Depress'd[9] he is already, and depos'd
'Tis doubt[10] he will be: letters came last night
To a dear friend of the good Duke of York's,
That tell black tidings.

Act III, Scene 4.

1. *a pale*: a paling, a fence – 2. *knots*: flowerbeds forming a complex pattern – 3. *suffered*: allowed – 4. *in eating him*: while eating him – 5. *Bushy, Green*: two of Richard's favourites, executed by Bolingbroke – 6. *at time of year*: when the season comes for it – 7. *over-proud*: too rich – 8. *bearing*: fruitful – 9. *depressed*: fallen low – 10. *'T'is doubt*: 't'is feared.

The "Grand Mechanism" in Shakespeare's historical tragedies:

Each of the great historical tragedies begins with a struggle for the throne, or for its consolidation. Each ends with the monarch's death and a new coronation. In each of the Histories the legitimate ruler drags behind him a long chain of crimes. He has rejected the feudal lords who helped him to reach for the crown; he murders, first, his enemies, then his former allies; he executes possible successors and pretenders to the crown. But he has not been able to execute them all. From banishment a young prince returns – the son, grandson, or brother of those murdered – to defend the violated law. The rejected lords gather round him, he personifies the hope for a new order and justice. But every step to power continues to be marked by murder, violence, treachery. And so, when the new prince finds himself near the throne, he drags behind him a chain of crimes as long as that of the until now legitimate ruler. When he assumes the crown, he will be just as hated as his predecessor. He has killed enemies, now he will kill former allies. And a new pretender appears in the name of violated justice. The wheel has turned full circle. A new chapter opens. A new historical tragedy. (...)

There are no good and bad kings; there are only kings on different steps of the same stairs. The names of the kings may change, but it is always a Henry who pushed a Richard down, or the other way round. Shakespeare's Histories are *dramatis personae* of the Grand Mechanism.

But what is this Grand Mechanism which starts operating at the foot of the throne and to which the whole kingdom is subjected? A mechanism whose cog-wheels are both great lords and hired assassins; a mechanism which forces people to violence, cruelty and treason; which constantly claims new victims? A mechanism according to whose laws the road to power is at the same time the way to death? This Grand Mechanism is for Shakespeare the order of history, in which the King is the Lord's Anointed.

"Not all the water in the rough rude sea
Can wash the balm from an anointed king;
The breath of worldly men cannot depose
The deputy elected by the Lord".

(*Richard II*, III, 2)

The sun circles round the earth, and with it the spheres, planets and stars all arranged in a hierarchic order. There is in the universe an order of the elements, an order of angelic choirs, and a corresponding order of rank on earth. There are superiors and vassals of the vassals. Royal power comes from God, and all power on earth is merely a reflection of the power wielded by the King.

"The heavens themselves, the planets, and this centre,
Observe degree, priority, and place,
Insisture, course, proportion, season, form,
Office and custom, in all line of order:
And therefore is the glorious planet Sol
In noble eminence enthron'd and sphered
Amidst the other; whose med'cinable eye
Corrects the ill aspects of planets evil,
And posts, like the commandment of a king,
Sans check, to good and bad: but when the planets,
In evil mixture, to disorder wander,
What plagues, and what portents, what mutiny,
What raging of the sea, shaking of earth,
Commotion in the winds, frights, changes, horrors,
Divert and crack, rend and deracinate
The unity and married calm of states
Quite from their fixture! O, when degree is shaked,
Which is the ladder to all high designs,
The enterprise is sick!"

(*Troilus and Cressida*, I, 3)

Richard II is a tragedy of dethronement. It is, however, not just Richard's dethronement, but that of the King. Dethronement, in fact, of the idea of regal power. We have seen how Shakespeare equalled a prince of royal blood – the King's brother – with a hired assassin. In *Richard II*, the Lord's Anointed, the King deprived of his crown, becomes a mere mortal. In the first acts of the tragedy the King was compared to the sun: others had to lower their eyes when faced with his dazzling Majesty. Now the sun has been hurled down from its orbit, and with it the entire order of the universe.

Jan Kott, *Shakespeare, Our Contemporary.*

Cf. Versification, p. 7. The Elizabethan stage v. The Picture Stage, p. 22; Figurative language p. 31.

Romeo and Juliet (1594?)

Juliet has secretly been married to Romeo and is awaiting him for their wedding-night together. Only the audience knows, however, that Romeo has just killed Tybalt, a Capulet, and has been banished.

**JULIET. Gallop apace[1], you fiery-footed steeds[2],
Towards Phoebus' lodging; such a wagoner
As Phaëton would whip you to the west,
And bring in cloudy night immediately.
Spread thy close[3] curtain, love-performing night[4],
That runaways' eyes may wink, and Romeo
Leap to these arms, untalked of and unseen.
Lovers can see to do their amorous rites
By their own beauties; or if love be blind,
It best agrees with night. Come civil[5] night,
Thou sober-suited matron all in black,
And learn[6] me how to lose a winning match[7],
Played for a pair of stainless maidenhoods.**

Hood my unmanned[8] blood, bating[9] in my cheeks,
With thy black mantle, till strange[10] love grow bold,
Think true love acted[11] simple modesty.
Come night, come Romeo, come thou day in night;
For thou wilt lie upon the wings of night,
Whiter than snow upon a raven's back.
Come gentle night, come loving black-browed night,
Give me my Romeo, and when he shall die,
Take him and cut him out in little stars,
And he will make the face of heaven so fine
That all the world will be in love with night
And pay no worship to the garish sun.
O I have bought the mansion of a love,
But not possessed it, and, though I am sold,
Not yet enjoyed. So tedious is this day
As is the night before some festival
To an impatient child that hath new robes
And may not wear them. *Act III, Scene 2.*

1. *apace*: quickly – 2. *steeds*: horses (drawing the chariot of Phoebus, the god of the sun) – 3. *close*: secret – 4. *love-performing night*: night made for love – 5. *civil*: serious – 6. *learn*: teach – 7. *lose a winning match*: by losing her virginity she will gain a husband (this line and the following were often omitted in Victorian times lest they should shock the audience.) – 8. *unmanned*: not trained (in hawking, one trained falcons by hooding them) – 9. *bating*: fluttering (for a falcon) – 10. *strange*: timid – 11. *true love acted*: the consummation of true love.

Shakespeare's imagery in Romeo and Juliet:

In *Romeo and Juliet* the beauty and ardour of young love are seen by Shakespeare as the irradiating glory of sunlight and starlight in a dark world. The dominating image is *light,* every form and manifestation of it: the sun, moon, stars, fire, lightning, the flash of gunpowder, and the reflected light of beauty and of love; while by contrast we have night, darkness, clouds, rain, mist and smoke.

Each of the lovers thinks of the other as light; Romeo's overpowering impression when he first catches sight of Juliet on the fateful evening at the Capulets' ball is seen in his exclamation,

"O, she doth teach the torches to burn bright!
It seems she hangs upon the cheek of night
Like a rich jewel in an Ethiop's ear."

To Juliet, Romeo is "day in night"; to Romeo, Juliet is the sun rising from the east, and when they soar to love's ecstasy, each alike pictures the other as stars in heaven, shedding such brightness as puts to shame the heavenly bodies themselves.

The intensity of feeling in both lovers purges even the most highly affected and euphuistic conceits of their artificiality, and transforms them into the exquisite and passionate expression of love's rhapsody.

Thus Romeo plays with the old conceit that two of the fairest stars in heaven, having some business on earth, have entreated Juliet's eyes to take their place till they return, and he conjectures,

"What if her eyes were there, they in her head?"

If so,

"The brightness of her cheek would shame those stars,
As daylight doth a lamp;"

and then comes the rush of feeling, the overpowering realisation and immortal expression of the transforming glory of love:

"her eyes in heaven
Would through the airy region stream so bright
That birds would sing and think it were not night."

And Juliet, in her invocation to night, using an even more extravagant conceit, such as Cowley or Cleveland at his wildest never exceeded, transmutes it into the perfect and natural expression of a girl whose lover to her not only radiates light, but is, indeed, very light itself:

"Give me my Romeo; and, when he shall die,
Take him and cut him out in little stars,
And he will make the face of heaven so fine,
That all the world will be in love with night,
And pay no worship to the garish sun."

Love is described by Romeo, before he knows what it really is, as

"a smoke raised with the fume of sighs;
Being purged, a fire sparkling in lovers' eyes;"

and the messengers of love are pictured by Juliet, when she is chafing under the nurse's delay, as one of the most exquisite effects in nature, seen especially on the English hills in spring the swift, magical, transforming power of light:

"love's heralds [she cries] should be thoughts,
Which ten times faster glide than the sun's beams,

Driving back shadows over louring hills." (...)

In addition to this more definite symbolic imagery, we find that radiant light, sunshine, starlight, moonbeams, sunrise and sunset, the sparkle of fire, a meteor, candles, torches, quick-coming darkness, clouds, mist, rain and night, form a pictorial background, or running accompaniment, to the play, which augments unconsciously in us this same sensation.

C. Spurgeon, *Shakespeare's Imagery.* *Cambridge University Press.*

Cf. Versification, p. 7. The Elizabethan stage v. the Picture stage, p. 22; Figurative language. p. 31.

The Court Fool, or King's Jester, is a common character in Shakesperian drama. Study his function and compare the treatment of the fool and that of madness in the following excerpts from Twelfth Night *&* King Lear :

Twelfth Night (1599-1600)

Viola, disguised as Cesario, has become Duke Orsino's page and fallen in love with her master. He has sent him – or rather her – to press his suit with Lady Olivia whom he loves. In Olivia's house, Viola meets Feste, the clown.

(Enter Viola, and Clown playing on pipe and tabor.)

VIOLA. Save thee, friend, and thy music! Dost thou live by thy tabor[1]?

CLOWN. No, sir, I live by the church[2].

VIOLA. Art thou a churchman?

CLOWN. No such matter, sir. I do live by the church, for I do live at my house, and my house house doth stand by the church.

VIOLA. So thou may'st say the king lies by[3] a beggar, if a beggar dwell near him; or the church stands by thy tabor[4], if thy tabor stand by the church.

CLOWN. You have said, sir. To see this age! A sentence is but a chev'ril[5] glove to a good wit – how quickly the wrong side may be turned outward!

VIOLA. Nay, that's certain: they that dally nicely with words may quickly make them wanton[6].

CLOWN. I would therefore my sister had had no name, sir.

VIOLA. Why, man?

CLOWN. Why, sir, her name's a word, and to dally with that word might make my sister wanton. But indeed, words are very rascals, since bonds[7] disgraced them.

VIOLA. Thy reason, man?

CLOWN. Troth, sir, I can yield you none without words, and words are grown so false, I am loath to prove reason with them.

VIOLA. I warrant thou art a merry fellow, and car'st for nothing.

CLOWN. Not so, sir, I do care for something; but in my conscience, sir, I do not care for you: if that be to care for nothing, sir, I would it would make you invisible.

VIOLA. Art not thou the Lady Olivia's fool?

CLOWN. No indeed sir, the Lady Olivia has no folly. She will keep no fool, sir, till she be married, and fools are as like husbands as pilchards are to herrings, the husband's the bigger. I am indeed not her fool, but her corrupter of words.

VIOLA. I saw thee late at the Count Orsino's.

CLOWN. Foolery, sir, does walk about the orb like the sun, it shines everywhere. I would be sorry, sir, but the fool should be as oft with your master as with my mistress: I think I saw your wisdom there.

VIOLA. Nay, and thou pass upon me[8], I'll no more with thee. Hold, there's expenses for thee. *(Giving a coin.)*

CLOWN. Now Jove, in his next commodity[9] of hair, send thee a beard!

VIOLA. By my troth, I'll tell thee, I am almost sick for one, *(Aside)* though I would not have it grow on my chin. – Is thy lady within?

CLOWN. Would not a pair of these[10] have bred, sir?

VIOLA. Yes, being kept together, and put to use.

CLOWN. I would play Lord Pandarus of Phrygia[11], sir, to bring a Cressida to this Troilus.

VIOLA. I understand you, sir, 'tis well begged. *(Giving another coin.)*

CLOWN. The matter, I hope, is not great, sir, begging but a beggar: Cressida was a beggar[12]. My lady is within, sir. I will conster[13] to them whence you come; who you are and what you would are out of my welkin[14]. I might say element, but the word is overworn. *(Exit.)*

VIOLA. This fellow is wise enough to play the fool,
And to do that well, craves a kind of wit:
He must observe their mood on whom he jests,
The quality of persons, and the time,
And like the haggard[15], check at every feather
That comes before his eye. This is a practice
As full of labour as a wise man's art:
For folly that he wisely shows is fit;
But wise[16] men, folly-fall'n, quite taint their wit[17].

Act III, Scene 1.

1. *by thy tabor:* thanks to thy tabor – 2. *by the church:* near the church – 3. *lies by:* lies with – 4. *the church stands by thy tabor:* is supported (financially) by thy tabor – 5. *chev'ril:* kid leather – 6. *wanton:* equivocal or licentious – 7. *bond:* written promise – 8. *thou pass upon me:* you make a fool of me – 9. *commodity:* consignment (something that is sent) – 10. *a pair of these:* refers to the coins – 11. *Lord Pandarus of Phrygia:* Pandarus was a messenger between Cressida and Troilus – 12. *begging but a beggar: Cressida was a beggar:* you want to woo a beggar (Cressida was sometimes said to have become a beggar): it is no great matter – 13. *conster:* construe (explain) – 14. *welkin:* element – 15. *haggard:* hawk – 16. *wise:* considered as wise and sane – 17. *taint their wit:* cannot be considered as intelligent.

King Lear (1605)

Abandoned by the two daughters who he believed loved him, Lear has lost his reason.

(The storm continues. Enter Lear and Fool.)

LEAR. Blow, winds, and crack your cheeks! rage! blow!
You cataracts and hurricanoes, spout
Till you have drenched our steeples, drowned the cocks[1]!
You sulphurous and thought-executing[2] fires,
Vaunt-couriers[3] of oak-cleaving thunderbolts,
Singe my white head! And thou, all-shaking thunder,
Strike flat[4] the thick rotundity o'th' world,
Crack Nature's moulds, all germens[5] spill at once
That makes ingrateful man!
FOOL. O nuncle[6], court holy water[7] in a dry house is better than this rain-water out o' door. Good nuncle, in; ask thy daughters blessing! Here's a night pities neither wise men nor fools.
LEAR. Rumble thy bellyful[8]! Spit, fire! spout, rain!
Nor rain, wind, thunder, fire are my daughters.
I tax not you, you elements, with unkindness;
I never gave you kingdom, called you children;
You owe me no subscription[9]. Then let fall
Your horrible pleasure. Here I stand your slave,
A poor, infirm, weak, and despised old man.
But yet I call you servile ministers,
That will with two pernicious daughters join
Your high-engendered[10] battles 'gainst a head
So old and white as this. O, ho! 'tis foul!
FOOL. He that has a house to put's head in has a good head-piece[11].
The codpiece[12] that will house
Before the head has any,
The head and he shall louse:
So beggars marry many.
The man that makes his toe
What he his heart should make[13]

Shall of a corn[14] cry woe,
And turn his sleep to wake.
For there was never yet fair woman but she made mouths in a glass[15].

Act III, scene 2.

1. *cocks:* the weathercocks on the steeples – 2. *thought-executing:* executing the orders of Jupiter – 3. *vaunt-couriers:* heralds – 4. *strike flat:* flatten, by striking – 5. *germens:* seeds – 6. *nuncle:* uncle, the usual address of a fool to his superiors – 7. *court holy water:* flattery – 8. *Rumble thy bellyful:* Lear keeps addressing the thunder – 9. *subscription:* loyalty – 10. *high-engendered:* formed high above – 11. *head-piece:* protection for the head or wisdom – 12. *codpiece:* part of the male dress covering the crotch; the stanza means: the man who prefers making love to finding a shelter for his head will become a beggar (louse = have lice), beggars marry many since they make love to many – 13. *the man... make:* the man who gives importance to small things – 14. *corn:* an excrescence on the feet (if you pay too much attention to your toes, they will make you suffer) – 15. *made mouths in a glass:* made faces in a mirror.

Three views of the fool:

● By the gods above, is there anything that is better off than that class of men whom we generally call morons, fools, halfwits, and zanies – the most beautiful names I know of! You see, I am telling you what at first blush may seem silly and absurd but is true many times over. For first of all, these folk are free from all fear of death – and this fear, by Jove, is no piddling evil! They are free from tortures of conscience. They are not frightened by tales of ghosts, or scared to death by specters and goblins. They are not tormented by dread of impending evils, and they are not blown up with hope of future good. In short, they are not vexed by the thousand cares to which this life is subject. They do not feel shame or fear, they are not ambitious they do not envy, they do not love. And finally, if they should approach even more closely to the irrationality of dumb animals they would not sin, according to the writers of theology. I wish you would think over for me, you wise fool, how by night and by day your soul is torn by so many carking cares; I wish you would gather into one heap all the discommodities of your life: then you will begin to understand from how many evils I have delivered my fools. Remember also that they are continually merry, they play, sing, and laugh; and what is more, they bring to others, wherever they may come, pleasure, jesting, sport, and laughter, as if they were created, by a merciful dispensation of the gods, for this one purpose – to drive away the sadness of human life.

Erasmus, *The Praise of Folly.*

● From the first signs of Goneril's cruelty, the Fool is used as a chorus, pointing us to the absurdity of the situation. He is indeed an admirable chorus, increasing our pain by his emphasis on a humour which yet will not serve to merge the incompatible in a unity of laughter. He is not all wrong when he treats the situation as matter for a joke. Much here that is always regarded as essentially pathetic is not far from comedy.

Lear is mentally a child; in passion a titan. The absurdity of his every act at the beginning of his tragedy is contrasted with the dynamic fury which intermittently bursts out, flickers – then flames and finally gives us those grand apostrophes lifted from man's stage of earth to heaven's rain and fire and thunder:

"Blow, winds, and crack your cheeks! rage! blow!
You cataracts and hurricanoes, spout
Till you have drench'd our steeples, drown'd the cocks!"
(III,ii.I)

Two speeches of this passionate and unrestrained volume of Promethean curses are followed by:

"No, I will be the pattern of all patience;
I will say nothing." (III. ii. 37)

Again we are in touch with potential comedy: a slight shift of perspective, and the incident is rich with humour. A sense of self-directed humour would have saved Lear. It is a quality he absolutely lacks.

Herein lies the profound insight of the Fool: he sees the potentialities of comedy in Lear's behaviour.

G. Wilson Knight, *The Wheel of Fire.*
Methuen and Co.

● Buffoonery is a philosophy and a profession at the same time. Touchstone and Feste are professional clowns. They wear jesters'attire, and are in the service of the prince. They have not ceased to be Harlequins and are not above pantomime. But they do not produce the performance any more; they do not even take part in it, but just comment on it. That is why they are jeering and bitter. The position of a jester is ambiguous and abounds in internal contradictions, arising out of the discrepancy between profession and philosophy. The profession of a jester, like that of an intellectual, consists in providing entertainment. His philosophy demands of him that he tell the truth and abolish myths. The Fool in *King Lear* does not even have a name, he is just a Fool, pure Fool. But he is the first fool to be aware of the fool's position:

"FOOL. Prithee, nuncle, keep a schoolmaster that can teach thy fool to lie: I would fain learn to lie.

KING LEAR. An you lie, sirrah, we'll have you whipp'd.

FOOL. I marvel what kin thou and thy daughters are: they'll have me whipp'd for speaking true, thou'lt have me whipp'd for lying; and sometimes I am whipp'd for holding my peace. I had rather be any kind o'thing than a fool: and yet I would not be thee, nuncle; thou hast pared thy wit o'both sides, and left nothing i'th' middle." (I, 4)

A fool who has recognized himself for a fool, who has accepted the fact that he is only a jester in the service of the prince, ceases to be a clown. But the clown's philosophy is based on the assumption that every one is a fool: and the greatest fool is he who does not know he is a fool: the prince himself. That is why the clown has to make fools of others; otherwise he would not be a clown. The clown is subject to alienations because he is a clown, but at the same time he cannot accept the alienation; he rejects it when he becomes aware of it. The clown has the social position of the bastard, as described many times by Sartre. The bastard is a bastard for as long as he accepts his bastard's position and regards it as inevitable. The bastard ceases to be a bastard when he does not consider himself a bastard any more. But at this point the bastard must abolish the division into bastards and legitimate offspring. he then enters into opposition against the foundations of social order, or at least exposes them. Social pressures want to limit the Clown to his part of a clown, to pin the label "clown" on him. But he does not accept this part. On the contrary: he constantly pins that label on others:

"KING LEAR. Dost thou call me fool, boy?

FOOL. All thy other titles thou hast given away; that thou wast born with.

KENT. This is not altogether fool, my lord.

FOOL. No, faith, lords and great men will not let me; if I had a monopoly out, they would have part on't: and ladies too, they will not let me have all fool to myself; they'll be snatching." (I, 4)

This is the opening of the "clowns' play", performed on "Job's stage". In his very first scene, the Fool offers Lear his fool's cap. For buffoonery is not only a philosophy, it is also a kind of theatre. To us it is the most contemporary aspect of *King Lear*. Only it has to be seen and interpreted properly. For this reason one must reject all the romantic and naturalistic accessories; the opera and melodrama about the old man who, driven out by his daughters, wanders about bareheaded in a storm and goes mad as a result of his misfortunes. But, as in the case of Hamlet, there is method in this madness. Madness is in *King Lear* a philosophy, a conscious crossing over to the position of the Clown. Leszek Kolakowski writes:

"The Clown is he who, although moving in high society, is not part of it, and tells unpleasant things to everybody in it; he, who disputes everything regarded as evident. He would not be able to do all this, if he were part of that society himself; then he could at most be a drawing-room scandal-monger. The Clown must stand aside and observe good society from outside, in order to discover the non-evidence of evidence, the non-finality of its finality. At the same time he must move in good society in order to get to know its sacred cows, and have occasion to tell the unpleasant things (...) The philosophy of Clowns is the philosophy that in every epoch shows up as doubtful what has been regarded as most certain; it reveals contradictions inherent in what seems to have been proved by visual experience; it holds up to ridicule what seems obvious common sense, and discovers truth in the absurd. (...)"

Lear and Gloster are adherents of eschatology; they desperately believe in the existence of absolutes. They invoke the gods, believe in justice, appeal to laws of nature. They have fallen off "Macbeth's stage", but remain its prisoners. Only the Fool stands outside "Macbeth's stage", just as he has stood outside "Job's stage". He is looking on apart and does not follow any ideology. He rejects all appearances, of law, justice, moral order. He sees brute force, cruelty and lust. He has no illusions and does not seek consolation in the existence of natural or supernatural order, which provides for the punishment of evil and the reward of good. Lear, insisting on his fictitious majesty, seems ridiculous to him. All the more ridiculous because he does not see how ridiculous he is. But the Fool does not desert his ridiculous, degraded king, and accompanies him on his way to madness. The Fool knows that the only true madness is to recognize this world as rational. The feudal order is absurd and can be described only in terms of the absurd. The world stands upside down:

"When usurers tell their gold i'the field;
And bawds and whores do churches build;
Then shall the realm of Albion
Come to great confusion:
Then comes the time, who lives to see't,
That going shall be us'd with feet."

(III, 2)

Hamlet escaped into madness not only to confuse informers and deceive Claudius. Madness to him was also a philosophy, a criticism of pure reason, a great, ironic clearing of accounts with the world, which has left its orbit. The Fool adopts the language Hamlet used in the scenes in which he feigned madness. There is nothing left in it now of Greek and Roman rhetoric, so popular in the Renaissance; nothing left of the cold and noble Senecan indifference to inevitable destiny. Lear, Gloster, Kent, Albany, even Edmund, still use rhetoric. Fool's language is different. It abounds in biblical travesties and inverted medieval parables. One can find in it splendid baroque surrealist expressions, sudden leaps of imagination, condensations and epitomes, brutal, vulgar and scatological comparisons. His rhymes are like limericks. The Fool uses dialectics, paradox and an absurd kind of humour. His language is that of our modern grotesque. The same grotesque that exposes the absurdity of apparent reality and of the absolute by means of a great and universal *reductio ad absurdum.*

"KING LEAR. O me, my heart, my rising heart! – but, down.
FOOL. Cry to it, nuncle, as the cockney did to the eels when she put'em i'the paste alive; she knapp'd 'em o'the coxcombs with a stick, and cried, 'Down, wantons, down!' 'Twas her brother that, in pure kindness to his horse, butter'd his hay." (II, 4)

The Fool appears on the stage when Lear's fall is only beginning. He disappears by the end of Act III. His last words are: "And I'll go to bed at noon." He will not be seen or heard again. A clown is not needed any more. King Lear has gone through the school of clown's philosophy. When he meets Gloster for the last time, he will speak the Fool's language and look at "Macbeth's stage" the way the Fool has looked at it:

"They told me I was everything; 'tis a lie, – I am not ague-proof." (IV, 6.)

Jan Kott, *Shakespeare, Our Contemporary.*
ibid.

Cf. Versification, p. 7; The Elizabethan stage v. The Picture stage, p. 22; Comedy, p. 24; Tragedy, p. 23; Figurative language, p. 31.

Shakespearian production
from the Restoration to the beginning of the 20th century

The Restoration, the 18th century

For eighteen years in the middle of the seventeenth century England had no public theatres. They were closed in 1642 by a Parliamentary Ordinance, instigated by the Puritans, and not re-opened until, in 1660, Charles II was restored to the throne. Throughout all these years, then, the art of playwriting obviously languished. Where could new plays be performed? The result was that when theatre-going was again made possible, the managers had to have recourse to plays that were already in existence. Overnight Shakespeare was granted the pre-eminence that has never since been denied him. (...)

Shakespeare was in constant demand. Certain changes introduced by the Restoration theatre managers helped matters along. Charles II had an eye for pretty women, and he insisted on the French custom of having women's parts played, whenever a good actress could be found, by an actress rather than by a teen-age boy. New mechanical devices for scene-shifting, lighting, etc., were invented. Effects could be obtained that brought the plays into far greater focus than had ever been possible sixty years earlier.

But at the same time began the mania for re-writing Shakespeare. (...)

The famous three unities–the action of a play should deal with but a single incident, occurring within the space of twenty-four hours, and in but one place–were being much discussed. Shakespeare had to be brought more closely into the current taste, so said Thomas Shadwell, and he and John Dryden concocted a *Tempest* in which "order" was established by introducing a man who had never seen a woman, to balance Miranda's never having seen a man. Everybody had his hand in Shakespeare's pocket. Dryden again with his re-writing of *Troilus and Cressida* in 1679, Davenant with *Macbeth* in 1673, Otway with *Romeo and Juliet* (or *Caius Marius,* as he entitled it) in 1680, Shadwell with *Timon of Athens* in 1679. This rage for improving Shakespeare continued well into the eighteenth century. (...)

For instance, *Much Ado about Nothing* in 1737 became, with a few scenes lifted from *Twelfth Night* and *The Two Gentlemen of Verona,* a sentimental something called *The Universal Passion*; in 1723 *As You Like It* became *Love in a Forest,* in which Jaques marries Celia. With most of the tragedies considerable liberties were also taken. *Romeo and Juliet,* which had lain idle for a century or more, was revived in 1748 by Garrick, in whose hands it fared, all in all, not badly. Except for the abridgement of a few scenes he left the lines pretty much as Shakespeare wrote them. But the concluding scene he was not at all satisfied with: a golden opportunity for both the actor and the actress to show what they could do was recklessly wasted. He therefore inserted, after Romeo has taken the poison, about sixty new lines. Juliet wakes up, exclaiming, "Where am I? Defend me! " and presently adds, "Bless me! how cold it is! " She and the dying Romeo then discuss all their miseries in great details ("Fathers have flinty hearts, no tears can melt'em", etc.) until Romeo is final-

Henry Fuseli: Lady Macbeth Seizing the Daggers, *1812.*
The Tate Gallery, London.
Garrick and Mrs Pritchard acting in Macbeth.

Thomas Rowlandson (?): Mrs Siddons rehearsing in the Green Room with her father and John Henderson.
Huntington Library of Art, San Marino, Cal.

ly allowed to expire. This scene was vastly admired. A contemporary critic called it "exceedingly judicious; it gives an opportunity of working the pathos to its tenderest pitch". (...)

Before damning the tastelessness of both audiences and managers in holding so fast to these revisions it would be well to look, briefly, at two important elements in the eighteenth century theatre as a whole. First, plays were acted, in London as well as in all the country theatres, on a repertory system. This meant that different members of the same company could be seen from time to time in the same parts: Macklin as Shylock, and a month later Henderson. And, second, it was a century of great actors and actresses–as great, perhaps, as the English stage has ever known. To compare two eminent performers in the same part was a matter of endless fascination to the theatre-going public. Clearly, then, if different versions of the same play were made use of, a proper comparison was not possible. It may be noted that it was not until the nineteenth century, when more theatres came to be opened, and the increasing population of London transformed it from "the town" to a modern city, that the public lost interest in the old arrangements of their favourite plays and in the game of debating the relative merits of David Garrick and Spranger Barry.

C. Beecher-Hogan, *Shakespearian Production During the Restoration and 18th Century. The Shakespeare Exhibition, Official catalogue.*

The 19th century

Paradoxically the public interest in the plays brought about another, entirely different kind of mutilation. For the longer dramas, such as *Hamlet,* cutting had always been common and accepted practice; but in general it may be said that throughout the course of the eighteenth century these cuts had not been made in order to make room for scenic effects. The simple use of side-wings and back-cloths familiar in most ordinary productions on the stage of that period meant that the fictional localities could be altered easily and without waste of time. Indeed, it might almost be averred that, although the theatres of 1750 were vastly different from the theatres of 1600 and although they used scenery, the lamp – and candle – illumination which shone upon stage and auditorium alike, the presence of the "apron" jutting out towards the spectators and the fairly usual employment of stock scenes, kept the playhouse of Garrick close in spirit and procedure to the playhouse of Burbage.

All this was changed when the passion for historical accuracy and detailed realism, combined with a craving for spectacle, invaded the theatrical world. Once more, we can see this trend beginning to throw its shadow forwards during the latter part of the eighteenth century; but it was not until the following century got under way that the incubus assumed monstrous proportions. We can see it growing with the work of the designer William Capon, who, in 1809, painted for Kemble a number of sets "for general use in our old English plays"; it becomes larger when, fourteen years later, J. R. Planché created new, historically correct dresses for Charles Kemble's production of *King John,* setting forth in the playbill (almost as though that had been a doctoral dissertation) a list of "Authorities" extending from illuminated manuscripts to the works of learned historians; and, finally, when the introduction of illumination by gas and electricity provided the producers with a means of control utterly unknown before, and when, as a result, the theatre was rudely cut into two parts – the darkened auditorium and the brightly-lit stage – we are confronted by the enormous spectacular shows exhibited to the public by Charles Kean, Sir Henry Irving and Sir Herbert Beerbohm Tree. Such spectacular shows involved the making of heavy cuts in the acting texts, so that, while the words were now usually Shakespeare's, often little of Shakespeare was left. The historical costumes necessitated the abandonment of inappropriate lines and even, as in Keans's *Winter's Tale,* the violent alteration of the dramatist's Bohemia into a supposedly more congruous Bithynia; the processional and supernumerary scenes required time for their silent display; the historical settings, increasingly heavy and three-dimensional, and demanding lengthy waits between scene and

Tree's Henry VIII, *His Majesty's Theatre, 1911. Mander & Mitchenson Theatre Collection.*

scene, made imperative the ruthless lopping of numerous speeches and episodes. During the last years of the century, this native trend was further intensified when the troupe sponsored by George II, duke of Saxe-Meiningen, visited London in 1881. Archaeological correctness appeared in their productions as well, but what most attracted the admiration of spectators and managers alike was their expert handling of stage crowds. Their actors may not have been very distinguished in their treatment of the lines, but over their crowds everyone went into raptures. And, quite naturally, imitation followed.

Just as the latter years of the eighteenth century had anticipated what was to come in the following age, however, the final decade of the nineteenth century tentatively introduced a kind of counter-movement which has seen mighty growth within our own period. The Grieves and the Telbins, the Lloyds and the Gordons, the Stanfields and the Hawes Cravens, the Alma Tademas and the Ford Madox Browns, the whole long line of scenic artists who had provided the stage with their richly spectacular settings, were still dominant in spirit or in practice as the century reached its close; yet in the midst of their glory their tradition was being confronted by two forces destined to play a considerable part in the years soon to come. The first of these forces was that symbolised in the work of Gordon Craig, an attempt to cast aside all the historical accuracies, all the dazzlingly colourful spectacular shows, all the animated and variegated crowd scenes, and to substitute in their place something simple and vast, appealing to the imagination instead of merely to the eyes, and, as it were, offering what might be styled a ritualistic approach rather than one speciously realistic. Before the year 1900 Gordon Craig's ideals were known only to a few; but the second force had already gone a considerable way towards establishing itself by the time the century ended. From 1700 to 1800, the form of the Elizabethan theatre had been almost wholly forgotten, and it was not until the appearance of Edmund Malone's studies that some men began to realise the difference between the stage for which Shakespeare wrote and the stage of their own era.

Seeing the famous sketch of the Swan theatre, scholars eagerly applied themselves to a study of the Elizabethan playhouse structure and, even more importantly, turned to analyse Shakespeare's dramatic method in the light of their findings, and very soon William Poel, in 1894, had established his Elizabethan Stage Society, an organisation based on a series of philosophical principles – that all the cutting of texts necessitated by the historical – spectacular productions of the actor-managers was essentially wrong, that the music and meaning of Shakespeare's lines were of all-importance, and that only by the presentation of these lines on a bare stage, without breaks between scene and scene and without the distraction of scenery, could the poet-dramatist's power truly become manifest. Thus the nineteenth century, which was still delighting in Irving's stupendous Lyceum shows, closed at least with a premonition of our modern reconstructed Globes and Fortunes, of our Stratford, Ontario, and our Chichester, of our simplified and often permanent sets, even of our theatres-in-the-round.

Allardyce Nicoll,
Shakesperian production in the 19 th century.
ibid.

Compare the following excerpt from Macbeth *with the corresponding passage in Davenant's version of the same play (written in 1673).*

Macbeth

At the end of Act I, scene 4, King Duncan prepares to receive the hospitality of Macbeth. In the following scene, Laby Macbeth reads the letter in which her husband announces his success in battle and the predictions of the three witches.

DUNCAN. True, worthy Banquo; he is full so valiant,
And in his commendations I am fed;
It is a banquet to me. Let's after him,
Whose care is gone before to bid us welcome:
It is a peerless kinsman. *(Flourish. Exeunt.)*

Scene 5
Inverness, Macbeth's, Castle.
(Enter Lady Macbeth, reading a letter.)

LADY MACBETH "They met me in the day of success; and I have learned by the perfectest report, they have more in them than mortal knowledge. When I burned in desire to question them further, they made themselves air, into which they vanished. Whiles I stood rapt in the wonder of it, came missives from the king, who all-hailed me 'Thane of Cawdor'; by which title, before, these weird sisters saluted me, and referred me to the coming on of time, with,

'Hail, king, that shalt be'! This have I thought good to deliver thee, my dearest partner of greatness, that thou mightst not lose the dues of rejoicing, by being ignorant of what greatness is promised thee. Lay it to thy heart, and farewell".

Glamis thou art, and Cawdor, and shalt be
What thou art promised: yet do I fear thy nature;
It is too full o' the milk of human kindness
To catch the nearest way: thou wouldst be great;
Art not without ambition, but without
The illness should attend it: what thou wouldst highly,
That wouldst thou holily; wouldst not play false,
And yet wouldst wrongly win: thou'ldst have, great Glamis,
That which cries "Thus thou must do, if thou have it;
And that which rather thou dost fear to do
Than wishest should be undone". Hie thee hither,
That I may pour my spirits in thine ear,
And chastise with the valour of my tongue
All that impedes thee from the golden round
Which fate and metaphysical aid doth seem
To have thee crown'd withal.

W. Shakespeare.

KING. True, Noble Banquo, he is full of worth;
And with his Commendations I am fed;
It is a Feast to me. Let's after him,
Whose care is gone before to bid us welcome:
He is a matchless Kinsman...
(Exeunt.)
(Enter LADY MACBETH, *and* LADY MACDUFF. LADY MACBETH *having a Letter in her hand.)*
LADY MACBETH. Madam, I have observ'd since you came hither,
You have been still disconsolate. Pray tell me,
Are you in perfect health?
LADY MACDUFF. Alas! how can I?
My Lord, when Honour call'd him to the War,
Took with him half of my divided soul,
Which lodging in his bosom, lik'd so well
The place, that 'tis not yet return'd.
LADY MACBETH. Methinks
That should not disorder you: for, no doubt
The brave Macduff left half his soul behind him,
To make up the defect of yours.
LADY MACDUFF. Alas!
The part transplanted from his breast to mine,
(As 'twere by sympathy) still bore a share
In all the hazards which the other half
Incurr'd, and fill'd my bosom up with fears.
LADY MACBETH. Those fears, methinks, should cease now he is safe.
LADY MACDUFF. Ah, Madam, dangers which have long prevail'd
Upon the fancy; even when they are dead
Live in the memory a-while.
LADY MACBETH. Although his safety has not power enough to put
Your doubts to flight, yet the bright glories which
He gain'd in Battel might dispel those Clowds.
LADY MACDUFF. The world mistakes the glories gain'd in war,
Thinking their Lustre true: alas, they are
But Comets, Vapours! by some men exhal'd
From others bloud, and kindl'd in the Region
Of popular applause, in which they live
A-while; then vanish: and the very breath
Which first inflam'd them, blows them out agen.
LADY MACBETH. I willingly would read this Letter; but
Her presence hinders me; I must divert her.
If you are ill, repose may do you good;
Y'had best retire; and try if you can sleep.
LADY MACDUFF. My doubtful thoughts too long have kept me waking.
Madam! I'll take your Counsel...
(*Exit* LADY MACDUFF.)
LADY MACBETH. Now I have leisure, peruse this Letter.
His last brought some imperfect news of things
Which in the shape of women greeted him
In a strange manner. This perhaps may give
More full intelligence. *(She reads.)*

They met me in the day of success; and I have been told they have more in them than mortal Knowledg. When I desir'd to question them further; they made themselves air. Whilst I entertain'd my self with the wonder of it, came Missives from the King, who call'd me Thane *of* Cawdor: *by which Title, these weyward Sisters had saluted me before, and referr'd me to the coming on of time; with, Hail King that shall be. This have I imparted to thee, (my dearest partner of Greatness) that thou might'st not lose thy rights of rejoycing, by being ignorant of what is promis'd. Lay it to thy heart, and farewel.*

Glamis thou art, and Cawdor, and shalt be
What thou art promis'd: yet I fear thy Nature
Has too much of the milk of humane kindness
To take the nearest way: thou would'st be great:
Thou do'st not want ambition: but the ill
Which should attend it: what thou highly covet'st
Thou covet'st holily! alas, thou art
Loth to play false; and yet would'st wrongly win!
Oh how irregular are thy desires?

W. Davenant, 1673.

Ben JONSON 1572-1637

1572 *Born in London.*
1583 *Began his education at Westminster School.*
1589 *Worked as an apprentice bricklayer for his stepfather.*
1597 *Became an actor in a strolling company.*
1598 Every Man in His Humour *performed.*
Imprisoned for killing a fellow-actor.
1599 Every Man Out of His Humour.
1599-1601 *Involved in "The War of the Theatres" (between rival companies), which opposed him to Marston and Dekker and prompted him to write several "comical satires".*
1603 *Became a well-known writer of masques for the court of James I.* Sejanus.
1605 Eastward Ho!
1606 Volpone.
1609 Epicoene or the Silent Woman.
1610 The Alchemist.
1614 Bartholemew Fair.
1616 *Publication, in a folio volume, of* The Works of Benjamin Jonson. *Made King's Poet by James I.*
1628 *Became paralyzed.*
1637 *Died in London, buried in Westminster Abbey.*

In spite of his poor education, Ben Jonson had a thorough classical training and was a strict follower of the ancient masters. This appears clearly in his respect for the unities of time and space in his plays. His early works exemplify the Elizabethan theory of humours: four humours (sanguine, choleric, phlegmatic, melancholic), mixed in different degrees, are present in each character - though one quality usually prevails. Jonson's characters therefore appear as unchanging types: in Every Man in His Humour, *the figures are caricatures, amusing embodiments of solicitude, cowardice, vanity or credulity.*

*A deeply moral man, Jonson attacked all forms of evil - especially hypocrisy, avarice and charlatanism (*Volpone *deals with people's "inheritance-hunting",* The Alchemist *with rogues who pretend they have discovered a gold-making formula in order to deceive a number of stupid and gullible characters,* Bartholomew Fair *is set among swindlers, harlots and hawkers at an English fair...) Full of common sense, Ben Jonson was the creator of the realistic play, showing ordinary people in settings and situations that were those of his time.*

Ben Jonson was also a poet. His works include epigrams and satirical and lyrical verse, whose regular form, balanced style and rhetorical development, restraining his wit, reveal a classical temper.

Volpone, or The Fox (1606)

Volpone, a wealthy Venitian, pretends to be dying in order to receive rich presents from those who come to visit him hoping to become his heirs. Mosca, his parasite, persuades each visitor (here, Corbaccio, an old gentleman) that Volpone has made him his legatee.

CORBACCIO. How does his apoplex?
Is that strong on him still?
MOSCA. Most violent.
His speech is broken, and his eyes are set,
His face drawn longer than 'twas wont –
CORBACCIO. How? how?
Stronger than he was wont?
MOSCA. No, sir: his face
Drawn longer than 'twas wont.
CORBACCIO. O, good!
MOSCA. His mouth
Is ever gaping, and his eyelids hang.
CORBACCIO. Good.
MOSCA. A freezing numbness stiffens all his joints,
And makes the colour of his flesh like lead.
CORBACCIO. 'Tis good.
MOSCA. His pulse beats slow and dull.
CORBACCIO. Good symptoms still.

MOSCA. And from his brain –
CORBACCIO. I conceive you; good.
MOSCA. Flows a cold sweat, with a continual rheum,
Forth the resolved[1] corners of his eyes.
CORBACCIO. Is it possible? Yet I am better, ha!
How does he with the swimming of his head?
MOSCA. Oh, sir, 'tis past the scotomy[2], he now
Hath lost his feeling, and hath left to snort!
You hardly can perceive him, that he breathes.
CORBACCIO. Excellent, excellent, sure I shall outlast him:
This makes me young again, a score of years.
MOSCA. I was a-coming for you, sir.
CORBACCIO. Has he made his will?
What has he given me?
MOSCA. No, sir.
CORBACCIO. Nothing? ha?
MOSCA. He has not made his will, sir.
CORBACCIO. Oh, oh, oh!
What then did Voltore, the lawyer, here?
MOSCA. He smelt a carcase, sir, when he but heard
My master was about his testament;
As I did urge him to it, for your good –
CORBACCIO. He came unto him, did he? I thought so.
MOSCA. Yes, and presented him this piece of plate.
CORBACCIO. To be his heir?
MOSCA. I do not know, sir..
CORBACCIO. True,
I know it too.
MOSCA. By your own scale, sir. *(Aside.)*
CORBACCIO. Well,
I shall prevent him yet. See, Mosca, look,
Here, I have brought a bag of bright *cecchines*[3],
Will quite weigh down his plate.
MOSCA. *(taking the bag.)* Yea, marry, sir.
This is true physic, this your sacred medicine;
No talk of opiates, to this great elixir!
CORBACCIO. 'Tis *aurum palpabile*[4], if not *potabile*[5].
MOSCA. It shall be ministered to him, in his bowl.
CORBACCIO. Ay, do, do, do.
MOSCA. Most blessed cordial!
This will recover him.
CORBACCIO. Yes, do, do, do.
MOSCA. I think it were not best, sir.
CORBACCIO. What?
MOSCA. To recover him.
CORBACCIO. O, no, no, no; by no means.
MOSCA. Why, sir, this
Will work some strange effect, if he but feel it.
CORBACCIO. 'Tis true, therefore forbear; I'll take my venture[6].
Give me't again.
MOSCA. At no hand[7], pardon me;
You shall not do yourself that wrong, sir. I
Will so advise you, you shall have it all.
CORBACCIO. How?
MOSCA. All, sir 'tis your right, your own: no man
Can claim a part: 'tis yours, without a rival,
Decreed by destiny.
CORBACCIO. How, how, good Mosca?
MOSCA. I'll tell you, sir. This fit he shall recover –
CORBACCIO. I do conceive you.
MOSCA. And, on first advantage[8]

Of his gained sense, will I re-importune him
Unto the making of his testament:
And show him this. *(Pointing to the money.)*
CORBACCIO. Good, good.
MOSCA. 'Tis better yet,
If you will hear, sir.
CORBACCIO. Yes, with all my heart.
MOSCA. Now, would I counsel you, make home with speed;
There frame a will; whereto you shall inscribe
My master your sole heir.
CORBACCIO. And disinherit
My son?
MOSCA. O, sir, the better: for that colour[9]
Shall make it much more taking.
CORBACCIO. O, but colour?
MOSCA. This will, sir, you shall send it unto me.
Now, when I come to enforce, as I will do,
Your cares, your watchings, and your many prayers,
Your more than many gifts, your this day's present,
And last, produce your will; where, without thought,
Or least regard, unto your proper issue,
A son so brave, and highly meriting,
The stream of your diverted love hath thrown you
Upon my master, and made him your heir:
He cannot be so stupid, or stone-dead,
But, out of conscience and mere gratitude –
CORBACCIO. He must pronounce me his?
MOSCA. 'Tis true.
CORBACCIO. This plot
Did I think on before.
MOSCA. I do believe it.
CORBACCIO. Do you not believe it?
MOSCA. Yes, sir.
CORBACCIO. Mine own project.
MOSCA. Which when he hath done, sir –
CORBACCIO. Published me his heir?
MOSCA. And you so certain to survive him –
CORBACCIO. Ay.
MOSCA. Being so lusty a man –
CORBACCIO. 'Tis true.
MOSCA. Yes, sir –
CORBACCIO. I thought on that too. See how he should be
The very organ to express my thoughts!
MOSCA. You have not only done yourself a good –
CORBACCIO. But multiplied it on my son?
MOSCA. 'Tis right, sir.
CORBACCIO. Still, my invention.
MOSCA. 'Las, sir, heaven knows,
It hath been all my study, all my care,
(I e'en grow grey withal), how to work things –
CORBACCIO. I do conceive, sweet Mosca.
MOSCA. You are he
For whom I labour here.
CORBACCIO. Ay, do, do, do:
I'll straight about it. *(Going.)*
MOSCA. Rook go with you[10], raven.
CORBACCIO. I know thee honest.
MOSCA. You do lie, sir – *(Aside.)*
CORBACCIO. And –
MOSCA. Your knowledge is no better than your ears, sir.
CORBACCIO. I do not doubt to be a father to thee.

MOSCA. Nor I to gull my brother[11] of his blessing.
CORBACCIO. I may have my youth restored to me, why not?
MOSCA. Your worship is a precious ass –
CORBACCIO. What say'st thou?
MOSCA. I do desire your worship to make haste, sir.
CORBACCIO. 'Tis done, 'tis done, I go. *(Exit.)*
VOLPONE. *(leaping from his couch.)* O, I shall burst;
Let out my sides, let out my sides –

Act I, Scene 4.

1. *resolved:* dissolved 2. *scotomy:* dizziness - 3. *cecchines:* sequins (Venitian coins) - 4. *aurum palpabile:* palpable gold - 5. *potabile:* potable (liquid gold was supposed to be a remedy) - 6. *my venture:* what I have ventured (the gold coins) - 7. *at no hand:* certainly not - 8. *on first advantage:* taking advantage - 9. *that colour:* that scheme - 10. *Rook go with you:* be rooked (a rook = a fool) - 11. *my brother:* Corbaccio's son and legal heir.

T.S. Eliot on Ben Jonson :

The Humour, even at the beginning, is not a type, as in Marston's satire, but a simplified and somewhat distorted individual with a typical mania. In the later work, the Humour definition quite fails to account for the total effect produced. The characters of Shakespeare are such as might exist in different circumstances than those in which Shakespeare sets them. The latter appear to be those which extract from the characters the most intense and interesting realization ; but that realization has not exhausted their possibilities. Volpone's life, on the other hand, is bounded by the scene in which it is played; in fact, the life is the life of the scene and is derivatively the life of Volpone; the life of the character is inseparable from the life of the drama. This is not dependence upon a background, or upon a substratum of fact. The emotional effect is single and simple. Whereas in Shakespeare the effect is due to the way in which the characters *act upon* one another, in Jonson it is given by the way in which the characters *fit in* with each other. The artistic result of *Volpone* is not due to any effect that Volpone, Mosca, Corvino, Corbaccio, Voltore have upon each other, but simply to their combination into a whole. And these figures are not personifications of passions; separately, they have not even that reality, they are constituents. It is a similar indication of Jonson's method that you can hardly pick out a line of Jonson's and say confidently that it is great poetry; but there are many extended passages to which you cannot deny that honour.

T.S. Eliot, *Selected Essays.*
Faber and Faber Publishers.

On the social background of Volpone:

The subject of *Volpone,* in the most obvious sense, is money – or rather, greed, and the corruption which greed works in the human soul. In recent years much work has been done – for instance, by L. C. Knights – on the presentation of this theme in Jacobean drama, and scholars have been inclined to connect its frequent appearance with the consciousness of the breakdown of one form of society, or of social cohesion, and the birth of another: the birth, in fact, of something that we can call capitalism. In other words, the dramatists had become aware that the older system of social unity, a system depending on mutual service and loyalty, and in its origin feudal and mediaeval, had given way to a newer form of social obligation, dependent on money, or credit, on what has been called the "cash-nexus". They were not interested in, and certainly did not understand, the economics of this change. What concerned them was its morality – the way in which an ancient set of beliefs about what was right and wrong between man and man had to yield, or to adapt itself, to a "bond" of a new kind – of Shylock's kind. And, on the whole, they did not like what they saw.

S. Musgrove,
Tragical Mirth : King Lear and Volpone.

Cf. Characters and characterization, p. 12; Comedy, p. 24, Wit, humour, satire and irony, p. 27.

2. From the Metaphysical Poets to the Commonwealth

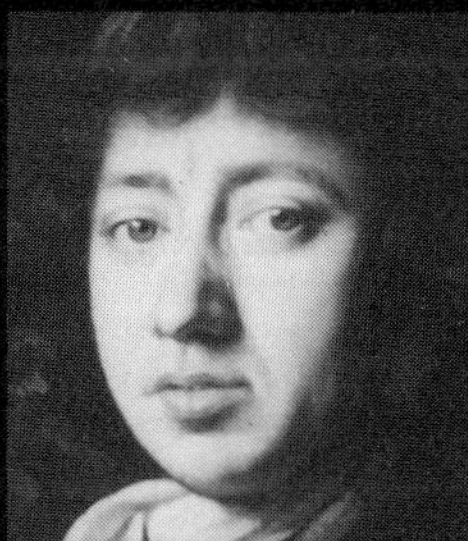

literature and society

William Faithorne: Oliver Cromwell, *1658, from the engraving for* The Emblem of England's Distraction.

This symbolical picture shows Oliver Cromwell, attended by Fame and trampling on Error and Faction. In the foreground, to the left is represented "They shall beat their speares into pruning hooks", and to the right "their swords into ploughshares". In the top left hand corner is depicted the Ark upon Mount Ararat and below it Abraham about to sacrifice Isaac with the ram caught in the thicket, while in the top right corner are Scylla and Charybdis.

G.M. Trevelyan.

For Books are not absolutely dead things, but doe contain a potencie of life in them to be as active as that soule was whose progeny they are; nay they do preserve as in a violl the purest efficacie and extraction of that living intellect that bred them. I know they are as lively, and as vigorously productive, as those fabulous Dragons teeth; and being sown up and down, may chance to spring up armed men. And yet on the other hand unlesse warinesse be us'd, as good almost kill a Man as kill a good Book; who kills a Man kills a reasonable creature, Gods Image; but hee who destroyes a good Booke, kills reason it selfe, kills the Image of God, as it were in the eye. Many a man lives a burden to the Earth; but a good Booke is the pretious life-blood of a master spirit, imbalm'd and treasur'd up on purpose to a life beyond life. 'Tis true, no age can restore a life, whereof perhaps there is no great losse; and revolutions of ages doe not oft recover the losse of a rejected truth, for the want of which whole Nations fare the worse. We should be wary therefore what persecution we raise against the living labours of publick men, how we spill that season'd life of man preserv'd and stor'd up in Books; since we see a kinde of homicide may be thus committed, sometimes a martyrdome, and if it extend to the whole impression, a kinde of massacre, whereof the execution ends not in the slaying of an elementall life, but strikes at that ethereall and fift essence, the breath of reason it selfe, slaies an immortality rather then a life.

John Milton, *Areopagitica.*

The Cromwellian revolution was not social and economic in its causes and motives; it was the result of political and religious thought and aspiration among men who had no desire to recast society or redistribute wealth. No doubt the choice of sides that men made in politics and religion was to some extent and in some cases determined by predispositions due to social and economic circumstance; but of this the men themselves were only half conscious. There were more lords and gentlemen on the side of the King, more yeomen and townsfolk on the side of Parliament. Above all, London was on the side of Parliament. Yet every class in town and country was itself divided.

The stage of economic and social development which had been reached in the England of 1640 was not the cause, but it was a necessary condition, of the political and religious movements that burst forth into sudden blaze. The astonishing attempt of Pym, Hampden, and the other parliamentary leaders to wrest power from the monarchy in good earnest, and to govern the State through an elected debating assembly of several hundred members, and the degree of success which that bold innovation actually attained in politics and war, presupposed not only an old parliamentary tradition but the existence of a powerful bourgeoisie, gentry, and yeomanry, long liberated from ecclesiastical and feudal control, and long accustomed to share with the monarchy in the work of government. So too

	Politics and Society	Literature and the Arts
1616		Death of Shakespeare.
1620	The Pilgrim Fathers settle in New England.	
1621		BURTON: *Anatomy of Melancholy.*
1623		DONNE: *Devotions upon emergent occasions.*
1625	Accession of Charles I.	BACON: Final version of the *Essays.*
1628	Petition of Right (Parliament's attempt to assert its rights).	
1629	Parliament dissolved by Charles I (no Parliament until 1640).	
1633		DONNE: *Poems.*
1634		MILTON: *Comus.*
1637		MILTON: *Lycidas.*
1640	The "Long" Parliament.	
1641	The Grand Remonstrance (statement of the king's errors, praise of the reforms achieved by the Long Parliament, list of needed reforms).	
1642	Beginning of the Civil War.	The theatres are closed.
1644		MILTON: *Areopagitica.*
1645	Execution of Laud, the Archbishop of Canterbury who supported royal supremacy and Roman Catholicism. Cromwell victorious at Naseby.	
1647	Surrender of Charles I to Parliament.	
1649	Execution of Charles I. Beginning of the Commonwealth.	
1650		1650-60 MARVELL writes his main poems.
1651	Charles II is defeated and flees to France.	HOBBES: *Leviathan.*
1651-2	Irish and Scottish rebellions crushed.	
1653	Cromwell becomes Lord Protector.	
1657	Cromwell declines the English crown.	
1658	Death of Cromwell. England governed by his son, then by Parliament.	MILTON starts writing *Paradise Lost.*
1660	Restoration: Charles II.	Beginning of PEPYS's *Diary.*
		(1667 MILTON: *Paradise Lost.*) (1678 BUNYAN: *The Pilgrim's Progress.*)

the rapid rise to national importance, and for a while to national predominance, of innumerable sects such as Baptists and Congregationalists could not have occurred except in a society where there was much personal and economic independence in the yeomen and artisan classes, and in a country where for nearly a century past the individual study of the Bible had been a great part of religion, and the chief stimulant of popular imagination and intellect. If there had been newspapers, magazines, and novels to compete with the Bible in manor-house, farm, and cottage, there would have been no Puritan revolution – and John Bunyan would never have written *Pilgrim's Progress.*

Indeed the Puritan Revolution was itself, in its basic impulse, a "Puritan's Progress". "I dreamed," wrote Bunyan, "and behold I saw a Man clothed with rags, standing in a certain place, with his face from his own house, a Book in his hand, and a great burden upon his back. I looked, and saw him open the book and read therein; and as he read, he wept and trembled; and not being able longer to contain, he broke out with a lamentable cry, saying What shall I do?." (...)

The great generation of men who between them produced the high English tragedy of Roundhead and Cavalier, were not brought up on the Bible and on the influences of the country life alone – though such a limitation would almost be true of Bunyan. The age of Milton, Marvell, and Herrick was an age of poetry and learning often in close alliance. Not only were simple and beautiful songs being written and set to music and sung by all classes, but in cultivated households more elaborate and scholarly poems circulated in manuscript before they found their way into print or passed into oblivion. When the music of Lawes was married to the immortal verse of Milton's *Comus* for the private theatricals of Lord Bridgewater's family (1634), English domestic culture touched perhaps the highest mark to which it ever attained. And the learning of the time, classical as well as Christian, was very widely spread.

Political and religious controversy was conducted in books and pamphlets forbiddingly learned to the modern eye, yet in spite of their heavy display of erudition, they caught the eager audience to which they made appeal.

G. M. Trevelyan, *English Social History,*
© 1942, 1944 by Longmans, Green; Longman Group Ltd.

"Loe, here are three men, standing in degree.
The least of these, the greatest ought to be,
The other two, of men and of the Devill,
Ought to be rooted out for ere as evill."

A puritan attack on Laud and his bishops. The woodcut shows Laud moving from the Bible unadorned towards the devilish superstition by way of his High Church practices, indicated by the Service Book.

© The Mansell Collection. G.M. Trevelyan, *ibid.*

political ideas during the revolution

It is only natural that in the England of Charles I and Cromwell, most of the philosophers and thinkers should have been interested in political and religious questions. As far as the nature of government was concerned, there were roughly three positions at the time of the revolution:

- *that of the Stuarts, who defended the doctrine of the Divine Right of the monarchs (cf text* **a**);
- *that of the "levellers", who advocated republicanism, manhood suffrage, toleration and the abolition of the House of Lords (cf text* **b**);
- *in between, the more moderate attitude of Cromwell.*

a

The state of monarchy is the supremest thing upon earth; for kings are not only God's lieutenants upon earth, and sit upon God's throne, but even by God himself they are called gods. There be three principal similitudes that illustrates the state of monarchy; one taken out of the word of God; and the two other out of the grounds of policy and philosophy. In the Scriptures kings are called gods and so their power after a certain relation compared to the divine power. Kings are also compared to fathers of families for a king is truly *"Parens Patriae"* [father of his country], the politic father of his people. And lastly, kings are compared to the head of this microcosm of the body of man.

Kings are justly called gods for that they exercise a manner or resemblance of divine power upon earth. For if you will consider the attributes to God, you shall see how they agree in the person of a king. God hath power to create or destroy, make or unmake at his pleasure, to give life or send death, to judge all and to be judged nor accountable to none, to raise low things and to make high things low at his pleasure, and to God are both soul and body due. And the like power have kings: they make and unmake their subjects; they have power of raising and casting down; of life and of death; judges over all their subjects, and in all causes, and yet accountable to none but God only. They have power to exalt low things, and abase high things, and make of their subjects like men at the chess – a pawn to take a bishop or a knight – and to cry up or down any of their subjects as they do their money. And to the king is due both the affections of the soul and the service of the body of his subjects...

From James I 's *Speech to the Parliament,*
21 March 1610.

b

We are well assured, yet cannot forget, that the cause of our choosing you to be Parliament-men, was to deliver us from all kind of bondage, and to preserve the commonwealth in peace and happiness. For effecting whereof, we possessed you with the same power that was in ourselves, to have done the same; for we might justly have done it ourselves without you, if we had thought it convenient, choosing you, as persons whom we thought fitly qualified and faithful, for avoiding some inconveniences.

But ye are to remember, this was only of us but a power of trust, which is ever revocable and cannot be otherwise, and to be employed to no other end than our own well being. Nor did we choose you to continue our trusts longer than the known established constitution of this commonly-wealth will justly permit, and that could be but for one year at the most: for by our law, a Parliament is to be called once every year, and oftener, if need be, as ye well know. We are your principals, and you our agents; it is a truth which you cannot but acknowledge. For if you or any other shall assume or exercise any power, that is not derived from our trust and choice thereunto, that power is no less than usurpation and an oppression, from which we expect to be freed, in whomsoever we find it; it being altogether inconsistent with the nature of just freedom, which ye also very well understand.

Richard Overton, *A Remonstrance of Many Thousand Citizens and other Freeborn People of England to their own House of Commons*, 1646.

The philosopher who undoubtedly dominated this period was Thomas HOBBES, *with his* Leviathan *(1647).*

His theories led him to be rejected both by the supporters of Cromwell (who thought he justified monarchical absolutism) as well as by the Stuarts (who saw in him an atheist, even a Republican).

Hobbes was a materialist who believed that all our feelings and thoughts are produced by the motions of external objects that influence our bodily senses:

external objects → sensations
→ motion in the brain and heart
→ imagination

Men are mainly motivated by fear and by a desire to dominate others. This is, according to Hobbes, a "general inclination of all mankind", something too deep-rooted to change. Governments must therefore be formed to counteract this inclination, by preventing too much liberty since that could only lead to strife and chaos.

This is why Hobbes advocated a social contract or covenant: men would delegate their rights to a man or an assembly responsible for order in the country and in return they would accept perfect discipline and obedience.

THE GENERATION OF A COMMONWEALTH

The only way to erect such a Common Power, as may be able to defend them from the invasion of Forraigners, and the injuries of one another, and thereby to secure them in such sort, as that by their owne industrie, and by the fruites of the Earth, they may nourish themselves and live contentedly; is, to conferre all their power and strength upon one Man, or upon one Assembly of men, that may reduce all their Wills, by plurality of voices, unto one Will: which is as much as to say, to appoint one man, or Assembly of men, to beare their Person; and every one to owne, and acknowledge himselfe to be Author of whatsoever he that so beareth their Person, shall Act, or cause to be Acted, in those things which concerne the Common Peace and Safetie; and therein to submit their Wills, every one to his Will, and their Judgements, to his Judgment. This is more than Consent, or Concord; it is a reall Unitie of them all, in one and the same Person, made by Covenant of every man with every man, in such manner, as if every man should say to every man, *I Authorise and give up my Right of Governing my selfe, to this Man, or to this Assembly of men, on this condition, that thou give up thy Right to him, and Authorise all his Actions in like manner.* This done, the Multitude so united in one Person, is called a COMMON-WEALTH, in latine CIVITAS. This is the Generation of that great LEVIATHAN, or rather (to speake more reverently) of that *Mortall God*, to which wee owe under the *Immortall God*, our peace and defence. (...)

The attaining to this Soveraigne Power, is by two wayes. One, by Naturall force; as when a man maketh his children, to submit themselves, and their children to his government, as being able to destroy them if they refuse; or by Warre subdueth his enemies to his will, giving them their lives on that condition. The other, is when men agree amongst themselves, to submit to some Man, or Assembly of men, voluntarily, on confidence to be protected by him against all others. This later, may be called a Politicall Common-wealth or Common-wealth by *Institution*; and the former, a Common-wealth by *Acquisition*. And first, I shall speak of a Common-wealth by Institution. (...)

THE SOVERAIGNS ACTIONS CANNOT BE JUSTLY ACCUSED BY THE SUBJECT.

Fourthly, because every Subject is by this Institution Author of all the Actions, and Judgments of the Soveraigne Instituted; it followes, that whatsoever he doth, it can be no injury to any of his Subjects; nor ought he to be by any of them accused of Injustice. For he that doth any thing by authority from another, doth therein no injury to him by whose authority he acteth: But by this Institution of a Common-wealth, every particular man is Author of all the Soveraigne doth; and consequently he that complaineth, of injury from his Soveraigne, complaineth of that whereof he himselfe is Author; and therefore ought not to accuse any man but himselfe; no nor himselfe of injury; because to do injury to ones selfe, is impossible. It is true that they that have Soveraigne power, may commit Iniquity; but not Injustice, or Injury in the proper signification.

WHAT SOEVER THE SOVERAIGNE DOTH,
IS UNPUNISHABLE BY THE SUBJECT

Fifthly, and consequently to that which was sayd last, no man that hath Soveraigne power can justly be put to death, or otherwise in any manner by his Subjects punished. For seeing every Subject is Author of the actions of his Soveraigne; he punisheth another, for the actions committed by himselfe.

T. Hobbes, *Leviathan*.

Sir Anthony Van Dyck: Charles I on horseback.
National Gallery Photograph.

literature and the arts

Painting

From the end of the reign of James I to the Restoration, painting moved from miniatures to large-scale portrait paintings, mostly marked by foreign influences.

Charles I's appreciation of the arts and his generosity attracted to the court many painters from the continent, especially from the Netherlands: Paul VAN SOMER, Daniel MYTENS, Cornelius JOHNSON, *and* VAN DYCK *who settled in London in 1632.* RUBENS *also came to England in 1629-30.*

VAN DYCK'S *baroque art was particularly suited to convey the graceful and light atmosphere of the time. He specialized in portraits of the Royal family and the Court, which give an impression of dignity and refinement characteristic of the Cavalier spirit. The same spirit is to be found in the works of the so-called "Cavalier Poets" of the first half of the 17th century – Herrick, Carew, Lovelace, etc.*

e.g. lines written by Lovelace from prison in 1642:

When (like committed Linnets) I
   With shriller throat shall sing
The sweetnes, Mercy, Majesty,
   And glories of my KING;
When I shall voyce aloud, how Good
   He is, how Great should be;
Inlarged Winds that curle the Flood,
   Know no such Liberty.

Stone Walls doe not a Prison make,
   Nor Iron bars a Cage;
Minds innocent and quiet take
   That for an Hermitage.
If I have freedome in my Love,
   And in my soule am free;
Angels alone that sore above
   Injoy such Liberty.

With the Commonwealth, a more austere strain appeared in portraiture. There was more simplicity, more solidity and directness in the works of William DOBSON, *"the moste distinguished purely British painter before Hogarth".*

William Dobson: Dobson, Sir Charles Cotterell, and Sir Balthazar Gerbier.
Duke of Northumberland, Alnwick Castle, Northumberland.

Architecture

In architecture, the first half of the century is dominated by Inigo JONES, *the architect of the Stuarts, whose style, influenced by the Italian and French Renaissance, was revolutionary for Great Britain.*

He can be considered as the first real English architect, in so far as he was concerned with a building as a whole (the carpentry, sculpture and painting interested him as much as the designing itself) – he had in fact devoted part of his early career to the designing of costumes and settings for court masques.

He brought back from Italy an interest in classical forms, which shows in the few buildings of his that still survive in England (e.g. The Banqueting Hall, Covent Garden...): the exteriors are simple, symmetrical, compact, influenced by ancient Roman style, while the interiors are richly decorated with painted ceilings.

His influence on other architects, however, will only become apparent in the 18th century: until the Restoration most domestic architecture was still in the Jacobean tradition: brick houses, highly decorated with gables and chimney-stacks.

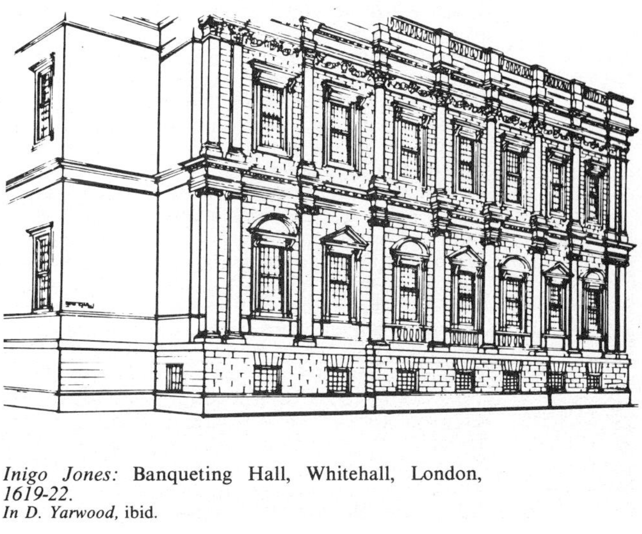

Inigo Jones: Banqueting Hall, Whitehall, London, *1619-22.*
In D. Yarwood, ibid.

The Metaphysical Poets

The first characteristic that I shall isolate in trying to discuss the admittedly vague and, it is often thought, unsatisfactory term "metaphysical poetry" is its concentration. The reader is held to an idea or a line of argument. He is not invited to pause upon a passage, "wander with it, and muse upon it, and reflect upon it, and bring home to it, and prophesy upon it, and dream upon it" as a "starting-post towards all the 'two-and-thirty Palaces' ". Keats's advice can be followed profitably with much poetry, particularly with Elizabethan and Romantic poetry ; but metaphysical poetry demands that we pay attention and read on (...).

A metaphysical poem tends to be brief, and is always closely woven. Marvell, under the metaphor of a garland, characterizes his own art finely in "The Coronet" when he speaks of a "curious frame" in which the flowers are "set with Skill and chosen out with Care". And Donne in a sermon, speaking of the Psalms as especially dear to him in that they were poems, stresses the same elements of deliberate art (curiosity), and economy of language, when he defines psalms as

"Such a form as is both curious, and requires diligence in the making, and then when it is made, can have nothing, no syllable taken from it, nor added to it".

Concentration and a sinewy strength of style is the mark of Ben Jonson as well as of Donne, and such adjectives as "strenuous" and "masculine" applied to him by his admirers point to a sense in which he too was in some degree a "strong-lined" man, and explain why so many younger writers were able to regard both him and Donne as equally their masters. Behind both, as behind much of the poetry of their followers, lies the classical epigram, and there is some truth in saying that a metaphysical poem is an expanded epigram. (...) The desire for concentration and concision marks also the verse forms characteristic of seventeenth-century lyric. It appears in the fondness for a line of eight syllables rather than a line of ten, and in the use of stanzas employing lines of varying length into which the sense seems packed, or of stanzas built on very short lines. A stanza of Donne or Herbert is not, like rhyme royal or a Spenserian stanza, an ideal mould, as it were, into which the words have flowed. It is more like a limiting frame in which words and thought are compressed, a 'box where sweets compacted lie'. The metaphysical poets favoured either very simple verse forms, octosyllabic couplets or quatrains, or else stanzas created for the particular poem, in which length of line and rhyme scheme artfully enforced the sense. In (...), "The Triple Foole", Donne suggests, in passing, this conception of the function of rhyme and metre :

I thought, if I could draw my paines,
Through Rimes vexation, I should them allay,
Griefe brought to numbers cannot be so fierce,
For, he tames it, that fetters it in verse.

The second characteristic of metaphysical poetry, its most immediately striking feature, is its fondness for conceits, and here, of course, Jonson and Donne part company. A conceit is a comparison whose ingenuity is more striking than its justness, or, at least, is more immediately striking. All comparisons discover likeness in things unlike: a comparison becomes a conceit when we are made to concede likeness while being strongly conscious of unlikeness. A brief comparison can be a conceit if two things patently unlike, or which we should never think of together, are shown to be alike in a single point in such a way, or in such a context, that we feel their incongruity. Here a conceit is like a spark made by striking two stones together. After the flash the stones are just two stones. Metaphysical poetry abounds in such flashes, as when Cartwright in his New Year's poem, promising to be a new man, declares that he will not be new as the year is new when it begins again its former cycle, and then thinks of two images of motion without progression, the circulation of the blood and a mill:

"Motion as in a Mill
Is busie standing still".

The wit of this depends on our being willing to suppress our memory of other features of mills, and particularly on our not allowing ourselves to think that mills are very usefully employed grinding corn while "standing still". (...)

Argument and persuasion, and the use of the conceit as their instrument, are the elements or body of a metaphysical poem. Its quintessence or soul is the vivid imagining of a moment of experience or of a situation out of which the need to argue, or persuade, or define arises. Metaphysical poetry is famous for its abrupt, personal openings in which a man speaks to his mistress, or addresses his God, or sets a scene, or calls us to mark this or see that.

H. Gardner, Introduction to *The Metaphysical Poets*. *Penguin Books Ltd.*

Cf. Figurative language, p. 31.

John DONNE 1571?-1631

1572 *Born in London.*
1584 *Sent to Oxford.*
1595 *Abandoned the Roman Catholic Church. Started writing poetry.*
1596-1597 *Volunteered to take part in the expedition to Cadiz and the Azores.*
1598-1602 *Secretary to the Lord Keeper.*
1601 *Secret marriage to Ann More, the Lord Keeper's niece: it led to Donne's imprisonment and years of great poverty.*
1610-1615 *Wrote a number of religious works, many of them attacking the Church of Rome.*
1615 *Ordained into the Church of England.*
1621 *Became Dean of St Paul's.*
1623 Devotions Upon Emergent Occasions
1631 *Died in London.*
1633 Songs and Sonnets *posthumously published.*

John Donne is the most prominent "metaphysical poet". The same vigour and fierceness can be felt both in his love poems and in his religious sonnets and sermons. Reacting against the Petrarchan tradition, he speaks of love either with cynicism and sensuality or with a rough and passionate violence.

His style is based on daring metaphors, hyperboles and conceits and on argumentative developments. It is, as Sir H. Grierson wrote "the peculiar blend of passion and thought, feeling and ratiocination which is (his) greatest achievement." T.S. Eliot saw this immediate link between thought and feeling as characteristic of the metaphysical poets and explained that it disappeared later in the 17th century when the "dissociation of sensibility" set in.

A Valediction[1]: forbidding mourning[2] (1633)

As virtuous men passe mildly away,
  And whisper to their soules, to goe,
Whilst some of their sad friends doe say,
  The breath goes now, and some say, no:

So let us melt, and make no noise,
  No teare-floods, nor sigh-tempests move,
T'were prophanation of our joyes
  To tell the layetie our love.

Moving of th'earth[3] brings harmes and feares,
  Men reckon what it did and meant,
But trepidation of the spheares[4],
  Though greater farre, is innocent[5].

Dull sublunary lovers love
  (Whose soule is sense) cannot admit
Absence, because it doth remove
  Those things which elemented[6] it.

But we by a love, so much refin'd,
  That our selves know not what it is,
Inter-assured of the mind,
  Care lesse, eyes, lips, and hands to misse.

Our two soules therefore, which are one,
Though I must goe, endure not yet
A breach, but an expansion,
Like gold to ayery thinnesse beate.

If they be two, they are two so
As stiffe twin compasses are two,
Thy soule the fixt foot, makes no show
To move, but doth, if the'other doe.

And though it in the center sit,
Yet when the other far doth rome,
It leanes, and hearkens after it,
And growes erect, as that comes home.

Such wilt thou be to mee, who must
Like th'other foot, obliquely runne ;
Thy firmnes makes my circle just,
And makes me end, where I begunne[7].

Songs and Sonnets.

1. *valediction:* farewell – 2. *mourning:* according to Walton, Donne wrote the poem for his wife, before he left for France in 1611 – 3. *moving of th'earth:* earthquakes – 4. *trepidation of the spheres:* the trepidation of the ninth sphere (the Crystalline, cf. p. 36) explained the precession of the equinoxes – 5. *innocent:* harmless (whereas earthquakes are destructive and portend future disasters) – 6. *elemented:* made, composed – 7. *makes me end where I begunne:* complete the circle.

Compare these two critical passages, one by Dr Johnson who applied the word "metaphysical" to the poets of Donne's age (though the word had already been used by Dryden before) and one by T.S. Eliot, whose essays led to a revival of interest in these poets.

Donne is here casting himself in the role of a melancholy lover. A Latin inscription, a parody of the psalms, implores his lady to whom he owes a saint-like devotion, to lighten the shadows which envelope his love-sick misery: *Illumina tenebras nostras domina.* Donne has all the usual trappings: a large hat with a floppy black brim, arms folded across his chest, black dress, his collar negligently left undone. Later in life melancholy took its religious form and in his *Corona* of Sonnets he offers to God:

"... this crown of prayers and praise,
Weav'd in my low devout melancholie."

R. Strong.

artist unknown, c. 1595: John Donne
The Marquess of Lothian.

● About the beginning of the seventeenth century appeared a race of writers that may be termed the "metaphysical poets"of whom, in a criticism on the works of Cowley, it is not improper to give some account.

The metaphysical poets were men of learning, and to show their learning was their whole endeavour; but unluckily resolving to show it in rhyme, instead of writing poetry they only wrote verses, and very often such verses as stood the trial of the finger better than of the ear; for the modulation was so imperfect, that they were only found to be verses by counting the syllabes.

If the father of criticism has rightly denominated poetry τεχυη μιμητικη, "an imitative art", these writers will, without great wrong, lose their right to the name of poets, for they cannot be said to have imitated anything; they neither copied nature nor life, neither painted the forms of matter, nor represented the operations of intellect.

Those, however, who deny them to be poets, allow them to be wits. (...)

But wit, abstracted from its effects upon the hearer, may be more rigorously and philosophically considered as a kind of "discordia concors", a combination of dissimilar images, or discovery of occult resemblances in things apparently unlike. Of wit, thus defined, they have more than enough. The most heterogeneous ideas are yoked by violence together; nature and art are ransacked for illustrations, comparisons, and allusions; their learning instructs, and their subtlety surprises; but the reader commonly thinks his improvement dearly bought, and, though he sometimes admires, is seldom pleased.

From this account of their compositions it will be readily inferred that they were not successful in representing or moving the affections. As they were wholly employed on something unexpected and surprising, they had no regard to that uniformity of sentiment which enables us to conceive and to excite the pains and the pleasure of other minds: they never inquired what, on any occasion, they should have said or done, but wrote rather as beholders than partakers of human nature; as beings looking upon good and evil, impassive and at leisure; as Epicurean deities, making remarks on the actions of men, and the vicissitudes of life, without interest and without emotion. Their courtship was void of fondness, and their lamentation of sorrow. Their wish was only to say what they hoped had been never said before.

Samuel Johnson, *Lives of the English Poets*
"The Life of Cowley."

● It is to be observed that the language of these poets is as a rule simple and pure; in the verse of George Herbert this simplicity is carried as far as it can go – a simplicity emulated without success by numerous modern poets. The "structure" of the sentences, on the other hand, is sometimes far from simple, but this is not a vice; it is a fidelity to thought and feeling. (...)

Donne, and often Cowley, employ a device which is sometimes considered characteristically 'metaphysical'; the elaboration (contrasted with the condensation) of a figure of speech to the furthest stage to which ingenuity can carry it. Thus Cowley develops the commonplace comparison of the world to a chess-board through long stanzas *(To Destiny),* and Donne, with more grace, in *A Valediction,* the comparison of two lovers to a pair of compasses. But elsewhere we find, instead of the mere explication of the content of a comparison, a development by rapid association of thought which requires considerable agility on the part of the reader. (...)

(It is) something (which had) happened to the mind of England between the time of Donne or Lord Herbert of Cherbury and the time of Tennyson and Browning; it is the difference between the intellectual poet and the reflective poet. Tennyson and Browning are poets, and they think; but they do not feel their thought as immediately as the odour of a rose. A thought to Donne was an experience; it modified his sensibility. When a poet's mind is perfectly equipped for its work, it is constantly amalgamating disparate experience; the ordinary man's experience is chaotic, irregular, fragmentary. The latter falls in love, or reads Spinoza, and these two experiences have nothing to do with each other, or with the noise of the typewriter or the smell of cooking; in the mind of the poet these experiences are always forming new wholes.

We may express the difference by the following theory: The poets of the seventeenth century, the successors of the dramatists of the sixteenth, possessed a mechanism of sensibility which could devour any kind of experience. They are simple, artificial, difficult, or fantastic, as their predecessors were; no less nor more than Dante, Guido Cavalcanti, Guinicelli, or Cino. In the seventeenth century a dissociation of sensibility set in, from which we have never recovered; and this dissociation, as is natural, was aggravated by the influence of the two most powerful poets of the century, Milton and Dryden. Each of these men performed certain poetic functions so magnificently well that the magnitude of the effect concealed the absence of others. The language went on and in some respects improved; the best verse of Collins, Gray, Johnson, and even Goldsmith satisfies some of our fastidious demands better than that of Donne or Marvell or King. But while the language became more refined, the feeling became more crude. (...)

The second effect of the influence of Milton and Dryden followed from the first, and was therefore slow in manifestation. The sentimental age began early in the eighteenth century, and continued. The poets revolted against the ratiocinative, the descriptive; they thought and felt by fits, unbalanced; they reflected.

T.S. Eliot, *The Metaphysical Poets* in *Selected Prose of T.S. Eliot, Harcourt, Brace, Jovanovitch Inc.*

Cf. Versification, p. 7 ; Figurative language, p. 31.

Andrew MARVELL 1621-1678

1621 *Born in Yorkshire, the son of a Calvinist clergyman.*
1638 *Became a scholar of Trinity College, Cambridge.*
1642-1646 *Travelled in Europe as a tutor.*
1650 An Horatian Ode Upon Cromwell's Return from Ireland.
1650-1653 *Became tutor to Mary Fairfax, the daughter of Cromwell's general, then to Cromwell's ward.*
1655 The First Anniversary of the Government under his Highness the Lord Protector.
1657 *Became Latin Secretary and worked with Milton.*
1659-1678 *Member of Parliament for Hull and served as secretary on embassies to Russia, Denmark, Sweden.*
1678 *Died in London.*
1681 *Publication of his* Miscellaneous Poems.

A Puritan, a faithful supporter of Cromwell, Marvell was deeply interested in politics and best-known as a satirist and controversialist (he was in favour of representative government) during his lifetime.

His lyric poetry, chiefly written in the 1650s, expresses his love for beauty and nature as well as a sensuousness that can be surprising in such a devout follower of the Puritan regime.

His few love poems and his few devotional pieces are perfect exponents of all the "metaphysical" qualities – passionate, paradoxical argument touched with humour and learned imagery... and above all the sudden soar of passion in bold and felicitous image, in clangorous lines.. Grierson.

Poems such as The Garden, Bermudas, *or* Upon Appleton House, *which convey his deep feeling for nature and his passion for country scenes, are probably his most original works at a time when it was rare for poetry to sing the beauties of nature for its own sake.*

To his Coy Mistress (1681)

Had we but world[1] enough, and time,
This coyness, Lady, were no crime.
We would sit down and think which way
To walk, and pass our long love's day.
Thou by the Indian Ganges'side
Shouldst rubies find: I by the tide
Of Humber[2] would complain. I would
Love you ten years before the Flood,
And you should, if you please, refuse
Till the conversion of the Jews.
My vegetable love[3] should grow
Vaster than empires, and more slow;
An hundred years should go to praise
Thine eyes, and on thy forehead gaze;
Two hundred to adore each breast ;
But thirty thousand to the rest;
An age at least to every part,
And the last age should show your heart;
For, Lady, you deserve this state[4],
Nor would I love at lower rate.
  But at my back I always hear
Time's winged chariot hurrying near;
And yonder all before us lie
Deserts of vast eternity.
Thy beauty shall no more be found;
Nor, in thy marble vault, shall sound
My echoing song: then worms shall try

That long preserved virginity,
And your quaint[5] honour turn to dust,
And into ashes all my lust.
The grave's a fine and private place,
But none, I think, do there embrace.
  Now, therefore, while the youthful hue
Sits on thy skin like morning dew,
And while thy willing soul transpires
At every pore with instant fires[6],
Now let us sport us while we may;
And now, like amorous birds of prey,
Rather at once our time devour,
Than languish in his slow-chapt[7] power.
Let us roll all our strength and all
Our sweetness up into one ball,
And tear our pleasures with rough strife
Thorough[8] the iron gates of life:
Thus, though we cannot make our Sun
Stand still, yet we will make him run.

Miscellaneous Poems.

1. *world:* space – 2. *the tide of Humber:* the river Humber (which runs through Hull, Marvell's native town) – 3. *vegetable love:* love that develops very slowly – 4. *state:* treatment – 5. *quaint:* fastidious – 6. *instant fires:* the sudden blushes on her cheeks – 7. *chaps:* jaws (slow-chapt power = power that devours slowly) – 8. *thorough:* through.

Compare Marvell's poem with the following two poems from Robert Herrick (another metaphysical poet) and W. H. Auden:

TO THE VIRGINS TO MAKE MUCH OF TIME

Gather ye rosebuds while ye may,
  Old Time is still a-flying;
And this same flower that smiles to-day,
  To-morrow will be dying.

The glorious lamp of heaven, the sun,
  The higher he's a-getting,
The sooner will his race be run,
  And nearer he's to setting.

That age is best which is the first,
  When youth and blood are warmer;
But being spent, the worse, and worst
  Times, still succeed the former.

Then be not coy, but use your time,
  And while ye may, go marry;
For, having lost but once your prime,
  You may forever tarry.

R. Herrick, 1648.

AS I WALKED OUT ONE EVENING

As I walked out one evening
  Walking down Bristol Street,
The crowds upon the pavement
  Were fields of harvest wheat.

And down by the brimming river
  I heard a lover sing
Under an arch of the railway:
  "Love has no ending.

"I'll love you, dear, I'll love you
  Till China and Africa meet,
And the river jumps over the mountain
  And the salmon sing in the street,

"I'll love you till the ocean
  Is folded and hung up to dry
And the seven stars go squawking
  Like geese about the sky.

The years shall run like rabbits,
  For in my arms I hold
The Flower of the Ages,
  And the first love of the world."

But all the clocks in the city
  Began to whirr and chime:
"O let not Time deceive you,
  You cannot conquer Time. →

"In the burrows of the Nightmare
  Where Justice naked is,
Time watches from the shadow
  And coughs when you would kiss.

"In headaches and in worry
  Vaguely life leaks away,
And Time will have his fancy
  To-morrow or to-day.

"Into many a green valley
  Drifts the appalling snow;
Time breaks the threaded dances
  And the diver's brilliant bow.

"O plunge your hands in water,
  Plunge them in up to the wrist;
Stare, stare in the basin
  And wonder what you've missed.

"The glacier knocks in the cupboard,
  The desert sighs in the bed,
And the crack in the tea-cup opens
  A lane to the land of the dead.

"Where the beggars raffle the banknotes
  And the Giant is enchanting to Jack,
And the Lily-white Boy is a Roarer,
  And Jill goes down on her back.

"O look, look in the mirror,
  O look in your distress;
Life remains a blessing
  Although you cannot bless.

"O stand, stand at the window
  As the tears scald and start;
You shall love your crooked neighbour
  With your crooked heart."

It was late, late in the evening,
  The lovers they were gone;
The clocks had ceased their chiming,
  And the deep river ran on.

W.H. Auden, 1940.
Collected Poems.
By permission of Faber and Faber.

See also, for the Carpe Diem *theme:*
John Donne: To His Mistress Going to Bed
Edmund Waller: Song *("Go, Lovely Rose!")*
Ben Jonson: Song *(from* Volpone, or the Fox: *"Come, my Celia...")*

for the use of hyperboles:
John Cleveland: Upon Phyllis Walking in a morning before sun-rising

Cf. Versification, p. 7; Figurative language, p. 31.

John MILTON 1608-1674

1608 *Born in London.*
1620-1625 *St Paul's School, London.*
1625-1632 *Christ's College, Cambridge. Wrote* On the Morning of Christ's Nativity *in 1629 and* L'Allegro *and* Il Penseroso *around 1631.*
1632-1638 *Private studies and reading at Hammersmith and Horton.* Comus *performed in 1634.*
1638 *Publication of* Lycidas. *Travelled in France and Italy.*
1639 *Became a private tutor.*
1641 *Wrote pamphlets on ecclesiastical controversy, advocating the abolition of bishops.*
1642 *Married Mary Powell.* The Reason of Church Government.
1643 The Doctrine and Discipline of Divorce.
1644 Aeropagitica; Of Education.
1645 Poems.
1649 On the Tenure of Kings and Magistrates *(a pamphlet in favour of the execution of Charles I). Appointed Secretary for the Foreign Tongues to the Council of State.*

John Milton's Protestant upbringing strengthened his austere and melancholy personality. He was the perfect Puritan and devoted many years to the service of Cromwell. From this period date his religious and political pamphlets in which he argued in favour of liberties (he pleaded for divorce in cases of incompatibility of temperament, not only of adultery), against the power of the bishops and for a more humanist education developing the intellect through poetry and philosophy. In the best-known of his pamphlets, Areopagitica *(cf p. 76), he asks Parliament to abolish the requirement that books should be officially approved before publication. In this defence of freedom of printing, he explains that books have a life of their own, that killing them is like killing reason, for dangerous books can only hurt a mind which is already damaged.*

Milton started writing poems when he was at University. His first important work, L'Allegro *and* Il Penseroso *opposes two moods: joy and melancholy. The pleasures of nature, of country and city life, are contrasted with comtemplative and solitary occupations.* Comus, *a masque (a form of court entertainment which included poetry, drama, songs and music) shows the triumph*

1651 A Defence of the English People *(a defence of the Commonwealth).*
1652 *Became blind.*
1656 *Second marriage.*
1659 A Treatise of Civil Power.
1663 *Third marriage.*
1667 Paradise Lost *published.*
1671 Paradise Regained; Samson Agonistes.
1673 Of True Religion.
1674 *Died in London.*

of chastity and purity over temptation and corruption. Lycidas, *a pastoral elegy, bewails the death of his friend Edward King and with many digressions, including attacks against the corruption of the Church, asserts the enduring power of poetry. It is the last work of importance Milton wrote before he turned to political activities, and it was only after twenty years that he started writing his great epic poem in twelve books,* Paradise Lost.

The poem relates the fall and rebellion of Satan, the creation of the world, Satan's revenge on Adam and Eve and their subsequent banishment from the earthly paradise. Throughout the poem, it is Satan with his energy and fearlessness who unconsciously appears as the most attractive character. This hero-villain is puzzling in a religious epic whose aim is to "justify the ways of God to man". The poem is written in very musical and powerful blank verse, making constant use of alliteration and verbal echoes to achieve a magnificent and sublime dimension.

Paradise Regained *deals with the temptation of Christ in the desert and his resistance to Satan.*

Paradise Lost (1667)

Satan has been expelled from Heaven by God and the angels. Still unrepentant, he surveys his new realm.

Is this the Region, this the Soil, the Clime,
Said then the lost Arch Angel, this the seat
That we must change for Heav'n, this mournful gloom
For that celestial light? Be it so, since hee
Who now is Sovran can dispose and bid
What shall be right: fardest from him is best
Whom reason hath equald, force hath made supream
Above his equals. Farewel happy Fields
Where Joy for ever dwells: Hail horrours, hail
Infernal world, and thou profoundest Hell
Receive thy new Possessor: One who brings
A mind not to be chang'd by Place or Time.
The mind is its own place, and in it self
Can make a Heav'n of Hell, a Hell of Heav'n.
What matter where, if I be still the same,
And what I should be, all but less then hee
Whom Thunder hath made greater? Here at least
We shall be free; th' Almighty hath not built
Here for his envy, will not drive us hence:
Here we may reign secure, and in my choyce
To reign is worth ambition though in Hell:
Better to reign in Hell, then serve in Heav'n.
But wherefore let we then our faithful friends,
Th' associates and copartners of our loss
Lye thus astonisht[1] on th' oblivious Pool[2],
And call them not to share with us their part
In this unhappy Mansion, or once more
With rallied Arms to try what may be yet
Regained in Heav'n, or what more lost in Hell?

Book I (l. 242-270)

1. *astonished:* dazed, in a stupor – 2. *the oblivious pool:* the lake of oblivion (in Hell).

Milton on his work:

● (...) I applied myself to that resolution which Ariosto followed against the persuasions of Bembo, to fix all the industry and art I could unite to the adorning of my native tongue; not to make verbal curiosities the end (that were a toilsome vanity), but to be an interpreter and relater of the best and sagest things among mine own citizens throughout this island, in the mother dialect. That what the greatest and choicest wits of Athens, Rome, or modern Italy, and those Hebrews of old, did for their country, I in my proportion with this over and above of being a Christian, might do for mine: not caring to be once named abroad, though perhaps I could attain to that, but content with these British Islands as my world (...)

The Reason of Church Government, 1642.

● And chiefly thou O Spirit that dost prefer
Before all temples the upright heart and pure,
Instruct me, for thou know'st; thou from the first
Wast present, and with mighty wings outspread
Dove-like sat'st brooding on the vast abyss
And madest it pregnant: what in me is dark
Illumine, what is low raise and support;
That to the highth of this great argument
I may assert eternal providence,
And justify the ways of God to men.

Paradise Lost, I, 17-26.

● THE VERSIFICATION OF PARADISE LOST

(This was inserted in 1668 "for the satisfaction of many that have desired it", in copies of the first edition of *Paradise Lost* still in the hands of the printer. Editor's note)

The measure is English heroic verse without rhyme, as that of Homer in Greek and of Virgil in Latin, rhyme being no necessary adjunct or true ornament of poem or good verse, in longer works especially, but the invention of a barbarous age to set off wretched matter and lame metre, graced indeed since by the use of some famous modern poets, carried away by custom, but much to their own vexation, hindrance, and constraint to express many things otherwise, and for the most part worse, than else they would have expressed them. Not without cause therefore some both Italian and Spanish poets of prime note have rejected rhyme both in longer and shorter works, as have also long since our best English tragedies, as a thing of itself to all judicious ears, trivial and of no true musical delight – which consists only in apt numbers, fit quantity of syllabes, and the sense variously drawn out from one verse into another, not in the jingling sound of like endings, a fault avoided by the learned ancients both in poetry and all good oratory. This neglect then of rhyme so little is to be taken for a defect, though it may seem so perhaps to vulgar readers, that it rather is to be esteemed an example set, the first in English, of ancient liberty recovered to heroic poem from the troublesome and modern bondage of rhyming.

Note on the Versification of *Paradise Lost,* 1668.

William Blake on Milton:

Those who restrain desire, do so because theirs is weak enough to be restrained; and the restrainer or reason usurps its place & governs the unwilling.

And being restrain'd, it by degrees becomes passive, till it is only the shadow of desire.

The history of this is written in *Paradise Lost,* & the Governor of Reason is call'd Messiah.

And the original Archangel, or possessor of the command of the heavenly host, is call'd the Devil or Satan, and his children are call'd Sin & Death.

But in the Book of Job, Milton's Messiah is call'd Satan.

For this history has been adopted by both parties.

It indeed appear'd to Reason as if Desire was cast out; but the Devil's account is, that the Messiah fell, & formed a heaven of what he stole from the Abyss.

This is shewn in the Gospel, where he prays to the Father to send the comforter, or Desire, that Reason may have Ideas to build on; the Jehovah of the Bible being no other than he who dwells in flaming fire.

Know that after Christ's death, he became Jehovah.

But in Milton, the Father is Destiny, the Son a Ratio of the five senses, & the Holy-ghost Vacuum!

Note: The reason Milton wrote in fetters when he wrote of Angels & God, and at liberty when of Devils & Hell, is because he was a true poet and of the Devil's party without knowing it.

The Marriage of Heaven and Hell, 1790.

P. B. Shelley on Milton:

Milton's Devil as a moral being is as far superior to his God, as one who perseveres in some person which he had conceived to be excellent, in spite of adversity and torture, is to one who in the cold security of undoubted triumph inflicts the most horrible revenge upon his enemy – not from any mistaken notion of bringing him to repent of a perseverance in enmity, but with the open and alleged design of exasperating him to deserve new torments...

Cf. Verse form and poetic genres, p. 2; Versification, p. 7.

Compare these two Romantic visions of Milton's Satan :

Milton was a constant source of inspiration for the Romantic painters, starting with Fuseli and Blake. William Blake (cf. p. 161) disapproved of Milton the Puritan but admired his creations: Satan, as well as Adam and Eve. His illustrations are more symbolic and stylized than representational. For both Fuseli and Blake, it was the figures that mattered more than the setting. ("Where man is not, nature is barren", wrote Blake in The Marriage of Heaven and Hell). *John Martin (cf. p. 55)'s illustrations, on the contrary, emphasize the fantastic and dramatic side, the immensity of the universe of* Paradise Lost, *to such a point that the characters become almost secondary.*

William Blake: Satan Arousing the Rebel Angels, *1808. The Victoria and Albert Museum.*

John Martin: Satan Summoning the Rebel Angels, *1827. The Victoria and Albert Museum.*

T. S. Eliot on Paradise Lost:

The appropriateness of the material of *Paradise Lost* to the genius and the limitations of Milton, is still more evident when we consider the visual imagery. I have already remarked, in a paper written some years ago, on Milton's weakness of visual observation, a weakness which I think was always present – the effect of his blindness may have been rather to strengthen the compensatory qualities than to increase a fault which was already present. Mr. Wilson Knight, who has devoted close study to recurrent imagery in poetry, has called attention to Milton's propensity towards images of engineering and mechanics; to me it seems that Milton is at his best in imagery suggestive of vast size. limitless space, abysmal depth, and light and darkness. No theme and no setting, other than that which he chose in *Paradise Lost,* could have given him such scope for the kind of imagery in which he excelled, or made less demand upon those powers of visual imagination which were in him defective.

Most of the absurdities and inconsistencies to which Johnson calls attention, and which, so far as they can justly be isolated in this way, he properly condemns, will I think appear in a more correct proportion if we consider them in relation to his general judgment. I do not think that we should attempt to *see* very clearly any scene that Milton depicts: it should be accepted as a shifting phantasmagory. To complain, because we first find the arch-fiend "chain'd on the burning lake", and in a minute or two see him making his way to the shore, is to expect a kind of consistency which the world to which Milton has introduced us does not require. (...)

We must, then, in reading *Paradise Lost,* not expect to see clearly; our sense of sight must be blurred, so that our *hearing* may become more acute. *Paradise Lost,* like *Finnegans Wake* (for I can think of no work which provides a more interesting parallel: two books by great blind musicians, each writing a language of his own based upon English) makes this peculiar demand for a readjustment of the reader's mode of apprehension. The emphasis is on the sound, not the vision, upon the word, not the idea; and in the end it is the unique versification that is the most certain sign of Milton's intellectual mastership.

T. S. Eliot, *Milton II.*
Selected Prose of T. S. Eliot.

Samuel PEPYS 1633-1703

1633 *Born in London.*
1654 *Graduated from Cambridge. Appointed secretary to Edward Mountagu.*
1660 *Began his diary.*
Accompanied Montagu's fleet bringing back Charles II from Holland.
Appointed Clerk of the Acts (i.e. Secretary to the Admiralty).
1660-1684 *Appointed to several successive offices (Surveyor-General of the Victualling, Secretary to the Admiralty Commission, Governor of Christ's Hospital, King's Secretary for Naval Affairs).*
1684-1686 *President of the Royal Society.*
1685 *MP for Harwich.*
1689 *Accused of Jacobitism after the fall of James II.*
Published Memoirs relating to the State of the Royal Navy.
1701 *Retired at Clapham.*
1703 *Died at Clapham.*

Pepys's Diary, *which made him famous, was only published in 1825, after being transcribed from the shorthand in which it had originally been written to ensure secrecy.*

With extreme candour and honesty, Pepys gives a description of his everyday life betwen 1660 and 1669. It is almost a confession, devoid as it is of the distortions of pride or modesty. The diary presents a superb self-portrait of a man of his time: active, hardworking, selfish, but with a keen interest in the world around him – whether the gossips of the town or the latest scientific discoveries. It is also a faithful and objective account of London life during the first ten years of the Restoration.

A plague broadsheet, 1665.

The Diary (1665)

12 August. The people die so, that now it seems they are fain to carry the dead to be buried by daylight, the nights not sufficing to do it in. And my Lord Mayor commands people to be within at 9 at night, all (as they say) that the sick may have liberty to go abroad for ayre.

16 August. Up; and after doing some necessary business about my accounts at home, to the office and there with Mr Hater wrote letters. And I did deliver to him my last will, one part of it to deliver to my wife when I am dead. Thence to the Exchange, which I have, not been a great while. But Lord, how sad a sight it is to see the streets empty of people, and very few upon the Change – jealous of every door that one sees shut up, lest it should be the plague – and about us, two shops in three, if not more, generally shut up.

3 September. Lords Day. Up, and put on my coloured silk suit, very fine, and my new periwigg, bought a good while since, but darst not wear it because the plague was in Westminster when I bought it. And it is a wonder what will be the fashion after the plague is done as to periwigs, for nobody will dare to buy any haire for fear of the infection – that it had been cut off of the heads of people dead of the plague. Church being done, my Lord Brouncker, Sir J. Mennes, and I up to the vestry at the desire of the Justices of the Peace, Sir Th. Bidolph and Sir W. Boreman and Alderman Hooker – in order to the doing something for the keeping of the plague from growing; but Lord, to consider the madness of people of the town, who will (because they are forbid) come in crowds along with the dead corps to see them buried. But we agreed on some orders for the prevention thereof.

16 October. But Lord, how empty the [city] streets are, and melancholy, so many poor sick people in the streets, full of sores, and so many sad stories overheard as I walk, everybody talking of this dead, and that man sick, and so many in this place, and so many in that. And they tell me that in Westminster there is never a physitian, and but one apothecary left, all being dead – but that there are great hopes of a great decrease this week: God send it.

Pepys's Diary.

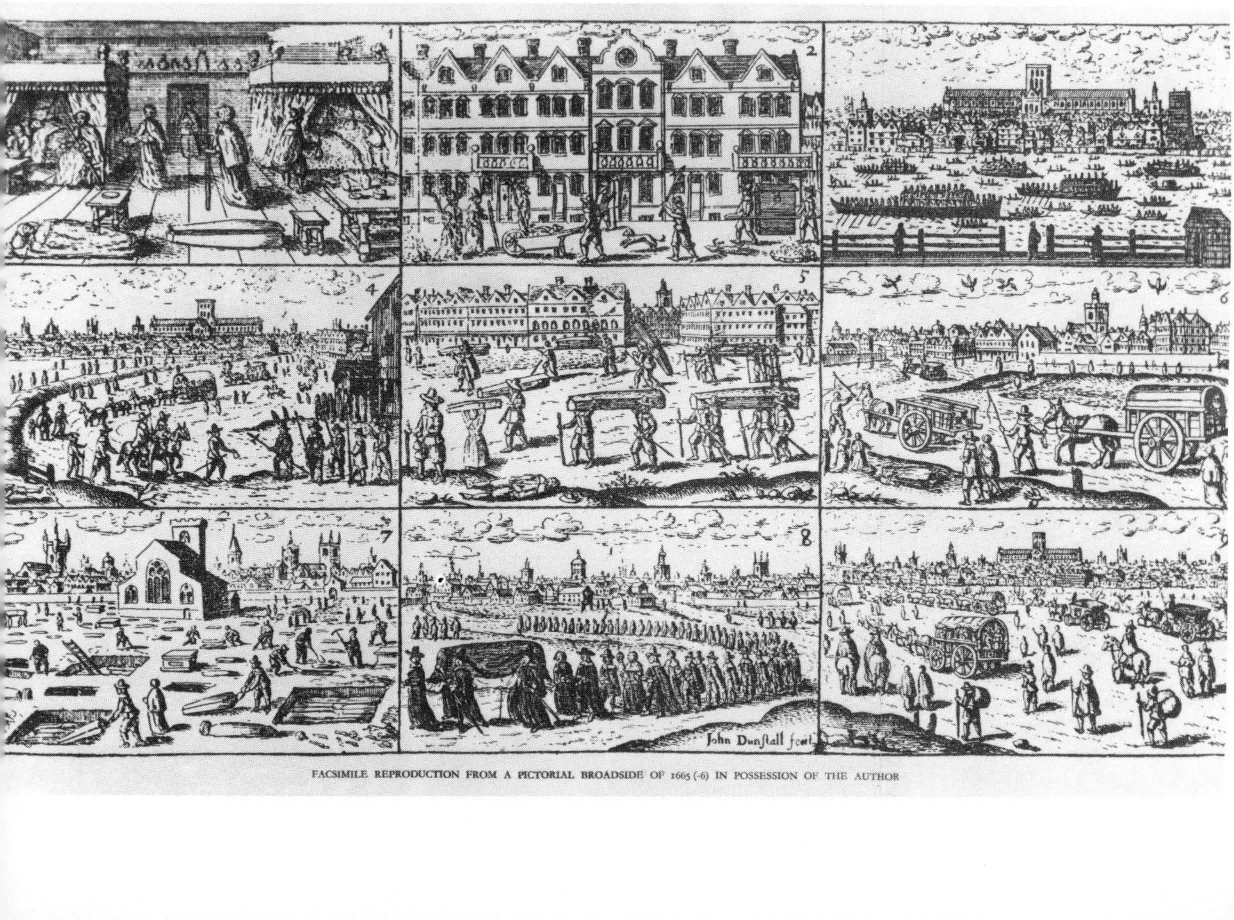

FACSIMILE REPRODUCTION FROM A PICTORIAL BROADSIDE OF 1665 (-6) IN POSSESSION OF THE AUTHOR

Compare the passage from Pepys's Diary *with the following excerpt from John Evelyn's* Diary, *written at the same time:*

16*th*. There died of the plague in London this week 1100; and in the week following, above 2000. Two houses were shut up in our parish.

2*nd August*. A solemn fast through England to deprecate God's displeasure against the land by pestilence and war; our Doctor preaching on 26 Levit. v. 41, 42, that the means to obtain remission of punishment was not to repine at it; but humbly to submit to it.

15*th August*. There perished this week 5000.

28*th*. The contagion still increasing, and growing now all about us, I sent my wife and whole family (two or three necessary servants excepted) to my brother's at Wotton, being resolved to stay at my house myself, and to look after my charge, trusting in the providence and goodness of God.

5*th September*. To Chatham, to inspect my charge, with 900l. in my coach.

7*th*. Came home, there perishing near 10,000 poor creatures weekly; however, I went all along the city and suburbs from Kent Street to St. James's, a dismal passage, and dangerous to see so many coffins exposed in the streets, now thin of people; the shops shut up, and all in mournful silence, not knowing whose turn might be next. I went to the Duke of Albemarle for a pest-ship, to wait on our infected men, who were not a few.

1*st October*. This afternoon, whilst at evening prayers, tidings were brought me of the birth of a Daughter at Wotton, after six Sons, in the same chamber I had first took breath in, and at the first day of that month, as I was on the last, 45 years before.

4*th*. The monthly fast.

11*th*. To London, and went through the whole City, having occasion to alight out of the coach in several places about business of money, when I was environed with multitudes of poor pestiferous creatures begging alms: the shops universally shut up, a dreadful prospect! I dined with my Lord General; was to receive 10,000 l., and had guards to convey both myself and it, and so returned home, through God's infinite mercy.

31*st*. Now blessed be God for His extraordinary mercies and preservation of me this year, when thousands, and ten thousands, perished, and were swept away on each side of me, there dying in our parish this year 406 of the pestilence!

John Evelyn (1620-1706) was a wealthy country gentleman and a Royalist. He held several minor offices after the Restoration and was devoted to public improvements, education and charity. He was a friend of Samuel Pepys. His diary covers most of his life and shows more reserve than Pepys's.

The Diseases and Casualties this Week.

Abortive	5	Imposthume	11
Aged	43	Infants	16
Ague	2	Killed by a fall from the Belfrey at Alhallows the Great	1
Apoplexie	1	Kingsevil	2
Bleeding	2	Lethargy	1
Burnt in his Bed by a Candle at St. Giles Cripplegate	1	Palsie	1
Canker	1	Plague	7165
Childbed	42	Rickets	17
Chrisomes	18	Rising of the Lights	11
Consumption	134	Scowring	5
Convulsion	64	Scurvy	2
Cough	2	Spleen	1
Dropsie	33	Spotted Feaver	101
Feaver	309	Stilborn	17
Flox and Small-pox	5	Stone	2
Frighted	3	Stopping of the stomach	9
Gowt	1	Strangury	1
Grief	3	Suddenly	1
Griping in the Guts	51	Surfeit	49
Jaundies	5	Teeth	121
		Thrush	5
		Timpany	1
		Tissick	11
		Vomiting	3
		Winde	3
		Wormes	15

Christned { Males — [illegible] / Females — 81 / In all — 176 } Buried { Males — [illegible] / Females — 4202 / In all — 8297 } Plague — 7165

Increased in the Burials this Week — 607

Parishes clear of the Plague — 4 Parishes Infected — 126

The Assize of Bread set forth by Order of the Lord Maior and Court of Aldermen,
A penny Wheaten Loaf to contain Nine Ounces and a half, and three half-penny White Loaves the like weight.

A bill of mortality, 1665.

John BUNYAN 1628-1688

1628 *Born near Bedford; his father was a tinker and John Bunyan was given little education and prepared for his father's trade.*
1644 *Entered the parliamentary army.*
1647 *Left the army and went through a period of fears and religious doubts which led to his conversion.*
1653 *Renounced the Church of England and became a Baptist dissenter.*
1656 *Started preaching, while still working as a tinker.*
1660-72 *Imprisoned for holding unauthorized religious meetings.*
1666 *While in jail, related his inner journey to conversion in* Grace Abounding to the Chief of Sinners.
1672-1688 *Became a renowned preacher.*
1678 The Pilgrim's Progress, *part I.*
1680 The Life and Death of Mr. Badman.
1684 The Pilgrim's Progress, *part II.*
1688 *Died in London.*

As a fundamentalist and a Puritan, Bunyan refused the hierarchical structure of the Anglican Church, believing that each Christian should develop his own relationship with God, using the Bible as his guide. It is such a spiritual pilgrimage that he attempted to relate in The Pilgrim's Progress, *a book which did not only have an immediate success when it was published, but which remained for about two centuries one of the most widely-read and popular works in English.*

It is an allegory that describes Christian's journey from the City of Destruction, a symbol of the corrupt and sinful world, to the Celestial City. The "hero" travels through many obstacles, temptations and pitfalls (e.g. The Slough of Despond, Vanity Fair, The Valley of Humiliation, the River of Death...) meeting numerous characters embodying various passions.

The book is reminiscent of medieval romances and allegories as well as of plays like Everyman, *but remains highly original. It is enhanced by Bunyan's vigorous and direct language, free of any affectation. The scenes are depicted in detail and with a realism often tinged with wit and humour.*

The Pilgrim's Progress (1678)

Now I beheld in my dream that they had not journeyed far, but the river and the way, for a time, parted. At which they were not a little sorry, yet they durst not go out of the way. Now the way from the river was rough, and their feet tender by reason of their travels. So the soul of the pilgrims was much discouraged, because of the way. [Numbers 21: 4[1]] Wherefore still as they went on, they wished for better way. Now a little before them there was on the left hand of the road a meadow and a stile to go over into it, and that meadow is called By-path Meadow. Then said Christian to his fellow, "If this meadow lieth along by our wayside, let's go over into it". Then he went to the stile to see, and behold a path lay along by the way on the other side of the fence. "'Tis according to my wish", said Christian. "Here is the easiest going; come, good Hopeful, and let us go over".

HOPEFUL. "But how if this path should lead us out of the way?"

CHRISTIAN. "That's not like", said the other. "Look, doth it not go along by the wayside"? So Hopeful, being persuaded by his fellow, went after him over the stile. When they were gone over and were got into the path, they found it very easy for their feet; and withal, they, looking before them, espied a man walking as they did (and his name was Vain Confidence). So they called after him, and asked him whither that way led. He said, "To the Celestial Gate". "Look", said Christian, "did not I tell you so? By this you may see we are right". So they followed, and he went before them. But behold the night came on, and it grew very dark; so that they that were behind lost the sight of him that went before.

He therefore that went before (Vain Confidence by name), not seeing the way before him, fell into a deep pit, which was on purpose there made by the prince of those grounds to catch vainglorious fools withal, and was dashed in pieces with his fall.

Now Christian and his fellow heard him fall. So they called to know the matter, but there was none to answer, only they heard a groaning. Then said Hopeful, "Where are we now"? Then was his fellow silent, as mistrusting that he had led him out of the way. And now it began to rain, and thunder, and lighten in a very dreadful manner, and the water rose amain[2].

Then Hopeful groaned in himself, saying, "Oh that I had kept on my way"!

CHRISTIAN. "Who could have thought that this path should have led us out of the way"?

HOPEFUL. "I was afraid on't at very first, and therefore gave you that gentle caution. I would have spoke plainer, but that you are older than I".

CHRISTIAN. "Good brother, be not offended. I am sorry I have brought thee out of the way, and that I have put thee into such eminent danger; pray, my brother, forgive me; I did not do it of an evil intent".

HOPEFUL. "Be comforted, my brother, for I forgive thee, and believe, too, that this shall be for our good".

CHRISTIAN. "I am glad I have with me a merciful brother. But we must not stand thus; let's try to go back again".

HOPEFUL. "But, good brother, let me go before".

CHRISTIAN. "No, if you please let me go first, that if there be any danger, I may be first therein, because by my means we are both gone out of the way".

HOPEFUL. "No", said Hopeful, "you shall not go first, for your mind, being troubled, may lead you out of the way again". Then for their encouragement, they heard the voice of one, saying, "Let thine heart be towards the highway, even the way that thou wentest: turn again". [Jeremiah 31: 21][3].

1. *Numbers 21: 4:* "And they journeyed from mount Hor by the way of the Red Sea, to compass the land of Edom: and the soul of the people was much discouraged because of the way." – 2. *amain:* quickly and violently – 3. *Jeremiah 31: 21:* "Set thee up waymarks, make thee high heaps: set thine heart toward the highway, even the way which thou wentest: turn again, O virgin of Israel, turn again to these thy cities".

Bunyan on his work:

By metaphors I speak; were not God's laws,
His Gospel laws, in olden time held forth
By types, shadows and metaphors? Yet loth
Will any sober man be to find fault
With them, lest he be found for to assault
The highest wisdom. No, he rather stoops
And seeks to find out what by pins and loops,
By calves and sheep, by heifers and by rams,
By birds and herbs, and by the blood of lambs,
God speaketh to him; and happy is he
That finds the light and grace that in them be. (...)
  This book will make a traveller of thee,
If by its counsel thou wilt ruled be;
It will direct thee to the Holy Land,
If thou wilt its directions understand.
Yea, it will make the slothful active be,
The blind, also, delightful things to see.
  Art thou for something rare and profitable?
Wouldest thou see a truth within a fable?
Art thou forgetful? Wouldest thou remember
From New Year's Day to the last of December?
Then read my fancies; they will stick like burrs,
And may be to the helpless comforters.
  This book is writ in such a dialect,
As may the minds of listless men affect.
It seems a novelty, and yet contains
Nothing but sound and honest gospel strains.

Apology.

About The Pilgrim's Progress *as an allegory:*

The Pilgrim's Progress is designed, in its broad lines, as an allegory. Let us define allegory here as Coleridge defined it, and then let us illustrate the definition in its simplest application. Coleridge says that allegory is the employment of a certain set of characters, actions, and circumstances in such a way that these convey to the mind, under the disguise of sense objects, certain moral qualities or conceptions, and so that all the parts combine to form a consistent whole. The large action of Bunyan's book is that of a pilgrimage, and we see the pilgrim going his way on a solid, earthy road, through mud, through green fields, over rocks; and conveyed under this earthy disguise is the notion of the complicated moral life of man, his occasions of serenity, his occasions of despair, the challenges of his mortal estate. It is an ancient, universal image that Bunyan has used – the image of life as a journey; he has given it a special inflection – the journey is not a mere wayfaring but a "pilgrimage", that is, a journey to a holy place. But our definition says that each of the parts, as well as the whole, conveys a moral idea. To illustrate the allegorical operation of one of the parts we may use the first image in the book – that of the "man clothed with rags, standing in a certain place, with his face from his own house, a book in his hand, and a great burden upon his back". Isaiah says (64:6): "all our righteousnesses are as filthy rags"; and the Psalmist says (38:4): "For mine iniquities are gone over mine head: as an heavy burden they are too heavy for me." We put an equal sign, as it were, between the man's previous complacent notions of his own goodness and the worthless rags that clothe him, and another equal sign between his guiltiness and his burden.

D. Van Ghent *The English Novel, Form and Function,*
By permission of Holt, Rinehart and Winston,
C.B.S. College Publishing.

Cf. Characters and Characterization, p. 12.

Compare the passage with the following excerpt from Everyman, *a 15th century Morality Play that relates how Everyman, called by Death, finds all his friends – except Good Deeds – unwilling to accompany him:*

FELLOWSHIP. Everyman, good morrow by this day.
Sir, why lookest thou so piteously?
If any thing be amiss, I pray thee, me say,
That I may help to remedy.
EVERYMAN. Yea, good Fellowship, yea,
I am in great jeopardy.
FELLOWSHIP. My true friend, show to me your mind;
I will not forsake thee, unto my life's end,
In the way of good company.
EVERYMAN. That was well spoken, and lovingly.
FELLOWSHIP. Sir, I must needs know your heaviness;
I have pity to see you in any distress;
If any have you wronged ye shall revenged be,
Though I on the ground be slain for thee, –
Though that I know before that I should die.
EVERYMAN. Verily, Fellowship, gramercy.
FELLOWSHIP. Tush! by thy thanks I set not a straw.
Show me your grief, and say no more.
EVERYMAN. If I my heart should to you break,
And then you to turn your mind from me,
And would not me comfort, when you hear me speak,
Then should I ten times sorrier be.
FELLOWSHIP. Sir, I say as I will do in deed.
EVERYMAN. Then be you a good friend at need:
I have found you true here before.
FELLOWSHIP. And so ye shall evermore;
For, in faith, and thou go to hell,
I will not forsake thee by the way!

This is one of the 28 watercolours Blake painted to illustrate The Pilgrim's Progress. *Though Blake was interested in Bunyan's works, he despised the allegory as a form ("Fable or allegory are a totally distinct and inferior kind of Poetry") and opposed it to vision ("Vision or Imagination is a Representation of what Eternally Exists, Really and Unchangeably") Nonetheless, he could admit that "Fable or Allegory is seldom without some Vision.* Pilgrim's Progress *is full of it..."*

William Blake: Christian reading in his book.
The Frick Collection, New York.

3. The Restoration and the Age of Pope

The stage of the Red Bull in 1673. Notice the candelabra and footlights. From The Wits, or Sport upon Sport, *by Francis Kirkman, 1673.*

literature and society

The Puritan experiment in government did not long survive Cromwell's death in 1658; less than two years later – in May, 1660 – Charles II returned from exile amid popular acclamation. "The shouting and joy expressed by all is past imagination,"recorded the diarist Samuel Pepys, and though, as one of those who went over to Holland to escort the King back, he cannot be considered a wholly impartial witness, there can be no doubt that a majority of the nation was weary both of the rigors of Puritan rule and of the instability in government that followed Cromwell's death. There remained, as time was to show, a strong Puritan core in England, but for the moment monarchist sentiment was in the ascendant, and the Cavaliers came back to enjoy an Indian summer until the bad judgment of Charles' brother and successor, James II, alienated finally the great Protestant heart of the country and so brought about the "Glorious Revolution" of 1688 and the accession of a king and queen not by divine right but on Parliament's terms. There was a strong traditionalist element in England which had never reconciled itself to the execution of Charles I and to the various forms which Cromwell's rule took, and this was true even of many who were on the Puritan side in the conflict. The popular welcome given to Charles on his return was largely due to the general belief that continuity and legality had now been re-established without loss of any of the real gains for Protestant freedom and variety won in the fight against royal absolutism and episcopal dictatorship in the 1640's. This view proved to be unduly optimistic; if it had been well-founded, the revolution of 1688 would have been unnecessary.

	Politics and Society	Literature and the Arts
1660	The Restoration: Charles II.	Beginning of Pepys' *Diary*.
1662	Creation of the Royal Society. Licensing Act (press censorship).	
1663		S. BUTLER: *Hudibras,*
1665	The Great Plague.	
1666	The Great Fire of London.	
1667		MILTON: *Paradise Lost.*

	Politics and Society	Literature and the Arts
1672		DRYDEN: *The Conquest of Granada.*
1678		BUNYAN: *The Pilgrim's Progress.* DRYDEN: *All for Love.*
1679	Habeas Corpus Act.	
1681		DRYDEN: *Absalom and Achitophel.*
1685	Accession of James II.	
1688	The Glorious Revolution: James II flees to France, then abdicates. William of Orange becomes William III.	
1689	Toleration Act. Bill of Rights.	
1690	Battle of the Boyne. James II defeated by William III in Ireland.	LOCKE: *Two Treatises of Civil Goverment.* *Essay Concerning Human Understanding.*
1692		PURCELL: *The Fairy Queen.*
1695	Licensing Act not renewed.	CONGREVE: *Love for Love.*
1698		COLLIER: *The Immorality & Profaneness of the English stage.*
1700		CONGREVE: *The Way of the World.*
1701	Settlement Act.	
1701-13	War of the Spanish Succession.	
1702	Accession of Queen Anne.	
1704		SWIFT: *A Tale of a Tub.*
1707	Act of Union with Scotland (First United Parliament of Great Britain).	FARQUHAR: *The Beaux' Stratagem.*
1709	Copyright Act.	STEELE: Beginning of *The Tatler.*
1710		Arrival of Händel in England. BERKELEY: *Principles of Human Knowledge.*
1711		ADDISON & STEELE: *The Spectator.*
1713	Peace of Utrecht.	BERKELEY: *Three Dialogues between Hylas and Philonous.*
1714	Hanoverian Succession: George I.	POPE: *The Rape of the Lock.*
1715	First Jacobite Uprising.	
1718	War with Spain.	
1719		DEFOE: *Robinson Crusoe.*
1724		SWIFT: *Drapier's Letters.*
1726		SWIFT: *Gulliver's Travels.*
1727	George II.	
1728		GAY: *The Beggar's Opera.* POPE: *The Dunciad.*
1729	Peace between France, Spain and Britain.	SWIFT: *A Modest Proposal...*
1730		THOMSON: *The Seasons.*
1732		HOGARTH: *The Harlot's Progress.*
1732-34		POPE: *Essay on Man.*
1735-39	War with Spain	HOGARTH: *The Rake's Progress.*

Artist unknown:
Charles II dancing with the Princess Palatine at a ball in the Hague, *1650.*
Windsor Castle. Ph. Edimedia.

The reaction against Puritan manners and morals was inevitable. It was all the more violent because many of the returned Cavaliers had spent their exile in France and become expert in French wit and French gallantry, and because the King himself, an indolent sensualist possessed of both wit and cunning, encouraged an atmosphere of hedonistic liveliness at Court. Charles set the tone for the Court Wits, and the Court Wits set the tone if not for all the literature of the period at least for a certain segment of it, notably dramatic comedy.

The Puritan government had stopped the performance of plays in September, 1642, and though there were occasional surreptitious performances at the various theaters after the passing of the ordinance of suppression, and though Sir William Davenant received permission to give some private dramatic performances (and perhaps also some more public performances) in the late 1650's, on the whole it can be said that the English theater did not exist between 1642 and 1660. With the restoration of King Charles came the restoration of the theater. But it was a different theater, playing to a different kind of audience, from that which had called forth the plays of Shakespeare. The modern theater, with its picture-frame stage, its actresses taking female parts, its moveable scenery designed to create a visual image of the locale of each scene, its artificial light, was developed during this period. This was partly because of the influence of France, where so many of Charles' hangers-on had spent their exile, and partly because the Restoration theater took over and developed the traditions of the *private* rather than the public Elizabethan and Jacobean theater, which had in some degree managed to survive the prohibition of public dramatic performances. The audience for Restoration drama was also more restricted both geographically and socially than it had been before the closing of the theaters. There was no dramatic activity of any consequence outside London, and the two theaters within the metropolis catered to wits and gallants who went to the play as much for the purpose of engaging in amorous intrigue or of displaying their own dress and manners as of seeing and enjoying a dramatic performance. The playhouse was regarded by the respectable citizens of London as a center of vice and exhibitionism, and they accordingly avoided it, while the dramatists in their turn took every opportunity of ridiculing the middle-class virtues and as often as not presented the citizenry as made up of foolish and jealous husbands whose wives were fair game for seduction by court gallants.

Restoration drama was thus a class drama to a degree that no earlier English drama – not even the "citizen comedy" of the Elizabethan theater had been.

David Daiches,
A Critical History of English Literature, Vol. 3,
Martin Secker and Warburg Ltd.

literature and philosophy

One philosopher, John Locke *(1632-1704) dominates the first half of the eighteenth century. At the basis of Locke's theory of knowledge is the principle that there are no a priori, innate ideas: everything comes from sense experience (which does not prevent reflection and reasoning from operating on these ideas coming from outside). Locke also explains how ideas that have nothing in common can become associated in our minds, in different ways for different people, therefore isolating them (cf Sterne's characters and their hobby-horses). In the following excerpt Locke develops his well-known theory of the mind as a blank page.*

All ideas come from sensation or reflection. – Let us then, suppose the mind to be, as we say, white paper, void of all characters, without any ideas; how comes it to be furnished? Whence comes it by that vast store which the busy and boundless fancy of man has painted on it with an almost endless variety? Whence has it all the materials of reason and knowledge? To this I answer, in one word, from experience; in that all our knowledge is founded, and from that it ultimately derives itself. Our observation, employed either about external sensible objects, or about the internal operations of our minds, perceived and reflected on by ourselves, is that which supplies our understandings with all the materials of thinking. These two are the fountains of knowledge, from whence all the ideas we have, or can naturally have do spring.

John Locke,
An Essay Concerning Human Understanding,
Book II.

Innate Ideas are in Every Man, Born with him; they are truly Himself. The Man who says that we have No Innate Ideas must be a Fool and Knave, Having No Con-Science or Innate Science.

William Blake.

Locke, après avoir ruiné les idées innées, après avoir bien renoncé à la vanité de croire qu'on pense toujours, établit que toutes nos idées viennent par les sens, examine nos idées simples et celles qui sont composées, suit l'esprit de l'homme dans toutes ses opérations, fait voir combien les langues que les hommes parlent sont imparfaites, et quel abus nous faisons des termes à tous moments.

Voltaire, *Lettres Philosophiques,* Lettre XIII.

".... from an unhappy association of ideas which have no connection in nature, it so fell out at length, that my poor mother could never hear the said clock wound up, – but the thoughts of some other things unavoidably popp'd into her head, – & vice versa: – which strange combination of ideas, the sagacious Locke, who certainly understood the nature of these things better than most men, affirms to have produced more wry actions than all other sources of prejudice whatsoever."

L. Sterne, *Tristram Shandy,* I, V.

Compare Locke's Essay, II, 33, 5.

His views about politics too are directly inspired by his study of human nature. Like Hobbes, Locke believes that certain selfish tendencies in man make a "contract" necessary. Yet he sees human beings as essentially reasonable so that it would be dangerous and futile to give up one's rights entirely to the ruler. Supreme power should rest with the people who must be able to remove and change the government if it acts contrary to the trust reposed in it. Hence the idea of a reciprocal *contract.*
Compare the following excerpts with the passage from Hobbes's Leviathan *(p. 79).*

Though perhaps at first some one good and excellent man, having got a pre-eminency amongst the rest, had this deference paid to his goodness and virtue, as to a kind of natural authority, that the chief rule, by a tacit consent, devolved into his hands, without any other caution, but the assurance they had of his uprightness and wisdom: yet when time... had brought in successors of another stamp the people finding their properties not secure under the government as then it was (whereas government has no other end but the preservation of property) could never be safe nor at rest nor think themselves in civil society until the legislature was placed in collective bodies of men, call them Senate, Parliament, or what you please. (...)

Here, it is likely, the common question will be made: Who shall be judge whether the prince or legislature act contrary to their trust? This, perhaps, ill-affected and factious men may spread amongst the people when the prince only makes use of his due prerogative. To this I reply: the people shall be judge, for who shall be judge whether the trustee or deputy acts well and according to the trust reposed in him but he who deputes him?

J. Locke, *Two Treatises of Civil Government,* 1690.

literature and the arts

"The amazed word shall henceforth find
None but my Lilly ever drew a Minde."

Lovelace *(the Cavalier poet)*

Sir Peter Lely: The Music Lesson, *1654.*
Lord Dulverton, Batsford Park, Glos.

Painting

The name most commonly associated with the reign of Charles II is that of Sir Peter LELY, *a Dutch painter who settled in England in 1641.*

In mere executive ability he was perhaps equal to Van Dyck. His drawing could be impeccable, he was capable of lovely colour, and he has hardly been surpassed in his painting of the texture of silks and satins. In the power of rendering the sleepy voluptuousness which was fashionable at the Court of Charles II (and elsewhere in Europe at the time) he was unrivalled. But he altogether lacks that flame of personal genius, that power of creating as well as recording an image, which warms the imagination when we contemplate a masterpiece by Van Dyck or Dobson. His style is international rather than English.

Ellis Waterhouse, Painting in Britain, 1530 to 1790, The Pelican History of Art, © *1953 Penguin Books.*

Though the Restoration brought no radical change in painting, a renewal of both themes and techniques was felt at the beginning of the 18th century.

Baroque and Rococco painting had flourished on the Continent, but hardly touched Great Britain (in spite of Rubens's ceiling of the Banqueting Hall at Whitehall.)

But the Court and the nobility who looked to France for the guidance of taste were aware that it had become fashionable for the staircases and ceilings of houses to be covered with vast mythological or allegorical paintings, and, by the time Baroque painting had lost its initial fire and faded into decorative platitude, it was introduced, in this watered form, into the British Isles.

ibid.

The best-known painters, in this genre, were Sir James THORNHILL, Antonio VERRIO *and* Louis LAGUERRE:

On painted ceilings you devoutly stare,
Where sprawl the saints of Verrio or Laguerre,
On gilded clouds in fair expansion lie,
And bring all Paradise before your eyes.

A. Pope, *To Richard Boyle, Earl of Burlington.*

New genres also appeared at this time: naval and marine paintings as well as landscapes. Portraits, however, remained the most popular form of painting; those of* Godfrey KNELLER *in particular announce the art of Hogarth: in contrast with the preciosity of Lely and his school, they are marked by directness, simplicity and a keen perception of character.

Sir Godfrey Kneller: Sir Christopher Wren, *1711. National Portrait Gallery, London.*

Architecture

Baroque architecture in England takes a diverse form. The curves are only occasionally to be seen, but the movement, violent and discordant, is present, evidenced in the strong massing of shapes, dramatic light and shade and large scale grandeur. The Baroque school was short-lived here; by 1730 it was over and the British returned to a Palladianism first introduced by Inigo Jones, its order and tranquillity more suited to the temperament of the people than the emotional violence and voluptuousness of Baroque.

Different in interpretation though it may be, the later work of Wren, that of Talman and, especially, the designs of Vanbrugh, Hawksmoor and Archer cannot be termed anything other than Baroque for the buildings display the chief characteristics of the concept. Wren's designs showed a tendency towards Baroque in his late seventeenth-century work. The west towers of *St Paul's Cathedral,* for instance and, even more, the domes and colonnades at *Greenwich* are plastic and vibrantly alive. But Wren's Baroque was always restrained and controlled; classicism was paramount over extravagance. The designs never got out of hand. In this, as always, Wren was essentially English.

D. Yarwood, The Architecture of Britain, *Batsford Ltd.*

Alexander Pope's To Richard Boyle, Earl of Burlington *(1731) marked a reaction against the baroque art of Vanbrugh. Pope advocated a return to more classical, more natural forms, and linked architecture to morality (the baroque, for example, conveying pride and a desire to impress people):*

To build, to plant, whatever you intend,
To rear the column, or the arch to bend,
To swell the terrace, or to sink the grot;
In all, let Nature never be forgot.
But treat the goddess like a modest fair,
Nor overdress, nor leave her wholly bare;
Let not each beauty everywhere be spied,
Where half the skill is decently to hide.
He gains all points, who pleasingly confounds,
Surprises, varies, and conceals the bounds.

Two names stand out:

Sir Christopher WREN, *one of England's best-known architects, who was in charge of all the major projects in London in the second half of the 17th century, such as the rebuilding of the City of London after the Great Fire of 1666.*

He built over 50 churches (among them St Paul's Cathedral) of a classical design generally, but all different and showing Wren's ability to adapt to the different sites.

Sir John Vanbrugh's *works are probably the best examples of baroque architecture in England: gigantic castles of massive and robust form with heavy groups of buildings contrasting one with another, and with highly decorated interiors. Castle Howard and Blenheim Palace are among his best-known work.*

Wren: St Bride, Fleet Street, *1680-1701.*
Vanbrugh: Blenheim Palace, Oxfordshire: the Great Court, *1705-22. In D. Yarwood, ibid.*

Music

The Restoration saw the revival of music together with that of the theatre: Charles II wanted to copy the light and gay music of the French court he had been familiar with during his exile and he surrounded himself with British and foreign musicians. The atmosphere became cosmopolitan (French and Italian music were particularly appreciated), choirs were formed and organs were heard again in churches.

Besides John BLOW *who composed a few operas (e.g.* Venus and Adonis, *1682), the outstanding figure was* Henry PURCELL *(1659-1695). Purcell was active in every field: theatre music, church music (many anthems and hymns showing the influence of John Blow, and cantatas with orchestra), instrumental music (especially for the harpsichord, the organ and wind instruments), secular and sacred songs (e.g. his* Odes to St Cecilia*) and operas (*Dido and Aeneas, *1689;* King Arthur, *1691;* The Fairy Queen, *1692;* The Indian Queen, *1695).*

Near the beginning of the 18th century, the court lost part of its brilliance and lustre with the arrival of the Hanoverian dynasty. Yet, because of the growing number of wealthy patrons, music gained in popularity: more and more people enjoyed going to the concert, and it was fashionable to visit such London gardens as Vauxhall or the Ranelagh in order to hear music performed. This pleasure appealed to all classes of society; it is thus possible to talk of a popularization of music at this period, explicable both by social snobbery and by the genuine development of a taste for music.

The German composer HAENDEL *(1685-1759) who settled in England in 1710 is the best representative of this period. He composed with great facility and diversity: instrumental music, cantatas, operas and especially oratorios (*Messiah, *1742).*

Haendel had brought the Italian operatic style to perfection, but in spite of his popularity, a reaction against Italian music and especially operas sung in Italian set in around 1720:

Thomas Rowlandson's satire of the Italian Opera.
Ph. Harvard Theatre Collection.

The English, unable to compete with foreign opera seria on its own ground, took revenge by creating the ballad opera, which at the same time ridiculed Italian music and originated a national comic type as distinctive and popular for the British as opera buffa was for the Italians or opéra comique for the French. The best-known of these works, and one which has survived to our own time, was *The Beggar's Opera,* written by John Gay with music arranged by John Christopher Pepusch (1667-1752) and first performed at London in 1728. The characters are pickpockets, bawds, jailbirds, and similar gentry (in keeping with Swift's suggested title "The Newgate Pastoral"), the language is low and racy, and the play is full of satirical thrusts both at the absurdities of Italian opera and at the reigning Whig politicians of the day. The songs, which alternate with spoken dialogue, are for the most part familiar ballad tunes, though there are some borrowings from other sources (for example, the march from Handel's *Rinaldo*). The motifs of political and musical satire are particularly congenial to the English in comic opera, as witness Gilbert and Sullivan; neither in the eighteenth nor the nineteenth century were the Londoners inclined to take opera seria with complete seriousness.

Donald Jay Grout, *A Short History of Opera*
Columbia U. Press, N.Y.

ACT II, SCENE XIII
LUCY, MACHEATH, POLLY

POLLY. Where is my dear husband? Was a rope ever intended for this neck! Oh, let me throw my arms about it, and throttle thee with love! Why dost thou turn away from me? – 'tis thy Polly – 'tis thy wife.

MAC. Was ever such an unfortunate rascal as I am!

LUCY. Was there ever such another villain!

POLLY. Oh, Macheath! was it for this we parted? Taken! imprisoned! tried! hanged! Cruel reflection! I'll stay with thee till death – no force shall tear thy dear wife from thee now. What means my love? – not one kind word! not one kind look! Think what thy Polly suffers to see thee in this condition.

AIR XVI. – "All in the Downs," etc.

Thus when the swallow, seeking prey,
Within the sash is closely pent,
His consort with bemoaning lay
Without sits pining for the event.
Her chattering lovers all around her skim;
She heeds them not, poor bird, her soul's with him.

MAC. I must disown her. *(Aside.)* The wench is distracted!

LUCY. Am I then bilked of my virtue? Can I have no reparation? Sure men were born to lie, and women to believe them! Oh, villain! villain!

POLLY. Am I not thy wife? Thy neglect of me, thy aversion to me, too severely proves it. Look on me – tell me, am I not thy wife?

LUCY. Perfidious wretch!

POLLY. Barbarous husband!

LUCY. Hadst thou been hanged five months ago, I had been happy.

POLLY. And I, too. If you had been kind to me till death, it would not have vexed me – and that's no very unreasonable request (though from a wife) to a man who hath not above seven or eight days to live.

LUCY. Art thou, then, married to another? Hast thou two wives, monster?

MAC. If women's tongues can cease for an answer – hear me.

LUCY. I won't. Flesh and blood can't bear my usage!

POLLY. Shall not I claim my own? Justice bids me speak.

AIR XVII. – "Have you heard of a frolicsome ditty," etc.

MAC.
How happy could I be with either,
Were t'other dear charmer away!
But, while ye thus tease me together,
To neither a word will I say;
But toll de roll, etc.

John Gay, *The Beggar's Opera.*

John DRYDEN 1631-1700

1631 *Born in Northamptonshire. Educated at Westminster School and Trinity College, Cambridge.*
1658 Heroic Stanzas *(in commemoration of the death of Cromwell).*
1660 Astrea Redux *(in honour of the return of Charles II).*
1663 *Started writing plays; he was to write comedies, tragedies and heroic dramas).*
1666 Annus Mirabilis, *a poem relating the events of the year 1666, including the Great Fire.*
1668 Of Dramatic Poesy: an Essay.
1670 *Appointed Historiographer Royal.* The Conquest of Granada *(heroic tragedy).*
1671 *Became Poet Laureate.*
1678 All For Love, *a tragedy.*
1681 Absalom and Achitophel *(satirical poem).*
1682 The Medal *(an attack on Shaftesbury);* Religio Laici *(a defence of the Anglican Church);* Mac Flecknoe *(a satire against the Protestant poet Shadwell).*
1685 *Converted to Roman Catholicism.*
1687 The Hind and the Panther, *a poem on the relations between the Church of Rome (the Hind), and the Church of England (the Panther).*
1688 *Deprived of pensions and office when William III succeeded James II.*
1700 *Died in London, buried in Westminster Abbey.*

As a man, Dryden seems to have been anxious to win the favour of the ruling power, celebrating Cromwell, then Charles II, and later converting to Roman Catholicism with the arrival of a Catholic sovereign, James II. He dropped out of favour with the Revolution of 1688.

Although he is best remembered as a poet and satirist, he devoted much of his time to writing plays. If not the initiator of the heroic tragedy, he wrote 28 successful tragedies between 1662 and 1675. He discussed the problems of drama in his essay Of Dramatic Poesy.

As a critic, Dryden shows a rational mind. He avoids excess and systematic opinions and prefers the dialectical method, always presenting the two sides of a question and balancing contrary arguments.

He was first of all an excellent translator of Juvenal and Horace. Satire was also fashionable with the French, and Dryden much admired Boileau. He adapted an Old Testament story to the political situation of his day and drew scathing portraits of the leaders of the Monmouth Rebellion in Absalom and Achitophel *or of his poetical rival Shadwell in* Mac Flecknoe.

Absalom and Achitophel (1681)

Of these the false Achitophel[1] was first;
A name to all succeeding ages curst:
For close[2] designs and crooked counsels fit,
Sagacious, bold, and turbulent of wit,
Restless, unfixed in principles and place,
In pow'r unpleased, impatient of disgrace:
A fiery soul, which, working out its way,
Fretted the pigmy body to decay,
And o'er-informed[3] the tenement of clay.
A daring pilot in extremity;
Pleased with the danger, when the waves went high,
He sought the storms; but, for a calm unfit,
Would steer too nigh the sands to boast his wit
Great wits are sure to madness near allied,
And thin partitions do their bounds divide;
Else why should he, with wealth and honour blest,
Refuse his age the needful hours of rest?
Punish a body which he could not please,
Bankrupt of life, yet prodigal of ease?
And all to leave what with his toil he won,
To that unfeathered two-legged thing, a son....
In friendship false, implacable in hate;

Resolved to ruin or to rule the state:
To compass this, the triple bond[4] he broke,
The pillars of the public safety shook,
And fitted Israel[5] for a foreign yoke[6];
Then, seized with fear, yet still affecting[7] fame,
Usurped a patriot's all-atoning name.
So easy still it proves, in factious times,
With public zeal to cancel private crimes.
How safe is treason, and how sacred ill,
Where none can sin against the people's will!
Where crowds can wink, and no offence be known,
Since in another's guilt they find their own!
Yet fame deserved no enemy can grudge;
The statesman we abhor, but praise the judge.
In Israel's courts ne'er sat an Abbethdin[8]
With more discerning eyes, or hands more clean,
Unbribed, unsought, the wretched to redress
Swift of despatch, and easy of access.
Oh! had he been content to serve the crown
With virtues only proper to the gown,
Or had the rankness of the soil been freed
From cockle[9] that oppressed the noble seed,
David for him his tuneful harp had strung,
And heav'n had wanted one immortal song
But wild ambition loves to slide, not stand,
And Fortune's ice prefers to Virtue's land
Achitophel, grown weary to possess
A lawful fame and lazy happiness,
Disdained the golden fruit to gather free,
And lent the crowd his arm to shake the tree.

l. 150-203.

The Monmouth Rebellion: Charles II had no legitimate children. The heir apparent was his Catholic brother. The Whig party, afraid to see him on the throne, encouraged the Duke of Monmouth – a bastard son of the king – to seize power, but he failed. Dryden's satire was meant to secure the condemnation of the Earl of Shaftesbury, the leader of the Whigs.
1. *Achitophel:* Anthony Ashey Cooper, 1st Earl of Shaftesbury, villain of the satire, who urged Absalom (Monmouth) to rebel against David (Charles II). Cf. 2 Samuel 16,17. – 2. *close:* secret – 3. *o'er informed:* overfilled – 4. *the triple bond:* the Alliance between England, Sweden and Holland against France – 5. *Israel:* England – 6. *a foreign yoke:* France – 7. *affecting:* desiring – 8. *Abbethdin:* Jewish High Judge – 9. *cockle:* a type of weed.

Dryden on satire:

Yet still the nicest and most delicate touches of Satire consist in fine Raillery. This, my Lord, is your particular Talent, to which even Juvenal could not arrive. 'Tis not Reading, 'tis not imitation of an Author, which can produce this fineness: it must be inborn; it must proceed from a Genius, and particular way of thinking, which is not to be taught; and therefore not to be imitated by him who has it not from Nature: How easie is it to call Rogue and Villain, and that wittily! But how hard to make a Man appear a Fool, a Blockhead, or a Knave, without using any of those opprobrious terms! To spare the grossness of the Names, and to do the thing yet more severely, is to draw a full Face, and to make the Nose and Cheeks stand out, and yet not to employ any depth of Shadowing. This is the Mystery of that Noble Trade, which yet no Master can teach to his Apprentice: He may give the Rules, but the Scholar is never the nearer in his practice. Neither is it true, that this fineness of Raillery is offensive. A witty Man is tickl'd while he is hurt in this manner, and a Fool feels it not. The occasion of an Offence may possibly be given, but he cannot take it. If it be granted that in effect this way does more Mischief; that a Man is secretly wounded, and though he be not sensible himself, yet the malicious World will find it for him: yet there is still a vast difference betwixt the slovenly Butchering of a Man, and the fineness of a stroke that separates the Head from the Body, and leaves it standing in its place. A man may be capable, as Jack Ketch's Wife said of his Servant, of a plain piece of Work, a bare Hanging; but to make a malefactor die sweetly was only belonging to her Husband. I wish I cou'd apply it to my self, if the Reader wou'd be kind enough to think it belongs to me. The character of Zimri in my *Absalom* is, in my opinion, worth the whole Poem: 'Tis not bloody, but 'tis ridiculous enough; and he for whom it was intended, was too witty to resent it as an injury. If I had railed,

I might have suffered for it justly; but I manag'd my own Work more happily, perhaps more dexterously. I avoided the mention of great Crimes, and apply'd myself to the representing of Blindsides, and little Extravagancies: to which, the wittier a Man is, he is generally the more obnoxious. It succeeded as I wish'd; the Jest went round, and he was laught at in his turn who began the Frolick.

A Discourse concerning the Original and Progress of Satire, 1693.

Samuel Johnson on Absalom and Achitophel:

Absalom and Achitophel is a work so well known, that particular criticism is superfluous. If it be considered as a poem political and controversial, it will be found to comprise all the excellences of which the subject is susceptible; acrimony of censure, elegance of praise, artful delineation of characters, variety and vigour of sentiment, happy turns of language, and pleasing harmony of numbers; and all these raised to such a height as can scarcely be found in any other English composition.

It is not, however, without faults; some lines are inelegant or improper, and too many are irreligiously licentious. The original structure of the poem was defective; allegories drawn to great length will always break; Charles could not run continually parallel with David.

The subject had likewise another inconvenience: it admitted little imagery or description, and a long poem of mere sentiments easily becomes tedious; though all the parts are forcible, and every line kindles new rapture, the reader, if not relieved by the interposition of something that soothes the fancy, grows weary of admiration, and defers the rest.

Lives of the English Poets, 1779-81.

Cf. Versification, p. 7; Wit, humour, satire and irony, p. 27.

Alexander POPE 1688-1744

1688 *Born in London, the son of a Catholic linen merchant.*
1709 Pastorals, *composed when he was 16.*
1711 An Essay on Criticism.
1712 The Rape of the Lock.
1713 Windsor Forest, *an eclogue.*
1714 The Rape of the Lock, *enlarged edition. Became a member of the "Scriblerus Club", a literary association which included, among others, Swift and Gay.*
1715-1720 *Translation of Homer's* Iliad.
1725-1726 *Translation of Homer's* Odyssey.
1728 *First edition of* The Dunciad, *a mock-epic, satirical work aimed at Theobald who had criticized Pope's edition of Shakespeare.*
1731-1735 *Epistles and satires* (*e.g. 1735:* Epistle to Dr. Arbuthnot).
1733-1734 Essay on Man.
1742 The New Dunciad *(Book IV).*
1743 *The Complete* Dunciad *(Books I-IV).*
1744 *Died in Twickenham.*

In spite of grave difficulties (he was a crippled invalid and, as a Catholic, could not attend public school or university), Pope was a born poet and embodied the spirit of his age in his philosophical and satirical works.

His first critical work, the Essay on Criticism, *advocated the quest of perfection in literary composition. Perfection meant absolute control of the content and form of one's work. This can involve a lack of originality, and if Pope perfected the heroic couplet, the resulting "poetic diction" can sometimes be monotonous. In the* Essay on Man, *Pope turned to philosophy. influenced by Deism, he asserted his faith in man and in the order of the universe. ("Whatever is, is right.") Man will find happiness in humility and love. This Augustan optimism is paralleled on a political level since he sees government as a form of natural order in harmony with the order of the whole universe.*

But Pope was also a satirist. In The Dunciad, *he criticized verbalism, triviality and pedantism in learning and ridiculed a whole gallery of characters. The satire is lighter in his famous mock-heroic poem,* The Rape of the Lock. *The occasion was to reconcile two Catholic families after Robert, Lord Peter had cut off a lock of hair from the head of Arabella Fermor. The trivial incident is presented in epic terms — with sylphs, battles and an exalted tone — and the poem ridicules the fashionable world of the time.*

The Rape of the Lock (1712)

The stealing of Miss Belle Fermor's hair was taken too seriously, and caused an estrangement between the two families, though they have lived long in great friendship before. A common acquaintance and well-wisher to both desired me to write a poem to make a jest of it, and laugh them together again. It was in this view that I wrote my Rape of the Lock, *which was well received and had its effect in the two families.* A. Pope

The following passage describes the actual snipping of the lock.

But when to Mischief Mortals bend their Will,
How soon they find fit Instruments of Ill!
Just then, *Clarissa* drew with tempting Grace
A two-edg'd Weapon from her shining Case;
So Ladies in Romance assist their Knight,
Present the Spear, and arm him for the Fight.
He takes the Gift with rev'rence, and extends
The little Engine on his Finger's Ends;
This just behind *Belinda's*[1] Neck he spread
As o'er the fragrant Steams she bends her Head:
Swift to the Lock a thousand Sprights repair,
A thousand Wings, by turns, blow back the Hair;
And thrice they twitch'd the Diamond in her Ear,
Thrice she look'd back, and thrice the Foe drew near.
Just in that instant, anxious *Ariel* sought
The close Recesses of the Virgin's thought;
As on the Nosegay in her Breast reclin'd,
He watch'd th'Ideas rising in her Mind,
Sudden he view'd, in spite of all her Art,
An Earthly Lover lurking at her Heart.
Amaz'd, confus'd, he found his Power expir'd,
Resign'd to Fate, and with a Sigh retir'd.

The *Peer* now spreads the glittering *Forfex*[2] wide,
T'inclose the Lock; now joins it, to divide.
Ev'n then, before the fatal Engine clos'd,
A wretched *Sylph* too fondly interpos'd;
Fate urged the Sheers, and cut the *Sylph* in twain,
(But Airy Substance soon unites again)
The meeting Points the sacred Hair dissever
From the fair Head, for ever and for ever!

Canto III.

1. *Belinda;* Arabella Fermor – 2. *forfex:* scissors.

Pope on the epic poem:

A RECEIT TO MAKE AN EPICK POEM

For the *Fable.*

Take out of any old Poem, History-books, Romance, or Legend (for instance *Geffry of Monmouth* or *Don Belianis of Greece*) those Parts of Story which afford most Scope for long Descriptions: Put these Pieces together, and throw all the Adventures you fancy into one Tale. Then take a Hero, whom you may chuse for the Sound of his Name, and put him into the midst of these Adventures: There let him *work,* for twelve Books; at the end of which you may take him out, ready prepared to conquer or to marry; it being necessary that the Conclusion of an Epick Poem be fortunate. (...)

For the *Manners.*

For those of the Hero, take all the best Qualities you can find in all the best celebrated Heroes of Antiquity; if they will not be reduced to a Consistency, lay'em all on a heap upon him. But be sure they are Qualities which your *Patron* would be thought to have; and to prevent any Mistake which the World may be subject to, select from the Alphabet those Capital Letters that compose his Name, and set them at the Head of a Dedication before your Poem. (...)

For the *Machines.*

Take of Deities, Male and Female, as many as you can use. Separate them into two equal parts, and keep *Jupiter* in the middle. Let *Juno* put him in a Ferment, and *Venus* mollifie him. Remember on all Occasions to make use of Volatile *Mercury.* If you have need of Devils, draw them out of *Milton's Paradise,* and extract your Spirits from *Tasso.* The Use of these Machines is evident; for since no Epick Poem can possibly subsist without them, the wisest way is to reserve them for your greatest Necessities. When you cannot extricate your Hero by any Human Means, or your self by your own Wit, seek Relief from Heaven, and the Gods will do your Business very readily. (...)

For the *Descriptions.*

For a Tempest. Take *Eurus, Zephyr, Auster,* and *Boreas,* and cast them together in one Verse. Add to these of Rain, Lightning, and of Thunder (the loudest you can) *quantum sufficit.* Mix your Clouds and Billows well together till they foam, and thicken your Description here and there with a Quicksand. Brew your Tempest well in your Head, before you set it a blowing.

For a Battel. Pick a large Quantity of Images and Descriptions from *Homer's* Iliads, with a Spice or two of *Virgil,* and if there remain any Overplus you may lay them by for a *Skirmish.* Season it well with *Similes,* and it will make an *Excellent Battel.* (...)

For the *Language.*

(I mean the *Diction*). Here it will do well to be an Imitator of *Milton,* for you'll find it easier to imitate him in this than any thing else. *Hebraisms* and *Grecisms* are to be found in him, without the trouble of Learning the Languages. (...)

Mock-heroic in The Rape of the Lock:

The parodies of epic convention in the poem are too numerous to be itemized, but among them may be singled out these: the dream message from the gods and the arming of the champion (I 23 ff, 121 ff); the sacrifice to the gods and the "charge" to the troops (II 35 ff, 73 ff); the single combat at Ombre, and the epic feast (III 25 ff, 105 ff); the journey to the underworld (IV 11 ff); the general combat, divine intervention, and the apotheosis of the lock (V 35 ff, 71 ff, 113 ff). The reader familiar with Paradise Lost will notice a particularly large number of mock-parallels with that poem – for example, between the situation of the fallen angels at the opening of Milton's first book and the punishments promised by Pope's Ariel to careless sylphs (II 125 ff). As for the sylphs themselves, they are a splendid re-creation in social terms of the divine powers who watch over the fortunes of epic heroes. And they are also Pope's way of rendering – in their luminosity, fragility, and grace – the womanliness of woman.

The "action" of the *Rape of the Lock* has many layers of complexity. The surface level is simply a narrative of Belinda's day: how she awakes, dresses for conquest, is conveyed down the Thames to Hampton Court, bests the Baron at Ombre, exults too proudly and therefore suffers an Aristotelean reversal of fortune in the loss of her lock, screams, collapses in a tantrum, receives good advice from Clarissa, but refuses to take it, and finally participates in the general huffing and puffing of polite indignation with which the poem ends. The progress of Belinda's day is denoted by successive references to the sun, the last of them (v 147) suggesting an implicit relation between the pattern of her day and the pattern of human life.

A second level in the action takes up the war between the sexes. Here we recognize that Pope's title has a possible literal as well as figurative significance, and that the poem is concerned with the elaborate forms that surround the courtship of man and woman. (...)

On a third level the movement of the poem is psychological. We first see Belinda fancy-free, i.e. surrounded with the influence of the sylphs (her own maidenly coquetries), whose protective power depends on her remaining fancy-free. At the critical moment, however, the sylphs are helpless to save the lock because Belinda's affections have become engaged: an earthly lover lurks at her heart, and as a consequence the lock of maidenliness is forfeit. (...)

The final level of meaning takes us to the general social criticism which forms the background of the poem. Here confusion of values is again the theme, but on a broader scale. Pope presents the absurdities of the fashionable world with affection, and with an eye to the delicate beauties that its best graces unfold. But he never allows us to forget that it is also a world whose ethical judgments are in sad disarray. Hearts and necklaces, lapdogs and lovers, statesmanship and tea, queens and Indian screens, the hunger of jurymen and justice, Bibles and billets-doux: the verse of the poem entangles these trifles and values together in order to reflect a similar entanglement in this society's mind. And it is just here, in the presentation of a moral muddle, that the mock-heroic structure proves itself invaluable. By juxtaposing the contemporary with the heroic, the poet can emphasize both the epic proportions to which this society has magnified its trifles (like the estrangement of families over a lock of hair) and also their real triviality.

Maynard Mack, *Mock-heroic in The Rape of the Lock,* in *The Introduction to the Augustans,* *Prentice Hall.*

Cf. Verse form and poetic Genres, p. 2; Versification, p.00; Figurative language, p. 3.

Aubrey Beardsley : The Rape of the Lock, *1895-96.*
Ph. Edimedia, coll. Snark.

The Rape of the Lock *was one of the last works Aubrey Beardsley illustrated. He was a draughtsman, influenced by the Pre-Raphaelites (Burne-Jones in particular), and by Japanese woodcuts. His art is marked by* "obsessions with the fantastic, the bizarre, the grotesque, the macabre, the perverse and the erotic (...) They reflect the Symbolists' disgust with the gross materialism of Western capitalist society and their desire to attack and undermine the accepted standards of taste, decency and morality of that society in order to expose the reality beneath". S. Wilson

Beardsley's originality and imagination and his love of ornamentation were particularly suited to Pope's fanciful poem.

Jonathan SWIFT 1667-1745

1667 *Born in Dublin.*
1682-1686 *Trinity College, Dublin.*
1689 *Became secretary to Sir William Temple. Met several political and literary personalities in his household, near London.*
1694 *Returned to Ireland to be ordained (as an Anglican priest).*
1696-1697 *Wrote* A Tale of a Tub *and* The Battle of the Books.
1699 *Death of William Temple.*
1700-1710 *Wrote several religious and political pamphlets (on the side of the Whigs). Became friendly with Addison and Steele.*
1711-1714 *Left the Whigs for the Tories and wrote more political pamphlets (e.g.* The Conduct of the Allies, *1711). He recorded his political activities in The* Journal to Stella. *Became one of the most active members of the Scriblerus Club, which gathered a number of "wits" (Pope, Arbuthnot, Gay).*
1713 *Appointed Dean of St Patrick's, Dublin.*
1714 *Back in Ireland, in exile, after he death of Queen Anne and the fall of the Tory ministry.*
1724 The Drapier's Letters.
1726 Gulliver's Travels.
1728 A Short View of the State of Ireland.
1729 A Modest Proposal.
1745 *Died in Dublin.*

The satirist of his age, Swift made use of savage and biting irony to defend the causes he believed in. At the beginning of his life these were chiefly literary, religious and political. The Battle of the Books *is his contribution to the quarrel between the Ancients and Moderns. He transforms the dispute into a burlesque battle between an ill-tempered spider (the Moderns) and a bee (the Ancients) that got entangled in its web in the King's Library. In* A Tale of a Tub, *the satire is turned against the Presbyterians and Roman Catholics. Three brothers – Martin (Luther), Jack (Calvin), and Peter (St Peter) – share an inheritance (Christianity) but all betray their father's will that the clothes bequeathed to them (the Bible) should not be altered.*

With his retirement to Ireland, in 1714, Swift's satire turned against the exploitation of his fellow-countrymen, and he tried to stir them out of their passivity. The Drapier's Letters *condemns the abuses of the Irish currency;* A Modest Proposal *offers cannibalism as a solution to the famine and poverty in Ireland.*

But little by little, Swift's mood slid into one of frustation and a bitter hatred of mankind. His evolution is paralleled by the hero's progress in Gulliver's Travels. *Among the miniature Lilliputians, he becomes wary, slowly awakening to their vanity and pride. The giants of Brobdingnag make him realize how corrupt the institutions of England are and he begins to lose his pride and self-esteem. The narrow-mindedness of the inhabitants of Laputa, where his next voyage takes him, brings the belief that human nature cannot be reformed. But it is in Gulliver's last voyage, in a country where men appear as deformed and repulsive animals (the Yahoos) contrasting with rational horses (the Houyhnhnms), that one can feel Swift's aversion to mankind reaching its climax.*

A Modest Proposal (1729)

... For preventing the children of poor people from being a burthen to their parents or country, and for making them beneficial to the public.

It is a melancholy object to those who walk through this great town, or travel in the country, when they see the streets, the roads, and cabin-doors crowded with beggars of the female sex, followed by three, four, or six children, *all in rags,* and importuning every passenger for an alms. These mothers, instead of being able to work for their honest livelihood, are forced to employ all their time in strolling, to beg sustenance for their helpless infants, who, as they grow up, either turn thieves for want of work, or leave their dear Native Country to fight for the Pretender in Spain, or sell themselves to the Barbadoes[1].

I think it is agreed by all parties that this prodigious number of children, in the arms, or on the backs, or at the heels of their mothers, and frequently of their fathers, is in the present deplorable state of the kingdom a very great additional grievance; and therefore whoever could find out a fair, cheap, and easy method of making these children sound useful members of the commonwealth would deserve so well of the public as to have his statue set up for a preserver of the nation.

But my intention is very far from being confined to provide only for the children of professed beggars; it is of a much greater extent, and shall take in the whole number of infants at a certain age who are born of parents in effect as little able to support them as those who demand our charity in the streets.

As to my own part, having turned my thoughts, for many years, upon this important subject, and maturely weighed the several schemes of other projectors, I have always found them grossly mistaken in their computation. It is true a child, just dropped from its dam[2], may be supported by her milk for a solar year with little other nourishment, at most not above the value of two shillings, which the mother may certainly get, or the value in scraps, by her lawful occupation of begging, and it is exactly at one year old that I propose to provide for them, in such a manner as, instead of being a charge upon their parents, or the parish, or wanting food and raiment for the rest of their lives, they shall, on the contrary, contribute to the feeding and partly to the clothing of many thousands.

There is likewise another great advantage in my scheme, that it will prevent those voluntary abortions, and that horrid practice of women murdering their bastard children, alas, too frequent among us, sacrificing the poor innocent babes, I doubt, more to avoid the expense than the shame, which would move tears and pity in the most savage and inhuman breast.

The number of souls in this kingdom being usually reckoned one million and a half, of these I calculate there may be about two hundred thousand couples whose wives are breeders, from which number I subtract thirty thousand couples who are able to maintain their own children, although I apprehend there cannot be so many under the present distresses of the kingdom, but this being granted, there will remain an hundred and seventy thousand breeders. I again subtract fifty thousand for those women who miscarry, or whose children die by accident or disease within the year. There only remain an hundred and twenty thousand children of poor parents annually born: The question therefore is, how this number shall be reared, and provided for, which, as I have already said, under the present situation of affairs, is utterly impossible by all the methods hitherto proposed, for we can neither employ them in handicraft, or agriculture; we neither build houses (I mean in the country), nor cultivate land: they can very seldom pick up a livelihood by stealing till they arrive at six years old, except where they are of towardly parts, although, I confess they learn the rudiments much earlier, during which time they can however be properly looked upon only as *probationers*, as I have been informed by a principal gentleman in the County of Cavan, who protested to me that he never knew above one or two instances under the age of six, even in a part of the kingdom so renowned for the quickest proficiency in that art.

I am assured by our merchants that a boy or a girl, before twelve years old, is no saleable commodity, and even when they come to this age, they will not yield above three pounds, or three pounds and half-a-crown at most on the Exhange, which cannot turn to account either to the parents or the kingdom, the charge of nutriment and rags having been at least four times that value.

I shall now therefore humbly propose my own thoughts, which I hope will not be liable to the least objection.

I have been assured by a very knowing American[3] of my acquaintance in London, that a young healthy child well nursed is at a year old a most delicious, nourishing and wholesome food, whether stewed, roasted, baked, or boiled, and I make no doubt that it will equally serve in a fricassee, or a ragout.

I do therefore humbly offer it to public consideration, that of the hundred and twenty thousand children already computed, twenty thousand may be reserved for breed, whereof only one fourth part to be males, which is more than we allow to sheep, black-cattle, or swine, and my reason is that these children are seldom the fruits of marriage, a circumstance not much regarded by our savages, therefore one male will be sufficient to serve four females. That the remaining hundred thousand may at a year old be offered in sale to the persons of quality, and fortune, through the kingdom, always advising the mother to let them suck plentifully in the last month, so as to render them plump, and fat for a good table. A child will make two dishes at an entertainment for friends, and when the family dines alone, the fore or hind quarter will make a reasonable dish, and seasoned with a little pepper or salt will be very good boiled on the fourth day, especially in winter.

I have reckoned upon a medium, that a child just born will weigh 12 pounds, and in a solar year if tolerably nursed increaseth to 28 pounds.

I grant this food will be somewhat dear, and therefore very proper for landlords, who, as they have already devoured most of the parents, seem to have the best title to the children.

Infants' flesh will be in season throughout the year, but more plentiful in March, and a little before and after, for we are told by a grave author an eminent French physician[4], that fish being a prolific[5] diet, there are more children born in Roman Catholic countries about nine months after Lent than at any other season; therefore reckoning a year after Lent, the markets will be more glutted than usual, because the number of Popish infants is at least three to one in this kingdom and therefore it will have one other collateral advantage by lessening the number of Papists among us.

I have already computed the charge of nursing a beggar's child (in which list I reckon all cottagers, labourers, and four-fifths of the farmers) to be about two shillings *per annum*, rags included, and I believe no gentleman would repine to give ten shillings for the carcass of a good fat child, which, as I have said, will make four dishes of excellent nutritive meat, when he hath only some particular friend or his own family to dine with him. Thus the Squire will learn to be a good landlord, and grow popular among his tenants, the mother will have eight shillings net profit, and be fit for work till she produces another child.

1. *sell themselves to the Barbadoes:* poverty in Ireland often led to emigration to the West Indies (generally to enter the French of Spanish armies). – 2. *dam:* "a human mother: in contempt or detestation" (Dr Johnson's Dictionary) Now used for the mothers of four-footed animals. – 3. *American:* probably an American Indian since people commonly thought they practised cannibalism. – 4 *an eminent French physician:* Rabelais. – 5. *prolific:* a prolific diet is likely to cause people to have many children.

In A Modest Proposal, *Swift parodies the numerous projects proposed to solve the Irish problem. Here is the beginning of one of them, Petty's* Political Arithmetic *(1687) which quite seriously recommends the transportation of part of the Irish population to England.*

How to enable the People of England
and Ireland to spend 5 Millions
worth of Commodities more than now:
And how to raise
the present Value of the Lands
and Goods of Ireland
from 2 to 3

This is to be done. (1) By bringing one Million of the present 1300 Thousand of the People out of Ireland into England, tho' at the Expence of a Million of Money. (2) That the remaining 300 Thousand left behind be all Herdsmen and Dairy-Women, Servants to the Owners of the Lands and Stock Transplanted into England; all aged between 16 and 60 years, and to quit all other Trades, but that of Cattle, and to import nothing but Salt and Tobacco. Neglecting all Housing, but what is fittest for these 300 Thousand People, and this Trade, tho' to the Loss of 2 Millions-worth of Houses. Now if a Million of People be worth 70l. per Head one with another, the whole are worth 70 Millions; then the said People, reckon'd as Money at 5 per Cent. Interest, will yield 3 Millions and a half per Ann. (3) And if Ireland send into England 1 Million and a half worth of Effects (receiving nothing back) Then England will be enriched from Ireland, and otherwise, 5 Millions per Ann. more than now: Which, at 20 Year's Purchase, is worth one Hundred Millions of Pounds Sterling, as was propounded...

Sir William Petty, *Treatise of Ireland: An Essay in Political Arithmetic*, in Clive T. Probyn, *Jonathan Swift: The Contemporary Background*, Manchester U.P.

This nineteenth-century print shows a well-dressed landlord receiving his rent from a poor tenant.
In K. Neill, An Illustrated History of the Irish People, *Gill and Macmillan.*

C.f. Wit , humour, satire and irony, p. 27.

Satire in the age of Swift
Another example of the use of irony for political satire is Defoe's The Shortest Way with Dissenters, *which pretends to advocate the extermination of all dissenters in order to show the stupidity of religious intolerance. Here is the end of the pamphlet:*

What's the Difference betwixt this, and being subjected to the Power of the Church of *Rome*, from whence we have reform'd? If one be an extreme on one Hand, and one on another, 'tis equally destructive to the Truth, to have Errors settled among us, let them be of what Nature they will.

Both are Enemies of our Church, and of our Peace, and why shou'd it not be as criminal to admit an Enthusiast as a Jesuit? Why shou'd the *Papist* with his Seven Sacraments be worse than the *Quaker* with no Sacraments at all? Why shou'd Religious-houses be more intollerable than Meeting-houses – *Alas the Church of England!* What with Popery on one Hand, and Schismaticks on the other; how has she been Crucify'd between two Thieves.

Now *let us Crucifie the Thieves*. Let her Foundations be establish'd upon the Destruction of her Enemies: The doors of Mercy being always open to the returning Part of the deluded People: Let the Obstinate be rul'd with the Rod of Iron.

Let all true Sons of so Holy an Oppressed Mother, exasperated by her Afflictions, harden their Hearts against those who have oppress'd her.

And may God Almighty put it into the Hearts of all the Friends of Truth, to lift up a Standard against Pride and Antichrist, that the Posterity of the Sons of Error may be rooted out from the Face of this Land for ever–

Gulliver's Travels (1726)

The following excerpt is from the Voyage to the Houyhnhnms.

Granville:
Gulliver's Travels.
Edimage, P. Jahan.

That, in some Fields of his Country, there are certain *shining Stones* of several Colours, whereof the *Yahoos* are violently fond; and when Part of these *Stones* are fixed in the Earth, as it sometimes happeneth, they will dig with their Claws for whole Days to get them out, and carry them away, and hide them by Heaps in their Kennels; but still looking round with great Caution, for fear their Comrades should find out their Treasure. My Master said, he could never discover the Reason of this unnatural Appetite, or how these *Stones* could be of any Use to a *Yahoo;* but now he believed it might proceed from the same Principle of *Avarice,* which I had ascribed to Mankind. That he had once, by way of Experiment, privately removed a Heap of these *Stones* from the Place where one of his *Yahoos* had buried it: Whereupon, the sordid Animal missing his Treasure, by his loud lamenting brought the whole Herd to the Place, there miserably howled, then fell to biting and tearing the rest; began to pine away, would neither eat nor sleep, nor work, till he ordered a Servant privately to convey the *Stones* into the same Hole, and hide them as before; which when his *Yahoo* had found, he presently recovered his Spirits and good Humour; but took Care to remove them to a better hiding Place; and hath ever since been a very serviceable Brute.

My Master farther assured me, which I also observed my self; That in the Fields where these *shining Stones* abound, the fiercest and most frequent Battles are fought, occasioned by perpetual Inroads of the neighbouring *Yahoos*.

He said, it was common when two *Yahoos* discovered such a *Stone* in a Field, and were contending which of them should be the Proprietor, a third would take the Advantage, and carry it away from them both; which my Master would needs contend to have some Resemblance with our *Suits at Law;* wherein I thought it for our Credit not to undeceive him; since the Decision he mentioned was much more equitable than many Decrees among us: Because the Plaintiff and Defendant there lost nothing beside the *Stone* they contended for; whereas our *Courts of Equity,* would never have dismissed the Cause while either of them had any thing left.

Part IV, Chapter 7.

There is a long tradition of Utopian/Dystopian writing in England. Some works – real Utopias – show an ideal country which can be considered as a model. This is for instance the case with Thomas More's Utopia *(1515), Francis Bacon's* New Atlantis *(1622), William Morris's* News from Nowhere *(1891).*

Other writers choose to describe an imaginary and nightmarish world to warn us against some of the dangers in our society. George Orwell's 1984 *(1949) is a well-known example of such a dystopia.*

Another possibility is to imagine an utterly different world, neither entirely good nor bad, but whose differences will bring out the absurdities or merits of what we take for granted in our own country (e.g. Samuel Butler's Erewhon*).*

Gulliver's Travels *combines these three varieties of Utopian writing.*

Compare the passage given above with the following excerpts from Utopia *and* Erewhon, *both dealing with the theme of money:*

● In the meantime gold and silver, whereof money is made, they do so use, as none of them doth more esteem it, than the very nature of the thing deserveth. And then who doth not plainly see how far it is under iron: as without the which men can no better live than without fire and water. Whereas to gold and silver nature hath given no use, that we may not well lack: if that the folly of men had not set it in higher estimation for the rareness sake. But of the contrary part, nature as a most tender and loving mother, hath placed the best and most necessary things open abroad: as the air, the water and the earth itself. And hath removed and hid farthest from us vain and unprofitable things. Therefore if these metals among them should be fast locked up in some tower, it might be suspected, that the prince and the council (as the people is ever foolishly imagining) intended by some subtlety to deceive the commons, and to take same profit of it to themselves. Furthermore if they should make thereof plate and such other finely and cunningly wrought stuff: if at any time they should have occasion to break it, and melt it again, and therewith to pay their soldiers' wages, they see and perceive very well, that men would be loath to part from those things, that they once began to have pleasure and delight in. To remedy all this they have found out a means, which, as it is agreeable to all their other laws and customs, so it is from ours, where gold is so much set by and so diligently kept, very far discrepant and repugnant: and therefore incredible, but only to them that be wise. For whereas they eat and drink in earthen and glass vessels, which indeed be curiously and properly made, and yet be of very small value: of gold and silver they make commonly chamber pots, and other like vessels, that serve for most vile uses, not only in their common halls, but in every man's private house. Furthermore of the same metals they make great chains, with fetters, and gyves wherein they tie their bondmen. Finally whosoever for any offence be infamed, by their ears hang rings of gold, upon their fingers they wear rings of gold, and about their necks chains of gold, and in conclusion their heads be tied about with gold. Thus by all means that may be they procure to have gold and silver among them in reproach and infamy. And therefore these metals, which other nations do as grievously and sorrowfully forgo, as in a manner from their own lives: if they should altogether at once be taken from the Utopians, no man there would think that he had lost the worth of one farthing. They gather also pearls by the seaside, and diamonds and carbuncles upon certain rocks, and yet they seek not for them: but by chance finding them, they cut and polish them. And therewith they deck their young infants. Which like as in the first years of their childhood, they make much and be fond and proud of such ornaments, so when they be a little more grown in years and discretion, perceiving that none but children do wear such toys and trifles: they lay them away even of their own shamefacedness, without any bidding of their parents: even as our children, when they wax big, do cast away nuts, brooches, and puppets. Therefore these laws and customs, which be so far different from all other nations, how divers fantasies also and minds they do cause, did I never so plainly perceive, as in the ambassadors of the Anemolians.

Thomas More, *Utopia.*

● During their absence certain reflections forced themselves upon me.

In the first place, it struck me as strange that the building should be so nearly empty; I was almost alone, and the few besides myself had been led by curiosity, and had no intention of doing business with the bank. But there might be more inside. I stole up to the curtain, and ventured to draw the extreme edge of it on one side. No, there was hardly any one there. I saw a large number of cashiers, all at their desks ready to pay cheques, and one or two who seemed to be the managing partners. I also saw my hostess and her daughters and two or three other ladies; also three or four old women and the boys from one of the neighbouring Colleges of Unreason; but there was no one else. This did not look as though the bank was doing a very large business; and yet I had always been told that every one in the city dealt with this establishment.

I cannot describe all that took place in these inner precincts, for a sinister-looking person in a black gown came and made unpleasant gestures at me for peeping. I happened to have in my pocket one of the Musical Bank pieces, which had been given me by Mrs Nosnibor, so I tried to tip him with it; but having seen what it was, he became so angry that I had to give him a piece of the other kind of money to pacify him. When I had done this he became civil directly. As soon as he was gone I ventured to take a second look, and saw Zulora in the very act of giving a piece of paper which looked like a cheque to one of the cashiers. He did not examine it, but putting his hand into an antique coffer hard by, he pulled out a quantity of metal pieces apparently at random, and handed them over without counting them; neither did Zulora count them, but put them into her purse and went back to her seat after dropping a few pieces of the other coinage into an alms box that stood by the cashier's side. Mrs Nosnibor and Arowhena then did likewise, but a little later they gave all (so far as I could see) that they had received from the cashier back to a verger, who I have no doubt put it back into the coffer from which it had been taken. They then began making towards the curtain; whereon I let it drop and retreated to a reasonable distance.

Samuel Butler, *Erewhon.*

See also William Morris, News from Nowhere, *chapters 6 and 15.*
Cf. Wit, humour, satire and irony, p. 27.

William CONGREVE 1670-1729

1670 *Born near Leeds.*
1674 *His family moved to Ireland.*
1686 *Entered Trinity College, Dublin; Swift was his school-fellow.*
1691 *Went to London to study law at the Middle Temple.*
1692 *Wrote a novel,* Incognita.
1693 *Successful production of* The Old Bachelor, *which Dryden had sponsored.*
1694 The Double Dealer.
1695 Love for Love.
1697 The Mourning Bride *(a tragedy).*
1698 *Controversy over Jeremy Collier's* A Short View of the Profaneness and Immorality of the English Stage.
1700 The Way of the World. *It did not meet with success and Congreve stopped writing for the stage. He led a respected life, holding several government sinecures.*
1729 *Died in London.*

Congreve's plays are typical of the Restoration Comedies of Manners exemplified by the works of Etherege, Wycherley, Vanbrugh or Farquhar. They are satires of society, ridiculing fops, fools, gallants and prudes alike, exposing all the "acquired follies" of man. At the centre of this type of comedy, one always finds the relationship between the sexes – witty and intellectual rather than emotional.

Yet, behind the brilliance of Congreve's concise and witty dialogues, there is less light-heartedness than in most of the plays of his time. His characters may be libertines, but they are always earnest and honest.

He preached the happy mean. His "wicked" *jeunes premiers,* and to a lesser degree his *premières,* are gentlemen and ladies. Bellmour, Mellefont, Valentine, and Mirabell... are never underhand or malicious, and have generosity. Cynthia, Angelica, and Millamant are charming women, warm-hearted, companionable, and direct. These are not scandal-mongers and sharpers, nor would-be wits and heartless jades.

They show up in solid relief against the dizzy world of Restoration comedy."

Bonamy Dobrée.

Sympathy and compassion always moderate the wit and irony, revealing a desire for order and an almost classical temper.

The Way of the World (1700)

Mrs. Millamant, Mirabell, Mincing

MIRABELL. I would beg a little private audience too. – You had the tyranny to deny me last night; though you knew I came to impart a secret to you that concerned my love.

MRS MILLAMANT. You saw I was engaged.

MIRABELL. Unkind. You had the leisure to entertain a herd of fools; things who visit you from their excessive idleness; bestowing on your easiness that time, which is the encumbrance of their lives. How can you find delight in such society? It is impossible they should admire you, they are not capable: or if they were, it should be to you as a mortification; for sure to please a fool is some degree of folly.

MRS MILLAMANT. I please myself. – Besides, sometimes to converse with fools is for my health.

MIRABELL. Your health! Is there a worse disease than the conversation of fools?

MRS MILLAMANT. Yes, the vapours; fools are physic for it, next to *assafoetida.*

MIRABELL. You are not in a course[1] of fools?

MRS MILLAMANT. Mirabell, if you persist in this offensive freedom – you'll displease me. – I think I must resolve after all, not to have you. – We shan't agree.

MIRABELL. Not in our physic it may be.

MRS MILLAMANT. And yet our distemper in all likelihood will be the same; for we shall be sick of one another. I shan't endure to be reprimanded, nor instructed; 'tis so dull to act always by advice, and so tedious to be told of one's faults – I can't bear it. Well, I won't have you Mirabell – I'm resolved – I think – you may go. – Ha, ha, ha. What would you give, that you could help loving me?

MIRABELL. I would give something that you did not know I could not help it.

MRS MILLAMANT. Come, don't look grave then. Well, what do you say to me?

MIRABELL. I say that a man may as soon make a friend by his wit, or a fortune by his honesty, as win a woman with plain-dealing and sincerity.

MRS MILLAMANT. Sententious Mirabell! Prithee don't look with that violent and inflexible wise face, like Solomon at the dividing of the child in an old tapestry hanging.

MIRABELL. You are merry, madam, but I would persuade you for a moment to be serious.

MRS MILLAMANT. What, with that face? No, if you keep your countenance, 'tis impossible I should hold mine. Well, afterall, there is something very moving in a lovesick face. Ha, ha, ha. – Well I won't laugh, don't be peevish. – Heigho! Now I'll be melancholy, as melancholy as a watchlight[2]. Well Mirabell, if ever you will win me woo me now. – Nay, if you are so tedious, fare you well; – I see they are walking away. (...)

Act II, Scene 6.

1. *a course:* a course of medicine – 2. *a watchlight:* very poor night-light.

A few opinions about Restoration comedy:

• Celui de tous les Anglais qui a porté le plus loin la gloire du théâtre comique est feu M. Congreve. Il n'a fait que peu de pièces, mais toutes sont excellentes dans leur genre. Les règles du théâtre y sont rigoureusement observées ; elles sont pleines de caractères nuancés avec une extrême finesse ; on n'y essuie pas la moindre mauvaise plaisanterie ; vous y voyez partout le langage des honnêtes gens avec des actions de fripon : ce qui prouve qu'il connaissait bien son monde (...)

Voltaire, *Lettres Philosophiques.*

• But when Vice is varnish'd over with Pleasure, and comes in the Shape of Convenience, the case grows somewhat dangerous; for then the Fancy may be gain'd, and the Guards corrupted, and Reason suborn'd against it self. And thus a *Disguise* often passes when the Person would otherwise be stopt. To put *Lewdness* into a Thriving condition, to give it an Equipage, of Quality, and to treat it with Ceremony and Respect, is the way to confound the Understanding, to fortifie the Charm, and to make the Mischief invincible. Innocence is often owing to Fear, and Appetite is kept under by Shame; But when these Restraints are once taken off, when Profit and Liberty lie on the same side, and a Man can Debauch himself into Credit, what can be expected in such a case, but that Pleasure should grow Absolute, and Madness carry all before it? The *Stage* seem eager to bring Matters to this Issue; They have made a considerable progress, and are still pushing their Point with all the Vigour imaginable. If this be not their Aim why is *Lewdness* so much consider'd in Character and Success? Why are their Favourites Atheistical, and their fine Gentleman debauched? To what purpose is *Vice* thus prefer'd, thus ornamented, and caress'd, unless for Imitation? (...)

The business of *Plays* is to recomend Virtue, and discountenance Vice; To shew the Uncertainty of Humane Greatness, the suddain Turns of Fate, and the Unhappy Conclusions of Violence and Injustice: 'Tis to expose the Singularities of Pride and Fancy, to make Folly and Falsehood contemptible, and to bring every Thing that is Ill Under Infamy, and Neglect.

Jeremy Collier (1650-1726), *A Short View of the Immorality and Profaneness of the English Stage,* 1698.

● The period in our own history of the grossest degradation of the drama is the reign of Charles II when all forms in which poetry had been accustomed to be expressed became hymns to the triumph of kingly power over liberty and virtue. Milton stood alone illuminating an age unworthy of him. At such periods the calculating principle pervades all the forms of dramatic exhibition, and poetry ceases to be expressed upon them. Comedy loses its ideal universality: wit succeeds to humour; we laugh from self-complacency and triumph instead of pleasure; malignity, sarcasm and contempt, succeed to sympathetic merriment; we hardly laugh, but we smile. Obscenity, which is ever blasphemy against the divine beauty in life, becomes, from the very veil which it assumes, more active if less digusting: it is a monster for which the corruption of society for ever brings forth new food, which it devours in secret.

Shelley, *A Defence of Poetry.*

Congreve on his plays:

● Those characters which are meant to be ridiculed in most of our comedies are of fools so gross, that in my hunble opinion, they should rather disturb than divert the well-natured and reflecting part of an audience; they are rather objects of charity than contempt; and instead of moving our mirth, they ought very often to excite our compassion.

Dedication of *The Way of the World.*

● But there is one thing, at which I am more concerned than all the false Criticisms that are made upon me; and that is, some of the Ladies are offended: I am heartily sorry for it, for I declare I would rather disoblige all the Criticks in the World, than one of the Fair Sex. They are concerned that I have represented some Women Vicious and Affected: How can I help it? It is the Business of a Comick Poet to paint the Vices and Follies of Humane kind; and there are but two Sexes that I know, *viz. Men,* and *Women,* which have a Title to Humanity: And if I leave one half of them out, the Work will be imperfect. I should be very glad of an opportunity to make my Complement to those Ladies who are offended: But they can no more expect it in a Comedy, than to be Tickled by a Surgeon, when he's letting them Blood. They who are Virtuous or Discreet, I'm sure cannot be offended, for such Characters as these distinguish them, and make their Beauties more shining and observ'd: And they who are of the other kind, may nevertheless pass for such, by seeming not to be displeased, or touched with the Satyr of this *Comedy.* Thus have they also wrongfully accused me of doing them a prejudice, when I have in reality done them a Service.

Dedication to Charles Montague, prefixed to first edition of *The Double-Dealer,* 1694.

Cf. Wit, humour, satire and irony, p. 27; Comedy, p. 24.

Richard Brinsley SHERIDAN 1751-1816

1751 *Born in Dublin; his father was an actor, his mother a playwright.*
1762-1768 *School at Harrow.*
1773 *Married Elizabeth Linley after escaping to France and fighting duels against his rivals.*

The 18th century was characterized by a decline of the theatre. The average theatre-goer favoured edifying and sentimental plays and valued acting and interpretation above the literary quality of the plays (cf p. 65-6) Sheridan and Goldsmith, however, brought about a revival of come-

1775 The Rivals *and* The Duenna *(a comic opera) performed.*
1776 *Bought Garrick's shares in the Drury Lane theatre.*
1777 The School for Scandal.
1779 The Critic.
1780 *Became member of Parliament for Stafford and devoted the rest of his life to public affairs.*
1782 *Under-Secretary of State for Foreign Affairs.*
1783 *Secretary to the Treasury.*
1787 *Well-known speech in the Commons against Warren Hastings.*
1809 *Drury Lane Theatre burnt, causing him financial problems.*
1813 *Arrested for debt.*
1816 *Died in London.*

dy, portraying the refined society of their time with wit and humour. Though Sheridan, the more brilliant of the two, lived in the second half of the eighteenth century, his spirit is more akin to that of the Restoration playwrights. But in spite of his virtuosity, epigrams and sparkling dialogues, his tone is usually less artificial than in the Restoration comedies.

His plays are comedies of manners. They mercilessly ridicule snobs, hypocrites, scandal-mongers and all those for whom morality and sentimentality are only social conventions.

In his first play, The Rivals, *the hero disguises himself as a poor lieutenant to seduce Lydia Languish who, brought up on sentimental novels, dreams of persecution and poverty.* The School for Scandal *exposes the hypocrisy of Sir Joseph Surface and the envenomed tongue of Lady Sneerwell who spends her time running characters down. As for* The Cricic, *it is a farce which makes use of a play within the play to satirize the sentimental dramas of the time. Beyond tragedy and literary criticism, it is the illusion of the stage which is laid bare.*

The School for Scandal (1777)

SIR PETER. (...) You forget what your situation was when I married you.

LADY TEAZLE. No, no, I don't; 'twas a very disagreeable one, or I should never have married you.

SIR PETER. Yes, yes, madam, you were then in somewhat an humbler style: – the daughter of a plain country squire. Recollect, Lady Teazle, when I saw you first, sitting at your tambour[1], in a pretty figured linen gown, with a bunch of keys at your side, your hair combed smooth over a roll[2], and you apartment hung round with fruits in worsted, of your own working.

LADY TEAZLE. Oh, yes! I remember it very well, and a curious life I led! my daily occupation to inspect the dairy, superintend the poultry, make extracts from the family receipt-book, and comb my Aunt Deborah's lapdog.

SIR PETER. Yes, yes, madame, 'twas so indeed.

LADY TEAZLE. And then, you know, my evening amusements! To draw patterns for ruffles, which I had not the materials to make up; to play Pope Joan[3] with the curate; to read a sermon to my aunt; or to be stuck down to an old spinet to strum my father to sleep after a fox-chase.

SIR PETER. I am glad you have so good a memory. Yes, madam, these were the recreations I took you from; but now you must have your coach – *vis-à-vis* – and three powdered footmen before your chair; and, in the summer, a pair of white cats[4] to draw you to Kensington Gardens. No recollection, I suppose, when you were content to ride double, behind the butler, on a dock'd coach-horse?

LADY TEAZLE. No – I swear I never did that; I deny the butler and the coach-horse.

SIR PETER. This, madam, was your situation; and what have I done for you? I have made you a woman of fashion, of fortune, of rank; – in short, I have made you *my wife.*

LADY TEAZLE. Well, then, – and there is but one thing more you can make me to add to the obligation, that is –

SIR PETER. My widow, I suppose?

LADY TEAZLE. Hem! hem!

SIR PETER. I thank you, madam – but don't flatter yourself; for, though your ill conduct may disturb my peace of mind, it shall never break my heart, I promise you: however, I am equally obliged to you for the hint.

LADY TEAZLE. Then why will you endeavour to make yourself so disagreeable to me, and thwart me in every little elegant expense?

SIR PETER. 'Slife[5], madam, I say, had you any of these little elegant expenses when you married me?

LADY TEAZLE. **Lud, Sir Peter! would you have me be out of the fashion?**

SIR PETER. **The fashion, indeed! what had you to do with the fashion when you married me?**

LADY TEAZLE. **For my part, I should think you would like to have your wife thought a woman of taste.**

SIR PETER. **Aye – there again – taste – Zounds[5] madam, you had no taste when you married me!**

LADY TEAZLE. **That's very true, indeed, Sir Peter; and, after having married you, I am sure I should never pretend to taste again. But now, Sir Peter, since we have finished our daily jangle, I presume I may go to my engagement at Lady Sneerwell's?**

SIR PETER. **Aye, there's another precious circumstance – a charming set of acquaintance you have made there!**

LADY TEAZLE. **Nay, Sir Peter, they are all people of rank and fortune, and remarkably tenacious of reputation.**

SIR PETER. **Yes, egad[5], they are tenacious of reputation with a vengeance; for they don't choose anybody should have a character but themselves! – Such a crew! Ah! many a wretch has rid on a hurdle who has done less mischief than these utterers of forged tales, coiners of scandal, and clippers of reputation.**

LADY TEAZLE. **What, would you restrain the freedom of speech?**

SIR PETER. **Oh! they have made you just as bad as any one of the society.**

LADY TEAZLE. **Why, I believe I do bear a part with a tolerable grace. But I vow I bear no malice against the people I abuse. When I say an ill-natured thing, 'tis out of pure good humour; and I take it for granted, they deal exactly in the same manner with me. But, Sir Peter, you know you promised to come to Lady Sneerwell's too.**

SIR PETER. **Well, well, I'llcall in just to look after my own character.**

LADY TEAZLE. **Then, indeed, you must make haste after me or you'll be too late. So good-bye to you.** ***(Exit Lady Teazle.)***

Act II, Scene 1.

1. *tambour:* frame for embroidery – 2. *a roll:* a pad of hair – 3. *Pope Joan:* a card game – 4. *cats:* ponies – 5. *'Slife, Zounds, egad:* oaths.

Thomas Rowlandson (1756-1827) was a satirist and caricaturist who left a picture of social life in town and country, a 'Human Comedy' even more comprehensive than that of Hogarth though without its moralistic overtones. W. Gaunt.

Thomas Rowlandson: Courtship. *1785-6.*
Private collection. Ph. Phaidon Press Ltd.

Matrimony. *c. 1785-6.*
ibid.

Compare the way Shakespeare and Lord Chesterfield deal with the same theme:

Thy husband is thy lord, thy life, thy keeper,
Thy head, thy sovereign; one that cares for thee,
And for thy maintenance commits his body
To painful labour, both by sea and land;
To watch the night in storms, the day in cold,
Whilst thou liest warm at home, secure and safe,
And craves no other tribute at thy hands,
But love, fair looks, and true obedience;
Too little payment for so great a debt.
Such duty as the subject owes the prince,
Even such a woman oweth to her husband:
And when she is froward, peevish, sullen, sour,
And not obedient to his honest will,
What is she but a foul contending rebel,
And graceless traitor to her loving lord?

W. Shakespeare, *The Taming of the Shrew,* V, II.

As women are a considerable, or at least a pretty numerous part of company; and as their suffrages go a great way toward establishing a man's character in the fashionable part of the world (which is of great importance to the fortune and figure he proposes to make in it), it is necessary to please them. I will therefore, upon this subject, let you into certain *Arcana* that will be very useful for you to know, but which you must, with the utmost care, conceal and never seem to know. Women, then, are only children of a larger growth; they have an entertaining tattle, and sometimes wit; but for solid reasoning, good sense, I never knew in my life one that had it, or who reasoned or acted consequentially for four-and-twenty hours together. Some little passion or humor always breaks upon their best resolutions. Their beauty neglected or controverted, their age increased, or their supposed understandings depreciated, instantly kindles their little passions, and overturns any system of consequential conduct, that in their most reasonable moments they might have been capable of forming. A man of sense only trifles with them, plays with them, humors and flatters them, as he does with a sprightly forward child; but he neither consults them about, nor trusts them with serious matters; though he often makes them believe that he does both; which is the thing in the world that they are proud of; for they love mightily to be dabbling in business (which by the way they always spoil); and being justly distrustful that men in general look upon them in a trifling light, they almost adore that man who talks more seriously to them, and who seems to consult and trust them; I say, who seems; for weak men really do, but wise ones only seem to do it. No flattery is either too high or too low for them. They will greedily swallow the highest, and gratefully accept of the lowest; and you may safely flatter any woman from her understanding down to the exquisite taste of her fan.

Lord Chesterfield, *Letters to his Son.*

A diplomat and politician as well as a patron of literature, the Earl of Chesterfield (1694-1773) is famous for the series of letters he wrote to his natural son. Their purpose was to direct his son's education with one single aim: success. With little respect for morals or feelings, he cynically advocated urbanity, grace and the development of intellectual qualities in order to advance one's career.

Cf. Wit, Humour, Satire and Irony, p. 27: Comedy p. 24.

4. The Rise of the Novel

literature and society

The social background

(In the years 1740-80) we find a generation of men wholly characteristic of the eighteenth-century ethos, a society with a mental outlook of its own, self-poised, self-judged, and self-approved, freed from the disturbing passions of the past, and not yet troubled with anxieties about a very different future which was soon to be brought upon the scene by the Industrial and the French Revolutions. The gods mercifully gave mankind this little moment of peace between the religious fanaticisms of the past and the fanaticisms of class and race that were speedily to arise and dominate time to come. In England it was an age of aristocracy and liberty; of the rule of law and the absence of reform; of individual initiative and institutional decay; of latitudinarianism above and Wesleyanism below; of the growth of humanitarianism and philanthropic feeling and endeavour; of creative vigour in all the trades and arts that serve and adorn the life of man.

It is a "classical" age, that is to say an age of unchallenged assumptions, when the philosophers of the street, such as Dr Johnson, have ample leisure to moralize on the human scene, in the happy belief that the state of society and the modes of thought to which they are accustomed are not mere passing aspects of an ever-shifting kaleidoscope, but permanent habitations, the final outcome of reason and experience. Such an age does not aspire to progress though it may in fact be progressing; it regards itself not as setting out but as having arrived; it is thankful for what it has, and enjoys life without "deep questioning which probes to endless dole". (...)

To the typical men of the period of Blackstone, Gibbon, and Burke, England appeared to be the best country possible in an imperfect world, requiring only to be left alone where providence and the Revolution of 1688 had so fortunately placed her. Their optimism about England was based on a general pessimism about the human race, not on a belief in perpetual and world-wide "progress" such as cheered simple hearts in the nineteenth century.

It is true that the men who were least content were those who looked closest at the realities of English life – Hogarth, Fielding, Smollett, and the philanthropists; they indeed exposed particular evils as unsparingly as Dickens himself. But even their strictures kept within the limits of the classical and conservative philosophy of the time. Nor was the self-complacency of that age altogether unjustified, though it was unfortunate because it sustained an atmosphere inimical to any general movement of reform. It was a society which, with all its grave faults, was brilliant above and stable below.

G.M. Trevelyan, *English Social History*.
© 1942, 1944 by Longmans Green, Longman Group Ltd.

Hogarth: Beer Street. *Ph. Hachette.*
Hogarth's Beer Street *reflects the wholesome influence of beer which encourages labour, commerce and art. See its counterpart,* Gin Lane, *p. 137.*

The new reading public

Evidence on the availability and use of leisure thus confirms the previous picture given of the composition of the reading public in the early eighteenth century. Despite a considerable expansion it still did not normally extend much further down the social scale than to tradesmen and shopkeepers, with the important exception of the more favoured apprentices and indoor servants. Still, there had been additions, and they had been mainly recruited from among the increasingly prosperous and numerous social groups concerned with commerce and manufacture. This is important, for it is probable that this particular change alone, even if it was of comparatively minor proportions, may have altered the centre of gravity of the reading public sufficiently to place the middle class as a whole in a dominating position for the first time.

In looking for the effects of this change upon literature, no very direct or dramatic manifestations of middle-class tastes and capacities are to be expected, for the dominance of the middle class in the reading public had in any case been long preparing. One general effect of some interest for the rise of the novel, however, seems to follow from the change in the centre of gravity of the reading public. The fact that literature in the eighteenth century was addressed to an ever-widening audience must have weakened the relative importance of those readers with enough education and leisure to take a professional or semi-professional interest in classical and modern letters; and in return it must have increased the relative importance of those who desired an easier form of literary entertainment, even if it had little prestige among the literati. (...)

The new literary balance of power, then, probably tended to favour ease of entertainment

	Politics and Society	**Literature and the Arts**
1739		HUME: *Treatise of Human Nature.*
1740	Rise of Methodism.	RICHARDSON: *Pamela.*
1742		FIELDING: *Joseph Andrews.* YOUNG: *Night Thoughts.*
1744		HOGARTH: *Marriage-à-la-Mode.*
1745	Second Jacobite Uprising (Charles Edward).	
1746	Defeat of Charles Edward at Culloden.	
1747		RICHARDSON: *Clarissa Harlowe.*
1748		SMOLLETT: *Roderick Random.*
1749		FIELDING: *Tom Jones.*
1750		GRAY: *Elegy.*
1752		DR JOHNSON: *The Rambler.*
1753		RICHARDSON: *Sir Charles Grandison.*
1755		DR JOHNSON: *Dictionary.*
1756	Seven Years' War.	
1757		BURKE: *The Sublime and Beautiful.*
1759		STERNE: *Tristram Shandy* (1759-1767).
1760	George III (1760-1820)	
1763	Treaty of Paris.	
1764		WALPOLE: *The Castle of Otranto.*
1765		PERCY: *Reliques of Ancient English Poetry.*
1766		GOLDSMITH: *The Vicar of Wakefield.*
1768		STERNE: *A Sentimental Journey.* Creation of the Royal Academy (Sir Joshua Reynolds).
1770	Invention of the Spinning Jenny.	
1771		SMOLLETT: *Humphry Clinker.* MACKENZIE: *The Man of Feeling.*
1773		GOLDSMITH: *She Stoops to Conquer.*
1776	American Independence Invention of the steam-engine (Watt).	SMITH: *The Wealth of Nations.* GIBBON: *Decline and Fall of the Roman Empire.*
1777		SHERIDAN: *The School for Scandal.*
1778		BURNEY: *Evelina.*
1779	Luddite riots.	DR JOHNSON: *Lives of the Poets.*
1780	Gordon Riots.	

at the expense of obedience to traditional critical standards, and it is certain that this change of emphasis was an essential permissive factor for the achievements of Defoe and Richardson. That these achievements were also related to other and more positive features of the tastes and attitudes of the main accessions to the reading public during the period also seems likely: the outlook of the trading class, for instance, was much influenced by the economic individualism and the somewhat secularized puritanism which finds expression in the novels of Defoe; and the increasingly important feminine component of the public found many of its interests expressed by Richardson.

I. Watt, *The Rise of the Novel*, 1957.
Chatto and Windus

literature and philosophy

Philosophically the particularizing approach to character resolves itself into the problem of defining the individual person. Once Descartes had given the thought processes within the individual's consciousness supreme importance, the philosophical problems connected with personal identity naturally attracted a great deal of attention. In England, for example, Locke, Bishop Butler, Berkeley, Hume, and Reid all debated the issue, and the controversy even reached the pages of the *Spectator*.

The parallel here between the tradition of realist thought and the formal innovations of the early novelists is obvious: both philosophers and novelists paid greater attention to the particular individual than had been common before.

Ian Watt, *The Rise of the Novel.*

Je n'ai jamais rencontré un de ses compatriotes, un des miens qui eût voyagé en Angleterre, sans lui demander : « Avez-vous vu le poète Richardson? » Ensuite : « Avez-vous vu le philosophe Hume? »

Diderot, *Éloge de Richardson.*

Hume divides "the contents of the mind", all labeled indiscriminately "ideas" by Locke and Berkeley, into two classes, "impressions" and "ideas". The impressions are intended to be the immediately given data of sense and of introspection, while the ideas are the images of memory and imagination.

Next he establishes that every simple idea that we have is a copy of a simple impression, and that, while we may form complex ideas which do not copy any impression, these are built up from simple ideas which are copies of impressions. Finally he proves that the impressions are temporally prior to the ideas which resemble them: first, by the simple fact of observation that they come earlier in time; and, secondly, by the argument that, while we may have impressions whithout subsequently having any resembling idea, we never have a (simple) idea without having previously had a resembling impression. This is Hume's statement of the empiricist thesis. It is a piece of descriptive psychology: all complex ideas are built up of simple ideas; all simple ideas are copies of previously experienced simple impressions; thus all our ideas are ultimately derived from impressions.

Sir Isaiah Berlin, *The Age of Enlightenment.*

(...) We shall here content ourselves with establishing one general proposition, *That all our simple ideas in their first appearance are derived from simple impressions, which are correspondent to them, and which they exactly represent.*

In seeking for phaenomena to prove the proposition, I find only those of two kinds; but, in each kind the pheanomena are obvious, numerous, and conclusive. I first make myself certain, by a new review, of what I have already asserted, that every simple impression is attented with a correspondent idea, and every simple idea with a correspondent impression. From this constant conjunction of resembling perceptions I immediately conclude that there is a great connexion betwixt our correspondent impressions and ideas, and that the existence of the one has a considerable influence upon that of the other. Such a constant conjunction, in such an infinite number of instances, can never arise from chance; but clearly proves a dependence of the impressions on the ideas, or of the ideas on the impressions. That I may know on which side this dependence lies, I consider the order of their *first appearance*; and find, by constant experience, that the simple impressions always take the precedence of their correspondent ideas, but never appear in the contrary order. To give a child an idea of scarlet or orange, of sweet or bitter, I present the objects, or, in other words, convey to him these impressions; but proceed not so absurdly as to endeavour to produce the impressions by exciting the ideas. Our ideas, upon their appearance, produce not their correspondent impressions, nor do we perceive any colour, or feel any sensation merely upon thinking of them. On the other hand, we find that any impression, either of the mind or body, is constantly followed by an idea which resembles it, and is only different in the degrees of force and liveliness. The constant conjunction of our resembling perceptions is a convincing proof that the one are the causes of the other; and this priority of the impressions is an equal proof that our impressions are the causes of our ideas, not our ideas of our impressions.

To confirm this, I consider another plain and convincing phaenomenon; which is, that wherever, by any accident, the faculties which give rise to any impressions are obstructed in their operations, as when one is born blind or deaf, not only the impressions are lost, but also their correspondent ideas; so that there never appear in the mind the least traces of either of them. Nor is this only true where the organs of sensation are entirely destroyed, but likewise where they have never been put in action to produce a particular impression. We cannot form to ourselves a just idea of the taste of a pine-apple without having actually tasted it.

David Hume, *A Treatise of Human Nature,* Book I.

literature and the arts

Painting

One of the main features of painting during the 18th century is that it became more distinctively British, less influenced by foreign schools. A new kind of picture appeared around 1720 and was to become extremely popular – the ***Conversation Piece:***

The essence of such pictures is that they represent a number of persons, a family or a group of friends, with a certain degree of informality and at ease among themselves, not stiffly posed for the benefit of the painter. They may be represented in their homes or in their gardens and the figures should be small in scale, generally some twelve to fifteen inches high. The eighteenth century applied the term "a conversation" to all informal groups, whether small in scale or on the size of life, and whether the figures were portraits or productions of the painter's fancy, but today the term is restricted in general use to small-scale portrait groups.

Ellis Waterhouse, *Painting in Britain, 1530-1790, The Pelican History of Art, Penguin Books Ltd.*

A conversation-piece by Philip Mercier: Viscount Tyrconnel and his Family, *1725/6.*
Lord Brownlow, Belton House.
Ph. M. Trelawny. © National Trust.

The "Conversation-Piece" in the novel:

My wife and daughters happening to return a visit to neighbour Flamborough's, found that family had lately got their pictures drawn by a limner, who travelled the country, and took likenesses for fifteen shillings a head. As this family and ours had long a sort of rivalry in point of taste, our spirit took the alarm at this stolen march upon us, and notwithstanding all I could say, and I said much, it was resolved that we should have our pictures done too. Having, therefore, engaged the limner, for what could I do? our next deliberation was to shew the superiority of our taste in the attitudes. As for our neighbour's family, there were seven of them, and they were drawn with seven oranges, a thing quite out of taste, no variety in life, no composition in the world. We desired to have something in a brighter style, and, after many debates, at length came to an unanimous resolution of being drawn together, in one large historical family piece. This would be cheaper, since one frame would serve for all, and it would be infinitely more genteel; for all families of any taste were now drawn in the same manner. As we did not immediately recollect an historical subject to hit us, we were contented each with being drawn as independent historical figures. My wife desired to be represented as Venus, and the painter was desired not to be too frugal of his diamonds in her stomacher and hair. Her two little ones were to be as Cupids by her side, while I, in my gown and band, was to present her with my books on the Whistonian controversy. Olivia would be drawn as an Amazon, sitting upon a bank of flowers, drest in a green joseph, richly laced with gold, and a whip in her hand. Sophia was to be a shepherdess, with as many sheep as the painter could put in for nothing; and Moses was to be drest out with an hat and white feather. Our taste so much pleased the 'Squire, that he insisted on being put in as one of the family in the character of Alexander the great, at Olivia's feet. This was considered by us all as an indication of his desire to be introduced into the family, nor could we refuse his request. The painter was therefore set to work, and as he wrought with assiduity and expedition, in less than four days the whole was compleated. The piece was large, and it must be owned he did not spare his colours; for which my wife gave him great encomiums. We were all perfectly satisfied with his performance; but an unfortunate circumstance had not occurred till the picture was finished, which now struck us with dismay. It was so very large that we had no place in the house to fix it. How we all came to disregard so material a point is inconceivable; but certain it is, we had been all greatly remiss. The picture, therefore, instead of gratifying our vanity, as we hoped, leaned, in a most mortifying manner, against the kitchen wall, where the canvas was stretched and painted, much too large to be got through any of the doors, and the jest of all our neighbours. One compared it to Robinson Crusoe's long-boat, too large to be removed; another thought it more resembled a reel in a bottle; some wondered how it could be got out, but still more were amazed how it ever got in.

O. Goldsmith, *The Vicar of Wakefield,* 1766.

The major painters of the period can roughly by divided into three groups.

The critics of society

HOGARTH *is the main figure in this group. It was men and manners rather than nature which interested him and his paintings contain harsh satire of society.*

They

- *are characterized by an interest in domestic or social scenes rather than the mere portrayal of "types",*
- *reflect Hogarth's interest in the theatre. Many of his paintings could be scenes on a stage, and he specialized in series of paintings with a moral subject:*

"I therefore turned my thoughts", he says, "to a still more novel mode, *viz.* painting modern moral subjects, a field not broken up in any country or in any age... I wished to compose pictures on canvas, similar to representations on the stage; and farther hope that they will be tried by the same test and criticized by the same criterion... In these compositions, those subjects which will both entertain and improve the mind, bid fair to be of the greatest utility, and must therefore be entitled to rank in the highest class."

Ellis Waterhouse, *ibid.*

J. HIGHMORE *(cf p. 145) and* F. HAYMAN *are two of his best-known followers*

Three scenes from Hogarth's The Harlot's Progress.
Ph. Bulloz.

1. The arrival from the country
A young and naive country girl arrives in London from the country (cf. the goose in the basket in the bottom right-hand corner which is addressed "To my loving cousin in Thames Street"). Her cousin is not there to meet the coach but a middle-aged woman (a bawd) adresses her, pretending to be a fine lady in search of a servant. Notice that instead of protecting her, the clergyman is busy reading a letter from his bishop (he wishes for preferment.)

2. The quarrel with her Jewish Protector
The young woman is now the mistress of a Jew and lives in a rich apartment. Her protector pays her a visit but while serving tea, she upsets the table on purpose in order to give her lover the opportunity to escape (his breeches are not even properly fastened). Notice the masquerade mask on the table (probably giving us a clue as to where she met her lover), the black page and the monkey (both very fashionable at the time), and the Old Testament paintings on the wall, all related to the theme of punishment.

3. Scene in Bridewell
The former prostitute is now beating hemp in Bridewell prison (some of it being used to make the rope with which people are hung). Notice the old man in fine clothes next to her: the cards on the floor in front of him show he was a sharper. Behind her, a woman is fingering her clothes which will eventually become hers.

Better to Work than Stand thus

The portrait painters

Sir Joshua REYNOLDS' *portraits are characterized by warmth, solidity and informality. They convey strength and a vivid impression of life.*

Thomas GAINSBOROUGH'S *art is lighter and more natural, giving an impression of elegance and transparence. But he was a landscape painter as well and was very successful in blending landscapes and portraits in a harmonious way.*

ROMNEY *and Sir* Thomas LAWRENCE *at the end of the century also became very fashionable portrait painters.*

Sir Joshua Reynolds: Georgiana, Countess Spencer, and her Daughter, *1760/1.*
Earl Spencer. Althorp, Northants. Ph. Bulloz.

Gainsborough: Mr and Mrs Andrews.
National Gallery, London. Ph. Bulloz.

The landscape painters

Some of Gainsborough's paintings as well as the luminous landscapes of Richard WILSON *reflect the rising taste for nature, the picturesque and the sublime, a taste that will reach its climax at the end of the century.*

Richard Wilson : Holt Bridge on the River Dee.

Architecture

In domestic architecture and the arts, the eighteenth century was Britain's "golden age". (...)

In Britain, the aristocracy functioned better as patron of the visual arts than even the monarchy had done in earlier years, for the monarch and his court had one viewpoint; the aristocracy was multiple. Some monarchs had good taste and were knowledgeable and interested in the arts; others had not and were not. The aristocracy, at their stage of development in the eighteenth century, were, on the whole, knowledgeable and had good taste. They were numerous and so could employ large numbers of architects, artists and craftsmen in all the allied trades and, due to their extensive European travels, knew exactly what they wished to create and possess. They demanded the highest standards, wishing to emulate the great palaces and houses which they had seen abroad and each to build one in the latest fashion greater than that of his acquaintances. To get what they wanted, unlike the middle classes and bureaucratic governments of the twentieth century, they did not count the cost. Indeed, it was not unknown for the head of an eighteenth-century aristocratic family to almost bankrupt the estate in order to create the mansion set in its parkland.

D. Yarwood, *The Architecture of Britain,* 1530 to 1790, *Batsford Ltd.*

PALLADIAN ARCHITECTURE, 1725-60

This style was, as its name suggests, based on the work of the Italian architect ANDREA PALLADIO, who had earlier inspired Inigo Jones and achieved such fame in England for his faithful interpretation of the architectural principles of Vitruvius. The chief patron of the Palladian school in England was LORD BURLINGTON, an architect himself but also a man of foresight and talent who assisted and inspired men of greater architectural gifts – such as WILLIAM KENT (1685-1748) and COLIN CAMPBELL (*d.* 1729). The influence of the Palladians on architecture was considerable but it was confined largely to the country mansion, where they set a pattern of layout that lasted well into the second half of the century. The house consisted of a central porticoed block, connected to side wings by low galleries or colonnades; the whole scheme was strictly symmetrical and conformed equally strictly to Palladio's (and Vitruvius') classical proportions, orders and details. In great contrast, but complementary and forming an essentially English combination, were the parkland and gardens, in which the mansion was set. Whereas the house was formal, controlled, symmetrical, the gardens were of a carefully contrived naturalness, with green swards interspersed at suitable intervals with spreading trees and flowering shrubs, lakes, ponds, classical temples and sculpture: the complete antithesis of the French or Italian formal gardens of the period.

D. Yarwood, *An Outline of English Architecture*, *Batsford Ltd.*

Lord Burlington: Chiswick House, London, *1727-36.*
In D. Yarwood, ibid.

Daniel DEFOE 1660-1731

1660 *Born in London (as Daniel Foe).*
1665-1666 *The Great Plague.*
1674-9(?) *Attended a non-conformist school to become a Presbyterian minister.*
1682 *Instead of becoming a minister, spent the following ten years trying different trades and travelling abroad.*
1697 An Essay upon Projects.
1701 The True-Born Englishman, *a satirical defense of William III.*
1702 The Shortest Way with Dissenters, *an ironical criticism of the Established Church. As a consequence, Defoe was imprisoned and exposed in the pillory.*
1703 *Became a secret agent for Harley, a Tory minister who had had him released from prison. Started writing in the* Review *as well as for different politicians, irrespective of their political ideas.*
1719 Robinson Crusoe.
1720 Captain Singleton.
1722 Moll Flanders, A Journal of the Plague Year, Colonel Jack.
1724 Roxana, A Tour thro' the whole Island of Great Britain.
1725 The Complete English Tradesman.
1731 *Died in London.*

It was only at the end of his life that Defoe turned to the novel, after years of journalistic and satirical writing. A Journal of the Plague Year *is a good example of this dual interest. It purports to be an eye-witness account of the epidemic of bubonic plague which had visited London in 1665. A mixture of recollection, historical study and imagination, the book almost reads as fiction though the accuracy and realism of the narration are never sacrificed.*

The same concern with realism underlies his works of fiction. Through simplicity of style and depiction of likely events, Defoe's aim is to create true-to-life and vivid pictures, giving an illusion of reality. This effect is enhanced by a minute psychological study of the motivations and reactions of the characters. But Defoe's principal aim is a moral one. Through Robinson Crusoe's struggles, through Moll's gradual downfall and eventual penitence, we are shown that...

... man's function is to apprehend the world, find ways to grapple with it, hang on while events frustrate him, defy society if it runs counter to his own needs... and eventually he comes through, while those around him may waste away. Defoe is interested only in the successes, and even God and fate cannot prevent the persistent individual from coming through.

F.R. Karl.

The Fortunes and Misfortunes of the famous Moll Flanders (1722)

Reduced to destitution, Moll Flanders has taken to stealing.

The next thing of moment was an attempt at a gentlewoman's gold watch. It happened in a crowd, at a meeting-house, where I was in very great danger of being taken. I had full hold of her watch, but giving a great jostle as if somebody had thrust me against her, and in the juncture giving the watch a fair pull, I found it would no come, so I let it go that moment, and cried as if I had been killed, that somebody had trod upon my foot, and that there was certainly pickpockets there, for somebody or other had given a pull at my watch; for you are to observe that on these adventures we always went very well dressed, and I had very good clothes, on, and a gold watch by my side, as like a lady as other folks.

I had no sooner said so but the other gentlewoman cried out, "A pickpocket," too, for somebody, she said, had tried to pull her watch away.

When I touched her watch I was close to her, but when I cried out I stopped as it were short, and the crowd bearing her forward a little, she made a noise too, but it was at some distance from me, so that she did not in the least suspect me; but when she cried out, "A pickpoket", somebody cried out, "Ay, and here has been another; this gentlewoman has been attempted too."

At that very instant, a little farther in the crowd, and very luckily too, they cried out, "A pickpocket," again, and really seized a young fellow in the very fact. This, though unhappy for the wretch, was very opportunely for my case, though I had carried it handsomely enough before; but now it was out of doubt, and all the loose part of the crowd ran that way, and the poor boy was delivered up to the rage of the street, which is a cruelty I need not describe, and which, however, they are always glad of, rather than be sent to Newgate, where they lie often a long time, and sometimes they are hanged, and the best they can look for, if they are convicted, is to be transported.

This was a narrow escape to me, and I was so frighted that I ventured no more at gold watches a great while. There were indeed many circumstances in this adventure which assisted to my escape; but the chief was, that the woman whose watch I had pulled at was a fool; that is to say, she was ignorant of the nature of the attempt, which one would have thought she should not have been, seeing she was wise enough to fasten her watch so that it could not be slipped up; but she was in such a fright that she had no thought about her; for she, when she felt the pull, screamed out, and pushed herself forward, and put all the people about her into disorder, but said not a word of her watch, or of a pickpocket, for at least two minutes, which was time enough for me, and to spare; for as I had cried out behind her, as I have said, and bore myself back in the crowd as she bore forward, there were several people, at least seven or eight, the throng being still moving on, that were got between me and her in that time, and then I crying out "A pickpocket" rather sooner than she, she might as well be the person suspected as I, and the people were confused in their inquiry; whereas, had she, with a presence of mind needful on such an occasion, as soon as she felt the pull, not screamed out as she did, but turned immediately round and seized the next body that was behind her, she had infallibly taken me.

This is a direction not of the kindest sort to the fraternity, but 'tis certainly a key to the clue of a pickpocket's motions; and whoever can follow it, will as certainly catch the thief as he will be sure to miss if he does not.

Defoe on Moll Flanders:

Throughout the infinite variety of this book, this fundamental is most strictly adhered to; there is not a wicked action in any part of it, but is first or last rendered unhappy and unfortunate; there is not a superlative villain brought upon the stage, but either he is brought to an unhappy end, or brought to be a penitent; there is not an ill thing mentioned but it is condemned, even in the relation, nor a virtuous, just thing but it carries its praise along with it. What can more exactly answer the rule laid down, to recommend even those representations of things which have so many other just objections lying against them? namely, of example of bad company, obscene language, and the like. (...)

All the exploits of this lady of fame, in her depredations upon mankind, stand as so many warnings to honest people to beware of them, intimating to them by what methods innocent people are drawn in, plundered, and robbed, and by consequence how to avoid them. Her robbing a little child, dressed fine by the vanity of the mother, to go to the dancing-school, is a good memento to such people hereafter, as is likewise her picking the gold watch from the young lady's side in the park.

Preface to *Moll Flanders.*

Cf. Novel and prose types, p. 11; Characters and characterization, p. 12; Narrative technique, p. 15; Presenting the characters words and thoughts, p. 20.

Hogarth: Gin Lane, *1750-1751.*
Ph. British Museum.
Engraved to support a measure against the unlimited sale of gin, this print shows the evils gin can lead to: poverty, murder and suicide. ... at a little country opera-house I got a gold watch from a lady's side, who was not only intolerably merry, but a little fuddled, which made my work much easier. *Moll Flanders.*

GIN LANE.
S. GRIPE PAWN-BROKER
KILMAN DISTILLER
GIN ROYAL
Gin cursed Fiend, with Fury fraught,
Makes human Race a Prey.
It enters by a deadly Draught,
And steals our Life away.
Virtue and Truth, driv'n to Despair,
It's Rage compells to fly.
But cherishes, with hellish Care,
Theft, Murder, Perjury.
Damn'd Cup! that on the Vitals preys,
That liquid Fire contains
Which Madness to the Heart conveys,
And rolls it thro' the Veins.

Defoe on the situation of women in England:

The capacities of women are supposed to be greater and their senses quicker than those of the men; and what they might be capable of being bred to is plain from some instances of female wit, which this age is not without; which upbraids us with injustice, and looks as if we denied women the advantages of education for fear they should vie with the men in their improvements.

To remove this objection, and that women might have at least a needful opportunity of education in all sorts of useful learning, I propose the draught of an Academy for that purpose.

I know 'tis dangerous to make public appearances of the sex. They are not either to be confined or exposed; the first will disagree with their inclinations, and the last with their reputations, and therefore it is somewhat difficult. (...)

Wherefore the academy I propose should differ but little from public schools, wherein such ladies as were willing to study should have all the advantages of learning suitable to their genius. But since some severities of discipline more than ordinary would be absolutely necessary to preserve the reputation of the house, that persons of quality and fortune might not be afraid to venture their children thither, I shall venture to make a small scheme by way of essay. (...)

An Essay upon Projects.

Virginia Woolf on Moll Flanders:

She has to depend entirely upon her own wits and judgement, and to deal with each emergency as it arises by a rule-of-thumb morality which she has forged in her own head. The briskness of the story is due partly to the fact that having transgressed the accepted laws at a very early age she has henceforth the freedom of the outcast. (...) Since she makes no scruple of telling lies when they serve her purpose, there is something undeniable about her truth when she speaks it. She has no time to waste upon the refinements of personal affection; one tear is dropped, one moment of despair allowed, and then "on with the story". She has a spirit that loves to breast the storm. She delights in the exercise of her own powers.

V. Woolf, *The Common Reader.*
V. Woolf's Literary Estate and the Hogarth Press.

... and Ian Watt on this excerpt from the novel:

It is very convincing. The gold watch is a real object, and it won't come, even with "a fair pull". The crowd is composed of solid bodies, pushing forwards and backwards, and lynching another pickpocket in the street outside. All this happens in a real, particular place. It is true that, as is his custom, Defoe makes no attempt to describe it in detail, but the little glimpses that emerge win us over completely to its reality. A dissenting meeting-house is a piquant choice for these activities, to be sure, but Defoe does not arouse suspicion that he is a literary man by drawing attention to its ironic inappropriateness.

If we have any doubts, they are concerned, not with the authenticity of the episode, but with its literary status. The vividness of the scene itself is curiously incidental. Defoe gets into the middle of the action, with "I had full hold of her watch", and then suddenly changes from laconic reminiscent summary to a more detailed and immediate presentation, as though only to back up the truth of his initial statement. Nor has the scene been planned as a coherent whole: we are soon interrupted in the middle of the scene by an aside explaining something that might have been explained before, the important fact that Moll Flanders was dressed like a gentlewoman herself: this transition adds to our trust that no ghost-writer has been imposing order on Moll Flanders's somewhat rambling reminiscences, but if we had seen Moll dressed "as like a lady as other folks" from the beginning, the action would have run more strongly, because uninterruptedly, into the next incident of the scene – the raising of the alarm.

Defoe goes on to stress the practical moral, which is that the gentlewoman should have "seized the next body that was behind her", instead of crying out. In so doing, Defoe lives up to the didactic purpose professed in the "Author's Preface", but at the same time he directs our attention to the important problem of what the point of view of the narrator is supposed to be. We presume that it is a repentant Moll, speaking towards the end of her life: it is therefore surprising that in the next paragraph she should gaily describe her "governess's" procuring activities as "pranks". Then a further confusion about the point of view becomes apparent: we notice that to Moll Flanders other pickpockets, and the criminal fraternity in general, are a "they", not a "we". She speaks as though she were not implicated in the common lot of criminals; or is it, perhaps, Defoe who has unconsciously dropped into the "they" he himself would naturally use for them? And earlier, when we are told that "the other gentlewoman" cried out, we wonder why the word "other"? Is Moll Flanders being ironical about the fact that she too was dressed like a gentlewoman, or has Defoe forgotten that, actually, she is not?

I. Watt, *The Rise of the Novel.*
Chatto and Winders.

Samuel RICHARDSON 1689-1761

1689 *Born in Derbyshire, and the son of a joiner.*
1706 *Apprenticed to a printer in London.*
1719 *Set up his own printing business – which was to be very successful.*
1739 *Started writing* Pamela. *The idea developed from a handbook he had composed on letter-writing – "a little volume of letters, in a common style, on such subjects as might be of use to country readers who are unable to indite for themselves."*
1740-1741 *Published* Pamela, or Virtue Rewarded.
1747-1748 *Published* Clarissa.
1753-1754 *Published* Sir Charles Grandison.
1761 *Died in London.*

Richardson was first of all a moralist, a low-church moralist for whom work and duty were the prevailing virtues. It is therefore no wonder that he set out writing in order to improve the morals of his time and to create a new "species of writing" that would entertain the reader without corrupting him (as he thought Defoe's works did), or deluding him (as romances did).

His novels are set in the limited world he knew – that of the upper middle-class or country squires – and deal with the attempted seduction of innocent yet prudent heroines. Clarissa *is undoubtedly the richest of the three novels. The heroine, a model of virtue and beauty, is the victim of her wealthy, greedy, ambitious family who try to push her into a financially advantageous marriage with Mr Solmes. Clarissa's refusal leads to her imprisonment and the growing pressure of her relatives will drive her to elope with Lovelace, a handsome and unscrupulous rake who finally seduces her while she is drugged. Lovelace then repents, hoping to marry Clarissa, but she refuses and dies of grief.*

Like the other two novels, Clarissa *is an epistolary novel, a succession of letters between the heroine and her friends or family, between Lovelace and his friends. This makes for slow development, heightened suspense, but also for a richer and more immediate analysis of the small events of everyday life and sometimes for multiple points of view when some of the events are narrated by different characters.*

For the first time, a type of literature appeared presenting heroes and heroines with whom readers could identify. At a time when a middle-class reading public was emerging, one can easily understand the overwhelming popularity of Richardson's works in England and on the continent. They were translated into French by the Abbé Prévost.

The History of Clarissa Harlowe (1747-8)

I went down this morning when breakfast was ready with a very uneasy heart, from what Hannah had informed me of yesterday afternoon; wishing for an opportunity, however, to appeal to my mother, in hopes to engage her interest in my behalf, and purposing to try to find one when she retired to her own apartment after breakfast: but, unluckily, there was the odious Solmes sitting asquat between my mother and sister, with *so much* assurance in his looks! But you know, my dear, that those we love not cannot do anything to please us.

Had the wretch kept his seat, it might have been well enough: but the bent and broad-shouldered creature must needs rise and stalk towards a chair; which was just by that which was set for me.

I removed it to a distance, as if to make way to my own: And down I sat, abruptly I believe; what I had heard all in my head.

But this was not enough to daunt him. The man is a very confident, he is a very bold, staring man! Indeed, my dear, the man is very confident!

He took the removed chair and drew it so near mine, squatting in it with his ugly weight, that he pressed upon my hoop. I was so offended (all I had heard, as I said, in my head) that I removed to another chair. I own I had too little command of myself. It gave my brother and sister too much advantage. I dare say they took it. But I did it involuntarily, I think. I could not help it. I knew not what I did.

I saw that my father was excessively displeased. When angry, no man's countenance ever shows it so much as my father's. Clarissa Harlowe! said he with a big voice – and there he stopped. Sir! said I, trembling and curtsying (for I *had* not then sat down again): and put my chair nearer the wretch, and sat down – my face, as I could feel, all in a glow.

Make tea, child, said my kind mamma: sit by me, love, and make tea.

I removed with pleasure to the seat the man had quitted; and being thus indulgently put into employment, soon recovered myself; and in the course of the breakfasting officiously asked two or three questions of Mr. Solmes, which I would not have done, but to make up with my father. *Proud spirits may be brought to!* whisperingly spoke my sister to me over her shoulder, with an air of triumph and scorn: but I did not mind her.

My mother was all kindness and condescension. I asked her once if she were pleased with the tea? She said softly (and again called me *dear*) she was pleased with all I did. I was very proud of this encouraging goodness: and all blew over, as I hoped, between my father and me; for he also spoke kindly to me two or three times.

Small incidents these, my dear, to trouble you with; only as they lead to greater, as you shall hear.

Before the usual breakfast-time was over my father withdrew with my mother, telling her he wanted to speak to her. Then my sister and next my aunt (who was with us) dropped away.

My brother gave himself some airs of insult, which I understood well enough; but which Mr. Solmes could make nothing of: and at last he arose from *his* seat. Sister, said he, I have a curiosity to show you. I will fetch it. And away he went; shutting the door close after him.

I saw what all this was for. I arose; the man hemming up for a speech, rising and beginning to set his splay feet [indeed, my dear, the man in all his ways is hateful to me!] in an approaching posture. I will save my brother the trouble of bringing to me his curiosity, said I. I curtsied – your servant, sir. The man cried, madam, madam, twice, and looked like a fool. But away I went – to find my brother to save my word. But my brother, indifferent as the weather was, was gone to walk in the garden with my sister. A plain case that he had left his *curiosity* with me, and designed to show me no other.

Volume I, Letter 16.

● *Compare this passage with the meeting between Sophia and Mr Blifil in Fielding's* Tom Jones *(Vol 1, Book VI, Chapter 7).*

● *About the social background of the novel, read Ian Watt's* The Rise of the Novel, *1957, Chatto and Windus.*

● *Cf: Novel and prose types, p. 11; Characters and characterization, p. 12; Narrative technique, p. 15; Presenting the characters words and thoughts, p. 20.*

Why should a foolish Marriage Vow
  Which long ago was made,
Oblige us to each other now
  When Passion is decay'd?

J. Dryden, *Marriage-A-la-mode.*

Hogarth: Marriage-à-la-mode, *three scenes, 1745.*
National Gallery.

A. The Marriage Contract *(scene 1).*
The Earl of Squanderfield, who needs money (cf, the Palladian mansion he is building), has arranged to marry his son to the daughter of a rich Alderman of the city of London. She will bring the money, he will bring the title. Counsellor Silvertongue, who works for the Earl, is already courting the bride who shows no joy whatsoever. The two chained dogs reflect the future condition of the couple (the same symbol is used in Rowlandson's paintings, on p. 123), and the pictures on the wall show terrible events (e.g. the martyrdom of St Sebastian, Prometheus tortured by the vulture...). Notice the Earl's coronets everywhere and his family tree.

B. The Breakfast Scene *(scene 2).*
It takes place early in the afternoon since both husband and wife went to bed very late: Lady Squanderfield because she gave a card and music party (cf. the room in the background), her husband because he spent the night with another woman (whose handkerchief the dog is sniffing). The steward – a Methodist (he is reading a pamphlet on "Regeneration") – is horrified.

C. The Death of the Countess *(scene 6).*
Lady Squanderfield, now a Countess after the death of the Earl, is grief-stricken. Counsellor Silvertongue, who had become her lover, killed her husband in a duel and has just been hanged at Tyburn (cf. the paper on the floor: Counsellor Silvertongue's last Dying Speech.*) The Countess killed herself by swallowing laudanum, and the doctor is now upbraiding the servant who got it for her. Already her ring is being taken off. Notice the dog who is taking advantage of the situation.*

A

B

C

Diderot on Richardson:

Par un roman, on a entendu jusqu'à ce jour un tissu d'événements chimériques et frivoles, dont la lecture était dangereuse pour le goût et pour les mœurs. Je voudrais bien qu'on trouvât un autre nom pour les ouvrages de Richardson, qui élèvent l'esprit, qui touchent l'âme, qui respirent partout l'amour du bien, et qu'on appelle aussi des romans (...)

Cet auteur ne fait point couler le sang le long des lambris; il ne vous transporte point dans des contrées éloignées; ne vous expose point à être dévoré par des sauvages; il ne se renferme point dans des lieux clandestins de débauche; il ne se perd jamais dans les régions de la féerie. Le monde où nous vivons est le lieu de la scène; le fond de son drame est vrai; ses personnages ont toute la réalité possible; ses caractères sont pris du milieu de la société; ses incidents sont dans les mœurs de toutes les nations policées; les passions qu'il peint sont telles que je les éprouve en moi; ce sont les mêmes objets qui les émeuvent, elles ont l'énergie que je leur connais; les traverses et les afflictions de ses personnages sont de la nature de celles qui me menacent sans cesse; il me montre le cours général des choses qui m'environnent. Sans cet art, mon âme se pliant avec peine à des biais chimériques, l'illusion ne serait que momentanée et l'impression faible et passagère.

Qu'est-ce que la vertu? C'est, sous quelque face qu'on la considère, un sacrifice de soi-même. Le sacrifice que l'on fait de soi-même en idée est une disposition préconçue à s'immoler en réalité.

Richardson sème dans les cœurs des germes de vertu qui y restent d'abord oisifs et tranquilles : ils y sont secrètement, jusqu'à ce qu'il se présente une occasion qui les remue et les fasse éclore. Alors ils se développent; on se sent porter au bien avec une impétuosité qu'on ne se connaissait pas. On éprouve, à l'aspect de l'injustice, une révolte qu'on ne saurait s'expliquer à soi-même. C'est qu'on a fréquenté Richardson; c'est qu'on a conversé avec l'homme de bien, dans des moments où l'âme désintéressée était ouverte à la vérité. (...)

C'est lui qui porte le flambeau au fond de la caverne; c'est lui qui apprend à discerner les motifs subtils et déshonnêtes qui se cachent et se dérobent sous d'autres motifs qui sont honnêtes et qui se hâtent de se montrer les premiers. Il souffle sur le fantôme sublime qui se présente à l'entrée de la caverne; et le More hideux qu'il masquait s'aperçoit.

Diderot, *Eloge de Richardson,* 1761.

Walter Scott on Richardson and Fielding:

In one passage (Dr Johnson) asserts, that "there is more knowledge of the human heart in one letter of Richardson's than in all *Tom Jones*". And in another, he thus explains the proposition: "There is all the difference in the world between characters of nature and characters of manners, and there is this difference between the characters of Fielding and those of Richarson. Characters of manners are very entertaining; but they are to be understood by a more superficial observer than characters of nature, where a man must dive into the recesses of the human heart". Again, in comparing these two distinguished authors, the critic uses this illustration, – "that there was as great a difference between them, as between a man who knew how a watch was made, and a man who could tell the hour by looking at the dial-plate". Dissenting as we do from the conclusions to be deduced from Dr. Johnson's simile, we would rather so modify it as to describe both authors as excellent mechanics; the time-pieces of Richardson showing a great deal of the internal work by which the index is regulated; while those of Fielding merely point to the day, being all that most men desire to know. Or, to take a more manageable comparison, the analogy betwixt the writings of Fielding and Richardson resembles that which free, bold and true sketches bear to paintings that have been very minutely laboured, and which, amid their excellence, still exhibit some of the heaviness that almost always attends the highest degree of finishing. This, indeed, is admitted by Johnson himself, in his reply to the observation of the Honourable Thomas Erskine, that Richardson was tedious. – "Why, sir, if you were to read Richardson for the story, your impatience would be so much fretted, that you would hang yourself. But you must read him for the sentiment". Were we to translate the controversy into plain language, it might be summed up in pronouncing the works of Richardson the more instructive, and the more deeply affecting, those of Fielding the more amusing.

Sir Walter Scott, *Samuel Richardson, Lives of the Novelists,* 1827.

About the epistolary method:

(...) *Much more* lively and affecting (...) must be the style of those who write in the height of a *present* distress, the mind tortured by the pangs of uncertainty (the events then hidden in the womb of fate); than the dry, narrative unanimated style of a person relating difficulties and danger surmounted, can be (...) the relater perfectly at ease; and if himself unmoved by his own story, not likely greatly to affect the reader.

Samuel Richardson, *Preface to Clarissa, The History of a Young Lady...,* 1747-8.

Little as Richardson may suspect it, he – and whoever else has the idea of making a story out of a series of letters, or a running diary written from day to day – is engaged in the attempt to show a mind in action, to give a dramatic display of the commotion within a breast. He desires to get into the closest touch with Clarissa's life, and to set the reader in the midst of it; and this is a possible expedient, though it certainly has its drawbacks.

He wishes to avoid throwing Clarissa's agitations into the past and treating them as a historical matter. If they were to become the subject of a record, compiled by her biographer, something would be lost; there would be no longer the same sense of meeting Clarissa afresh, every morning, and of witnessing the new development of her wrongs and woes, already a little more poignant than they were last night. Even if he set Clarissa to write the story in after days, preserving her life for the purpose, she could not quite give us this recurring suspense and shock of sympathy; the lesson of her fortitude would be weakened. Reading her letters, you hear the cry that was wrung from her at the moment; you look forward with her in dismay to the ominous morrow; the spectacle of her bearing under such terrible trials is immediate and urgent. You accompany her step by step, the end still in the future, knowing no more than she how the next corner is to be turned. This is truly to share her life, to lead it by her side, to profit by her example; at any rate her example is eloquently present. Richardson or another, whoever first thought of making her tell her story while she is still in the thick of it, invented a fashion of dramatizing her sensibility that is found to be serviceable occasionally, even now, though scarcely for an enterprise on Clarissa's scale.

Percy Lubbock, *The Craft of Fiction.*

Henry FIELDING 1707-1754

1707 *Born in Somerset. Brought up among country squires.*
1719-1724 *Eton.*
1728 *His first play produced. Started studying law.*
1730-1737 *Wrote several comedies (*Tom Thumb, *1730;* The Modern Husband, *1732;* The Miser, *1733;* Pasquin, *1736...) and opened a theatre in the Haymarket which had to close after the Licensing Act of 1737.*
1739-1741 *Editor of* The Champion, *in which he criticized Walpole.*
1740 *Called to the Bar.*
1741 Shamela.
1742 Joseph Andrews.
1743 Miscellanies *(which included* Jonathan Wild*).*
1745-1746 *Editor of* The True Patriot.
1747-1748 *Editor of* The Jacobite's Journal.
1748 *Became a magistrate for Westminster.*
1749 Tom Jones.
1751 Amelia.
1753 *Active campaign (as a magistrate) against crime in London.*
1754 *Sailed to Lisbon where he died.*
1755 A Voyage to Lisbon *published.*

Fielding, who started his career as a playwright, turned to the novel by accident when he decided to ridicule the novels of Richardson. In Joseph Andrews, *it is Joseph (Pamela's imaginary brother) who is this time the victim of Lady Booby's infatuation. He leaves, meets Parson Adams, and both run into all kinds of adventures on the road: the victims of robbers, innkeepers and country gentlemen, they make their way through the novel until Joseph is finally united with Fanny. The novel which had started as a parody of* Pamela, *"continued in the spirit of Cervantes" (I. Watt) and became a satire of romance and sentimentality more generally.*

In his preface to Joseph Andrews, *Fielding explained he wanted to write "comic epics in prose", which would give a comprehensive view of society, using light incidents and characters of inferior rank. What he achieved was picaresque novels, bursting with a comic sense of life as they relate the humourous adventures of the hero. Fielding's novels open on to the outside world, they slice across all classes and show a gallery of boisterous and vivid characters, involved in endless comic or burlesque situations, often described in a mock-heroic tone.*

Fielding saw himself as a moralist too: hypocrisy, affectation, selfishness and malevolence are constantly ridiculed in his novels.

His masterpiece is Tom Jones *which describes the adventures of Sophia (who has run away from home to avoid a hateful marriage) and Tom, a foundling who after numerous incidents and mishaps (he becomes the lover of an elderly lady, is imprisoned, etc.) eventually marries Sophia.*

Joseph Andrews (1742)

Joseph has just been attacked by thieves.

The Thief, who had been knocked down, had now recovered himself; and both together fell to be-labouring poor Joseph with their sticks, till they were convinced they had put an end to his miserable Being: They then stript him entirely naked, threw him into a Ditch, and departed with their Booty.

The poor Wretch, who lay motionless a long time, just began to recover his Senses as a Stage-Coach came by. The Postillion hearing a Man's Groans, stopt his Horses, and told the Coachman "he was certain there was a dead man lying in the Ditch, for he heard him groan". "Go on, Sirrah", says the Coachman, "we are confounded late, and have no time to look after dead Men". A Lady, who heard what the Postillion said, and likewise heard the Groan, called eagerly to the Coachman, "to stop and see what was the matter". Upon which he bid the Postillion "alight, and look into the Ditch". He did so, and returned, "that there was a Man sitting upright as naked as ever he was born". – "O J-sus", cry'd the Lady, "A naked Man! Dear Coachman, drive on and leave him". Upon this the Gentleman got out of the Coach; and Joseph begged them, "to have Mercy upon him: For that he had been robbed, and almost beaten to Death". "Robbed", cries an old Gentleman; "Let us make all the haste imaginable, or we shall be robbed too". A young man, who belonged to the Law answered, "he wished they had past by without taking any Notice: But that now they might be proved to have been last in his Company; if he should die, they might be called to some account for his Murther. He therefore thought it advisable to save the poor Creature's Life, for their own sakes, if possible; at least, if he died, to prevent the Jury's finding that they fled for it[1]. He was therefore of Opinion, to take the Man into the Coach, and carry him to the next Inn". The Lady insisted, "that he should not come into the Coach. That if they lifted him in, she would herself alight: for she had rather stay in that Place to all Eternity, than ride with a naked Man". The Coachman objected, "that he could not suffer him to be taken in, unless somebody would pay a Shilling for his Carriage the four Miles". Which the two Gentlemen refused to do; but the Lawyer, who was afraid of some Mischief happening to himself if the Wretch was left behind in that Condition, saying, "no Man could be too cautious in these Matters, and that he remembered very extraordinary Cases in the Books", threatened the Coachman, and bid him deny taking him up at his Peril; "for that if he died, he should be indicted for his Murther, and if he lived, and brought an Action against him, he would willingly take a Brief in it". These words had a sensible effect on the Coachman, who was well acquainted with the Person who spoke them; and the old Gentleman abovementioned, thinking the naked Man would afford him frequent Opportunities of shewing his Wit to the Lady, offered to join with the Company in giving a Mug of Beer for his Fare; till partly alarmed by the Threats of the one, and partly by the Promises of the other, and being perhaps a little moved with Compassion at the poor Creature's Condition, who stood bleeding and shivering with the Cold, he at length agreed; and Joseph was now advancing to the Coach, where seeing the Lady, who held the Sticks of her Fan before her Eyes, he absolutely refused, miserable as he was, to enter, unless he was furnished with sufficient Covering, to prevent giving the least Offence to Decency. So perfectly modest was this young Man; such mighty Effects had the spotless Example of the amiable Pamela, and the excellent Sermons of Mr. Adams wrought upon him.

Chapter 12.

1. *they fled for it:* fleeing the scene of a crime was punishable by law, even if one had been acquitted of the crime.

Fielding on the novel:

(...) the actions should be such as may not only be within the compass of human agency, and which human agents may probably be supposed to do; but they should be likely for the very actors and characters themselves to have performed; for what may be only wonderful and surprising in one man, may become improbable, or indeed impossible, when related of another.

This last requisite is what the dramatic critics call conversation of character; and it requires a very extraordinary degree of judgment, and a most exact knowledge of human nature. (...)

Our modern authors of comedy have fallen almost universally into the error here hinted at; their heroes generally are notorious rogues, and their heroines abandoned jades, during the first four acts, but in the fifth, the former become very worthy gentlemen, and the latter women of virtue and discretion: nor is the writer often so kind as to give himself the least trouble to reconcile or account for this monstrous change and incongruity. (...)

Within these few restrictions, I think, every writer may be permitted to deal as much in the wonderful as he pleases; nay, if he thus keeps within the rules of credibility, the more he can surprise the reader the more he will engage his attention, and the more he will charm him. As a genius of the highest rank observes in his fifth chapter of the Bathos: "The great art of all poetry is to mix truth with fiction, in order to join the credible with the surprising."

For though every good author will confine himself within the bounds of probability, it is by no means necessary that his characters, or his incidents, should be trite, common, or vulgar; such as happen in every street, or in every house, or which may be met with in the home articles of a newspaper. Nor must he be inhibited from showing many persons and things, which may possibly have never fallen within the knowledge of great part of his readers. If the writer strictly observes the rules above-mentioned, he hath discharged his part; and is then intitled to some faith from his reader, who is indeed guilty of critical infidelity if he disbelieves him.

The History of Tom Jones.

Compare the passage with Smollett's Roderick Random, *chapter XII.*

Shamela (1741)

Thursday Night, Twelve o' Clock

Mrs Jervis and I are just in Bed, and the Door unlocked; if my Master should come – Odsbobs! I hear him just coming in at the Door. You see I write in the present Tense, as Parson Williams says. Well, he is in Bed between us, we both shamming a Sleep, he steals his Hand into my Bosom, which I, as if in my Sleep, press close to me with mine, and then pretend to awake. – I no sooner see him, but I scream out to Mrs Jervis, she feigns likewise but just to come to herself; we both begin, she to becall, and I to bescratch very liberally. After having made a pretty free Use of my Fingers, without any great Regard to the Parts I attack'd, I counterfeit a Swoon. Mrs Jervis then cries out, O, Sir, what have you done, you have murdered poor Pamela: she is gone, she is gone.

O what a Difficulty it is to keep one's Countenance, when a violent Laugh desires to burst forth.

Letter 6.

*J. Highmore:*Pamela in the bedroom with Mrs Jewkes and Mr. B. *The Tate Gallery, London.*
Like his friend Hogarth, Joseph Highmore (1692-1780) portrayed eighteenth-century scenes of social life, but his paintings are less satirical and more delicate. Devoid of Hogarth's inventive spirit, he was particularly good at illustrations. His twelve paintings following scenes from Pamela *are among his best works.*

Compare the text with the passage from Pamela *which it parodies. With the help of Mrs Jewkes, Squire B. has disguised himself as a maid – Mrs Anne – in order to enter Pamela's bedroom. Pamela sleeps in the same bed as Mrs Jewkes, the housekeeper.*

I heard her, as I thought, breathe quick and short: "Indeed", said I, "Mrs Jewkes, the poor maid is not well. What ails you, Mrs Anne?" And still no answer was made.

I tremble to relate it! the pretended she came into bed, but trembled like an aspen-leaf; and I, poor fool that I was! pitied her much. – But well might the barbarous deceiver tremble at his vile dissimulation, and base designs.

What words shall I find, my dear mother (for my father should not see this shocking part), to describe the rest, and my confusion, when the guilty wretch took my left arm, and laid it under his neck, and the vile procuress held my right; and then he clasped me round the waist!

Said I, "Is the wench mad! Why, how now, Confidence"? thinking still it had been Nan. But he kissed me with frightful vehemence; and then his voice broke upon me like a clap of thunder, "Now, Pamela", said he, "is the dreadful time of reckoning come, that I have threatened". I screamed out in such a manner, as never anybody heard the like.

Richardson, *Pamela*, Book I.

Richardson and Fielding on the morality of Pamela *and* Shamela:

(...) I thought the story, if written in an easy and natural manner, suitable to the simplicity of it, might possibly introduce a new species of writing, that might possibly turn young people into a course of reading different from the pomp and parade of romance-writing, and dismissing the improbable and marvellous, with which novels generally abound, might tend to promote the cause of religion and virtue.

Samuel Richardson, *Preface to Clarissa.*

(...) nor do I, indeed, conceive the good purposes served by inserting characters of such angelic perfection, or such diabolical depravity, in any work of invention; since, from contemplating either, the mind of man is more likely to be overwhelmed with sorrow and shame than to draw any good uses from such patterns; for in the former instance he may be both concerned and ashamed to see a pattern of excellence in his nature, which he may reasonably despair of ever arriving at; and in contemplating the latter he may be no less affected with those uneasy sensations, at seeing the nature of which he is a partaker degraded into so odious and detestable a creature.

Fielding, *Tom Jones*, Book X, ch. 1.

Fielding's opinion of Pamela as expressed by Parson Oliver in Shamela:

The Book is by no means innocent: For,

First, There are many lascivious Images in it, very improper to be laid before the Youth of either sex.

2dly, Young Gentlemen are here taught, that to marry their Mother's Chambermaids, and to indulge the Passion of Lust, at the Expense of Reason and Common Sense, is an Act of Religion, Virtue and Honour; and indeed the surest Road to Happiness.

3dly, All Chambermaids are strictly enjoyned to look out after their Masters; they are taught to use little Arts to that purpose: And lastly, are countenanced in Impertinence to their Superiours.

4thly, In the Character of Mrs Jewkes Vice is rewarded; whence every Housekeeper may learn the Usefulness of Pimping and bawding for her Master.

Cf. Characters and Characterization, p. 12; Narrative technique, p. 15; Presenting the characters' words and thoughts, p. 20; Wit, humour, satire and irony, p. 27.

Laurence STERNE 1713-1768

1713 *Born in Ireland.*
1723-1731 *Went to school in Yorkshire until his father's death.*
1733-1737 *Studied at Jesus College, Cambridge.*

Laurence Sterne (1713-68) produced a remarkable and eccentric novel in his *Tristram Shandy*, which breaks all the rules, even of language and punctuation, and deliberately excludes all suggestions of a plot, so that – despite

1738-1759 *Took orders and became vicar of Sutton-on-the-Forest (Yorkshire).*
1760-1761 *Publication of Volumes I to VI of* Tristram Shandy.
1762 *Travelled abroad (France and Italy) because of ill health.*
1765-1767 *Publication of Volumes VII to IX of* Tristram Shandy.
1768 A Sentimental Journey. *Died in London*

the considerable length of the book – nobody gets anywhere, nothing really happens, and the hero does not succeed even in getting himself born until half-way through! The author deliberately hinders all movement: just when we think a story is about to develop, Sterne introduces an incredible digression – a long piece of Latin (with translation on the opposite page), a blank sheet, a page with a marbled design on it, a collection of asterisks – anything to obstruct or mystify. Yet characters emerge: the learned Mr. Shandy, the gentle old soldier Uncle Toby and Trim, his corporal (these last two spend much time reconstructing the Battle of Namur on a bowling-green). There are lewd jokes, patches of sentimentality – often saved, just in time, from becoming mawkish by an ironical stroke – and grotesque Rabelaisian episodes.

A. Burgess, *English Literature.*
Longman Group Ltd.

The Life and Opinions of Tristram Shandy, Gent. (1761)

Chapter XXXIX

As *Susannah* was informed by an express from Mrs *Bridget*, of my uncle *Toby's* falling in love with her mistress, fifteen days before it happened, ——— the contents of which express, *Susannah* communicated to my mother the next day, ——— it has just given me an opportunity of entering upon my uncle *Toby's* amours a fortnight before their existence.

I have an article of news to tell you, Mr. *Shandy*, quoth my mother, which will surprise you greatly. ———

Now my father was then holding one of his second beds of justice, and was musing within himself about the hardships of matrimony, as my mother broke silence. ———

"——— My brother Toby, quoth she, is going to be married to Mrs. *Wadman*".

——— Then he will never, quoth my father, be able to lie *diagonally*, in his bed again as long as he lives.

It was a consuming vexation to my father, that my mother never asked the meaning of a thing she did not understand.

——— That she is not a woman of science, my father would say ——— is her misfortune ———but she might ask a question. ———

My mother never did. ——— In short, she went out of the world at last without knowing whether it turned *round* or stood *still*. ——— My father had officiously told her above a thousand times which way it was, ——— but she always forgot.

For these reasons a discourse seldom went on much further betwixt them, than a proposition, ——— a reply, and a rejoinder; at the end of which, it generally took breath for a few minutes, (as in the affair of the breeches) and then went on again.

If he marries, 'twill be the worse for us, ——— quoth my mother.

Not a cherry-stone, said my father, ——— he may as well batter away his means upon that, as any thing else.

——— To be sure, said my mother: so here ended the proposition, ——— the reply, ——— and the rejoinder, I told you of.

It will be some amusement to him, too, ——— said my father.

A very great one, answered my mother, if he should have children. ———

——— Lord have mercy upon me. ——— said my father to himself. ———

☆ ☆ ☆ ☆ ☆ ☆ ☆ ☆ ☆ ☆ ☆ ☆ ☆ ☆ ☆
☆ ☆ ☆ ☆ ☆ ☆ ☆ ☆ ☆ ☆ ☆ ☆ ☆ ☆ ☆
☆ ☆ ☆ ☆ ☆ ☆ ☆ ☆ ☆ ☆ ☆ ☆ ☆ ☆ ☆
☆ ☆ ☆ ☆ ☆ ☆ ☆ ☆ ☆ ☆ ☆ ☆ ☆ ☆ ☆
☆ ☆ ☆ ☆ ☆ ☆ ☆ ☆ ☆ ☆ ☆ ☆ ☆ ☆ ☆

Chapter XL.

I am now beginning to get fairly into my work; and by the help of a vegitable diet, with a few of the cold seeds[1], I make no doubt but I shall be able to go on with my uncle *Toby's* story, and my own, in a tolerable straight line. Now,

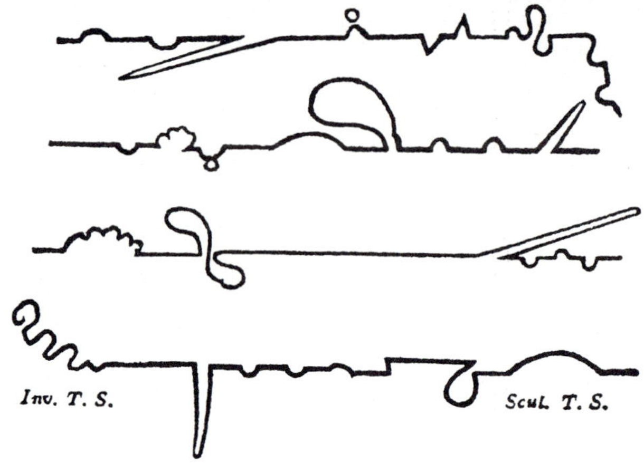

These were the four lines I moved in through my first, second, third, and fourth volumes. — In the fifth volume I have been very good, ______the precise line I have described in it being this:

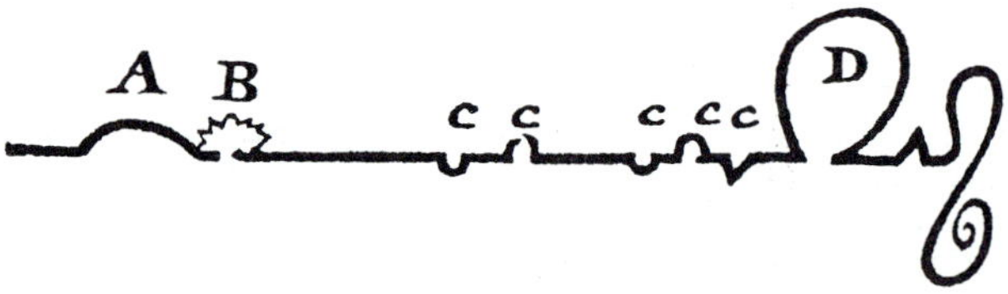

By which it appears, that except at the curve, marked. A where I took a trip to *Navarre,* ______ and the indented curve B. which is the short airing when I was there with the Lady *Baussiere* and her page, ______ I have not taken the least frisk of a digression, till *John de la Casse's* devils led me the round you see marked D. ______ for as for *c c c c c* they are nothing but parentheses, and the common *ins* and *outs* incident to the lives of the greatest ministers of state; and when compared with what men have done, ______ or with my own trangressions at the letters A B D ______ they vanish into nothing.

In this last volume I have done better still ______ for from the end of *Le Fever's* episode, to the begining of my uncle *Toby's* campaigns, ______ I have scarce stepped a yard out of my way.

If I mend at this rate, it is not impossible ______ by the good leave of his grace of *Benevento's* devils[2] ______ but I may arrive hereafter at the excellency of going on even thus; ____

which is a line drawn as straight as I could draw it, by a writing-master's ruler, (borrowed for thath purpose) turning neither to the right hand or to the left.

This *right line,* ______ the path-way for Christians to walk in! say divines ______ ______ The emblem of moral rectitude! says *Cicero.* ______

______ The *best line*! say cabbage-planters ______ is the shortest line, says *Archimedes,* which can be drawn from one given point to another. ______

I wish your ladyships would lay this matter to heart in your next birth-day suits[3]!

Pray can you tell me, ______ that is, without anger, before I write my chapter upon straight lines ______ by what mistake ______ who told them so ______ or how it has come to pass, that your men of wit and genius have all along confounded this line, with the line of gravitation?

Vol. VI, ch. 39-40.

1. *the cold seeds*: e.g. cucumbers - 2. *his grace of Benevento's devils*: cf. *Tristram Shandy*, Volume V, chapter 16: a reference to "John de la Casse, the lord archbishop of Benevento" (an Italian poet of the 16th century) who wrote very slowly since he maintained that the moment a personage of venerable character took pen in hand, "all the devils in hell broke out of their holes to cajole him". - 3. *birth-day clothes*: rich clothes worn at birthday celebrations.

Digressions and associations of ideas – a few 17th and 18th century opinions:

• But without Steddinesse, and Direction to some End, a great Fancy is one kind of Madnesse; such as they have, that entring into any discourse, are snatched from their purpose, by every thing that comes in their thought, into so many, and so long digressions, and Parentheses, that they utterly lose themselves.

Thomas Hobbes, *Leviathan, 1651. Part I, ch. 8.*

• Some of our ideas have a natural correspondence and connection one with another; it is the office and excellency of our reason to trace these and hold them together in that union and correspondence which is founded in their peculiar beings. Besides this there is another connection of ideas wholly owing to chance or custom; ideas that in themselves are not all of kin come to be so united in some men's minds that it is very hard to separate them; they always keep in company and the one no sooner comes into the understanding but its associate appears with it.

J. Locke, *Essay concerning Human Understanding,* 1690.

Tristram Shandy *was for a long time considered as a comic illustration of Locke's doctrines.*

• Vous voyez, lecteur, que je suis en beau chemin, et qu'il ne tiendrait qu'à moi de vous faire attendre un an, deux ans, trois ans, le récit des amours de Jacques, en le séparant de son maître et en leur faisant courir à chacun tous les hasards qu'il me plairait. Qu'est-ce qui m'empêcherait de marier le maître et de le faire cocu? d'embarquer Jacques pour les îles? d'y conduire son maître? de les ramener tous les deux en France sur le même vaisseau? Qu'il est facile de faire des contes! Mais ils en seront quittes l'un et l'autre pour une mauvaise nuit, et vous pour ce délai.

Diderot, *Jacques le Fataliste et son maître,* 1796.

Sterne on digressions:

For in this long digression which I was accidentally led into, as in all my digressions (one only excepted) there is a master-stroke of digressive skill, the merit of which has all along, I fear, been overlooked by my reader, – not for want of penetration in him, – but because 'tis an excellence seldom looked for, or expected indeed, in a digression; – and it is this: That tho' my digressions are all fair, as you observe, – and that I fly off from what I am about, as far and as often too as any writer in *Great-Britain*; yet I constantly take care to order affairs so, that my main business does not stand still in my absence.

I was just going, for example, to have given you the great out-lines of my uncle *Toby's* most whimsical character; – when my aunt *Dinah* and the coachman came a-cross us, and led us a vagary some millions of miles into the very heart of the planetary system: Notwithstanding all this you perceive that the drawing of my uncle *Toby's* character went on gently all the time; – not the great contours of it, – that was impossible, – but some familiar strokes and faint designations of it, were here and there touch'd in, as we went along, so that you are much better acquainted with my uncle *Toby* now than you was before.

By this contrivance the machinery of my work is of a species by itself; two contrary motions are introduced into it, and reconciled, which were thought to be at variance with each other. In a word, my work is digressive, and it is progressive too, – and at the same time....

Digressions, incontestably, are the sunshine; – they are the life, the soul of reading; – take them out of this book for instance, – you might as well take the book along with them; – one cold eternal winter would reign in every page of it; restore them to the writer; – he steps forth like a bridegroom, – bids All hail; brings in variety, and forbids the appetite to fail.

Tristram Shandy, I, ch. 22.

Cf. Narrative technique, p. 15; Wit, humour, satire and irony, p. 27.

5. Romanticism

the artist and society

THE ROMANTIC ARTIST

Than the poets from Blake and Wordsworth to Shelley and Keats there have been few generations of creative writers more deeply interested and more involved in study and criticism of the society of their day. Yet a fact so evident, and so easily capable of confirmation, accords uneasily in our own time with that popular and general conception of the 'romantic artist' which, paradoxically, has been primarily derived from study of these same poets. In this conception, the Poet, the Artist, is by nature indifferent to the crude worldliness and materialism of politics and social affairs; he is devoted, rather, to the more substantial spheres of natural beauty and personal feeling. The elements of this paradox can be seen in the work of the Romantic poets themselves, but the supposed opposition between attention to natural beauty and attention to government, or between personal feeling and the nature of man in society, is on the whole a later development. What were seen at the end of the nineteenth century as disparate interests, between which a man must choose and in the act of choice declare himself poet or sociologist, were, normally, at the beginning of the century, seen as interlocking interests: a conclusion about personal feeling became a conclusion about society, and an observation of natural beauty carried a necessary moral reference to the whole and unified life of man. The subsequent dissociation of interests certainly prevents us from seeing the full significance of this remarkable period, but we must add also that the dissociation is itself in part a product of the nature of the Romantic attempt. Meanwhile, as some sort of security against the vestiges of the dissociation, we may usefully remind ourselves that Wordsworth wrote political pamphlets, that Blake was a friend of Tom Paine and was tried for sedition, that Coleridge wrote political journalism and social philosophy, that Shelley, in addition to this, distributed pamphlets in the streets, that Southey was a constant political commentator, that Byron spoke on the frame-riots and died as a volunteer in a political war; and, further, as must surely be obvious from the poetry of all the men named, that these activities were neither marginal nor incidental, but were essentially related to a large part of the experience from which the poetry itself was made. It is, moreover, only when we are blinded by the prejudice of the dissociation that we find such a complex of activities in any way suprising. For these two generations of poets lived through the crucial period in which the rise both of democracy and of industry was effecting qualitative changes in society: changes which by their nature were felt in a personal as well as in a general way. In the year of the French Revolution, Blake was 32, Wordsworth 19, Coleridge 17 and Southey 15. In the year of Peterloo, Byron was 31, Shelley 27, Keats 24. The dates are sufficient reminder of a period of political turmoil and controversy fierce enough to make it very difficult for even the least sensitive to be indifferent. Of the slower, wider, less observable changes that we call the Industrial Revolution, the landmarks are less obvious; but the lifetime of Blake, 1757 to 1827, is, in general, the decisive period. The changes that we receive as record were experienced, in these years, on the senses: hunger, suffering, conflict, dislocation; hope, energy, vision, dedication. The pattern of change was not background, as we may now be inclined to study it; it was, rather, the mould in which general experience was cast.

It is possible to abstract a political commentary from the writings of these poets, but this is not particularly important. The development of Wordsworth, Coleridge and Southey from differing degrees of revolutionary ardour in their youth to differing degrees of Burkean conservatism in their maturity is interesting. A distinction between the revolutionary principles of Shelley and the fine libertarian opportunism of Byron is useful. A reminder that Blake and Keats cannot be weakened to some ideal vagueness, but were, as men and poets, passionately committed to the tragedy of their period, is timely. In every case, however, the political criticism is now less interesting than the wider social criticism: those first apprehensions of the essential significance of the Industrial Revolution, which all felt and none revoked. Beyond this, again, is a different kind of response, which is a main root of the idea of culture. At this very time of political, social and economic change there is a radical change also in ideas of art, of the artist, and of their place in society. It is this significant change that I wish to adduce.

There are five main points: first, that a major change was taking place in the nature of the relationship between a writer and his readers; second, that a different habitual attitude towards the 'public' was establishing itself; third that the production of art was coming to be regarded as one of a number of specialized kinds of production, subject to much the same conditions as general production; fourth, that a theory of the 'superior reality' of art, as the seat of imaginative truth, was receiving increasing emphasis; fifth, that the idea of the independent creative writer, the autonomous genius, was becoming a kind of rule. In naming these points, it is of course necessary to add at once that they are clearly very closely interrelated, and that some might be named as causes, and some as effects, were not the historical process so complex as to render a clear division impossible.

Raymond Williams,
Culture & Society, 1780-1950,
Chatto & Windus.

	Politics and Society	Literature and the Arts
1780	Gordon riots in London.	
1783	End of the American War of Independence.	
1785		COWPER: *The Task.*
1786		BURNS: *Poems.* BECKFORD: *Vathek.*
1789	The Storming of the Bastille.	BLAKE: *Songs of Innocence, The Book of Thel.*
1792		M. WOLLSTONECRAFT: *The Rights of Woman.*
1793	Execution of Louis XVI. Beginning of the war between England and France.	GODWIN: *Political Justice.* BLAKE: *The Marriage of Heaven & Hell.*
1794		BLAKE: *Songs of Experience.* A. RADCLIFFE: *The Mysteries of Udolpho.*
1796		LEWIS: *The Monk.*
1798	Irish rebellion.	WORDSWORTH & COLERIDGE: *Lyrical Ballads.* MALTHUS: *An Essay on the Principle of Population.*
1801	Act of Union with Ireland.	
1802	Peace of Amiens between France and Britain.	
1803	The war starts again.	
1804	Napoleon becomes Emperor.	
1805	Trafalgar.	
1812		BYRON: *Childe Harold.*
1813		J. AUSTEN: *Pride and Prejudice.*
1814		W. SCOTT: *Waverley.*
1815	Waterloo.	J. AUSTEN: *Emma.*
1816		COLERIDGE: *Kubla Khan.* *Christabel.*
1818		KEATS: *Endymion.*
1819	Peterloo massacre (dispersion of a Parliamentary reform meeting in Manchester).	BYRON: *Don Juan.*
1820	Accession of George IV.	SHELLEY : *Prometheus Unbound.*
1821	Greek declaration of Independence.	DE QUINCEY: *Confessions of an English Opium-eater.*
1823		LAMB: *Essays of Elia.*
1829	Catholic Emancipation Act.	
1830	Accession of William IV.	
1832	Reform Bill.	
1833	Abolition of slavery in the British colonies.	CARLYLE: *Sartor Resartus.*
1836		DICKENS: *The Pickwick Papers.*
1837	Accession of Queen Victoria.	CARLYLE : *The French Revolution.*
		(1847 CH. BRONTË: *Jane Eyre.* E. BRONTË: *Wuthering Heights*).

romanticism and political ideas

Never since the Commonwealth had a political event raised such issues as the French revolution did.

The Jacobin theorists foresaw a complete transformation of society through revolution: history would "start again" and man, stripped of the artificial environment that set him in a given class from his birth, would become free and natural again. It is a similar hope that rings in the following lines from Shelley's Prometheus Unbound *(1819):*

And those foul shapes, abhorred by god and man, –
Which, under many a name and many a form
Strange, savage, ghastly, dark and execrable,
Were Jupiter, the tyrant of the world;
And which the nations, panic-stricken, served
With blood, and hearts broken by long hope, and love
Dragged to his altars soiled and garlandless,
And slain amid men's unreclaiming tears,
Flattering the thing they feared, which fear was hate, –
Frown, mouldering fast, o'er their abandoned shrines:
The painted veil, by those who were, called life,
Which mimicked, as with colours idly spread,
All men believed or hoped, is torn aside;
The loathsome mask has fallen, the man remains,
Sceptreless, free, uncircumscribed, but man;
Equal, unclassed, tribeless, and nationless,
Exempt from awe, worship, degree, the king
Over himself; just, gentle, wise (...)

Edmund BURKE, *however, violently condemned the French revolution on the grounds that history is based on convention and inheritance, that it cannot suddenly become "a blank page", that it is impossible to make a clean sweep of one's past and follow abstract principles.*

Compare the following passages from Burke's Reflections on the Revolution in France *(1790) and from* Thomas PAINE'S *answer:* The Rights of Man *(1791).*

You will observe, that from Magna Charta to the Declaration of Right, it has been the uniform policy of our Constitution to claim and assert our liberties, as an *entailed inheritance* derived to us from our forefathers and to be transmitted to our posterity, as an estate specially belonging to the people of this kingdom without any reference whatever to any other more general or prior right. By this means, our Constitution preserves an unity in so great a diversity of its parts. We have an inheritable Crown, an inheritable peerage, and a House of Commons, and a people inheriting privileges, franchises, and liberties from a long line of ancestors.

This policy appears to me to be the result of profound reflection, or, rather, the happy effect of following nature, which is wisdom without reflection and above it. A spirit of innovation is generally the result of a selfish temper and confined views. People will not look forward to posterity who never look backward to their ancestors. Besides, the people of England well know that the idea of inheritance furnishes a sure principle of conservation and a sure principle of transmission, without at all excluding a principle of improvement. (...)

If civil society be the offspring of convention, that convention must be its law. That convention must limit and modify all the descriptions of constitution which are formed under it. Every sort of legislative, judicial, or executory power are its creatures. They can have no being in any other state of things, and how can any man claim, under the conventions of civil society, rights which do not so much as suppose its existence? Rights which are absolutely repugnant to it? (...)

Government is not made in virtue of natural rights, which may and do exist in total independence of it, and exist in much greater clearness; and in a much greater degree of abstract perfection: but their abstract perfection is their practical defect. By having a right to everything, they want everything. Government is a contrivance of human wisdom to provide for human *wants.* Men have a right that these wants should be provided for by this wisdom. Among these wants is to be reckoned the want, out of civil society, of a sufficient restraint upon their passions. Society requires not only that the passions of individuals should be subjected but that, even in the mass and body as well as in the individuals, the inclinations of men should frequently be thwarted, their will controlled, and their passions brought into subjection. This can only be done *by a power out of themselves* and not, in the exercise of its function, subject to that will and to those passions which it is its office to bridle and subdue. In this sense, the restraints on men, as well as their liberties, are to be reckoned among their rights. But as the liberties and the restrictions vary with times and circumstances and admit of infinite modifications, they cannot be settled upon any abstract rule, and nothing is so foolish as to discuss them upon that principle.

E. Burke, "Reflections on the Revolution in France", in *Political Writers of 18th Century England,* ed. by J. Hart, *A.A. Knopf.*

There never did, there never will, and there never can exist a parliament, or any description of men, or any generation of men, in any country, possessed of the right or the power of binding and controlling posterity to the end of time, or of commanding forever how the world shall be governed, or who shall govern it; and, therefore, all such clauses, acts or declarations, by which the makers of them attempt to do what they have neither the right nor the power to do, nor the power to execute, are in themselves null and void.

Every age and generation must be as free to act for itself, *in all cases,* as the ages and generation which preceded it. The vanity and presumption of governing beyond the grave is the most ridiculous and insolent of all tyrannies.

Man has no property in man; neither has any generation a property in the generations which are to follow. The Parliament of the people of 1688, or of any other period, had no more right to dispose of the people of the present day, or to bind or to control them *in any shape whatever,* than the Parliament or the people of the present day have to dispose of, bind, or control those who are to live a hundred or a thousand years hence.

Every generation is, and must be, competent to all the purposes which its occasions require. It is the living, and not the dead, that are to be accommodated. When man ceases to be, his power and his wants cease with him, and, having no longer any participation in the concerns of this world, he has no longer any authority in directing who shall be its governors, or how its government shall be organized, or how administered.

I am not contending for, nor against, any form of government, not for, nor against, any party here or elsewhere. That which a whole nation chooses to do, it has a right to do. Mr. Burke says, No. Where then *does* the right exist? I am contending for the rights of the *living,* and against their being willed away, and controlled and contracted for, by the manuscript assumed authority of the dead; and Mr. Burke is contending for the authority of the dead over the rights and freedom of the living.

Thomas Paine, *The Rights of Man, ibid.*

literature and the arts

Painting

During the Romantic age, the links between literature and painting were particularly close: BLAKE *was an engraver as well as a poet, Constable is often compared to Wordsworth, and Turner to Coleridge.*

The Gothic fashion at the end of the 18th century is best reflected in the works of J.H. Füssli (or FUSELI*) (1741-1825): his paintings convey a very strange and eerie atmosphere of dreams and phantasms, depicting sinister creatures, monsters and visions of terror. Although Swiss by birth, Fuseli spent many years in England where his influence was felt by painters such as William Blake, the most original representative of the visionary and imaginative movement. (cf p. 161)*

But the main characteristic of Romantic painting is its concentration on landscapes. Picturesque scenes depicting hilly, mountainous and irregular views had become increasingly popular in the second half of the 18th century. Alpine landscapes in particular were greatly appreciated (see the works of Cozens and Girtin.) But it was with CONSTABLE *and* TURNER *that landscape painting reached its perfection.*

Fuseli: The Nightmare *(or Night-Mare?), 1781.*
Frankfurter Goethemuseum. Ph. Edimedia, coll. Snark.

It is a remarkable instance of the individualism of English painting that two contemporaries such as Constable and Turner should be so entirely distinct. We have to contrast Constable, the home-keeping artist, content ever to remain in the south of England, with Turner the widely-travelled; the strictly non-literary attitude of the one with the poetic ambitions of the other; the concentration of energy as opposed to a wide diffusion and expansion. If a certain kinship may be found between Constable and Wordsworth it is not like that which places Turner in the heart of the Romantic movement with all its impulsion towards wild nature, infinities of space, and moments of tremendous violence. It was possible for Ruskin, very perceptively, to group a whole series of Turner's paintings under the heading of "Flood and fire and wreck and battle and pestilence" – how sharp becomes the contrast with the placidity of water meadows and the mild variations of English spring and summer to be found in the work of Constable.

William Gaunt, *A Concise History of English Painting*, *Thames & Hudson. Ltd.*

John CONSTABLE *(1776-1837) was deeply attached to his native Suffolk and, breaking away from the conventions of landscape painting, he tried to convey the atmosphere, the temperament of the countryside he loved. His favourite themes are meadows and waterways, old farms and mills, all treated with richness of detail and an emphasis on movement — nature alive. For that purpose, he dwelt on effects of light and especially on skies. A sky, he said, ought to be* "the key-note, the standard of scale and chief organ of sentiment in a landscape."

Cf. George Eliot (p. 221): 6 September 1859, Weymouth *(George Henry Lewes to John Blackwood).* « G.E. is in high spirits, having found a Mill and Millstream to his [sic] heart's content; and we are going to hire a labourer's cottage for a day or two, and live a poetical primitive life, the results of which will appear in Maggie – who by the way becomes more fascinating than ever, and Tom more intensely boyish. »

Constable: Landscape: Noon, The Hay-Wain.
National Gallery.

Joseph Mallord Turner *(1775-1851), on the contrary, was fascinated by more grandiose and pathetic scenes.*

There are two main influences on the outlook of the mature Turner, one being that of poetry. How far he participated in the feelings of Milton and the many landscapes described in *Paradise Lost*, of Thomson of the *Seasons*, of Byron and Scott, may be gathered from the quotations which accompanied his contributions to the Royal Academy varied by quotations from his own somewhat incoherent epic, *The Fallacies of Hope*. Without the Romantic background of poetry he would not so well have appreciated the falls of the Reichenbach, the unleashed violence of an avalanche in the Alps, the dreaming grandeur of the castles of the Rhine, the splendour of mountains.

The other influence was that of light. The dusky atmosphere of the Thames in London may well have been the source of the "Turner sunset" and yet it was in Italy, which he first visited in 1819, that he encountered the full splendour of light which he was to transform into the glowing visions of later years, visions in which sky, sea, and water became a luminous entity, as at Venice which he surrounded with such gorgeous vapour in the works he produced when over sixty years of age. The later paintings, in which he advanced far beyond the understanding of his contemporaries, are grandly elemental in their expression of dynamic force and movement on the one hand and on the other calm infinities of space.

William Gaunt, *ibid.*

Turner: The Devil's Bridge, Pass of St Gothard, *1802.*
London, British Museum.

Fonthill Abbey, *designed by James* WYATT *in 1799 for William Beckford (the author of* Vathek*).*
Victoria and Albert Museum, London.

Architecture

Two trends appeared at the end of the 18th century:

- *A classical reaction against the Baroque and Rococco styles, even though they had never really flourished in England where Palladianism was more popular. There was a desire for more simplicity and purer lines, which went with a renewal of interest in Greek and Roman styles, which it became fashionable to study and imitate.*

This period also saw the development of terrace architecture, that is to say whole streets or squares planned to form an architectural unit. Several such terraces and crescents had been built in Bath around 1750 and this style reached London at the end of the century (e.g. Fitzroy Square, Regent's Street). CHAMBERS, ADAM *and* NASH *are the outstanding architects of that time.*

- *Meanwhile, a more "romantic" current could be felt: the love of exotic styles (Indian, Greek, Chinese) as well as of Gothic architecture. The Pagoda in Kew Gardens was built in 1761, the Brighton Pavilion, a mixture of oriental and gothic influences in 1816-1820. As for Gothic architecture, it was closely related to the so-called "Gothic literature" (cf. p. 184) The first novel of that genre for instance, Horace Walpole's* Castle of Otranto, *was partly prompted by Strawberry Hill, the medieval Gothic mansion that Walpole had built in Twickenham:*

The lower part of the castle was hollowed into several intricate cloisters; and it was not easy for one under so much anxiety to find the door that opened into the cavern. An awful silence reigned throughout those subterraneous regions, except now and then some blasts of wind that shook the doors she had passed, and which, grating on the rusty hinges, were re-echoed through that long labyrinth of darkness.

Horace Walpole, *The Castle of Otranto.*

In landscape gardening, an art that thrived all through the 18th century, the same taste for the "sublime" appeared before the turn of the century. Compare these two opinions on scenery, the first one written in 1712 and the second almost a century later:

(...) Though there are several of these wild scenes, that are more delightful than any artificial shows; yet we find the works of nature still more pleasant, the more they resemble those of art (...)

Hence it is that we take delight in a prospect which is well laid out, and diversified with fields and meadows; woods and rivers; in those accidental landskips of trees, clouds and cities, that are sometimes found in the veins of marble; in the curious fret-work of rocks, and grottos; and, in a word, in any thing that hath such a variety or regularity as may seem the effect of design, in what we call the works of Chance.

J. Addison, *The Spectator,* 23 June 1712.

There is another species of scenery, in which every object is wild, abrupt, and fantastic; – in which endless intricacies discover, at every turn, something new and unexpected; so that we are at once amused and surprised, and curiosity is constantly gratified, but never satiated. This sort of scenery we call *romantic*; not only because it is similar to that usually described in romances, but because it affords the same kind of pleasure, as we feel from the incidents usually related in such of them as are composed with sufficient skill to afford any pleasure at all.

R.P. Knight,
An Analytical Enquiry into the Principles of Taste, 1808.

William COLLINS 1721-1759

1721 *Born in Chichester, the son of a tradesman.*
1742 *Publication of* Persian Eclogues.
1743 *Graduated from Oxford.*
1747 *Publication of* Odes on Several Descriptive and Allegoric Subjects.
1749 *Wrote his* Ode on the popular Superstitions of the Highlands. *(published 1788)*
1759 *Died in Chichester, after becoming insane.*

The poetic production of William Collins is small, interrupted as it was by his insanity. He belonged to a group of pre-romantics (Thomson, Joseph Warton) who were ahead of their time in their exaltation of sensibility and imagination.

His chief achievements are his Odes (to peace, liberty or pity, on the poetical character, on passions). Their form (the Pindaric Ode) is conventional; his large use of personification and allegory is often artificial; but his originality lies in the sincerity of his inspiration. For Collins, poetry springs from imagination and emotion. He is attracted by wild natural landscapes, by ruins and by melancholy scenes which excite his sensibility and inspire him with a sense of mystery and awe.

Collins was also one of the first poets to show an interest in the supernatural and in popular legends and folklore, as evidenced by his Ode on the popular Superstitions of the Highlands. *This was, however, only published in 1788, by which time the works of Ossian had already made those themes popular.*

Ode to Evening (1747)

If aught of oaten stop[1], or pastoral song,
May hope, chaste Eve, to soothe thy modest ear,
　　Like thy own brawling springs,
　　Thy springs, and dying gales;
O Nymph reserv'd, while now the bright-hair'd sun
Sits on yon western tent, whose cloudy skirts,
　　With brede[2] ethereal wove,
　　O'erhang his wavy bed:
Now air is hush'd, save where the weak-eyed bat
With short shrill shriek flits by on leathern wing;
　　Or where the beetle winds
　　His small but sullen horn,
As oft he rises 'midst the twilight path,
Against the pilgrim borne in heedless hum:
　　Now teach me, Maid compos'd,
　　To breathe some soften'd strain,
Whose numbers[3], stealing thro' thy darkning vale,
May not unseemly with its stillness suit;
　　As, musing slow, I hail
　　Thy genial loved return!
For when thy folding star[4] arising shews
His paly circlet, at his warning lamp
　　The fragrant Hours, and Elves
　　Who slept in buds the day,
And many a Nymph who wreathes her brows with sedge,
And sheds the fresh'ning dew, and lovelier still,
　　The pensive Pleasures sweet,
　　Prepare thy shadowy car[5].
Then let me rove some wild and heathy scene,
Or find some ruin 'midst its dreary dells,
　　Whose walls more awful nod
　　By thy religious gleams.

Or if chill blust'ring winds, or driving rain
Prevent my willing feet, be mine the hut,
That, from the mountain's side,
Views wilds, and swelling floods[6],
And hamlets brown, and dim-discover'd spires,
And hears their simple bell, and marks o'er all
The dewy fingers draw
The gradual dusky veil.
While Spring shall pour his showers, as oft he wont,
And bathe thy breathing[7] tresses, meekest Eve!
While Summer loves to sport
Beneath thy ling'ring light;
While sallow Autumn fills thy lap with leaves;
Or Winter, yelling thro' the troublous air,
Affrights thy shrinking train,
And rudely rends thy robes;
So long, regardful of thy quiet rule,
Shall Fancy, Friendship, Science, smiling Peace,
Thy gentlest influence own,
And hymn thy fav'rite name!

Odes on Several Descriptive and Allegoric Subjects.

1. *Oaten stop*: oaten flute (made of oats) – 2. *brede*: braid – 3. *numbers*: verses – 4. *folding-star*: the evening star, which appears when it is time to put the sheep back in their folds – 5. *car*: chariot – 6. *floods*: streams – 7. *breathing*: fragrant.

Study the poem in the light of John Ruskin's famous definition of "pathetic fallacy":

(...) Of the cheating of the fancy we shall have to speak presently; but in this chapter, I want to examine the nature of the other error, that which the mind admits when affected strongly by emotion. Thus, for instance, in Alton Locke,

"They rowed her in across the rolling foam –
The cruel, crawling foam."

The foam is not cruel, neither does it crawl. The state of mind which attributes to it these characters of a living creature is one in which the reason is unhinged by grief. All violent feelings have the same effect. They produce in us a falseness in all our impressions of external things, which I would generally characterize as the "pathetic fallacy".

§ 6. Now we are in the habit of considering this fallacy as eminently a character of poetical description, and the temper of mind in which we allow it, as one eminently poetical, because passionate. But I believe, if we look well into the matter, that we shall find the greatest poets do not often admit this kind of falseness, – that it is only the second order of poets who much delight in it.

Thus, when Dante describes the spirits falling from the bank of Acheron "as dead leaves flutter from a bough," he gives the most perfect image possible of their utter lightness, feebleness, passiveness, and scattering agony of despair, without, however, for an instant losing his own clear perception that *these* are souls, and *those* are leaves; he makes no confusion of one with the other. But when Coleridge speaks of

"The one red leaf, the last of its clan,
That dances as often as dance it can,"

he has a morbid, that is to say, a so far false, idea about the leaf; he fancies a life in it, and will, which there are not; confuses its powerlessness with choice, its fading death with merriment, and the wind that shakes it with music. Here, however, there is some beauty, even in the morbid passage. (...)

§ 8. The temperament which admits the pathetic fallacy, is, as I said above, that of a mind and body in some sort too weak to deal fully with what is before them or upon them; borne away, or over-clouded, or over-dazzled by emotion; and it is a more or less noble state, according to the force of the emotion which has induced it. For it is no credit to a man that he is not morbid or inaccurate in his perceptions, when he has no strength of feeling to warp them; and it is in general a sign of higher capacity and stand in the ranks of being, that the emotions should be strong enough to vanquish, partly, the intellect, and make it believe what they choose. But it is still a grander condition when the intellect also rises, till it is strong enough to assert its rule against, or together with, the utmost efforts of the passions; and the whole man stands in an iron glow, white hot, perhaps, but still strong, and in no wise evaporating; even if he melts, losing none of his weight.

So, then, we have the three ranks: the man who perceives rightly, because he does not feel, and to whom the primrose is very accurately the primrose, because he does not love it. Then, secondly, the man who perceives wrongly, because he feels, and to whom the primrose is anything else than a primrose: a star, or a sun, or a fairy's shield, or a forsaken maiden. And then, lastly, there is the man who perceives rightly in spite of his feelings, and to whom the primrose is for ever nothing else than itself – a little flower apprehended in the very plain and leafy fact of it, whatever and how many soever the associations and passions may be that crowd around it. And, in general, these three classes may be rated in comparative order, as the men who are not poets at all, and the poets of the second order, and the poets of the first.

Modern Painters, vol. 3, 1863.

The literary background; the growing interest in melancholy, imagination and the picturesque: Joseph Warton's Essay on the Genius and Writings of Pope *(1756) was something of a manifesto for Gray, Cowper, Thomson, Collins and the pre-romantics:*

(...) a clear head and acute understanding are not sufficient alone to make a poet; that the most solid observations on human life expressed with the utmost elegance and brevity are morality, and not poetry; that the *Epistles* of Boileau in rhyme are no more poetical than the *Characters* of La Bruyère in prose; and that it is a creative and glowing *imagination, acer spiritus ac vis,* and that alone, that can stamp a writer with this exalted and very uncommon character which so few possess and of which so few can properly judge.

For one person who can adequately relish and enjoy a work of imagination, twenty are to be found who can taste and judge of observations on familiar life and the manners of the age. (...)

The sublime and the pathetic are the two chief nerves of all genuine poesy.

From Akenside's The Pleasures of Imagination *(1744):*

(...) the glad impulse of congenial powers,
Or of sweet sound, or fair-proportioned form,
The grace of motion, or the bloom of light,
Thrills through Imagination's tender frame,
From nerve to nerve; all naked and alive
They catch the spreading rays; till now the soul
At length discloses every tuneful spring,
To that harmonious movement from without,
Responsive. Then the inexpressive strain
Diffuses its enchantment; Fancy dreams
Of sacred fountains and Elysian groves,
And vales of bliss; the intellectual power
Bends from his awful throne a wondering ear,
And smiles: the passions, gently soothed away,
Sink to divine repose, and love and joy
Alone are waking; love and joy serene
As airs that fan the summer...

Cf. Verse form and poetic genres, p. 2; Versification, p. 7; Figurative language, p. 31.

William BLAKE 1757-1827

1757 *Born in London.*
1771 *Apprenticed to an engraver because of his extremely visual mind.*
1779-1780 *Studied at the Royal Academy; met Fuseli.*
1783 Poetical Sketches.
1788 *Developed his engraving method.*
1789 *Engraved The* Songs of Innocence *and* The Book of Thel.
1790 *Wrote* The Marriage of Heaven and Hell.
1791 The French Revolution.
1793 *Engraved* America *and* Visions of the Daughters of Albion.
1794 *Engraved* Europe, Songs of Experience, The Book of Urizen.
1795 *Engraved* The Book of Los, The Song of Los.

William Blake was a rebel who turned against the Augustan beliefs of his time: faith in nature, reason and society. All rules, all laws were hateful to him – they distorted man and killed the spirit. He saw them everywhere: in the works of Newton and Locke, and in the conventions and tyranny of the state and the church.

Politically, he was a radical who had high hopes of the French and American revolutions (he belonged to the circle of Tom Paine, William Godwin, Mary Wollstonecraft) but was later disillusioned when he saw tyranny prevail in France under Napoleon and despaired of any rational system ever improving humanity. This may account for the more visionary and Christian quality of the poems he wrote after 1800.

Religiously, he saw God the Father, the vengeful God of the Old Testament whom he called

1796 *Started illustrating Young's* Night Thoughts.
1797 *Started writing* The Four Zoas.
1800-1803 *Worked with Hayley.*
1804 *Engraved* Milton *and* Jerusalem.
1823-1825 *Worked on his engravings for* The Book of Job.
1825-1826 *Worked on illustrations of Dante.*
1827 *Died in London.*

Urizen, as the symbol of authority, repression and fear, whereas Christ — Orc — embodied the freedom of man and all that is good. Around these characters, Blake created a vast and complex mythology.

What he advocated was the reign of intuition, inspiration and imagination. He saw the world of children, which he described in the Songs of Innocence, *as an unfallen world of pastoral bliss symbolizing a state of grace. The* Songs of Experience *describe the contrary state, that of the England of his time in which children were exploited, love was not free, misery and fear prevailed.*

Though some of his poems may seem obscure, one should remember his defence of difficulty: "that which can be made Explicit is not worth my care."

Blake was an engraver as much as a poet and always conceived of poems and illustrations as one.

The Little Black Boy (1789)

My mother bore me in the southern wild,
And I am black, but O! my soul is white;
White as an angel is the English child,
But I am black, as if bereav'd of light.

My mother taught me underneath a tree,
And sitting down before the heat of day,
She took me on her lap and kissed me,
And pointing to the east, began to say:

"Look on the rising sun: there God does live,
And gives his light, and gives his heat away;
And flowers and trees and beasts and men receive
Comfort in morning, joy in the noonday.

And we are put on earth a little space,
That we may learn to bear the beams of love;
And these black bodies and this sunburnt face
Is but a cloud, and like a shady grove.

For when our souls have learn'd the heat to bear,
The cloud will vanish; we shall hear his voice,
Saying: 'Come out from the grove, my love & care,
And round my golden tent like lambs rejoice'."

Thus did my mother say, and kissed me;
And thus I say to little English boy:
When I from black and he from white cloud free,
And round the tent of God like lambs we joy,

I'll shade him from the heat, till he can bear
To lean in joy upon our father's knee;
And then I'll stand and stroke his silver hair,
And be like him, and he will then love me.

Songs of Innocence.

Blake printed his own poems, combining word and picture in etchings which he then coloured.
© British Museum.

"As Poetry admits not a Letter that is Insignificant, so Painting admits not a Grain of Sand or a Blade of Grass Insignificant – much less an Insignificant Blur or Mark."

W. Blake, *A Vision of the Last Judgment.*

The Chimney Sweeper (1794)

A little black thing among the snow.
Crying "'weep! 'weep!" in notes of woe!
"Where are thy father & mother? say?"
"They are both gone up to the church to pray.

"Because I was happy upon the heath,
"And smil'd among the winter's snow,
"They clothed me in the clothes of death,
"And taught me to sing the notes of woe.

"And because I am happy & dance & sing,
"They think they have done me no injury,
"And are gone to praise God & his Priest & King,
"Who make up a heaven of our misery."

Songs of Experience.

Blake on imagination;

• "Mental Things are alone Real; what is call'd Corporal, Nobody Knows of its Dwelling Place: it is in Fallacy, and its Existence an Imposture. Where is the Existence Out of Mind or Thought? Where is it but in the Mind of a Fool?"

A Vision of the Last Judgment.

• Fable or Allegory are a totally distinct and inferior kind of Poetry. Vision or Imagination is a representation of what eternally exists, really and unchangeably. Fable or Allegory is formed by the daughters of Memory. Imagination is surrounded by the daughters of Inspiration...

The Nature of... Imagination is very little known, and the eternal nature and permanence of its ever existent images is considered as less permanent than the things of vegetative and generative Nature; yet the oak dies as well as the lettuce, but its eternal image and individuality never dies, but renews by its seed, just so the imaginative image returns by the seed of contemplative Thought.

This world of Imagination is the world of Eternity; it is the divine bosom into which we shall all go after the death of the vegetated body. This world of Imagination is infinite and eternal, whereas the world of Generation, or Vegetation, is finite and temporal. There exist in that eternal world the permanent realities of every thing which we see reflected in the vegetable glass of Nature...

I assert for myself that I do not behold the outward Creation and that to me it is hindrance and not action; it is as the dirt upon my feet, no part of me. "What", it will be question'd, "when the sun rises, do you not see a round disk of fire somewhat like a guinea?" O no, no, I see an innumerable company of the heavenly host crying, "Holy, Holy, Holy is the Lord God Almighty." I question not my corporeal or vegetative eye any more than I would question a window concerning a sight. I look thro' it and not with it...

From Blake's M.S. Book about his picture of *The Last Judgment.*
Reprinted in Rafroidi, English Romantic Poets, *OCDL.*

... and on his verse:

When this verse was first dictated to me, I considered a monotonous cadence like that used by Milton and Shakespeare and all writers of English blank verse, derived from the modern bondage of rhyming, to be a necessary and indispensable part of verse. But I soon found out that in the mouth of a true orator such monotony was not only awkward, but as much a bondage as rhyme itself. I therefore have produced a variety in every line, both of cadences and number of syllabes. Every word and every letter is studied and put into its fit place; the terrific numbers are reserved for the mild and gentle parts, and the prosaic for inferior parts; all are necessary to each other. Poetry fettered fetters the human race. Nations are destroyed or flourish in proportion as their poetry, painting and music are destroyed or flourish. The primeval state of man was wisdom, art and science.

Preface to *Jerusalem,* begun 1804.

Northrop Frye on the Songs of Experience and Innocence:

In the *Songs of Innocence* (...) the divine imagination is an infant, symbolized in Christianity by the infant Jesus, the gentle and innocent Lamb of God. God from this perspective is a loving Father who sees the sparrow fall. Nature is a kindly old nurse, and a vigilant Providence appoints guardian angels to take care of the children. As is appropriate to the state of Beulah, it is especially in sleep and repose that these guardians are invoked. Here we find the harmonious society which the single organism represents in this world. All the forces of nature help to find lost children; glowworms are beacons to bewildered ants; and as in Isaiah, the lion lies down with the lamb and all animals are childrens' pets. (...)

Childhood to Blake is a state or phase of imaginative existence, the phase in which the world of imagination is still a brave new world and yet reassuring and intelligible. In the protection which the child feels from his parents and his evening prayer against darkness there is the image of a cosmos far more intelligently controlled than ours. The spontaneity of life which such protection makes possible is the liberty of the expanding imagination which has nothing to do but complete its own growth. No one can watch babies, kittens, puppies or even the first green shoots of plants for very long without beginning to smile; and the smile is a partial vision of the state of existence which this infant life is in. It was to the same vision that Jesus was appealing when he put a child in the midst of his disciples. (...)

The reader needs no commentary to help him understand the terrible indictment of this latter world in the *Songs of Experience.* Contempt and horror have never spoken more clearly in English poetry. But Blake never forgets to see behind all the cruelty of man the fact of his fall. Just as no one can watch a baby without smiling, so no one can see a child tortured for its own "good" or neglected for someone else's: no one can see its parents, blackened and twisted by the St. Anthony's fire of moral virtue, stumbling out of a darkened church and blinking like bats in the sun: no one can see prostitution or war or race hatred or poverty, without groping for some cause of what seems to be utterly pointless evil. The reason can supply irrefutable proofs that in such things the world is behaving illogically and contrary to its own best interests. The reason will not take us far. Only vision helps us here, and vision shows us the tree of mystery and morality growing inside the human skull; it shows us the prophet calling to the earth to redeem herself and earth answering with a groan to be delivered; it shows us our accusing enemy who frightens us out of Paradise behind the menacing blaze of a tiger's eyes.

This is the only world the child can grow into, and yet the child must grow. The *Songs of Experience* are satires, but one of the things that they satirize is the state of innocence. They show us the butcher's knife which is waiting for the unconscious lamb. Conversely, the *Songs of Innocence* satirize the state of experience, as the contrast which they present to it makes its hypocrisies more obviously shameful. Hence the two sets of lyrics show two *contrary* states of the soul, and in their opposition there is a double-edged irony, cutting into both the tragedy and the reality of fallen existence.

N. Frye, *Fearful Symmetry.*
Princeton University Press.

Cf. Thomas Hood's The Song of the Shirt *(1843); Versification, p. 7.*

Fancy and Imagination

The distinction between fancy and imagination is one of the fundamental romantic theories. Here is how Coleridge explained the difference in his Biographia Literaria, *ch.13.*

(...) The Imagination then, I consider either as primary, or secondary. The primary Imagination I hold to be the living Power and prime Agent of all human Perception, and as a repetition in the finite mind of the eternal act of creation in the infinite I am. The secondary Imagination I consider as an echo of the former, coexisting with the conscious will, yet still as identical with the primary in the *kind* of its agency, and differing only in *degree,* and in the *mode* of its operation. It dissolves, diffuses, dissipates, in order to re-create; or where this process is rendered impossible, yet still at all events it struggles to idealize and to unify. It is essentially *vital,* even as all objects (*as* objects) are essentially fixed and dead.

Fancy, on the contrary, has no other counters to play with, but fixities and definites. The Fancy is indeed no other than a mode of Memory emancipated from the order of time and space; while it is blended with, and modified by that empirical phenomenon of the will, which we express by the word choice. But equally with the ordinary memory the Fancy must receive all its materials ready made from the law of association.

Fancy and imagination; an example from painting.

Consider these two architectural fantasies: in Marlow's *Capriccio* a scene by a Venetian Canal is deliberately and carefully juxtaposed with St Paul's, London; in Gandy's watercolour we are meant to note the care with which the artist has reproduced "Architecture from the school of Constantinople of the 6th and 7th centuries" though in fact the Byzantine references are hardly the most prominent. I think Coleridge would have seen in the Marlow the exercise of the faculty which he called *fancy,* which deals with "finities and definites. The fancy is no other than a mode of memory emancipated from the order of time and space". In the Gandy, on the other hand, memories of Roslin Chapel blend in with whatever he had been able to learn of the Byzantines, so that the picture illustrates Coleridge's Imagination, which "dissolves, diffuses, dissipates, in order to re-create." Gandy was also trying to illustrate a passage from Harrington's translation of Ariosto:

"This was a church most solemn and devout
And rais'd by art on arches all about
And straight she saw the stately tomb erected
Of marble pure....
The very marble was so clear and bright
That though the sun no light into it gave
The Tomb itself did lighten all the cave."

As Sir John Summerson has pointed out it is the reversal of normal lighting which makes this picture so uncanny. He compares the lighting of *Christabel,* and sees this as a visual analogue of that poem, as well as of the "intricate archaeological romance of Sir Walter Scott".

J. Purkis. *The World of the English Romantic Poets.*

William Marlow: Capriccio, St Paul's and a Venetian Canal, *c. 1795.*
London, The Tate Gallery.

Joseph Michael Gandy:
The Tomb of Merlin, *1815.*
© The British Architectural Library/IRIBA.

William WORDSWORTH 1770-1850

1770 *Born at Cockermouth, Cumberland.*
1787-1791 *St John's College, Cambridge. Travelled in France and Switzerland.*
1791-1792 *Lived in France where he fell in love (he had a daughter). He supported the revolution.*
1793 An Evening Walk, Descriptive Sketches.
1795 *Met Godwin and Coleridge.*
1798 Lyrical Ballads, *written with Coleridge (second edition with preface in 1800). Travelled to Germany.*
1799 *Settled in the Lake District with his sister Dorothy.*
1802 *Married Mary Hutchinson.*
1805 *Wrote* The Prelude *(pub. 1850).*
1807 Poems in Two Volumes.
1814 The Excursion.
1815 Poems, The White Doe of Rylstone.
1817 *Met Keats.*
1819 Peter Bell, The Waggoner.
1820 *Travelled in Europe.* Duddon Sonnets.
1822 Ecclesiastical Sonnets.
1842 Poems, chiefly of Early and Late Years.
1843 *Appointed Poet Laureate.*
1850 *Died in Westmorland.* The Prelude *published.*

William Wordsworth began as an optimistic and revolutionary artist, seeking universal harmony. In the preface to the Lyrical Ballads, *he and Coleridge expounded their principles: the artificial poetic diction of the eighteenth century should give way to a more natural and less intellectual language, that of ordinary men and women. As for the creative process, the manifesto asserted the importance of imagination, intuition and feelings in reaction against the Augustan spirit.*

These principles directly derived from Wordsworth's somewhat Pantheistic conception of Nature. Only in nature can man find peace, truth, and beauty – the manifestation of God. With vividness and freshness, Wordsworth can convey the beauty of a scene, bring to light the sublime behind the ordinary, awaken the reader's consciousness. He believed that a natural state, unspoilt by intellectual systems and theories, could only generate truth and goodness. Simple country people, children, not yet corrupted, are privileged in his poetry (e.g. his Ode: Intimations of Immortality, *about the child's communion with the world that surrounds him and the sense of loss that accompanies his growth.)*

The Prelude *is an autobiographical poem which relates the development of the poet's mind, of his perception of the universe. It reflects the main originality of Wordsworth: he transformed the subject of poetry; from an exterior subject, it became the poet himself, his own subjectivity and feelings.*

After 1810, Wordsworth became far less innovative, defended the establishment, and his poetry became more conventional, announcing that of the mid-Victorians.

The Prelude (1805, pub. 1850)

One summer evening (led by her[1]) I found
A little boat tied to a willow tree
Within a rocky cave, its usual home.
Straight I unloosed her chain, and stepping in
Pushed from the shore. It was an act of stealth
And troubled pleasure, nor without the voice
Of mountain-echoes did my boat move on;
Leaving behind her still, on either side,
Small circles glittering idly in the moon,
Until they melted all into one track
Of sparkling light. But now, like one who rows,
Proud of his skill, to reach a chosen point
With an unswerving line, I fixed my view
Upon the summit of a craggy ridge,
The horizon's utmost boundary; for above
Was nothing but the stars and the grey sky.
She was an elfin pinnace; lustily
I dipped my oars into the silent lake,
And, as I rose upon the stroke, my boat
Went heaving through the water like a swan;
When, from behind that craggy steep till then
The horizon's bound, a huge peak, black and huge,
As if with voluntary power instinct,
Upreared its head. I struck and struck again,
And growing still in stature the grim shape
Towered up between me and the stars, and still,
For so it seemed, with purpose of its own
And measured motion like a living thing,
Strode after me. With trembling oars I turned,
And through the silent water stole my way
Back to the covert of the willow tree;
There in her mooring-place I left my bark, –
And through the meadows homeward went, in grave
And serious mood; but after I had seen
That spectacle, for many days, my brain
Worked with a dim and undetermined sense
Of unknown modes of being; o'er my thoughts
There hung a darkness, call it solitude
Or blank desertion. No familiar shapes
Remained, no pleasant images of trees,
Of sea or sky, no colours of green fields;
But huge and mighty forms, that do not live
Like living men, moved slowly through the mind
By day, and were a trouble to my dreams.

Book I, l. 357-400.

1. *her:* nature.

J.M.W. Turner: Buttermere Lake, with Part of Cromackwater, Cumberland, a Shower, *1798.*
London, The Tate Gallery.

There is – in the several ridges that enclose these vales, and divide them from each other, I mean in the forms and surfaces, first of the swelling grounds, next of the hills and rocks, and lastly of the mountains – an ascent of almost regular gradation, from elegance and richness, to their highest point of grandeur and sublimity. It follows therefore from this, first, that these rocks, hills, and mountains must present themselves to view in stages rising above each other, the mountains clustering together towards the central point; and next, that an observer familiar with the several vales, must, from their various position in relation to the sun, have had before his eyes every possible embellishment of beauty, dignity, and splendour, which light and shadow can bestow upon objects so diversified.

W. Wordsworth, *Guide to the Lakes.*

From the preface to the Lyrical Ballads:

The principal object, then, which I proposed to myself in these poems was to choose incidents and situations from common life and to relate or describe them, throughout, as far as was possible, in a selection of language really used by men; and, at the same time, to throw over them a certain colouring of imagination, whereby ordinary things should be presented to the mind in an unusual way; and, further, and above all, to make these incidents and situations interesting by tracing in them, truly though not ostentatiously, the primary laws of our nature: chiefly, as far as regards the manner in which we associate ideas in a state of excitement. Low and rustic life was generally chosen, because in that condition, the essential passions of the heart find a better soil in which they can attain their maturity, are less under restraint, and speak a plainer and more emphatic language; because in that condition of life our elementary feelings co-exist in a state of greater simplicity, and, consequently, may be more accurately contemplated, and more forcibly communicated; because the manners of rural life germinate from those elementary feelings; and, from the necessary character of rural occupations, are more easily comprehended; and are more durable; and lastly, because in that condition the passions of men are incorporated with the beautiful and permanent forms of nature. The language, too, of these men is adopted (purified indeed from what appear to be its real defects, from all lasting and rational causes of dislike or disgust) because such men hourly communicate with the best objects from which the best part of language is originally derived; and because, from their rank in society and the sameness and narrow circle of their intercourse, being less under the influence of social vanity they convey their feelings and notions in simple and unelaborated expressions. Accordingly, such a language, arising out of repeated experience and regular feelings, is a more permanent, and a far more philosophical language, than that which is frequently substituted for it by poets, who think that they are conferring honour upon themselves and their art, in proportion as they separate themselves from the sympathies of men, and indulge in arbitrary and capricious habits of expression, in order to furnish food for fickle tastes, and fickle appetites, of their own creation. (...)

What is a poet? To whom does he address himself? And what language is to be expected from him? He is a man speaking to men: a man, it is true, endued with more lively sensibility, more enthusiasm and tenderness, who has a greater knowledge of human nature, and a more comprehensive soul, than are supposed to be common among mankind; a man pleased with his own passions and volitions, and who rejoices more than other men in the spirit of life that is in him; delighting to contemplate similar volitions and passions as manifested in the goings-on of the universe, and habitually impelled to create them where he does not find them. To these qualities he has added a disposition to be affected more than other men by absent things as if they were present; an ability of conjuring up in himself passions, which are indeed far frombeing the same as those produced by real events, yet (especially in those parts of the general sympathy which are pleasing and delightful) do more nearly resemble the passions produced by real events, than any thing which, from the motions of their own minds merely, other men are accustomed to feel in themselves; whence, and from practice, he has acquired a greater readiness and power in expressing what he thinks and feels, and especially those thoughts and feelings which, by his own choice, or from the structure of his own mind, arise in him without immediate external excitement.

But, whatever portion of this faculty we may suppose even the greatest poet to possess, there cannot be a doubt but that the language which it will suggest to him, must, in liveliness and truth, fall far short of that which is uttered by men in real life, under the actual pressure of those passions, certain shadows of which the poet thus produces, or feels to be produced, in himself. However exalted a notion we would wish to cherish of the character of a poet, it is obvious, that, while he describes and imitates passions, his situation is altogether slavish and mechanical, compared with the freedom and power of real and substantial action and suffering. So that it will be the wish of the poet to bring his feelings near to those of the persons whose feelings he describes, nay, for short spaces of time perhaps, to let himself slip into an entire delusion, and even confound and identify his own feelings with theirs; modifying only the language which is thus suggested to him, by a consideration that he describes for a particular purpose, that of giving pleasure. Here, then, he will apply the principle on which I have so much insisted, namely, that of selection; on this he will depend for removing what would otherwise be painful or disgusting in the passion; he will feel that there is no necessity to trick out or to elevate nature: and, the more industriously he applies this principle, the deeper will be his faith that no words, which his fancy or imagination can suggest, will be to be compared with those which are the emanations of reality and truth.

Cf. Versification. p. 7; Figurative language, p. 31.

Samuel Taylor COLERIDGE 1772-1834

1772 *Born in Devon; his father was a vicar and schoolmaster.*
1782-1791 *After his father's death when he was nine, was sent to Christ's Hospital, London, a charity school. Charles Lamb was another student there.*
1791-1794 *Jesus College, Cambridge (left to enlist in the Cavalry, gave up and returned to Cambridge, but never graduated). With Southey, planned a communistic society in the USA (a "Pantisocracy").*
1795 *Met Wordsworth; married Sarah Fricker.*
1796 Poems on Various Subjects. *Started taking opium.*
1797-1798 *Close collaboration with Wordsworth. Wrote the first part of* Christabel *and possibly* Kubla Khan. The Rime of the Ancient Mariner *appeared in* Lyrical Ballads. *Toured Germany.*
1799 *Fell in love with Sara Hutchinson.*
1800 Wallenstein; *wrote the second part of* Christabel; *settled in the Lake District.*
1801 *Beginning of his addiction to opium.*
1802 Dejection: an Ode.
1804-1806 *Lived in Malta and Italy.*
1806 *Separation from his wife.*
1808 *Started lecturing on literature.*
1816 *Publication of* Kubla Khan, Christabel, The Pains of Sleep.
1817 Biographia Literaria *and* Sibylline Leaves *published.*
1818-1834 *Gave lectures on literature and philosophy.*
1834 *Died in Highgate.*

Coleridge's poetic production is limited and many of his poems were left unfinished, partly because of ill-health, partly because of his addiction to opium.

They all reflect the same attraction for the mysterious, the supernatural, the irrational. They have the quality of dreams or hallucinations. The Rime of the Ancient Mariner, *very much influenced by traditional ballads, relates the curse that falls on a ship after the killing of an albatross. The poem is imbued with spirituality and religiosity: the Fall, punishment, remorse, redemption through prayer and love...* Christabel, *set in a Gothic background — a cold night, a deep forest, a castle — contrasts the innocence of Christabel with the evil and supernatural powers of the mysterious Geraldine. A disturbing atmosphere and a feeling of menace pervade the whole poem. As for* Kubla Khan, *Coleridge explained he had dreamt it under the influence of an anodyne and on awakening, had remembered and immediately transcribed it. Interrupted, however, he could not remember the whole dream and all that remained was a vision of the scene where the Khan Kubla had commanded a castle to be built.*

All of Coleridge's poems show the influence of German legends and ballads. They are also based on a belief in the "oneness" of the whole universe, in the unity of man's soul with the divine. Coleridge turned to philosophy and criticism at the end of his life. Reacting against the mechanistic theories of the 18th century, he developed his theory according to which Imagination is the essential force behind creation, a force that fuses form and matter, creating a whole whose parts cannot be studied separately.

The Rime of the Ancient Mariner (1798)

An old mariner meets a wedding-guest and tells him how his ship was driven by a storm to the south pole. An albatross came through the fog and was greeted with joy, but the ancient mariner inhospitably killed it.

Part II

The Sun now rose upon the right:
Out of the sea came he,
Still hid in mist, and on the left
Went down into the sea.

And the good south wind still blew behind,
But no sweet bird did follow,
Nor any day for food or play
Came to the mariners' hollo!

His shipmates cry out against the ancient Mariner, for killing the bird of good luck.

And I had done a hellish thing,
And it would work 'em woe:
For all averred, I had killed the bird
That made the breeze to blow.
Ah wretch! said they, the bird to slay,
That made the breeze to blow!

But when the fog cleared off, they justify the same, and thus make themselves accomplices in the crime.

Nor dim nor red, like God's own head,
The glorious Sun uprist:
Then all averred, I had killed the bird
That brought the fog and mist.
'Twas right, said they, such birds to slay,
That bring the fog and mist.

The fair breeze continues; the ship enters the Pacific Ocean, and sails northward, even till it reaches the Line.

The fair breeze blew, the white foam flew,
The furrow followed free;
We were the first that ever burst
Into that silent sea.

The ship hath been suddenly becalmed.

Down dropped the breeze, the sails dropped down,
'Twas sad as sad could be;
And we did speak only to break
The silence of the sea!

All in a hot and copper sky,
The bloody Sun, at noon,
Right up above the mast did stand,
No bigger than the Moon.

Day after day, day after day,
We stuck, nor breath nor motion;
As idle as a painted ship
Upon a painted ocean.

And the Albatross begins to be avenged.

Water, water, every where,
And all the boards did shrink;
Water, water, every where,
Nor any drop to drink.

The very deep did rot: O Christ!
That ever this should be!
Yea, slimy things did crawl with legs
Upon the slimy sea.

About, about, in reel and rout
The death-fires[1] danced at night;
The water, like a witch's oils,
Burnt green, and blue and white.

A Spirit had followed them; one of the invisible inhabitants of this planet, neither departed souls nor angels; concerning whom the learned Jew, Josephus, and the Platonic Constantinopolitan, Michael Psellus, may be consulted. They are very numerous, and there is no climate or element without one or more.

And some in dreams assured were
Of the Spirit that plagued us so;
Nine fathom deep he had followed us
From the land of mist and snow.

And every tongue, through utter drought,
Was withered at the root;
We could not speak, no more than if
We had been choked with soot.

The shipmates, in their sore distress, would fain throw the whole guilt on the ancient Mariner: in sign whereof they hang the dead sea-bird round his neck.

Ah! well a-day! what evil looks
Had I from old and young!
Instead of the cross, the Albatross
About my neck was hung.

The marginal glosses were added by Coleridge in 1816.
1. *the death-fires:* St Elmo's fire (flame-like effect, caused by electricity, that could sometimes be seen on a ship. It was supposed to portend ill luck.)

Gustave Doré's vision of the ice-bound ship (1875). Ph. Hachette.

"The ice was here, the ice was there,
The ice was all around:
It cracked and growled, and roared and howled,
Like noises in a swound!

"At length did cross an Albatross,
Thorough the fog it came;
As if it had been a Christian soul,
We hailed it in God's name."

Coleridge on The Rime of The Ancient Mariner:

... in my own judgment the poem had too much [moral]... the only or chief fault was the obtrusion of the moral sentiment so openly on the reader as a principle or cause of action in a work of pure imagination.

In reply to Mrs Barbauld.

... on poetic diction:

My own differences from certain supposed parts of Mr. Wordsworth's theory ground themselves on the assumption, that his words had been rightly interpreted, as purporting that the proper diction for poetry in general consists altogether in a language taken, with due exceptions, from the mouths of men in real life, a language which actually constitutes the natural conversation of men under the influence of natural feelings. My objection is, first, that in *any* sense this rule is applicable only to *certain* classes of poetry; secondly, that even to these classes it is not applicable, except in such a sense, as hath never by any one (as far as I know or have read) been denied or doubted; and lastly, that as far as, and in that degree in which it is *practicable*, yet as a *rule* it is useless, if not injurious, and therefore either need not, or ought not to be practised. The poet informs his reader, that he had generally chosen *low and rustic* life; but not *as* low and rustic, or in order to repeat that pleasure of doubtful moral effect, which persons of elevated rank and of superior refinement oftentimes derive from a happy *imitation* of the rude unpolished manners and discourse of their inferiors. For the pleasure so derived may be traced to three exciting causes. The first is the naturalness, in *fact*, of the things represented. The second is the apparent naturalness of the *representation*, as raised and qualified by an imperceptible infusion of the author's own knowledge and talent, which infusion does, indeed, constitute it an *imitation* as distinguished from a mere *copy*. The third cause may be found in the reader's conscious feeling of his superiority awakened by the contrast presented to him; even as for the same purpose the kings and great barons of yore retained sometimes *actual* clowns and fools, but more frequently shrewd and witty fellows in that *character*. These, however, were not Mr. Wordsworth's objects.

Biographia Literaria, ch. XVII.

Cf. The Preface to the Lyrical Ballads, *p. 170.*

... on his aim in the Lyrical Ballads:

During the first year that Mr. Wordsworth and I were neighbours, our conversations turned frequently on the two cardinal points of poetry, the power of exciting the sympathy of the reader by a faithful adherence to the truth of nature, and the power of giving the interest of novelty by the modifying colours of imagination. The sudden charm, which accidents of light and shade, which moonlight or sunset diffused over a known and familiar landscape, appeared to represent the practicability of combining both. These are the poetry of nature. The thought suggested itself (to which of us I do not recollect) that a series of poems might be composed of two sorts. In the one, the incidents and agents were to be, in part at least, supernatural; and the excellence aimed at was to consist in the interesting of the affections by the dramatic truth of such emotions, as would naturally accompany such situations, supposing them real. And real in *this* sense they have been to every human being who, from whatever source of delusion, has at any time believed himself under supernatural agency. For the second class, subjects were to be chosen from ordinary life; the characters and incidents were to be such, as will be found in every village and its vicinity, where there is a meditative and feeling mind to seek after them, or to notice them, when they present themselves.

In this idea originated the plan of the *Lyrical Ballads*; in which it was agreed, that my endeavours should be directed to persons and characters supernatural, or at least romantic; yet so as to transfer from our inward nature a human interest and a semblance of truth sufficient to procure for these shadows of imagination that willing suspension of disbelief for the moment, which constitutes poetic faith. Mr. Wordsworth, on the other hand, was to propose to himself as his object, to give the charm of novelty to things of every day, and to excite a feeling analogous to the supernatural, by awakening the mind's attention from the lethargy of custom, and directing it to the loveliness and the wonders of the world before us; an inexhaustible treasure, but for which, in consequence of the film of familiarity and selfish solicitude we have eyes, yet see not, ears that hear not, and hearts that neither feel nor understand.

Biographia Literaria, ch. XIV.

Cf. Verse form and poetic genres, p. 2; Versification, p. 7; Figurative language, p. 31.

The Ballad

An entry in Dr Johnson's Dictionary *(1755):*

ballad. A song.

Ballad once signified a solemn and sacred song, as well as trivial, when Solomon's Song was called the *ballad of ballads;* but now it is applied to nothing but trifling verse. (Watts).

... and Wordsworth on the tempering and restraining effect of the ballad:

The end of poetry is to produce excitement in co-existence with an overbalance of pleasure. Now, by the supposition, excitement is an unusual and irregular state of the mind; ideas and feelings do not in that state succeed each other in accustomed order. But, if the words by which this excitement is produced are in themselves powerful, or the images and feelings have an undue proportion of pain connected with them, there is some danger that the excitement may be carried beyond its proper bounds. Now the co-presence of something regular, something to which the mind has been accustomed in various moods and in a less excited state, cannot but have great efficiency in tempering and restraining the passion by an intertexture of ordinary feeling, and of feeling not strictly and necessarily connected with the passion.

Preface to the Lyrical Ballads, 1802.

Further references

The end of E. A. Poe's The Narrative of Arthur Gordon Pym of Nantucket, *1838:*

March 9. The white ashy material fell now continually around us, and in vast quantities. The range of vapor to the southward had arisen prodigiously in the horizon, and began to assume more distinctness of form. I can liken it to nothing but a limitless cataract, rolling silently into the sea from some immense and far-distant rampart in the heaven. The gigantic curtain ranged along the whole extent of the southern horizon. It emitted no sound.

March 21. A sullen darkness now hovered above us – but from out the milky depths of the ocean a luminous glare arose, and stole up along the bulwarks of the boat. We were nearly overwhelmed by the white ashy shower which settled upon us and upon the canoe, but melted into the water as it fell. The summit of the cataract was utterly lost in the dimness and the distance. Yet we were evidently approaching it with a hideous velocity. At intervals there were visible in it wide, yawning, but momentary rents, and from out these rents, within which was a chaos of flitting and indistinct images, there came rushing and mighty, but soundless winds, tearing up the enkindled ocean in their course.

March 22. The darkness had materially increased, relieved only by the glare of the water thrown back from the white curtain before us. Many gigantic and pallidly white birds flew continuously now from beyond the veil, and their scream was the eternal *Tekeli-li!* as they retreated from our vision. Hereupon Nu-Nu stirred in the bottom of the boat; but upon touching him, we found his spirit departed. And now we rushed into the embraces of the cataract, where a chasm threw itself open to receive us. But there arose in our pathway a shrouded human figure, very far larger in its proportions than any dweller among men. And the hue of the skin of the figure was of the perfect whiteness of the snow.

An opium dream, from T. De Quincey's Confessions of an English Opium-Eater, *1822:*

The dream commenced with a music which now I often heard in dreams – a music of preparation and of awakening suspense; a music like the opening of the Coronation Anthem, and which, like *that,* gave the feeling of a vast march – of infinite cavalcades filing off – and the tread of innumerable armies. The morning was come of a mighty day – a day of crisis and of final hope for human nature, then suffering some mysterious eclipse, and labouring in some dread extremity. Somewhere, I knew not where – somehow, I knew not how – by some beings, I knew not whom – a battle, a strife, an agony, was conducting – was evolving like a great drama, or piece of music; with which my sympathy was the more insupportable from my confusion as to its place, its cause, its nature, and its possible issue. I, as is usual in dreams (where, of necessity, we make ourselves central to every movement), had the power, and yet had not the power, to decide it. I had the power, if I could raise myself, to will it; and yet again had not the power, for the weight of twenty Atlantics was upon me, or the oppression of inexpiable guilt. "Deeper than ever plummet sounded", I lay inactive. Then, like a chorus, the passion deepened. Some greater interest was at stake; some mightier cause than ever yet the sword had pleaded, or trumpet had proclaimed. Then came sudden alarms: hurryings to and fro: trepidations of innumerable fugitives, I knew not whether from the good cause or the bad: darkness and lights: tempest and human faces; and at last, with the sense that all was lost, female, forms, and the features that were worth all the world to me, and but a moment allowed, – and clasped hands, and heart-breaking partings, and then – everlasting farewells! and with a sigh, such as the caves of hell sighed when the incestuous mother uttered the abhorred name of death, the sound was reverberated – everlasting farewells! and again, and yet again reverberated – everlasting farewells!

And I awoke in struggles, and cried aloud – "I will sleep no more!".

George Noel Gordon, Lord BYRON 1788-1824

1788 *Born in London.*
1791 *Succeeded to the title of Baron.*
1801-1805 *Harrow.*
1805 *Trinity College, Cambridge.*
1806 Fugitive Pieces.
1807 Poems on Several Occasions; Hours of Idleness.
1809 *Took his seat in the House of Lords;* English Bards and Scotch Reviewers.*Away for a year in the near East.*
1812 Childe Harold, *Cantos I and II.*
1813 The Giaour; The Bride of Abydos.
1814 The Corsair; Lara.
1815 *Married Isabella Milbanke (who left him in 1816).*
1816 Childe Harold, *Canto III. Left England, never to return.*
The Siege of Corinth, The Prisoner of Chillon.
1817 Manfred *(a drama),* The Lament of Tasso *(a dramatic soliloquy).*
1818 Beppo, Childe Harold, *Canto IV.*
1819 Mazeppa *(a drama);* Don Juan, *Cantos I and III.*
1821 *Active in the Carbonari insurrection;* Marino Faliero *(a drama);* Sardanapalus *(a drama);* Don Juan, *Cantos III-IV;* Cain *(a drama).*
1822 The Vision of Judgment.
1823 Don Juan, *Cantos VI-XIV;* The Island; Werner *(a tragedy). Joined the Greek insurgents.*
1824 Don Juan, *Cantos XV-XVI;* The Deformed Transformed *(a drama). Died of fever at Missolonghi.*

Byron was above all a legendary figure, the Romantic rebel and cynic who shocked and fascinated Regency society by his scandalous life, and who died heroically for Greek independence. He attacked political and religious hypocrisy, had a total disregard for moral values (his homosexual and incestuous propensities forced him to leave England) and he ended up wandering Southern Europe, in an attempt to flee the respectable and conventional world he despised.

Though an admirer of Dryden and Pope far more than of Romantic poetry (which he satirized), he had the Romantics' conception of poetic creation as emotional outlet ("it comes over me in a kind of rage") and the Romantics' vision of the rebel as hero.

His early poems, written before 1815, were Eastern tales *(e.g. the Giaour's love for a slave-girl, the adventures of a pirate in* The Corsair *and* Lara, *the attack of Corinth by the Turks in* The Siege of Corinth).

But it was Childe Harold *that made him enormously popular on the Continent as well as in England ("I awoke one morning and found myself famous".). Written in Spenserian stanzas, the poem records the melancholy of the "Byronic hero", the emotions awakened in him by nature and art, his disgust with the world and his own self as he wanders all over Europe.*

Byron also wrote several dramas (both Manfred *(cf p. 53) and* Cain *show tormented heroes who defy God and the laws of society) and satirical works, of which* Don Juan *is the best known. It relates the picaresque and amorous adventures of the 18th century character and satirizes several aspects of British and European society (e.g. the Napoleonic wars).*

Childe Harold's Pilgrimage (1816)

13

Where rose the mountains, there to him were friends;
Where rolled the ocean, thereon was his home;
Where a blue sky, and glowing clime, extends,
He had the passion and the power to roam;
The desert, forest, cavern, breaker's foam,
Were unto him companionship; they spake
A mutual language, clearer than the tome
Of his land's tongue, which he would oft forsake
For Nature's pages glassed[1] by sunbeams on the lake.

14

Like the Chaldean[2], he could watch the stars,
Till he had peopled them with beings bright
As their own beams; and earth, and earth-born jars,
And human frailties, were forgotten quite:
Could he have kept his spirit to that flight
He had been happy; but this clay will sink
Its spark immortal, envying it the light
To which it mounts, as if to break the link
That keeps us from yon heaven which woos us to its brink.

15

But in Man's dwellings he became a thing
Restless and worn, and stern and wearisome,
Drooped as a wild-born falcon with clipped wing,
To whom the boundless air alone were home:
Then came his fit again[3], which to o'ercome,
As eagerly the barred-up bird will beat
His breast and beak against his wiry dome
Till the blood tinge his plumage – so the heat
Of his impeded Soul would through his bosom eat.

16

Self-exiled Harold wanders forth again,
With nought of Hope left, but with less of gloom;
The very knowledge that he lived in vain,
That all was over on this side the tomb,
Had made Despair a smilingness assume,
Which, though 'twere wild, – as on the plundered wreck
When mariners would madly meet their doom
With draughts intemperate on the sinking deck,
Did yet inspire a cheer, which he forbore to check.

Canto III.

1. *glassed*: reflected, or looking like glass 2. *Chaldean*: Babylonian (the Chaldeans had well-known astrologers) – 3. "Then came his fit again": from *Macbeth*, III, IV, 21 "Then comes my fit again".

From Byron's Preface to Childe Harold's Pilgrimage:

I now leave "Childe Harold" to live his day such as he is; it had been more agreeable, and certainly more easy, to have drawn an amiable character. It had been easy to varnish over his faults, to make him do more and express less, but he never was intended as an example, further than to show, that early perversion of mind and morals leads to satiety of past pleasures and disappointment in new ones, and that even the beauties of nature and the stimulus of travel (except ambition, the most powerful of all excitements) are lost on a soul so constituted, or rather misdirected. Had I proceeded with the Poem, this character would have deepened as he drew to the close; for the outline which I once meant to fill up for him was, with some exceptions, the sketch of a modern Timon, perhaps a poetical Zeluco.

From Byron's Journal:

I wish I could settle to reading again, – my life is monotonous, and yet desultory. I take up books, and fling them down again. I began a comedy, and burnt it because the scene ran into *reality* – a novel – for the same reason. In rhyme, I can keep more away from facts; but the thought always runs through, through...

Nov. 17th 1813.

Byron and the romantic mood of ennui:

It is significant that Goethe's Werther, Chateaubriand's René, Senancour's Obermann, all adopt the same attitude as "Childe Harold". Melancholy, said Victor Hugo, is a note of the romantic movement. The identity of tone is not due to imitation. It is created by the romantic and revolutionary atmosphere of France, Germany, and England. Under the name of *ennui*, Horace Walpole described the same feeling, seventy years earlier:

"Oh! my dear Sir" (so he writes to John Chute, Aug. 20, 1743), "don't you find that nine parts in ten of the world are of no use but to make you wish yourself with that tenth part? I am so far from growing used to mankind by living amongst them, that my natural ferocity and wildness does but every day grow worse. They tire me, they fatigue me: I don't know what to do with them; I fling open the windows and fancy I want air:... I literally seem to have murdered a man whose name was Ennui, for his ghost is ever before me".

The feeling is an expression of the rising revolt against the order and repression, the complacent optimism, the starvation of many needs and moods of the imagination, which characterised the 18th century. It spread far and wide; it struck its roots deep. It assumed various forms, and the refuges in which men sought ways of escape were diverse. On the artistic and literary side, it underlay the Romantic movement. As it descended from the *salon* to the streets, and deepened from dissatisfaction with society into fierce hostility to its existing order, it became the parent of revolution. When Byron, therefore, embodied this prevailing mood in the character of his hero, he expressed a feeling with which, in one or other of its multitudinous forms, all men of more than average sensibility were, like himself, saturated.

R. E. Prothero, "Centenary Reflections on Childe Harold's Pilgrimage and Don Juan, 1924", *The Poetry of Byron* in *Quarterly Review*, CCXLI, 1924.

Cf. Versification, p. 7; Figurative language, p. 31.

J.M.W. Turner: Childe Harold's Pilgrimage, Italy, *(1832).*
Tate Gallery. Ph. Anderson-Giraudon.

Percy Bysshe SHELLEY 1792-1822

1792 *Born in Sussex.*
1804-1810 *Eton.*
1810 Zastrozzi *(a Gothic novel) and* Original Poetry by Victor and Cazire. *Entered University College, Oxford.*
1811 *Sent down from Oxford for publishing* The Necessity of Atheism. *Eloped with and married Harriet Westbrook.*
1812 *Active on the side of the radicals in Ireland. Met Godwin.*
1813 Queen Mab.
1814 *Parted from his wife and eloped with Mary Godwin.*
A Refutation of Deism.
1816 Alastor. *With Mary Godwin, joined Byron in Switzerland. Harriet drowned herself. Married Mary.*
1817 Laon and Cythna *suppressed but published the next year as* The Revolt of Islam.
1818 *Left for Italy, where he remained till his death.*
1819 Rosalind and Helen.
Wrote "Ode to the West Wind".
1820 The Cenci *(a tragedy);* Prometheus Unbound. *Wrote* "Ode to Liberty", "To a Skylark", "Letter to Maria Gisborne".
1821 Adonais *(an elegy on the death of Keats);* Epipsychidion. *Wrote* A Defence of Poetry *(pub. 1840).*
1822 Hellas *(a lyrical drama).*
Drowned in the bay of Spezia.

Shelley was the most lyrical of the romantic poets. He was also a revolutionary and an atheist, a disciple of the radical William Godwin who had written An Enquiry Concerning Political Justice. *An idealist, he believed in the perfectibility and goodness of human nature and yearned for a world of perfect love. In his* Defence of Poetry *he asserts the role of the poet as legislator of mankind; in touch with the infinite, he alone can transmit his visions of beauty and truth to the rest of the world. This gives the poet a moral function, quite separate from formal ethics.*

Shelley's early poems clearly illustrate these principles. Queen Mab *is a passionate condemnation of all institutions and laws, whether religious, policital or moral.* Alastor *describes the poet's contemplation and seclusion, his vain search for "the sublimest and most perfect natures" and his subsequent despair and death. In his lyrical drama* Prometheus Unbound, *Shelley makes the Titan who stole the fire from the Gods triumph over Jupiter. In spite of his suffering, Prometheus stops hating Jupiter, and so brings about the God's destruction. With Asia, his wife, who represents the power of love and beauty, his mother, Earth, and Demogorgon, the Primal Power of the world, he finally can start an era of love, devoid of "Thrones, altars, judgement-seats and prisons."*

Prometheus Unbound *represents the climax of Shelley's hopes and optimism. Apart from* Epipsychidion, *an hymn to free love leading to a more visionary life, his later poems (e.g.* Ode to the West Wind, To a Skylark, Adonais*) gradually grow more pessimistic.*

Prometheus Unbound (1820)

***Scene** A Ravine of Icy Rocks in the Indian Caucasus. Prometheus is discovered bound to the Precipice. Panthea and Ione are seated at his feet. Time, night. During the Scene, morning slowly breaks.*

PROMETHEUS. Monarch of Gods and Daemons[1], and all Spirits
But One[2], who throng those bright and rolling worlds
Which Thou and I alone of living things
Behold with sleepless eyes! regard this Earth
Made multitudinous with thy slaves, whom thou
Requitest for knee-worship, prayer, and praise,
And toil, and hecatombs of broken hearts,
With fear and self-contempt and barren hope.
Whilst me, who am thy foe, eyeless[3] in hate,
Hast thou made reign and triumph, to thy scorn,[4]
O'er mine own misery and thy vain revenge.
Three thousand years of sleep-unsheltered hours,
And moments aye[5] divided by keen pangs
Till they seemed years, torture and solitude,
Scorn and despair, – these are mine empire: –
More glorious far than that which thou surveyest
From thine unenvied throne, O Mighty God!

Almighty, had I deigned to share the shame
Of thine ill tyranny, and hung not here
Nailed to this wall of eagle-baffling mountain,
Black, wintry, dead, unmeasured; without herb,
Insect, or beast, or shape or sound of life.
Ah me! alas, pain, pain ever, forever!

No change, no pause, no hope! Yet I endure.
I ask the Earth, have not the mountains felt?
I ask yon Heaven, the all-beholding Sun,
Has it not seen? The sea, in storm or calm,
Heaven's ever-changing Shadow, spread below,
Have its deaf waves not heard my agony ?
Ah me! alas, pain, pain ever, forever!

The crawling glaciers pierce me with the spears
Of their moon-freezing crystals, the bright chains
Eat with their burning cold into my bones.
Heaven's winged hound[6], polluting from thy lips
His beak in poison not his own, tears up
My heart; and shapeless sights come wandering by,
The ghastly people of the realm of dream,
Mocking me: and the Earthquake-fiends are charged
To wrench the rivets from my quivering wounds
When the rocks split and close again behind:
While from their loud abysses howling throng
The genii of the storm, urging the rage
Of whirlwind, and afflict me with keen hail.
And yet to me welcome is day and night,
Whether one breaks the hoar frost of the morn,
Or starry, dim, and slow, the other climbs
The leaden-coloured east; for then they lead
The wingless, crawling hours, one among whom
– As some dark Priest hales[7] the reluctant victim
Shall drag thee, cruel King, to kiss the blood
From these pale feet, which then might trample thee
If they disdained not such a prostrate slave.

Act I.

1. *Daemons*: Supernatural beings who can communicate with gods and men – 2. *One*: Demogorgon – 3. *eyeless*: blind – 4. *to thy scorn*: to scorn you – 5. *aye*: constantly – 6. *Hound*: the vulture that tortures Prometheus – 7. *hales*: drags.

Shelley on poetry.
From the Preface to Prometheus Unbound:

The only imaginary being resembling in any degree Prometheus, is Satan; and Prometheus is, in my judgement, a more poetical character than Satan because, in addition to courage and majesty and firm and patient opposition to omnipotent force, he is susceptible of being described as exempt from the taints of ambition, envy, revenge, and a desire for personal aggrandisement, which in the Hero of *Paradise Lost*, interfere with the interest. The character of Satan engenders in the mind a pernicious casuistry which leads us to weigh his faults with his wrongs and to excuse the former because the latter exceed all measure. In the minds of those who consider that magnificent fiction with a religious feeling, it engenders something worse. But Prometheus is, as it were, the type of the highest perfection of moral and intellectual nature, impelled by the purest and the truest motives to the best and noblest ends.

Let this opportunity be conceded to me of acknowledging that I have, what a Scotch philosopher characteristically terms, "a passion for reforming the world," what passion incited him to write and publish his book, he omits to explain. For my part I had rather be damned with Plato and Lord Bacon, than go to Heaven with Paley and Malthus. But it is a mistake to suppose that I dedicate my poetical compositions solely to the direct enforcement of reform, or that I consider them in any degree as containing a reasoned system on the theory of human life. Didactic poetry is my abhorrence; nothing can be equally well expressed in prose that is not tedious and supererogatory in verse. My purpose has hitherto been simply to familiarise the highly refined imagination of the more select classes of poetical readers with beautiful idealisms of moral excellence; aware that until the mind can love, and admire, and trust, and hope, and endure, reasoned principles of moral conduct are seeds cast upon the highway of life which the unconscious passenger tramples into dust, although they would bear the harvest of his happiness. Should I live to accomplish what I purpose, that is, produce a systematical history of what appear to me to be the genuine elements of human society, let not the advocates of injustice and superstition flatter themselves that I should take Aeschylus rather than Plato as my model.

Cf. Byron's Prometheus:

Titan! to whose immortal eyes
  The sufferings of mortality,
  Seen in their sad reality,
Were not as things that gods despise;
What was thy pity's recompense?
A silent suffering, and intense;
The rock, the vulture, and the chain,
All that the proud can feel of pain,
The agony they do not show,
The suffocating sense of woe...

l. 1-10.

Cf. Versification, p. 7, Figurative language, p. 31.

Fuseli's vision of Prometheus (cf. p. 155):

... from A Defence of Poetry *(Shelley wrote this work in 1821, as an answer to T. L. Peacock's* The Four Ages of Poetry. *Peacock was trying to show that as rationality developed – as it did in the 18th and 19th centuries – poetry was bound to degenerate. Shelley shows that, on the contrary, one of the main functions of poetry is to bring about the awakening of a nation):*

The most unfailing herald, companion, and follower of the awakening of a great people to work a beneficial change in opinion or institution, is Poetry. At such periods there is an accumulation of the power of communicating and receiving intense and impassioned conceptions respecting man and nature. The persons in whom this power resides, may often, as far as regards many portions of their nature, have little apparent correspondence with that spirit of good of which they are the ministers. But even whilst they deny and abjure, they are yet compelled to serve, the Power which is seated upon the throne of their own soul. It is impossible to read the compositions of the most celebrated writers of the present day without being startled with the electric life which burns within their words. They measure the circumference and sound the depths of human nature with a comprehensive and all-penetrating spirit, and they are themselves perhaps the most sincerely astonished at its manifestations, for it is less their spirit than the spirit of the age. Poets are the hierophants of an unapprehended inspiration, the mirrors of the gigantic shadows which futurity casts upon the present, the words which express what they understand not; the trumpets which sing to battle, and feel not what they inspire; the influence which is moved not, but moves. Poets are the unacknowledged legislators of the World.

Henry Fuseli: Prometheus Rescued by Heracles, *c. 1810.*

John KEATS 1795-1821

1795 *Born in London.*
1804 *Death of his father. Brought up by his grandmother.*
1810-1811 *Death of his mother. Apprenticed to an apothecary and surgeon.*
1815 *Entered Guy's Hospital to study medicine.*
1816 *Met Leigh Hunt.*
Wrote several poems.
1817 Poems *published. Travelled in England.*
1818 Endymion *published. Death of his brother Tom. Engaged to Fanny Brawne.*
1819 *Wrote most of his greatest poems: "La belle Dame Sans Merci", "Ode to Psyche", "Ode to a Nightingale", "Ode on a Grecian Urn", "Ode on Melancholy", "Ode on Indolence", "Ode to Autumn". Finished* Hyperion. *Met Coleridge. Became ill (tuberculosis).*
1820 *Serious hemorrhages.*
Lamia, Isabella, The Eve of St Agnes and Other Poems *published. Sailed for Italy.*
1821 *Died in Rome.*

John Keats, often considered as the most sensuous of the Romantic poets, thought that poetry "should be great and unobstrusive, a thing which enters into one's soul, and does not startle it or amaze it with itself, but with its subject". Rejecting reason and didacticism, he thought the poet should reach a condition of "Negative Capability", in which his mind, unaffected by ideas or opinions, would be open to sensations, doubts and mysteries. He would then be receptive to imagination, which enhanced and idealized sensations – that of beauty in particular. For Keats was the apostle of beauty. ("A thing of beauty is a joy for ever".). He saw in it the only source of truth and happiness, the only way of reaching joy and brotherhood, of fighting the evils of his time.

This almost pagan love for sensuous beauty (Keats was attracted by Greece and the classical past) appears in all his major poems. The Eve of St Agnes *tells of Madeline's passionate love for Porphyro among a gothic and mysterious background protecting them from the hostile world outside. His* Odes *deal with the relationship between time and beauty, the fear of corruption and destruction. He asserts the timelessness of the song of the nightingale which will be heard generation after generation; he sees the figures on the Grecian urn as eternal forms of beauty; in the* Ode to Melancholy, *it is the awareness of the possible erosion of pleasure which leads to melancholy.*

John William Waterhouse: La Belle Dame Sans Merci, *1893.*
Waterhouse was a Pre-Raphaelite painter in whose pictures "a romantic, dreamy mood prevails". (C. Wood)
Keats inspired many of the Pre-Raphaelite painters:

"The magical, metaphysical meaning which Keats found in the song of the nightingale *(Ode to a Nightingale)* was applied by the aesthetes, from Gautier downwards, to female beauty, ... (...). Keats himself gave a hint of a similar application of it in *La Belle Dame sans merci*, a poem which in the magical, painful mystery it expresses (the subject is obviously that of Tannhäuser) contains in embryo the whole world of the Pre-Raphaelites and the Symbolists, from Swinburne's *Laus Veneris* to certain pictures by Moreau."
M. Praz, *The Romantic Agony.*

Cf. C. V. Stanford's musical setting of "La Belle Dame Sans Merci".
Cf. Verse form and poetic genres, p. 2; Versification, p. 7; Figurative language, p. 31.

La Belle Dame Sans Merci *First Version* (1819)

O what can ail thee Knight-at-arms
Alone and palely loitering?
The sedge has withered from the Lake
And no birds sing!

O what can ail thee, Knight-at-arms!
So haggard and so woe-begone?
The Squirrel's granary is full
And the harvest's done.

I see a lily on thy brow
With anguish moist and fever dew,
And on thy cheeks a fading rose
Fast withereth too –

"I met a Lady in the Meads,
Full beautiful, a faery's child,
Her hair was long, her foot was light,
And her eyes were wild –

I made a Garland for her head,
And bracelets too, and fragrant Zone[1];
She look'd at me as she did love
And made sweet moan –

I set her on my pacing steed
And nothing else saw all day long,
For sidelong would she bend and sing
A faery's song –

She found me roots of relish sweet,
And honey wild and manna dew,
And sure in language strange she said
I love thee true –

She took me to her elfin grot
And there she wept and sigh'd full sore,
And there I shut her wild wild eyes
With kisses four.

And there she lullèd me asleep
And there I dream'd – Ah! woe betide!
The latest dream I ever dreamt
On the cold hill side.

I saw pale Kings, and Princes too,
Pale warriors, death-pale were they all;
They cried – 'La belle Dame sans Merci
Thee hath in thrall!'

I saw their starv'd lips in the gloam
With horrid warning gapèd wide,
And I awoke and found me here
On the cold hill's side.

And this is why I sojourn here
Alone and palely loitering;
Though the sedge is wither'd from the lake
And no birds sing".

1. *zone*: girdle.

Keats on poetry:

Truth, Beauty and imagination

I am certain of nothing but of the holiness of the Heart's affections and the truth of Imagination – What the imagination seizes as Beauty must be truth – whether it existed before or not – for I have the same Idea of all our Passions as of Love they are all in their sublime, creative of essential Beauty – In a Word, you may know my favorite Speculation by my first Book and the little song I sent in my last – which is a representation from the fancy of the probable mode of operating in these Matters – The Imagination may be compared to Adam's dream – he awoke and found it truth. I am the more zealous in this affair, because I have never yet been able to perceive how any thing can be known for truth by consequitive reasoning – and yet it must be – Can it be that even the greatest Philosopher ever arrived at his goal without putting aside numerous objections – However it may be, O for a Life of Sensations rather than of Thoughts! It is 'a Vision in the form of Youth' a Shadow of reality to come – and this consideration has further conv[i]nced me for it has come as auxiliary to another favorite Speculation of mine, that we shall enjoy ourselves here after by having what we called happiness on Earth repeated in a finer tone and so repeated – And yet such a fate can only befall those who delight in sensation rather than hunger as you do after Truth – Adam's dream will do here and seems to be a conviction that Imagination and its empyreal reflection is the same as human Life and its spiritual repetition.

Letter to B. Bailey, Nov. 1817.

Negative Capability

(...) at once it struck me, what quality went to form a Man of Achievement especially in Literature & which Shakespeare posessed so enormously – I mean *Negative Capability*, that is when man is capable of being in uncertainties, Mysteries, doubts, without any irritable reaching after fact & reason – Coleridge, for instance, would let go by a fine isolated verisimilitude caught from the Penetralium of mystery, from being incapable of remaining content with half knowledge. This pursued through Volumes would perhaps take us no further than this, that with a great poet the sense of Beauty overcomes every other consideration, or rather obliterates all consideration.

Letter to G. and T. Keats, Dec. 1817.

Compare the poem with the end of Coleridge's Kubla Khan *(published in 1816):*

Weave a circle round him thrice
And close your eyes with holy dread,
For he on honey-dew hath fed,
And drunk the milk of paradise.

Ann RADCLIFFE 1764-1823

1764 *Born in London.*
1787 *Married. Was to lead a peaceful & uneventful life.*
1789 The Castles of Athlin and Dunbayne.
1790 A Sicilian Romance.
1791 A Romance of the Forest.
1794 The Mysteries of Udolpho.
1797 The Italian, or the Confessional of the Black Penitents.
1823 *Died in London.*

With *A Sicilian Romance* (1790), Ann Radcliffe (1764-1823) launched a succession of novels of more merit and stronger influence than the rest of those produced by the gothic school. She had a genuine feeling for nature, no small skill in creating an extravagant type of character, and more control of the intractable material of horror than any other contemporary writer of such fiction. The Alps fascinated her, as *The Romance of the Forest* (1791) shows, and scenery in its wilder aspects provides an impressive setting for her masterpiece *The Mysteries of Udolpho* (1794), which has the gloomy castle of Udolpho in the Apennines as its chief scene of action, Emily the heroine being held there by the villain Montoni, her aunt's husband. Mrs. Radcliffe's technical superiority lay in her ability to maintain suspense by a procession of scenes, incidents, and descriptions which no doubt carried her early readers thrillingly and tremulously through many hundreds of pages without the wrench of periodic anti-climax, though not without cunningly positioned points of rest for tried nerves.

A. C. Ward. *Illustrated History of English Literature.* Longman Group Ltd.

The Mysteries of Udolpho (1794)

Emily de St Aubert, an orphan, is taken by Madame Cheron, her aunt, to the castle of Udolpho, in the Appenines. There she is held prisoner by Signor Montoni, Madame Cheron's husband and the leader of a band of thieves.

As they passed up, the wind, which poured through the narrow cavities in the wall, made the torch flare, and it threw a stronger gleam upon the grim and sallow countenance of Barnardine, and discovered more fully the desolation of the place – the rough stone walls, the spiral stairs black with age, and a suit of ancient armour, with an iron visor, that hung upon the walls, and appeared a trophy of some former victory.

Having reached a landing-place, "You may wait here, lady", said he, applying a key to the door of a chamber, "while I go up and tell the signora you are coming".

"That ceremony is unnecessary", replied Emily; "my aunt will rejoice to see me".

"I am not sure of that", said Barnardine, pointing to the room he had opened; "come in here, lady, while I step up".

Emily, surprised and somewhat shocked, did not dare to oppose him further; but, as he was turning away with the torch, desired he would not leave her in darkness. He looked around, and, observing a tripod lamp that stood on the stairs, lighted and gave it to Emily, who stepped forward into a large old chamber, and he closed the door. As she listened anxiously to his departing steps, she thought he descended, instead of ascended, the stairs: but the gusts of wind that whistled round the portal would not allow her to hear distinctly any other sound. Still, however, she listened, and perceiving no step in the room above, where he had affirmed Madame Montoni to be, her anxiety increased, though she considered that the thickness of the floor in this strong building might prevent any sound reaching her from the upper chamber. The next moment, in a pause of the wind, she distinguished Barnardine's step descending to the court, and then thought she heard his voice; but the rising gust again overcoming other sounds, Emily, to be certain on this point, moved softly to the door, which, on attempting to open it, she discovered was fastened. All the horrid apprehensions that had lately assailed her, returned at this instant with redoubled force; and no longer appeared like the exaggerations of a timid spirit, but seemed to have been sent to warn her of her fate. She now did not doubt that Madame Montoni had been murdered, perhaps in this very chamber; or that she herself was brought hither for the same purpose. The countenance, the manners, and the recollected words of Barnardine when he had spoken of her aunt, confirmed her worst fears. For some moments she was incapable of considering of any means by which she might attempt an escape. Still she listened, but heard footsteps neither on the stairs nor in the room above; she thought, however, that she again distinguished Barnardine's voice below, and went to a grated window, that opened upon the court, to inquire further. Here she plainly heard his hoarse accents mingling with the blast that swept by, but they were lost again so quickly that their meaning could not be interpreted; and then the light of a torch, which seemed to issue from the portal below, flashed across the court, and the long shadow of a man, who was under the archway, appeared upon the pavement. Emily, from the hugeness of this sudden portrait, concluded it to be that of Barnardine; but other deep tones which passed in the wind soon convinced her he was not alone, and that his companion was not a person very liable to pity.

When her spirits had overcome the first shock of her situation, she held up the lamp to examine if the chamber afforded a possibility of an escape. It was a spacious room, whose walls, wainscoted with rough oak, showed no casement but the grated one which Emily had left, and no other door than that by which she had entered. The feeble rays of the lamp, however, did not allow her to see at once its full extent; she perceived no furniture, except, indeed, an iron chair fastened in the centre of the chamber, immediately over which, depending on a chain from the ceiling, hung an iron ring. Having gazed upon these for some time with wonder and horror, she next observed iron bars below, made for the purpose of confining the feet, and on the arms of the chair were rings of the same metal. As she continued to survey them, she concluded that they were instruments of torture; and it struck her that some poor wretch had once been fastened in this chair, and had there been starved to death. She was chilled by the thought; but what was her agony when, in the next moment, it occurred to her that her aunt might have been one of these victims, and that she herself might be the next! An acute pain seized her head, she was scarcely able to hold the lamp; and, looking round for support, was seating herself, unconsciously, in the iron chair itself: but suddenly perceiving where she was, she started from it in horror, and sprung towards a

remote end of the room. Here again she looked round for a seat to sustain her, and perceived only a dark curtain, which, descending from the ceiling to the floor, was drawn along the whole side of the chamber. Ill as she was, the appearance of this curtain struck her, and she paused to gaze upon it in wonder and apprehension.

It seemed to conceal a recess of the chamber; she wished, yet dreaded, to lift it, and to discover what its veiled; twice she was withheld by a recollection of the terrible spectacle her daring hand had formerly unveiled in an apartment of the castle, till, suddenly conjecturing that it concealed the body of her murdered aunt, she seized it in a fit of desperation, and drew it aside. Beyond appeared a corpse stretched on a kind of low couch, which was crimsoned with human blood, as was the floor beneath. The features, deformed by death, were ghastly and horrible, and more than one livid wound appeared in the face. Emily, bending over the body, gazed, for a moment, with an eager, frenzied eye; but, in the next, the lamp dropped from her hand, and she fell senseless at the foot of the couch.

Part II, Chapter 26.

The Gothic novel...

The commonest of all plots of the eighteenth-century Gothic novel involves a frail protagonist in terrible danger. She (more commonly than he) is placed in a hostile, threatening, mysterious environment, usually so prodigiously large that it dwarfs her; she is made prisoner; she is threatened by individuals who should protect her, parents and parent-figures. It is a nightmare, and perhaps the reason for its potent appeal is that it enables the reader to live vicariously through nightmare. It is not so terrible as it would be if one were asleep. It is not nearly so terrible as it would be in life. Facing up to one's fears is a needful process, and emotionally satisfying. Besides, there is something comforting, again almost magical, in anticipating the worst. It is a common intuition that the known evil never comes. If all eighteenth-century popular fiction – not merely the Gothic – rests ultimately on the simple black-and-white fables common to oral literature in many cultures, it may well be because in these reiterated adventures by surrogate figures there is reassurance and even the illusion of protection.

M. Butler,
Romantics, Rebels and Reactionaries,
Oxford University Press.

For a parody of Gothic novels, see Northanger Abbey, *by Jane Austen (chapter 21 in particular).*

Cf. Novel and prose types, p. 11.

... and its 18th century background. Compare these two opinions about the effect of the terrifying on our passions:

The first step to get this noble and manly steadiness is what I have above mentioned, carefully to keep children from frights of all kinds when they are young. Let not any fearful apprehensions be talked into them, nor terrible objects surprise them. This often so shatters and discomposes the spirits that they never recover it again, but during their whole life, upon the first suggestion or appearance of any terrifying idea, are scattered and confounded; the body is enervated, and the mind disturbed, and the man scarce himself, or capable of any composed or rational action. Whether this be from an habitual motion of the animal spirits, introduced by the first strong impression, or from the alteration of the constitution by some more unaccountable way, this is certain, that so it is. Instances of such who in a weak timorous mind have borne, all their whole lives through, the effects of a fright when they were young, are everywhere to be seen, and therefore as much as may be to be prevented.

John Locke,
Some Thoughts Concerning Education, 1693.

SECT. XXVII. – THE SUBLIME AND BEAUTIFUL COMPARED

On closing this general view of beauty, it naturally occurs, that we should compare it with the sublime; and in this comparison there appears a remarkable contrast. For sublime objects are vast in their dimensions, beautiful ones comparatively small: beauty should be smooth and polished; the great, rugged and negligent; beauty should shun the right line, yet deviate from it insensibly; the great in many cases loves the right line, and when it deviates it often makes a strong deviation: beauty should not be obscure; the great ought to be dark and gloomy; beauty should be light and delicate; the great ought to be solid, and even massive. They are indeed ideas of a very different nature, one being founded on pain, the other on pleasure...

Edmund Burke, *On the Sublime and Beautiful,* 1757.

Piranesi: Carcere d'invenzione, *1745-61.*
Bibliothèque des Arts Décoratifs, Paris. Ph. Giraudon.
Burke's conception of the sublime as excess is reflected in the paintings of the Italian architect and engraver Piranesi (1720-1778). He was very much admired in England, where Horace Walpole praised his views of Rome, which he called "sublime dreams". His most original work is his Carceri d'invenzione *– engravings of imaginary, vast and maze-like prisons.*

Jane AUSTEN 1775-1817

1775 *Born in Hampshire.*
1793-1795 *Wrote parodies and tales.*
1797 *Finished writing* First Impressions, *an early form of* Pride and Prejudice.
1801 *Settled in Bath.*
1803 Susan *(first version of* Northanger Abbey*) accepted by a London publisher, though not published.*
1806 *Moved to Southampton after her father's death, then to Hampshire in 1809.*
1811 *Publication of* Sense and Sensibility *(anonymously, like the rest of her works).*
1813 Pride and Prejudice *published.*
1814 Mansfield Park *published.*
1816 Emma *published.*
1817 *Died in Winchester.*
1818 *Posthumous publication of* Northanger Abbey *and* Persuasion.

The first major woman novelist, Jane Austen did not belong to any of the literary movements of her time: she ridiculed romance and sentimentality in most of her novels and parodied the Gothic fashion in Northanger Abbey. *Her range of vision is limited, for she shows the interaction between human beings in small provincial communities, usually focused around the heroine's finding a husband and her self-discovery in the process. But the form is always perfect, the dialogue witty and the light cast upon the characters is ruthlessly searching. For Jane Austen is a satirist who is interested in manners in so far as they reflect morals.*

One after another she creates her fools, her prigs, her worldlings, her Mr. Collinses, her Sir Walter Elliotts, her Mrs. Bennets. She encircles them with the lash of a whip-like phrase which, as it runs round them, cuts out their silhouettes for ever. But there they remain; no excuse is found for them and no mercy shown them. (...)

Sometimes it seems as if her creatures were born merely to give Jane Austen the supreme delight of slicing their heads off. She is satisfied; she is content; she would not alter a hair on anybody's head, or move one brick or one blade of grass in a world which provides her with such exquisite delight. (...)

The discrimination is so perfect, the satire so just, that, consistent though it is, it almost escapes our notice. No touch of pettiness, no hint of spite, rouse us from our contemplation. Delight strangely mingles with our amusement. Beauty illumines these fools.

V. Woolf, *The Common Reader.*

Pride and Prejudice (1813)

After staying a few days with his cousins – the Bennetts – Mr Collins, a pompous clergyman, decides to ask one of the three daughters, Elizabeth, to marry him.

"May I hope, Madam, for your interest with your fair daughter Elizabeth, when I solicit for the honour of a private audience with her in the course of this morning?"

Before Elizabeth had time for any thing but a blush of surprise, Mrs. Bennet instantly answered,

"Oh dear! – Yes – certainly. – I am sure Lizzy will be very happy – I am sure she can have no objection. – Come, Kitty, I want you up stairs." And gathering her work together, she was hastening away, when Elizabeth called out,

"Dear Ma'am, do not go. – I beg you will not go. – Mr. Collins must excuse me. – He can have nothing to say to me that any body need not hear. I am going away myself."

"No, no, nonsense, Lizzy. – I desire you will stay where you are." – And upon Elisabeth's seeming really, with vexed and embarrassed looks, about to escape, she added, "Lizzy, I *insist* upon your staying and hearing Mr. Collins."

Elizabeth would not oppose such an injunction – and a moment's consideration making her also sensible that it would be wisest to get it over as soon and as quietly as possible, she sat down again, and tried to conceal by incessant employment the feelings which were divided between distress and diversion. Mrs. Bennet and Kitty walked off, and as soon as they were gone Mr. Collins began.

"Believe me, my dear Miss Elizabeth, that your modesty, so far from doing you any disservice, rather adds to your other perfections. You would have been less amiable in my eyes had there *not* been this little unwillingness; but allow me to assure you that I have your respected mother's permission for this address. You can hardly doubt the purport of my discourse, however your natural delicacy may lead you to dissemble; my attentions have been too marked to be mistaken. Almost as soon as I entered the house I singled you out as the companion of my future life. But before I am run away with by my feelings on this subject, perhaps it will be advisable for me to state my reasons for marrying – and moreover for coming into Hertfordshire with the design of selecting a wife, as I certainly did."

The idea of Mr. Collins, with all his solemn composure, being run away with by his feelings, made Elizabeth so near laughing that she could not use the short pause he allowed in any attempt to stop him farther, and he continued:

"My reasons for marrying are, first, that I think it a right thing for every clergyman in easy circumstances (like myself) to set the example of matrimony in his parish. Secondly, that I am convinced it will add very greatly to my happiness; and thirdly – which perhaps I ought to have mentioned earlier, that it is the particular advice and recommendation of the very noble lady whom I have the honour of calling patroness. Twice has she condescended to give me her opinion (unasked too!) on this subject; and it was but the very Saturday night before I left Hunsford – between our pools at quadrille, while Mrs. Jenkinson was arranging Miss de Bourgh's foot-stool, that she said, "Mr. Collins, you must marry. A clergyman like you must marry. – Chuse properly, chuse a gentlewoman for *my* sake; and for your *own*, let her be an active, useful sort of person, not brought up high, but able to make a small income go a good way. This is my advice. Find such a woman as soon as you can, bring her to Hunsford, and I will visit her." Allow me, by the way, to observe, my fair cousin, that I do not reckon the notice and kindness of Lady Catherine de Bourgh as among the least of the advantages in my power to offer. You will find her manners beyond any thing I can describe;

Compare the following critical judgements on Walter Scott:

- Who shall tell us a story?
Sir Walter Scott of course.
Scott is a novelist over whom we shall violently divide. For my own part I do not care for him, and find it difficult to understand his continued reputation. His reputation in his day – that is easy to understand. There are important historical reasons for it, which we should discuss if our scheme was chronological. But when we fish him out of the river of time and set him to write in that circular room with the other novelists, he presents a less impressive figure. He is seen to have a trivial mind and a heavy style. He cannot construct. He has neither artistic detachment nor passion, and how can a writer who is devoid of both, create characters who will move us deeply? Artistic detachment – perhaps it is priggish to ask for that. But passion – surely passion is lowbrow enough, and think how all Scott's laborious mountains and scooped out glens and carefully ruined abbeys call out for passion, passion, and how it is never there! If he had passion he would be a great writer – no amount of clumsiness or artificiality would matter then. But he only has a temperate heart and gentlemanly feelings, and an intelligent affection for the countryside: and this is not basis enough for great novels. And his integrity – that is worse than nothing, for it was a purely moral and commercial integrity. It satisfied his highest needs and he never dreamt that another sort of loyalty exists.

E.M. Forster, *Aspects of the Novel.*

- The "hero" of a Scott novel is always a more or less mediocre, average English gentleman. He generally possesses a certain, though never outstanding, degree of practical intelligence, a certain moral fortitude and decency which even rises to a capacity for self-sacrifice, but which never grows into a sweeping human passion, is never the enraptured devotion to a great cause. Not only are the Waverleys, Mortons, Osbaldistons and so on correct, decent, average representatives of the English petty aristocracy of this kind, but so, too, is Ivanhoe, the "romantic" knight of the Middle Ages.
In later criticism this choice of hero was sharply criticized, for example by Taine. Such later critics saw here a symptom of Scott's own mediocrity as an artist. Precisely the opposite is true. That he builds his novels round a "middling", merely correct and never heroic "hero" is the clearest proof of Scott's exceptional and revolutionary epic gifts, although from a psychological-biographical point of view, no doubt his own personal, petty aristocratic-conservative prejudices did play an important part in the choice of these heroes.
What is expressed here, above all, is a renunciation of Romanticism, a conquest of Romanticism, a higher development of the realist literary traditions of the Enlightenment in keeping with the new times. As a form of opposition to the degrading, all-levelling prose of rising capitalism the "demonic hero" makes his appearance even in the writings of politically and ideologically progressive writers who frequently, though unjustly, have been treated as Romantics. This hero type, particularly as he appears in the poetry of Byron, is the literary expression of the social eccentricity and superfluity of the best and sincerest human talents in this period of prose, a lyrical protest against the dominion of this prose. But it is one thing to acknowledge the social roots or even the historical necessity and justification of this protest and another to make of it a lyrical-subjectivist absolute. On this latter basis an objective portrayal is impossible. The great realistic writers of a somewhat later period who portrayed this type, such as Pushkin or Stendhal, overcame Byronism differently from Scott and in a higher form. They interpreted the problem of the eccentricity of this type in a social-historical, objective-epic way: that is, they saw the present historically and revealed all the social determinants of the tragedy (or tragicomedy) of this protest. Scott's criticism and rejection of this type does not go as deep as this. His recognition or rather sense of the eccentricity of this type has the result of eliminating him from the sphere of historical portrayal. Scott endeavours to portray the struggles and antagonisms of history by means of characters who, in their psychology and destiny, always represent social trends and historical forces. Scott also extends this approach to the processes of declassing, always regarding them socially and not individually. His understanding for the problems of the present is not sufficiently deep for him to portray the problem of declassing as it affects the present. Therefore he avoids this subject and preserves in his portrayals the great historical objectivity of the true epic writer.
For this reason alone, then, it is completely wrong to see Scott as a Romantic writer, unless one wishes to extend the concept of Romanticism to embrace all great literature in the first third of the nineteenth century.

G. Lukacs, *The Historical Novel.*

- Scott presents great crises of historical life in his novels. Accordingly, hostile social forces, bent on one another's destruction, are everywhere colliding. Since those who lead these warring forces are always passionate partisans of their respective sides, there is the danger that their struggle will become a merely external picture of mutual destruction incapable of arousing the human sympathies and enthusiasms of the reader. It is here that the compositional importance of the mediocre hero comes in. Scott always chooses as his principal figures such as may, through character and fortune, enter into human contact with both camps. The appropriate fortunes of such a mediocre hero, who sides passionately with neither of the warring camps in the great crisis of his time can provide a link of this kind without forcing the composition. Let us take the best known example. Waverley is an English country squire from a family which is pro-Stuart, but which does no more than quietly sympathize in a politically ineffective fashion. During his stay in Scotland as an English officer, Waverley, as a result of personal friendships and love entanglements, enters the camp of the rebellious Stuart supporters. As a result of his old family connections and the uncertain nature of his participation in the uprising, which allows him to fight bravely, but never to become fanatically partisan, his relations with the Hanoverian side are sustained. In this way Waverley's fortunes create a plot which not only gives us a pragmatic picture of the struggle on both sides, but brings us humanly close to the important representatives of either side.

This manner of composition is not the product of a "search for form" or some ingeniously contrived "skill", it stems rather from the strengths and limitations of Scott's literary personality. In the first place Scott's conception of English history is, as we have seen, that of a "middle course" asserting itself through the struggle of extremes. The central figures of the Waverley type represent for Scott the age-old steadfastness of English development amidst the most terrible crises. In the second place, however, Scott, the great realist, recognizes that no civil war in history has been so violent as to turn the entire population without exception into fanatical partisans of one or other of the contending camps. Large sections of people have always stood between the camps with fluctuating sympathies now for this side, now for the other. And these fluctuating sympathies have often played a decisive role in the actual outcome of the crisis. In addition, the daily life of the nation still goes on amidst the most terrible civil war. The "middle-of-the-road heroes" of Scott also represent this side of popular life and historical development.

G. Lukacs, *ibid.*

Cf. Characters and characterization, p. 12.

Victorian painting also reflects the passion of the Victorians for history:
In the Royal Academy of 1878 William Frederick Yeames exhibited what was destined to become one of the most famous of all Victorian evocations of the British past, *And When Did You Last See Your Father?* So celebrated did this picture become that it was translated into a wax tableau in Madame Tussaud's, where it stands to this day. Yeames's achievement lay in crystallizing for all time in one potent image the whole saga of romantic, doomed Cavaliers and stern, relentless Puritans, a subject which occupied a central position amongst the themes and obsessions of the Victorian literary and artistic mind. The child, a figure clearly derived from Gainsborough's Blue Boy, stands on a footstool about to answer an inquiry made by the Puritan who leans across the table towards him. The latter is wanting to discover the whereabouts of the boy's father.

Roy Strong, *The Victorian Painter and British History,*
Thames and Hudson, © 1978 R. Strong.

William Frederick Yeames: And When Did You Last See Your Father? *1878.*
Merseyside Art Galleries, Liverpool. Ph. J. Mills.

Caspard David Friedrich: Tree with Ravens, *1822.*
Paris, Louvre. Ph. Lauros-Giraudon.

One of the best-known representatives of German romanticism, Caspar David Friedrich (1774-1840) was particularly interested in rendering the drama and power in nature.

his meditations. With time and labour, the crag took human shape; and there it stands colossal, dark and frowning, half statue, half rock: in the former sense, terrible and goblin-like; in the latter, almost beautiful, for its colouring is of mellow grey, and moorland moss clothes it; and heath, with its blooming bells and balmy fragrance, grows faithfully close to the giant's foot.

Currer Bell,
Editor's Preface, *Wuthering Heights*, 1850 edition.

Wuthering Heights *and German romanticism :*

Wuthering Heights, then, is the product of romantic imagination, working probably under influences from German literature, and marvellously fused with local knowledge and a realistic power which, within its own range, has seldom been surpassed. Its few great faults are soon enumerated. The tendency to extravagance and monstrosity may, as we have seen, be taken to some extent as belonging more to a literary fashion than to the artist. Tieck and Hoffmann are full of raving and lunatic beings who sob, shout, tear out their hair by the roots, and live in a perpetual state of personal violence both towards themselves and their neighbours. Emily Brontë probably received from them an additional impulse towards a certain wildness of manner and conception which was already natural to her Irish blood, to a woman brought up amid the solitudes of the moors and the ruggedness of Yorkshire life fifty years ago, and natural also, alas! to the sister of the opium-eater and drunkard, Branwell Brontë. (...)

Yet, at the same time, *Wuthering Heights* is a book of the later Romantic movement, betraying the influences of German Romantic imagination, as Charlotte's work betrays the influences of Victor Hugo and George Sand. The Romantic tendency to invent and delight in monsters, the *exaltation du moi* which has been said to be the secret of the whole Romantic revolt against classical models and restraints; the love of violence in speech and action, the preference for the hideous in character and the abnormal in situation – of all these there are abundant examples in *Wuthering Heights*.

Mrs. Humpry Ward.

On the function of Nelly in the novel:

Essentially, *Wuthering Heights* exists for the mind as a tension between two kinds of reality: the raw, inhuman reality of anonymous natural energies, and the restrictive reality of civilized habits, manners and codes. The first kind of reality is given to the imagination in the violent figures of Catherine and Heathcliff, portions of the flux of nature, children of rock and heath and tempest, striving to identify themselves as human, but disrupting all around them with their monstrous appetite for an inhuman kind of intercourse, and finally disintegrated from within by the very energies out of which they are made (...)

Set over against the wilderness of inhuman reality is the quietly secular, voluntarily limited, safely human reality that we find in the gossipy concourse of Nelly Dean and Lockwood, the one an old family servant with a strong grip on the necessary emotional economies that make life endurable, the other a city visitor in the country, a man whose very disinterestedness and facility of feeling and attention indicate the manifold emotional economies by which city people particularly protect themselves from any disturbing note of the ironic discord between civilized life and the insentient wild flux of nature in which it is islanded (...)

The inhuman excess of Heathcliff's and Catherine's passion, an excess that is carried over into the second half of the book by Heathcliff's revenge, an excess everywhere present in language – in verbs and modifiers and metaphors that seethe with a brute fury – this excess is held within a most rigorous pattern of repeated motifs and of what someone has called the "chinese box" of Nelly Dean's and Lockwood's interlocution. The form of the book, then – a form that may be expressed as a tension between the impulse to excess and the impulse to limitation or economy – *is* the content. The form, in short, is the book itself. Only in the fully wrought, fully realized, work of art does form so exhaust the possibilities of the material that it identifies itself with these possibilities...

If the story of Catherine and Heathcliff had not been a story told by an old woman as something that had had its inception many years ago, if the old woman who tells the story had not been limited in imagination and provincial in her sympathies, if the story had been dramatized immediately in the here-and-now and not at a temporal remove and through a dispassioned intermediator, it is doubtful that it would resonate emotionally for us or carry any conviction – even any "meaning". Because of the very fact that the impulses it represents are taboo, they can conveniently be observed only at a remove, as someone else's, as of the past, and from the judicial point of view of conventional manners. The "someone else's" and the "long ago" are the mind's saving convention for making a distance with itself such as will allow it perspective. Thus the technical *displacement* of Heathcliff's and Catherine's story into past time and into the memory of an old woman functions in the same way as dream displacements: it both censors and indulges, protects and liberates.

D. Van Ghent
The English Novel, Form and Function.
By permission of Holt, Rinehart and Winston, CBS College Publishing.

Cf. Narrative technique, p. 15.

---

6. The Victorian Age

literature and society

Thackeray was born in 1811, Dickens in 1812, Trollope in 1815, Charlotte Brontë in 1816, Emily Brontë in 1818, George Eliot in 1819. Mrs Gaskell had been born in 1810, and lesser novelists born in the Regency period include Charles Reade (1814) and Charles Kingsley (1819). Together, they are the names that first come to mind when we think of the Victorian novelists. They do not form a coherent body; and Emily Brontë will prove an exception to all generalizations we care to make about the rest of them. Yet if we set them beside the chief novelists born in the generation after the Regency, Samuel Butler (1835), George Meredith (1828), Thomas Hardy (1840), we shall see that they have much more in common with one another than they have with the younger man. What they have in common is a special climate of ideas and feelings, a set of fundamental assumptions. It was this special climate, these assumptions, that the later novelists of the century were to question, even though the great mass of the reading public still took them for granted.

And this points to another main difference between the novelists of the first half of the Victorian age and those of the second half. The former were at one with their public to a quite remarkable degree; they were conditioned by it, as of course any novelist must be, but for the most part were willingly conditioned by it. They identified themselves with their age and were its spokesmen. The later novelists, however, were writing in some sense against their age; they were critical, even hostile, to its dominant assumptions. Their relation to the reading public was nearer to that of the twentieth-century novelist than to the early Victorians. (...)

(The early Victorian novelists) accepted the society in which they lived without question; or rather, when they criticized it, they criticized it as many of their readers were doing. They voiced their doubts and fears; the assumptions of their age they fully shared. When the reaction against the age set in, among intellectuals in the nineties, among the general public in the first twenty years of the present century, the Victorians were commonly charged with smugness, complacency, hypocrisy, and foolish optimism. It is now possible for us to see the Victorians more justly. They were as conscious as we are, looking back, of the tensions and contradictions of their times, the havoc caused by the industrial revolution, the presence of mass poverty, the existence side by side of what Disraeli called the two nations; and in the forties they feared revolution. The forces set in motion by the industrial revolution they did not know how to control, and the working of what seemed the iron laws of economics outraged the consciences of the best and most intelligent of the time. They were, then, thoroughly aware of the evils of their age; yet they could hardly not believe that these evils, awkward though they were to surmount, would prove to be merely temporary; for on all sides was the plainest possible evidence of enormous increase in material wealth and the physical amenities of civilization. There seemed no good reason why this progress should not continue indefinitely. There were, of course, dissident

	Politics and Society	Literature and the Arts
1837	Accession of Queen Victoria.	CARLYLE: *The French Revolution.* DICKENS: *The Pickwick Papers.*
1838	Birth of the Chartist movement.	DICKENS: *Oliver Twist.*
1839	Chartist riots in Birmingham & Sheffield.	
1841		NEWMAN: *Tract 90.*
1846	Abolition of the Corn laws.	RUSKIN: *Modern Painters.*
1847		C. BRONTË: *Jane Eyre.* E. BRONTË: *Wuthering Heights.* THACKERAY: *Vanity Fair.*
1848	End of the Chartist Movement.	
1849		MACAULAY: *History of England* (1849-61).
1850		TENNYSON: *In Memoriam.* WORDSWORTH: *The Prelude* (pub. posth.). DICKENS: *David Copperfield.*
1851	The Great Exhibition in London.	

	Politics and Society	Literature and the Arts
1847-50-53	Factory Acts : regulation of the hours of work (60-hour week for women & children).	
1854-6	Crimean War.	
1855		BROWNING: *Men & Women.*
1857	Indian Mutiny.	
1859		DARWIN: *The Origin of Species.* G. ELIOT: *Adam Bede.* G. MEREDITH: *The Ordeal of Richard Feverel.*
1860		G. ELIOT: *The Mill on the Floss.*
1861		DICKENS: *Great Expectations.* J.S. MILL: *Utilitarianism.*
1865		M. ARNOLD: *Essays in Criticism.* L. CARROLL: *Alice's Adventures in Wonderland.*
1866		SWINBURNE: *Poems and Ballads.*
1867	Second Reform Act further extending franchise. Canada becomes a Dominion.	A. TROLLOPE: *The Last Chronicle of Barset.*
1868		R. BROWNING: *The Ring and the Book.*
1870	Forster's Education Act (Elementary schools free & compulsory).	
1871	Trade Unions Act (granting legal status to trade unions).	
1872	Secret ballot for Parliamentary elections.	S. BUTLER: *Erewhon.* G. ELIOT: *Middlemarch.* L. CARROLL: *Through the Looking-Glass.*
1874		HARDY: *Far from the Madding Crowd.*
1875	Public Health Act.	
1876	Queen Victoria Empress of India.	
1879		G. MEREDITH: *The Egoist.*
1881		H. JAMES: *Portrait of a Lady.* *Washington Square.*
1884	Third Reform Act (enfranchising agricultural labourers).	
1886		R.L. STEVENSON: *Kidnapped ;* *Dr Jekyll and Mr Hyde.*
1887	Queen Victoria's Golden Jubilee.	
1889	Dockers'strike.	
1891	Foundation of the Labour Party.	HARDY: *Tess of the d'Urbervilles.* O. WILDE: *The Picture of Dorian Gray.* W. MORRIS: *News from Nowhere.*
1893	Irish Home Rule rejected by Parliament.	
1895		HARDY: *Jude the Obscure.* WELLS: *The Time Machine.*
1898		O. WILDE: *The Ballad of Reading Gaol.* G.B. SHAW: *Plays Pleasant & Unpleasant.*
1899	Beginning of the Boer War.	O. WILDE: *The Importance of Being Earnest.*
1900	Australian Commonwealth.	CONRAD: *Lord Jim.*
1901	Death of Queen Victoria.	KIPLING: *Kim.*

voices: Carlyle, Ruskin, Newman, and, later, Matthew Arnold. But broadly, the early Victorians accepted the idea of progress without much question. The age represented the triumph of protestantism, and perhaps its great achievement was the universal acceptance of the idea of respectability. It *was* a great achievement, no matter how dingy may be our present associations with the word-lace curtains, aspidistras, and a prudential self-regarding morality summed up in such sayings as "Honesty is the best policy" and "Nothing for nothing, and remarkably little for sixpence". (...)

What we often think of as typically Victorian, especially in its attitude towards sex, had become dominant years before the Queen came to the throne. The taboo on the frank recognition and expression of sex had come into existence slowly and, as it were, almost unawares. It was in 1818 that Thomas Bowdler published his *Family Shakespeare*, in which, as he stated, "nothing is added to the original text, but those words and expressions are omitted which cannot with propriety be read aloud in a family".

One symbol of this aspect of Victorian respectability was the banishment of Fielding. He was read, and much admired; but he was no longer public reading. *Tom Jones* was kept on the top shelf of the study, or relegated to the billiard-room or the smoking-room out of the way of women and children. Thackeray wistfully said that Fielding was the last writer to be "permitted to depict to his utmost power a man", and the taboo on sex represented the triumph of woman. (...)

From one point of view, the notion of respectability may be regarded as the apotheosis of wishful thinking; from another and more rewarding, as a violent and heroic attempt to correct vices and weaknesses of the age. One may ask why the triumph of the Evangelical Movement, with its emphasis on the responsibility of the individual human being, should have been delayed until Victoria came to the throne and should then have been so sudden and apparently irresistible. One reason was the rapid progress of the industrial revolution, with its wholesale shifting of population and its enormous speeding up of communications. In a sense, the industrial revolution changed nothing; but it did bring to public attention, in the most startling way, evils that had always existed. There had always been overcrowding, there had always been drunkenness, there had always been sweatshops in cellars, and exploitation of children in industry. But now they existed on so colossal a scale that awareness of them had become unavoidable, and the viciousness and misery they bred were such as no man of goodwill could contemplate without horror. It is significant that industrial reform and legislation to curb the worst excesses of the factory system were often first promoted by mill-owners themselves, who had not made the industrial system so much as inherited it. It had grown up piecemeal and at haphazard, and out of the public view. Its consequences, as soon as seen, were plain to all, though how they might be amended was another matter.

W. Allen, *The English Novel.*

The Queen is most anxious to enlist every one who can speak or write to join in checking this mad, wicked folly of "Woman's Rights", with all its attendant horrors, on which her poor feeble sex is bent, forgetting every sense of womanly feeling and propriety. God created men and women different - then let them remain each in their own position.

Queen Victoria,
Letter to Sir Theodore Martin, 1870.

a Victorian philosopher: T. Carlyle

During the second half of the 19th century a reaction set in against the principle of laissez-faire and the utilitarianism of Jeremy BENTHAM *and* James MILL.

Thomas CARLYLE *(1795-1881) led this new spirit of reform, this desire for individual fulfilment and liberation.*
1836: Sartor Resartus
1837: The French Revolution
1841: Heroes and Hero-Worship
1843: Past and Present

He sees, with a terrible clarity, the spiritual emptiness of the characteristic social relationships of his day, "with Cash Payment as the sole nexus" between man and man "and there are so many things which cash will not pay". The perception disqualifies him, wholly, from acquiescence in this construction of relationships; and he is therefore, without argument, a radical and a reformer. In this, however, he is isolated, feels himself isolated: the existing framework of relationships, the existing society, is against him, necessarily, because he is against it. He feels himself, in this situation, cut off from all fruitful social relationships, he has, in Burke's words, but by a force of circumstance which Burke overlooked, "nothing of politics but the passions they excite". What he lacks, or feels himself to lack, is power; and yet he is conscious of power;

conscious, too, of the superiority of his insight (which is not to be reduced to a merely personal conceit) into the real problems of the day. Under this tension – the conclusion is not necessary, but it has been reached again and again – he construes the generally desirable as what he personally desires; he creates the image of the hero, "the strong man who stands alone", the leader, the leader possessed by vision, who shall be listened to, revered, obeyed.

R. Williams, *Culture and Society*, *Chatto & Windus.*

Compare this excerpt from Past and Present *with Dickens's view of society in* Hard Times *(see p. 213) :*

Industrial work, still under bondage to Mammon, the rational soul of it not yet awakened, is a tragic spectacle. Men in the rapidest motion and self-motion; restless, with convulsive energy, as if driven by Galvanism, as if possessed by a Devil; tearing asunder mountains, – to no purpose, for Mammonism is always Midas-eared! This is sad, on the face of it. Yet courage: the beneficent Destinies, kind in their sternness, are apprising us that this cannot continue. Labour is not a devil, even while encased in Mammonism; Labour is ever an imprisoned god, writhing unconsciously or consciously to escape out of Mammonism! (...) Show me a People energetically busy; heaving, struggling, all shoulders at the wheel; their heart pulsing, every muscle swelling, with man's energy and will; – I show you a People of whom great good is already predicable; to whom all manner of good is yet certain, if their energy endure. By very working, they will learn; they have, Antæus-like, their foot on Mother Fact: how can they but learn? (...) And yet I will venture to believe that in no time, since the beginnings of Society, was the lot of those same dumb millions of toilers so entirely unbearable as it is even in the days now passing over us. It is not to die, or even to die of hunger, that makes a man wretched; many men have died; all men must die, – the last exit of us all is in a Fire-Chariot of Pain. But it is to live miserable we know not why; to work sore and yet gain nothing; to be heart-worn, weary, yet isolated, unrelated, girt-in with a cold universal Laissez-faire: it is to die slowly all our life long, imprisoned in a deaf, dead, Infinite Injustice, as in the accursed iron belly of a Phalaris' Bull! This is and remains forever intolerable to all men whom God has made. Do we wonder at French Revolutions, Chartisms, Revolts of Three Days? The times, if we will consider them, are really unexampled. (...)

Liberty? The true liberty of a man, you would say, consisted in his finding out, or being forced to find out the right path, and to walk thereon. To learn, or to be taught, what work he actually was able for; and then by permission, persuasion, and even compulsion, to set about doing of the same! That is his true blessedness, honour, "liberty"and maximum of wellbeing: if liberty be not that, I for one have small care about liberty. You do not allow a palpable madman to leap over precipices; you violate his liberty, you that are wise; and keep him, were it in strait-waistcoats, away from the precipices! Every stupid, every cowardly and foolish man is but a less palpable madman: his true liberty were that a wiser man, that any and every wiser man, could, by brass collars, or in whatever milder or sharper way, lay hold of him when he was going wrong, and order and compel him to go a little righter. O, if thou really art my *Senior,* Seigneur, my *Elder,* Presbyter or Priest, – if thou art in very deed my *Wiser,* may a beneficent instinct lead and impel thee to "conquer" me, to command me! If thou do know better than I what is good and right, I conjure thee in the name of God, force me to do it; were it by never such brass collars, whips and handcuffs, leave me not to walk over precipices!

T. Carlyle, *Past and Present.*

literature and the arts

Painting

The nineteenth century saw the flowering of sentimental "genre" painting (i.e. the portrayal of scenes from everyday life) depicting the themes that were dearest to the Victorians: nature, children and animals as well as numerous family scenes. Many pictures also reflected their interest in history (cf p. 194).

Besides this popular trend the Victorian age was dominated by

- W.M. TURNER *(cf p. 157) who painted until 1851,*
- *The* PRE-RAPHAELITES *in the second half of the nineteenth century:*

Inspired like the Chartists by the spirit of revolt, the Pre-Raphaelite Brotherhood was a militant group, the first organized revolt against the Royal Academy, the objects of its attack being on the one hand the dark and pretentious history picture and on the other trivial anecdotes, and in particular what the Brotherhood termed the "monkeyana"of Landseer. The remedy and the ideal was seen in a double aspect; as the "truth to nature", expounded in *Modern Painters* by Ruskin and as a return to the purity of art before the High Renaissance period, along the lines suggested by the earlier 'Pre-Raphaelite' movement of the German "Nazarenes". There were many possibilities of complication in this duality which were to appear the more complex because of the very different temperaments of the leaders of the movement, Dante Gabriel ROSSETTI (1828-82), William Holman HUNT (1827-1910), and John Everett MILLAIS (1829-96). "Truth to nature", a conception which Constable (much more specifically than Turner) had applied to landscape painting, suggested such realism as might be gained in painting from nature, that is, in the open air, and indeed for a while this was a Pre-Raphaelite practice, showing in theory a certain correspondence with the aims of Realism and later of Impressionism in France. Yet whereas French painters were mainly concerned with the general truth of light and atmospheric effect, the Pre-Raphaelites looked for it in minuteness and precision of detail. They differed also in devoting themselves to figure subjects in the main, with an ethical and narrative content. A further difference was the tendency encouraged by Rossetti in particular to look back sentimentally and nostalgically to the past, which took on a dream-like attraction.

William Gaunt, *ibid.*

Life imitates art far more than Art imitates life. We have all seen in our own day in England how a certain curious and fascinating type of beauty, invented and emphasised by two imaginative painters, has so influenced Life that whenever one goes to a private view or to an artistic salon one sees, here the mystic eyes of Rossetti's dream, the long ivory throat, the strange square-cut jaw, the loosened shadowy hair that he so ardently loved, there the sweet maidenhood of "The Golden Stair", the blossom-like mouth and weary loveliness of the "Laus Amoris", the passion-pale face of Andromeda, the thin hands and lithe beauty of the Vivian in "Merlin's Dream".

O. Wilde, *The Decay of Lying.*

John Ruskin on: "Millais and Turner".

Suppose, for instance, two men, equally honest, equally industrious, equally impressed with a humble desire to render some part of what they saw in nature faithfully; and, otherwise, trained in convictions such as I have above endeavoured to induce. But one of them is quiet in temperament, has a feeble memory, no invention and excessively keen sight. The other is impatient in temperament, has a memory which nothing escapes, an invention which never rests, and is comparatively near-sighted.

Set them both free in the same field in a mountain valley. One sees everything, small and large, with almost the same clearness; mountains and grasshoppers alike; the leaves on the branches, the veins in the pebbles, the bubbles in the stream; but he can remember nothing and invent nothing. Patiently he sets himself to his mighty task; abandoning at once all thoughts of seizing transient effects, or giving general impressions of that which his eyes present to him in microscopical dissection, he chooses some small portion out of the infinite scene, and calculates with courage the number of weeks which must elapse before he can do justice to the intensity of his perceptions, or the fulness of matter in his subject.

Meantime, the other has been watching the change of the clouds, and the march of the light along the mountain sides; he beholds the entire scene in broad, soft masses of true gradation, and the very feebleness of his sight is in some sort an advantage to him, in making him more sensible of the aerial mystery of distance, and hiding from him the multitudes of circumstances which it would have been impossible for him to represent. But there is not one change in the casting of the jagged shadows along the hollows of the hills, but it is fixed on his mind for ever; not a flake of spray has broken from the sea of cloud about their bases, but he has watched it as it melts away, and could recall it to its lost place in heaven by the slightest effort of his thoughts. Not only so, but thousands and thousands of such images, of older scenes, remain congregated in his mind, each mingling in new associations with those now visibly passing before him, and these again confused with other images of his own ceaseless, sleepless imagination, flashing by in sudden troops. Fancy how his paper will be covered with stray symbols and blots, and undecipherable shorthand: – as for his sitting down to "draw from Nature", there was not one of the things which he wished to represent, that stayed for so much as five seconds together: but none of them escaped for all that: they are sealed up in that strange storehouse of his; he may take one of them out perhaps, this day twenty years, and paint it in his dark room, far away. Now observe, you may tell both of these men, when they are young, that they are to be honest, that they have an important function, and that they are not to care what Raphael did. This you may wholesomely impress on them both. But fancy the exquisite absurdity of expecting either of them to possess any of the qualities of the other.

I have supposed the feebleness of sight in the last, and of invention in the first painter, that the contrast between them might be more striking; but, with very slight modification, both the characters are real. Grant to the first considerable inventive power, with exquisite sense of colour; and give to the second, in addition to all his other faculties, the eye of an eagle; and the first is John Everett Millais, the second Joseph Mallord William Turner.

Pre-Raphaelitism, 1851.

Turner: Slavers Throwing Overboard the Dead and Dying: Typhoon Coming on, *1839. Museum of Fine Arts,* Boston.
Sir J. E. Millais: Ophelia, *1852. Tate Gallery, London. Photo Edimedia, coll. Snark.*

Architecture

Despite continued demolition of nineteenth-century work, we still possess a great deal because so much was built. Indeed, more buildings were constructed in the nineteenth century than in all the previous ages added together; this is one of the reasons for the low standard of much of the work. It was in the years 1830-1900 that the effects of the Industrial Revolution snowballed; the movement of peoples from country to town accelerated and the higher birth-rate and better medical care raised the total number of people to an undreamt of level. To provide houses, factories, schools, colleges and civic buildings for this increased population a tremendous building drive was necessary.

Two major results of this – problems which still trouble us today – were the mass-production development of the building industry and speculative expansion. (...)

In style the Victorian age was one in which previous designs were revived. There was not a single earlier style which architects did not emulate and adapt to their use. The two fundamental types of building – classical and Gothic – were used in all their forms. Classical architecture was designed in Greek, Roman, Italian and French-Renaissance clothing, while Gothic appeared in all its guises from Romanesque and Lancet to Perpendicular and Tudor. Many architects designed in both classical and Gothic form, suiting the style to the building. Although there was no rule, classical forms were preferred for civic and public building – government offices, town halls, university colleges – and Gothic for ecclesiastical and domestic work. This was particularly so before 1855-60, after which time the Gothic Revival became stronger than the classical faction and Gothic town halls, station façades and academic buildings appeared all over the country.

D. Yarwood, *The Architecture of Britain,* Batsford Ltd.

Sir George Gilbert Scott:
St Pancras Station Midland Hotel, *1865-75.*
In D. Yarwood, An Outline of English Architecture, *Batsford Ltd.*

Robert BROWNING 1812-1889

1812 *Born in Camberwell, London.*
1828-1829 *Studied at London University.*
1833 *Anonymous publication of* Pauline.
1834 *Travelled to Russia.*
1835 *Publication of* Paracelsus.
1837 *Production of* Strafford: An Historical Tragedy.
1840 Sordello *published.*
1841-1842 Dramatic Lyrics.
1845 *Met Elizabeth Barrett;* Dramatic Romances and Lyrics *published.*
1846 *Eloped with Elisabeth Barrett and settled in Italy (until 1861).*
1855 Men and Women *published.*
1861 *Death of Elizabeth Barrett. Returned to London.*
1864 Dramatis Personae *published.*
1868-1869 The Ring and the Book *published.*
1876 Pacchiarotto *published.*
1879 Dramatic Idylls *published.*
1881 *Foundation of the English Browning Society.*
1889 *Died in Venice; buried in Westminster Abbey.*
1890 Asolando: Fancies and Facts *appeared posthumously.*

Robert Browning's chief literary inspiration was the poetry of Shelley which deeply influenced his first poems. But his admiration for the "subjective poet" soon gave way to a desire for greater objectivity which led him to his "dramatic monologues".

Browning insisted that in these monologues, it was not his voice but that of imaginary characters that could be heard. "What I have printed gives no *knowledge of me" he wrote to Elizabeth Barrett, and again: "I only make men and women speak, give you truth broken into prismatic hues". Behind the diversity of all the characters who reveal themselves to us (e.g. a Spanish monk, a Renaissance bishop, an imaginary Greek poet, an Arab doctor) some kinship can be felt. Most of them are frustrated beings, full of contradictions, intent on some personal quest, but rarely reaching fulfilment. They all see life as a pilgrimage or a quest, so that we feel a continuity between all the voices. In the monologues, the speakers comment and reflect upon their own actions with sinuous digressions and complex reasonings which befit the creations of this "poet of half-lights, of ambiguous situations, of spiritual failure". (L.G. Salingar). Browning's most ambitious work,* The Ring and the Book *is made up of twelve monologues representing different opinions in a Roman murder trial, thus anticipating James's technique of multiplicity of points of view.*

My Last Duchess (1842)

FERRARA[1]

That's my last Duchess painted on the wall,
Looking as if she were alive. I call
That piece a wonder, now: Fra Pandolf's[2] hands
Worked busily a day, and there she stands.
Will't please you sit and look at her? I said
"Fra Pandolf" by design, for never read
Strangers like you that pictured countenance,
The depth and passion of its earnest glance,
But to myself they turned (since none puts by
The curtain I have drawn for you, but I)
And seemed as they would ask me, if they durst,
How such a glance came there; so, not the first,
Are you to turn and ask thus, Sir, 'twas not
Her husband's presence only, called that spot
Of joy into the Duchess' cheek: perhaps
Fra Pandolf chanced to say "Her mantle laps
Over my lady's wrist too much", or "Paint
Must never hope to reproduce the faint
Half-flush that dies along her throat", such stuff
Was courtesy, she thought, and cause enough

For calling up that spot of joy. She had
A heart – how shall I say? – too soon made glad,
Too easily impressed; she liked whate'er
She looked on, and her looks went everywhere.
Sir, 'twas all one! My favour at her breast,
The dropping of the daylight in the West,
The bough of cherries some officious fool
Broke in the orchard for her, the white mule
She rode with round the terrace – all and each
Would draw from her alike the approving speech,
Or blush, at least. She thanked men, – good! but thanked
Somehow – I know not how – as if she ranked
My gift of a nine-hundred-years-old name
With anybody's gift. Who'd stoop to blame
This sort of trifling? Even had you skill
In speech – (which I have not) – to make your will
Quite clear to such an one, and say, "Just this
Or that in you disgusts me; here you miss,
Or there exceed the mark" – and if she let
Herself be lessoned so, nor plainly set
Her wits to yours, forsooth, and made excuse,
– E'en then would be some stooping: and I choose
Never to stoop. Oh sir, she smiled, no doubt,
Whene'er I passed her; but who passed without
Much the same smile? This grew; I gave commands;
Then all smiles stopped together. There she stands
As if alive. Will't please you rise? We'll meet
The company below, then. I repeat,
The Count your master's[3] known munificence
Is ample warrant that no just pretence
Of mine for dowry will be disallowed;
Though his fair daughter's self, as I avowed
At starting, is my object. Nay, we'll go
Together down, sir. Notice Neptune, though,
Taming a sea-horse, thought a rarity,
Which Claus of Innsbruck[4] cast in bronze for me!

Dramatic Lyrics.

1. *Ferrara:* the Duke of Ferrara (the speaker in this monologue). His first wife had died in 1561, probably of poisoning, and in 1564, he sought the hand of the Count of Tyrol's niece. 2. *Fra Pandolf:* the painter of the portrait – 3. *the Count your master:* Ferrara is addressing the Count of Tyrol's envoy – 4. *Claus of Innsbruck:* a sculptor, whose name Browning invented.

Another example of dramatic monologue: Tennyson's Ulysses.

ULYSSES. It little profits that an idle king,
By this still hearth, among these barren crags,
Matched with an aged wife, I mete and dole
Unequal laws unto a savage race,
That hoard, and sleep, and feed, and know not me.

I cannot rest from travel: I will drink
Life to the lees: all times I have enjoyed
Greatly, have suffered greatly, both with those
That loved me, and alone; on shore, and when
Through scudding drifts the rainy Hyades
Vexed the dim sea: I am become a name;
For always roaming with a hungry heart
Much have I seen and known; cities of men
And manners, climates, councils, governments,
Myself not least, but honoured of them all;
And drunk delight of battle with my peers,
Far on the ringing plains of windy Troy.
I am a part of all that I have met;
Yet all experience is an arch wherethrough
Gleams that untravelled world, whose margin fades
For ever and for ever when I move.
How dull it is to pause, to make an end,
To rust unburnished, not to shine in use!

As though to breathe were life. Life piled on life
Were all too little, and of one to me
Little remains: but every hour is saved
From that eternal silence, something more,
A bringer of new things; and vile it were
For some three suns to store and hoard myself,
And this grey spirit yearning in desire
To follow knowledge like a sinking star,
Beyond the utmost bound of human thought.

This is my son, mine own Telemachus,
To whom I leave the sceptre and the isle –
Well-loved of me, discerning to fulfil
This labour, by slow prudence to make mild
A rugged people, and through soft degrees
Subdue them to the useful and the good.
Most blameless is he, centred in the sphere
Of common duties, decent not to fail
In offices of tenderness, and pay
Meet adoration to my household gods,
When I am gone. He works his work, I mine.

There lies the port; the vessel puffs her sail:
There gloom the dark broad seas. My mariners,
Souls that have toiled, and wrought, and thought with me –
That ever with a frolic welcome took
The thunder and the sunshine, and opposed
Free hearts, free foreheads – you and I are old;
Old age hath yet his honour and his toil;
Death closes all: but something ere the end,
Some work of noble note, may yet be done,
Not unbecoming men that strove with Gods.
The lights begin to twinkle from the rocks:
The long day wanes: the slow moon climbs: the deep
Moans round with many voices. Come, my friends,
'Tis not too late to seek a newer world.
Push off, and sitting well in order smite
The sounding furrows; for my purpose holds
To sail beyond the sunset, and the baths
Of all the western stars, until I die.
It may be that the gulfs will wash us down:
It may be we shall touch the Happy Isles,
And see the great Achilles, whom we knew.
Though much is taken, much abides; and though
We are not now that strength which in old days
Moved earth and heaven; that which we are, we are;
One equal temper of heroic hearts,
Made weak by time and fate, but strong in will
To strive, to seek, to find, and not to yield.

1833-published 1842

Sir Edward Burne-Jones: Clara Von Borke.
The Tate Gallery.
Tennyson's poems were a constant source of inspiration for the Pre-Raphaelites (cf. pp. 203-204), perhaps because of their common interest in symbolism, sentimentality and a return to the past (e.g. Arthurian legends).

Alfred Tennyson (1809-1892) was a typically Victorian poet. Though aware of the dangers of materialism and of some of the trends of the society he was living in, his beliefs were those of his time: faith in God, in the family, in the moral tenets and the respectability of the Victorians. Tennyson's style is characterized by sensuousness, a musical flow and a sense of rhythm. His main works are Poems, Chiefly Lyrical *(1830),* Poems *(1832-1842),* In Memoriam *(1850),* Maud *(1855),* Idylls of the King *(1859).*

Cf. Versification, p. 7.

About the dramatic monologue:

(1) The sort of dramatic monologue Browning wrote is a poem of which the versified part is devoted almost entirely to the imaginary utterance of some person other than the author. (2) There is a distinct attempt to reproduce the characteristics of actual speech, even in the unusual case where the utterance is supposed to have been written, or the form of the poem is that of simple lyric. (3) The utterance is used to do a job natural to extended speech, namely, to express a state of mind, disposition, attitude, or set of beliefs. It is not used to express action for its own sake, and, where it does express action, the interest is that this is a characteristic action for the speaker. (4) The state of mind, or whatever, is treated seriously, in the sense that it is given a full and fairly eloquent expression; it is not obviously discredited. (5) It matters for a full understanding of the text that the reader should take it as the utterance of some person other than the author.

M. Mason, "Browning and the Dramatic Monologue" in *Writers and their Background, ed. by Armstrong.*

The standard account of the dramatic monologue is that Browning and Tennyson conceived it as a reaction against the romantic confessional style. This is probably true. Both poets had been stung by unfriendly criticism of certain early poems in which they had too much revealed themselves; and both poets published, in 1842, volumes which were a new departure in their careers and which contained dramatic monologues. The personal sting was probably responsible for Tennyson's decade of silence before 1842; it was almost certainly responsible for the disclaimer attached by Browning to his 1842 *Dramatic Lyrics:* "so many utterances of so many imaginary persons, not mine". Yet the reserve of the two poets cannot explain the coincidence that, working independently, they both arrived at the same form and produced at first try dramatic monologues so perfect (Browning's *My Last Duchess* and Tennyson's *Ulysses* and *St Simeon Stylites)* that they were never themselves to surpass them.

R. Langbaum, "Sympathy Versus Judgment", in *Poety of Experience.*
Chatto and Windus.

Gerard Manley HOPKINS 1844-1889

1844 *Born in Essex.*
1860 *Travelled in Germany.*
1863 *Studied in Oxford.*
1866 *Converted to Roman Catholicism, under the influence of Pater and Newman.*
1868 *Burnt his poems and entered the Jesuit Order.*
1875 The Wreck of the Deutschland; *started writing poetry again.*
1877 *Ordained.*
1878 *Started preaching (was to be a priest in London, Oxford, Liverpool, Glasgow).*
1884 *Became Professor of Greek at University College, Dublin.*
1885 *The "terrible" sonnets,*
1889 *Died of typhoid fever in Dublin.*
1918 *Hopkins's poems edited by Robert Bridges.*

A fervent religious poet, Hopkins saw the manifestation of God everywhere in nature. His poems are striking for their daring and energy, their intensity and immediacy; this is partly due to a highly individual language: the use of violent, striking words, rich metaphors, unexpected syntax. The effect is one of vividness and passion, making each poem an "experience".

A romantic at heart, Hopkins was deeply influenced by Keats's poetry and his conception of "Negative Capability" (cf p. 184) the poet's power of detachment from facts and reason. Like Keats, Hopkins tried to reach a perception of the essence of things and he distinguished between "inscape" (the true nature of things, their "self") and "instress" (its effect upon his imagination).

But his main achievement concerns rhythm; in an attempt to revive the patterns of Old English poetry, he created what he called "Sprung Rhythm".

For Hopkins a single stress made a single metrical foot, and it could equally well (sense permitting) stand alone in that foot or be accompanied by any number of light, unstressed syllables. The character of the movement of such verse is that of expressive common speech (...) The objective is (...) expressiveness, in preference to mere tunefulness.

F.N. Lees.

The Windhover[1] (1877, pub. 1918)

To Christ our Lord

I CAUGHT this morning morning's minion[2], kingdom
  of daylight's dauphin, dapple-dawn-drawn[3] Falcon, in his riding
  Of the rolling level underneath him steady air, and striding
High there, how he rung upon the rein[4] of a wimpling[5] wing
In his ecstasy! then off, off forth on swing,
  As skate's heel sweeps smooth on a bow-bend: the hurl and gliding
  Rebuffed the big wind. My heart in hiding
Stirred for a bird, – the achieve[6] of, the mastery of the thing!

Brute beauty and valour and act, oh, air, pride, plume, here
Buckle[7]! AND[8] the fire that breaks from thee then, a billion
Times told lovelier, more dangerous, O my chevalier!

  No wonder of it; sheer plod makes plough down sillion[9]
Shine, and blue-bleak embers, ah my dear[10],
  Fall, gall themselves, and gash gold-vermilion[11].

1. *The Windhover:* the kestrel (a small hawk) which often hovers in the wind – 2. *minion:* darling – 3. *dapple-dawn-drawn:* drawn by the dappled dawn – 4. *rung upon the rein:* in horse-riding to ring on the rein is to guide a horse that circles at the end of its rein – 5. *wimpling:* rippling – 6. *achieve:* achievement – 7. *buckle:* several meanings are possible here a) prepare for battle b) collapse, give way as if under pressure c) buckle on, fasten – 8. *AND:* the capital letters express the importance of the change that is taking place – 9. *sillion:* furrow – 10. *ah my dear:* cf Herbert's *Love,* II. in which the same words are used to address Christ – 11. *gash gold-vermillion:* probably evoke the Crucifixion.

G.M. Hopkins on Sprung Rhythm (from the author's Preface to his poems):

The poems in this book are written some in Running Rhythm, the common rhythm in English use, some in Sprung Rhythm, and some in a mixture of the two (...)

Common English rhythm, called Running Rhythm above, is measured by feet of either two ot three syllables (...)

Every foot has one principal stress or accent, and this or the syllable it falls on may be called the Stress of the foot and the other part, the one or two unaccented syllables, the Slack. Feet (and the rhythms made out of them) in which the Stress comes first are called Falling Feet and Falling Rhythms, feet and rhythm in which the Slack comes first are called Rising feet and Rhythms, and if the Stress is between two Slacks there will be Rocking Feet and Rhythms. (...)

But because verse written strictly in these feet and by these principles will become same and tame the poets have brought in licences and departures from rule to give variety, and especially when the natural rhythm is rising, as in the common ten-syllable or five-foot verse, rhymed or blank. These irregularities are chiefly Reversed Feet and Reversed or Counter-point Rhythm, which two things are two steps or degrees of licence in the same kind. By a reversed foot I mean the putting the stress where, to judge by the rest of the measure, the slack should be and the slack where the stress, and this is done freely at the beginning of a line and, in the course of a line, after a pause; only scarcely ever in the second foot or place and never in the last, unless when the poet designs some extraordinary effect; for these places are characteristic and sensitive and cannot well be touched. But the reversal of the first foot and of some middle foot after a strong pause is a thing so natural that our poets have generally done it, from Chaucer down, without remark and it commonly passes unnoticed and cannot be said to amount to a formal change of rhythm, but rather is that irregularity which all natural growth and motion shews. If however the reversal is repeated in two feet running, especially so as to include the sensitive second foot, it must be due either to great want of ear or else is a calculated effect, the superinducing or *mounting* of a new rhythm upon the old; and since the new or mounted rhythm is actually heard and at the same time the mind naturally supplies the natural or standard foregoing rhythm, for we do not forget what the rhythm is that by rights we should be hearing, two rhythms are in some manner running at once and we have something answerable to counterpoint in music, which is two or more strains of tune-going on together, and this is Counterpoint Rhythm[1]. Of this kind of verse Milton is the great master and the choruses of *Samson Agonistes* are written throughout in it – but with the disadvantage that he does not let

1 First heard in *God's Grandeur:*

/ x | / x | x / | x / x /
"Generations have trod, have trod, have trod".

the reader clearly know what the ground-rhythm is meant to be and so they have struck most readers as merely irregular. And in fact if you counterpoint throughout, since one only of the counter rhythms is actually heard, the other is really destroyed or cannot come to exist and what is written is one rhythm only and probably Sprung Rhythm, of which I now speak.

Sprung Rhythm, as used in this book, is measured by feet of from one to four syllabes, regulary, and for particular effects any number of weak or slack syllables may be used. It has one stress, which falls on the only syllable, if there is only one, or, if there are more, then scanning as above, on the first, and so gives rise to four sorts of feet, a monosyllable and the so-called accentual Trochee, Dactyl, and the First Paeon[2]. And there will be four corresponding natural rhythms; but nominally the feet are mixed and any one may follow any other. And hence Sprung Rhythm differs from Running Rhythm in having or being only one nominal rhythm, a mixed or 'logaoedic' one, instead of three, but on the other hand in having twice the flexibility of foot, so that any two stresses may either follow one another running or be divided by one, two, or three slack syllables. But strict Sprung Rhythm cannot be counterpointed. In Sprung Rhythm, as in logaoedic rhythm generally, the feet are assumed to be equally long or strong and their seeming inequality is made up by pause or stressing.

Remark also that it is natural in Sprung Rhythm for the lines to be *rove over*, that is for the scanning of each line immediately to take up that of the one before, so that if the first has one or more syllables at its end the other must have so many the less at its beginning; and in fact the scanning runs on without break from the beginning, say, of a stanza to the end and all the stanza is one long strain, though written in lines asunder.(...)

Note on the nature and history of Sprung Rhythm.

Sprung Rhythm is the most natural of things. For (1) it is the rhythm of common speech and of written prose, when rhythm is perceived in them. (2) It is the rhythm of all but the most monotonously regular music, so that in the words of choruses and refrains and in songs written closely to music it arises. (3) It is found in nursery rhymes, weather saws, and so on; because, however these may have been once made in running rhythm, the terminations having dropped off by the change of language, the stresses come together and so the rhythm is sprung. (4) It arises in common verse when reversed or counterpointed, for the same reason.

But nevertheless in spite of all this and though Greek and latin lyric verse, which is well known, and the old English verse seen in *Pierce Ploughman* are in sprung rhythm, it has in fact ceased to be used since the Elizabethan age.

2. E.g. in *The Wreck of the Deutschland* (only the stressed syllables are marked in MSS):

a) Monosyllabic feet:

×¦ / | / | / ‖ × × / | / | /
"The your scythe cringe, and the blear share come".
(XI,8).

b) Paeons:

/ × × × | / × × × / × ‖ × ×¦
"Startle the poor sheep back! is the shipwrack then a
/ × × | / × × × × | / × ×
harvest, does tempest carry the grain for th ee"?
(XXXI,8).

Cf. Versification, p. 7; Figurative Language, p. 31.

Charles DICKENS 1812-1870

1812 *Born at Portsmouth.*
1824 *His father was arrested for debt and the whole family went to live in the Marshalsea Prison. Charles took a job in a blacking factory.*
1824-1826 *School at Wellington School Academy, London.*
1827 *Worked in an attorney's office, taught himself shorthand and became a law-reporter in the court of Doctors'Commons.*
1832-1834 *Worked as a reporter for several papers.*

Perhaps the most widely popular works in the English language, Charles Dickens's novels are remarkable for their vitality and their gift for entertaining, moving and reforming.

Dickens's first novel immediately revealed his genius for characterization and caricature. With one sentence, one expression, he can make his characters come alive. The collection of grotesque and eccentric figures who people his novels with their obsessions and phobias, these 'humours' whom a word can sum up — meekness, self-complacency, utilitarianism — are what one remembers best. They even outshine the heroes who tend

1836 Sketches by Boz *published. Became popular. Commissioned to write* The Pickwick Papers *in monthly instalments: it was to turn out immensely popular. Married Catherine Hogarth.*
1837-1839 Oliver Twist.
1838-1839 Nicholas Nickelby.
1840-1841 The Old Curiosity Shop; Barnaby Rudge.
1842: *Travelled to the United States.*
1843-1844 Martin Chuzzlewit, A Christmas Carol.
1844-1845 *Travelled to Italy and France.*
1846-1848 Dombey and Son.
1849-1850 David Copperfield.
1852-1853 Bleak House.
1854 Hard Times.
1855-1857 Little Dorrit.
1857-1858 *Started giving public readings of his works. Separated from his wife.*
1859 A Tale of Two Cities.
1860-1861 Great Expectations.
1864-1865 Our Mutual Friend.
1967-1868 *Tour of public readings in the USA.*
1870 *Died at Gad's Hill; buried in Westminster Abbey.* The Mystery of Edwin Drood *(unfinished) was published posthumously.*

to remain dull and unconvincing.

This pervading spirit of comedy is often linked to a deep social awareness. Affected by his childhood experiences, Dickens grew into a humanitarian, something of a social reformer. His novels take us to the most miserable London underworld, with its jails, opium-dens, slums and workhouses. In this setting he exposes the failure of the Victorian social system: ineffective justice and bureaucracy, the power of money, the cruelty and stupidity of the school-system, and above all, the exploitation of children. For children are the perfect victims, uniting weakness and helplessness, which Dickens had set out to defend. Oppressed childhood is a recurrent theme in his works, partly because so many social ills had to do with children during the Victorian era (child-labour, the poor-houses, schooling...) but also because the child's distorted vision of the grown-up world was so congenial to Dickens's personality, so much in keeping with his own exuberant and exaggerated vision of life. Yet Dickens is no revolutionary: rather than advocating radical changes in society, he appeals to individual good-will and humanity, merely pointing out the wrongs of a "laissez-faire" policy, acting – to use W. Allen's expression – as "the conscience of his age".

The serial publication of his novels made for a close relationship with his public, a need to maintain suspense from each instalment to the next and to take his readers' feelings into consideration – vhich may partly account for his sometimes over-indulgent use of sentimentality and melodrama.

Hard Times (1854)

Coketown

Coketown, to which Messrs Bounderby and Gradgrind now walked, was a triumph of fact; it had no greater taint of fancy in it than Mrs Gradgrind herself. Let us strike the keynote, Coketown, before pursuing our tune.

It was a town of red brick, or of brick that would have been red if the smoke and ashes had allowed it; but as matters stood it was a town of unnatural red and black like the painted face of a savage. It was a town of machinery and tall chimneys, out of which interminable serpents of smoke trailed themselves for ever and ever, and never got uncoiled. It had a black canal in it, and a river that ran purple with ill-smelling dye, and vast piles of buildings full of windows where there was a rattling and a trembling all day long, and where the piston of the steam-engine worked monotonously up and down like the head of an elephant in a state of melancholy madness. It contained several large streets all very like one another, and many small streets still more like one another, inhabited by people equally like one another, who all went in and out at the same hours, with the same sound upon the same pavements, to do the same work, and to whom every day was the same as yesterday and to-morrow, and every year the counterpart of the last and the next.

These attributes of Coketown were in the main inseparable from the work by which it was sustained; against them were to be set off, comforts of live which found their way all over the world, and elegancies of life which made, we will not ask how much of the fine lady, who could scarcely bear to hear the place mentioned. The rest of its features were voluntary, and they were these.

You saw nothing in Coketown but what was severely workful. If the members of a religious persuasion built a chapel there – as the members of eighteen religious persuasions had done – they made it a pious warehouse of red brick, with sometimes (but this is only in highly ornamented examples) a bell in a birdcage on the top of it. The solitary exception was the New Church; a stuccoed edifice with a square steeple over the door, terminating in four short pinnacles like florid wooden legs. All the public inscriptions in the town were painted

alike, in severe characters of black and white. The jail might have been the infirmary, the infirmary might have been the jail, the town-hall might have been either, or both, or anything else, for anything that appeared to the contrary in the graces of their construction. Fact, fact, fact everywhere in the material aspect of the town; fact, fact, fact, everywhere in the immaterial. The M'Choakumchild school was all fact, and the school of design was all fact, and the relations between master and man were all fact, and everything was fact between the lying-in hospital and the cemetery, and what you couldn't state in figures, or show to be purchaseable in the cheapest market and saleable in the dearest, was not, and never should be, world without end, Amen...

A sunny midsummer day. There was such a thing sometimes, even in Coketown.

Seen from a distance in such weather, Coketown lay shrouded in a haze of its own, which appeared impervious to the sun's rays. You only knew the town was there, because you knew there could have been no such sulky blotch upon the prospect without a town. A blur of soot and smoke, now confusedly tending this way, now that way, now aspiring to the vault of Heaven, now murkily creeping along the earth, as the wind rose and fell, or changed its quarter: a dense formless jumble, with sheets of cross light in it, that showed nothing but masses of darkness: – Coketown in the distance suggestive of itself, though not a brick of it could be seen.

The wonder was, it was there at all. It had been ruined so often, that it was amazing how it had borne so many shocks. Surely there never was such fragile china-ware as that of which the millers of Coketown were made. Handle them never so lightly and they fell to pieces with such ease that you might suspect them of having been flawed before. They were ruined, when they were required to send labouring children to school; they were ruined when inspectors were appointed to look into their works; they were ruined, when such inspectors considered it doubtful whether they were quite justified in chopping people up with their machinery; they were utterly undone, when it was hinted that perhaps they need not always make quite so much smoke. Besides Mr Bounderby's gold spoon which was generally received in Coketown, another prevalent fiction was very popular there. It took the form of a threat. Whenever a Coketowner felt he was ill-used – that is to say, whenever he was not left entirely alone, and it was proposed to hold him accountable for the consequences of any of his acts – he was sure to come out with the awful menace, that he would "sooner pitch his property into the Atlantic". This had terrified the Home Secretary within an inch of his life, on several occasions.

However, the Coketowners were so patriotic after all, that they never had pitched their property into the Atlantic yet, but, on the contrary, had been kind enough to take mighty good care of it. So there it was, in the haze yonder; and it increased and multiplied.

Book I, Chapter 5.

Coketown and the Victorian manufacturing towns

Dickens:

When I did *Hard Times* I called the scene Coketown. Everybody knew what was meant, but every cotton-spinning town said it was the other cotton-spinning town...

Letter to C. Fechter, 1866.

F. Engels:

So, too, Bradford, which, but seven miles from Leeds at the junction of several valleys, lies upon the banks of a small, coal-black, foul-smelling stream. On week-days the town is enveloped in a grey cloud of coal smoke, but on a fine Sunday it offers a superb picture, when viewed from the surrounding heights. Yet within reigns the same filth and discomfort as in Leeds. The older portions of the town are built upon steep hillsides, and are narrow and irregular. In the lanes, alleys, and courts lie filth and *débris* in heaps; the houses are ruinous, dirty, and miserable, and in the immediate vicinity of the river and the valley bottom I found many a one, whose ground-floor, half-buried in the hillside, was totally abandoned. In general, the portions of the valley bottom in which working-men's cottages have crowded between the tall factories, are among the worst built and dirtiest districts of the whole town. In the newer portions of this, as of every other factory town, the cottages are more regular, being built in rows, but they share here, too, all the evils incident to the customary method of providing working-men's dwellings, evils of which we shall have occasions to speak more particularly in discussing Manchester.

The Condition of the Working-Class, 1845.

Carlyle:

"Call ye that a Society", cries he again, "where there is no longer any Social Idea extant; not so much as the Idea of a common Home, but only of a common overcrowded Lodging-house? Where each, isolated, regardless of his neighbour, turned against his neighbour, clutches what he can get, and cries 'Mine!' and calls it Peace, because, in the cut-purse and cut-throat Scramble, no steel knives, but only a far cunninger sort, can be employed? Where Friendship, Communion, has become an incredible tradition; and your holiest Sacramental Supper is a smoking Tavern Dinner, with Cook for Evangelist? Where your Priest has no tongue but for plate-licking: and your high Guides and Governors cannot guide; but on all hands hear it passionately proclaimed: *Laissez faire*; Leave us alone of *your* guidance, such light is darker than darkness; eat you your wages, and sleep!"

"Thus, too", continues he, "does an observant eye discern everywhere that saddest spectacle: The Poor perishing, like neglected, foundered Draught-Cattle, of Hunger and Over-work; the Rich, still more wretchedly, of Idleness, Satiety, and Over-growth. The Highest in rank, at length, without honour from the Lowest; scarcely, with a little mouth-honour, as from tavern-waiters who expect to put it in the bill. Once-sacred Symbols fluttering as empty Pageants, whereof men grudge even the expense; a World becoming dismantled: in one word, the CHURCH fallen speechless, from obesity and apoplexy; the STATE shrunken into a Police-Office, straitened to get its pay!"

Carlyle, *Sartor Resartus*, 1833-1834.

See Mrs Gaskell's description of Milton in North and South *(chapter 7).*

Gustave Doré's vision of "bricks and mortar":

Gustave Doré: Over London, by Rail, *in* London, *1872. Bibliothèque Nationale, Est., Paris. Ph. Hachette.*

Dickens's philosophy in Hard Times:

In *Hard Times* the pedantry of the obstructing society is associated with a utilitarian philosophy and an infantile trust in facts, statistics, and all impersonal and generalized forms of knowledge. We may wonder why Dickens denounces this philosophy so earnestly and caricatures it so crudely, instead of letting its absurdities speak for themselves. But it is clear that *Hard Times*, of all Dickens's stories, comes nearest to being what in our day is sometimes called the dystopia, the book which, like *Brave New World* or *1984*, shows us the nightmare world that results from certain perverse tendencies inherent in society getting free play. The most effective dystopias are likely to be those in which the author isolates certain features in his society that most directly threaten his own social function as a writer. Dickens sees in the cult of facts and statistics a threat, not to the realistic novelist, and not only to a life based on concrete and personal relations, but to the unfettered imagination, the mind that can respond to fairy tales and fantasy and understand their relevance to reality. The insistence on the importance of fairy tales, nursery rhymes, and similar genres in education often meets us in Dickens, and implies that Dickens's fairy-tale plots are regarded by Dickens himself as an essential part of his novels.

N. Frye,
"*Dickens and the Comedy of Humors*",
Experience in the Novel,
edited by R. Harvey Pearce,
© *1968 Columbia University Press, N. Y.*

Dickens on his narrative art: fancy and invention. Study Dickens's narrative method in the passage in the light of the following quotations from his Letters:

It does not seem to me to be enough to say of any description that it is the exact truth. The exact truth must be there; but the merit or art in the narrator, is the manner of stating the truth. As to which thing in literature, it always seems to me that there is a world to be done. And in these times, when the tendency is to be frightfully literal and catalogue-like – to make the thing, in short, a sort of sum in reduction that any miserable creature can do in that way – I have an idea (really founded on the love of what I profess), that the very holding of popular literature through a kind of popular dark age, may depend on such fanciful treatment.

Invention, thank God, seems the easiest thing in the world; and I seem to have such a preposterous sense of the ridiculous (...) as to be constantly requiring to restrain myself from launching into extravagances in the height of my enjoyment.

I work slowly and with great care, and never give way to my invention recklessly, but constantly restrain it; (...) (but) I think it is my infirmity to fancy or perceive relations in things which are not apparent generally. Also, I have such an inexpressible enjoyment of what I see in a droll light, that I dare say I pet it as if it were a spoilt child.

Cf. Narrative technique, p. 15; Figurative language, p. 31.

David Copperfield (1849-1850)

Mr Micawber, in whose family David Copperfield had lived for a time as a lodger, found himself in financial difficulties and was arrested and sent to the King's Bench Prison. He has just been released.

"May I ask, ma'am, what you and Mr Micawber intend to do, now that Mr Micawber is out of his difficulties, and at liberty? Have you settled yet?"

"My family", said Mrs Micawber, who always said those two words with an air, though I never could discover who came under the denomination, "my family are of opinion that Mr Micawber should quit London, and exert his talents in the country. Mr Micawber is a man of great talent, Master Copperfield".

I said I was sure of that.

"Of great talent", repeated Mrs Micawber. "My family are of opinion, that, with a little interest, something might be done for a man of his ability in the Custom House. The influence of my family being local, it is their wish that Mr Micawber should go down to Plymouth. They think it indispensable that he should be upon the spot".

"That he may be ready ?" I suggested.

"Exactly", returned Mrs Micawber. "That he may be ready – in case of anything turning up".

"And do you go too, ma'am?"

The events of the day, in combination with the twins, if not with the flip, had made Mrs Micawber hysterical, and she shed tears as she replied:

"I never will desert Mr Micawber. Mr Micawber may have concealed his difficulties from me in the first instance, but his sanguine temper may have led him to expect that he would overcome them. The pearl necklace and bracelets which I inherited from mama, have been disposed of for less than half their value; and the set of coral, which was the wedding gift of my papa, has been actually thrown away for nothing. But I never will desert Mr Micawber. No!" cried cread Mrs Micawber, more affected than before, cried "I never will do it! It's of no use asking me!"

I felt quite uncomfortable – as if Mrs Micawber supposed I had asked her to do anything of the sort! – and sat looking at her in alarm.

"Mr Micawber has his faults. I do not deny that he is improvident. I do not deny that he has kept me in the dark as to his resources and his liabilities both", she went on, looking at the wall; "but I never will desert Mr Micawber!"

Mrs Micawber having now raised her voice into a perfect scream, I was so frightened that I ran off to the club-room, and disturbed Mr Micawber in the act of presiding at a long table, and leading the chorus of

"Gee up, Dobbin,
Gee ho, Dobbin,
Gee up, Dobbin,
Gee up, and gee ho-o-o!"

– with the tidings that Mrs Micawber was in an alarming state, upon which he immediately burst into tears, and came away with me with his waistcoat full of the heads and tails of shrimps, of which he had been partaking.

"Emma, my angel!" cried Mr Micawber, running into the room; "what is the matter?"

"I never will desert you, Micawber!" she exclaimed.

"My life!" said Mr Micawber, taking her in his arms. "I am perfectly aware of it".

"He is the parent of my children! He is the father of my twins! He is the husband of my affections", cried Mrs Micawber, struggling; "and I ne – ver – will – desert Mr Micawber!"

Chapter 12

Phiz: Mr Micawber delivers some valedictory Remarks.

Hablôt K. Browne (1815-1882) chose the pen-name Phiz to rhyme with Dickens's Sketches by Boz. *His first work for Dickens was his illustrations of* The Pickwick Papers. *He then went on illustrating many of Dickens's novels as well as sporting novels by Surtees and some of Smedley's romances. The other well-known Dickens illustrator was George Cruikshank.*

Northrop Frye on Dickens's Comedy of Humors:

Most of the people who move across the pages of Dickens are neither realistic portraits, like the characters of Trollope, nor "caricatures", so far as that term implies only a slightly different approach to realistic portraiture. They are humors, like the characters in Ben Jonson, who formulated the principle that humors were the appropriate characters for a New Comedy plot. The humor is a character identified with a characteristic, like the miser, the hypochondriac, the braggart, the parasite, or the pedant. He is obsessed by whatever it is that makes him a humor, and the sense of our superiority to an obsessed person, someone bound to an invariable ritual habit, is, according to Bergson, one of the chief sources of laughter.

(...)

In Dickens we find humors on both sides of the social conflict, genial, generous, and lovable humors as well as absurd or sinister ones. But the humors in the congenial society merely diversify it with amiable and harmless eccentricities; the humors of the obstructing society help to build up that society, with all its false standards and values. (...)

The simplest form of humor is the tagged humor, who is associated with the repetition of a set phrase. Thus we have Mrs Micawber, whose tag is that she will never desert Mr Micawber, and Major Bagnet in *Bleak House*, who admires his wife but asserts that he never tells her so because "discipline must be maintained". We notice that our sense of superiority to such characters is edged with antagonism: when the repeated trait is intended to be endearing we are more likely to find it irritating. (...)

Sometimes a humor's obsessed behavior and repetitive speech suggest a puppet or mechanical doll, whose response is invariable whatever the stimulus. We may feel with some of these characters that the mechanical quality is simply the result of Dickens's not having worked hard enough on them, but occasionally we realize that Dickens himself is encouraging us to see them as inanimate objects.

N. Frye, *ibid.*

Cf. Characters and characterization, p. 12.

William Makepeace THACKERAY 1811-1863

1811	*Born in Calcutta.*
1817	*Sent to school in England.*
1829	*Trinity College, Cambridge.*
1830-1831	*Travelled to Germany.*
1831-1832	*Studied law.*
1834-1837	*Settled in Paris where he got married and began to work as a journalist.*
1837-1838	The Yellowplush Correspondence *(for* Fraser's Magazine).
1840	The Paris Sketch Book*; his wife became insane.*
1842	*Started writing for* Punch.
1843	The Irish Sketch Book.
1844	The Luck of Barry Lyndon *(for Fraser's).*
1846-1847	The Snobs of England, *written for* Punch, *later published as* The Book of Snobs.
1847-1848	Vanity Fair *(in serial numbers).*
1848-1850	The History of Pendennis *(in serial numbers).*
1852	The History of Henry Esmond.
1852-1853	*Gave lectures in the USA (returned there in 1855-6).*

During his long career as a journalist, Thackeray turned his hand to several kinds of writing — parodies (of Disraeli, Scott, Dickens, of romantic fiction and the fashion for idealizing criminals); historical novels (e.g. Esmond*); satirical works (e.g.* The Book of Snobs *which ridicules pretensions to gentility); criticism and travel sketches — but his reputation (he was long considered the equal of Dickens) is chiefly based on his novels.*

Vanity Fair*, the best-known of them, is described in its subtitle as "a novel without a hero": though the book is centred on the contrast between the clever, exuberant and unscrupulous Becky Sharp and the virtuous but stupid and helpless Amelia, its aim is to give a panorama of the upper middle-class society of London during a span of several years. The picture is presented with realism, without the least idealization or sentimentality. Indeed, Thackeray is often cruel in his satire of snobs and hypocrites, or when he exposes the stupidity and mediocrity of his characters. Yet Thackeray shared the Victorian beliefs in love, marriage and the family. They always meet with his approval. For the novelist's voice*

1853 The English Humourists of the Eighteenth Century.
1853-1855 The Newcomes *(serial numbers).*
1857-1859 The Virginians *(serial numbers).*
1859-1862 *Editor of* Cornhill Magazine.
1863 *Died in London.*

can always be heard, constantly intruding in the narration to criticize, moralize or generalize.

Vanity Fair (1847-1848)

At Pinkerton's Academy, the ambitious Becky Sharp met Amelia Sedley who invited her home on their leaving school.

Rebecca is in presence of the enemy

A VERY stout, puffy man, in buckskins and Hessian boots, with several immense neckcloths, that rose almost to his nose, with a red-striped waistcoat and an apple-green coat with steel buttons almost as large as crown pieces (it was the morning costume of a dandy or blood of those days), was reading the paper by the fire when the two girls entered, and bounced off his arm-chair, and blushed excessively, and hid his entire face almost in his neckcloths at this apparition.

"It's only your sister, Joseph," said Amelia, laughing and shaking the two fingers which he held out. "I've come home *for good*, you know; and this is my friend, Miss Sharp, whom you have heard me mention."

"No, never, upon my word," said the head under the neckcloth, shaking very much, – "that is, yes, – what abominably cold weather, Miss;" – and herewith he fell to poking the fire with all his might, although it was in the middle of June.

"He's very handsome," whispered Rebecca to Amelia, rather loud.

"Do you think so?" said the latter. "I'll tell him."

"Darling! not for worlds," said Miss Sharp, starting back as timid as a fawn. She had previously made a respectful virginlike curtsey to the gentleman, and her modest eyes gazed so perseveringly on the carpet that is was a wonder how she should have found an opportunity to see him.

"Thank you for the beautiful shawls, brother," said Amelia to the fire-poker. "Are they not beautiful, Rebecca?"

"Oh, heavenly!" said Miss Sharp, and her eyes went from the carpet straight to the chandelier.

Joseph still continued a huge clattering at the poker and tongs, puffing and blowing the while, and turning as red as his yellow face would allow him. "I can't make you such handsome presents, Joseph," continued his sister, "but while I was at school, I have embroidered for you a very beautiful pair of braces."

"Good Gad! Amelia," cried the brother, in serious alarm, "what do you mean?" and plunging with all his might at the bell-rope, that article of furniture came away in his hand, and increased the honest fellow's confusion. "For Heaven's sake see if my buggy's at the door! I *can't* wait. I must go. D – that groom of mine! I must go."

At this minute the father of the family walked in, rattling his seals like a true British merchant. "What's the matter, Emmy?" says he.

"Joseph wants me to see if his – his *buggy* is at the door. What is a buggy, papa?"

"It is a one-horse palanquin," said the old gentleman, who was a wag in his way.

Joseph at this burst out into a wild fit of laughter; in which, encountering the eye of Miss Sharp, he stopped all of a sudden, as if he had been shot.

"This young lady is your friend? Miss Sharp, I am very happy to see you. Have you and Emmy been quarrelling already with Joseph, that he wants to be off?"

"I promised Bonamy, of our service, sir," said Joseph, "to dine with him."

"O fie! didn't you tell your mother you would dine here?"

"But in this dress it's impossible."

"Look at him, isn't he handsome enough to dine anywhere, Miss Sharp?"

On which, of course, Miss Sharp looked at her friend, and they both set off in a fit of laughter, highly agreeable to the old gentleman.

"Did you ever see a pair of buckskins like those at Miss Pinkerton's?" continued he, following up his advantage.

"Gracious heavens! father," cried Joseph.

"There now, I have hurt his feelings. Mrs. Sedley, my dear, I have hurt your son's feelings. I have alluded to his buckskins. Ask Miss Sharp if I haven't. Come, come, Joseph, be friends with Miss Sharp, and let us all go to dinner."

"There's a pillau[1], Joseph, just as you like it, and Papa has brought home the best turbot in Billingsgate."

"Come, come, sir, walk downstairs with Miss Sharp, and I will follow with these two young women," said the father, and he took an arm of wife and daughter and walked merrily off. If Miss Rebecca Sharp had determined in her heart upon making the conquest of this big beau, I don't think, ladies, we have any right to blame her; for though the task of husband-hunting is generally, and with becoming modesty, intrusted by young persons to their mammas, recollect that Miss Sharp had no kind parent to arrange these delicate matters for her, and that if she did not get a husband for herself, there was no one else in the wide world who would take the trouble off her hands. What causes young people to "come *out*," but the noble ambition of matrimony? What sends them trooping to watering-places? What keeps them dancing till five o'clock in the morning through a whole mortal season? What causes them to labour at pianoforte sonatas, and to learn four songs from a fashionable master at a guinea a lesson, and to play the harp if they have handsome arms and neat elbows, and to wear Lincoln Green toxophilite[2] hats and feathers, but that they may bring down some "desirable" young man with those killing bows and arrows of theirs? What causes respectable parents to take up their carpets, set their houses topsy-turvy, and spend a fifth of their year's income in ball suppers and iced champagne? Is it sheer love of their species, and an unadulterated wish to see young people happy and dancing? Psha! they want to marry their daughters; and, as honest Mrs. Sedley has, in the depths of her kind heart, already arranged a score of little schemes for the settlement of her Amelia, so also had our beloved but unprotected Rebecca determined to do her very best to secure the husband, who was even more necessary for her than for her friend.

Chapter 3.

1. *a pillau*: pilau, an oriental dish (rice boiled with fowl, meat or fish) – 2. *a toxophilite*: someone who enjoys the practice of archery.

Thackeray: Mr. Joseph Entangled.
Ph. Bibl. Nat. Paris.

One of Thackeray's own illustrations for the novel.

Thackeray on his aim in Vanity Fair:

Of course you are quite right about Vanity Fair and Amelia, it is mentioned in this very number. My object is not to make a perfect character or anything like it. Don't you see how odious all the people are in the book (with the exception of Dobbin) – behind whom all there lies a dark moral I hope. What I want is to make a set of people living without God in the world (only that is a cant phrase) greedy pompous mean perfectly self-satisfied for the most part and at ease about their superior virtue.

Letter to his mother, 1847.

If I had put in more fresh air as you call it my object would have been defeated – It is to indicate, in cheerful terms, that we are for the most part an abominably foolish and selfish people "desperately wicked" and all eager after vanities.... I want to leave everybody dissatisfied and unhappy at the end of the story – we ought all to be with our own and all other stories. Good God don't I see (in that may-be cracked and warped looking glass in which I am always looking) my own weaknesses wickednesses lusts follies shortcomings?... We must lift up our voices about these and howl to a congregation of fools: so much at least has been my endeavour.

Letter to Robert Bell.

Thackeray's narrative technique:

● ... may the writer take the reader into his confidence about his characters?... better not. It is dangerous, it generally leads to a drop in the temperature, to intellectual and emotional laxity, and worse still to facetiousness, and to a friendly invitation to see how the figures hook up behind. "Doesn't A look nice – she always was my favourite", "Let's think of why B does that – perhaps there's more in him than meets the eyes – yes, see – he has a heart of gold – having given you this peep at it I'll pop it back – I don't think he's noticed". "And C – he always was the mystery man." Intimacy is gained but at the expense of illusion and nobility. It is like standing a man a drink so that he may not criticize your opinions. With all respect to Fielding and Thackeray it is devastating, it is bar-parlour chattiness, and nothing has been more harmful to the novels of the past.

E. M. Forster, *Aspects of the Novel*, 1927.
Edward Arnold Publishers Ltd.

● I know that Thackeray, so far from trying to conceal himself, comes forward and attracts attention and nudges the reader a great deal more than he need; he likes the personal relation with the reader and insists on it. But do what he might to disguise it, so long as he is ranging over his story at a height, chronicling, summarizing, foreshortening, he *must* be present to the reader as a narrator and a showman. It is only when he descends and approaches a certain occasion and sets a scene with due circumspection – rarely and a trifle awkwardly, as we saw – that he can for the time being efface the thought of his active part in the affair. (...)

Who is disposing the scattered facts, whose is this new point of view? It is the omniscient author, and the point of view is his – such would be the common answer, and it is the answer we get in Vanity Fair. By convention the author is allowed his universal knowledge of the story and the people in it. But still it is a convention, and a prudent novelist does not strain it unnecessarily. Thackeray in Vanity Fair is not at all prudent; his method, so seldom strictly dramatic, is one that of its nature is apt to force this question of the narrator's authority, and he goes out of his way to emphasize the question still further. He flourishes the fact that the point of view is his own, not to be confounded with that of anybody in the book. And so his book, as one may say, is not complete in itself, not really self-contained; it does not meet and satisfy all the issues it suggests. Over the whole of one side of it there is an inconclusive look, something that draws the eye away from the book itself, into space. It is the question of the narrator's relation to the story.

P. Lubbock, *The Craft of Fiction*, 1921.

Cf. Characters and characterization, p. 12; Narrative technique, p. 15.

George ELIOT 1819-1880

1819 *Mary Ann Evans born on a Warwickshire farm.*
1824-1835 *Strict religious schooling.*
1841 *Renounced the Anglican faith.*
1846 *Published a translation of Strauss'* Life of Jesus.
1849 *After her father's death, left for the Continent, then settled in London.*
1851-1853 *Became assistant editor of* The Westminster Review. *Met Herbert Spencer, Dickens, J. S. Mill and Henry Lewes, editor of the* Leader, *with whom she lived till his death in 1878.*

George Eliot was a radical, an intellectual who was influenced by the writings of Darwin and by German philosophy. She became a Methodist when she was young, but soon lost her Christian beliefs altogether, choosing instead to see life as fully determined by one's own choices and actions.

She was chiefly a moralist, who insisted that the function of the novel was to teach and to encourage social and political reforms, though the aesthetic aim should not be forgotten in favour of preaching. Most of her fiction studies the development of character within a small country community, often in the Midlands that she knew. Within

1854 *Published a translation of Feuerbach's* The Essence of Christianity.
1858 Scenes of Clerical Life *published under the pen name George Eliot.*
1859 Adam Bede
1860 The Mill on the Floss
1861 Silas Marner
1863 Romola
1866 Felix Holt
1871 Middlemarch
1876 Daniel Deronda
1880 *Died in London.*

this realistic background (her novels evoke the atmosphere of elections, Dissenters' meetings, life on a farm or in a rectory) she gives us a penetrating study of her characters' motivations and feelings, their hesitations and choices between temptation and dignity. She also shows how the social environment shapes and conditions the individual.

It is George Eliot's moral concern for her characters, – her sympathy and compassion – that is most vivid throughout her works, in Adam Bede's love for Hetty, condemned to death for the murder of her illegetimate child, in the happy childhood and subsequent sufferings of Tom and Maggie Tulliver in The Mill on the Floss *or in Dorothea's yearnings and frustrations in* Middlemarch.

The Mill on the Floss (1860)

The following scene between Tom and Maggie Tulliver takes place while the whole family, including aunts, uncles and cousins, has gathered at the Mill for dinner.

"Maggie," said Mrs. Tulliver, beckoning Maggie to her and whispering in her ear as soon as this point of Lucy's staying was settled, "go and get your hair brushed – do, for shame. I told you not to come in without going to Martha first; you know I did."

"Tom, come out with me," whispered Maggie, pulling his sleeve as she passed him; and Tom followed willingly enough.

"Come upstairs with me, Tom," she whispered when they were outside the door. "There's something I want to do before dinner."

"There's no time to play at anything before dinner," said Tom, whose imagination was impatient of any intermediate prospect.

Oh, yes, there is time for this – *do* come, Tom."

Tom followed Maggie upstairs into her mother's room and saw her go at once to a drawer, from which she took out a large pair of scissors.

"What are they for, Maggie?" said Tom, feeling his curiosity awakened.

Maggie answered by seizing her front locks and cutting them straight across the middle of her forehead.

"Oh, my buttons, Maggie, you'll catch it!" exclaimed Tom. "You'd better not cut any more off."

Snip! went the great scissors again while Tom was speaking; and he couldn't help feeling it was rather good fun; Maggie would look so queer.

"Here, Tom, cut it behind for me," said Maggie, excited by her own daring and anxious to finish the deed.

"You'll catch it, you know," said Tom, nodding his head in an admonitory manner and hesitating a little as he took the scissors.

"Never mind – make haste!" said Maggie, giving a little stamp with her foot. Her cheeks were quite flushed.

The black locks were so thick – nothing could be more tempting to a lad who had already tasted the forbidden pleasure of cutting the pony's mane. I speak to those who know the satisfaction of making a pair of shears meet through a duly resisting mass of hair. One delicious grinding snip, and then another and another, and the hinder-locks fell heavily on the floor, and Maggie stood cropped in a jagged, uneven manner, but with a sense of clearness and freedom, as if she had emerged from a wood into the open plain.

"Oh, Maggie," said Tom, jumping round her and slapping his knees as he laughed. "Oh, my buttons, what a queer thing you look! Look at yourself in the glass – you look like the idiot we throw our nut-shells to at school."

Maggie felt an unexpected pang. She had thought beforehand chiefly of her own deliverance from her teasing hair and teasing remarks about it, and something also of the triumph she should have over her mother and her aunts by this very decided course of action: she didn't want her hair to look pretty – that was out of the question – she only wanted people to think her a clever little girl and not to find fault with her. But now, when Tom began to laugh at her and say she was like the idiot, the affair had quite a new aspect. She looked in the glass, and still Tom laughed and clapped his hands, and Maggie's flushed cheeks began to pale, and her lips to tremble a little.

"Oh, Maggie, you'll have to go down to dinner directly", said Tom. "Oh, my!"

"Don't laugh at me, Tom", said Maggie in a passionate tone, with an outburst of angry tears, stamping, and giving him a push.

"Now, then, spitfire!" said Tom. "What did you cut it off for, then? I shall go down; I can smell the dinner going in."

He hurried downstairs and left poor Maggie to that bitter sense of the irrevocable which was almost an everyday experience of her small soul. She could see clearly enough, now the thing was done, that it was very foolish and that she should have to hear and think more about her hair than ever, for Maggie rushed to her deeds with passionate impulse and then saw not only their consequences but what would have happened if they had not been done with all the detail and exaggerated circumstance of an active imagination. Tom never did the same sort of foolish things as Maggie, having a wonderful instinctive discernment of what would turn to his advantage or disadvantage; and so it happened that though he was much more wilful and inflexible than Maggie, his mother hardly ever called him naughty. But if Tom did make a mistake of that sort, he espoused it and stood by it: he "didn't mind". If he broke the lash of his father's gig-whip by lashing the gate, he couldn't help it – the whip shouldn't have got caught in the hinge. If Tom Tulliver whipped a gate, he was convinced, not that the whipping of gates by all boys was a justifiable act, but that he, Tom Tulliver, was justifiable in whipping that particular gate, and he wasn't going to be sorry. But Maggie, as she stood crying before the glass, felt it impossible that she should go down to dinner and endure the severe eyes and severe words of her aunts, while Tom and Lucy and Martha, who waited at table, and perhaps her father and her uncles, would laugh at her – for if Tom had laughed at her, of course everyone else would. And if she had only let her hair alone, she could have sat with Tom and Lucy and had the apricot pudding and the custard! What could she do but sob? She sat as helpless and despairing among her black locks as Ajax among the slaughtered sheep.

Book I, Chapter 7.

George Eliot on realism:

If the ethics of art do not admit the truthful presentation of a character essentially noble but liable to great error – error that is anguish to its own nobleness – *then,* it seems to me, the ethics of art are too narrow, and must be widened to correspond with a widening psychology.

To J. Blackwood, 9 July 1860.

Art is the nearest thing to life; it is a mode of amplifying experience and extending our contact with our fellow-men beyond the bounds of our personal lot. All the more sacred is the task of the artist when he undertakes to paint the life of the People. Falsification here is far more pernicious than in the more artificial aspects of life. It is not so very serious that we should have false ideas about evanescent fashions – about the manners and conversation of beaux and duchesses; but it *is* serious that our sympathy with the perennial joys and struggles, the toil, the tragedy, and the humour in the life of our more heavily-laden fellow-men, should be perverted, and turned towards a false object instead of the true one.

This perversion is not the less fatal because the misrepresentation which gives rise to it has what the artist considers a moral end. The thing for mankind to know is, not what are the motives and influences which the moralist thinks *ought* to act on the labourer or the artisan, but what are the motives and influences which *do* act on him. We want to be taught to feel, not for the heroic artisan or the sentimental peasant, but for the peasant in all his coarse apathy, and the artisan in all his suspicious selfishness...

"The Natural History of German Life", in *Westminster Review,* LXVI (July 1856); reprinted in *Essays,* ed. Pinney.

Character and environment in the novels of George Eliot:

The organic or living form of her novels, within the expected framework, is different from anything that had gone before. It resembles, in some respects, Jane Austen's form in so far as the central characters are deeply rooted in their social environment which determines their story as much as does their individual character. The difference is that the social environment is wider, more complex, made up of a greater variety of minor characters drawn from any more social and economic levels, and also that the display of this outer circle or environment is more conscious. Jane Austen took her social *milieu* for granted; its manners and traditions were, for her, as little open to question as the laws of nature. George Eliot was aware of the ethical, religious and social conventions of the world she paints as a product of history, evolved in time and changing with time. She was consciously interested in the pressure all these exert on individual lives and in the existence of a problem concerned with resisting or succumbing to that pressure. She shares the modern consciousness of man in a changing and developing society. Consequently, the organic form of her novels – an inner circle (a small group of individuals involved in a moral dilemma) surrounded by an outer circle (the social world within which the dilemma has to be resolved) – is more significant than in any preceding fiction. Furthermore, her perception of individual human beings is more complex than that of her predecessors. She never suggests a simple division of characters into good and bad. The individual, like the environment, has evolved and is still evolving; his or her behaviour at any given moment is the inevitable result of all that has gone before; therefore, while the action can itself be judged, both in relation to its consequences and to its aesthetic beauty (an action that pleases or displeases) the doer is not presented judicially but compassionately.

Joan Bennett, *George Eliot: Her Mind and Her Art.* *Cambridge University Press.*

Cf. Characters and characterization, p. 12; Narrative technique, p. 15.

Thomas HARDY 1840-1928

1840 *Born near Dorchester; his father was a stonemason.*
1856-1861 *Apprenticed to an architect. Started writing verse.*
1862-1867 *Worked for an ecclesiastical architect in London. Read extensively. Became an agnostic.*
1871 *Publication of* Desperate Remedies, *his first novel.*
1872 Under the Greenwood Tree.
1874 Far From the Madding Crowd *published for the* Cornhill Magazine.
1878 The Return of the Native.
1880 The Trumpet-Major.
1881 A Laodicean.
1886 The Mayor of Casterbridge.
1887 The Woodlanders.
1891 Tess of the d'Urbervilles.
1895 Jude the Obscure: *its publication caused a scandal and he turned to poetry.*
1898 Wessex Poems.
1903-1908 The Dynasts.
1916 Selected Poems
1928 *Died in Dorchester.*

Thomas Hardy's novels are all set in the imaginary rural county of Wessex (in fact his native Dorset). With sombre realism, they describe the rough and simple peasants among a desolate but majestic landscape. His characters live close to nature; they have bonds with the earth, the stones, the past, and exist in a sort of timelessness. This harmony is usually destroyed, however, by change and by man's high aspirations. For hopes are always thwarted, and man is never free. A disciple of Darwin, Spencer and Mill, Hardy believed in determinism and turned it into a pessimistic philosophy of life: fate controls everything, suffering is inevitable and part of one's appointed course, man is caught in the ironies of life which lead him to destruction.

In The Return of the Native, *it is Clym Yeobright, the intellectual who symbolizes modernism, who loses his illusions when he marries the selfish Eustacia. Their unhappiness ends tragically when Eustacia is drowned with her lover.*

Tess of the d'Urbervilles *relates the seduction of the pure and innocent Tess by Alec d'Urberville, an obdurate and hypocritical intellectual.*

Jude the Obscure *is Hardy's darkest novel. The hero who aspires to knowledge is gradually destroyed by love and circumstances and dies among squalor and misery.*

Some of Hardy's poems reveal the same pessimism, but he also wrote lyrical poems about love and nature. The Dynasts, *an epic-drama that gives a panoramic view of the Napoleonic wars, is his most ambitious poetic work.*

Tess of the d'Urbervilles (1891)

Twice wronged by Alec d'Urberville, Tess was driven to murder him. She now finds herself at Stonehenge with Angel Clare, who had abandoned her when she confessed her affair with Alec, but has now come back repentant. It is her last moment of liberty before she is arrested and hanged.

Though the sky was dense with cloud a diffused light from some fragment of a moon had hitherto helped them a little. But the moon had now sunk, the clouds seemed to settle almost on their heads, and the night grew as dark as a cave. However, they found their way along, keeping as much on the turf as possible that their tread might not resound, which it was easy to do, there being no hedge or fence of any kind. All around was open loneliness and black solitude, over which a stiff breeze blew.

They had proceeded thus gropingly two or three miles further when on a sudden Clare became conscious of some vast erection close in his front, rising sheer from the grass. They had almost struck themselves against it.

"What monstrous place is this?" said Angel.

"It hums," said she. "Hearken!"

He listened. The wind, playing upon the edifice, produced a booming tune, like the note of some gigantic one-stringed harp. No other sound came from it, and lifting his hand and advancing a step or two, Clare felt the vertical surface of the structure. It seemed to be of solid stone, without joint or molding. Carrying his fingers onward he found that what he had come in contact with was a colossal rectangular pillar; by stretching out his left hand he could feel a similar one adjoining. At an indefinite height overhead something made the black sky blacker, which had the semblance of a vast architrave uniting the pillars horizontally. They carefully entered beneath and between; the surfaces echoed their soft rustle; but they seemed to be still out of doors. The place was roofless. Tess drew her breath fearfully, and Angel, perplexed, said –

"What can it be?"

Feeling sideways they encountered another tower-like pillar, square and uncompromising as the first; beyond it another and another. The place was all doors and pillars, some connected above by continuous architraves.

"A very Temple of the Winds," he said.

The next pillar was isolated; others composed a trilithon; others were prostrate, their flanks forming a causeway wide enough for a carriage; and it was soon obvious that they made up a forest of monoliths grouped upon the grassy expanse of the plain. The couple advanced further into this pavilion of the night till they stood in its midst.

"It is Stonehengel" said Clare.

"The heathen temple, you mean?"

"Yes. Older than the centuries; older than the D'Urbervilles! Well, what shall we do, darling? We may find shelter further on."

But Tess, really tired by this time, flung herself upon an oblong slab that lay close at hand, and was sheltered from the wind by a pillar. Owing to the action of the sun during the preceding day the stone was warm and dry, in comforting contrast to the rough and chill grass around, which had damped her skirts and shoes.

"I don't want to go any further, Angel," she said stretching out her hand for his. "Can't we bide here?"

"I fear not. This spot is visible for miles by day, although it does not seem so now."

"One of my mother's people was a shepherd hereabouts, now I think of it. And you used to say at Talbothays that I was a heathen. So now I am at home."

Phase the Seventh, Chapter 58.

Thomas Hardy on the novel:

The real, if unavowed, purpose of fiction is to give pleasure by gratifying the love of the uncommon in human experience, mental or corporeal.

This is done all the more perfectly in proportion as the reader is illuded to believe the personages true and real like himself.

Solely to this latter end a work of fiction should be a precise transcript of ordinary life: but,

The uncommon would be absent and the interest lost, Hence,

The writer's problem is, how to strike the balance between the uncommon and the ordinary so as on the one hand to give interest, on the other to give reality.

In working out this problem, human nature must never be made abnormal, which is introducing incredibility. The uncommonness must be in the events, not in the characters; and the writer's art lies in shaping that uncommonness while disguising its unlikelihood, if it be unlikely.

Notebook entry, July 1881.

The business of the poet and novelist is to show the sorriness underlying the grandest things, and the grandeur underlying the sorriest things. (...)

Nature is played out as a Beauty, but not as a Mystery. ... I don't want to see the original realities – as optical effects, that is. I want to see the deeper reality underlying the scenic, the expression of what are sometimes called abstract imaginings.

The "simply natural" is interesting no longer. The much decried, mad, late-Turner rendering is now necessary to create my interest. The exact truth as to material fact ceases to be of importance in art – it is a student's style – the style of a period when the mind is serene and unawakened to the tragical mysteries of life; when it does not bring anything to the object that coalesces with and translates the qualities that are already there, – half hidden, it may be –, and the two are depicted as the All. (...)

The whole secret of fiction and the drama – in the constructional part – lies in the adjustement of things unusual to things eternal and universal. The writer who knows exactly how exceptional, and how nonexceptional, his events should be made, possesses the key to the art. (...)

The best tragedy – highest tragedy in short – is that of the worthy encompassed by the inevitable. The tragedies of immoral and worthless people are not of the best.

Essays, Notes and *Letters.*

Compare the relationship between man and nature in the passage from **Tess of the d'Urbervilles** ***and in the following excerpt from George Meredith's*** **The Ordeal of Richard Feverel.**

On a barren corner of the wooded highland looking inland stood grey topless ruins set in nettles and rank grass-blades. Richard mechanically sat down on the crumbling flints to rest, and listened to the panting of the dog. Sprinkled at his feet were emerald lights: hundreds of glow-worms studded the dark dry ground.

He sat and eyed them, thinking not at all. His energies were expended in action. He sat as a part of the ruins, and the moon turned his shadow westward from the south. Overhead, as she declined, long ripples of silver cloud were imperceptibly stealing toward her. They were the van of a tempest. He did not observe them or the leaves beginning to chatter. When he again pursued his course with his face to the Rhine, a huge mountain appeared to rise sheer over him, and he had it in his mind to scale it. He got no nearer to the base of it for all his vigorous outstepping. The ground began to dip; he lost sight of the sky. Then heavy thunderdrops struck his cheek, the leaves were singing, the earth breathed, it was black before him and behind. All at once the thunder spoke. The mountain he had marked was bursting over him.

Up started the whole forest in violet fire. He saw the country at the foot of the hills to the bounding Rhine gleam, quiver, extinguished. Then there were pauses; and the lightning seemed as the eye of heaven, and the thunder as the tongue of heaven, each alternately addressing him; filling him with awful rapture. Alone there – sole human creature among the grandeurs and mysteries of storm – he felt the representative of his kind, and his spirit rose, and marched, and exulted, let it be glory, let it be ruin! Lower down the lightened abysses of air rolled the wrathful crash: then white thrusts of light were darted from the sky, and great curving ferns, seen steadfast in pallor a second, were supernaturally agitated, and vanished. Then a shrill song roused in the leaves and the herbage. Prolonged and louder it sounded, as deeper and heavier the deluge pressed. A mighty force of water satisfied the desire of the earth. Even in this, drenched as he was by the first outpouring, Richard had a savage pleasure. Keeping in motion, he was scarcely conscious of the wet, and the grateful breath of the weeds was refreshing.

The novels of George Meredith (1828-1909) blend poetry and a deep psychological analysis. He is no painter of society but, like Henry James, an explorer of the characters' minds, of their progress towards self-discovery. His women are spirited and proud, his men are often endowed with selfishness (like Sir Willoughby in The Egoist) *and a high opinion of their own honour. Meredith's style, based on a sometimes excessive use of wit, epigrams and metaphors, often makes his works difficult to read. His main novels are* The Ordeal of Richard Feverel *(1859),* Evan Harrington *(1861),* The Adventures of Harry Richmond *(1871),* Beauchamp's Career *(1876) and* The Egoist *(1879). Meredith also wrote poetry.*

Cf. Narrative technique, p. 15.

Two visions of Stonehenge.
See what Hardy said of Turner on p. 226.

J. Constable: Stonehenge.
London, Victoria and Albert Museum. Ph. Lauros-Giraudon.

J. M. W. Turner: Stonehenge, *1820?-1830?*
© British Museum.

Henry JAMES 1843-1916

1843 *Born in New York, in an intellectual family (his father was a friend of Emerson's, and his elder brother William became a well-known philosopher).*
1855-1959 *School and studies in Albany, New York, Geneva, London, Paris and Bonn.*
1862-1863 *Harvard Law School.*
1864 *Started writing stories for periodicals.*
1869-1874 *Several travels and stays in Europe.*
1874-1875 Roderick Hudson.
1875-1876 *Met Flaubert, Zola and Turgenev in Paris. Wrote* The American.
1876 *Settled in London, but often visited France and Italy during the rest of his life (went back to the United States in 1882 and 1905).*
1879 *Became famous with* Daisy Miller.
1880-1882 The Europeans, Washington Square, The Portrait of a Lady.
1886 The Bostonians, The Princess Casamassima.
1890-1895 *Unsuccessfully turned to the theatre.*
1897-1898 What Maisie Knew, *wrote* The Turn of the Screw.
1899 The Awkward Age.
1902-1904 *Publication of* The Ambassadors, The Wings of the Dove, The Golden Bowl.
1915 *Became a British citizen.*
1916 *Died in Chelsea.*

Henry James's large production includes novels, short stories, plays, travel books and criticism, but it was his fiction that made him famous. Two themes are dominant in his novels:

The first is what he himself called the "international subject", which meant in effect the relationship between America and Americans on the one hand and Europe and Europeans on the other. (...)

The other dominant theme is related to this: it is that of the innocent, eager for life, corrupted or despoiled by the sophisticated, in whom the good things sought by the innocent appear to reside. In practice in James's fiction, the innocent tend to be American, their exploiters European.

W. Allen.

Yet it is his method which is truly original: his attempt to study the relationships between individuals, the workings of the human heart and moral decisions through a subtle and intricate psychological analysis that often requires active and penetrating participation on the part of the reader. James conceived a novel as an aesthetically harmonious whole, in which each part was to contribute to the general picture, as in painting. He also developed the theory of a character as a "centre of consciousness", who – like a polished mirror – reflects life in a credible way, showing both lucidity and bias. James's ideas on fiction were published in his prefaces to the novels (The Art of the Novel) *as well as in* The House of Fiction.

The Portrait of a Lady (1881)

It may be affirmed without delay that Isabel was probably very liable to the sin of self-esteem ; she often surveyed with complacency the field of her own nature; she was in the habit of taking for granted, on scanty evidence, that she was right; she treated herself to occasions of homage. Meanwhile her errors and delusions were frequently such as a biographer interested in preserving the dignity of his subject must shrink from specifying. Her thoughts were a tangle of vague outlines which had never been corrected by the judgement of people speaking with authority. In matters of opinion she had had her own way, and it had led her into a thousand ridiculous zigzags. At moments she discovered she was grotesquely wrong, and then she treated herself to a week of passionate humility. After this she held her head higher than ever again; for it was of no use, she had an unquenchable desire to think well of herself. She had a theory that it was only under this provision life was worth living; that one should be one of the best, should be conscious of a fine organisation (she couldn't help knowing her organisation was fine), should move in a realm of light, of natural wisdom, of happy impulse, of inspiration gracefully chronic. It was almost as unnecessary to cultivate doubt of one's self as to cultivate doubt of one's best friend: one should try to be one's own best friend and to give one's self, in this manner, distinguished company. The girl had a certain nobleness of imagination which rendered her a good many services and played her a great many tricks. She spent half her time in thinking of beauty and bravery and magnanimity; she had a fixed determination to regard the world as a place of brightness, of free expansion, of irresistible action: she held it must be detestable to be afraid or ashamed. She had an infinite hope that she should never do anything wrong. She had resented so strongly, after discovering them, her mere errors of feeling (the discovery always made her tremble as if she had escaped from a trap which might have caught her and smothered her) that the chance of inflicting a sensible injury upon another person, presented only as a contingency, caused her at moments to hold her breath. That always struck her as the worst thing that could happen to her. On the whole, reflectively, she was in no uncertainty about the things that were wrong. She had no love of their look, but when she fixed them hard she recognised them. It was wrong to be mean, to be jealous, to be false, to be cruel; she had seen very little of the evil of the world, but she had seen women who lied and who tried to hurt each other. Seeing such things had quickened her high spirit; it seemed indecent not to scorn them. Of course the danger of a high spirit was the danger of inconsistency – the danger of keeping up the flag after the place has surrendered; a sort of behaviour so crooked as to be almost a dishonour to the flag. But Isabel, who knew little of the sorts of artillery to which young women are exposed, flattered herself that such contradictions would never be noted in her own conduct. Her life should always be in harmony with the most pleasing impression she should produce; she would be what she appeared, and she would appear what she was. Sometimes she went so far as to wish that she might find herself some day in a difficult position, so that she should have the pleasure of being as heroic as the occasion demanded. Altogether, with her meagre knowledge, her inflated ideals, her confidence at once innocent and dogmatic, her temper at once exacting and indulgent, her mixture of curiosity and fastidiousness, of vivacity and indifference, her desire to look very well and to be if possible even better, her determination to see, to try, to know, her combination of the delicate, desultory, flame-like spirit and the eager and personal creature of conditions: she would be an easy victim of scientific criticism if she were not intended to awaken on the reader's part an impulse more tender and more purely expectant.

Chapter 6.

Henry James on his fiction :

• Trying to recover here, for recognition, the germ of my idea, I see that it must have consisted not at all in any conceit of a "plot", nefarious name, in any flash, upon the fancy, of a set of relations, or in any one of those situations that, by a logic of their own, immediately fall, for the fabulist, into movement, into a march or a rush, a patter of quick steps; but altogether in the sense of a single character, the character and aspect of a particular engaging young woman, to which all the usual elements of a "subject", certainly of a setting, were to need to be superadded. (...)

I have always fondly remembered a remark that I heard fall years ago from the lips of Ivan Turgenieff in regard to his own experience of the usual origin of the fictive picture. It began for him almost always with the vision of some person or persons, who hovered before him, soliciting him, as the active or passive figure, interesting him and appealing to him just as they were and by what they were. He saw them, in that fashion, as *disponibles,* saw them subject to the chances, the complications of existence, and saw them vividly, but then had to find for them the right relations, those that would most bring them out; to imagine, to invent and select and piece together the situations most useful and favourable to the sense of the creatures themselves, the complications they would be most likely to produce and to feel.

"To arrive at these things is to arrive at my 'story'," he said, "and that's the way I look for it. The result is that I'm often accused of not having 'story' enough. I seem to myself to have as much as I need – to show my people, to exhibit their relations with each other; for that is all my measure. If I watch them long enough I see them come together, I see them *placed* (...)"

Preface to *The Portrait of a Lady.*

• "Place the centre of the subject in the young woman's own consciousness", I said to myself, "and you get as interesting and as beautiful a difficulty as you could wish. Stick to *that* – for the centre; put the heaviest weight into *that* scale, which will be so largely the scale of her relation to herself. Make her only interested enough, at the same time, in the things that are not herself, and this relation needn't fear to be too limited. Place meanwhile in the other scale the lighter weight (which is usually the one that tips the balance of interest) : press least hard, in

J. Mac Neill Whistler: The White Girl, *1862.*
The National Gallery of Arts, Washington D. C.

Almost a contemporary of James and, like him, an American who spent a great part of his life in Europe, J.A. Whistler (1834-1903) early asserted his theory that painting should be independent of ideas, literature and outside relationships (a reaction against Victorian painting) and appeal to the eyes through the mere harmony of colours and elements. He is best-known for his portraits (like James, Whistler could convey a mood or an expression with a few touches) and later his "nocturnes".

short, on the consciousness of your heroine's satellites, especially the male; make it an interest contributive only to the greater one. See, at all events, what can be done in this way. What better field could there be for a due ingenuity? The girl hovers, inextinguishable, as a charming creature, and the job will be to translate her into the highest terms of that formula, and as nearly as possible moreover into *all* of them. To depend upon her and her little concerns wholly to see you through will necessitate, remember, your really 'doing' her."

ibid.

• I have already betrayed, as an accepted habit, and even to extravagance commented on, my preference for dealing with my subject-matter, for "seeing my story," through the opportunity and the sensibility of some more or less detached, some not strictly involved, though thoroughly interested and intelligent witness or reporter, some person who contributes to the case mainly a certain amount of criticism and interpretation of it. Again and again, on review, the shorter things in especial that I have gathered into this Series have ranged themselves not as my own impersonal account of the affair in hand, but as my account of somebody's impression of it – the terms of this person's access to it and estimate of it contributing thus by some fine little law to intensification of interest. The somebody is often, among my shorter tales I recognize, but an unnamed, unintroduced and (save by right of intrinsic wit) unwarranted participant, the impersonal author's concrete deputy or delegate, a convenient substitute or apologist for the creative power otherwise so veiled and disembodied. My instinct appears repeatedly to have been that to arrive at the facts retailed and the figures introduced by the given help of some other conscious and confessed agent is essentially to find the whole business – that is, as I say, its effective interest – enriched *by the way.* I have in other words constantly inclined to the idea of the particular attaching case *plus* some near individual view of it; that nearness quite having thus to become an imagined observer's, a projected, charmed painter's or poet's – however avowed the "minor" quality in the latter – close and sensitive contact with it. Anything, in short, I now reflect, must have seemed to me better – better for the process and the effect of representation, my irrepressible ideal – than the mere muffled majesty of irresponsible "authorship"...

Preface to *The Golden Bowl,* 1904.

Cf. Characters and characterization, p. 12; Narrative technique, p. 15.

Joseph CONRAD 1857-1924

1857 *Józef Teodor Konrad Korzeniowski born in the Ukraine.*
1861 *His father, a Polish nationalist, imprisoned by the Russians (and exiled to Northern Russia in 1862).*
1869 *Death of his father.*
1874 *Went to Marseille and became an apprentice in the merchant marine.*
1877-1878 *Period of adventure (smuggling, gambling, love affair) which ended with his attempted suicide.*
1878-1894 *Worked in the British merchant marine and eventually became a captain.*
1889 *Started* Almayer's Folly.
1890 *Voyage to the Congo (which inspired* Heart of Darkness*).*
1894 *Left the merchant marine to become a full-time writer.*
1897 The Nigger of the "Narcissus".
1899 Heart of Darkness.
1900 Lord Jim.
1902 Typhoon.
1904 Nostromo.
1906 The Secret Agent.
1910 Under Western Eyes.
1914 Victory.
1922 The Rover.
1924 *Died near Canterbury.*

Conrad's fiction is closely related to his lifelong love of the sea and to his travelling experiences. They provided him with the settings of most of his novels: Eastern, exotic places and the sea.

Superficially, he is the novelist of adventure, romance and violence; but it is the nature of man that interests him – how a character can react to an ordeal or a strange and hostile environment. His romantic adventures serve only to reveal moral conflicts, man's courage and need for self-respect, the way he copes with responsibility, and more generally, the waverings between chance and will, illusion and reality. This relationship between the material and the spiritual appears clearly in one of his best works, Lord Jim, *which relates the wandering and tortured life of a ship mate who, through panic, abandoned the ship which he believed to be on the point of sinking. He spends his life drifting, pursued by his guilt, looking for a redemption which he will find through sacrifice.*

Conrad was not only a moralist but also an artist looking for technical perfection. Though English was not his native language (he was 23 when he started learning it), he had acquired a remarkable mastery of it by the time he wrote his first novel. His exact and precise vocabulary and the balance and rhythm of his sentences create a general effect of eloquence. Yet it is Conrad's narrative technique which is truly innovative: a slow and involved development, often relying on multiple points of views and distorted chronologies, gradually reveals the characters' nature and motivations. A device repeated in many of his novels is the use of a narrator – Marlow – who is half-witness, half-participant, and through whose eyes the story is seen and other points of view are relayed.

Heart of Darkness (1899)

"The story of *Heart of Darkness* is told by Marlow, who once had the job of taking a rickety steam-boat up the Congo to bring back from a distant trading-post an ivory-trader called Kurtz. Marlow and Kurtz are Europeans who react differently to the primitive lure of Africa: the narrator holds on to his European values even when in the very heart of darkness, but Kurtz surrenders his European heritage, exploits the natives by making them think him a god, and abandons the moral values in which he has been educated by participating in certain unspecified but 'unspeakable rites'. On the journey back down the Congo Kurtz dies, and on his death-bed cries, enigmatically, 'The Horror! The horror!'. Everything turns on the interpretation of this cry, with its 'strange and terrible message of ambivalence toward the life of civilisation': is it a deathbed renunciation of an evil life, as the narrator and some critics would like to believe, or is it (as Marlow suspects) simply exultant, a confirmation of the unspeakable and an unrepenting rejection of the European values Marlow cherishes?"

K.K. Ruthren, *The Savage God*, 1968 Critical Quarterly.
Manchester University Press.

Here is Marlow's first vision of the natives and of an accountant at one of the stations.

"My purpose was to stroll into the shade for a moment; but no sooner within than it seemed to me I had stepped into the gloomy circle of some Inferno. The rapids were near, and an uninterrupted, uniform, headlong, rushing noise filled the mournful stillness of the grove, where not a breath stirred, not a leaf moved, with a mysterious sound – as though the tearing pace of the launched earth had suddenly become audible.

"Black shapes crouched, lay, sat between the trees leaning against the trunks, clinging to the earth, half coming out, half effaced within the dim light, in all the attitudes of pain, abandonment, and despair. Another mine on the cliff went off, followed by a slight shudder of the soil under my feet. The work was going on. The work! And this was the place where some of the helpers had withdrawn to die.

"They were dying slowly – it was very clear. They were not enemies, they were not criminals, they were nothing earthly now, – nothing but black shadows of disease and starvation, lying confusedly in the greenish gloom. Brought from all the recesses of the coast in all the legality of time contracts, lost in uncongenial surroundings, fed on unfamiliar food, they sickened, became inefficient, and were then allowed to crawl away and rest. These moribund shapes were free as air – and nearly as thin. I began to distinguish the gleam of the eyes under the trees. Then, glancing down, I saw a face near my hand. The black bones reclined at full length with one shoulder against the tree, and slowly the eyelids rose and the sunken eyes looked up at me, enormous and vacant, a kind of blind, white flicker in the depths of the orbs, which died out slowly. The man seemed young – almost a boy – but you know with them it's hard to tell. I found nothing else to do but to offer him one of my good Swede's ship's biscuits I had in my pocket. The fingers closed slowly on it and held – there was no other movement and no other glance. He had tied a bit of white worsted round his neck – Why? Where did he get it? Was it a badge – an ornament – a charm – a propitiatory act? Was there any idea at all connected with it? It looked startling round his black neck, this bit of white thread from beyond the seas.

"Near the same tree two more bundles of acute angles sat with their legs drawn up. One, with his chin propped on his knees, stared at nothing, in an intolerable and appalling manner: his brother phantom rested its forehead, as if overcome with a great weariness; and all about others were scattered in every pose of contorted collapse, as in some picture of a massacre or a pestilence. While I stood horror-struck, one of these creatures rose to his hands and knees, and went off on all-fours towards the river to drink. He lapped out of his hand, then sat up in the sunlight, crossing his shins in front of him, and after a time let his woolly head fall on his breastbone.

"I didn't want any more loitering in the shade, and I made haste towards the station. When near the buildings I met a white man, in such an unexpected elegance of get-up that in the first moment I took him for a sort of vision. I saw a high starched collar, white cuffs, a light alpaca jacket, snowy trousers, a clear necktie, and varnished boots. No hat. Hair parted, brushed, oiled, under a green-lined parasol held in a big white hand. He was amazing, and had a penholder behind his ear.

"I shook hands with this miracle, and I learned he was the Company's chief accountant, and that all the book-keeping was done at this station. He had come out for a moment, he said, "to get a breath of fresh air". The expression sounded wonderfully odd, with its suggestion of sedentary desk-life. I wouldn't have mentioned the fellow to you at all, only it was from his lips that I first heard the name of the man who is so indissolubly connected with the memories of that time. Moreover, I respected the fellow. Yes; I respected his collars, his vast cuffs, his brushed hair. His appearance was certainly that of a hairdresser's dummy; but in the great demoralization of the land he kept up his appearance. That's backbone. His starched collars and got-up shirt-fronts were achievements of character. He had been out nearly three years; and later, I could not help asking him how he managed to sport such linen. He had just the faintest blush, and said modestly, 'I've been teaching one of the native women about the station. It was difficult. She had a distaste for the work.' Thus this man had verily accomplished something. And he was devoted to his books, which were in apple-pie order."

Chapter 1.

Joseph Conrad on the art of the novelist:

■ A work that aspires, however humbly, to the condition of art should carry its justification in every line. And art itself may be defined as a single-minded attempt to render the highest kind of justice to the visible universe, by bringing to light the truth, manifold and one, underlying its every aspect. It is an attempt to find in its forms, in its colours, in its light, in its shadows, in the aspects of matter and in the facts of life, what of each is fundamental, what is enduring and essential – their one illuminating and convincing quality – the very truth of their existence. (...)

The artist appeals to that part of our being which is not dependent on wisdom; to that in us which is a gift and not an acquisition – and, therefore, more permanently enduring. He speaks to our capacity for delight and wonder, to the sense of mystery surrounding our lives; to our sense of pity, and beauty, and pain, to the latent feeling of fellowship with all creation – and to the subtle but invincible conviction of solidarity that knits together the loneliness of innumerable hearts, to the solidarity in dreams, in joy, in sorrow, in aspirations, in illusions, in hope, in fear, which binds men to each other, which binds together all humanity – the dead to the living and the living to the unborn. (...)

All art (...) appeals primarily to the senses, and the artistic aim when expressing itself in written words must also make its appeal through the senses, if its high desire is to reach the secret spring of responsive emotions. It must strenuously aspire to the plasticity of sculpture, to the colour of painting, and to the magic suggestiveness of music – which is the art of arts. And it is only through complete, unswerving devotion to the perfect blending of form and substance; it is only through an unremitting never-discouraged care for the shape and ring of sentences that an approach can be made to plasticity, to colour, and that the light of magic suggestiveness may be brought to play for an evanescent instant over the commonplace surface of words: of the old, old words, worn thin, defaced by ages of careless usage. (...)

To snatch in a moment of courage, from the remorseless rush of time, a passing phase of life, is only the beginning of the task. The task approached in tenderness and faith is to hold up unquestioningly, without choice and without fear, the rescued fragment before all eyes in the light of a sincere mood. It is to show its vibration, its colour, its form ; and through its movement, its form, and its colour, reveal the substance of its truth – disclose its inspiring secret: the stress and passion within the core of each convincing moment. In a single-minded attempt of that kind, if one be deserving and fortunate, one may perchance attain to such clearness of sincerity that at last the presented vision of regret or pity, of terror or mirth, shall awaken in the hearts of the beholders that feeling of unavoidable solidarity; of the solidarity in mysterious origin, in toil, in joy, in hope, in uncertain fate, which binds men to each other and all mankind to the visible world.

Preface to *The Nigger of the "Narcissus".*

● The *whole* of the truth lies in the presentation; therefore the expression should be studied in the interest of veracity. This is the only morality of art apart from *subject.*

I have travelled a good way from my original remark – not enough left to the imagination in the phrasing. I beg leave to illustrate my meaning from extracts... "When the whole horror of his position forced itself with an agony of apprehension upon his frightened mind, Pa'Tûa for a space lost his reason."... In this sentence the reader is borne down by the full expression. The words: *with an agony of apprehension* completely destroy the effect – therefore interfere with the truth of the statement. The word *frightened* is fatal. It seems as if it had been written without any thought at all. It takes away all sense of reality – for if you read the sentence *in its place on the page* you will see that the word *frightened* (or indeed any word of that sort) is inadequate to express the true state of that man's mind. No word is adequate. The imagination of the reader should be left free to arouse his feeling.

"...When the whole horror of his position forced itself upon his mind, Pa'Tûa for a space lost his reason..." This is truth; this it is which, thus stated, carries conviction because it is a *picture* of a mental state. And look how finely it goes on with a perfectly legitimate effect... "He screamed aloud, and the hollow of the rocks took up his cries"... It is magnificent! It is suggestive. It is truth effectively stated. But "and hurled them back to him mockingly" is nothing at all. It is a phrase anybody can write to fit any sort of situation; it is the sort of thing I write twenty times a day and (with the fear of overtaking fate behind me) spend half my nights in taking out of my work.

Letter to Sir Hugh Clifford, 1899.

Cf. Narrative technique, p. 15.

Another view on imperialism:

THE WHITE MAN'S BURDEN

Take up the White Man's burden –
  Send forth the best ye breed –
Go bind your sons to exile –
  To serve your captives' need;
To wait in heavy harness,
  On fluttered folk and wild –
Your new-caught, sullen peoples,
  Half-devil and half-child.

Take up the White Man's burden –
  In patience to abide,
To veil the threat of terror
  And check the show of pride;
By open speech and simple,
  An hundred times made plain,
To seek another's profit,
  And work another's gain.

Take up the White Man's burden –
  The savage wars of peace –
Fill full the mouth of Famine
  And bid the sickness cease;
And when your goal is nearest
  The end for others sought,
Watch Sloth and heathen Folly
  Bring all your hope to nought.

Take up the White Man's burden –
  No tawdry rule of kings,
But toil of serf and sweeper –
  The tale of common things.
The ports ye shall not enter,
  The roads ye shall not tread,
Go make them with your living,
  And mark them with your dead!

Take up the White Man's burden –
  And reap his old reward:
The blame of those ye better,
  The hate of those ye guard –
The cry of hosts ye humor
  (Ah, slowly!) toward the light: –
"Why brought ye us from bondage,
  "Our loved Egyptian night?"

Take up the White Man's burden –
  Ye dare not stoop to less –
Nor call too loud on Freedom
  To cloak your weariness;
By all ye cry or whisper,
  By all ye leave or do,
The silent, sullen peoples
  Shall weigh your Gods and you.

Take up the White Man's burden –
  Have done with childish days –
The lightly proffered laurel,
  The easy, ungrudged praise.
Comes now, to search your manhood
  Through all the thankless years,
Cold-edged with dear-bought wisdom,
  The judgment of your peers!

Rudyard Kipling, *The Five Nations*, 1899.
Rudyard Kipling's Verse.

Rudyard Kipling (1865-1936) was born and bred in India and worked there as a journalist. He is well-known for his short stories about India, its people, the jungle and the sea: Tales from the Hills *(1888),* The Jungle Book *(1894),* Just So Stories *(1902), but also wrote some novels –* Kim *(1901),* Stalky & Co. *(1899) – and some verse. Kipling had faith in the good work that Britain could do for its empire and thought that developing other civilisations was its responsibility and "burden".*

Oscar WILDE 1854-1900

1854 *Born in Dublin.*

1871-1874 *Brilliant studies at Trinity College, Dublin.*

1874-1879 *Magdalen College, Oxford; gained a reputation as founder of "Aestheticism".*

1876-1877 *Travelled to Greece and Italy; published several poems.*

1881-1882 Poems *published; lecture tour to the USA.*

1883 *British lecture tour.*

1884-1886 *Gave lectures and wrote essays on the theatre.*

1887-1888 *Several stories published in magazines (published in 1891 as* Lord Arthur Savile's Crime and Other Stories).

[illegible] *Wrote essays (published in 1891 as* Intentions*), among them* The Decay of Lying.

1890 The Picture of Dorian Gray, *first published in a magazine.*

More than the writer, it was the man Oscar Wilde who affronted, shocked but also fascinated the society of his time. He was a flamboyant character who moved among the aristocracy with ready wit and affected manner and dress.

He was at the centre of the aesthetic movement influenced by some of the Pre-Raphaelite doctrines of William Morris and Ruskin as well as by the theories of Pater, Baudelaire, Huysmans (cf A Rebours*) and Gautier. Reacting against Victorianism, the aesthetes and decadents claimed that the enjoyment of beauty was the only aim of life. What mattered was art and sensibility rather than morality and duty – all art should be useless and beautiful: "it appeared to Dorian Gray that the true nature of the senses had never been understood, and that they had remained savage and animal merely because the world had sought to starve them into submission or to kill them by pain, instead of aiming at making them elements of a new spirituality, of which a fine instinct for beauty was to be the dominant characteristic."*

1891 *Wrote* Salomé *in Paris (refused a licence in England; pub. in Paris in 1893).*
1892 *Production of* Lady Windermere's Fan.
1893 *Production of* A Woman of No Importance.
1895 *Production of* An Ideal Husband *and* The Importance of Being Earnest. *Arrested for homosexual practices and sentenced to two years' hard labour.*
1895-1897 *Reading gaol (where he wrote* De Profundis *and* The Ballad of Reading Gaol.)
1897-1900 *Travelled in France and Italy.*
1900 *Died in Paris.*

O. Wilde wrote many poems in which he tried to reach perfect beauty through symbolism, and essays and stories, but is better known for his novel and plays.

The Picture of Dorian Gray *is the story of a young man entirely given to the pleasures of beauty and art, without any moral restraint. Throughout his hedonistic life, he keeps his youth and beauty and it is the picture of him painted by his friend which slowly deteriorates and shows the marks of time and corruption. The book was considered as scandalous because of the latent homosexuality of the hero.*

His comedies, in which he shows himself the heir of the Restoration playwrights, have remained enormously popular. Their main theme is the battle of the sexes and their most typical character the outrageous dandy whose witticisms, paradoxes and epigrams often hide generosity and humanity.

Lady Windermere's Fan (1892)

Drawing-room in Lord Windermere's house. Door R.U. opening into ball-room, where band is playing. Door L. through which guests are entering. Door L.U. opens on to illuminated terrace. Palms, flowers, and brilliant lights. Room crowded with guests. Lady Windermere is receiving them.

Duchess of Berwick (*up C.*): So strange Lord Windermere isn't here. Mr. Hopper is very late, too... You have kept those five dances for him, Agatha? (*Comes down*)

Lady Agatha: Yes, mamma.

Duchess of Berwick (*sitting on sofa*): Just let me see your card. I'm so glad Lady Windermere has revived cards. They're a mother's only safeguard. You dear simple little thing! (*Scratches out two names.*) No nice girl should ever waltz with such particularly younger sons! It looks so fast! The last two dances you might pass on the terrace with Mr. Hopper.

(Enter Mr. Dumby and Lady Plymdale from the ball-room)

Lady Agatha: Yes, mamma.

Duchess of Berwick (*fanning herself*): The air is so pleasant there.

Parker: Mrs. Cowper-Cowper. Lady Stutfield. Sir James Royston. Mr. Guy Berkeley. (*These people enter as announced.*)

Dumby: Good evening, Lady Stutfield. I suppose this will be the last ball of the season?

Lady Stutfield: I suppose so, Mr. Dumby. It's been a delightful season, hasn't it?

Dumby: Quite delightful! Good evening, Duchess. I suppose this will be the last ball of the season?

Duchess of Berwick: I suppose so, Mr. Dumby. It has been a very dull season, hasn't it?

Dumby: Dreadfully dull! Dreadfully dull !

Mrs. Cowper-Cowper: Good evening, Mr. Dumby. I suppose this will be the last ball of the season?

Dumby: Oh, I think not. There'll probably be two more. (*Wanders back to Lady Plymdale.*)

Parker: Mr. Rufford. Lady Jedburgh and Miss Graham. Mr. Hopper. (*These people enter as announced.)*

Hopper: How do you do, Lady Windermere? How do you do, Duchess? (*Bows to Lady Agatha.*)

Duchess of Berwick: Dear Mr. Hopper, how nice of you to come so early. We all know how you are run after in London.

Hopper: Capital place, London! They are not nearly so exclusive in London as they are in Sydney.

Duchess of Berwick: Ah! we know your value, Mr. Hopper. We wish there were more like you. It would make life so much easier. Do you know, Mr. Hopper, dear Agatha and I are so much interested in Australia. It must be so pretty with all the dear little kangaroos flying about. Agatha has found it on the map. What a curious shape it is! Just like a large packing-case. However, it is a very young country, isn't it?

Hopper: Wasn't it made at the same time as the others, Duchess?

Duchess of Berwick: How clever you are, Mr. Hopper. You have a cleverness quite of your own. Now I mustn't keep you.

Hopper: But I should like to dance with Lady Agatha, Duchess.

Duchess of Berwick: Well, I *hope* she has a dance left. Have you a dance left, Agatha?

Lady Agatha: Yes, mamma.

Duchess of Berwick: The next one?

Lady Agatha: Yes, mamma.

Hopper: May I have the pleasure? (*Lady Agatha bows.*)

Duchess of Berwick: Mind you take great care of my little chatter-box, Mr. Hopper.

Act II, 1.

Oscar Wilde on art:

● The public imagine that, because they are interested in their immediate surroundings, Art should be interested in them also, and should take them as her subject-matter. But the mere fact that they are interested in these things makes them unsuitable subjects for Art. The only beautiful things, as somebody once said, are the things that do not concern us. As long as a thing is useful or necessary to us, or affects us in any way, either for pain or for pleasure, or appeals strongly to our sympathies, or is a vital part of the environment in which we live, it is outside the proper sphere of art. To art's subject-matter we should be more or less indifferent.

The Decay of Lying.

● The nineteenth century dislike of Romanticism is the rage of Caliban not seeing his own face in a glass.

The moral life of man forms part of the subject-matter of the artist, but the morality of art consists in the perfect use of an imperfect medium. No artist desires to prove anything. Even things that are true can be proved.

No artist has ethical sympathies. An ethical sympathy in an artist is an unpardonable mannerism of style.

No artist is ever morbid. The artist can express everything.

Thought and language are to the artist instruments of an art.

Vice and virtue are to the artist materials for an art.

From the point of view of form, the type of all the arts is the art of the musician. From the point of view of feeling, the actor's craft is the type.

All art is at once surface and symbol.

The artist is the creator of beautiful things.

To reveal art and conceal the artist is art's aim.

The critic is he who can translate into another manner or a new material his impression of beautiful things.

The highest, as the lowest, form of criticism is a mode of autobiography.

Those who find ugly meanings in beautiful things are corrupt without being charming. This is a fault.

Those who find beautiful meanings in beautiful things are the cultivated. For these there is hope.

They are the elect to whom beautiful things mean only Beauty.

There is no such thing as a moral or an immoral book.

Books are well written, or badly written. That is all.

The nineteenth century dislike of Realism is the rage of Caliban seeing his own face in a glass.

Those who go beneath the surface do so at their peril.

Those who read the symbol do so at their peril.

It is the spectator, and not life, that art really mirrors.

Diversity of opinion about a work of art shows that the work is new, complex, and vital.

When critics disagree the artist is in accord with himself.

We can forgive a man for making a useful thing as long as he does not admire it. The only excuse for making a useless thing is that one admires it intensely.

All art is quite useless.

The Picture of Dorian Gray, The Preface.

Cf. Comedy, p. 24; Wit, humour, satire and irony, p. 27.

Though Oscar Wilde and James McN. Whistler eventually quarrelled, they knew each other well for many years and had constant battles of wit. (e.g.:
O. Wilde: "I wish I'd said that, Jimmy.
Whistler: - You will, Oscar, you will.")
Their aesthetic theories (cf p. 236) were very close.

J. Whistler: Cremorne Gardens No 2, *1875.*
New York, Metropolitan Museum.

Henry Moore: Mother and Child, *1924.*
City Art Gallery, Manchester.

Barbara Hepworth: Two Figures, *1964.*
Ph. British Information Services, London.

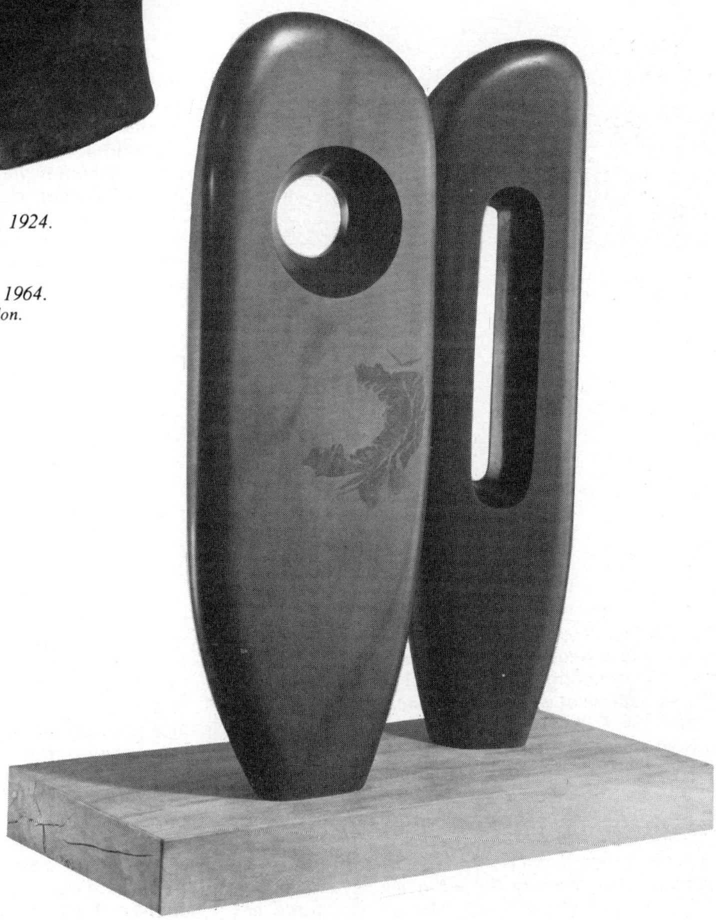

The forties were marked by the emergence of two major painters, both conveying an intense vision of reality: Graham SUTHERLAND *and* Francis BACON.

As painters of Romantic character Graham Sutherland and Francis Bacon (b. 1910) may be grouped together. Since 1945 Sutherland's work has shown a surprising variety though the sense of strangeness remains a constant factor, appearing in his studies of a bat or a toad, or in his half-natural, half-mechanical constructions with an eerie fascinating life of their own. Francis Bacon, a self-taught painter who began to exhibit his work in the 1930s, has given an impressive modern variant on the moment of terror which Fuseli conceived, the distortion which Goya saw in human expression, the horror which lurks in modern life. It is part of the effect that he has made that he has shown how often reality is unlike the conventional idea of it – as indeed photography has indicated.

W. Gaunt, *ibid.*

The period after the second World War witnessed a renewal of interest in non-figurative art (cf. the paintings of Victor Pasmore for example) as well as pop art.

Peter BLAKE'S *paintings are typical of pop art, making use of collages, photographs and everyday objects to give a sense of relief and to reflect popular culture.*

David HOCKNEY, *another painter whose early works achieved the same aim through using graffiti and dealing mainly with popular themes such as advertising, pop music and everyday life, evolved towards more figurative paintings in the 1960s, with richer colours and more autobiographical themes.*

Francis Bacon: Acrobats, *1967.*
Paris, Galerie Claude Bernard.

Music

C.H.H. Parry's Prometheus Unbound *(1880), though a fairly traditional cantata, marked the conclusive revival of English choral music. A number of factors had paved the way for this renewal: the development of popular concerts (the Promenade Concerts were to appear in 1895) and music festivals, the creation of numerous amateur choirs and schools of music, and the popularity of Gilbert and Sullivan's operettas after 1870 (e.g.* H.M.S. Pinafore, The Pirates of Penzance, The Mikado*). Besides* Hubert PARRY *(whose works include a few symphonies, but mainly comprise choral works showing the influence of the romantics), two other composers can be considered as pioneers:* Alexander MACKENZIE *and* Charles V. STANFORD.

But it was during the first decade of the 20th century that English music fully came into its own again with Edward ELGAR *(1857-1934) whose works could express nostalgia as well as the humour and gaiety of Edwardian London. (*Enigma Variations, *1899;* Cockaigne Overture, Pomp and Circumstance, *1900;* The Dream of Gerontius, *an oratorio, 1900).*

Elgar's influence was deeply felt throughout the first half of the century, which was dominated by three composers:

- R. Vaughan WILLIAMS *(1872-1957): mainly a composer of orchestral music, religious vocal works and operas* (Hugh the Drover, The Shepherds of the Delectable Mountain, Riders to

D. Hockney: Mr and Mrs Clark and Percy, *1970-71.*
London, The Tate Gallery.

the Sea), *his production is coloured by his interests in folk song and Tudor polyphony.*

• Gustav HOLST *(1874-1935), who also contributed to the revival of national English music through his interest in folklore and Elizabethan madrigals (1914-16:* The Planets*).*

• John IRELAND *(1879-1962), whose best works – under the influence of Brahms, Ravel and Debussy – are for the piano.*

After 1930, the musical production broke into several directions, though two composers stand out: Michael Tippet and Benjamin Britten.

The works of Michael TIPPETT *(1905) (concertos, symphonies and operas, and the oratorio* A Child of Our Time, *1944) reveal his human compassion as well as his interest in rhythm.*

Benjamin BRITTEN *(1913-1977) is now certainly the best-known twentieth century British composer. His production is enormous and diversified. It contains chamber and orchestral music, but his best works are vocal:*

– melodies and songs (he often worked with W.H. Auden and composed much of his music for the well-known tenor Peter Pears),

*– operas, which made him famous (*Paul Bunyan, *1941;* Peter Grimes, *written in 1945, is about sailors' lives in a small Norfolk fishing village and the popular and poetic music was an immediate success;* The Rape of Lucrecia, *1946;* The Turn of the Screw, *1954;* A Midsummer Night's Dream, *1960,*

– other choral works, such as his well-known War Requiem.

William Butler YEATS 1865-1939

1865 *Born near Dublin.*
1882 *Wrote his first poems.*
1884 *Entered the Dublin School of Art.*
1886 *Gave up his studies in art to become a professional writer.*
1887 *Settled in London. Interested in the occult. Met W. Morris, O. Wilde and G. B. Shaw.*
1889 *Publication of his first poems,* The Wanderings of Oisin and Other Poems. *Fell in love with Maud Gonne.*
1890 *Joined the Order of the Golden Dawn, a secret society.*
1891 *Founded the Irish Literary Society, the Rhymers' Club and, in Dublin, the National Literary Society.*
1892 The Countess Kathleen *(a verse play) published.*
1894 *Met French Symbolist poets in Paris.*
1895 Collected Poems.
1896 *Met John Millington Synge and Lady Gregory. Many theatrical and political activities.*
1899 The Wind Among the Reeds.
1902 *Production of* Cathleen ni Hoohilan.
1904 *Opened the Abbey Theatre (of which he became director in 1905 with Synge and Lady Gregory).*
1906 Poems 1899-1905.
1908 Collected Works.
1911 *Met Ezra Pound.*
1914 Responsibilities.
1917 The Wild Swans at Coole.
1921 Michael Robartes and The Dancer; Four Plays for Dancers.
1923 *Nobel Prize.*
1926 A Vision.
1928 The Tower.
1933 The Winding Stair.
1938 New Poems; Purgatory *produced at the Abbey Theatre.*
1939 *Died in France.*

Yeats's early poems and plays blend his interest in magic and his deep attachment to his country. They evoke Irish mythology and traditions and the "Celtic Twilight", and show the influence of the French symbolists and the aesthetic movement whose followers he met in the Rhymers' Club.

A second group of poems deals with Irish nationalism and the revolution, with the heroism and corruption the 1916 Easter rising led to.

But his major achievement lies in the cosmos and symbolism of his later poetry. He conceived of his works as an organic whole, in which each poem should contribute some element to the general "system" that would explain the entire universe. The result is the creation of an elaborate framework, mostly inspired by his occult interests and often reminiscent of Blake's mythology (Yeats had edited his poems). But Blake's gods and biblical figures give way to patterns such as gyres, or the Great Wheel, which represents all the possible phases of history and all the incarnations of man. This system provided him with a rich imagery, full of symbolic meanings (e.g. Byzantium, which symbolizes ideal and everlasting art) and with a philosophy that made the renewal of man possible at a time when he saw the world threatened by decadence and the Apocalypse.

The Second Coming (1919)

Turning and turning in the widening gyre[1]
The falcon cannot hear the falconer.
Things fall apart; the centre cannot hold;
Mere anarchy is loosed upon the world,
The blood-dimmed tide is loosed, and everywhere
The ceremony of innocence is drowned;
The best lack all conviction, while the worst
Are full of passionate intensity.

Surely some revelation is at hand;
Surely the Second Coming is at hand.
The Second Coming! Hardly are those words out
When a vast image out of *Spiritus Mundi*[2]
Troubles my sight; somewhere in sands of the desert

A shape with lion body and the head of a man[3]
A gaze blank and pitiless as the sun,
Is moving its slow thighs, while all about it
Reel shadows of the indignant desert birds.
The darkness drops again; but now I know
That twenty centuries of stony sleep
Were vexed to nightmare by a rocking cradle,
And what rough beast, its hour come round at last,
Slouches towards Bethlehem to be born.

Michael Robartes and the Dancer.

1. *gyre*: see below. – 2. *Spiritus Mundi*: "a general storehouse of images which have ceased to be a property of any personality or spirit" – 3. *line 14*: cf *Revelation, 13:*
1 (...) And I stood upon the sand of the sea, and saw a beast rise up out of the sea, having seven heads and ten horns, and upon his horns ten crowns, and upon his heads the name of blasphemy.
2 And the beast which I saw was like unto a leopard, and his feet were as the feet of a bear, and his mouth as the mouth of a lion: and the dragon gave him his power, and his seat, and great authority.
3 And I saw one of his heads as it were wounded to death; and his deadly wound was healed: and all the world wondered after the beast.
4 And they worshipped the dragon which gave power unto the beast: and they worshipped the beast, saying, Who is like unto the beast? who is able to make war with him?
5 And there was given unto him a mouth speaking great things and blasphemies; and power was given unto him to continue forty and two months.

The images of the gyre in the poetry of Yeats: *T. R. Henn,* The Lonely Tower, *Methuen.*

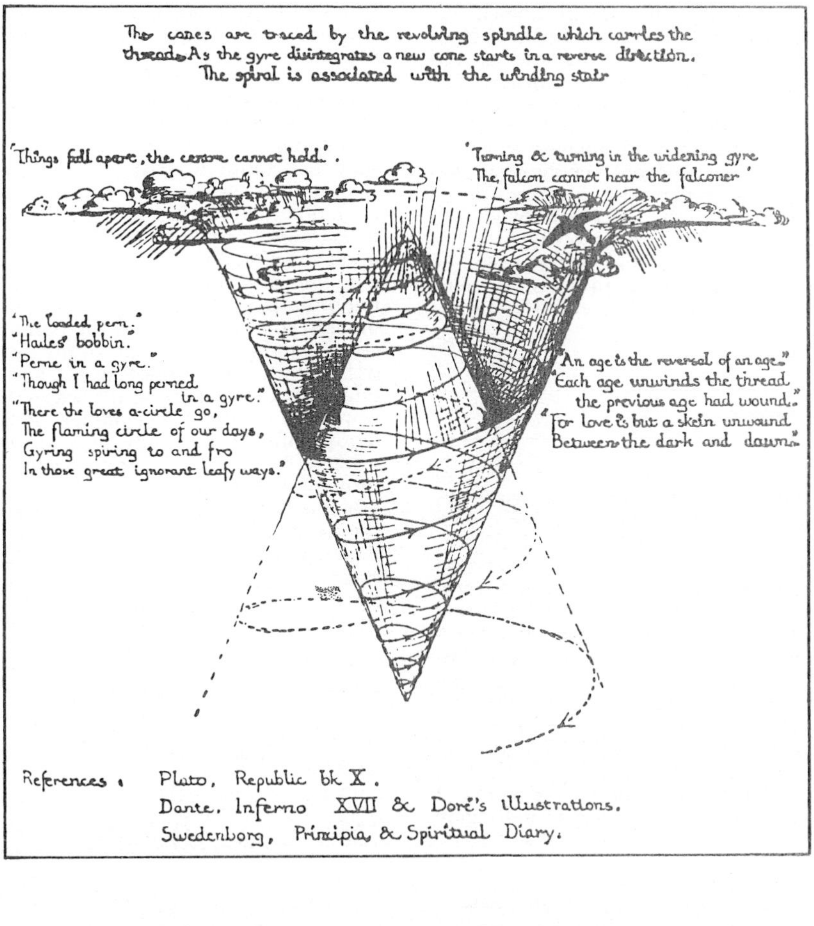

Yeats's notes to the poem:

The human soul is always moving outward into the objective world or inward into itself; & this movement is double because the human soul would not be conscious were it not suspended between contraries, the greater the contrast the more intense the consciousness. The man, in whom the movement inward is stronger than the movement outward, the man who sees all reflected within himself, the subjective man, reaches the narrow end of a gyre at death, for death is always, they contend, even when it seems the result of accident, preceded by an intensification of the subjective life; and has a moment of revelation immediately after death, a revelation which they describe as his being carried into the presence of all his dead kindred, a moment whose objectivity is exactly equal to the subjectivity of death. The objective man on the other hand, whose gyre moves outward, receives at this moment the revelation, not of himself seen from within, for that is impossible to objective man, but of himself as if he were somebody else. This figure is true also of history, for the end of an age, which always receives the revelation of the character of the next age, is represented by the coming of one gyre to its place of greatest expansion and of the other to that of its greatest contraction. At the present moment the life gyre is sweeping outward, unlike that before the birth of Christ which was narrowing, and has almost reached its greatest expansion. The revelation which approaches will however take its character from the contrary movement of the interior gyre. All our scientific, democratic, fact-accumulating, heterogeneous civilisation belongs to the outward gyre and prepares not the continuance of itself but the revelation as in a lightning flash, though in a flash that will not strike only in one place, and will for a time be constantly repeated, of the civilisation that must slowly take its place.

ibid.

Yeats on his poetry:

Do not try to make a politician of me, even in Ireland I shall never I think be that again – as my sense of reality deepens, and I think it does with age, my horror at the cruelty of governments grows greater, and if I did what you want, I would seem to hold one form of government more responsible than any other, and that would betray my convictions. Communist, Fascist, nationalist, clerical, anti-clerical, are all responsible according to the number of their victims. I have not been silent; I have used the only vehicle I possess – verse. If you have my poems by you, look up a poem called *The Second Coming*. It was written some sixteen or seventeen years ago and foretold what is happening. I have written of the same thing again and again since...

Forgive me my dear and do not cast me out of your affection. I am not callous, every nerve trembles with horror at what is happening in Europe, "the ceremony of innocence is drowned".

Letter to Ethel Mannin, Postmark 8 April 1936.
The Letters of W.B. Yeats.

... and on symbolism:

If people were to accept the theory that poetry moves us because of its symbolism, what change should one look for in the manner of our poetry ? A return to the way of our fathers, a casting out of descriptions of nature for the sake of nature, of the moral law for the sake of the moral law, a casting out of all anecdotes and of that brooding over scientific opinion that so often extinguished the central flame in Tennyson, and of that vehemence that would make us do or not do certain things; or, in other words, we should come to understand that the beryl stone was enchanted by our fathers that it might unfold the pictures in its heart, and not to mirror our own excited faces, or the boughs waving outside the window. With this change of substance, this return to imagination, this understanding that the laws of art, which are the hidden laws of the world, can alone bind the imagination, would come a change of style, and we would cast out of serious poetry those energetic rhythms, as of a man running, which are the invention of the will with its eyes always on something to be done or undone; and we would seek out those wavering, meditative, organic rhythms, which are the embodiment of the imagination, that neither desires nor hates, because it has done with time, and only wishes to gaze upon some reality, some beauty; nor would it be any longer possible for anybody to deny the importance of form, in all its kinds, for although you can expound an opinion, or describe a thing, when your words are not quite well chosen, you cannot give a body to something that moves beyond the senses, unless your words are as subtle, as complex, as full of mysterious life, as the body of a flower or of a woman. The form of sincere poetry, unlike the form of the "popular poetry", may indeed be sometimes obscure, or ungrammatical as in some of the best of the *Songs of Innocence and Experience*, but it must have the perfections that escape analysis, the subtleties that have a new meaning every day, and it must have all this whether it be but a little song made out of a moment of dreamy indolence, or some great epic made out of the dreams of one poet and of a hundred generations whose hands were never weary of the sword.

The Symbolism of Poetry

Versification, p. 7; Figurative language, p. 31.

Thomas Stearns ELIOT 1888-1965

1888 *Born in St Louis, Missouri.*
1906-1910 *Studied language, literature and philosophy at Harvard.*
1910-1914 *Led a cosmopolitan life in Europe (England, France, Germany).*
1915 *Married and settled in London).* The Love Song of J. Alfred Prufrock. *(Until 1925, led the drab life of a clerk in London.)*
1919 Gerontion.
1920 The Sacred Wood *(essays on poetry).*
1922 The Waste Land.
1925 The Hollow Men.
1927 *British nationality and conversion to Anglo-Catholicism.*
1930 Ash Wednesday.
1933 The Use of Poetry and the Use of Criticism *(essays).*
1934 Choruses from "The Rock".
1935 Murder in the Cathedral *(a play).*
1939 The Family Reunion *(a play).*
1940 The Idea of a Christian Society.
1943 Four Quartets.
1948 *Nobel Prize.*
1950 The Cocktail Party *(a play).*
1954 The Confidential Clerk *(a play).*
1957 Essays on Poets and Poetry.
1965 *Died in London.*

Eliot's first poems combine satire of society, its decadence and hypocrisy, and a sense of disillusion and nostalgia.

With The Waste Land, *the satire becomes harsher. The chaos and downfall of civilization are shown through a series of images reminiscent of the technique of 'collage'. Through echoing themes and rhythms and constant allusions to the past and various cultures, Eliot makes of the* Waste Land *a sort of epic of the development and breakdown of civilization.*

The later poems reveal a completely different mood: optimism, faith and peace.

W. Lewis : Portrait of T. S. Eliot.
Durban Art Gallery South Africa.
For the relationship between Eliot and Lewis see p. 253.

Marina[1] (1930)

Quis hic locus, quae
regio, quae mundi plaga[2]?

What seas what shores what grey rocks and what islands
What water lapping the bow
And scent of pine and the woodthrush singing through the fog
What images return
O my daughter.

Those who sharpen the tooth of the dog[3], meaning
Death
Those who glitter with the glory of the hummingbird, meaning
Death
Those who sit in the sty of contentment, meaning
Death
Those who suffer the ecstasy of the animals, meaning
Death

Are become unsubstantial, reduced by a wind,
A breath of pine, and the woodsong fog
By this grace dissolved in place

What is this face, less clear and clearer
The pulse in the arm, less strong and stronger –
Given or lent[4]? more distant than stars and nearer than the eye

Whispers and small laughter between leaves and hurrying feet
Under sleep, where all the waters meet.

Bowsprit cracked with ice and paint cracked with heat.
I made this, I have forgotten
And remember.
The rigging weak and the canvas rotten
Between one June and another September.
Made this unknowing, half conscious, unknown, my own.
The garboard strake[5] leaks, the seams need caulking.
This form, this face, this life
Living to live in a world of time beyond me; let me
Resign my life for this life, my speech for that unspoken,
The awakened, lips parted, the hope, the new ships.

What seas what shores what granite islands towards my timbers
And woodthrush calling through the fog
My daughter.

Collected Poems.

1. *Marina:* the daughter of Pericles. She was born at sea, carried off by pirates when she was sixteen and later restored to her father – 2. *epigraph:* "What place is this, what region, what part of the world"? = the words of Hercules in Seneca's *Hercules Furens* as his sanity returns after killing his wife and children in a fit of madness. Eliot explained he used the contrasting examples of Pericles and Hercules to achieve a "criss cross" – 3. *the dog:* a symbol of evil. The images that follow are allusions to the seven deadly sins – 4. *lines 17-19:* an allusion to the questions of Pericles to his daughter when he finds her again. – 5. *the garboard strake:* a plank near the keel of a ship.

Among the most direct influences on T.S. Eliot, may be noted the Metaphysical Poets (cf p. 82 and Eliot's criticism on p. 85), the Imagists and Vorticism in painting.

IN A STATION OF THE
METRO

THE APPARITION OF THESE
FACES IN THE CROWD:
PETALS ON A WET, BLACK BOUGH.

Ezra Pound, 1916.

Imagism
The movement flourished during the second decade of the century, around T.E. Hulme and Ezra Pound mainly. Here is what is considered as the manifesto of the imagists. Compare their principles to the main characteristics of the metaphysical poets (cf p. 82).

The poets in this volume do not represent a clique. Several of them are personally known to the others, but they are united by certain common principles, arrived at independently. These principles are not new; they have fallen into desuetude. They are the essentials of all great poetry, indeed of all great literature, and they are simply these:

1 – To use the language of common speech, but to employ always the exact word, not the nearly-exact, nor the merely decorative word.

2 – To create new rhythms – as the expression of new moods – and not to copy old rhythms, which merely echo old moods. We do not insist upon 'free verse' as the only method of writing poetry. We fight for it as for a principle of liberty. We believe that the individuality of a poet may often be better expressed in free verse than in conventional forms. In poetry, a new cadence means a new idea.

3 – To allow absolute freedom in the choice of subject. It is not good art to write badly about aeroplanes and automobiles; nor is it necessarily bad art to write well about the past. We believe passionately in the artistic value of modern life, but we wish to point out that there is nothing so uninspiring nor so old-fashioned as an aeroplane of the year 1911.

4 – To present an image (hence the name: 'Imagist'). We are not a school of painters, but we believe that poetry should render particulars exactly and not deal in vague generalities, however magnificent and sonorous. It is for this reason that we oppose the cosmic poet, who seems to us to shirk the real difficulties of his art.

5 – To produce poetry that is hard and clear, never blurred not indefinite.

6 – Finally, most of us believe that concentration is of the very essence of poetry.

Preface to *Some Imagist Poets,* 1915
Written by Richard Aldington,
slightly revised by Amy Lowell.
Houghton Mifflin Co.

Vorticism

Vorticism was a movement in art (linked to cubism and futurism) that appeared in 1912, around Wyndham Lewis. They wanted to react against the escapism of the Pre-Raphaelites who took refuge in romance and the past. What Eliot most admired in Vorticism was

– the strength and vitality conveyed through angles, lines and the impression of a "vortex",

– the link between the past and modern civilization (e.g. in The Surrender of Barcelona, *the 14th century scene is painted in a mechanistic way).*

The Vorticists had a horror of escapism, and they explained in their manifesto that "once this consciousness towards the new possibilities of expression in present life has come... it will be more the legitimate property of Englishmen than of any other people in Europe. It should also, as it is by origin theirs, inspire them more forcibly and directly. They are the inventors of this bareness and hardness, and should be the great enemies of Romance". In other words, Vorticism intended to view with deliberate dispassion the subject-matter it had chosen to interpret. It wanted to take upon itself what it saw as the essential character of the machine environment, and become equally dynamic, rigid and implacable. Ezra Pound, who first coined the name "vortex" and actually christened the movement sometime during the early months of 1914, maintained in *Blast No 1* that the vortex is the point of maximum energy. It represents, in mechanics, "the greatest efficiency". We use the words greatest efficiency in the precise sense – as they would be used in a text book of *Mechanics.* Pound and his artist allies admired the compressed power of the machine, its ability to perform its function with clean precision and without any messy emotionalism or fuss. They wanted to transfer those attributes to their own art, so that the essence of the machine age which surrounded them could be defined in pictorial and sculptural terms.

Richard Cork *What was Vorticism?*
© 1980 City of Manchester Cultural Services.
Lund Humphries Publishers Ltd.

W. Lewis, The Surrender of Barcelona, *1934-1937.*
The Tate Gallery.
Eliot wrote of W. Lewis that "he combined the energy of the caveman and the thought of the modern man."

T.S. Eliot on poetry :

1 – ... the historical sense involves a perception, not only of the pastness of the past, but of its presence; the historical sense compels a man to write not merely with his own generation in his bones, but with a feeling that the whole of the literature of Europe from Homer and within it the whole of the literature of his own country has a simultaneous existence and composes a simultaneous order...

No poet, no artist of any art, has his complete meaning alone. His significance, his appreciation is the appreciation of his relation to the dead poets and artists.

The conscious present is an awareness of the past.

2 – The progress of an artist is a continual self-sacrifice, a continual extinction of personality.

Poetry is not a turning loose of emotion, but an escape from emotion; it is not the expression of personality, but an escape from personality.

The emotion of art is impersonal. And the poet cannot reach this impersonality without surrendering himself wholly to the work to be done. And he is not likely to know what is to be done unless he lives in what is not merely the present, but the present moment of the past...

3 – The only way of expressing emotion in the form of art is by finding an "objective correlative"; in other words, a set of objects a situation, a chain of events which shall be the formula of that particular emotion; such that when the external facts, which must terminate in sensory experience, are given, the emotion is immediately evoked.

4 – It is one of the greatest merits of Dante's poem that the vision is so nearly complete; it is evidence of this greatness that the significance of any single passage, of any of the passages that are selected as "poetry", is incomplete unless we ourselves apprehend the whole.

The Sacred Wood.

Wystan Hugh AUDEN 1907-1973

1907 *Born in York.*
1915-1925 *Prep school (where he met Christopher Isherwood), then Gresham's School. Started writing poetry.*
1925-1928 *Studied at Christ Church, Oxford. Met Stephen Spender and Cecil Day Lewis.*
1928-1929 *Stay in Berlin. Discovered psychoanalytical theories, Rilke and popular German poetry.*
1930 Poems.
1933 The Dance of Death.
1935 *Worked as a teacher and wrote numerous articles and film scripts.*
1936 Look, Stranger.
Travelled to Iceland with Louis Mac Neice (later published Letters from Iceland*).*
Married Thomas Mann's daughter, whom he had never seen, to allow her to leave Germany.
1937 *Served on the Republican side in the Spanish Civil War.*
1938 *Went to China with Christopher Isherwood.*

A socialist and Freudian who turned to philosophy and Christianity at the end of his life, a musician and the inheritor of German cultural traditions, W. H. Auden was a prolific writer striking for the diversity of his inspiration and for his constant involvement with the problems of his time, an involvement reflected in his predilection for topical and occasional verse.

Auden's early poems, written before the war, made him immediately famous. The picture they give is that of industrial Britain during the crisis, the plight of the poorer classes, the social and intellectual degradation that endangers all humanist values. The influence of Marxism, of Brecht, Eliot and psychoanalysis is apparent in these first works. They are also characterized by sharpness, virtuosity and inventiveness, and by variety of tone – a mixture of lightness and seriousness. This diversity is emphasized by Auden's use of a wide range of vocabulary – from slang to the technical and philosophical. His verse also reflects his interest in music, using as he does all kinds of metrical patterns, from the popular ballad rhythm to alliterative verse and a mixture of prose and verse.

1939 *With Isherwood, decided to leave Europe and settle in the USA. Professor of literature in New York.*
1940 *Conversion to Anglo-Catholicism.* Another Time.
1941 New Year Letter.
1940-1945 *Various teaching jobs. Became interested in opera (collaborated with Britten).*
1944 For the time Being.
1946 *Became an American citizen.*
1948 *Pulitzer Prize.* The Age of Anxiety.
1955 The Shield of Achilles.
1960 Homage to Clio.
1973 *Died in Vienna.*

His later works include more meditative and philosophical poems as well as two collections of essays: The Enchafed Flood *(1951) and* The Dyer's Hand *(1963).*

Roman Wall Blues (1937)

Over the heather the wet wind blows,
I've lice in my tunic and a cold in my nose.

The rain comes pattering out of the sky,
I'm a Wall soldier, I don't know why.

The mist creeps over the hard grey stone,
My girl's in Tungria; I sleep alone.

Aulus goes hanging around her place,
I don't like his manners, I don't like his face.

Piso's a Christian, he worships a fish[1];
There'd be no kissing if he had his wish.

She gave me a ring but I diced it away;
I want my girl and I want my pay.

When I'm a veteran with only one eye
I shall do nothing but look at the sky.

Selected Poems.

1. *He worships a fish:* because ichthus (a Greek word for fish) was a rebus for Christ.

W. H. Auden on his poetry:

- Poetry is not magic. In so far as poetry, or any other of the arts, can be said to have an ulterior purpose, it is, by telling the truth, to disenchant and disintoxicate.

"Writing", *The Dyer's Hand,* 1963.

- The characteristic style of "Modern" poetry is an intimate tone of voice, the speech of one person addressing one person, not a large audience; whenever a modern poet raises his voice he sounds phony. And its characteristic hero is neither the "Great Man" nor the romantic rebel, both doers of extraordinary deeds, but the man or woman in any walk of life who, despite all the impersonal pressures of modern society, manages to acquire and preserve a face of his own.

"The Poet and the City",
The Massachusetts Review, Spring 1962.

Stephen Spender on W.H. Auden's poetry:

Auden held certain views very strongly at Oxford. These have impressed themselves on me the more because he reversed most of them shortly after he left. Here are a few of his characteristic pronouncements:

A poet must have no opinions, no decided views which he seeks to put across in his poetry.

Above all, poetry must in no way be concerned with politics.

Politicians are just lackeys and public servants whom we should ignore.

The subject of a poem is only a peg on which to hang the poetry.

A poet must be clinical, dispassionate about life. The poet feels much less strongly about things than do other people.

Poems should not have titles.

Never use exclamation marks, and avoid abstractions.

At this time Auden was convinced that modern poetry should not be written in conventional verse patterns.

Stephen Spender, *W. H. Anden and his Poetry*, The Atlantic Monthly, 1953.

Compare Auden's portrait of a soldier with Stephen Spender's in the following poem:

I THINK CONTINUALLY
OF THOSE WHO WERE TRULY GREAT

I think continually of those who were truly great.
Who, from the womb, remembered the soul's history
Through corridors of light where the hours are suns,
Endless and singing. Whose lovely ambition
Was that their lips, still touched with fire,
Should tell of the Spirit, clothed from head to foot in song.
And who hoarded from the Spring branches
The desires falling across their bodies like blossoms.

What is precious, is never to forget
The essential delight of the blood drawn from ageless springs
Breaking through rocks in worlds before our earth.
Never to deny its pleasure in the morning simple light
Nor its grave evening demand for love.

Never to allow gradually the traffic to smother
With noise and fog the flowering of the Spirit.

Near the snow, near the sun, in the highest fields,
See how these names are fêted by the waving grass
And by the streamers of white cloud
And whispers of wind in the listening sky.
The names of those who in their lives fought for life,
Who wore at their hearts the fire's centre.
Born of the sun, they travelled a short while toward the sun,
And left the vivid air signed with their honor.

1933

Stephen Spender, *Collected Poems 1928-1953.*

Together with W.H. Auden, C. Day Lewis and Louis Mac Neice, Spender (1909) was one of the "New Country" group, whose verse was published in New signatures, *1932 and* New Country, *1933. These poets believed that they should be involved in contemporary life, and actively engaged in politics...* "(Spender) was never a true Marxist, but a romantic liberal longing for a new age of heroism. What he saw around him in the world of the 1930's made him increasingly melancholy and pessimistic." Cox & Dyson, *Modern Poetry.*

Cf. Verse form and poetic genres, p. 2; Versification, p. 7.

Graham Sutherland: Devastation, 1941. An East End Street. *London, The Tate Gallery.* © *ADAGP.*

Dylan THOMAS 1914-1953

1914 *Born in Swansea in Wales.*
1925-1931 *Educated at Swansea Grammar School.*
1931-1932 *Worked as a reporter for a Welsh paper.*
1934 Eighteen Poems.
1936 Twenty-five poems
1939 The Map of Love.
1940 Portrait of the Artist as a Young Dog.
1940-1944 *Worked for the BBC and on film scenarios.*
Became a well-known script-writer and broadcaster.
1946 Deaths and Entrances.
1950 *Gave poetry readings in the USA (where he was to return in 1952 and 1953).*
Twenty-six Poems.
1952 Collected Poems.
1953 Under Milk Wood *performed in Cambridge and New York.*
Died in New York, buried in Wales.

Dylan Thomas was deeply influenced both by his Welsh background (as seen through the wealth of his imagination and his interest in oral poetry) and by a large number of European writers and works, especially the Bible, the metaphysical poets, Rimbaud, Eliot, Joyce and Hopkins.

A recurrent theme in Dylan Thomas's works is the cycle of life: birth and growth, sexuality and most of all death, which haunted him throughout his life. All his poems can be read, to use his own words, as "statements on the way to the grave". Even his love for nature, for the beauty of all creation, seems all the more intense as the horror of the "dying of the light" is always present. His poems also read like the works of a religious and visionary mind that sees man in the grip of cosmic powers. Hence the moving power and exuberance of his poetry, which are emphasized by the vitality of the language (making use of puns, wit, kennings, striking phrases and unusual structures) and the strong rhythmic patterns of his verse, often reminiscent of Hopkins's "sprung rhythm".

Besides his poetry, Dylan Thomas also wrote autobiographical stories — Portrait of the Artist as a Young Dog *— and* Under Milk Wood, *"a play for voices" about one day in the lives of the inhabitants of a small Welsh town.*

Poem in October (1945)

IT WAS my thirtieth year to heaven[1]
Woke to my hearing from harbour and neighbour wood
And the mussel pooled[2] and the heron
Priested shore[3]
The morning beckon
With water praying and call of seagull and rook
And the knock of sailing boats on the net webbed wall[4]
Myself to set foot
That second
In the still sleeping town and set forth.

My birthday began with the water-
Birds and the birds of the winged trees flying my name
Above the farms and the white horses[5]
And I rose
In rainy autumn
And walked abroad in a shower of all my days.
High tide and the heron dived when I took the road
Over the border[6]
And the gates
Of the town closed as the town awoke.

A springful of larks in a rolling
Cloud and the roadside bushes brimming with whistling
Blackbirds and the sun of October
Summery
On the hill's shoulder,

Here were fond climates and sweet singers suddenly
Come in the morning where I wandered and listened
To the rain wringing
Wind blow cold
In the wood faraway under me.

Pale rain over the dwindling harbour
And over the sea wet church the size of a snail
With its horns through mist and the castle
Brown as owls
But all the gardens[7]
Of spring and summer were blooming in the tall tales[8]
Beyond the border[9] and under the lark full cloud.
There could I marvel
My birthday
Away but the weather turned around[10].

It turned away from the blithe country
And down the other air and the blue altered sky
Streamed again a wonder of summer
With apples
Pears and red currants
And I saw in the turning so clearly a child's
Forgotten mornings when he walked with his mother
Through the parables
Of sun light
And the legends of the green chapels

And the twice told fields of infancy
That his tears burned my cheeks and his heart moved in mine.
These were the woods the river and sea
Where a boy
In the listening
Summertime of the dead whispered the truth of his joy
To the trees and the stones and the fish in the tide.
And the mystery
Sang alive
Still in the water and singingbirds.

And there could I marvel my birthday
Away but the weather turned around. And the true
Joy of the long dead child sang burning
In the sun.
It was my thirtieth
Year to heaven stood there then in the summer noon
Though the town below lay leaved with October blood[11].
O may my heart's truth
Still be sung
On this high hill in a year's turning.

Death Entrances, The Collected Poems of Dylan Thomas.

1. *first stanza* (structure): my thirtieth birthday ... woke to my hearing (= made me hear) the morning beckon to set foot in... – 2. *the mussel pooled*: the pools full of mussels – 3. *the heron priests shore*: the herons on the shore are compared to priests – 4. *net webbed wall*: wall covered by fishing nets that resemble webs – 5. *white horses*: the foam on the waves – 6. *over the border*: the border of time – 7. *But all the gardens*: the gardens of the mind – 8. *a tall tale*: a tale impossible to believe – 9. *beyond the border*: in the realm of memory – 10. *the weather turned around*: my memories changed (he will now evoke another part of his childhood) – 11. *October blood*: an allusion to the war.

Dylan Thomas on his poetry:

• Poetry is the rhythmic, inevitably narrative, movement from an overclothed blindness to a naked vision that depends in its intensity on the strength of the labour put into the creation of the poetry. My poetry is, or should be, useful to me for one reason: it is the record of my individual struggle from darkness towards some measure of light, and what of the individual struggle is still to come benefits by the sight and knowledge of the faults and fewer merits in that concrete record. My poetry is, or should be, useful to others for its individual recording of that same struggle with which they are necessarily acquainted...

Reply to "An Enquiry",
New Verse, II, October, 1934
Reprinted in Constantine FitzGibbon,
The Life of Dylan Thomas, 1965.

• A poem by myself *needs* a host of images, because its centre is a host of images. I make only one image – though "make" is not the word; I let, perhaps an image be "made" emotionally in me and then apply to it what intellectual and critical forces I possess – let it breed another, let that image contradict the first, make, of the third image bred out of the other two together, a fourth contradictory image, and let them all, within my imposed formal limits, conflict. Each image holds within it the seed of its own destruction, and my dialectical method, as I understand it, is a constant building up and breaking down of the images that come out of the central seed, which is itself destructive and constructive at the same time...

Out of the inevitable conflict of images – inevitable, because of the creative, recreative, destructive and contradictory nature of the motivating centre, the womb of war – I try to make that momentary peace which is a poem.

Letter to Henry Treece, 23 March 1938.
Selected Letters of Dylan Thomas.

Cf. Figurative language, p. 31; Versification, p 7; Hopkins on sprung rhythm, p. 211.

Augustus John: Dylan Thomas *c. 1938.*
The National Museum of Wales, Cardiff.
Ph. The Bridgeman Art Library, London/Ziolo.
Cf. p. 244.

• To your third question – Do I deliberately utilize devices of rhyme, rhythm, and word-formation in my writing – I must, of course, answer with an immediate, Yes. I am a painstaking, conscientious, involved and devious craftsman in words, however unsuccessful the result so often appears, and to whatever wrong uses I may apply my technical paraphernalia. I use everything and anything to make my poems work and move in the direction I want them to: old tricks, new tricks, puns, portmanteau-words, paradox, allusion, paranomasia [punning], paragram ["a kind of play upon words consisting in the alteration of one letter or a group of letters of a word" (*O.E.D.*)], catachresis [improper use of words], slang, assonantal rhymes, vowel rhymes, sprung rhythm. Every device there is in language is there to be used if you will. Poets have got to enjoy themselves sometimes, and the twisting and convolutions of words, the inventions and contrivances, are all part of the joy that is part of the painful, voluntary work.

Notes on the Art of Poetry,
in J. Scully (ed.), *Modern poets on Modern poetry,*
The Texas Quarterly of 1961.

Ted HUGHES born 1930

1930 *Born in Yorkshire.*
1954 *Graduated from Cambridge, where he had met Thom Gunn.*
1954-1956 *Worked as a gardener, a night-watchman, and a reader for studios.*
1956 *Married Sylvia Plath (who was to die in 1963) and went to America where he wrote and taught.*
1957 The Hawk in the Rain.
1960 Lupercal.
1967 Wodwo.
1970 Crow.
1976 Season Songs.
1979 Moortown.
1983 River.
1984 *Named Poet Laureate.*
1986 Flowers and Insects.
1988 Tales of the Early World.
1989 Wolfwatching; Moortown Diary.

Ted Hughes's main theme is violence and power. He is fascinated by the cruelty and roughness of the physical world. "What excites my imagination is the war between vitality and death", he wrote. He often finds this energy among the animal world as evidenced by the titles of some of his best-known poems: The Jaguar, The Thought-Fox, A Dream of Horses, The Hawk in the Rain. *But ruthlessness also characterizes the world of men – war and heroism are recurrent themes in his poetry.*

There are, for Ted Hughes, privileged moments of violence which, though they may be linked to pain or death, are the only ways of asserting one's energy and existence, of proving the triumph of one's will.

Ted Hughes values such moments for their intensity; but he has to isolate them from past and future, cause and effect, reflection and evaluation before he can savour them to the full. Hence the absence of compassion, anger, humility, nostalgia disgust and the other attitudes belonging to the perspectives of time.

A. E. Dyson.

The Horses (1957)

I climbed through woods in the hour-before-dawn dark.
Evil air, a frost-making stillness,

Not at leaf, not a bird, –
A world cast in frost. I came out above the wood

Where my breath left tortuous statues in the iron light.
But the valleys were draining the darkness

Till the moorline – blackening dregs of the brightening grey –
Halved the sky ahead. And I saw the horses:

Huge in the dense grey – ten together –
Megalith-still. They breathed, making no move,

With draped manes and tilted hind-hooves,
Making no sound.

I passed: not one snorted or jerked its head.
Grey silent fragments

Of a grey silent world.

I listened in emptiness on the moor-ridge.
The curlew's tear turned its edge on the silence.

Slowly detail leafed from the darkness. Then the sun
Orange, red, red erupted

Silently, and splitting to its core tore and flung cloud
Shook the gulf open, showed blue,

And the big planets hanging –.
I turned

Stumbling in the fever of a dream, down towards
The dark woods, from the kindling tops,

And came to the horses.
                                        There, still they stood,
But now steaming and glistening under the flow of light,

Their draped stone manes, their tilted hind-hooves
Stirring under a thaw while all around them

The frost showed its fires. But still they made no sound.
Not one snorted or stamped,

Their hung heads patient as the horizons,
High over valleys, in the red levelling rays –

In din of the crowded streets, going among the years, the faces,
May I still meet my memory in so lonely a place

Between the streams and the red clouds, hearing curlews,
Hearing the horizons endure.

The Hawk in the Rain.

Ted Hughes about his poetry:

• (A poem is) an assembly of living parts moved by a single spirit. The living parts are the words, the images, the rhythms. The spirit is the life which inhabits them when they all work together. It is impossible to say which comes first, parts or spirit. But if any of the parts are dead... if any of the words, or images or rhythms do not jump to life as you read them... then the creature is going to be maimed and the spirit sickly. So, as a poet, you have to make sure that all those parts over which you have control, the words and rhythms and images, are alive.

Capturing Animals.

• What do I write about?

After thinking the poems over, I have decided to say this: What excites my imagination is the war between vitality and death, and my poems may be said to celebrate the exploits of the warriors of either side. Also, they are attempts to prove the realness of the world, and of myself in this world, by establishing the realness of my relation to it. Another way of saying this might be – the poems celebrate the pure solidity of my illusion of the world. Again – and probably this is the first near-truth I have put down yet – they are the only way I can unburden myself of that excess which, for their part, bulls in June bellow away.

In each poem, besides the principal subject – and in my poems this is usually pretty easy to see, as, for instance, the jaguar in the poem called The Jaguar – there is what is not so easy to talk about, even generally, but which is the living and individual element in every poet's work. What I mean is the way he brings to peace all the feelings and energies which, from all over the body, heart, and brain, send up their champions onto the battleground of that first subject. The way I do this, as I believe, is by using something like the method of a musical composer. I might say that I turn every combatant into a bit of music, then resolve the whole uproar into as formal and balanced a figure of melody and rhythm as I can. When all the words are hearing each other clearly, and every stress is feeling every other stress, and all are contented – the poem is finished.

I have gone to some length, I see, to give what is perhaps a generalization about the composition of poetry, as well as a description of my own particular experience. I hope, though, to have defined the making of a special kind of verse. There is a great mass of English poetry in which the musical element – the inner figure of stress – is not so important as other elements. To me – no matter what metaphysical persuasion or definable philosophy a poem may seem to subscribe to – what is unique and precious in it is its heart, that inner figure of stresses. And in composing these poems I have been concerned to give to them – as well as good faces, clear brains and strong hands – sound hearts.

in *Worlds, Seven Modern Poets, Penguin Education.*

Cf. Figurative language, p. 31.

Philip LARKIN 1922-1985

1922 *Born in Coventry.*
1940-1943 *A student at St John's College, Oxford. Several Poems published in magazines. Awarded a first-class degree in English language and literature.*
1943 *Became Librarian at Wellington (Shropshire).*
1945 The North Ship (*poems*).
1946 Jill (*novel*). *Became Assistant Librarian at the University College of Leicester.*
1947 A Girl in Winter (*novel*).
1950 *Sub-librarian at Queen's University, Belfast.*
1951 XX Poems.
1955 *Took up post as Librarian at the University of Hull.*
The Less Deceived (*poems*).
1961-1971 *Wrote jazz reviews for* The Daily Telegraph.
1964 The Whitsun Weddings (*poems*).
1970 All What Jazz: A record diary 1961-1968 (*prose*).
1974 High Windows (*poems*).
1983 Required Writing: Miscellaneous pieces 1955-1982 (*prose*).
1984 *Refused to become Poet Laureate after the death of John Betjeman.*
1985 *Died in Hull.*
1988 Collected Poems.

Philip Larkin's poetry is marked by honesty and by the rejection of pretention and of inflated language and feelings. In the 1950s, he was linked with The Movement, a group of poets (including Thom Gunn, Kingsley Amis, John Wain, Donald Davie, D.J. Enright) who reacted against the loose neo-Romanticism and the political involvement of the 1940s and advocated clarity, control and precision instead. But Larkin's achievement is much more wide-ranging. His poetry combines a terse, highly-controlled form with restrained but deep emotion. Always defending "fidelity to experience," he observes the dreariness of everyday provincial and suburban life in the England of the 1950s, 1960s and 1970s. His poems deal with the passage of time and the transience of beauty, the failure of relationships and love, the collapse of ideals and hopes, the misery of old age and suffering. They express the sense of loss and loneliness which he sees in the shabbiness and routine of working- and middle-class lives, the desolation of people who hold no beliefs, possess little identity and are trapped in circumstances over which they have no control. The detached narrative voice takes on a wide range of tones and moods, in which compassion, tenderness and melancholy are tempered by quiet irony and humour.

The Whitsun Weddings (1964)

That Whitsun, I was late getting away:
  Not till about
One-twenty on the sunlit Saturday
Did my three-quarters-empty train pull out,
All windows down, all cushions hot, all sense
Of being in a hurry gone. We ran
Behind the backs of houses, crossed a street
Of blinding windscreens, smelt the fish-dock; thence
The river's level drifting breadth began,
Where sky and Lincolnshire and water meet.

All afternoon, through the tall heat that slept
  For miles inland,
A slow and stopping curve southwards we kept.
Wide farms went by, short-shadowed cattle, and
Canals with floatings of industrial froth;
A hothouse flashed uniquely: hedges dipped
And rose: and now and then a smell of grass
Displaced the reek of buttoned carriage-cloth
Until the next town, new and nondescript,
Approached with acres of dismantled cars.

At first, I didn't notice what a noise
  The weddings made
Each station that we stopped at: sun destroys
The interest of what's happening in the shade,
And down the long cool platforms whoops and skirls
I took for porters larking with the mails,

And went on reading. Once we started, though,
We passed them, grinning and pomaded, girls
In parodies of fashion, heels and veils,
All posed irresolutely, watching us go,

As if out on the end of an event
  Waving goodbye
To something that survived it. Struck, I leant
More promptly out next time, more curiously,
And saw it all again in different terms:
The fathers with broad belts under their suits
And seamy foreheads; mothers loud and fat;
An uncle shouting smut; and then the perms,
The nylon gloves and jewellery-substitutes,
The lemons, mauves, and olive-ochres that

Marked off the girls unreally from the rest.
  Yes, from cafés
And banquet-halls up yards, and bunting-dressed
Coach-party annexes, the wedding-days
Were coming to an end. All down the line
Fresh couples climbed aboard: the rest stood round;
The last confetti and advice were thrown,
And, as we moved, each face seemed to define
Just what it saw departing: children frowned
At something dull; fathers had never known

Success so huge and wholly farcical;
  The women shared
The secret like a happy funeral;
While girls, gripping their handbags tighter, stared
At a religious wounding. Free at last,
And loaded with the sum of all they saw,
We hurried towards London, shuffling gouts of steam.
Now fields were building-plots, and poplars cast
Long shadows over major roads, and for
Some fifty minutes, that in time would seem

Just long enough to settle hats and say
  I nearly died,
A dozen marriages got under way.
They watched the landscape, sitting side by side
— An Odeon went past, a cooling tower,
And someone running up to bowl — and none
Thought of the others they would never meet
Or how their lives would all contain this hour.
I thought of London spread out in the sun,
Its postal districts packed like squares of wheat:

There we were aimed. And as we raced across
  Bright knots of rail
Past standing Pullmans, walls of blackened moss
Came close, and it was nearly done, this frail
Travelling coincidence; and what it held
Stood ready to be loosed with all the power
That being changed can give. We slowed again,
And as the tightening brakes took hold, there swelled
A sense of falling, like an arrow-shower
Sent out of sight, somewhere becoming rain.

1964 Faber and Faber.

Philip Larkin on his poetry:

I write poems to preserve things I have seen / thought / felt... both for myself and for others, though I feel that my prime responsibility is to the experience itself, which I am trying to keep from oblivion for its own sake. Why I should do this I have no idea, but I think the impulse to preserve lies at the bottom of all art...

As a guiding principle I believe that every poem must be its own sole freshly-created universe, and therefore have no belief in "tradition" or a common myth-kitty or casual allusions in poems to other poems or poets, which last I find unpleasantly like the talk of literary under-strappers letting you see they know the right people.

Poets of the 1950s,
edited by D.J. Enright, 1955

... What I want readers to carry away from the poem in their minds is not the poem, but the experience; I want them to live something through the poem, without necessarily being conscious of the poem as a poem.

"Speaking of Writing- XIII,"
The Times, 20.2.1974

Compare "The Whitsun Weddings" with the following poems by Thomas Hardy and John Betjeman:

FAINTHEART IN A RAILWAY TRAIN

At nine in the morning there passed a church,
At ten there passed me by the sea,
At twelve a town of smoke and smirch,
At two a forest of oak and birch,
  And then, on a platform, she:

A radiant stranger, who saw not me.
I said, "Get out to her do I dare?"
But I kept my seat in my search for a plea,
And the wheels moved on. O could it but be
  That I had alighted there!

Thomas Hardy, *Collected Poems.*

Thomas Hardy (cf. p. 224), whose poetry also associates a tightness of form with a melancholy sensitivity, was the poet who most influenced Philip Larkin.

GREAT CENTRAL RAILWAY
SHEFFIELD VICTORIA TO BANBURY

"Unmitigated England"
  Came swinging down the line
That day the February sun
  Did crisp and crystal shine.
Dark red at Kirkby Bentick stood
  A steeply gabled farm
'Mid ash trees and a sycamore
  In charismatic calm.
A village street — a manor house —
  A church — then, tally ho!
We pounded through a housing scheme
  With tellymasts a-row,
Where cars of parked executives
  Did regimented wait
Beside administrative blocks
  Within the factory gate.
She waved to us from Hucknall South
  As we hooted round a bend,
From a curtained front-room window did
  The diesel driver's friend.
Through cuttings deep to Nottingham
  Precariously we wound;
The swallowing tunnel made the train
  Seem London's Underground.
Above the fields of Leicestershire
  On arches we were borne
And the rumble of the railway drowned
  The thunder of the Quorn;
And silver shone the steeples out
  Above the barren boughs;
Colts in a paddock ran from us
  But not the solid cows,
And quite where Rugby Central is
  Does only Rugby know.
We watched the empty platform wait
  And sadly saw it go.
By now the sun of afternoon
  Showed ridge and furrow shadows
And shallow unfamiliar lakes
  Stood shivering in the meadows.
Is Woodford church or Hinton church
  The one I ought to see?
Or were they both too much restored
  In 1883?
I do not know. Towards the west
  A trail of glory runs
And we leave the old Great Central line
  For Banbury and buns.

John Betjeman's *Collected Poems*, 1958,
John Murray.

John Betjeman (1906-1984), another major influence on Philip Larkin, is a social historian whose poems convey a sense of place and atmosphere — a fascination for Edwardian life and Gothic revival architecture, and a nostalgia for the vanishing England of his youth. There is often detachment and irony in his reflection upon the absurdities and emptiness of upper-middle-class life, but he also evokes childhood, love, death, pain and fear with compassion and moving simplicity. Larkin saw in his poems a thread of "unfeigned and uninflated fascination by human beings."

The paintings of L.S. Lowry (1887-1976) also convey the dreariness and monotony of working-class lives. According to William Gaunt, he "stands alone as a 'provincial Brueghel' in his depiction of scurrying crowds against backgrounds of factories, chimneys, dingy canals, and the little terrace houses of the industrial town."

L.S. Lowry, Railway Platform, 1953. *Oil on canvas*
Collection: Lefevre Gallery, London.

Thom GUNN born 1929

1929 *Born in Gravesend.*
1948-1950 *Served in the British Army.*
1953 *BA from Trinity College, Cambridge.*
1954-1958 *Studied at Stanford University, California. Has lived in California ever since.*
1954 Fighting Terms.
1957 The Sense of Movement.
1961 My Sad Captains and Other Poems.
1967 Touch.
1971 Moly.
1976 Jack Straw's Castle and Other Poems.
1982 The Passage of Joy.
The Occasions of Poetry (*essays*).
1992 The Man with Night Sweats.

Thom Gunn's poetry is distinguished by the fusion of conventional, tight, disciplined form with modern themes typical of the American counterculture, such as violence, LSD or the Hell's Angels. This creates a tension and a balance between rule and energy, order and violence, which, discussing Moly, *Gunn called "a debate between the passion for definition and the passion for flow."*

His early poems were influenced by the existential insistence on man's freedom to choose his actions and to reject the norms of society. This is why they show a fascination with will and energy, with deliberate choice and toughness, with the man of action who comes to embody a whole generation of "rebels without a cause" — young toughs and tearaways in black leather jackets, whose actions serve only to hide existential anguish. For Gunn shows that there can be a tender and reflective side, a quest for an identity, hiding behind instinctive animal violence.

Thom Gunn's later poetry is more serene and more concerned with nature, beauty and human relationships and, under the influence of modern American poetry, often written in syllabic and free verse.

On the Move (1957)

"Man, you gotta Go"

The blue jay scuffling in the bushes follows
Some hidden purpose, and the gust of birds
That spurts across the field, the wheeling swallows,
Have nested in the trees and undergrowth.
Seeking their instinct, or their poise, or both,
One moves with an uncertain violence
Under the dust thrown by a baffled sense
Or the dull thunder of approximate words.

On motorcycles, up the road, they come:
Small, black, as flies hanging in heat, the Boys,
Until the distance throws them forth, their hum
Bulges to thunder held by calf and thigh.
In goggles, donned impersonality,
In gleaming jackets trophied with the dust,
They strap in doubt — by hiding it, robust —
And almost hear a meaning in their noise.

Exact conclusion of their hardiness
Has no shape yet, but from known whereabouts
They ride, direction where the tires press.
They scare a flight of birds across the field:
Much that is natural, to the will must yield.
Men manufacture both machine and soul,
And use what they imperfectly control
To dare a future from the taken routes.

It is a part solution, after all.
One is not necessarily discord
On earth; or damned because, half animal,
One lacks direct instinct, because one wakes
Afloat on movement that divides and breaks.
One joins the movement in a valueless world,
Choosing it, till, both hurler and the hurled,
One moves as well, always toward, toward.

A minute holds them, who have come to go:
The self-defined, astride the created will
They burst away; the towns they travel through
Are home for neither bird nor holiness,
For birds and saints complete their purposes.
At worst, one is in motion; and at best,
Reaching no absolute, in which to rest,
One is always nearer by not keeping still.

The Sense of Movement, 1957,
Faber

Thom Gunn said that "On the Move" was much influenced by Sartre's lecture « L'Existentialisme est un humanisme », *and particularly by the following passage dealing with escapism:*

When a man commits himself to anything, fully realising that he is not only choosing what he will be, but is thereby at the same time a legislator deciding for the whole of mankind — in such a moment a man cannot escape from the sense of complete and profound responsibility. There are many, indeed, who show no such anxiety. But we affirm that they are merely disguising their anguish or are in flight from it.

J.-P. Sartre, *Existentialism and Humanism*,
tr. Philip Mairet. *Methuen, 1948.*

Thom Gunn on The Sense of Movement:

It is this malaise that I am trying to explore in most of the poems in *The Sense of Movement...* it seems to me a specifically contemporary subject; seeking to understand one's deliberate aimlessness, having the courage of one's lack of convictions, reaching a purpose only by making the right rejections. Poems are actions, of a sort, and by actions I may attempt to define the direction which is not mystical, or political, or necessarily one that has ever been taken before.

Poetry Book Society Bulletin N° 14, May 1957.

Compare "On the Move" with "Thrushes" by Ted Hughes (cf p. 260)

THRUSHES

Terrifying are the attent sleek thrushes on the lawn,
More coiled steel than living — a poised
Dark deadly eye, those delicate legs
Triggered to stirrings beyond sense — with a start, a bounce, a stab
Overtake the instant and drag out some writhing thing.
No indolent procrastinations and no yawning stares.
No sighs or head-scratchings. Nothing but bounce and stab
And a ravening second.

Is it their single-mind-sized skulls, or a trained
Body, or genius, or a nestful of brats
Gives their days this bullet and automatic
Purpose? Mozart's brain had it, and the shark's mouth
That hungers down the blood-smell even to a leak of its own
Side and devouring of itself: efficiency which
Strikes too streamlined for any doubt to pluck at it
Or obstruction deflect.

With a man it is otherwise. Heroisms on horseback,
Outstripping his desk-diary at a broad desk.
Carving at a tiny ivory ornament
For years: his act worships itself — while for him,
Though he bends to be blent in the prayer, how loud and above what
Furious spaces of fire do the distracting devils
Orgy and hosannah, under what wilderness
Of black silent waters weep.

Ted Hughes, *Lupercal*, 1960.
Faber and Faber.

Seamus HEANEY born 1939

1939 *Born in Northern Ireland, in a family of farmers.*
1957-1961 *Student at Queen's University, Belfast.*
1962-1963 *Taught at St Thomas's Secondary School, Belfast.*
1963-1966 *Lecturer in English at St Joseph's College.*
1965 11 Poems. *Married to Marie Devlin (two sons, one daughter).*
1966-1972 *Lecturer in English at Queen's University, Belfast.*
1966 Death of a Naturalist.
1969 Door in the Dark.
1972 Wintering Out.
1975 North.
1976-1982 *Lecturer at Carysfort College, Dublin.*
1979 Field Work.
1980 Poems: 1965-1975.
1982-1986 *Visiting professor at Harvard University.*
1984 Station Island.
1987 The Haw Lantern.

An Ulster Catholic, Seamus Heaney writes about the Ireland that he knows: the hard life of Irish farmers and craftsmen, the recollected experiences of childhood, the cities and their inner strife. But he is not just an observer with a keen eye for detail; his poems give depth to the most simple rural activities, revealing the life force that underlies earthly things and the hidden meaning beneath the familiar world. Hence the constant parallelisms and symbiosis between people and the land, between the life of today and the world of legend and myth and between material and intellectual life. Seamus Heaney sees poetry as a "door in the dark" which can lead to our origins, our centre of being, and help us reach self-definition.

The violence of Northern Ireland also appears in these poems through the threats which often intrude in the rural landscapes and day-to-day experiences — for example, the menacing frogspawn in Death of a Naturalist. *But this violence is not specific to modern Ireland; the poet sees it as universal, to be related to history and myth.*

Seamus Heaney's poems are memorable for their technical precision and control. He delights in the sound of words and their histories, making wide use of Old Irish words, archaisms, assonance, rich and sensuous adjectives, and arresting metaphors. For language too is closely linked to Irish nature — being rich, enigmatic, capable of renewal, and marked by the Irish as well as the British traditions of the country.

Death of a Naturalist (1966)

All year the flax-dam festered in the heart
Of the townland; green and heavy headed
Flax had rotted there, weighted down by huge sods.
Daily it sweltered in the punishing sun.
Bubbles gargled delicately, bluebottles
Wove a strong gauze of sound around the smell.
There were dragon-flies, spotted butterflies,
But best of all was the warm thick slobber
Of frogspawn that grew like clotted water
In the shade of the banks. Here, every spring
I would fill jampotfuls of the jellied
Specks to range on window-sills at home,
On shelves at school, and wait and watch until
The fattening dots burst into nimble-
Swimming tadpoles. Miss Walls would tell us how
The daddy frog was called a bullfrog
And how he croaked and how the mammy frog
Laid hundreds of little eggs and this was
Frogspawn. You could tell the weather by frogs too
For they were yellow in the sun and brown
In rain.

Then one hot day when fields were rank
With cowdung in the grass the angry frogs
Invaded the flax-dam; I ducked through hedges
To a coarse croaking that I had not heard
Before. The air was thick with a bass chorus.
Right down the dam gross-bellied frogs were cocked
On sods; their loose necks pulsed like sails. Some hopped:
The slap and plop were obscene threats. Some sat
Poised like mud grenades, their blunt heads farting.
I sickened, turned, and ran. The great slime kings
Were gathered there for vengeance and I knew
That if I dipped my hand the spawn would catch it.

1966, Faber and Faber.

Seamus Heaney on his poems:

I assume that to be able to make his personal cry resonant for his generation and the generations that succeed him, the poet will have to be gifted with an ear that is deeply tuned to the genius of his language. I assume that poetic craft and technique, once they have been learned will disappear into the voice and appear as sureness of tone from poem to poem and that there will always be a nicely held tension between poetry's need to be true to the impurities of life and its need to remember that it intends to be pure language.

"Current Unstated Assumptions about Poetry," *Critical Inquiry*, 7, 4, 1981.

Catholicism as a set of doctrines and beliefs is not what being a Roman Catholic means in Northern Ireland. It's almost a racist term, a label for a set of cultural suppositions. I think if you look at my poems with that in mind then you will see that when I think about my territory and my hinterland and my past I am thinking in terms of Ireland as a whole and the history of the famine and the rebellion. Within Northern Ireland having that set of myths for yourself and your nation is what it means to be a Catholic.

My poetry is not sectarian but it has been deeply affected by the smells of sectarianism. Poetry works by association and subtlety and the cultural load implicit in word. You don't have to bludgeon people like you have to do in a leading article. I would think that the cultural, rather than the religious, load implicit in that term Catholic is in my work. No, it would not surprise me that someone outside Ireland didn't know I was a Catholic.

I think a poem is often diminished and destroyed by attaching the idea that a moral must be deduced from it. I suppose that I am affected by the notion of the poem as a symbol, the poem as a scanner or receiving station for the language, the poem as a centre which attracts energies and allows energies to pass through it while still remaining a perfect whole, the

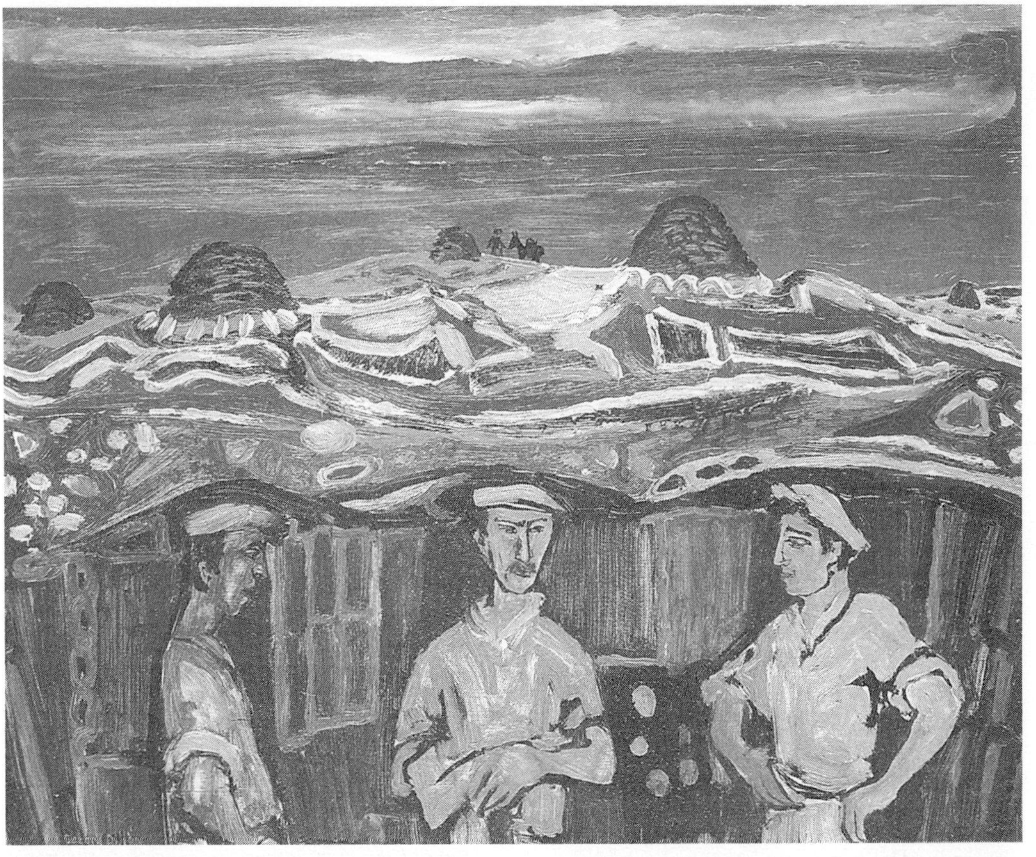

Gerard Dillon (1916-1971), Three Men in a Bog. *Oil on canvas.*
Reproduced in Free Spirit.
Exh. Dublin. Irish Exhibition of Living Art. 1956, no. 36.

"Many of Dillon's earlier pictures were informed by a unique perception of life in rural Ireland. (...) [In Three Men in a Bog *] Dillon insists upon a tripartite division of the image. In the foreground, the three turf-cutters find themselves in a deep trench, their subterranean labour casting them in a dull glow of pinks and blues. The whole symbolic context of the figures is one enormous richness in Irish art. It has recently been explored by Seamus Heaney who, in poems like* The Tollund Man *and* Bogland, *sees the bog as a preserver and embalmer of a long forgotten culture. It is the earth whence humanity sprang and to which it will return — the womb and the grave."*

Kenneth McConkey, A Free Spirit, Irish Art, 1860-1960. The Antique Collectors Club, in association with Pyms Gallery.

poem as an entrancement, ideally, rather than the poem as a message. Personally I find myself wilting at the thought of instructing people or interpreting experience for them in a way that could be done in prose.

Of course there is a responsibility to be aware of your age but that responsibility is exercised between the moments of writing. That is a personal view although I think it is a very general thing with writers. The activity of making a poem or surrendering to an impulse and working out the implications of an image is what excites me. The activity of making the thing or of being possessed by the thing is different for many poets from the activity of being responsible or aware. Now what I would say is that unless you are responsible and aware between these moments of activity then the moments are going to be less meaningful, perhaps less moral, in the widest sense, than they could be. It is not enough to have the will to be moral in your writing.

The Guardian, 2 Nov. 1974

James JOYCE 1882-1941

1882 *Born in Dublin.*
1888-1898 *Educated in Jesuit schools.*
1899-1902 *University College, Dublin. Wrote several essays on the theatre, including* The Day of the Rabblement, 1901.
1902-1903 *Poor life in Paris. Wrote poems and reviews.*
1903 *Death of his mother.*
1904 *Met Nora Barnacle; both left for Zurich. Taught in Pola.*
First poems published.
1905-1915 *Lived in Trieste.*
1906 *Finished writing* The Dubliners *(pub. 1914).*
1909 *Translated Synge and Yeats.*
1912 *Last trip to Dublin.*
1913 *Met Ezra Pound.*
1915 *Left for Zurich.*
1916-1917 A Portrait of the Artist as a Young Man *published in New York and London.*
1918 Exiles.
1920 *Moved to Paris.*
1922 Ulysses *published in Paris (had been working on it since 1914).*
Began to have serious eye troubles.
1923 *Started* Finnegans Wake.
1936 Collected Poems.
1939 Finnegans Wake *published.*
1941 *Died in Zurich.*
1944 *Posthumous publication of* Stephen Hero.

Joyce entirely renewed the novel and deeply influenced the first half of the twentieth century. He was Irish, Dublin did form the background of all his works, but he was a self-exile, more interested in universality and myth. The Irish revolution and the problems of his native country never appear in his novels.

Dubliners *is a collection of stories, each throwing some light on one aspect of the degradation of Dublin and the failure of its inhabitants. We are made to feel that the only spiritual salvation lies in European culture.*

Joyce's first novel, A Portrait of the Artist as a Young Man, *makes large use of symbolism and irony while relating an adolescent's education and development, his obsession whith sin, his longing for wider experiences, his discovery of beauty and love.*

But it is Ulysses *which is undoubtedly Joyce's masterpiece. It is the record of a single day in the life of Leopold Bloom, in Dublin. Through his wanderings about the city which parallel those of Homer's hero we discover his relationship with Marion, his wife, and Stephen Dedalus, a young poet. Like the* Odyssey, *the book is divided into episodes so that we are constantly reminded of the contrast between a heroic past and the degraded present – for Dublin appears as a ruined city, sheltering drifting and helpless characters. The novel becomes an epic, the trivial events of the day take on a universal value and Bloom, Molly and Stephen become archetypal characters.*

One of the most innovative aspects of the novel is its use of the interior monologue. Plot and time disappear, merging into the stream of consciousness: smells, thoughts, the prickings of conscience, impressions and memories surface pell-mell, giving a more objective view of reality. The virtuosity of Joyce's language, full of puns, word-creations, references and allusions attempts to convey the complex texture of reality, the leitmotivs and ambiguities that alone can give the true feel of existence.

Joyce's last novel, Finnegans Wake, *relates the thoughts that flicker through the mind of a sleeping Dublin innkeeper. The allusions, the parodies, the simultaneous use of several languages, the constant creation of portmanteau-words, make it an extremely difficult and hermetic work.*

Ulysses (1922)

Bloom, who canvasses for advertisements, enters the newspaper office.

IN THE HEART OF THE HIBERNIAN METROPOLIS

Before Nelson's pillar trams slowed, shunted, changed trolley, started for Blackrock, Kingstown and Dalkey, Clonskea, Rathgar and Terenure, Palmerston park and upper Rathmines, Sandymount Green, Rathmines, Ringsend and Sandymount Tower, Harold's Cross. The hoarse Dublin United Tramway Company's timekeeper bawled them off:

– Rathgar and Terenure!

– Come on, Sandymount Green!

Right and left parallel clanging ringing a double-decker and a single-deck moved from their railheads, swerved to the down line, glided parallel.

– Start, Palmerston park!

THE WEARER OF THE CROWN

Under the porch of the general post office shoeblacks called and polished. Parked in North Prince's street His Majesty's vermilion mailcars, bearing on their sides the royal initials, E. R., received loudly flung sacks of letters, postcards, lettercards, parcels, insured and paid, for local, provincial, British and overseas delivery.

GENTLEMEN OF THE PRESS

Grossbooted draymen rolled barrels dullthudding out of Prince's stores and bumped them up on the brewery float. On the brewery float bumped dullthudding barrels rolled by grossbooted draymen out of Prince's stores.

– There it is, Red Murray said. Alexander Keyes.

– Just cut it out, will you? Mr Bloom said, and I'll take it round to the *Telegraph* office.

The door of Ruttledge's office creaked again. Davy Stephens, minute in a large capecoat, a small felt hat crowning his ringlets, passed out with a roll of papers under his cape, a king's courier.

Red Murray's long shears sliced out the advertisement from the newspaper in four clean strokes. Scissors and paste.

– I'll go through the printing works, Mr Bloom said, taking the cut square.

– Of course, if he wants a par, Red Murray said earnestly, a pen behind his ear, we can do him one.

– Right, Mr Bloom said with a nod. I'll rub that in.

We.

WILLIAM BRAYDEN,
ESQUIRE, OF OAKLANDS, SANDYMOUNT

Red Murray touched Mr Bloom's arm with the shears and whispered:

– Brayden.

Mr Bloom turned and saw the liveried porter raise his lettered cap as a stately figure entered between the newsboards of the *Weekly Freeman and National Press* and the *Freeman's Journal and National Press.* Dullthudding Guinness's barrels. It passed stately up the staircase steered by an umbrella, a solemn beardframed face. The broadcloth back ascended each step: back. All his brains are in the nape of his neck, Simon Dedalus says. Welts of flesh behind on him. Fat folds of neck, fat, neck, fat, neck.

– Don't you think his face is like Our Saviour? Red Murray whispered.

The door of Ruttledge's office whispered: ee: cree. They always build one door opposite another for the wind to. Way in. Way out.

Our Saviour: beardframed oval face: talking in the dusk Mary, Martha. Steered by an umbrella sword to the footlights: Mario the tenor.

– Or like Mario, Mr Bloom said.

– Yes, Red Murray agreed. But Mario was said to be the picture of Our Saviour.

Jesus Mario with rougy cheeks, doublet and spindle legs. Hand on his heart. In *Martha.*

Co-ome thou lost one,
Co-ome thou dear one.

THE CROZIER AND THE PEN

– His grace phoned down twice this morning, Red Murray said gravely.

They watched the knees, legs, boots vanish. Neck.

A telegram boy stepped in nimbly, threw an envelope on the counter and stepped off posthaste with a word.

– *Freeman!*

Mr Bloom said slowly:

– Well, he is one of our saviours also.

A meek smile accompanied him as he lifted the counterflap, as he passed in through the sidedoor and along the warm dark stairs and passage, along the now reverberating boards. But will he save the circulation? Thumping, thumping.

He pushed in the glass swingdoor and entered, stepping over strewn packing paper. Through a lane of clanking drums he made his way towards Nannetti's reading closet.

WITH UNFEIGNED REGRET IT IS WE
ANNOUNCE THE DISSOLUTION OF A MOST RESPECTED
DUBLIN BURGESS

Hynes here too: account of the funeral probably. Thumping thump. This morning the remains of the late Mr Patrick Dignam. Machines. Smash a man to atoms if they got him caught. Rule the world today. His machineries are pegging away too. Like these, got out of hand: fermenting. Working away, tearing away. And that old grey rat tearing to get in.

HOW A GREAT DAILY ORGAN IS TURNED OUT

Mr Bloom halted behind the foreman's spare body, admiring a glossy crown.

Strange he never saw his real country. Ireland my country. Member for College green. He boomed that workaday worker tack for all it was worth. It's the ads and side features sell a weekly not the stale news in the official gazette. Queen Anne is dead. Published by authority in the year one thousand and. Demesne situate in the townland of Rosenallis, barony of Tinnachinch. To all whom it may concern schedule pursuant to statute showing return of number of mules and jennets exported from Ballina. Nature notes. Cartoons. Phil Blake's weekly Pat and Bull story. Uncle Toby's page for tiny tots. Country bumpkin's queries. Dear Mr Editor, what is a good cure for flatulence? I'd like that part. Learn a lot teaching others. The personal note M. A. P. Mainly all pictures. Shapely bathers on golden strand. World's biggest balloon. Double marriage of sisters celebrated. Two bridegrooms laughing heartily at each other. Cuprani too, printer. More Irish than the Irish.

Joyce on his intention in Ulysses:

It is an epic of two races (Israelite-Irish) and at the same time the cycle of the human body as well as a little story of a day (life). The character of Ulysses always facinated me – even when a boy. Imagine, fifteen years ago I started writing it as a short story for *Dubliners*! For seven years I have been writing at this book – blast it! It is also a sort of encyclopaedia. My intention is to transpose the myth *sub specie temporis nostri*. Each adventure (that is, every hour, every organ, every art being interconnected and interrelated in the structural scheme of the whole) should not only condition but even create its own technique. Each adventure is so to say one person although it is composed of persons – as Aquinas relates of the angelic hosts...

Letter to Carlo Linati.
Letters of James Joyce.

Valery Larbaud on the structure of Ulysses:

Larbaud décrit ensuite le schéma même, semble-t-il, que Joyce lui avait remis:
« Voilà les grandes lignes du plan qu'on peut représenter graphiquement de la façon suivante: en haut, trois panneaux: la Télémachie; au-dessous, les douze épisodes; et, en bas, les trois épisodes du Retour. En tout : dix-huit panneaux, – les dix-huit nouvelles.
A partir de là, sans perdre complètement de vue l'*Odyssée*, Joyce trace un plan particulier à l'intérieur de chacun de ses dix-huit panneaux, ou épisodes.
Ainsi chaque épisode traitera d'une science ou d'un art particulier, contiendra un symbole particulier, représentera un organe donné du corps humain, aura sa couleur particulière, sa technique propre, et en tant qu'épisode, correspondra à une des heures de la journée.
Ce n'est pas tout, et dans chacun des panneaux ainsi divisés, l'auteur inscrit de nouveaux symboles plus particuliers, des correspondances.
Pour être plus clair, prenons un exemple: l'épisode IV des aventures. Son titre est Eole: le lieu où il se passe est la salle de rédaction d'un journal; l'heure à laquelle il a lieu est midi; l'organe auquel il correspond: le poumon; l'art dont il traite: la rhétorique; sa couleur: le rouge; sa figure symbolique: le rédacteur en chef; sa technique: l'enthymème; ses correspondances: un personnage qui correspond à l'Eole d'Homère; l'inceste comparé au journalisme; l'île flottante d'Eole: la presse; le personnage nommé Dignam, mort subitement trois jours avant et à l'en-

terrement duquel Léopold Bloom est allé (ce qui constitue l'épisode de la descente aux Hadès): Elpenor ».

Valéry Larbaud, « Ce vice impuni, la lecture, Domaine anglais », *Œuvres Complètes*, Tome III. *Gallimard, Paris 1951.*

Portmanteau words – Humpty Dumpty's explanation of the poem *Jabberwocky* (cf. p. 49) *in* Through the Looking-Glass:

"You seem very clever at explaining words, Sir", said Alice. "Would you kindly tell me the meaning of the poem called *Jabberwocky*?"

"Let's hear it", said Humpty Dumpty. "I can explain all the poems, that ever were invented – and a good many that haven't been invented just yet".

This sounded very hopeful, so Alice repeated the first verse: –

'Twas brillig, and the slithy toves
Did gyre and gimble in the wabe:
All mimsy were the borogoves,
And the mome raths outgrabe.

"That's enough to begin with", Humpty Dumpty interrupted: "there are plenty of hard words there. *Brillig* means four o'clock in the afternoon – the time when you begin *broiling* things for dinner".

"That'll do very well", said Alice: "and *slithy*?"

"Well, *slithy* means 'lithe and slimy'. 'Lithe'is the same as 'active'. You see it's like a portmanteau – there are two meanings packed up into one word".

"I see it now", Alice remarked thoughtfully: "and what are *toves*?"

"Well, *toves* are something like badgers – they're something like lizards – and they're something like corkscrews".

"They must be very curious-looking creatures".

"They are that", said Humpty Dumpty: "also they make their nests under sun-dials – also they live on cheese".

"And what's to *gyre* and to *gimble*?"

"To *gyre* is to go round and round like a gyro scope. To *gimble* is to make holes like a gimblet".

"And *the wabe* is the grass-plot round a sundial, I suppose?" said Alice, surprised at her own ingenuity.

"Of course it is. It's called *wabe*, you know, because it goes a long way before it, and a long way behind it – "

"And a long way beyond it on each side", Alice added.

"Exactly so. Well then, *mimsy* is 'flimsy and miserable' (there's another portmanteau for you). And a *borogove* is a thin shabby-looking bird with its feathers sticking out all round – something like a live mop".

"And then *mome raths*?" said Alice. "I'm afraid I'm giving you a great deal of trouble."

"Well, a *rath* is a sort of green pig: but *mome* I'm not certain about. I think it's short for 'from home' – meaning that they'd lost their way, you know".

"And what does *outgrabe* mean"

"Well, *outgribing* is something between bellowing and whistling, with a kind of sneeze in the middle: however, you'll hear it done, maybe – down in the wood yonder – and, when you've once heard it, you'll be *quite* content."

Lewis Carroll,
Through the Looking-Glass, Chapter 6.

Lewis Carroll (Charles Dodgon's pseudonym, 1832-1898) was an Oxford Mathematician who wrote books for children. Behind that humour, fantasy and nonsense, his works are characterized by a deep interest in logic.
1865 Alice's Adventures in Wonderland.
1872 Through the Looking-Glass.
1876 The Hunting of the Snark.
1889 Sylvie and Bruno.

Original illustration by Tenniel
Ph. Hachette/Landin.

Can Joyce be translated?
Compare the following excerpt from Finnegans Wake *with the two translations that follow:*

It was of a night, late, lang time agone, in an auldstane eld, when Adam was delvin and his madameen spinning watersilts, when mulk mountynotty man was everybully and the first leal ribberrobber that ever had her ainway everybuddy to his lovesaking eyes and everybilly lived alove with everybiddy else, and Jarl van Hoother had his burnt head high up in his lamphouse, laying cold hands on himself. And his tow little jiminies, cousins of ourn, Tristopher and Hilary, were kickaheeling their dummy on the oil cloth flure of his homerigh, castle and earthenhouse. And, be dermot, who come to the keep of his inn only the niece-of-his-in-law, the prankquean. And the prankquean pulled a rosy one and made her wit foreninst the dour. And she lit up and fireland was ablaze. And spoke she to the dour in her petty perusienne: Mark the Wans, why do I am alook alike a poss of porterpease? And that was how the skirtmisshes began. But the dour handworded her grace in dootch nossow: Shut! So her grace o'malice kidsnapped up the jiminy Tristopher and into the shandy westerness she rain, rain, rain. And Jarl van Hoother warlessed after her with soft dovesgall: Stop deef stop come back to my earin stop. But she swaradid to him: Unlikelihud. And there was a brannewail that same sabboath night of falling angles somewhere in Erio. And the prankquean went for her forty years' walk in Tourlemonde and she washed the blessings of the lovespots off the jiminy with soap sulliver suddles and she had her four owlers masters for to tauch him his tickles and she convorted him to the onesure allgood and he became a luderman. So then she started to rain and to rain and, be redtom, she was back again at Jarl van Hoother's in a brace of samers and the jiminy with her in her pinafrond, lace at night, at another time.

ibid.

● C'était d'une nuit, tard, bien des années passées, de trèsancienne ancienneté, qu'Adam allait bêchant et sa madamina flots de limon filant, que, immassif montanœud, homme allait par monts et par bœufs et le prime léal troussecôte à l'avoir oncques eue toutenfleur pour l'amour de ses yeux, et ravi toucocun vivait avec coquinautre, et Jarl Van Hoother levait sa tête brûlée haut en sa lanternerie ses mains froides à tâté de lui. Et ses deux petits cigalots, nos orphecousins, Tristophe et Hilare, faisaient sabasculer leur poupequin sur la toile sirée du flancher de son homerigh castel érédíterre. Et saperliflopette, qui arrive à l'huis de son hostel, fi fe n'est la nièfe de sa belle-fourmille, l'espiègle-reine. Et l'espièglereine, sans brune ni douce, s'esprima frontre la cochère. Et elle jeta feu et flamme, et tout le pays de s'embraser. Et ainsi dit à la cochère, parlant mesquine persienne: Marck Fermier, parquoi suis-je à clef acquis semble un pot de porteau s'il te glaise? Et c'est comme cela que l'aquerelle se lança. Mais la cochère à sa grace mot à main révergonda: Ferme! Sur quoi sa grace, o la malice! hydraffla le cigalot Tristophe et vers l'ouestan shandreux coulut, coulut, coulut. Et Jarl Van Hoother gerrugit atrêve elle en ireroucoulant suave: Halte fourde retourne à mon orie halte. Mais elle lui sanscritta: Pleuplausible. Et il y eut un branlehouhaha cette nuit-là de sabbat d'angles hulle part culbutant dans l'Eirio. Et l'espièglereine s'en alla sa quarantannée de promenage en Tourlemonde et lessiva les bénissures du cigalot avec des pluiettes de persavaube et le confia à quatre maîtres hibourniens afin qu'ils lui baptrennent ses chatouilles et le convortit à l'omnibon surécertain et il se fit lutarien. Alors elle se mit en coulure, coulure et, reparlotte, la voilà de rebours chez Jarl van Hoother [illegible] même avec le cigalot dans ses ramures, têtard de nuit, une nouvelle fois.

Traduction André Du Bouchet,
Gallimard 1962.

● C'était par une nuit, il y a tard, long évanoui passé, dans une vieille terre, lorsqu'Adam bêchait la terre et que sa petite madame filait la soie des rivières, que tout le monde était moult heureux, que la première loyale voleuse de côte qu'il y eût jamais empluviait tout le monde au charme de ses yeux, que chacun vivait en aime avec son prochain, et que Jarl van Hoother avait sa tête flamme sur les haut de sa lampe, posant ses mains froides sur lui. Et ses deux petits gémeaux, des cousins à nous, Tristophe & Hilare, talonnaient leur maman à l'endroit où blesse l'appât de son autodétermination, château et dépendances. Et honnêtement qui vint tenir son auberge si ce n'est la nièce par alliance, la prinsexe. Et la prinsexe s'est mise au rose et décidée, face à la porte. Elle a une illumination et la patrie s'en feu. Puis elle s'adressa à la porte des Porter dans son petite parler parisienne: « Marc I, pourquoi mes fesses ressemblent-elles comme deux petits pois à un grain de Porter? » Et c'est ainsi que commencèrent les scaramouches. Mais l'inflexible répondit à sa grâce en son hollangue Orangée : « Va te faire ! » Alors sa grâce O'Malice enleva d'un coup le gémeau Tristophe et s'enpluie pluie pluie vers l'ouestitude de sa cabane. Alors Jarl van Hoother lui télégraphia par colombophie sans fiel: « Stoppe là stop reviens dans mon Eire stop. » Mais elle lui rétorque: « Improbabilité! » Alors il se fit un tonnerre de plainte nuit en ce même sabbath – murs d'angles qui s'écroulent quelque part en l'Eire. Et la prinsexe partit faire son Tourlemonde, pour quarante années, effaça les bénédictions à l'endroit du gémeau avec sa salive de bulles de savon, ordonna à ses quatre anciens maîtres de lui enseigner ses tâches, et le convertit au seul dieu sûr pour qu'il devienne un dévoyé. C'est alors qu'elle commença de s'enpluir pluie et par hasard elle revint chez Jarl van Hoother après un couple d'étés, tenant le gémeau dans son tablier, tard la nuit, dans une autre époque.

Traduction Philippe Lavergne.
Éditions Gallimard 1982.

Virginia WOOLF 1882-1941

1882 *Born in London. Her father, Leslie Stephen, was a well-known historian, critic and philosopher.*
1904 *Death of her father.*
1906 *First meetings of the Bloomsbury Group, which she attended.*
1912 *Married Leonard Woolf, another member of the group.*
1914-1918 *Mental breakdown.*
1915 The Voyage Out.
1917 *Founded the Hogarth Press.*
1922 Jacob's Room.
1925 Mrs Dalloway, The Common Reader.
1927 To the Lighthouse.
1928 Orlando, A Room of one's Own.
1931 The Waves.
1932 The Second Common Reader.
1937 The Years.
1941 *Committed suicide by drowning. Posthumous publication of* Between the Acts.

A member of the Bloomsbury Group (like E.M. Forster the novelist, J.M. Keynes the economist, G.E. Moore the philosopher, Vanessa Bell the painter, Roger Fry the painter and critic, Lytton Strachey the historian), Virginia Woolf shared their interest in friendship and the arts which they believed "formed the rational ultimate end of social progress". She was a feminist (cf A Room of one's Own*) though not exempt from snobbery, for she was always conscious of her birth and upbringing. The world of her books is indeed limited to upper-class intellectuals, and over-sensitive aesthetes.*

Events are of no importance in her novels, wich have no plots: Mrs Dalloway *is the story of one day in the life of a fashionable woman who is giving a party that evening, in* To the Lighthouse, *a projected trip to a lighthouse and the completion of a picture are the only two themes. Yet the impression of a vivid and lively world is constant, a world reflected through the characters' moods, thoughts and ideas. For if her characters seem so strongly alive, it is because they are over-aware of the reality of each moment, of the passing of time. They try to catch the "myriad impressions" that each instant evokes – a whole range of memories, pictures or words. The expression "stream of consciousness" is often used to describe her technique though it should be qualified since her novels never render the raw experience of living, as Joyce's do.* "The nature of her characters alone made the use of the full stream of consciousness impossible. Her characters are highly articulate and quite abnormally self-aware, watching their thoughts and feelings the whole time as Leopold and Marion Bloom never do". W. Allen *Besides, several centres of consciousness are used in each of her novels, creating a more impressionistic effect. This is not to say that her novels lack unity. The characters are linked through a community of feeling and intuition and by a device which consists of showing their reactions to the same experiences (e.g. an aeroplane writing something in the sky) or to an object or element (e.g. the lighthouse).*

Mrs Dalloway (1925)

In Mrs Dalloway, *we follow Clarissa Dalloway's thoughts through one day. She is making preparations for a party she is giving in the evening. In this passage, she has gone out to buy flowers.*

So she would still find herself arguing in St James's Park, still making out that she had been right – and she had too – not to marry him. For in marriage a little licence, a little independence there must be between people living together day in day out in the same house; which Richard[1] gave her, and she him. (Where was he this morning, for instance?

Some committee, she never asked what.) But with Peter[2] everything had to be shared; everything gone into. And it was intolerable, and when it came to that scene in the little garden by the fountain, she had to break with him or they would have been destroyed, both of them ruined, she was convinced; though she had borne about her for years like an arrow sticking in her heart the grief, the anguish: and then the horror of the moment when someone told her at a concert that he had married a woman met on the boat going to India! Never should she forget all that. Cold, heartless, a prude, he called her. Never could she understand how he cared. But those Indian women did presumably – silly, pretty, flimsy nincompoops. And she wasted her pity. For he was quite happy, he assured her – perfectly happy, though he had never done a thing that they talked of; his whole life had been a failure. It made her angry still.

She had reached the Park gates. She stood for a moment, looking at the omnibuses in Piccadilly.

She would not say of anyone in the world now that they were this or were that. She felt very young; at the same time unspeakably aged. She sliced like a knife through everything; at the same time was outside, looking on. She had a perpetual sense, as she watched the taxicabs, of being out, out, far out to sea and alone ; she always had the feeling that it was very, very dangerous to live even one day. Not that she thought herself clever, or much out of the ordinary. How she had got through life on the few twigs of knowledge Fräulein Daniels gave them she could not think. She knew nothing; no language, no history; she scarcely read a book now; except memoirs in bed, and yet to her it was absolutely absorbing; all this; the cabs passing; and she would not say of Peter, she would not say of herself, I am this, I am that.

Her only gift was knowing people almost by instinct, she thought, walking on. If you put her in a room with someone, up went her back like a cat's; or she purred. Devonshire House, Bath House, the house with the china cuckatoo[3], she had seen them all lit up once; and remembered Sylvia, Fred, Sally Seton – such hosts of people; and dancing all night; and the wagons plodding past to market; and driving home across the Park. She remembered once throwing a shilling into the Serpentine. But everyone remembered; what she loved was this, here, now, in front of her; the fat lady in the cab. Did it matter then, she asked herself, walking towards Bond Street, did it matter that she must inevitably cease completety; all this must go on without her; did she resent it; or did it not become consoling to believe that death ended absolutely? but that somehow in the streets of London, on the ebb and flow of things, here, there, she survived, Peter survived, lived in each other, she being part, she was positive, of the trees at home; of the house there, ugly, rambling all to bits and pieces as it was; part of people she had never met; being laid out like a mist between the people she knew best, who lifted her on their branches as she had seen the trees lift the mist, but it spread ever so far, her life, herself.

1. *Richard*: Clarissa's husband – 2. *Peter*: someone Clarissa knew and loved, but did not marry – 3. *Devonshire House, Bath House, the house with the china cuckatoo* = houses along Piccadilly, where Clarissa is walking.

Virginia Woolf and the post-impressionists :

If, as Virginia Woolf suggested, art is a world "where no stories are told" then meaning must derive from the relations between areas of colour, lines, marks, "geared down" from reality in that manner which is such a major characteristic of English Post-Impressionism.

This is the process which Virginia Woolf also analyses so succintly in the person and work of Lily Briscoe in *To The Lighthouse;* Lily, who constantly "tried to make of the moment something permanent". This is exactly the aim of the Camden Town painters from 1912 onwards; how to achieve Cezanne's sense of "duration" in the image, without losing sight of that lived social experience which so profoundly nourished their art. It is at this point that a definite local Post-Impressionist style clearly emerges. By the time Fry's Second Post-Impressionist Exhibition opened in London in October 1912, including pictures by Gore, Bell and Grant, this style was already firmly established.

Simon Watney, *English Post-Impressionism.*

Malcolm Drummond: In the Park (St James's Park).
Southampton Art Gallery, Southampton.

Virginia Woolf on time:

An hour, once in lodges in the queer element of the human spirit, may be stretched to fifty or a hundred times its clock length; on the other hand, an hour may be accurately represented on the timepiece of the mind by one second. This extraordinary discrepancy between time on the clock and time in the mind is less known than it should be and deserves fuller investigation... When a man has reached the age of thirty... time when he is thinking becomes inordinately long, time when he is doing becomes inordinately short.

Orlando, 1928.
ibid.

Cf. Narrative technique, p. 15; Presenting the characters' words and thoughts, p. 20.

... and on modern fiction:

Admitting the vagueness which afflicts all criticism of novels, let us hazard the opinion that for us at this moment the form of fiction most in vogue more often misses than secures the thing we seek. Whether we call it life or spirit, truth or reality, this, the essential thing, has moved off, or on, and refuses to be contained any longer in such ill-fitting vestments as we provide. Nevertheless, we go on persevering, conscientiously, constructing our two and thirty chapters after a design which more and more ceases to resemble the vision in our minds. So much of the enormous labour of proving the solidity, the likeness to life, of the story is not merely labour thrown away but labour misplaced to the extent of obscuring and blotting out the light of the conception. The writer seems constrained, not by his own free will but by some powerful and unscrupulous tyrant who has him in thrall, to provide a plot, to provide comedy, tragedy, love interest, and an air of probability embalming the whole so impeccably that if all his figures were to come to life they would find themselves dressed down to the last button of their coats in the fashion of the hour. The tyrant is obeyed; the novel is done to a turn. But sometimes, more and more often as time goes by, we suspect a momentary doubt, a spasm of rebellion, as the pages fill themselves in the customary way. Is life like this? Must novels be like this?

Look within and life, it seems, is very far from being "like this". Examine for a moment an ordinary mind on an ordinary day. the mind receives a myriad impressions – trivial, fantastic, evanescent, or engraved with the sharpness of steel. From all sides they come, an incessant show of innumerable atoms; and as they fall, as they shape themselves into the life of Monday or Tuesday, the accent falls differently from of old; the moment of importance came not here but there; so that, if a writer were a free man and not so slave, if he could write what he chose, not what he must, if he could base his work upon his own feeling and not upon convention, there would be no plot, no comedy, no tragedy, no love interest or catastrophe in the accepted style, and perhaps not a single button sewn on as the Bond Street tailors would have it. Life is not a series of gig lamps symmetrically arranged; life is a luminous halo, a semi-transparent envelope surrounding us from the beginning of consciousness to the end. Is it not the task of the novelist to convey this varying, this unknown and uncircumscribed spirit, whatever aberration or complexity it may display, with as little mixture of the alien and external as possible? We are not pleading merely for courage and sincerity; we are suggesting that the proper stuff of fiction is a little other than custom would have us believe it.

It is, at any rate, in some such fashion as this that we seek to define the quality which distinguishes the work of several young writers, among whom Mr James Joyce is the most notable, from that of their predecessors. They attempt to come closer to life, and to preserve more sincerely and exactly what interests and moves them, even if to do so they must discard most of the conventions which are commonly observed by the novelist. Let us record the atoms as they fall upon the mind in the order in which they fall, let us trace the pattern, however disconnected and incoherent in appearance, which each sight or incident scores upon the consciousness.

"Modern fiction", 1919.
Reprinted in *the Common Reader*, 1925.
ibid.

Cf. Characters and characterization, p. 12; Narrative technique, p. 15.

David Herbert LAWRENCE 1885-1930

1885 *Born in Nottinghamshire. His father was a miner and a heavy drinker; his mother, of a higher social status, was more cultured and ambitious.*
1906-1908 *Studied at Nottingham University College.*
1908 *Taught in Croydon.*
1910 *Finished* The White Peacock, *started the first version of* Sons and Lovers.
1911 *Pneumonia forced him to give up teaching.*
1912 *Met Frieda von Richthofen and eloped with her to Germany and Italy. Finished* Sons and Lovers.
1914-1915 *Wrote* The Rainbow *(published in 1915 but outraged the public so much that the copies were seized). Poverty and illness.*
1916 *Finished* Women in Love *(pub. 1920, in the U.S.A.).*
1917 *Publication of collected poems* Look, We Have Come Through!

Deeply conditioned by his childhood in a mining town, D.H. Lawrence was a class-conscious writer who grew to hate modern civilisation and what it stood for: materialism, repression, a divorce from nature, an existence that was too polished and refined.

His works are a celebration of intuition, emotions, sexual relationship and love in which he finds the only source of vitality capable of redeeming man. He is comparable to Blake in his passionate dismissal of the power of reason or the intellect to get to the mystery of life, to the unconscious mind. Hence his admiration for simple, instinctive, non-intellectual people: his favourite characters are farmers, gypsies, gamekeepers. Central to all of D.H. Lawrence's works is the idea that the shame which is felt by modern man, paralyzing his impulses, is to be ascribed to women – mothers, wives or lovers – who tend to bring about the dissociation between minds and bodies, and should therefore be held subordinate.

The teacher or preacher in Lawrence can al-

1919-1922 *Travelled in Italy and Sicily.*
1922-1925 *Travelled to Ceylon, Australia, then New Mexico. Wrote* Kangaroo; The Plumed Serpent; The Woman Who Rode Away; St Mawr.
Birds, Beasts and Flowers *(poems) pub. in 1923.*
1925-1930 *Back in England but often travelled on the continent.*
1928 Lady Chatterley's Lover *published and seized.*
1928 Pornography and Obscenity.
1930 *Died of tuberculosis in Vence.*

ways be felt, particularly in his vehement, often overcharged style that makes constant use of symbolism.

Women in Love (1916, pub. 1920)

Coal-dust

Going home from school in the afternoon, the Brangwen girls descended the hill between the picturesque cottages of Willey Green till they came to the railway crossing. There they found the gate shut, because the colliery train was rumbling nearer. They could hear the small locomotive panting hoarsely as it advanced with caution between the embankments. The one-legged man in the little signal-hut by the road stared out from his security, like a crab from a snail-shell.

Whilst the two girls waited, Gerald Crich trotted up on a red Arab mare. He rode well and softly, pleased with the delicate quivering of the creature between his knees. And he was very picturesque, at least in Gudrun's eyes, sitting soft and close on the slender red mare, whose long tail flowed on the air. He saluted the two girls, and drew up at the crossing to wait for the gate, looking down the railway for the approaching train. In spite of her ironic smile at his picturesqueness, Gudrun liked to look at him. He was well set and easy, his face with its warm tan showed up his whitish, coarse moustache, and his blue eyes were full of sharp light as he watched the distance.

The locomotive chuffed slowly between the banks, hidden. The mare did not like it. She began to wince away, as if hurt by the unknown noise. But Gerald pulled her back and held her head to the gate. The sharp blasts of the chuffing engine broke with more and more force on her. The repeated sharp blows of unknown, terrifying noise struck through her till she was rocking with terror. She recoiled like a spring let go. But a glistening, half-smiling look came into Gerald's face. He brought her back again, inevitably.

The noise was released, the little locomotive with her clanking steel connecting-rod emerged on the highroad, clanking sharply. The mare rebounded like a drop of water from hot iron. Ursula and Gudrun pressed back into the hedge, in fear. But Gerald was heavy on the mare, and forced her back. It seemed as if he sank into her magnetically, and could thrust her back against herself.

"The fool!" cried Ursula loudly. "Why doesn't he ride away till it's gone by?"

Gudrun was looking at him with black-dilated, spellbound eyes. But he sat glistening and obstinate, forcing the wheeling mare, which spun and swerved like a wind, and yet could not get out of the grasp of his will, nor escape from the mad clamour of terror that resounded through her, as the trucks thumped slowly, heavily, horrifying, one after the other, one pursuing the other, over the rails of the crossing.

The locomotive, as if wanting to see what could be done, put on the brakes, and back came the trucks rebounding on the iron buffers, striking like horrible cymbals, clashing nearer and nearer in frightful strident concussions. The mare opened her mouth and rose slowly, as if lifted up on a wind of terror. Then suddenly her fore-feet struck out, as she convulsed herself utterly away from the horror. Back she went, and the two girls clung to each other, feeling she must fall backwards on top of him. But he leaned forward, his face shining with fixed amusement, and at last he brought her down, sank her down, and was bearing her back

to the mark. But as strong as the pressure of his compulsion was the repulsion of her utter terror, throwing her back away from the railway, so that she spun round and round on two legs, as if she were in the centre of some whirlwind. It made Gudrun faint with poignant dizziness, which seemed to penetrate to her heart.

Chapter 9.

Study the passage in the light of the following opinions and writings of D.H.Lawrence about his work:

• True, we must all develop into mental consciousness. But mental consciousness is not a goal; it is a cul-de-sac. It provides us only with endless *appliances* which we can use for the all-too-difficult business of coming to our spontaneous-creative fulness of being. It provides us with means to adjust ourselves to the external universe. It gives us further means for subduing the external, materio-mechanical universe to our great end of creative life. And it gives us plain indications of how to avoid falling into automatism, hints for the *applying* of the will, the loosening of false, automatic fixations, the brave adherence to a profound soul-impulse. This is the use of the mind – a great indicator and instrument. The mind as author and director of life is anathema. (...)

The mind is the dead end of life. But it has all the mechanical force of the non-vital universe. It is a great dynamo of super-mechanical force. Given the *will* as accomplice, it can even arrogate its machine-motions and automatizations over the whole of life, till every tree becomes a clipped tea-pot and every man a useful mechanism. So we see the brain, like a great dynamo and accumulator, accumulating *mechanical* force and presuming to apply this mechanical force-control to the living unconscious, subjecting everything spontaneous to certain machine-principles called ideals or ideas.

And the human will assists in this humiliating and sterilizing process. We don't know what the human will is. But we do know that it is a certain faculty belonging to every living organism; the faculty for self-determination.

"Psychoanalysis and the Unconscious",
quoted in F.R. Leavis, *D.H.Lawrence: Novelist.*

• You mustn't look in my novel for the old stable ego of character. There is another ego, according to whose action the individual is unrecognizable, and passes through, as it were, allotropic states which it needs a deeper sense than any we've been used to exercise, to discover – states of the same single radically unchanged element. (Like as diamond and coal are the same pure single element of carbon. The ordinary novelist would trace the history of the diamond – but I say, "Diamond, what! This is carbon!" And my diamond might be coal or soot, and my theme is carbon).

Letter to Edward Garnett.

• Let us hesitate no longer to announce that the sensual passions and mysteries are equally sacred with the spiritual mysteries and passions. Who would deny it any more? The only thing unbearable is the degradation, the prostitution of the living mysteries in us. Let man only approach his own self with a deep respect, even reverence for all that the creative soul, the God-mystery within us, puts forth. Then we shall all be sound and free. Lewdness is hateful because it impairs our integrity and our proud being.

The creative, spontaneous soul sends forth its promptings of desire and aspiration in us. These promptings are our true fate, which is our business to fulfil. A fate dictated from outside, from theory or from circumstance, is a false fate.

This novel pretends only to be a record of the writer's own desires, aspirations, struggles; in a word, a record of the profoundest experiences in the self. Nothing that comes from the deep, passional soul is bad, or can be bad. So there is no apology to tender, unless to the soul itself, if it should have been belied.

Man struggles with his unborn needs and fulfilment. New unfoldings struggle up in torment in him, as buds struggle forth from the midst of a plant. Any man of real individuality tries to know and to understand what is happening, even in himself, as he goes along. This struggle for verbal consciousness should not be left out in art. It is a very great part of life. It is not superimposition of a theory. It is the passionate struggle into conscious being.

We are now in a period of crisis. Every man who is acutely alive is acutely wrestling with his own soul. The people that can bring forth the new passion, the new idea, this people will endure. Those others, that fix themselves in the old idea, will perish with the new life strangled unborn within them. Men must speak out to one another.

In point of style, fault is often found with the continual, slightly modified repetition. The only answer is that it is natural to the author; and that every natural crisis in emotion or passion or understanding comes from this pulsing, frictional to-and-fro which works up to culmination.

Foreword to *Women in Love,* 1920.
ibid.

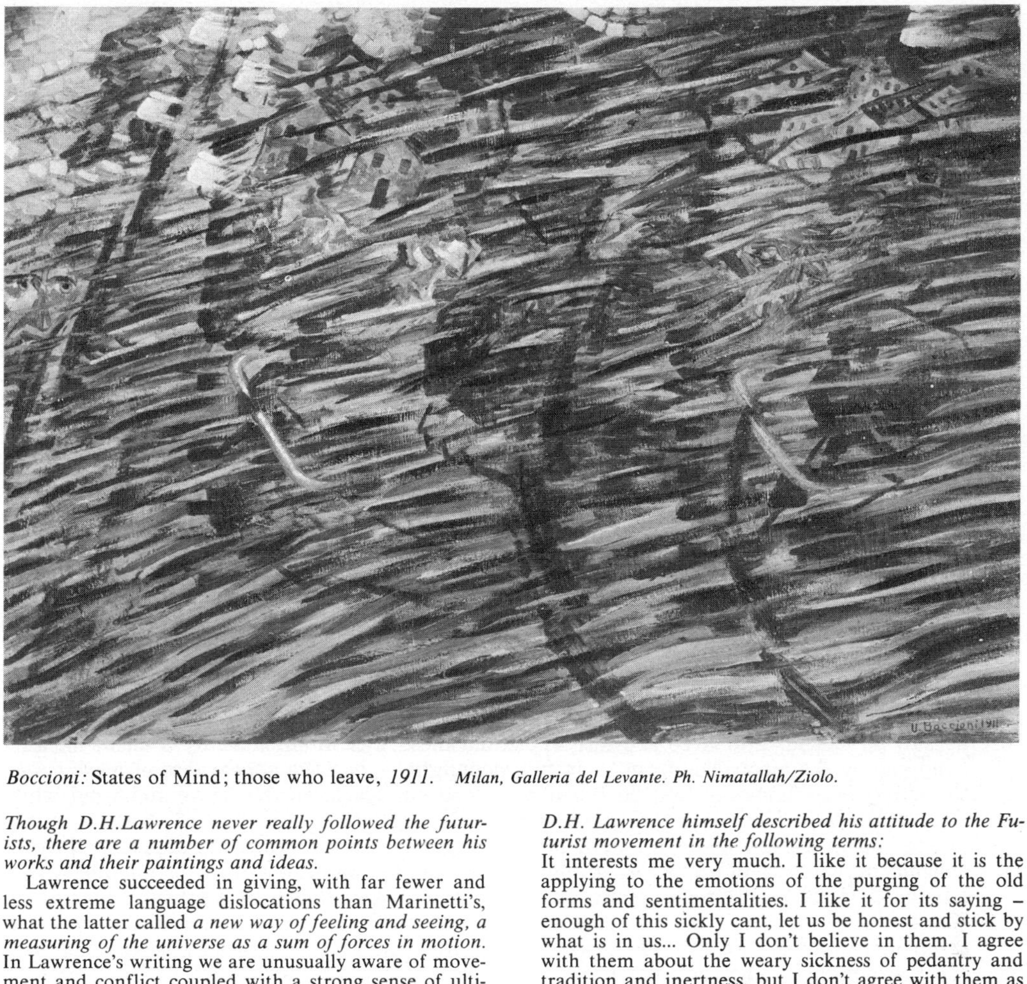

Boccioni: States of Mind; those who leave, *1911.* *Milan, Galleria del Levante. Ph. Nimatallah/Ziolo.*

Though D.H.Lawrence never really followed the futurists, there are a number of common points between his works and their paintings and ideas.

Lawrence succeeded in giving, with far fewer and less extreme language dislocations than Marinetti's, what the latter called *a new way of feeling and seeing, a measuring of the universe as a sum of forces in motion.* In Lawrence's writing we are unusually aware of movement and conflict coupled with a strong sense of ultimate unity. The association of this skill with amoral sensationalism in both Lawrence and the futurists appears to arise from their common effort to relate in an intensive sensory experience that which is not rationally relatable. M. Freeman, *Lawrence and Futurism.*

D.H. Lawrence himself described his attitude to the Futurist movement in the following terms:
It interests me very much. I like it because it is the applying to the emotions of the purging of the old forms and sentimentalities. I like it for its saying – enough of this sickly cant, let us be honest and stick by what is in us... Only I don't believe in them. I agree with them about the weary sickness of pedantry and tradition and inertness, but I don't agree with them as to the cure and the escape. They will progress down the purely male or intellectual or scientific line. They will even use their intuition for intellectual or scientific purposes. Letter to A.W. McLeod, 1914.

Edward Morgan FORSTER 1879-1970

1879 *Born in London.*
1888 *His great-aunt's death left him wealthy.*
1897-1901 *Student at King's College, Cambridge. Met Goldsworthy Lowes Dickinson who initiated him into the cult of friendship and frankness. Among the undergraduates, he also met J.M. Keynes, Lytton Strachey, Leonard Woolf and Roger Fry who,*

The works of E.M. Forster always express a conflict between two worlds: that of the individual, of instinct and spontaneity, and the world of convention and hypocrisy which destroys the vitality in men. In A Room With a View *it is England which represents the latter culture and is opposed to Italy; in* Howards End, *two families are contrasted, symbolising refinement and culture in face of narrow-mindedness and utilitarianism.*

What Forster advocates is the healing of the

together with Virginia Woolf, were later to form the Bloomsbury Group.

1901 *Travelled to Italy and Greece.*

1905 *Travelled to Germany,* Where Angels Fear to Tread.

1907 The Longest Journey.

1908 A Room with a View.

1910 Howards End.

1911 The Celestial Omnibus and Other Stories.

1912-1913 *Travelled to India.*

1915-1918 *Worked in Alexandria for the Red Cross.*

1920 *Back in India.*

1924 A Passage to India.

1927 Aspects of the Novel.

1946 *Settled in Cambridge.*

1951 Two Cheers for Democracy.

1970 *Died in the Midlands.*

breach: "only connect", he says in Howards End. *This liberalism is to be related to the ideas of the Bloomsbury Group, their belief in a complete freedom between races, between men and women, their defence of all minorities such as homosexuals, their faith in personal relationships. Forster even went as far as saying: "If I had to choose between betraying my country and betraying my friend, I hope I should have the guts to betray my country."*

His last and most famous novel, A Passage to India, *is set in Chandrapore and analyses the racial, cultural and religious differences between the English rulers and the Indian community.*

Forster also wrote essays and literary criticism. Aspects of the Novel, *a study of the theory and methods of fiction, has now become a classic* *(cf p. 13).*

A Passage to India (1924)

He had always liked this mosque. It was gracious, and the arrangement pleased him. The courtyard – entered through a ruined gate – contained an ablution tank of fresh clear water, which was always in motion, being indeed part of a conduit that supplied the city. The courtyard was paved with broken slabs. The covered part of the mosque was deeper than is usual ; its effect was that of an English parish church whose side has been taken out. Where he sat, he looked into three arcades whose darkness was illuminated by a small hanging lamp and by the moon. The front – in full moonlight – had the appearance of marble, and the ninety-nine names of God on the frieze stood out black, as the frieze stood out white against the sky. The contest between this dualism and the contention of shadows within pleased Aziz, and he tried to symbolize the whole into some truth of religion or love. A mosque by winning his approval let loose his imagination. The temple of another creed, Hindu, Christian, or Greek, would have bored him and failed to awaken his sense of beauty. Here was Islam, his own country, more than a Faith, more than a battle-cry, more, much more... Islam, an attitude towards life both exquisite and durable, where his body and his thoughts found their home.

His seat was the low wall that bounded the courtyard on the left. The ground fell away beneath him towards the city, visible as a blur of trees, and in the stillness he heard many small sounds. On the right, over in the club, the English community contributed an amateur orchestra. Elsewhere some Hindus were drumming – he knew they were Hindus, because the rhythm was uncongenial to him – and others were bewailing a corpse – he knew whose, having certified it in the afternoon. There were owls, the Punjab mail... and flowers smelt deliciously in the station master's garden. But the mosque – that alone signified, and he returned to it from the complex appeal of the night, and decked it with meanings the builder had never intended. Some day he too would build a mosque, smaller than this but in perfect taste, so that all who passed by should experience the happiness he felt now. And near it, under a low dome, should be his tomb, with a Persian inscription:

"Alas, without me for thousands of years
  The Rose will blossom and the Spring will bloom,
  But those who have secretly understood my heart –
  They will approach and visit the grave where I lie."

He had seen the quatrain on the tomb of a Deccan king and regarded it as profound philosophy – he always held pathos to be profound. The secret understanding of the heart! He repeated the phrase with tears in his eyes, and as he did so one of the pillars of the mosque seemed to quiver. It swayed in the gloom and detached itself. Belief in ghosts ran in his blood, but he sat firm. Another pillar moved, a third, and then an Englishwoman stepped out into the moonlight. Suddenly he was furiously angry and shouted: "Madam! Madam! Madam!"

"Oh! Oh!" the woman gasped.

"Madam, this is a mosque; you have no right here at all; you should have taken off your shoes; this is a holy place for Moslems."

"I have taken them off."

"You have?"

"I left them at the entrance."

"Then I ask your pardon."

Still startled, the woman moved out, keeping the ablution tank between them. He called after her: "I am truly sorry for speaking."

"Yes, I was right, was I not? If I remove my shoes, I am allowed?"

"Of course; but so few ladies take the trouble, especially if thinking no one is there to see."

"That makes no difference. God is here."

"Madam!"

"Please let me go."

"Oh, can I do you some service now or at any time?"

"No, thank you, really none – good night."

"May I know your name?"

She was now in the shadow of the gateway, so that he could not see her face, but she saw his, and she said with a change of voice: "Mrs Moore."

"Mrs – " Advancing, he found that she was old. A fabric bigger than the mosque fell to pieces, and he did not know whether he was glad or sorry. She was older than Hamidullah Begum, with a red face and white hair. Her voice had deceived him.

"Mrs Moore, I am afraid I startled you. I shall tell my community – our friends – about you. That God is here – very good, very fine indeed."

Chapter 2.

Study the excerpt from A Passage to India *in the light of this passage from* What I Believe *(in* Two Cheers for Democracy) *which is probably the best summary of the Bloomsbury Group's views concerning personality:*

I believe in aristocracy, though – if that is the right word, and if a democrat may use it. Not an aristocracy of power, based upon rank and influence, but an aristocracy of the sensitive, the considerate and the plucky. Its members are to be found in all nations and classes, and all through the ages, and there is a secret understanding between them when they meet. They represent the true human tradition, the one permanent victory of our queer race over cruelty and chaos. Thousands of them perish in obscurity, a few are great names. They are sensitive for others as well as for themselves, they are considerate without being fussy, their pluck is not swankiness but the power to endure, and they can take a joke. (...)

The aristocrats, the elect, the chosen, the Best People – all the words that describe them are false, and all attempts to organize them fail. Again and again Authority, seeing their value, has tried to net them and to utilize them as the Egyptian Priesthood or the Christian Church or the Chinese Civil Service or the Group Movement, or some other worthy stunt. But they slip through the net and are gone; when the door is shut, they are no longer in the room; their temple, as one of them remarked, is the holiness of the Heart's affections, and their kingdom, though they never possess it, is the wide-open world.

With this type of person knocking about, and constantly crossing one's path if one has eyes to see or hands to feel, the experiment of earthly life cannot be dismissed as a failure. But it may well be hailed as a tragedy, the tragedy being that no device has been found by which these private decencies can be transmitted to public affairs. As soon as people have power they go crooked and sometimes dotty as well, because the possession of power lifts them into a region where normal honesty never pays.

E.M. Forster, "What I believe", *Two cheers for Democracy.*
E. Arnold Publishers Ltd.

---

*The novel takes its title from a poem by Walt Whitman (*Passage to India, *1871):*

Passage to India!
Lo, soul, sees't thou not God's purpose from the first?
The earth to be spanned, connected by network,
The races, neighbors, to marry and be given in marriage,
The oceans to be crossed, the distant brought near,
The lands to be welded together.

Cf. Characters and characterization, p. 12; Narrative technique, p. 15.

George ORWELL 1903-1950

1903 *Eric Arthur Blair born in Bengal, the son of a British civil servant.*
1917-1921 *Educated at Eton.*
1922-1927 *Joined the Indian Imperial Police.*
1927-1930 *Lived among the poor in Paris and London.*
1933 Down and Out in Paris and London, *published under the pseudonym George Orwell.*
1935 A Clergyman's Daughter, Burmese Days.
1936 Keep the Apidistra Flying. *Went to the North of England to study the life of the unemployed, which led to* The Road to Wigan Pier.
1937 *Fought against fascism in Spain.*
1938 *Wrote* Homage to Catalonia *about the Spanish Civil war. Ill with tuberculosis.*
1939 Coming up for Air.
1941-1943 *Worked for the BBC.*
1943-1944 *Wrote* Animal Farm *(published 1945).*
1946 *Settled on the island of Jura in the Hebrides.*
1948 *Finished* 1984. *Entered a sanatorium.*
1950 *Died in London.*

Orwell stands out as a committed and patriotic writer who always expressed individualistic ideas with honesty and conviction.

He is best known for his two political allegories. Animal Farm *tells of the rebellion of the animals of a farm against the tyrannical farmer. Their newly-organized democracy, however, soon gives way to the pigs' oligarchy, and the book becomes a clear mockery of the Russian revolution.* 1984 *is a dystopia, the story of Winston's struggle against a totalitarian regime. More than communism, it is any form of oppression, or threat to freedom, which he attacks. In* Such, such, were the Joys, *Orwell wrote: "What I have most wanted to do throughout the past ten years is to make political writing into an art. My starting point is always a feeling of partisanship, a sense of injustice. When I sit down to write a book, I do not say to myself, 'I am going to produce a work of art'. I write it because there is some lie that I want to expose, some fact to which I want to draw attention, and my initial concern is to get a hearing." The rest of his essays and novels, always verging on journalism, are good illustrations of his comment:* Down and Out in Paris and London *is a study of poverty, working conditions and the social system,* The Road to Wigan Pier *looks at the problems of unemployment and its effects on men,* Homage to Catalonia *exposes the deceits that underlie all politics. A clear and straightforward prose underlines the sincerity of Orwell's writings.*

Nineteen Eighty-Four (1948)

In 1984 Winston Smith, a civil servant and Party member in the English Totalitarian State (now known as Air Strip No. 1), conceives political doubts, drifts into tacit rebellion, is detected after a short and touching period of happiness with a girl member of the Party and is horribly "rehabilitated." Henceforth he will be spiritually, emotionally, intellectually infantile, passive and obedient, as though he had undergone a spiritual leucotomy.

V.S. Pritchett.

O'Brien smiled slightly. "You are a flaw in the pattern, Winston. You are a stain that must be wiped out. Did I not tell you just now that we are different from the persecutors of the past? We are not content with negative obedience, nor even with the most abject submission. When finally you surrender to us, it must be of your own free will. We do not destroy the heretic because he resists us: so long as he resists us we never destroy him. We convert him, we capture his inner mind, we reshape him. We burn all evil and all illusion out of him: we bring him over to our side, not in appearance, but genuinely, heart and soul. We make him one of ourselves before we kill him. It is intolerable to us that an erroneous thought should exist anywhere in the world, however secret and powerless it may be. Even in the instant of death we cannot permit any deviation. In the old days the heretic walked to the stake still a heretic, proclaiming his heresy, exulting in it. Even the victim of the Russian purges could carry rebellion locked up in his skull as he walked down the passage waiting for the bullet. But we make the brain perfect before we blow it out. The command of the old despotisms was 'Thou shalt not.' The command of the totalitarians was 'Thou shalt.' Our command is '*Thou art*'. No one whom we bring to this place ever stands out against us. Everyone is washed clean. Even those three miserable traitors in whose innocence you once believed – Jones, Aaronson, and Rutherford – in the end we broke them down. I took part in their interrogation myself. I saw them gradually worn down, whimpering, grovelling, weeping – and in the end it was not with pain or fear, only with penitence. By the time we had finished with them they were only the shells of men. There was nothing left in them except sorrow for what they had done, and love of Big Brother. It was touching to see how they loved him. They begged to be shot quickly, so that they could die while their minds were still clean."

His voice had grown almost dreamy. The exaltation, the lunatic enthusiasm, was still in his face. He is not pretending, thought Winston; he is not a hypocrite; he believes every word he says. What most oppressed him was the consciousness of his own intellectual inferiority. He watched the heavy yet graceful form strolling to and fro, in and out of the range of his vision. O'Brien was a being in all ways larger than himself. There was no idea that he had ever had, or could have, that O'Brien had not long ago known, examined, and rejected. His mind *contained* Winston's mind. But in that case how could it be true that O'Brien was mad? It must be he, Winston, who was mad. O'Brien halted and looked down at him. His voice had grown stern again.

Part III, Chapter 2.

Compare the conditioning described in the text and that of Huxley's Brave New World.

The Director of Hatcheries and Conditioning explains to students how human beings are graded in the incubators according to the social destiny the State decides for them.

"We also predestine and condition. We decant our babies as socialized human beings, as Alphas or Epsilons, as future sewage workers or future..."He was going to say "future World Controllers", but correcting himself, said "future Directors of Hatcheries" instead.

The D.H.C. acknowledged the compliment with a smile.

They were passing Metre 320 on Rack II. A young Beta-Minus mechanic was busy with screw-driver and spanner on the blood-surrogate pump of a passing bottle. The hum of the electric motor deepened by fractions of a tone as he turned the nuts. Down, down... A final twist, a glance at the revolution counter, and he was done. He moved two paces down the line and began the same process on the next pump.

"Reducing the number of revolutions per minute," Mr Foster explained. "The surrogate goes round slower; therefore passes through the lung at longer intervals; therefore gives the embryo less oxygen. Nothing like oxygen-shortage for keeping an embryo below par." And he rubbed his hands.

"But why do you want to keep the embryo below par?" asked an ingenuous student.

"Ass!" said the Director, breaking a long silence. "Hasn't it occured to you that an Epsilon embryo must have an Epsilon environment as well as an Epsilon heredity?"

It evidently hadn't occured to him. He was covered with confusion.

"The lower the caste," said Mr Foster, "the shorter the oxygen. The first organ affected was the brain. After that the skeleton. At seventy per cent of normal oxygen you got dwarfs. At less than seventy, eyeless monsters.

"Who are no use at all," concluded Mr Foster.

A. Huxley, *Brave New World,* ch. 1.
Chatto and Windus.

Francis Bacon: Study after Velazquez's Portrait of Pope Innocent X, *1953.*
Ph. Edimedia © Archives Snark; N. Y. private collection.

Another vision of nightmare.
Bacon's paintings succeed in expressing with strength and immediacy man's anguish, terror and isolation. Many of them were inspired by photographs, Bacon's best-known photographic basis probably being the picture of the screaming nursemaid in Eisenstein's Battleship Potemkin.

Huxley on the nightmares of Brave New World *and* 1984:

The first hints of a philosophy of the ultimate revolution – the revolution which lies beyond politics and economics, and which aims at the total subversion of the individual's psychology and physiology – are to be found in the Marquis de Sade, who regarded himself as the continuator, the consummator, of Robespierre and Babeuf. The philosophy of the ruling minority in *Nineteen Eighty-Four* is a sadism which has been carried to its logical conclusion by going beyond sex and denying it. Whether in actual fact the policy of the boot-on-the-face can go on indefinitely seems doubtful. My own belief is that the ruling oligarchy will find less arduous and wasteful ways of governing and of satisfying its lust for power, and that these ways will resemble those which I described in *Brave New World*. Within the next generation I believe that the world's rulers will discover that infant conditioning and narco-hypnosis are more efficient, as instruments of government, than clubs and prisons, and that the lust for power can be just as completely satisfied by suggesting people into loving their servitude as by flogging and kicking them into obedience. In other words, I feel that the nightmare of *Nineteen Eighty-Four* is destined to modulate into the nightmare of a world having more resemblance to that which I imagined in *Brave New World.* The change will be brought about as a result of a felt need for increased efficiency. Meanwhile, of course, there may be a large-scale biological and atomic war – in which case we shall have nightmares of other and scarely imaginable kinds.

Letter to George Orwell
The Letters of Aldous Huxley, ed. by G. Smith,

The great-nephew of Matthew Arnold and the brother of the scientist Julian Huxley, Aldous Huxley (1894-1963) was brought up in a highly intellectual atmosphere. His first novels – Antic Hay *(1923),* Crome Yellow *(1921),* Those Barren Leaves *(1925) – are satires of the aimless life of the rich and cultured in the twenties. Two of his novels stand out:* Point Counter Point *(1928) shows divided man incapable of reaching happiness. The novel is made up of several almost independent plots which develop like musical counterpoint.* Brave New World *(1932) imagines a world entirely controlled by science and aiming at general happiness. Huxley's later works are more meditative and influenced by Eastern philosophy.*

Graham GREENE 1904-1991

1904 *Born at Berkhamsted.*
1925 *Graduated from Balliol College, Oxford.*
Started to work as a journalist (in Nottingham, then as sub-editor on The Times).
1926 *Converted to Roman Catholicism.*
1929 The Man Within, *his first novel, published. Left* The Times *to live by his writing.*
1932 Stamboul Train.
1935 *Travelled to Liberia.*
Became a film critic for The Spectator.
1936 A Gun for Sale.
1938 Brighton Rock.
Visited Mexico to report on the religious persecutions there.
1939 The Confidential Agent.
1940 The Power and the Glory.
1940-1941 *Worked for the Ministry of Information and for* The Spectator.
1941-1943 *Sent to West Africa by the Foreign Office.*
1943 The Ministry of Fear.

Graham Greene's large production can be divided into two groups of novels. The first, which he called "entertainments", includes works such as Stambul Train *or* The Third Man, *novels which, with their suspense, action and closely-knit plots, resemble thrillers. They are not devoid of moral and psychological depth, however, and the local atmosphere, as always in Greene's novels, is brilliantly caught, with an eye for the unexpected and telling detail.*

The second group of works are inspired by his Catholic faith. They deal with the problems of grace and redemption, of temptation and treason and involve tortured and divided characters, torn by the forces of good and evil. The setting is often sordid and seedy humanity, the uprooted and depraved beings who live apart from God but whom grace can nevertheless touch – thus the "whisky priest" who is he hero of The Power and the Glory, *though a sinner and a drunkard, is still capable of heroism.*

It is Greene's compassion, his sympathy towards all human beings (also reflected in his growing interest in political problems) which we finally remember.

1948 The Heart of the Matter.
1950 The Third Man.
1951 The End of the Affair.
1954-1955 *Travelled to Indochina.*
1955 The Quiet American.
1958 Our Man in Havana.
Became director of The Bodley Head Press.
1960 A Burnt-Out Case.
1967 *Settled in France.*
1969 Travels with my Aunt.
1973 The Honorary Consul.
1978 The Human Factor.
1980 Dr Fischer of Geneva.
1982 Monsignor Quixote.
1985 The Tenth Man.
1988 The Captain and the Enemy.
1990 The Last Word and Other Stories.
1991 *Died in Switzerland.*

Brighton Rock (1938)

The Boy (also called Pinkie) and Spicer are in on the same racket and are being attacked by a rival gang.

"Well, this is good-bye", the Boy said.

"You remember the address," Spicer said. "The 'Blue Anchor', you remember, Union Street. Send me any news. I don't suppose there'll be any for *me* to send."

The Boy put his hand up as if to pat Spicer on the back and let it fall again: the group of men stood in a bunch waiting. "Maybe – " the Boy said: he looked round: there wasn't any end to what he had begun. A passion of cruelty stirred in his belly. He put up his hand again and patted Spicer on the back. "Good luck to you," he said in a high broken adolescent voice and patted him again.

The men with one accord came round them. He heard Spicer scream, "Pinkie," and saw him fall: a boot with heavy nails was lifted, and then he felt pain run like blood down his own neck.

The surprise at first was far worse than the pain (a nettle could sting as badly). "You fools," he said, "it's not me, it's him you want," and turned and saw the faces ringing him all round. They grinned back at him: every man had his razor out: and he remembered for the first time Colleoni laughing up the telephone wire. The crowd had scattered at the first sign of trouble; he heard Spicer call out, "Pinkie. For Christ's sake", an obscure struggle reached its climax out of his sight. He had other things to watch: the long cut-throat razors which the sun caught slanting low down over the downs from Shoreham. He put his hand to his pocket to get his blade, and the man immediately facing him leant across and slashed his knuckles. Pain happened to him, and he was filled with horror and astonishment as if one of the bullied brats at school had stabbed first with the dividers.

They made no attempt to come in and finish him. He sobbed at them, "I'll get Colleoni for this." He shouted "Spicer" twice before he remembered that Spicer couldn't answer. The mob were enjoying themselves, just as he had always enjoyed himself. One of them leant forward to cut his cheek, and when he put up his hand to shield himself they slashed his knuckles again. He began to weep, as the four-thirty went by in a drumbeat of hooves beyond the rail.

Then someboby from the stand shouted "Bogies" and they all moved together, coming quickly at him in a bunch. Somebody kicked him on the thigh, he clutched a razor in his hand and was cut to the bone. Then they scattered as the police ran up the edge of the course, slow in their heavy boots, and he broke through them. A few followed him, out of the wire gate and straight down the side of the Down towards the houses and the sea. He wept as he ran, lame in one leg from the kick, he even tried to pray. You could be saved between the stirrup and the ground, but you couldn't be saved if you didn't repent and he hadn't time, scrambling down the chalk down, to feel the least remorse. He ran awkwardly, tripping, bleeding down his face and from both hands.

Part IV, chapter 1.

Peter Blake : Self-Portrait with Badges, *1961.*
London, The Tate Gallery.
The paintings of Peter Blake (born 1931) also reflect an interest in the contemporary scene by their use of pop imagery – the pictures, objects, magazines and emblems of popular culture.

Anthony Burgess on Brighton Rock:

(...) it was not until the appearance of *Brighton Rock* that the true voice of the novelist, the Catholic novelist, was heard. It is sometimes said that Greene's Catholicism is not strictly orthodox, that he adheres to the Jansenist heresy. If this means that he broods more on man's inborn depravity than on his ability to be regenerated, this is true: he is more interested in presenting evil than good. The hero of *Brighton Rock* is a young lapsed Catholic who runs a "bookmaker's protection" racket in the seaside resort of the title. He is dedicated to evil – betrayal, violence, murder – but with a full awareness of the eternal – or eschatological – meaning of his acts. At one point he says, rather improbably, *Credo in unum Satanum.* He is pursued by a blowsy decent stout-drinking woman who is convinced that he murdered her one-day seaside friend and who is much concerned with the righting of wrongs. Greene makes the paradox clear: she is animated only by relative values – since right and wrong are man-made – while the young ruffian is bound to the absolutes of good and evil. If one accepts evil one is at least expressing a belief in an ultimate reality: the Devil presupposes God. If one is scornful of these concepts and satisfied with the standards of merely human law, then one belongs to a lower order of mankind. The boy gangster – despite his unremitting pursuit of evil – can be seen with the eyes of eternity; his pursuer – despite her decency and desire for justice – cannot. In a sense, it is better for one's soul to pursue evil rather than right. It is a dangerous paradox, but it produced a superb novel.

A. Burgess, *The Novel Now.*

Compare the passage, p. 287, with the excerpt from A. Burgess's A Clockwork Orange *(1962) p. 300*

Cf. Narrative Technique, p. 15.

Samuel BECKETT 1906-1989

1906 *Born near Dublin.*
1923-1927 *Studied modern literature at Trinity College, Dublin.*
1928-1930 *Lecteur at the "Ecole Normale Supérieure". Met James Joyce.*
1930-1931 *Gave French lectures at Trinity College. M.A. in philosophy.*
1932-1937 *Travelled through Europe.*
1934* More Pricks than Kicks *(short stories).*
1937 *Settled in Paris.*
1938 Murphy.
1942-1945 *Active in the Resistance. Wrote* Watt.
1946-1950 *Wrote his trilogy:* Molloy *(pub. 1951),* Malone Dies *(pub. 1951),* The Unamable *(pub. 1953); and* Waiting for Godot *(pub. 1952).*
1953 *First performance of* Waiting for Godot.
1957 Endgame.
1958 Krapp's Last Tape.
1961 Happy Days; Play.
1966 Eh Joe.
1969 *Nobel Prize for literature.*
1972 Not I; Breath and Other Short Plays.
1973 First Love (*novel*).
1974 Mercier and Camier (*novel*).
1976 Ends and Odds.
1980 Company (*novel*).
1981 Rockaby and Other Short Pieces.
1984 Collected Shorter Plays.
1989 Died in Paris.

**** Beckett wrote in English or French, translating his own works. The dates given above are those of the first performances or publications in either language.***

Samuel Beckett's novels are plotless and his characters anti-heroes: miserable, lonely and uprooted, they are victims in a world that has lost its meaning. Caught in existential absurdity, they end up reflecting on their own being, trying to relate mind, body and the exterior world of objects. Yet, Beckett, the heir of James Joyce, succeeds in creating comedy through his use of language: jokes, puns, twisted clichés, hilarious and outrageous comments, and unexpected syntax that reflects the mind's meanderings, and the use of parody – many of his novels can in fact be read as parodies of philosophical reflection.

It was mainly through his plays, however, that Beckett became well-known. They reveal the same tragic solitude in man, so well exemplified by Vladimir and Estragon, the two clownish tramps of Waiting for Godot *who keep quarrelling and bickering but are spiritually linked by their common distress. Their resigned wait for Godot, whom nobody knows and who will probably never appear, is the only scrap of hope they can hang on to. In* Endgame, *the absurdity of the wait gives way to the claustrophobic atmosphere of a closed room where four characters – one in a wheelchair and two in dustbins – have found a last refuge from the outside world.*

Malone Dies (1951)

And it is no doubt all the same to Macmann whether it is spring or whether it is autumn, unless he prefers summer to winter or inversely, which is improbable. But it must not be thought he will never move again, out of this place and attitude, for he has still the whole of his old age before him, and then that kind of epilogue when it is not very clear what is happening and which does not seem to add very much to what has already been acquired or to shed any light on its confusion, but which no doubt has its usefulness, as hay is left out to dry before being garnered. He will therefore rise, whether he likes it or not, and proceed by other places to another place, and then by others still to yet another, unless he comes back here where he seems to be snug enough, but one never knows, does one? And so on, on, for long years. Because in order not to die you must come and go, come and go, unless you happen to have someone who brings you food wherever you happen to be, like myself. And you can remain for two, three and even four days without stirring hand or foot, but what are four days when you have all old age before you, and then the lingers of evaporation, a drop in the ocean. It is true you know nothing of this, you flatter yourself you are hanging by a thread like all mankind, but that is not the point. For there is no point, no point in not knowing this or that, either you know all or you know nothing, and Macmann knows nothing. But he is concerned only with his ignorance of certain things, of those that appal him among others, which is only human. But it is bad policy, for on the fifth day rise you must, and rise in fact you do, but with how much greater pains than if you had made up your mind to it the day before, or better still two days before, and why add to your pains, it's bad policy, assuming you do add to them, and nothing is less certain. For on the fifth day, when the problem is how to rise, the fourth and third do not matter any more, all that matters is how to rise, for you are half out of your mind. And sometimes you cannot, get to your feet I mean, and have to drag yourself to the nearest plot of vegetables, using the tufts of grass and asperities of the earth to drag yourself forward, or to the nearest clump of brambles, where there are sometimes good things to eat, if acid, and which are superior to the plots in this, that you can crawl into them and hide, as you cannot in a plot of ripe potatoes for example, and in this also, that often you frighten the little wild things away, both furred and feathered. For it is not as if he possessed the means of accumulating, in a single day, enough food to keep him alive for three weeks or a month, and what is a month compared to the whole of second childishness, a drop in a bucket. But he does not, possess them I mean, and could not employ them even if he did, he feels so far from the morrow. And perhaps there is none, no morrow any more, for one who has waited so long for it in vain. And perhaps he has come to that stage of his instant when to live is to wander the last of the living in the depths of an instant whithout bounds, where the light never changes and the wrecks look all alike. Bluer scarcely than white of egg the eyes stare into the space before them, namely the fullness of the great deep and its unchanging calm. But at long intervals they close, with the gentle suddenness of flesh that tightens, often without anger, and closes on itself. Then you see the old lids all red and worn that seem hard set to meet, for there are four, two for each lachrymal. And perhaps it is then he sees the heaven of his old dream, the heaven of the sea and of the earth too, and the spasms of the waves from shore to shore all stirring to their tiniest stir, and the so different motion of men for example, who are not tied together, but free to come and go as they please. And they make full use of it and come and go, their great balls and sockets rattling and clacking like knackers, each on his way. And when one dies the others go on, as if nothing had happened.

I feel.

I feel it's coming. How goes it, thanks, it's coming. I wanted to be quite sure before I noted it. Scrupulous to the last, finical to a fault, that's Malone, all over. I mean sure of feeling that my hour is at hand. For I never doubted it would come, sooner or later, except the days I felt it was past. For my stories are all in vain, deep down I never doubted, even the days abounding in proof to the contrary, that I was still alive and breathing in and out the air of earth. At hand, that is in two or three days, in the language of the days when they taught me the names of the days and I marvelled at their being so few and flourished my little fists, crying out for more, and how to tell the time, and what are two or three days, more or less, in the long run, a joke. But not a word and on with the losing game, it's good for the health. And all I have to do is go on as though doomed to see the midsummer moon. For I believe I have now reached what is called the month of May, I don't know why, I mean why I believe that, for May comes from Maia, hell, I remember that too, goddess of increase and plenty, yes, I believe I have entered on the season of increase and plenty, of increase at last, for plenty comes later, with the harvest. So quiet, quiet, I'll be still here at All Saints, in the middle of the chrysanthemums, no, this year I shall not hear them howling over their charnels. But this sensation of dilation is hard to resist. All strains towards the nearest deeps, and notably my feet, which even in the ordinary way are so much further from me than all the rest, from my head I mean, for that is where I am fled, my feet are leagues away. And to call them in, to be cleaned for example, would I think take me over a month, exclusive of the time required to locate them. Strange, I don't feel my feet any more, my feet feel nothing any more, and a mercy it is. And yet I feel they are beyond the range of the most powerful telescope. Is that what is known as having a foot in the grave? And similarly for the rest. For a mere local phenomenon is something I would not have noticed, having been nothing but a series or rather a succession of local phenomena all my life, without any result. But my fingers too write in other latitudes and the air that breathes through my pages and turns them without my knowing, when I doze off, so that the subject falls far from the verb and the object lands somewhere in the void, is not the air of this second-last abode, and a mercy it is. And perhaps on my hands it is the shimmer of the shadows of leaves and flowers and the brightness of a forgotten sun.

John Calder Publisher, London.

Beckett on his works:

"What is more true than anything else? To swim is true, and to sink is true. One is not more true than the other. One cannot speak anymore of being, one must speak only of the mess. When Heidegger and Sartre speak of a contrast between being and existence, they may be right, I don't know, but their language is too philosophical for me. I am not a philosopher. One can only speak of what is in front of him, and that now is simply the mess." (...)

"What I am saying does not mean that there will henceforth be no form in art. It only means that there will be new form, and that this form will be of such a type that it admits the chaos and does not try to say that the chaos is really something else. The form and the chaos remain separate. The latter is not reduced to the former. That is why the form itself becomes a preoccupation, because it exists as a problem separate from the material it accommodates. To find a form that accommodates the mess, that is the task of the artist now." (...)

Interview of S. Beckett by T. Driver
in *Columbia University Forum*, summer 61.
Columbia University Press, N.Y.

"I've only read Kafka in German – serious reading – except for a few things in French and English – only "The Castle" in German. I must say it was difficult to get to the end. The Kafka hero has a coherence of purpose. He's lost but he's not spiritually precarious, he's not falling to bits. My people seem to be falling to bits. Another difference. You notice how Kafka's form is classic, it goes on like a steamroller – almost serene. It seems to be threatened the whole time – but the consternation is in the form. In my work there is consternation behind the form, not in the form.

"At the end of my work there's nothing but dust – the namable. In the last book – *L'Innommable* – there's complete disintegration. No 'I,' no 'have,' no 'being.' No nominative, no accusative, no verb. There's no way to go on."

S. Beckett, an interview by L. Shenker
in *The New York Times,* 5 May 1956.

Anthony Burgess on the novels of Beckett:

"My characters have nothing", says Beckett, and this is true. Again, he says: "I'm working with impotence, ignorance. I don't think impotence has been exploited in the past... My little exploration is that whole zone of being that has always been set aside by artists as something unusable – as something by definition incompatible with art." All of the wretches who give their names to Beckett's novels – Watt, Molloy, Malone (of *Malones Dies*) – as well as those who never reach the glory of a title, are reductions of mankind – tramps, outcasts, poverty-stricken old men. They wear rags, they are diseased, they smell, they are rejected by us, thrown out of doss-houses, told to get off the bus. They are not only disgusting, they are absurd. And yet they are human beings like ourselves, humiliated by charity, demanding something better than condescension or contempt. The point about them is that they manage to survive, finding the odd hole in the ground to sleep in, the odd crust to gnaw. Ultimately they are stoical, expecting nothing from God, aware that the stars they sleep under are indifferent, insentient matter. Indeed, neither religion nor philosophy can offer any comfort. Beckett does not believe in God, though he seems to imply that God has committed an unforgivable sin by not existing. All that stripped, poverty-eaten, diseased, stinking humanity possesses is the ability to do better than God – namely, to exist; also, it has a voice, though the outer world cannot hear it.: "... within, motionless, I can live, and utter me, for no ears but my own..."

A. Burgess, *The Novel Now,* Faber & Faber 1967.

Cf. Narrative technique, p. 15.

Lawrence DURRELL 1912-1990

1912 *Born in India (but his family went to live in England and he was educated in Canterbury).*
1937 *Beginning of his friendship with Henry Miller.*
1938 The Black Book *published in France and the USA.*

Durrell's first novel, The Black Book, *followed his discovery of Henry Miller's* Tropic of Cancer. *It is a violent, Lawrentian outburst against what Durrell called "The English Death" — conformism and inhibitions. In spite of H. Miller's and T.S. Eliot's support, the book was found too outrageous and banned in England.*

1939 *Lectured and worked as Foreign Service Press Officer in Athens, Cairo and Alexandria. From then on, held several official positions in different countries, mainly around the Mediterranean (Dodecanese Islands, Belgrade) and in Argentina.*
1945 Prospero's Cell.
1952 *Taught English in Cyprus, then went back to Corfu, where his family lived.*
1956 *Settled in Provence.*
1957 Bitter Lemons.
1957-1960 The Alexandria Quartet (Justine, Balthazar, Mountolive, Clea).
1958 Stiff Upper Lip, The Dark Labyrinth.
1960 Collected Poems.
1968 Tunc.
1970 Nunquam.
1975-1985 *Novels of the* Avignon Quintet (Monsieur, or the Prince of Darkness; Livia, or Buried Alive; Constance, or Solitary Practices; Sebastian, or Ruling Passions; Quinx, or The Ripper's Tale.)
1979 Collected Poems.
1990 *Died in France.*

Though Durrell also wrote poems, plays, travel books (evoking the exotic and unreal atmosphere of Cyprus, Corfu or Rhodes) and some humorous accounts of life in diplomatic circles, he is better-known for the four novels that form The Alexandria Quartet.

They are the poetic description of a city – Alexandria – and its inhabitants. Like a magnet, the town seems to attract freaks and marginal people, the homeless and the loveless, among whom all kinds of intrigues, affairs, mysteries and murders are enacted. The landscape of the city becomes closely linked to the emotions – "I have tried to see people through landscapes", wrote Durrell. But most of all, the tetralogy is built upon the theory of relativity. What we see of the others is linked to our position in time and space – alter them and the vision will be different. Hence Durrell's attempt to create "space-time continuums", by writing four novels which view the same events and characters from different standpoints. The four books, therefore, are not sequentially related but complementary.

Mountolive (1958)

He drove up across the crackling desert in his pennoned car, rejoicing in the sweet whistle of its cooled engine, and the whickering of wind at the side-screens. It had been some time since he had been able to travel across the desert alone like this – it reminded him of older and happier journeys. Flying across the still white air with the speedometer hovering in the sixties, he hummed softly to himself, despite his distaste, the refrain:

Jamais de la vie,
Jamais dans la nuit
Quand ton cœur se démange de chagrin...

How long was it since he had caught himself singing like this? An age. It was not really happiness, but an overmastering relief of mind. Even the hateful song helped him to recover the lost image of an Alexandria he had once found charming. Would it, could it be so again?

It was already late afternoon by the time he reached the desert fringe and began the slow in-curving impulse which would lead him to the city's bristling outer slums. The sky was covered with clouds. A thunderstorm was breaking over Alexandria. To the east upon the icy green waters of the lake poured a rainstorm – flights of glittering needles pocking the waters; he could dimly hear the hush of rain above the whisper of the car. He glimpsed the pearly city through the dark cloud-mat, its minarets poked up against the cloud bars of an early sunset; linen soaked in blood. A sea-wind chaffered and tugged at the sea-limits of the estuary. Higher still roamed packages of smoking, blood-stained cloud throwing down a strange radiance into the streets and squares of the white city. Rain was a rare and brief winter phenomenon in Alexandria. Presently the sea-wind would rise, alter inclination, and peel the sky clear in a matter of minutes, rolling up the heavy cumulus like a carpet. The glassy freshness of the winter sky would resume its light, polishing the city once more till it glittered against the desert like quartz, like some beautiful artifact. He was no longer impatient. Dusk was beginning to swallow the sunset. As he neared the ugly ribbons of cabins and warehouses by the outer harbour, his tyres began to smoke and seethe upon the wet tarmac, its heat now slaked by a light rain. Time to throttle down...

He entered the penumbra of the storm slowly, marvelling at the light, at the horizon drawn back like a bow. Odd gleams of sunshine scattered rubies upon the battleships in the basin (squatting under their guns like horned toads). It was the ancient city again; he felt its pervading melancholy under the rain as he crossed it on his way to the Summer Residence. The brilliant unfamiliar lighting of the thunder-storm re-created it, giving it a spectral, story-book air – broken pavements made of tinfoil, snail-shells, cracked horn, mica; earth-

brick buildings turned to the colour of ox-blood; the lovers wandering in Mohammed Ali Square, disoriented by the unfamiliar rain, disconsolate as untuned instruments; the clicking of violet trams along the sea-front among the tatting of palm-fronds. The desuetude of an ancient city whose streets were plastered with the wet blown dust of the surrounding desert. He felt it all anew, letting it extend panoramically in his consciousness – the moan of a liner edging out towards the sunset bar, or the trains which flowed like a torrent of diamonds towards the interior, their wheels chattering among the shingle ravines and the powder of temples long since abandoned and silted up...

Mountolive saw it all now with a world-weariness which he at last recognized as the stripe which maturity lays upon the shoulders of an adult – the stigma of the experiences which age one. The wind spouted in the harbour. The corridors of wet rigging swayed and shook like the foliage of some great tree. Now the tears were trickling down the windscreen under the diligent and noiseless wipers. ... A little period in this strange contused darkness, fitfully lit by lightning, and then the wind would come – the magistral north wind, punching and squeezing the sea into its own characteristic plumage of white crests, knocking open the firmament until the faces of men and women once more reflected the open winter sky. He was in plenty of time.

Chapter 15.

Compare Durrell's vision of Alexandria with Malcolm Lowry's description of Quauhnahuac, Mexico:

M. Laruelle wondered if it was going to rain: it sometimes, though rarely, did at this time of year, as last year for instance, it rained when it should not. And those were storm clouds in the south. He imagined he could smell the rain, and it ran in his head he would enjoy nothing better than to get wet, soaked through to the skin, to walk on and on through this wild country in his clinging white flannels getting wetter and wetter and wetter. He watched the clouds: dark swift horses surging up the sky. A black storm breaking out of its season! That was what love was like, he thought; love which came too late. Only no sane calm succeeded it, as when the evening fragrance or slow sunlight and warmth returned to the surprised land! M. Laruelle hastened his steps still farther. And let such love strike you dumb, blind, mad, dead – your fate would not be altered by your simile. *Tonnerre de dieu...* It slaked no thirst to say what love was like which came too late.

The town was almost directly to his right now and above him, for M. Laruelle had been walking gradually downhill since leaving the Casino de la Selva. From the field he was crossing he could see, over the trees on the slope of the hill, and beyond the dark castled shape of Cortez Palace, the slowly revolving Ferris wheel, already lit up, in the square of Quauhnahuac; he thought he could distinguish the sound of human laughter rising from its bright gondolas and, again, that faint intoxication of voices singing, diminishing, dying in the wind, inaudible finally. A despondent American tune, the *St Louis Blues,* or some such, was borne across the fields to him, at times a soft wind-blown surge of music from which skimmed a spray of gab-

Lawrence Durrell: Alexandria.
Ph. Edimedia © J. Guillot, Connaissance des Arts.
"When I was about twenty I lived on a Greek island with a young painter. It was then that I started to look at things through water-colour."

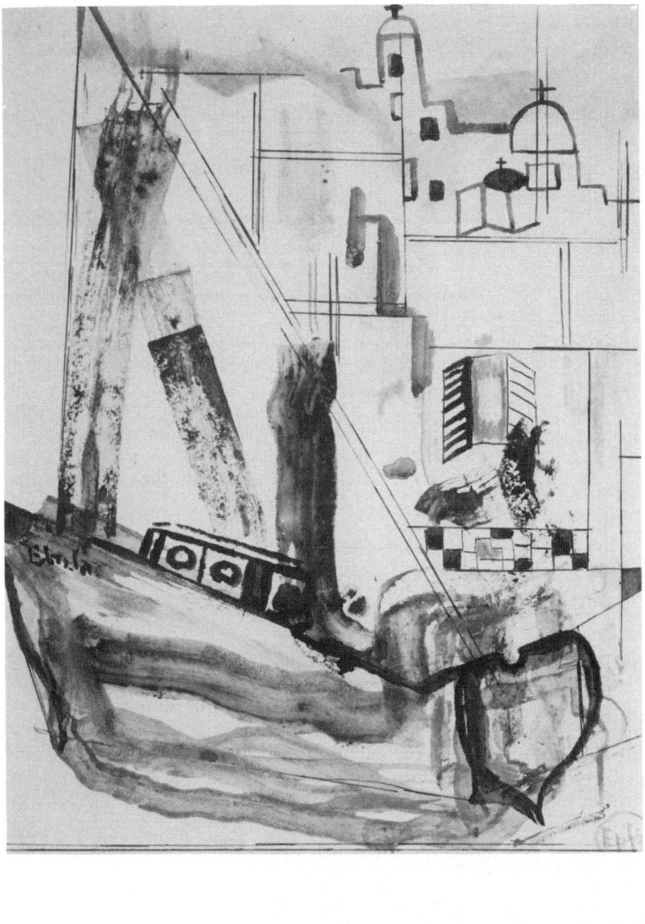

bling, that seemed not so much to break against as to be thumping the walls and towers of the outskirts; then with a moan it would be sucked back into the distance. He found himself in the lane that led away through the brewery to the Tomalin road. He came to the Alcapancingo road. A car was passing and as he waited, face averted, for the dust to subside, he recalled that time motoring with Yvonne and the Consul along the Mexican lake-bed, itself once the crater of a huge volcano, and saw again the horizon softened by dust, the buses whizzing past through the whirling dust, the shuddering boys standing on the backs of the lorries holding on for grim death, their faces bandaged against the dust (and there was a magnificence about this, he always felt, some symbolism for the future, for which such truly great preparation had been made by a heroic people, since all over Mexico one could see those thundering lorries with those young builders in them, standing erect, their trousers flapping hard, legs planted wide, firm) and in the sunlight, on the round hill, the lone section of dust advancing, the dust-darkened hills by the lake like islands in driving rain. The Consul, whose old house M. Laruelle now made out on the slope beyond the *barranca*, had seemed happy enough too then, wandering around Cholula with its three hundred and six churches and its two barber shops, the "Toilet" and the "Harem", and climbing the ruined pyramid later, which he had proudly insisted was the original Tower of Babel. How admirably he had concealed what must have been the babel of his thoughts!

Malcolm Lowry, *Under the Volcano.*

Like Lawrence Durrell, Malcolm Lowry – 1909-1957 – spent a large part of his life abroad, either travelling (he worked for a time as a deckhand) or writing in France, the United States, Mexico and British Columbia. Under the Volcano *(1947), his masterpiece, relates the last day in the life of Geoffrey Firmin, the British Consul in a small Mexican town. He has drunk himself to death, deliberately looking for damnation, trying to escape the decaying world that surrounds him. The Mexican setting becomes a background of hell for the tortured and exiled Firmin who will eventually be murdered. His other works include* Ultramarine *(1933-5) and* Hear Us O Lord From Heaven Thy Dwelling Place *(published 1962).*

William GOLDING 1911-1993

1911 *Born in Cornwall (his father was a schoolmaster, his mother a suffragette).*
1930-1932 *Studied science at Oxford, then turned to English literature.*
1935-1939 *After taking his B.A., worked as an actor and producer for a small London theatre.*
1940-1945 *Served in the Navy.*
1945 *Resumed his teaching, started before the war, at Bishop Wordsworth's School in Salisbury.*
1954 Lord of the Flies.
1955 The Inheritors.
1956 Pincher Martin.
1959 Free Fall.
1961 *Became a full-time writer.*
1964 The Spire.
1965 The Hot Gates *(essays).*
1967 The Pyramid.
1971 The Scorpion God.
1979 Darkness Visible.
1980 Rites of Passage.

William Golding is a moralist, interested in the metaphysics of behaviour and in trying to find out the true nature of man behind the polish of civilization. What he finds is savagery and evil; hence his interest in primitive man and the struggle for survival.

Lord of the Flies, *his first novel, is a reinterpretation of R. M. Ballantyne's* Coral Island. *The optimism of the latter work (in which children, stranded on a desert island, built a sensible and idyllic community), gives way to a disillusioned vision of life: cruelty, anarchy and the irrational prevail, leading to tragedy and the dissolution of the group.*

Each of Golding's subsequent novels will explore a moral and intellectual problem – sometimes at the cost of characterization.

Lord of the Flies introduces a structural principle that becomes Golding's hallmark: a polarity expressed in terms of a moral tension. Thus, there is the rational (the fire-watchers) pitted against the irrational (the hunters) in *Lord of the Flies;* Neanderthal man absorbed by the fitter

1983 *Nobel Prize for literature.*
1984 The Paper Men.
1988 Close Quarters.
1989 Fire Down Below.
1993 *Died in Somerset.*

species of Homo sapiens *(The Inheritors);* fallen man confronting God *(Pincher Martin);* science and humanism *(Free Fall);* and the vision versus the reality *(The Spire).* Consequently, a Golding novel is reminiscent of a skeletal framework that is deliberately and at times deceptively simple.

B. F. Dick, *William Golding.*

Golding shows great stylistic economy of means and the form of his novels is always inventive and daring (for instance, the inverted chronology of Free Fall *or the unexpected ending of* Pincher Martin *that calls for a complete reassessment of the whole novel.)*

The Inheritors (1955)

Lok was running as fast as he could. His head was down and he carried his thorn bush horizontally for balance and smacked the drifts of vivid buds aside with his free hand. Liku rode him laughing, one hand clutched in the chestnut curls that lay on his neck and down his spine, the other holding the little Oa tucked under his chin. Lok's feet were clever. They saw. They threw him round the displayed roots of the beeches, leapt when a puddle of water lay across the trail. Liku beat his belly with her feet.

"Faster! Faster!"

His feet stabbed, he swerved and slowed. Now they could hear the river that lay parallel but hidden to their left. The beeches opened, the bush went away and they were in the little patch of flat mud where the log was.

"There, Liku."

The onyx marsh water was spread before them, widening into the river. The trail along by the river began again on the other side on ground that rose until it was lost in the trees. Lok, grinning happily, took two paces towards the water and stopped. The grin faded and his mouth opened till the lower lip hung down. Liku slid to his knee then dropped to the ground. She put the little Oa's head to her mouth and looked over her.

Lok laughed uncertainly.

"The log has gone away."

He shut his eyes and frowned at the picture of the log. It had lain in the water from this side to that, grey and rotting. When you trod the centre you could feel the water that washed beneath you, horrible water, as deep in places as a man's shoulder. The water was not awake like the river or the fall but asleep, spreading there to the river and waking up, stretching on the right into wildernesses of impassable swamp and thicket and bog. So sure was he of this log the people always used that he opened his eyes again, beginning to smile as if he were waking out of a dream; but the log was gone.

Fa came trotting along the trail. The new one was sleeping on her back. She did not fear that he would fall because she felt his hands gripping her hair at the neck and his feet holding the hair farther down her back but she trotted softly so that he should not wake. Lok heard her coming before she appeared under the beeches.

"Fa! The log has gone away!"

She came straight to the water's edge, looked, smelt, then turned accusingly to Lok. She did not need to speak, Lok began to jerk his head at her.

"No, no. I did not move the log to make the people laugh. It has gone."

He spread his arms wide to indicate the completeness of that absence, saw that she understood, and dropped them again.

Liku called him.

"Swing me."

She was reaching for a beech bough that came down out of the tree like a long neck, saw light and craned up with an armful of green and brown buds. Lok abandoned the log that was not there and swung her into the crook. He heaved sideways, he pulled, gaining a little backwards with each step as the bough creaked.

"Ho!"

He let the branch go and dropped on to his hams. The bough shot away and Liku shrieked delightedly.

"No! No!"

But Lok hauled again and again and the armful of leaves bore Liku shrieking and laughing and protesting along the edge of the water. Fa was looking from the water to Lok and back. She was frowning again.

Ha came along the trail, hurrying but not running, more thoughtful than Lok, the man for an emergency. When Fa began to call out to him he did not answer her immediately but looked at the empty water and there away to the left where he could see the river beyond the arch of beeches. Then he searched the forest with ear and nose for intruders and only when he was sure of safety did he put down his thorn bush and kneel by the water.

"Look!"

His pointing finger showed the gashes under water where the log had moved. The edges were still sharp and pieces of broken earth lay in the gashes, not yet disintegrated by the water that covered them. He traced the curving gashes away down into the water until they disappeared in that obscurity. Fa looked across to the place where the broken trail began again. There was earth churned up there where the other end of the log had lain. She asked a question of Ha and he answered her with his mouth.

"One day. Perhaps two days. Not three."

Liku was still shrieking with laughter.

Chapter 1.

The Neanderthal man: H.G. Wells v. W. Golding

• The *Inheritors* is a devastating subversion of H.G. Wells's view of *homo sapiens* as maker, hero, liberal conqueror. The world of Neanderthal man approaches a golden dream of innocence; *homo sapiens* comes along to disrupt it – evil is built in him, part of his nature; he is led instinctively to the worship of Beelsebub.

A. Burgess, *The Novel Now.*

• We know very little of the Neanderthal man, but this... seems to suggest an extreme hairiness; an ugliness, or repulsive strangeness in his appearance over and above his low forehead, his beetle brows, his ape neck, and his inferior stature... Says Sir Harry Johnston, in a survey of the rise of modern man in his *Views and Reviews* : "The dim racial remembrance of such gorilla-like monsters, with cunning brains, shambling gait, hairy bodies, strong teeth, and possibly cannibalistic tendencies, may be the germ of the ogre in folklore..."

H.G. Wells, *The Outline of History.*

• Wells' *Outline of History* is the rationalist's gospel *in excelsis*... And when I re-read it as an adult I came across his picture of Neanderthal man, our immediate predecessors, as being the gross brutal creatures who were possibly the basis of the mythological bad man, whatever he may be, the ogre. I thought to myself that this is just absurd. What we're doing is externalising our inside.

W. Golding, *The Meaning of It All.*

W. Golding on evil:

Before the second world war I believed in the perfectibility of social man; that a correct structure of society would produce goodwill; and that therefore you could remove all social ills by a reorganization of society. It is possible that today I believe something of the same again; but after the war I did not because I was unable to. I had discovered what one man could do to another. (...)

Anyone who moved through those years without understanding that man produces evil as a bee produces honey, must have been blind or wrong in the head. (...)

It seems to me that in nineteenth-century and early twentieth-century society of the West, similar taboos grew up round the nature of man. He was supposed not to have in him, the sad fact of his own cruelty and lust. When these capacities emerged into action they were thought aberrant. Social systems, political systems were composed, detached from the real nature of man. They were what one might call political symphonies. They would perfect most men, and at the least, reduce aberrance. (...)

To many of you, this will seem trite, obvious and familiar in theological terms. Man is a fallen being. He is gripped by original sin. His nature is sinful and his state perilous. I accept the theology and admit the triteness; but what is trite is true; and a truism can become more than a truism when it is a belief passionately held.

William Golding, "Fable", *The Hot Gates*, 1965.

ibid.

Cf. Narrative technique, p. 15.

Alan SILLITOE born 1928

1928 *Born in Nottingham; his father was a tannery labourer.*
1942 *Left school to work in a bicycle factory.*
1946 *Entered the R.A.F. Sent to Malaya as a radio operator.*
1947-1948 *Spent a year in hospital with tuberculosis. Started writing short stories.*
1949-1952 *Lived in the south of France.*
1952-1958 *Worked as a teacher and translator in Majorca.*
1958 Saturday Night and Sunday Morning: *Authors' Club Prize.*
1959 The Loneliness of the Long-distance Runner: *Hawthornden Prize.*
1960 The General; The Rats and other Poems.
1961 Key to the Door.
1963 The Ragman's Daughter.
1964 The Road to Volgograd *(travel book about Russia).*
1967 A Tree on Fire.
1970 A Start in Life.
1976 The Widower's Son.
1979 The Story Teller.
1981 The Second Chance and Other Stories.
1982 Her Victory.
1984 The Lost Flying Boat; Down from the Hill.
1985 Life Goes On.
1989 The Open Door.
1990 Last Loves.
1991 Leonard's War: a love story.

Alan Sillitoe belongs to the post-war generation of the "angry young men". His novels reflect a deep class-consciousness: "The poor know of only two classes in society. Their sociology is much simplified. There are them *and* us*... Them are those who robbed you of your innocence, live on your backs, buy the house from over your head, eat you up or tread you down." (A. Sillitoe,* Poor People).

His first novel, Saturday Night and Sunday Morning, *relates the adventures of a young factory worker, Arthur Seaton, whose life centres round beer, cigarettes and women. He is conscious of a sense of injustice too; he resents the rich, the establishment, the boss and the unions alike. He grumbles and fights his days away in a spirit of rebellion, yet never really attacks the system at its roots, never finds himself politically involved. It is the truculence and liveliness of his world that dominate the novel.*

The message of The Loneliness of the Long-distance Runner, *a novella, goes one step further. Colin Smith, the hero of the story, is a young delinquent in a Borstal. He has come to love long-distance running which liberates him from his hatred, but will finally deliberately lose an important competition which means a lot to the Director of the Borstal and himself, in order to show that he refuses to play the rules of society. Colin Smith lucidly sees how his symbolic refusal and the fall into disgrace that will ensue are a step towards asserting his freedom and dignity.*

Saturday Night and Sunday Morning (1958)

Once a rebel, always a rebel. You can't help being one. You can't deny that. And it's best to be a rebel so as to show 'em it don't pay to try to do you down. Factories and labour exchanges and insurance offices keep us alive and kicking – so they say – but they're booby-traps and will suck you under like sinking-sands if you aren't careful. Factories sweat you to death, labour exchanges talk you to death, insurance and income tax offices milk money from your wage packets and rob you to death. And if you're still left with a tiny bit of life in your guts after all this boggering about, the army calls you up and you get shot to death. And if you're clever enough to stay out of the army you get bombed to death. Ay, by God, it's a hard life if you don't weaken, if you don't stop that bastard government from grinding your face in the muck, though there ain't much you can do about it unless you start making dynamite to blow their four-eyed clocks[1] to bits.

They shout at you from soapboxes: "Vote for me, and this and that", but it amounts to the same in the end whatever you vote for because it means a government that puts stamps all over your phizzog[1] until you can't see a hand before you, and what's more makes you buy 'em so's they can keep on doing it. They've got you by the guts, by backbone and skull, until they think you'll come whenever they whistle.

But listen, this lathe is my everlasting pal because it gets me thinking, and that's their big mistake because I know I'm not the only one. One day they'll bark and we won't run into a pen like sheep. One day they'll flash their lamps and clap their hands and say: "Come on, lads. Line-up and get your money. We won't let you starve." But maybe some of us will want to starve, and that'll be where the trouble'll start. Perhaps some'll want to play football, or go fishing up Grantham Cut. That big fat-bellied union ponce[2] 'll ask us not to muck things up. Sir Harold Bladdertab'll promise us a bigger bonus when things get put right. Chief Inspector Popcorn will say: "Let's have no trouble, no hanging around the gates there." Blokes with suits and bowler hats will say: "These chaps have got their television sets, enough to live on, council houses, beers and pools – some have even got cars. We've made them happy. What's wrong? Is that a machine-gun I hear starting up or a car backfiring?"

Der-der-der-der-der-der-der-der-der-der-der-der-der. I hope I'm not here to see it, but I know I will be. I'm a bloody billygoat trying to screw the world, and no wonder I am, because it's trying to do the same to me.

Chapter 15.

1. *clock, phizzog:* face – 2. *ponce:* man who lives with a prostitute and on her earnings, now a general term of abuse.

About the "Angry Young Men":

The novels of Kingsley Amis, John Braine, William Cooper, Thomas Hinde, Peter Towry, John Wain, and Keith Waterhouse are frequently more significant as demonstrations of certain social phenomena than as works of fiction. (...)

The term Angry Young Men[1] has been arbitrarily imposed upon these novelists' protagonists, but the word "snivelling" would perhaps have been more appropriate. For those accustomed to real protest, this kind is strange indeed. It consists of pot shots at vainglorious individuals and at institutions which reward hypocrisy. It also means gnashing one's teeth, burning holes in mattresses, fighting in pubs, testing one's endurance with gin and beer, making ridiculous faces; it allows for little wit, little intelligence, little analysis of society in anything but black and white. In brief, it cuts off nearly every area of life that gives sustenance to human beings, and, accordingly, it makes a circus sideshow of the comic novel. Although these novelists are often akin in theme to their eighteenth-century predecessors – in common, they ask how an "honest" lowerclassman can move into genteel society with its sophisticated and frequently phony tastes and retain his innocence – their over-all performance dissipates the seriousness of the intent.

1. I repeat this popular phrase simply in order to group several writers whose "heroes" share certain characteristics, although the term is itself not descriptive of all the work of the novelists in question. I use it only for the sake of convenience, rather than as an artificial tag from which the writer cannot escape. The words themselves gained currency in connection with John Osborne's Jimmy Porter in his play *Look Back in Anger* (1956), but they had appeared as early as 1951 in the title of Leslie Allen Paul's autobiography, *Angry Young Man* with the growing popularity of Kingsley Amis's *Lucky Jim*, the phrase Angry Young Men has become part of the language despite Amis's and Osborne's angry disclaimer of it.

Primarily, the protagonists of these novelists are not really angry. They are, however, disgruntled – with themselves, with their social status, with their work, with their colleagues, with the shabbiness of daily life, with their frustrated aspirations for self-fulfillment, with the competitive spririt, with the inaccessibility of women and drink, with all the small activities whose pursuit takes up their depleted energies.

F. Karl, *A Reader's Guide to the Contemporary English Novel.*

Compare the "anger" of Arthur Seaton with that of Joe Lampton in John Braine's Room at the Top:

The Aston-Martin started with a deep, healthy roar. As it passed the café in the direction of St Clair Road I noticed the young man's olive linen shirt and bright silk neckerchief. The collar of the shirt was tucked inside the jacket; he wore the rather theatrical ensemble with a matter-of-fact nonchalance. Everything about him was easy and loose but not tired or sloppy. He had an undistinguished face with a narrow forehead and mousy hair cut short with no oil on it. It was a rich man's face, smooth with assurance and good living.

He hadn't ever had to work for anything he wanted; it had all been given him. The salary which I'd been so pleased about, an increase from Grade Ten to Grade Nine, would seem a pittance to him. The suit in which I fancied myself so much – my best suit – would seem cheap and nasty to him. He wouldn't have a *best* suit; all his clothes would be the best.

For a moment I hated him. I saw myself, compared with him, as the Town Hall clerk, the subordinate pen-pusher, half-way to being a zombie, and I tasted the sourness of envy. Then I rejected it. Not on moral grounds; but because I felt then, and still do, that envy's a small and squalid vice – the convict sulking because a fellow-prisoner's been given a bigger helping of skilly. This didn't abate the fierceness of my longing. I wanted an Aston-Martin, I wanted a three-guinea linen shirt, I wanted a girl with a Riviera suntan – these were my rights, I felt, a signed and sealed legacy.

As I watched the tail-end of the Aston-Martin with its shiny new G.B. plate go out of sight I remembered the second-hand Austin Seven which the Efficient Zombie, Dufton's Chief Treasurer, had just treated himself to. That was the most the local government had to offer me; it wasn't enough. I made my choice then and there: I was going to enjoy all the luxuries which that young man enjoyed. I was going to collect that legacy. It was as clear and compelling as the sense of vocation which doctors and missionaries are supposed to experience, though in my instance, of course, the call ordered me to do good to myself not others.

If Charles had been with me things would have been different. We had evolved a special mode of conversation to dispel envy and its opposite, forelock-tugging admiration. "The capitalist beast", Charles would have said. "Give the girl her clothes back, Lufford." I would have said, "she's turning blue." "Those big pop eyes of yours are glinting with lust", Charles would have said. "Is it the girl of the car"?

We would have continued in this vein for some time, becoming more and more outrageous, until we'd dissolve into laughter. It was an incantation, a ritual; the frank admission of envy somehow cleansed us of it. And very healthy-minded it all was; but I think that it fulfilled its purpose too thoroughly and obscured the fact that the material objects of our envy were attainable.

How to attain them I didn't know. I was like an officer fresh from training-school, unable for the moment to translate the untidiness of fear and cordite and corpses into the obvious and irresistible method of attack. I was going to take the position, though, I was sure of that. I was moving into the attack, and no one had better try to stop me. General Joe Lampton, you might say, had opened hostilities.

John Braine (born 1922) is best known for his two novels Room at the Top *(1957) and* Life at the Top *(1962). Their hero, Joe Lampton, who comes from a working-class background, gradually climbs up the social ladder, marries the boss's daughter and will be able to look down on the middle class. The happiness that he finds "at the top" is, however, a very partial one.*

Anthony BURGESS 1917-1993

1917 *Born in Manchester.*
1940 *BA from Manchester University.*
1940-1946 *Served in the British Army Education Corps.*
1942 *Married L. Isherwood (died 1968).*
1946-1973 *Held various teaching jobs in England and abroad.*
1960 The Doctor is Sick; The Right to an Answer.
1961 The Worm and the Ring; Devil of a State.
1962 A Clockwork Orange; The Wanting Seed.
1963 Inside Mr. Enderby; Honey for the Bears.
1964 Nothing like the Sun; The Malayan Trilogy.
1965 A Vision of Battlements.
1966 Tremor of Intent.

Anthony Burgess is a prolific writer who has written in a large variety of styles and genres. His themes range from history to anticipation of the future, from fantasy to the realistic portrait of society.

His interest in Irish writers — Joyce in particular — and his knowledge of linguistics and music partly account for his verbal inventiveness and his brilliant and witty style.

Burgess's main heroes are failures, outsiders who do not fit into a society where they feel alienated and entrapped. The main concern of their study is a moral one: questions of good and evil, guilt and punishment, original sin and innocence. Enderby is obsessed by Pelagius and St Augustine, by determinism and free will. A Clockwork Orange, *takes place in a future world dominated by juvenile delinquent groups. Alex, the protagonist, becomes the object of a behavioural experiment aimed at curing him of his violent tendencies. He is released unable to terrorize any more, but*

1968 *Married L. Marcellari (one son).* Enderby Outside.
1971 MF.
1974 Napoleon Symphony; The Clockwork Testament.
1978 1985.
1979 Man of Nazareth.
1980 Earthly Powers.
1982 The End of the World News.
1984 Enderby's Dark Lady.
1985 The Kingdom of the Wicked.
1986 The Pianoplayers.
1989 Any Old Iron.

the conclusion of the novel is clearly that it is better to be free and act evilly than to be artificially forced to do good in a totalitarian society. A similar theme is developed in Earthly Powers *which follows the lives of two men through fifty years of the 20th century and leads to their final conviction that evil is necessary as God's way of preserving the free will of humanity.*

A Clockwork Orange (1962)

The novel is written in Nadsat,[1] the language spoken by Alex, a kind of slang combining elements of Russian and of Cockney.

It was round by the Municipal Power Plant that we came across Billyboy and his five droogs. Now in those days, my brothers, the teaming up was mostly by fours or fives, these being like auto-teams, four being a comfy number for an auto, and six being the outside limit for gang-size. Sometimes gangs would gang up so as to make like malenky armies for big night-war, but mostly it was best to roam in these like small numbers. Billyboy was something that made me want to sick just to viddy his fat grinning litso, and he always had this von of very stale oil that's been used for frying over and over, even when he was dressed in his best platties, like now. They viddied us just as we viddied them, and there was like a very quiet kind of watching each other now. This would be real, this would be proper, this would be the nozh, the oozy, the britva, not just fisties and boots. Billyboy and his droogs stopped what they were doing, which was just getting ready to perform something on a weepy young devotchka they had there, not more than ten, she creeching away but with her platties still on, Billyboy holding her by one rooker and his number-one, Leo, holding the other. They'd probably just been doing the dirty slovo part of the act before getting down to a malenky bit of ultra-violence. When they viddied us a-coming they let go of this boo-hooing little ptitsa, there being plenty more where she came from, and she ran with her thin white legs flashing through the dark, still going "Oh oh oh." I said, smiling very wide and droogie: "Well, if it isn't fat stinking billygoat Billyboy in poison. How art thou, thou globby bottle of cheap stinking chip-oil? Come and get one in the yarbles, if you have yarbles, you eunuch jelly, thou." And then we started.

There were four of us to six of them, like I have already indicated, but poor old Dim, for all his dimness, was worth three of the others in sheer madness and dirty fighting. Dim had a real horrorshow length of oozy or chain round his waist, twice wound round, and he unwound this and began to swing it beautiful in the eyes or glazzies. Pete and Georgie had good sharp nozhes, but I for my own part had a fine starry horrorshow cut-throat britva which, at that time,I could flash and shine artistic. So there we were dratsing away in the dark, the old Luna with men on it just coming up, the stars stabbing away as it might be knives anxious to join in the dratsing. With my britva I managed to slit right down the front of one of Billyboy's droog's platties, very very neat and not even touching the plott under the cloth. Then in the dratsing this droog of Billyboy's suddenly found himself all opened up like a peapod, with his belly bare and his poor old yarbles showing, and then he got very very razdraz, waving and screaming and losing his guard and letting in old Dim with his chain snaking whissssssshhhhhhhhh, so that old Dim chained him right in the glazzies, and this droog of Billyboy's went tottering off and howling his heart out. We were doing very horrorshow, and soon we had Billyboy's number-one down underfoot, blinded with *old* Dim's chain and crawling and howling about like an animal, but with one fair boot on the gulliver he was out and out and out.

Of the four of us Dim, as usual, came out the worst in point of looks, that is to say his litso was all bloodied and his platties a dirty mess, but the others of us were still cool and whole. It was stinking fatty Billyboy I wanted now, and there I was dancing about with my britva like I might be a barber on board a ship on a very rough sea, trying to get in at him with a few fair slashes on his unclean oily litso. Billyboy had a nozh, a long flick-type, but he was a malenky bit too slow and heavy in his movements to vred anyone really bad. And, my brothers, it was real satisfaction to me to waltz — left two three, right two three — and carve left cheeky and right cheeky, so that like two curtains of blood seemed to pour out at the same time, one on either side of his fat filthy oily snout in the winter starlight. Down this blood poured in like red curtains, but you could viddy Billyboy felt not a thing, and he went lumbering on like a filthy fatty bear, poking at me with his nozh.

Then we slooshied the sirens and knew the millicents were coming with pooshkas pushing out of the police-auto-windows at the ready. That little weepy devotchka had told them, no doubt, there being a box for calling the rozzes not too far behind the Muni Power Plant. "Get you soon, fear not," I called, "stinking billygoat. I'll have your yarbles off lovely." Then off they ran, slow and panting, except for Number One Leo out snoring on the ground, away north towards the river, and we went the other way.

Heinemann, 1962.

1. From the "Glossary of Nadsat Language": *droog:* friend; *malenky:* little, tiny; *viddy:* to see or look; *litso:* face; *von:* smell; *platties:* clothes; *nozh:* knife; *oozy:* chain; *britva:* razor; *devotchka:* girl; *creech:* to shout or scream; *rook, rooker:* hand, arm; *slovo:* word; *ptitsa:* "chick"; *yarbles:* testicles; *horrorshow:* good, well; *glazz:* eye; *starry:* ancient; *dratsing:* fighting; *plott:* body; *razdraz:* upset; *gulliver:* head; *vred:* to harm or damage; *sloosh, slooshy:* to hear, to listen; *millicent:* policeman; *pooshka:* "cannon"; *rozz:* policeman.

Anthony Burgess on A Clockwork Orange*:*

I imagined an experimental institution in which a generic delinquent, guilty of every crime of rape to murder, was given aversion therapy and rendered incapable of contemplating, let alone perpetrating, an anti-social act without a sensation of profound nausea.

The book was called *A Clockwork Orange* for various reasons. I had always loved the Cockney phrase "queer as a clockwork orange," that being the queerest thing imaginable, and I had saved up the expression for years, hoping some day to use it as a title. When I began to write the book, I saw that this title would be appropriate for a story about the application of Pavlovian, or mechanical, laws to an organism which, like a fruit, was capable of colour and sweetness. But I had also served in Malaya, where the word for a human being is *orang*. The name of the anti-hero is Alex, short for Alexander, which means "defender of men." *Alex* has other connotations — *a lex*: a law (unto himself); *a lex(is)*: a vocabulary (of his own); a (Greek) *lex*: without a law. *Alex* is a rich and noble name, and I intended its possessor to be sympathetic, pitiable, and insidiously identifiable with us, as opposed to them. But, in a manner, I digress.

Alex is not only deprived of the capacity to choose to commit evil. A lover of music, he has responded to the music, used as a heightener of emotion, which has accompanied the violent films he has been made to see. A chemical substance injected into his blood induces nausea while he is watching the films, but the nausea is also associated with the music. It was not the intention of his State manipulators to induce this bonus or *malus:* it is purely an accident that, from now on, he will automatically react to Mozart or Beethoven as he will to rape or murder. The State has succeeded in its primary aim: to deny Alex free moral choice, which, to the State, means choice of evil. But it had added an unforeseen punishment: the gates of heaven are closed to the boy, since music is a figure of celestial bliss. The State has committed a double sin: it has destroyed a human being, since humanity is defined by freedom of moral choice; it has also destroyed an angel.

The novel has not been well understood. Readers, and viewers of the film made from the book, have assumed that I, a most unviolent man, am in love with violence. I am not, but I am committed to freedom of choice, which means that if I cannot choose to do evil nor can I choose to do good. It is better to have our streets infested with murderous young hoodlums than to deny individual freedom of choice. This is a hard thing to say, but the saying of it was imposed on me by the moral tradition which, as a member of western civilization, I inherit. Whatever the conditions needful to the sustension of society, the basic human endowment must not be denied. The evil, or merely wrong, products of free will may be punished or held off with deterrents, but the faculty itself may not be removed.The unintended destruction of Alex's capacity for enjoying music symbolizes the State's imperfect understanding (or volitional ignorance) of the whole nature of man, and of the consequences of its own decisions. We may not be able to trust man — meaning ourselves — very far, but we must trust the State far less.

Hutchinson, 1978.

Muriel SPARK born 1918

1918 *Born in Edinburgh.*
1937 *Married S. O. Spark (one son; marriage dissolved in 1944).*
1944 *Worked in the Foreign Office Political Intelligence Department.*
1947-1949 *Edited* The Poetry Review *in London.*
1954 *Converted to Roman Catholicism.*
1957 The Comforters.
1959 Memento Mori.
1960 The Ballad of Peckham Rye; The Bachelors.
1961 The Prime of Miss Jean Brodie.
1963 The Girls of Slender Means.
1965 *Went to live in New York.* The Mandelbaum Gate.
1967 Collected Stories I; Collected Poems I.
1970 The Driver's Seat.
1971 Not to Disturb.
1974 The Abbess of Crewe.
1976 The Takeover.
1981 Loitering with Intent.
1984 The Only Problem.
1988 A Far Cry from Kensington.
1990 Symposium.

*A convert to Roman Catholicism, Muriel Spark explores metaphysical and moral issues such as the freedom of the will or good and evil. Most of her novels focus on the bizarre and obsessional behaviour of small sets of upper-class characters — impoverished young women in a hostel (*The Girls of Slender Means*), elderly people (*Memento Mori*), servants on a Swiss estate (*Not to Disturb*) — whose oddities and foibles are shrewdly observed and seen in the context of the social roles they are expected to play.*

Muriel Spark's novels are characterized by complex plots in which the supernatural often intrudes into the prosaic everyday setting, thus provoking thought and spiritual insight. By introducing ghosts, disembodied voices, spiritualism or satanism into the commonplace, she shows how some characters are capable of seeing beyond sensory observation and of acquiring "vision." But it is through entertainment that she attempts to arouse the reader's awareness — hence the dry, witty, economical prose and dialogue, and the cool and distant authorial omniscience.

In The Comforters, *Muriel Spark studies the process of artistic creation.* Memento Mori *analyzes the effect, upon a group of elderly people, of mysterious telephone calls reminding them that they are going to die.* The Prime of Miss Jean Brodie *describes the powerful personality of Miss Brodie, a teacher at a school for girls in Edinburgh, and her fascist-like control of a small set of pupils.* The Abbess of Crewe, *an allegory of Watergate, relates a nun's intrigues to become elected abbess of her convent. Muriel Spark's later novels focus on the relation between art and reality (*Loitering with Intent*) and on the struggle to reconcile pain and tragedy with a belief in the benevolence of God (*The Only Problem*).*

The Prime of Miss Jean Brodie (1961)

Six years previously, Miss Brodie had led her new class into the garden for a history lesson underneath the big elm. On the way through the school corridors they passed the headmistress's study. The door was wide open, the room was empty.

"Little girls," said Miss Brodie, "come and observe this."

They clustered round the open door while she pointed to a large poster pinned with drawing-pins on the opposite wall within the room. It depicted a man's big face. Underneath were the words "Safety First."

"This is Stanley Baldwin who got in as Prime Minister and got out again ere long," said Miss Brodie. "Miss Mackay retains him on the wall because she believes in the slogan 'Safety First'. But Safety does not come first. Goodness, Truth and Beauty come first. Follow me."

This was the first intimation, to the girls, of an odds between Miss Brodie and the rest of the teaching staff. Indeed, to some of them, it was the first time they had realized it was possible for people glued together in grown-up authority to differ at all. Taking inward note of this, and with the exhilarating feeling of being in on the faint smell of row, without being endangered by it, they followed dangerous Miss Brodie into the secure shade of the elm.

Often, that sunny autumn, when the weather permitted, the small girls took their lessons seated on three benches arranged about the elm.

"Hold up your books," said Miss Brodie quite often that autumn, "prop them up in your hands, in case of intruders.

If there are any intruders, we are doing our history lesson... our poetry... English grammar."

The small girls held up their books with their eyes not on them, but on Miss Brodie.

"Meantime I will tell you about my last summer holiday in Egypt... I will tell you about care of the skin, and of the hands... about the Frenchman I met in the train to Biarritz... and I must tell you about the Italian paintings I saw. Who is the greatest Italian painter?"

"Leonardo da Vinci, Miss Brodie."

"That is incorrect. The answer is Giotto, he is my favourite."

Some days it seemed to Sandy that Miss Brodie's chest was flat, no bulges at all, but straight as her back. On other days her chest was breast-shaped and large, very noticeable, something for Sandy to sit and peer at through her tiny eyes while Miss Brodie on a day of lessons indoors stood erect, with her brown head held high, staring out of the window like Joan of Arc as she spoke.

"I have frequently told you, and the holidays just past have convincend me, that my prime has truly begun. One's prime is elusive. You little girls, when you grow up, must be on the alert to recognize your prime at whatever time of your life it may occur. You must then live it to the full. Mary, what have you got under your desk, what are you looking at?"

Mary sat lump-like and too stupid to invent something. She was too stupid ever to tell a lie; she didn't know how to cover up.

"A comic, Miss Brodie," she said.

"Do you mean a comedian, a droll?"

Everyone tittered.

"A comic paper," said Mary.

"A comic paper, forsooth. How old are you?"

"Ten, ma'am."

"You are too old for comic papers at ten. Give it to me."

Miss Brodie looked at the coloured sheets. "*Tiger Tim's* forsooth," she said, and threw it into the waste-paper basket. Perceiving all eyes upon it she lifted it out of the basket, tore it up beyond redemption and put it back again.

"Attend to me, girls. One's prime is the moment one was born for. Now that my prime has begun — Sandy, your attention is wandering. What have I been talking about?"

"Your prime, Miss Brodie."

Macmillan 1961.

Muriel Spark on her novels:

I like to think that my novels have something of the compression and tidiness of verse. When I started writing them I was a great admirer of MacNeice, and I felt closer to him that to any practising novelist.

In the early 1950s there was no Robbe-Grillet, and scarcely anyone had heard of Beckett. Hardly anyone was trying to write novels with the compression and obliqueness I was aiming at. (...)

I'm tremendously against the kind of literature which is making a constant appeal to our emotional sympathy. What happens when the sympathies and the indignation of a modern audience are aroused by a play or novel of the kind I'm talking about? I suspect a great number of the audience or of the readers feel their moral responsibilities are sufficiently fulfilled by the emotions they've been induced to feel. A man may go to bed feeling less guilty after seeing such a play. (...)

So I think the only effective art of our particular time is the satirical; the harsh, witty, ironic, elegant and derisive. What I'd really like to see is the *desegregation* of art — the liberation of our minds from the comfortable cells of lofty sentiment (what you call profundity) in which they are confined and in which they can never really feel satisfied. (...)

As writers our real job is to bring about an environment of honesty and self-knowledge, a sense of the absurd and a general looking-lively to defend ourselves from the ridiculous oppressions of our time. And above all to entertain our readers in the process.

The Observer Colour Supplement, 7 November 1971.

Doris LESSING born 1919

1919 *Born in Persia.*
1925 *Moved to Southern Rhodesia with her family. Attended a convent school in Salisbury.*
1938 *Joined a left-wing political group.*
1939 *Married Frank Wisdom (a son and a daughter; divorced in 1943.)*
1945 *Married Gottfried Lessing (a son; divorced in 1949).*
1949 *Moved to London.*
1950 The Grass is Singing.
1951 This Was the Old Chief's Country (*short stories*).
1952 * Martha Quest.
1953 Five: Short Novels.
1954 * A Proper Marriage.
1956 Retreat to Innocence. *Left the Communist party in protest at the invasion of Hungary.*
1958 * A Ripple from the Storm.
1962 The Golden Notebook.
1963 A Man and Two Women (*short stories*).
1964 African Stories.
1965 * Landlocked.
1969 * The Four-Gated City.
1971 Briefing for a Descent into Hell.
1972 The Temptation of Jack Orkney and Other Stories.
1973 The Summer before the Dark.
1975 The Memoirs of a Survivor.
1979 Shikasta.
1980 The Marriages between Zones Three, Four and Five.
1981 The Sirian Experiments.
1982 The Making of the Representative for Planet 8.
1984 The Diaries of Jane Somers.
1985 The Good Terrorist.
1988 The Fifth Child.

* The "Children of Violence" series.

Doris Lessing's novels explore the themes of violence, racism, communism, loneliness, feminism and psychology. The basic idea behind these themes is the need for the individual to overcome historical, social and political preconditioning in order to achieve personal freedom. Her sober, unsentimental prose depicts strong-willed heroines who struggle to maintain their independence and reach wholeness of vision in a socially bleak and male-oriented society. The Children of Violence *is a* bildungsroman *in which we follow Martha Quest's attempt to escape her restricted upbringing, and then the development of her awareness of others through emotional crises and her involvement with left-wing political groups.* The Golden Notebook *juxtaposes excerpts from a novel Anna Wulf is trying to write and different aspects of her life and personality related in four different notebooks whose colours are symbolic. The "golden notebook" represents Anna's attempt to reconcile this "fragmented consciousness" and to achieve wholeness through art.*

Doris Lessing's later works reflect her interest in mysticism and Sufism, in speculative fiction (a form of science-fiction), and in works of "inner space fiction" revealing the influence of Carl Jung and R.D. Laing.

The Golden Notebook (1962)

I was the odd man out in this group because I was the only one who was free. Free in the sense that I had chosen to come to the Colony in the first place and could leave it when I liked. And why did I not leave it? I hated the place, and had done so since I first came to it in 1939 to marry and become a tobacco farmer's wife. I met Steven in London the year before, when he was on holiday. The day after I arrived on the farm I knew I liked Steven but could never stand the life. But instead of returning to London I went into the city and became a secretary. For years my life seems to have consisted of activities I began to do provisionally, temporarily, with half a heart, and which I then stayed with. For instance I became "a communist" because the left people were the only people in the town with any kind of moral energy, the only people who took it for granted that the colour bar was monstrous. And yet there were always two personalities in me, the "communist" and Anna, and Anna judges the communist all the time. And vice-versa. Some kind of lethargy I suppose. I knew the war was coming and it would be hard to get a passage home, yet I stayed. Yet I did not enjoy the life, I don't enjoy pleasure, but I went to sundowner parties and dances and I played tennis and enjoyed the sun. It seems such a long time ago that I can't *feel* myself doing any of these things. I can't "remember" what it was like to be Mr Campbell's secretary or to dance every night, etc. It happened to someone else. I can see myself though, but even that wasn't true until I found an old photograph the other day which showed a small, thin, brittle black-and-white girl, almost doll-like. I was more sophisticated than the colonial girls of course; but far less experienced — in a colony people have far more room to do as they like. Girls can do things there that I'd have to fight to do in England. My sophistication was literary and social. Compared with a girl like Maryrose, for all her apparent fragility and vulnerability, I was a baby. The photograph shows me standing on the Club steps, holding a racket. I look amused and critical; it's a sharp little face. I never acquired that admirable Colonial quality — good humour. (Why is it admirable? Yet I enjoy it.) But I can't remember what I felt except that I repeated to myself every day, even after that war began, that now I must book my passage home. About then I met Willi Rodde and got involved with politics. Not for the first time. I was too young of course to have been involved with Spain, but friends had been; so communism and the left was nothing new to me. I did not like Willi. He did not like me. Yet we began to live together, or as much as is possible in a small town where everyone knows what you do. We had rooms in the same hotel and shared meals. We were together for nearly three years. Yet we neither liked nor understood each other. We did not even enjoy sleeping together. Of course then I was inexperienced, having slept only with Steven, and that briefly. But even then I knew, as Willi knew, that we were incompatible. Having learned about sex since, I know that the word incompatible means something very real. It doesn't mean, not being in love, or not being in sympathy, or not being patient, or being ignorant. Two people can be sexually incompatible who are perfectly happy in bed with other people, as if the very chemical structures of their bodies were hostile. Well, Willi and I understood this so well that our vanity wasn't involved. Our emotions were, about this point only. We had a kind of pity for each other; we were both afflicted permanently with a feeling of sad helplessness because we were unable to make each other happy in this way. But nothing stopped us from choosing other partners. We did not. That I did not isn't surprising, because of that quality in me I call lethargy, or curiosity, which always keeps me in the situation long after I should leave it. Weakness? Until I wrote that word I never thought of it as applying to me. But I suppose it does. Willi, however, was not weak. On the contrary he was the most ruthless person I have ever known.

Having written that, I am astounded. What do I mean? He was capable of great kindness. And now I remember that all those years ago, I discovered that no matter what adjective I applied to Willi, I could always use the opposite. Yes. I have looked in my old papers. I find a list, headed *Willi*:

Ruthless	Kind
Cold	Warm
Sentimental	Realistic

And so on, down the page; and underneath I wrote: "From the process of writing these words about Willi I have discovered I know nothing about him. About someone one understands, one doesn't have to make lists of words."

But really what I discovered, though I didn't know it then, was that in describing any personality all these words are meaningless. To describe a person one says: "Willi, sitting stiffly at the head of the table, allowed his round spectacles to glitter at the people watching him and said, formally, but with a gruff clumsy humour..." Something like that. But the point is, and it is the point that obsesses me (and how odd this obsession should be showing itself, so long ago, in helpless lists of opposing words, not knowing what it would develop into), once I say that words like good/bad, strong/weak, are irrelevant, I am accepting amorality, and I do accept it the moment I start to write "a story," "a novel," because I simply don't care. All I care about is that I should describe Willi and Maryrose so that a reader can feel their reality. And after twenty years of living in and around the left, which means twenty years' preoccupation with this question of morality in art, that is all I am left with. So what I am saying is, in fact, that the human personality, that unique flame, is so sacred to me, that everything else becomes unimportant? Is that what I am saying? And if so, what does it mean?

Simon & Shuster, 1962.

Doris Lessing on The Golden Notebook:

[I] wanted to write a short formal novel which would enclose the rest in order to suggest what I think a great many writers feel about the formal novel; namely, that it's not doing its job any more. So I thought that the only way to do this would be to write the short formal novel and put in the experience it came out of, showing how ridiculous the formal novel is... (...) [I] split up the rest into four parts to express a split person. I felt that if the artist's sensibility is to be equated with the sensibility of the educated person, then it is logical to use different styles to express different kinds of people... Also this particular form enabled me to say things about time, about memory — which interests me very much; what we choose to remember — about the human personality because a personality is very much what is remembered... If I had used a conventional style, the old-fashioned novel... I would not have been able to do this kind of playing with time, memory and the balancing of people.

"Footnote to *The Golden Notebook*,"
Queen, 21 August 1962.

... and on the responsibilities of a writer:

I believe that the pleasurable luxury of despair, the acceptance of disgust, is as much a betrayal of what a writer should be as the acceptance of the simple economic view of man; both are aspects of cowardice, both failings — away from a central vision, the two easy escapes of our time into false innocence... The point of rest should be the writer's recognition of man the responsible individual, voluntarily submitting his will to collective, but never finally; and insisting on making his own personal and private judgments before every act of submission.

Declaration, *ed. Tom Maschler, London*
MacGibbon and Kee, 1957.

Iris MURDOCH born 1919

1919 *Born in Dublin.*
1938-1942 *Studied "Greats" at Oxford.*
1942-1944 *Assistant Principal in the Treasury.*
1944-1946 *Worked for the United Nations Relief and Rehabilitation Administration.*
1947-1948 *Studentship in philosophy at Newham College, Cambridge.*
1948 *Appointed Fellow of St Anne's College, Oxford.*
1953 Sartre: Romantic Rationalist (*Philosophy*).
1954 Under the Net.
1956 *Married John Bayley.* The Flight from the Enchanter.
1957 The Sandcastle.
1958 The Bell.
1961 A Severed Head.
1962 An Unofficial Rose.
1963 The Unicorn.
1964 The Italian Girl.
1965 The Red and the Green.
1966 The Time of the Angels.
1968 The Nice and the Good.
1969 Bruno's Dream.
1970 A Fairly Honourable Defeat.
1971 The Accidental Man.

Iris Murdoch's novels explore philosophical ideas; they show the complexity of moral life and the need to preserve one's existential freedom and independence in order to preserve the "opacity" of the self. The difficulty of living morally is that it means accepting the reality and difference of others. In a world devoid of any guidance from above, people build "nets" and systems in order to structure their own lives, unaware that by thus trying to avoid contingent features of reality they relinquish their own freedom. Hence the recurrent figure of the manipulative character who tries to control the lives of others. A moralist, Iris Murdoch deals with such themes as liberty and responsibility, the nature of good and evil, the role of art, the relationship between imagination and reality and between religion and power, and the different attitudes towards love and sex.

Many of the novels seem artificial because of their intricate plots — rich in twists and reversals — and their bizarre and fantastic characters. They include macabre and weird scenes, supernatural events, and complex relationships which the novelist Anthony Burgess compared to "a contrived sexual dance in which partners are always changing." But besides adding a symbolic dimension to her themes, these gothic elements are, for Iris Murdoch, what life is really like:

1973 The Black Prince.
1974 The Sacred and Profane Love Machine.
1975 A Word Child.
1976 Henry and Cato.
1977 The Fire and the Sun (*Philosophy*).
1978 The Sea, The Sea.
1980 Nuns and Soldiers.
1983 The Philosopher's Pupil.
1985 The Good Apprentice.
1987 The Book and the Brotherhood.
1989 The Message to the Planet.
1992 Metaphysics as a Guide to Morals (*Philosophy*).

"In real life the fantastic and the ordinary, the plain and the symbolic, are often indissolubly joined together, and I think the best novels explore and exhibit life without disjoining them."

The Unicorn (1963)
Marian Taylor has accepted a job as governess at Gaze Castle, in a remote and lonely part of the British Isles. The following passage describes her arrival at Gaze Castle.

The car slowed down to rattle very slowly over a long wooden bridge across a channel of large almost spherical speckled stones. A little trickle of water, the colour of brown sherry, forced an erratic way among the stones and spread out on the seaward side into a shallow rippled expanse bordered with tangles of glistening yellow seaweed. A few white-washed one-room cottages huddled in a disorderly group near to the road. Marian noticed that some of them were roofless. No people were to be seen. Below and beyond, framed on each side by the perpendicular black cliffs, whose great height was now apparent, was the sea, total gold. The house, Riders, had come into view again behind them. The car began to climb the other side of the valley.

Marian was suddenly overcome by an appalling crippling panic. She was very frightened at the idea of arriving. But it was more than that. She feared the rocks and the cliffs and the grotesque dolmen and the ancient secret things. Her two companions seemed no longer reassuring but dreadfully alien and even sinister. She felt, for the first time in her life, completely isolated and in danger. She became in an instant almost faint with terror.

She said, as a cry of help, "I'm feeling terribly nervous."

"I know you are," said Scottow. He smiled, not looking at her, and again the words had an intimate protective ring. "Don't be. You'll soon feel at home here. We're a very harmless lot."

Behind her she heard again the high-pitched sound of the boy's laugh.

The car bumped over a jangling cattle-grid and through an immense crenellated archway. A lodge cottage with blank gaping windows and a sagging roof stood in a wilderness of wind-torn shrubs. The uneven gravel track, devastated by rain and weeds, wound away to the left, circling upward toward the house. After the dry rocks, the earth here was suddenly moist and black, covered patchily with wiry grass of a vivid green. Red flowering fuchsia blotched the hillside among dark dishevelled clumps of rhododendron. The track turned again and the house was near. Marian descried the stone balustrade of a terrace which surrounded it on all sides, lifting it high out of the peaty earth. There was a grey stone wall some distance beyond and indications of an overgrown garden with a few bedraggled fir trees and a monkey puzzle. The car came to a standstill and Scottow switched off the engine.

Marian was appalled at the sudden quietness. But the insane panic had left her. She was frightened now in an ordinary way, sick in her stomach, shy, tongue-tied, horribly aware of the onset of a new world.

Scottow and Jamesie carried her bags. Not looking up at the staring windows, she followed up the steps to the terrace of cracked weedy paving-stones, on to the big ornate stone porch and through swinging glass doors. Inside there was a new kind of silence, and it was dark and rather cold and there was a sweetish smell of old curtains and old damp. Two maids with tall white lace caps and black streaky hair and squints came forward to take her luggage.

Jamesie had vanished into the darkness. Scottow said, "I expect you would like to wash and so on. There's no hurry. Of course, we don't usually change for dinner here, not seriously, I mean. The maids will show you to your room. Perhaps you'd like to find your way again in half an hour or so, and I'll be waiting about on the terrace."

The maids were already whisking the luggage away up the stairs. Marian followed them through the semi-darkness. The floors were mostly uncarpeted, tilting, creaking, echoing, but there were soft hangings above her head, curtains in archways and vague cobwebby textiles which hung down at doors and corners and tugged her passing sleeve. At last she was ushered into a big room full of evening light. The maids disappeared.

She crossed to the window. She had the big view across the valley to Riders and the sea. The sea was peacock blue now and the cliffs were jet black, receding to where the distant islands were again to be seen against a tawny sky. She looked and sighed, forgetting herself.

The case containing her brand-new field-glasses was slung about her neck. Still absorbed in looking, she fumbled them out. They were yet a delightful toy. She focused them upon the valley. Startlingly close the wooden bridge sprang into view, and slowly the magic circle moved up the hill toward the opposite house. She came to a wall, discerning the uneven texture of the stone where the sinking sun struck it obliquely and cast small shadows; and then unexpectedly there was a stone balustrade, like the one at Gaze, and behind it a shuttered window. She moved the glasses slowly, pausing at a group of gay deck-chairs and white table with a bottle on it. The next moment she was looking at a man. He was standing on the terrace and looking straight into her eyes with lifted binoculars trained on Gaze. Marian dropped her glasses and moved hastily back from the window. The panic returned.

Chatto & Windus, 1963.

Iris Murdoch on her novels:

Why are people not good, and why, without being evil or even having bad intentions, do they do bad things? Schopenhauer, whom I admire, is good on this topic of tragedy. Some people who are not bad find themselves so situated that they are unable to stop themselves from doing the greatest possible harm they can to others. It's an evident feature of human psychology that people have secret dream lives. The secrecy of people is very interesting, and the novelist is overcoming the secrecy and attempting to understand.

Tom Philips, Dame Iris Murdoch, © *National Portrait Gallery.*

Readers sometimes say to me that I portray odd characters; but the secret thoughts and obsessions and fantasies of others would amaze one, only people don't tell them, partly because they're ashamed and partly because secrecy is very natural and proper.

Novelists in Interview, John Haffenden
Methuen, 1985

We need to be enabled to think in terms of degrees of freedom, and to picture, in a non-metaphysical, non-totalitarian, and non-religious sense, the transcendence of reality. A simple-minded faith in science, together with the assumption that we are all rational and totally free, engenders a dangerous lack of curiosity about the real world, a failure to appreciate the difficulties of knowing it. We need to return from the self-centred concept of sincerity to the other-centred concept of truth. We are not isolated free-choosers, monarchs of all we survey, but benighted creatures sunk in a reality whose nature we are constantly and overwhelmingly tempted to deform by fantasy. Our current picture of freedom encourages a dream-like facility; whereas what we require is a renewed sense of the difficulty and complexity of the moral life and the opacity of persons. We need more concepts in terms of which to picture the substance of our being; it is through an enriching and deepening of concepts that moral progress takes place.

(...)

Reality is not a given whole. An understanding of this, a respect for the contingent, is essential to imagination as opposed to fantasy. Our sense of form, which is an aspect of our desire for consolation, can be a danger to our sense of reality as a rich receding background. Against the consolations of form, the clean crystalline work, the simplified fantasy-myth, we must pit the destructive power of the now so unfashionable naturalistic idea of character.

Real people are destructive of myth, contingency is destructive of fantasy and opens the way for imagination. (...) Literature must always represent a battle between real people and images; and what it requires now is a much stronger and more complex conception of the former.

"Against Dryness: A polemical Sketch,"
Encounter, Jan. 1961.

John FOWLES born 1926

1926 *Born in Essex.*
1945-1946 *Served in the Royal Marines.*
1950 *BA in French from Oxford University.*
1950-1963 *Held various teaching positions in France, Greece and England.*
1963 The Collector.
1965 The Magus.
1969 The French Lieutenant's Woman.
1974 The Ebony Tower *(short stories).*
1977 Daniel Martin.
1982 Mantissa.
1985 A Maggot.

John Fowles once wrote that his chief concern was "to preserve the freedom of the individual against those pressures-to-conform that threaten our century." Confronted with the social and psychological constraints of their environment, human beings must exercise free will and independent thought to remain authentic and capable of change and evolution. Hence John Fowles's fascination with the mysterious and the occult, with masks and mystification, since curiosity about the unknown can only lead to an active quest for answers — one manifestation of man's freedom.

In The Collector, *a young clerk kidnaps an art student and imprisons her in a windowless room. The novel explores the domination and suffocation of the Few — the creative and independent people who reject conventions — by the Many — the more apathetic masses who resent social and intellectual superiority.*

The Magus *is set on an isolated Greek island where the hero, Nicholas, has taken a job. There he meets Maurice Conchis, who sets the stage for an elaborate series of theatricals and "godgames," a web of truths and lies that confuse and instruct the young man. He keeps looking for clues that might give him an insight into reality, but only sees its chaotic, unpredictable and deceptive nature. He concludes that the only way of achieving freedom is to invent your own world, to become a magus yourself.*

The French Lieutenant's Woman *examines Victorian society from a 20th century perspective. It reflects the characters' attempt to free themselves from social restraints and prohibitions — as illustrated by the mysterious character Sarah who put herself "beyond the pale" by giving herself to a French Lieutenant. The novel has multiple endings — another way of preserving the characters' freedom from the author and of replacing the tyranny of fiction by the aleatory. The novel questions the meaning of Victorian values through the use of parody, anachronism and constant allusions to and quotations from Tennyson, Hardy, Darwin and Marx.*

In A Maggot, *the death of a servant and the disappearance of his master lead to a search marked by lies, false identities and mysteries. The novel develops the metaphor of the "larval stage of a winged creature," but also explores the word's 18th century meaning of — a whim or quirk — by following a group of 18th century characters, among them Rebecca Lee, the mother of Ann Lee, the founder of the Shaker religion.*

The French Lieutenant's Woman (1969)

Mrs Poulteney, a strict and rigid Victorian lady, is looking for a companion and has asked the vicar to find her "a refined person who has come upon adverse circumstances."

Ah Maud, you milk-white fawn, you are all unmeet for a wife.
TENNYSON. *Maud (1855)*

Mrs Poulteney's face, that afternoon when the vicar made his return and announcement, expressed a notable ignorance. And with ladies of her kind, an unsuccessful appeal to knowledge is more often than not a successful appeal to disapproval. Her face was admirably suited to the latter sentiment; it had eyes that were not Tennyson's "homes of silent prayer" at all, and lower cheeks, almost dewlaps, that pinched the lips together in condign rejection of all that threatened her two life principles: the one being (I will borrow Treitschke's sarcastic formulation) that "Civilization is Soap" and the other, "Respectability is what does not give me offense." She bore some resemblance to a white Pekinese; to be exact, to a stuffed Pekinese, since she carried concealed in her bosom a small bag of camphor as a prophylactic against cholera ... so that where she was, was always also a delicate emanation of mothballs.

"I do not know her."

The vicar felt snubbed; and wondered what would have happened had the Good Samaritan come upon Mrs Poulteney instead of the poor traveler.

"I did not suppose you would. She is a Charmouth girl."

"A girl?"

"That is, I am not quite sure of her age, a woman, a lady of some thirty years of age. Perhaps more. I would not like to hazard a guess." The vicar was conscious that he was making a poor start for the absent defendant. "But a most distressing case. Most deserving of your charity."

"Has she an education?"

"Yes indeed. She was trained to be a governess. She was a governess."

"And what is she now?"

"I believe she is without employment."

"Why?"

"That is a long story."

"I should certainly wish to hear it before proceeding."

So the vicar sat down again, and told her what he knew, or some (for in his brave attempt to save Mrs Poulteney's soul, he decided to endanger his own) of what he knew, of Sarah Woodruff.

"The girl's father was a tenant of Lord Meriton's, near Beaminster. A farmer merely, but a man of excellent principles and highly respected in that neighborhood. He most wisely provided the girl with a better education than one would expect."

"He is deceased?"

"Some several years ago. The girl became a governess to Captain John Talbot's family at Charmouth."

"Will he give a letter of reference?"

"My dear Mrs Poulteney, we are discussing, if I understood our earlier conversation aright, an object of charity, not an object of employment." She bobbed, the nearest acknowledgment to an apology she had ever been known to muster. "No doubt such a letter can be obtained. She left his home at her own request. What happened was this. You will recall the French barque — I think she hailed from Saint Malo — that was driven ashore under Stonebarrow in the dreadful gale of last December? And you will no doubt recall that three of the crew were saved and were taken in by the people of Charmouth? Two were simple sailors. One, I understand, was the lieutenant of the vessel. His leg had been crushed at the first impact, but he clung to a spar and was washed ashore. You must surely have read of this."

"Very probably. I do not like the French."

"Captain Talbot, as a naval officer himself, most kindly charged upon his household the care of the ... foreign officer. He spoke no English. And Miss Woodruff was called upon to interpret and look after his needs."

"She speaks French?" Mrs Poulteney's alarm at this appalling disclosure was nearly enough to sink the vicar. But he ended by bowing and smiling urbanely.

"My dear madam, so do most governesses. It is not their fault if the world requires such attainments of them. But to return to the French gentleman. I regret to say that he did not deserve that appellation."

"Mr Forsythe!"

She drew herself up, but not too severely, in case she might freeze the poor man into silence.

"I hasten to add that no misconduct took place at Captain Talbot's. Or indeed, so far as Miss Woodruff in concerned, at any subsequent place or time. I have Mr Fursey-Harris's word for that. He knows the circumstances far better than I." The person referred to was the vicar of Charmouth. "But the Frenchman managed to engage Miss Woodruff's affections. When his leg was mended he took himself to Weymouth, there, or so it was generally supposed, to find a passage home. Two days after he had gone Miss Woodruff requested Mrs Talbot, in the most urgent terms, to allow her to leave her post. I am told that Mrs Talbot tried to extract the woman's reasons. But without success."

"And she let her leave without notice?"

The vicar adroitly seized his chance. "I agree — it was most foolish. She should have known better. Had Miss Woodruff been in wiser employ I have no doubt this sad business would not have taken place." He left a pause for Mrs Poulteney to grasp the implied compliment.

Little, Brown & Co. 1969

John Fowles on the novelist's function in The French Lieutenant's Woman:

For the drift of the Maker is dark, an Isis hid
by the veil ...
TENNYSON, *Maud* (1855)

I do not know. This story I am telling is all imagination. These characters I create never existed outside my own mind. If I have pretended until now to know my characters' minds and innermost thoughts, it is because I am writing in (just as I have assumed some of the vocabulary and "voice" of) a convention universally accepted at the time of my story: that the novelist stands next to God. He may not know all, yet he tries to pretend that he does. But I live in the age of Alain Robbe-Grillet and Roland Barthes; if this is a novel, it cannot be a novel in the modern sense of the word.

So perhaps I am writing a transposed autobiography; perhaps I now live in one of the houses I have brought into the fiction; perhaps Charles is myself disguised. Perhaps it is only a game. Modern women like Sarah exist, and I have never understood them. Or perhaps I am trying to pass off a concealed book of essays on you. Instead of chapter headings, perhaps I should have written "On the Horizontality of Existence," "The Illusions of Progress," "The History of the Novel Form," "The Aetiology of Freedom," "Some Forgotten Aspects of the Victorian Age" ... what you will.

Perhaps you suppose that a novelist has only to pull the right strings and his puppets will behave in a lifelike manner; and produce on request a thorough analysis of their motives and intentions. Certainly I intended at this stage (*Chap. Thirteen — Unfolding of Sarah's true state of mind*) to tell all — or all that matters. But I find myself suddenly like a man in the sharp spring night, watching from the lawn beneath that dim upper window in Marlborough House; I know in the context of my book's reality that Sarah would never have brushed away her tears and leaned down and delivered a chapter of revelation. She would instantly have turned, had she seen me there just as the old moon rose, and disappeared into the interior shadows.

But I am a novelist, not a man in a garden — I can follow her where I like? But possibility is not permissibility. Husbands could often murder their wives — and the reverse — and get away with it. But they don't.

You may think novelists always have fixed plans to which they work, so that the future predicted by Chapter One is always inexorably the actuality of Chapter Thirteen. By novelists write for countless different reasons: for money, for fame, for reviewers, for parents, for friends, for loved ones; for vanity, for pride, for curiosity, for amusement: as skilled furniture makers enjoy making furniture, as drunkards like drinking, as judges like judging, as Sicilians like emptying a shotgun into an enemy's back. I could fill a book with reasons, and they would all be true, though not true of all. Only one same reason is shared by all of us: *we wish to create worlds as real as, but other than the world that is.* Or was. This is why we cannot plan. We know a world is an organism, not a machine. We also know that a genuinely created world must be independent of its creator; a planned world (a world that fully reveals its planning) is a dead world. It is only when our characters and events begin to disobey us that they begin to live. When Charles left Sarah on her cliff edge,[1] I ordered him to walk straight back to Lyme Regis. But he did not; he gratuitously turned and went down to the Dairy.

Oh, but you say, come on — what I really mean is that the idea crossed my mind as I wrote that it might be more clever to have him stop and drink milk ... and meet Sarah again. That is certainly one explanation of what happened; but I can only report — and I am the most reliable witness — that the idea seemed to me to come clearly from Charles, not myself. It is not only that he has begun to gain an autonomy; I must respect it, and disrespect all my quasi-divine plans for him, if I wish him to be real.

In other words, to be free myself, I must give him, and Tina, and Sarah, even the abominable Mrs Poulteney,[2] their freedom as well. There is only one good definition of God: the freedom that allows other freedoms to exist. And I must conform to that definition.

The novelist is still a god, since he creates (and not even the most aleatory avant-garde modern novel has managed to extirpate its author completely); what has changed is that we are no longer the gods of the Victorian image, omniscient and decreeing; but in the new theological image, with freedom our first principle, not authority.

I have disgracefully broken the illusion? No. My characters still exist, and in a reality no less, or no more, real than the one I have just broken. Fiction is woven into all, as a Greek observed some two and a half thousand years ago. I find this new reality (or unreality) more valid; and I would have you share my own sense that I do not fully control these creatures of my mind, any more than you control — however hard you try, however much of a latterday Mrs Poulteney you may be — your children, colleagues, friends, or even yourself.

But this is preposterous? A character is either

---

1. Charles, who is engaged to marry Ernestina, has just met Sarah on Ware Commons.
2. Mrs Poulteney has forbidden Sarah to walk on Ware Commons — a place also called Lovers' Lane and which she associates with infamy.

"real" or "imaginary"? If you think that, *hypocrite lecteur*, I can only smile. You do not even think of your own past as quite real; you dress it up, you gild it or blacken it, censor it, tinker with it ... fictionalize it, in a word, and put it away on a shelf — your book, your romanced autobiography. We are all in flight from the real reality. That is a basic definition of *Homo sapiens*.

So if you think all this unlucky (but it *is* Chapter Thirteen) digression has nothing to do with your Time, Progress, Society, Evolution and all those other capitalized ghosts in the night that are rattling their chains behind the scenes of this book ... I will not argue. But I shall suspect you.

Ibid.

Graham SWIFT born 1949

1949 *Born in London.*
1967-1970 *Studied at Queen's College, Cambridge.*
1980 The Sweet Shop Owner.
1981 Shuttlecock.
1982 Learning to Swim and Other Stories.
1984 Waterland.
1988 Out of This World.
1992 Ever After.

A major theme in Graham Swift's novels is the relationship between man and his past, between the routine of ordinary domestic life and the drama and majesty of history. Many of his characters are therefore concerned with discovering the truth about their past and the way it has shaped their present lives.

In Graham Swift's best-known novel, Waterland, *Tom Crick, the protagonist, is a history teacher who is about to lose his job and tries to bring the past to life in his classroom. Several levels of history become intertwined in his rambling discourse to his class: the French revolution, the history of the Fens with its canals, its eels, and the Atkinson brewery, and his own personal past which includes a saga of incest, murder and insanity. The novel thus illustrates the close links between the different meanings of the word "history" that appear in the epigraph: 1. inquiry, investigation, learning; 2. a) a narrative of past events, history; b) any kind of narrative: account, tale, story.*

Waterland (1984)

This is the opening chapter of the novel.

ABOUT THE STARS AND THE SLUICE

"And don't forget," my father would say, as if he expected me at any moment to up and leave to seek my fortune in the wide world, "whatever you learn about people, however bad they turn out, each one of them has a heart, and each one of them was once a tiny baby sucking his mother's milk..."

Fairy-tale words; fairy-tale advice. But we lived in a fairy-tale place. In a lock-keeper's cottage, by a river, in the middle of the Fens. Far away from the wide world. And my father, who was a superstitious man, liked to do things in such a way as would make them seem magical and occult. So he would always set his eel traps at night. Not because eel traps cannot be set by day, but because the mystery of darkness appealed to him. And one night, in midsummer, in 1937, we went with him, Dick and I, to set traps near Stott's Bridge. It was hot and windless. When the traps had been set we lay back on the river-bank. Dick was fourteen and I was ten. The pumps were tump-tumping, as they do, incessantly, so that you scarcely notice them, all over the Fens, and frogs were croaking in the ditches. Up above, the sky swarmed with stars which seemed to multiply as we looked at them. And as we lay, Dad said: "Do you know what the stars are? They are the silver dust of God's blessing. They are little broken-off bits of heaven. God cast them down to fall on us. But when he saw how wicked we were, he changed his mind and ordered the stars to stop. Which is why they hang in the sky but seem as though at any time they might drop..."

For my father, as well as being a superstitious man, had a knack for telling stories. Made-up stories, true stories; soothing stories, warning stories; stories with a moral or with no point at all; believable stories and unbelievable stories; stories which were neither one thing nor the other. It was a knack which ran in his family. But it was a knack which my mother had too — and perhaps he really acquired it from her. Because when I was very small it was my mother who first told me stories, which, unlike my father, she got from books as well as out of her head, to make me sleep at night.

And since my mother's death, which was six months before we lay by the eel traps under the stars, my father's yen for the dark, his nocturnal restlessness, had grown more besetting. As if he were constantly brooding on some story yet to be told. So I would see him sometimes, inspecting his vegetable patch by the moonlight, or talking to his roosting chickens, or pacing up and down by the lock-gates or the sluice, his movements marked by the wandering ember of his cigarette.

We lived in a lock-keeper's cottage by the River Leem, which flows out of Norfolk into the Great Ouse. And no one needs telling that the land in that part of the world is flat. Flat, with an unrelieved and monotonous flatness, enough of itself, some might say, to drive a man to unquiet and sleep-defeating thoughts. From the raised banks of the Leem, it stretched away to the horizon, its uniform colour, peat-black, varied only by the crops that grew upon it — grey-green potato leaves, blue-green beet leaves, yellow-green wheat; its uniform levelness broken only by the furrowed and dead-straight lines of ditches and drains, which, depending on the state of the sky and the angle of the sun, ran like silver, copper or golden wires across the fields and which, when you stood and looked at them, made you shut one eye and fall prey to fruitless meditations on the laws of perspective.

And yet this land, so regular, so prostrate, so tamed and cultivated, would transform itself, in my five- or six-year-old mind, into an empty wilderness. On those nights when my mother would be forced to tell me stories, it would seem that in our lock-keeper's cottage we were in the middle of nowhere; and the noise of the trains passing on the lines to King's Lynn, Gildsey and Ely was like the baying of a monster closing in on us in our isolation.

A fairy-tale land, after all.

My father kept the lock on the River Leem, two miles from where it empties into the Ouse. But because a lock-keeper's duties are irregular and his pay, set against the rent-free cottage in which he lives, is scant, and because, in any case, by the nineteen-thirties, the river-traffic on the Leem had dwindled, my father also grew vegetables, kept chickens and trapped eels. It was only in times of heavy rain or thaw that these secondary occupations were abandoned. Then he would have to watch and anticipate the water-level. Then he would have to raise the sluice which cut across the far side of the stream like a giant guillotine.

For the river in front of our cottage divided into two channels, the nearer containing the navigation lock, the farther the sluice, with, in between, a solidly built brick-faced pier, a tiny island, on which stood the cabin housing the sluice engine. And even before the river had visibly risen, even before its colour had changed and it began to show the milky brown of the Norfolk chalk hills from which it flowed, Dad would know when to cross the lock-gates to the cabin and begin — with a groaning of metal and throbbing of released water — to crank up the sluice.

But under normal conditions the sluice remained lowered, almost to the river bottom, its firm blade holding back the slow-flowing Leem, making it fit for the passage of boats. Then the water in the enclosure above it, like the water in the lock-pen, would be smooth and placid and it would give off that smell which is characteristic of places where fresh water and human ingenuity meet, and which is smelt over and over again in the Fens. A cool, slimy but strangely poignant and nostalgic smell. A smell which is half man and half fish. And at such times Dad would have plenty of leisure for his eel traps and vegetables, and little to do with the sluice, save to combat rust, grease the cog-wheels and clear away from the water the accumulations of flotsam.

For, flood or no flood, the Leem brought down its unceasing booty of debris. Willow branches; alder branches; sedge; fencing; crates; old clothes; dead sheep; bottles; potato sacks; straw bales; fruit boxes; fertiliser bags. All floated down on the westerly current, lodged against the sluice-gate and had to be cleared away with boat-hooks and weed-rakes.

And thus it was that one night, in midsummer, when God's withheld benedictions were shining in the sky, though this was several years after Dad told us about the stars, but only two or three since he began to speak of hearts and mother's milk, and the tump-tump of the pumps was drowned now, in the evening, by the roar of ascending bombers — it was, to be precise, July, 1943 — that something floated down the Leem, struck the ironwork of the sluice and, tugged by the eddies, continued to knock and scrape against it till morning. Something extraordinary and unprecedented, and not to be disposed of like a branch or potato sack or even a dead sheep. For this something was a body. And the body belonged to Freddie Parr, who lived less than a mile away and was my age, give or take a month.

William Henemann.

Graham Swift on his novels:

I believe it would be a bad day for a writer if he could say, "I know exactly what I'm doing," and I am wary of making statements about my work. If I have any abiding allegiance in my writing it is to the power of the imagination, and I hope my imagination will always surprise and stretch me and take me along unsuspected paths, just as I hope it will continue to bring me up against certain things which I will have to recognise as my own peculiar territory — though that too is a process of discovery, not of preconception.

I have no wariness about the potential of fiction as such, or the privilege and joy (despite many an agony!) of writing it. Where else can you have such licence of expression? Where else can you combine so richly and intimately the world of ideas with the world of concrete reality? And where else can you know — or at least hope — that for each individual reader, each act of collaboration between author and reader, the experience will be something different? I have enormous faith in that invisible collaborative experience, though when I write I never think of the reader. Fiction seems to me only to do in a specialised, concentrated way what we all need to do: to enter, in our minds, experiences other than our own. That is no small or simple thing — all our moral and social pretensions rest upon it. So I have no wariness about fiction's importance either.

Contemporary Writers; Graham Swift.

John Millington SYNGE 1871-1909

1871 *Born near Dublin.*
1889-1892 *A student at Trinity College, Dublin.*
1893 *Went to Germany to study music.*
1895 *Studied languages in Paris.*
1896 *Met Yeats who advised him to go to the Aran Islands.*
1898 *First visit to the Aran Islands.*
1903 The Shadow of the Glen *performed in Dublin.*
1904 Riders to the Sea *performed in Dublin.*
1905 The Well of the Saints *performed at the Abbey Theatre, Dublin.*
1907 The Playboy of the Western World *caused a riot when it was performed at the Abbey Theatre.*
1908 *Publication of* The Tinker's Wedding.
1909 *Died in Dublin.*
1910 Deirdre of the Sorrows *performed.*

Synge was one of the leading figures of the Irish dramatic revival at the beginning of the twentieth century. Encouraged by Yeats, he turned back to the ancient Irish myths and legends in an attempt to re-awaken the heroic vein so central to Irish folklore and to recreate a cultural unity in Ireland.

His plays combine this national and popular inspiration with realism, his favourite theme being the harsh, dull and lonely life of the Aran Islands peasants. Among the hostile and primitive setting, they are shown as crude and violent (hence the criticisms his works provoked at the time) though they never lack sensitivity and humour. A yearning for heroism and adventure as well as a gift for verbal imagination and poetry are the necessary outlets in their lives which constantly hover between imagination and reality.

The Playboy of the Western World (1907)

Christy Mahon arrives in a village in Mayo, pretending that he has killed his father and is a fugitive from justice. The villagers' admiration and their help will turn to scorn when the father comes looking for his son.

PEGEEN Were you off east, young fellow, fighting bloody wars for Kruger and the freedom of the Boers?

CHRISTY I never left my own parish till Tuesday was a week.

PEGEEN *(coming from counter).* He's done nothing, so. *(To Christy)* If you didn't commit murder or a bad, nasty thing, or false coining, or robbery, or butchery, or the like of them, there isn't anything would be worth your troubling for to run from now. You did nothing at all.

CHRISTY *(his feelings hurt).* That's an unkindly thing to be saying to a poor orphaned traveller, has a prison behind him, and hanging before, and hell's gap gaping below.

PEGEEN *(with a sign to the men to be quiet).* You're only saying it. You did nothing at all. A soft lad the like of you wouldn't slit the windpipe of a screeching sow.

CHRISTY *(offended).* You're not speaking the truth.

PEGEEN *(in mock rage).* Not speaking the truth, is it? Would you have me knock the head of you with the butt of the broom?

CHRISTY *(twisting round on her with a sharp cry of horror).* Don't strike me. I killed my poor father, Tuesday was a week, for doing the like of that.

PEGEEN *(with blank amazement).* Is it killed your father?

CHRISTY *(subsiding).* With the help of God I did surely, and that the Holy Immaculate Mother may intercede for his soul.

PHILLY *(retreating with Jimmy).* There's a daring fellow.

JIMMY Oh, glory be to God! →

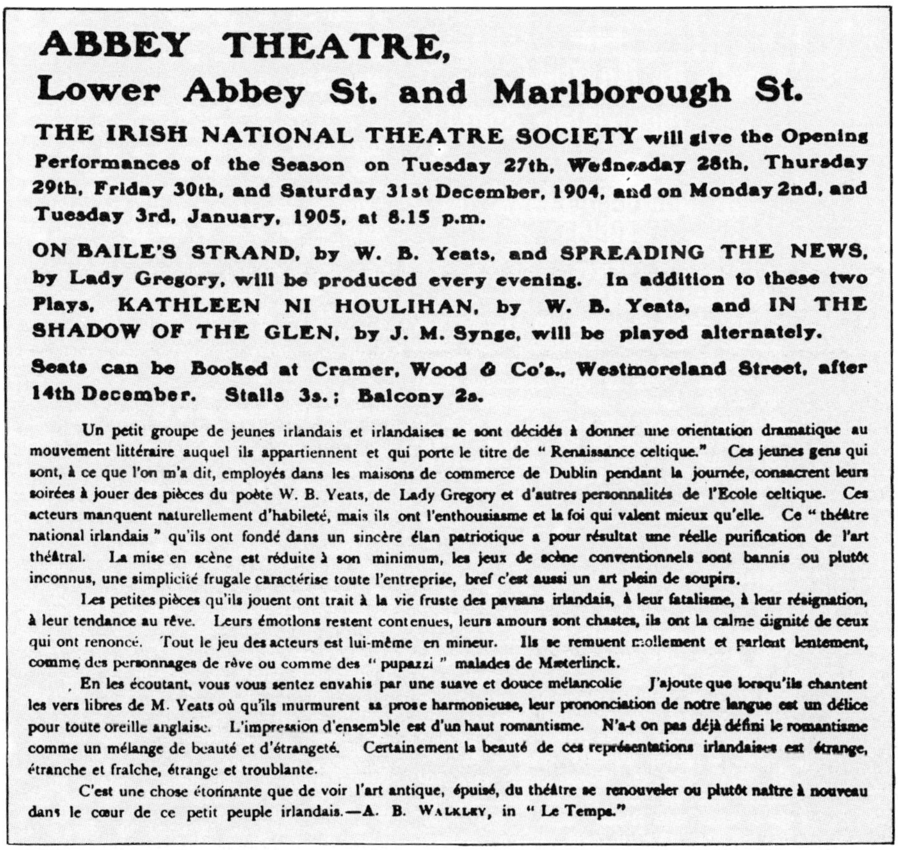

ABBEY THEATRE,

Lower Abbey St. and Marlborough St.

THE IRISH NATIONAL THEATRE SOCIETY will give the Opening Performances of the Season on Tuesday 27th, Wednesday 28th, Thursday 29th, Friday 30th, and Saturday 31st December, 1904, and on Monday 2nd, and Tuesday 3rd, January, 1905, at 8.15 p.m.

ON BAILE'S STRAND, by W. B. Yeats, and SPREADING THE NEWS, by Lady Gregory, will be produced every evening. In addition to these two Plays, KATHLEEN NI HOULIHAN, by W. B. Yeats, and IN THE SHADOW OF THE GLEN, by J. M. Synge, will be played alternately.

Seats can be Booked at Cramer, Wood & Co's., Westmoreland Street, after 14th December. Stalls 3s.; Balcony 2s.

Un petit groupe de jeunes irlandais et irlandaises se sont décidés à donner une orientation dramatique au mouvement littéraire auquel ils appartiennent et qui porte le titre de "Renaissance celtique." Ces jeunes gens qui sont, à ce que l'on m'a dit, employés dans les maisons de commerce de Dublin pendant la journée, consacrent leurs soirées à jouer des pièces du poète W. B. Yeats, de Lady Gregory et d'autres personnalités de l'Ecole celtique. Ces acteurs manquent naturellement d'habileté, mais ils ont l'enthousiasme et la foi qui valent mieux qu'elle. Ce "théâtre national irlandais" qu'ils ont fondé dans un sincère élan patriotique a pour résultat une réelle purification de l'art théâtral. La mise en scène est réduite à son minimum, les jeux de scène conventionnels sont bannis ou plutôt inconnus, une simplicité frugale caractérise toute l'entreprise, bref c'est aussi un art plein de soupirs.

Les petites pièces qu'ils jouent ont trait à la vie fruste des paysans irlandais, à leur fatalisme, à leur résignation, à leur tendance au rêve. Leurs émotions restent contenues, leurs amours sont chastes, ils ont la calme dignité de ceux qui ont renoncé. Tout le jeu des acteurs est lui-même en mineur. Ils se remuent mollement et parlent lentement, comme des personnages de rêve ou comme des "pupazzi" malades de Mæterlinck.

En les écoutant, vous vous sentez envahis par une suave et douce mélancolie J'ajoute que lorsqu'ils chantent les vers libres de M. Yeats où qu'ils murmurent sa prose harmonieuse, leur prononciation de notre langue est un délice pour toute oreille anglaise. L'impression d'ensemble est d'un haut romantisme. N'a-t on pas déjà défini le romantisme comme un mélange de beauté et d'étrangeté. Certainement la beauté de ces représentations irlandaises est étrange, étranche et fraîche, étrange et troublante.

C'est une chose étonnante que de voir l'art antique, épuisé, du théâtre se renouveler ou plutôt naître à nouveau dans le cœur de ce petit peuple irlandais.—A. B. WALKLEY, in "Le Temps."

Contemporary reactions to Synge's plays: An Abbey Theatre Announcement (1904).
Page 316: The performance of The Playboy, *The Evening Herald, 3.1.1905.*

MICHAEL *(with great respect).* That was a hanging crime, mister honey. You should have had good reason for doing the like of that.

CHRISTY *(in a very reasonable tone).* He was a dirty man, God forgive him, and he getting old and crusty, the way I couldn't put up with him at all.

PEGEEN And you shot him dead?

CHRISTY *(shaking his head).* I never used weapons. I've no licence, and I'm a law-fearing man.

MICHAEL It was with a hilted knife maybe? I'm told, in the big world, it's bloody knives they use.

CHRISTY *(loudly, scandalized).* Do you take me for a slaughter-boy?

PEGEEN You never hanged him, the way Jimmy Farrell hanged his dog from the licence[1], and had it screeching and wriggling three hours at the butt of a string, and himself swearing it was a dead dog, and the peelers swearing it had life?

CHRISTY I did not then. I just riz the loy[2] and let fall the edge of it on the ridge of his skull, and he went down at my feet like an empty sack, and never let a grunt or groan from him at all.

MICHAEL *(making a sign to Pegeen to fill Christy's glass).* And what way weren't you hanged, mister? Did you bury him then?

CHRISTY *(considering).* Aye. I buried him then. Wasn't I digging spuds in the field?

MICHAEL And the peelers never followed after you the eleven days that you're out?

"THE PLAYBOY."

LAST NIGHT'S PERFORMANCE

Leads to Further Disorderly Scenes

THE POLICE PRESENT IN FORCE

ANOTHER PROTEST.

Long before 8 o'clock the theatre was packed. The first unpleasant note came before the rise of the curtain on "Riders to the Sea," when an aged gentleman stood up in the balcony and commenced to deliver an address. He said he had come to utter a protest against Mr. Synge's "Playboy" and to demonstrate his respect for the virtue of the West of Ireland. He further stated that he intended to leave the house before the objectionable piece opened.

He was not allowed to carry out his intention, as he suggested, and in a couple of minutes he was outside the theatre on the far side of the street, with a couple of dozen policemen around him. The police were hissed for removing him.

"Riders to the Sea" was again received with wrapt attention, and at its close all the artistes were heartily applauded [illegible]

After a fifteen minutes' interval Mr. W. B. Yeats and Mr. Synge came into the stalls, and the boys at the back rose up in a mass and hissed them. Then when the curtain went up there was an attempt to renew the disorder, but a stentorian voice overhead called for a fair hearing for the work, and, to the tune of "By the Banks of the Zuyder Zee," whistled by the young men at the rere, the comedy was commenced.

For some time things went harmoniously, the only noise being hisses and boohs for Messrs. Yeats and Synge as they left the auditorium for the stage. Mr. Synge returned again in a few minutes, and received a very mixed reception.

RENEWED UPROAR.

There was peace again until the entrance of "Christopher Mahon." Hoarse shouts were raised as he appeared at the doorway, and during his time on the stage it was not possible to hear a fourth of his lines. "Get off, you fraud," and "What do you know of the West of Ireland?" were the cries that punctuated the hissing, groaning, and tramping; and great cheers were raised when Christie retired. When he reappeared he was met with cries of "Lynchehaun" and "Rotten," and amidst a perfect storm of hisses and clatter of feet the curtain fell. All this time Mr. Yeats was continuously running up and down a few flights of steps near the stage door, making exits and entrances without number, and these peripatetic movements became so marked that during the interval there were vigorous requests for "a cake walk by Mr. W. B. Yeats," but that gentleman appeared only to take a quiet seat in the stalls.

When the comedy was resumed the house appeared more inclined to disorder, and in one or two instances it was noticed that the dialogue was expunged at some of the objectionable parts. At each of these places the cry at once came—"Who cut the comedy?" and when Mr. Synge was again seen in the stalls he was told to take his "miserable effort to England at once."

But the first great outburst of disorder came when "Christopher Mahon" proceeded to tell [illegible] father. "Lynchehaun" came freely to many tongues in the house, and as the narrative proceeded it was punctuated with interjections of "Hit him," "Brain him," and "Get him arrested by the bobbies who are behind the scenes." Various melodies were subsequently whistled by the occupants of the pit, and, strange to say, the curtain fell amidst all-round applause.

CHRISTY *(shaking his head).* Never a one of them, and I walking forward facing hog, dog, or devil on the highway of the road.

PHILLY *(nodding wisely).* It's only with a common week-day kind of murderer them lads would be trusting their carcase, and that man should be a great terror when his temper's roused.

MICHAEL He should then. *(To Christy)* And where was it, mister honey, that you did the deed?

CHRISTY *(looking at him with suspicion).* Oh, a distant place, master of the house, a windy corner of high distant hills.

PHILLY *(nodding with approval).* He's a close man, and he's right, surely.

PEGEEN That'd be a lad with the sense of Solomon to have for a pot-boy, Michael James, if it's the truth you're seeking one at all.

PHILLY The peelers is fearing him, and if you'd that lad in the house there isn't one of them would come smelling around if the dogs itself were lapping poteen from the dungpit of the yard.

JIMMY Bravery's a treasure in a lonesome place, and a lad would kill his father, I'm thinking, would face a foxy divil with a pitchpike on the flags of hell.

PEGEEN It's the truth they're saying, and if I'd that lad in the house, I wouldn't be fearing the loosed khaki cutthroats, or the walking dead.

CHRISTY *(swelling with surprise and triumph).* Well, glory be to God!

MICHAEL *(with deference).* Would you think well to stop here and be pot-boy, mister honey, if we gave you good wages, and didn't destroy you with the weight of work?

SHAWN *(coming forward uneasily).* That'd be a queer kind to bring into a decent, quiet household with the like of Pegeen Mike.

PEGEEN *(very sharply).* Will you wisht? Who's speaking to you?

SHAWN *(retreating).* A bloody-handed murderer the like of...

PEGEEN *(snapping at him).* Whisht, I am saying; we'll take no fooling from your like at all. *(To Christy with a honeyed voice)* And you, young fellow, you'd have a right to stop, I'm thinking, for we'd do our all and utmost to content your needs.

CHRISTY *(overcome with wonder).* And I'd be safe this place from the searching law?

MICHAEL You would, surely. If they're not fearing you, itself, the peelers in this place is decent, drouthy poor fellows, wouldn't touch a cur dog and not give warning in the dead of night.

PEGEEN *(very kindly and persuasively).* Let you stop a short while anyhow. Aren't you destroyed walking with your feet in bleeding blisters, and your whole skin needing washing like a Wicklow sheep.

CHRISTY *(looking round with satisfaction).* It's a nice room, and if it's not humbugging me you are, I'm thinking that I'll surely stay.

Act I.

1. *from the licence:* to avoid paying for the dog licence – 2. *loy:* long thin-bladed spade.

Synge and Yeats on The Playboy of the Western World:

This impulse to protect the criminal is universal in the West. It seems partly due to the association between justice and the hated English jurisdiction, but more directly to the primitive feeling of these people, who are never criminals yet always capable of crime, that a man will not do wrong unless he is under the influence of a passion which is as irresponsible as a storm on the sea. If a man has killed his father, and is already sick and broken with remorse, they can see no reason why he should be dragged away and killed by the law.

Such a man, they say, will be quiet all the rest of his life, and if you suggest that punishment is needed as an example, they ask, "Would anyone kill his father if he was able to help it?"

J.M. Synge.

I am certain that, in the long run, his grotesque plays with their lyric beauty, their violent laughter, *The Playboy of the Western World* most of all, will be loved for holding so much of the mind of Ireland. Synge has written of *The Playboy:* "Any one who has lived in real intimacy with the Irish peasantry will know that the wildest sayings in this play are tame indeed compared with the fancies one may hear at any little hillside cottage of Geesala, or Carraroe, or Dingle Bay". It is the strangest, the most beautiful expression in drama of that Irish fantasy which overflowing through all Irish literature that has come out of Ireland itself (compare the fantastic Irish account of the Battle of Clontarf with the sober Norse account) is the unbroken character of Irish genius.

Yeats, *J.M. Synge and the Ireland of his Time.*

George Bernard SHAW 1856-1950

1856 *Born in Dublin (his mother was a singer and he had a good musical education).*
1876 *Settled in London and started writing.*
1879-1883 *Unsuccessfully tried to become a novelist.*
1884 *Became a member of the Fabian society. Began to be well-known as a musical critic.*
1892 *Production of his first play,* Widower's House.
1894 Arms and the Man; Candida.
1898 Plays Pleasant and Unpleasant *published.*
1901 Three Plays for Puritans *published.*
1901-1903 Man and Superman.
1904 John Bull's other Island.
1905 Major Barbara.
1911 Androcles and the Lion.
1912 Pygmalion.
1914 *Very much criticised for his condemnation of war.*
1913-1916 Heartbreak House.
1923 Saint Joan.
1925 *Nobel Prize for literature.*
1929 The Apple Cart.
1950 *Died in Hertforshire.*

A legendary Irish figure, well-known for his verve and audacity, G.B. Shaw was the satirist of his time. With Beatrice and Sidney Webb, he founded the Fabian Society in 1884. They were socialists who advocated progressive social reforms, by democratic means, rather than by revolution. In his plays, true to the tradition of Ibsen, he attacked hypocrisy, snobbery and all kinds of social flaws: the affected language of the upper classes in Pygmalion, *military heroism in* Arms and the Man, *the problem of slums in* Widowers' House, *prostitution in* Mrs Warren's Profession.

G.B.S. was Challenge incarnate – a rampant note of interrogation, eternally asking us uncomfortable questions about our most cherished habits. Why, for instance, we ate meat; Why we vivisected animals; Why we owned property; Why we tolerated such a brainless drama – such unimaginative art – such low wages – such long hours of labour – such inconvenient houses – such adulteration – such dirty cities – such illogical morals – such dead religions – in short, such a chaotic civilisation? And he did not wait for us to answer his innumerable questions; he answered them himself, or provoking a defence by a process of irritation, he smashed our replies with the nicest of dialectical art; tempting us in the pauses of our bewilderment with a new vision of life.

Holbrook Jackson, *The Eighteen Nineties,* Pelican Book. *The Society of Authors as the literary representative of the Estate of Holbrook Jackson.*

His characters are full of vitality and frankness, casting an ironic look at life and symbolizing Shaw's own faith in the possible improvement of mankind.

But Shaw is also the heir of Farquhar, Sheridan and Wilde in his use of a language based on wit, paradox and aphorism. The virulence of his invective reflects the courage of the man who always questioned the accepted values of his time.

Saint Joan (1923)

Joan has just agreed to sign "a solemn recantation of her heresy".

THE INQUISITOR You understand this, Joan?

JOAN *(listless)* It is plain enough, sir.

THE INQUISITOR And it is true?

JOAN It may be true. If it were not true, the fire would not be ready for me in the market-place.

LADVENU *(taking up his pen and a book, and going to her quickly lest she should compromise herself again)* Come, child: let me guide your hand. Take the pen. *(She does so; and they begin to write, using the book as a desk)* J.E.H.A.N.E. So. Now make your mark by yourself.

JOAN *(makes her mark, and gives him back the pen, tormented by the rebellion of her soul against her mind and body)* There!

LADVENU *(replacing the pen on the table, and handing the recantation to Cauchon with a reverence)* Praise be to God, my brothers the lamb has returned to the flock; and the shepherd rejoices in her more than in ninety and nine just persons. *(He returns to his seat).*

THE INQUISITOR *(taking the paper form Cauchon)* We declare thee by this act set free from the danger of excommunication in which thou stoodest. *(He throws the paper down to the table).*

JOAN I thank you.

THE INQUISITOR But because thou hast sinned most presumptuously against God and the Holy Church, and that thou mayst repent thy errors in solitary contemplation, and be shielded from all temptation to return to them, we, for the good of thy soul, and for a penance that may wipe out thy sins and bring thee finally unspotted to the throne of grace, do condemn thee to eat the bread of sorrow and drink the water of affliction to the end of thy earthly days in perpetual imprisonment.

JOAN *(rising in consternation and terrible anger)* Perpetual imprisonment! Am I not then to be set free?

LADVENU *(mildly shocked)* Set free, child, after such wickedness as yours! What are you dreaming of?

JOAN Give me that writing. *(She rushes to the table; snatches up the paper; and tears it into fragments)* Light your fire: do you think I dread it as much as the life of a rat in a hole? My voices were right.

LADVENU Joan! Joan!

JOAN Yes: they told me you were fools *(the word gives great offence)*, and that I was not to listen to your fine words nor trust to your charity. You promised me my life; but you lied *(indignant exclamations)*. You think that life is nothing but not being stone dead. It is not the bread and water I fear: I can live on bread: when have I asked for more? It is no hardship to drink water if the water be clean. Bread has no sorrow for me, and water no affliction. But to shut me from the light of the sky and the sight of the fields and flowers; to chain my feet so that I can never again ride with the soldiers nor climb the hills; to make me breathe foul damp darkness, and keep from me everything that brings me back to the love of God when your wickedness and foolishness tempt me to hate Him: all this is worse than the furnace in the Bible that was heated seven times. I could do without my warhorse; I could drag about in a skirt; I could let the banners and the trumpets and the knights and soldiers pass me and leave me behind as they leave the other women, if only I could still hear the wind in the trees, the larks in the sunshine, the young lambs crying through the healthy frost, and the blessed blessed church bells that send my angel voices floating to me on the wind. But without these things I cannot live; and by your wanting to take them away from me, or from any human creature, I know that your counsel is of the devil, and that mine is of God.

THE ASSESSORS *(in great commotion)* Blasphemy! blasphemy! She is possessed. She said our counsel was of the devil. And hers of God. Monstrous! The devil is in our midst, etc., etc.

D'ESTIVET *(shouting above the din)* She is a relapsed heretic, obstinate, incorrigible, and altogether unworthy of the mercy we have shewn her. I call for her excommunication.

THE CHAPLAIN *(to the Executioner)* Light your fire, man. To the stake with her.

Scene 6.

From G.B. Shaw's Preface to Saint Joan:

THE CONFLICT BETWEEN GENIUS AND DISCIPLINE

With all this in mind, consider the career of Joan. She was a village girl, in authority over sheep and pigs, dogs and chickens, and to some extent over her father's hired laborers when he hired any, but over no one else on earth. Outside the farm she had no authority, no prestige, no claim to the smallest deference. Yet she ordered everybody about, from her uncle to the king, the archbishop, and the military General Staff. Her uncle obeyed her like a sheep, and took her to the castle of the local commander, who, on being ordered about, tried to assert himself, but soon collapsed and obeyed. And so on up to the king, as we have seen. This would have been unbearably irritating even if her orders had been offered as rational solutions of the desperate difficulties in which her social superiors found themselves just then. But they were not so offered. Nor were they offered as the expression of Joan's arbitrary will. It was never "I say so" but always "God says so".

JOAN AS THEOCRAT

Leaders who take that line have no trouble with some people, and no end of trouble with others. They need never fear a lukewarm reception. Either they are messengers of God, or they are blasphemous impostors. In the Middle Ages the general belief in witchcraft greatly intensified this contrast, because when an apparent miracle happened (as in the case of the wind changing at Orleans) it proved the divine mission to the credulous, and proved a contract with the devil to the sceptical. All through, Joan had to depend on those who accepted her as an incarnate angel against those who added to an intense resentment of her presumption a bigoted abhorrence of her as a witch. To this abhorrence we must add the extreme irritation of those who did not believe in the voices, and regarded her as a liar and impostor. (...)

And as she met all remonstrances and all criticisms, not with arguments or persuasion, but with a flat appeal to the authority of God and a claim to be in God's special confidence, she must have seemed, to all who were not infatuated by her, so insufferable that nothing but an unbroken chain of overwhelming successes in the military and political field could have saved her from the wrath that finally destroyed her.

UNBROKEN SUCCESS ESSENTIAL IN THEOCRACY

To forge such a chain she needed to be the King, the Archbishop of Rheims, the Bastard of Orleans, and herself into the bargain; and that was impossible. From the moment when she failed to stimulate Charles to follow up his coronation with a swoop on Paris she was lost. The fact that she insisted on this whilst the king and the rest timidly and foolishly thought they could square the Duke of Burgundy, and effect a combination with him against the English, made her a terrifying nuisance to them; and from that time onward she could do nothing but prowl about the battlefields waiting for some lucky chance to sweep the captains into a big move. But it was to the enemy that the chance came: she was taken prisoner by the Burgundians fighting before Compiègne, and at once discovered that she had not a friend in the political world. Had she escaped she would probably have fought on until the English were gone, and then had to shake the dust of the court off her feet, and retire to Domrémy as Garibaldi had to retire to Caprera.

ibid.

In Murder in the Cathedral, *T.S. Eliot relates the story of another martyr, Thomas à Beckett, archbishop of Canterbury, killed by four knights because he had opposed Henry II's measures against the clergy. In Eliot's play, Thomas Beckett prepares himself to his fate, trying to suppress his desire for fame and canonization. Compare his attitude with that of Joan.*
The following passage describes Beckett's dismissal of the first Tempter.

TEMPTER What, my Lord, now that you recover
Favour with the King, shall we say that summer's over
Or that the good time cannot last?
Fluting in the meadows, viols in the hall,
Laughter and apple-blossom floating on the water,
Singing at nightfall, whispering in chambers,
Fires devouring the winter season,
Eating up the darkness, with wit and wine and wisdom!
Now that the King and you are in amity,
Clergy and laity may return to gaiety,
Mirth and sportfulness need not walk warily.
THOMAS You talk of seasons that are past. I remember
Not worth forgetting.
TEMPTER And of the new season.
Spring has come in winter. Snow in the branches
Shall float as sweet as blossoms. Ice along the ditches
Mirror the sunlight. Love in the orchard
Send the sap shooting. Mirth matches melancholy.
THOMAS We do not know very much of the future
Except that from generation to generation
The same things happen again and again.
Men learn little from others' experience.
But in the life of one man, never
The same time returns. Sever
The cord, shed the scale. Only
The fool, fixed in his folly, may think
He can turn the wheel on which he turns.
TEMPTER My Lord, a nod is as good as a wink.
A man will often love what he spurns.
For the good times past, that are come again
I am your man.
THOMAS Not in this train
Look to your behaviour. You were safer
Think of penitence and follow your master.
TEMPTER Not at this gait!
If you go so fast, others may go faster.
Your Lordship is too proud!
The safest beast is not the one that roars most loud,
This was not the way of the King our master!
You were not used to be so hard upon sinners
When they were your friends. Be easy, man!
The easy man lives to eat the best dinners.
Take a friend's advice. Leave well alone,
Or your goose may be cooked and eaten to the bone.
THOMAS You come twenty years too late.
TEMPTER Then I leave you to your fate.
I leave you to the pleasures of your higher vices,
Which will have to be paid for at higher prices.
Farewell, my Lord, I do not wait upon ceremony,
I leave as I came, forgetting all acrimony,
Hoping that your present gravity
Will find excuse for my humble levity.
If you will remember me, my Lord, at your prayers,
I'll remember you at kissing-time below the stairs.
THOMAS Leave-well-alone, the springtime fancy,
So one thought goes whistling down the wind.
The impossible is still temptation,
The impossible, the undesirable,
Voices under sleep, waking a dead world,
So that the mind may not be whole in the present. *(Enter Second Tempter.)*

T. S. Eliot, *Murder in the Cathedral.*

Harold PINTER born 1930

1930	*Born in London, in a Jewish family of the East End.*
1939-1944	*Evacuated to Cornwall.*
1948	*Given a grant to study at the Royal Academy of Dramatic Art.*
1949	*Attended the Central School of Speech and Drama.*
1951-1952	*Toured Ireland with an acting company, playing Shakespeare.*
1957	*Production of* The Room.
1958	*Production of* The Birthday Party.
1959	A Slight Ache *broadcast by the BBC.*
1960	*Production of* The Dumb Waiter, The Caretaker. A Night Out *and* The Dwarfs *broadcast by the BBC.*
1961	The Collection *performed.*
1962	*Wrote the screenplay of Losey's film* The Servant.
1963	The Lover *televised.*
1965	The Homecoming *produced.*
1968	The Tea-Party *and* The Basement *(originally for the radio) produced on stage.*
1969	*Production of* Landscape *and* Silence.
1971	*Production of* Old Times.
1975	*Production of* No Man's Land.
1978	Betrayal.
1980	The Hothouse.
1981	Family Voices.
1982	Other Places.
1984	One for the Road.
1988	Mountain Language.
1989	The Heat of the Day.
1990	The Dwarfs (*a novel*).

Influenced by Kafka, Beckett and Ionesco, Harold Pinter is a playwright who blends humour and tragedy, the banal and the unusual. His characters are often grotesque – prostitutes, tramps, over-possessive mothers – and the situations absurd: a quiet lodger in a boarding-house who, for no given reason, is cross-examined and carried away by two sinister characters in The Birthday Party; *two hired killers who are waiting for their instructions and finally discover one of them is the next intended victim in* The Dumb Waiter. *The dominant atmosphere is one of menace. Hunted and anxious, the characters take refuge in a confined world – a room, a basement – where they fear the intrusion of an alien element which would threaten their predictable existence. Threats lurk everywhere behind the apparent monotony of their lives, revealing their inability to communicate.*

Feeling trapped and terrified, people react by threatening the others in their turn, as if invading their territories gave them an illusion of power, of getting a grasp on reality. It is this wish to dominate which underlies the racism of so many of the characters.

Pinter's plays are striking for their economy of means: few characters and little setting are sufficient to create an immediate feeling of tension. But it is mainly the language that conveys this tension: the use of everyday speech, trite expressions, clichés and silences hides man's anxiety and his difficulty to relate to others.

Request Stop (1959)

A queue at a Request Bus Stop. A Woman at the head, with a Small Man in a raincoat next to her, two other Women and a Man.

WOMAN *(to Small Man)* I beg your pardon, what did you say?
(Pause)
All I asked you was if I could get a bus from here to Shepherds Bush.
(Pause)
Nobody asked you to start making insinuations.
(Pause)
Who do you think you are?
(Pause)
Huh. I know your sort, I know your type. Don't worry, I know all about people like you.
(Pause)
We can all tell where you come from. They're putting your sort inside every day of the week. All I've got to do, is report you, and you'd be standing in the dock in next to no time. One of my best friends is a plain clothes detective.
(Pause)
I know all about it. Standing there as if butter wouldn't melt in your mouth. Meet you in a dark alley it'd be... another story. *(To the others, who stare into space.)* You heard what this

man said to me. All I asked him was if I could get a bus from here to Shepherds Bush. *(To him)* I've got witnesses, don't you worry about that.

(Pause)

Impertinence.

(Pause)

Ask a man a civil question he treats you like a threepenny bit. *(To him)* I've got better things to do, my lad, I can assure you. I'm not going to stand here and be insulted on a public highway. Anyone can tell you're a foreigner. I was born just around the corner. Anyone can tell you're just up from the country for a bit of a lark. I know your sort.

(Pause. She goes to a Lady)

Excuse me, Lady. I'm thinking of taking this man up to the magistrate's court, you heard him make that crack, would you like to be a witness?

(The Lady steps into the road.)

LADY Taxi...

WOMAN We know what sort she is. *(Back to position)* I was the first in this queue.

(Pause)

Born just round the corner. Born and bred. These people from the country haven't the faintest idea of how to behave. Peruvians. You're bloody lucky I don't put you on a charge. You ask a straightforward question –

(The others suddenly thrust out their arms at a passing bus. They run off left after it. The Woman, alone, clicks her teeth and mutters. A man walks from the right to the stop, and waits. She looks at him out of the corner of her eye. At length she speaks shyly, hesitantly, with a slight smile.)

Excuse me. Do you know if I can get a bus from here... to Marble Arch?

Review Sketches, Plays : Two Methuen Ltd.
By permission of Associated Book Publishers Ltd.

Harold Pinter on his plays:

● INTERVIEWER Peter Hall, who has directed many of your plays, says that they rely on precise verbal form and rhythm, and when you write "pause" it means something other than "silence", and three dots are different form a full stop. Is his sensitivity to this kind of writing responsible for your working well together?

PINTER Yes, it is, very much so. I do pay great attention to those points you just mentioned. Hall once held a dot and pause rehearsal for the actors in *The Homecoming*. Although it sounds bloody pretentious it was apparently very valuable.

INTERVIEWER Why do you think the conversations in your plays are so effective?

PINTER I don't know, I think possibly it's because people fall back on anything they can lay their hands on verbally to keep away from the danger of knowing, and of being known.

INTERVIEWER There's a sense of terror and a threat of violence in most of your plays. Do you see the world as an essentially violent place?

PINTER The world *is* a pretty violent place, it's as simple as that, so any violence in the plays comes out quite naturally. It seems to me an essential and inevitable factor.

I think what you're talking about began in *The Dumb Waiter*, which from my point of view is a relatively simple piece of work. The violence is really only an expression of the question of dominance and subservience, which is possibly a repeated theme in my plays. I wrote a short story a long time ago called "The Examination", and my ideas of violence carried on from there. That short story dealt very explicitly with two people in one room having a battle of an unspecified nature, in which the question was one of who was dominant at what point and how they were going to be dominant and what tools they would use to achieve dominance and how they would try to undermine the other person's dominance. A threat is constantly there: it's got to do with this question of being in the uppermost position, or attempting to be. That's something of what attracted me to do the screenplay of *The Servant*, which was someone else's story, you know. I wouldn't call this violence so much as a battle for positions, it's a very common, everyday thing.

"Harold Pinter: An Interview" in *Writers at Work: The Paris Review Interviews, Third Series* ed. by George Plimpton.

● I feel that instead of any inability to communicate there is a deliberate evasion of communication. Communication itself between people is so frightening that rather than do that there is continual cross-talk, a continual talking about other things rather than what is at the root of their relationship.

Arnold WESKER born 1932

1932 *Born in an East-End Russian-Jewish family. His father was a tailor, his mother often earned some money by helping in kitchens.*
1945 *Joined an amateur theatrical group.*
1948-1952 *Several jobs and national service in the R.A.F.*
1952-1958 *Worked on a variety of jobs (plumber's mate, farm labourer, pastrycook in Paris).*
1956 *Wrote* The Kitchen *(perf. 1959); saw* Look Back in Anger *(J. Osborne) and wrote* Chicken Soup with Barley *(perf. 1958).*
1958 *Wrote* Roots *(perf. 1959).*
1959 *Wrote* I'm Talking about Jerusalem *(perf. 1960).*
1960 *Wrote* Chips with Everything *(perf. 1962).*
1961 *Spent a month in prison for his anti-nuclear activities. Became director of « Centre 42 » (to popularize the arts). Wrote* Menace, *a TV play.*
1964 *Wrote* Their Very Own and Golden City.
1965 *Production of* The Four Seasons.
1968 *Wrote* The Friends *(perf. 1970).*
1970 *Wrote* The Old Ones; *dissolution of "Centre 42".*
1973 The Wedding Feast.
1974 The Merchant.
1978 Love Letters on Blue Paper.
1981 Caritas.
1982 Mothers: Four Portraits.
1983 Annie, Anna, Annabella.
1984 Sullied Hand; Yardsale.
1985 One More Ride on the Merry-Go-Round.
1986 Whatever Happened to Betty Lemon; When God Wanted a Son.
1988 The Mistress.
1990 Three Women Talking; Letter to a Daughter.
1991 Blood Libel.
1992 Wild Spring.

Arnold Wesker is a working class dramatist, a socialist who writes with passion and honesty of the people he knows best: Norfolk labourers, cooks, Jewish communists, members of Trade-Unions.

His chief aim is to use his plays as weapons against the social evils and the hypocrisy he exposes; at the same time he has tried to encourage a popular culture (mainly through "Centre 42") to help working-class people enjoy life and art.

The example of his trilogy can best give an idea of his main themes. The first play, Chicken Soup with Barley, *presents the working-class situation from 1936 to the present day. Their hopes, enthusiasm and militancy before the war give way to disillusion and a loss of faith in the 1950s with the Welfare State. In the two plays that follow, Wesker shows us individual reactions to this problem.* Roots *relates the slow evolution of a young woman, Beatie Bryant, towards social awareness and self realization, while* I'm Talking About Jerusalem *is about the failure of Dave and Ada's attempt to create a sort of socialist community (on lines derived from William Morris).*

It is always through realism, the presentation of real people in real situations, that Wesker conveys his moral and political message.

My people are not caricatures. They are real (though fiction), and if they are portrayed as caricatures the point of all these plays will be lost. The picture I have drawn is a harsh one, yet my tone is not one of disgust – nor should it be in the presentation of the plays. I am at one with these people: it is only that I am annoyed, with them and myself.

A. Wesker.

Chicken Soup with Barley (1956)

In Act I, the Kahn family has been shown as active and militant, particularly against the rise of fascism in 1936. This scene takes place at the beginning of Act II. The time is now June 1946. Sarah and Harry Kahn are talking with their daughter Ada and their son Ronnie.

ADA (...) When Dave comes back we shall leave London and live in the country. That'll be our socialism. Remember this, Ronnie: the family should be a unit, and your work and your life should be part of one existence, not something hacked about by a bus queue and office hours. A man should see, know, and love his job. Don't you want to feel your life? Savour it gently? In the country we shall be somewhere where the air doesn't smell of bricks and the kids can grow up without seeing grandparents who are continually shouting at each other.

SARAH Ada, Ada.

RONNIE And no more political activity?

ADA No more political activity.

RONNIE I bet Dave won't agree to that. Dave fought in Spain. He won't desert humanity like that.

ADA Humanity! Ach!

RONNIE Listen to her! With a Labour majority in the House? And two of our own Party members? It's only just beginning.

ADA It's always only just beginning for the Party. Every defeat is victory and every victory is the beginning.

RONNIE But it is, it is the beginning. Plans for town and country planning. New cities and schools and hospitals. *(Jumping up on chair to Harry's facetious applause).* Nationalization! National health! Think of it, the whole country is going to be organized to cooperate instead of tear at each other's throat. That's what I said to them in a public speech at school and all the boys cheered and whistled and stamped their feet — and blew raspberries.

ADA I dot not believe in the right to organize people. And anyway I'm not so sure that I love them enough to *want* to organize them.

SARAH *(sadly)* This — from *you*, Ada? You used to be such an organizer.

ADA I'm tired, Mother. I spent eighteen months waiting for Dave to return from Spain and now I've waited six years for him to come home from a war against Fascism and I'm tired. Six years in and out of offices, auditing books and working with young girls who are morons — lipsticked, giggling morons. And Dave's experience is the same — fighting with men who he says did not know what the war was about. Away from their wives they behaved like animals. In fact they wanted to get away from their wives in order to behave like animals. Give them another war and they'd run back again. Oh yes! the service killed any illusions Dave may have once had about the splendid and heroic working class.

HARRY *(pedantically)* This is the talk of an intellectual, Ada.

ADA God in heaven save me from the claptrap of a threepenny pamphlet. How many friends has the Party lost because of lousy, meaningless titles they gave to people. *He* was a bourgeois intellectual, *he* was a Trotskyist, *he* was a reactionary Social Democrat. Whisht! Gone!

HARRY But wasn't it true? Didn't these people help to bolster a rotten society?

ADA The only rotten society is an industrial society. It makes a man stand on his head and then convinces him he is good-looking. I'll tell you something. It wasn't the Trotskyist or the Social Democrat who did the damage. It was progress! There! Progress! And nobody dared fight progress.

Act II, Scene 1.

Another look back on the past.
Compare the excerpt from the Wesker trilogy with the following passage from John Arden's The Waters of Babylon:

PAUL *(to Krank, sobbing)* You said to me, you said to me, that you were two years in the Buchenwald Concentration Camp. Did you not say it?

KRANK Certainly I said it. It was the truth.

PAUL But he says...

KRANK Well, what does he say?

PAUL *(with a tremendous effort)* He says to me, that you were in Buchenwald, yes, but Sigismanfred, you were no prisoner.

KRANK Henry Ginger, words of truth, how should Henry Ginger know? He was not there?

HENRY GINGER No, I wasn't, no. But what about them as was, what about Constantin; what about Ranewski; or Joachim Klarakiewicz, what about Braunstein, you know him, a little Jew with three warts under his jowl; what about Jean-Pierre Dumaurice, I think he was a Frenchman?

KRANK So? What about them?

HENRY GINGER All of them was once in Buchenwald. Now then, you see, all of them are living in London. They've told me some curious things, Mr. Krank. When you was in Buchenwald? You used to be...

PAUL You used to be...

KRANK I used to be a German soldier in Buchenwald. I helped to garrison the camp. And my principal occupation was to clean the officers' boots: but nevertheless, I was a German soldier, a volunteer, I used to wear the grey uniform, all right now, Paul, you have heard Henry Ginger's truth, all right, you shoot me.

PAUL *(terribly upset)* Why, I do not want to shoot you. What is the good to shoot you? All I want – I want to shoot myself. You have been my friend. I *must* understand this. *(He lowers the gun.)*

KRANK You know, there's nothing difficult, psychological, obscure.
It's a most easy story, no very long. I will tell you.
1939, my part of Poland is invaded by the Russians,
So I find it convenient to join the Russian Army
I clean the officers' boots. Amusing. Then, 1941.
My part of the Russian Army is destroyed by the Germans.
So I find it convenient – so, once again, I find...
I clean the officers' boots. Amusing? I did not ask

To be posted to Buchenwald. That was the time of the world
That I know to myself I have no year, town, or family,
The house of Krank is to be always an empty house.
Eighty people in it, lodgers? For me it is empty.
In Buchenwald was I prisoner, was I convenient soldier...
So many thousands of people all lost in that cold field.
Who knows what I was?

PAUL We know what you were.

KRANK But I don't know what *you* are.
Or you, Henry Ginger, or all the rest of you,
With your pistols, and your orations,
And your bombs in my private house,
And your fury, and your national pride and honour.
This is the lunacy.
(Exit Henry Ginger furtively.)
This was the cause, the carrying through
Of all the insensate war
This is the rage and purposed madness of your lives,
That *I*, Krank, do not know. I *will* not know it,
Because, if I know it, from that tight day forward,
I am a man of time, place, society, and accident:
Which is what I must not be. Do you understand me?

PAUL No.

KRANK *(violently)* The world is running mad in every direction.
It is quicksilver, shattered, here, here, here, here,
All over the floor. Go on, hurtle after it,
Chase it, dear Paul. But I choose to follow
Only such fragments as I can easily catch,
I catch them, I keep them such time as I choose,
Then roll them away down and follow another.
Is that philosophy? It is a reason, anyway,
Why I am content to hold such a disgusting lodging house,
And why I'd be content to get you and your bombs out of it.

PAUL I do not know what to think of you. I was going to shoot you, but how can I shoot a man who does not understand why I am shooting him?

Act III.

First published in Penguin Books Ltd 1964.

About John Arden :

Arden permits himself, in his treatment of the characters and situations in his plays, to be less influenced by moral preconceptions than any other writer in the British theatre today. (...)

Where do we stand in a situation which seems to deny the very possibility of heroism or villainy? The question may not be all that worrying on a purely personal level – one could argue that such concepts as heroism and villainy have little meaning in Pinter's work, for example – but Arden brings us face to face with it in its baldest form by writing plays which appear to be about general social, moral, and political issues: colour prejudice and prostitution, social clashes on a housing estate, pacifism, the treatment of old age. Arden the man no doubt feels strongly about all these subjects, or he would hardly choose to write about them, but his dramatist's instinct absolutely prevents him from stacking things in favour of the characters whose opinions most closely resemble his own; in an interview he has expressed "grave objections to being presented with a character on the stage whom you know to be the author's mouthpiece". (...)

In other words, in all Arden's plays the characters we meet are first and foremost just people: not concepts cast into a vaguely human mould, with built-in labels saying "good" or "bad", "hero" or "villain", to help us into the right grooves.

J. Russel Taylor, *Anger & After.*

Methuen and Co. Ltd.
By permission of Associated Book Publishers Ltd.

John Arden (born 1930) also aimed at illustrating everyday life in poetic terms, drawing on English cultural traditions and folklore; hence the verse and ballads that blend with the prose of his plays.

Tom STOPPARD born 1937

1937 *Born in Czechoslovakia.*

1939-1946 *Family moved to Singapore, where his father died, then to Darjeeling where he attended a multi-racial school.*

1946 *Moved to Nottinghamshire after his mother's remarriage to Kenneth Stoppard.*

1954-1960 *Worked as a journalist, specializing in theatre and film.*

Tom Stoppard's style of drama has been called "philosophical farce," for his plays deal with serious issues in the context of comedy. He uses brilliant dialogue and verbal exuberance — puns, paradox, stichomythia, slapstick — to comment on philosophical and existential issues: the function of art, the existence of God, the relationship between words and reality, the illusory nature of perception, free will versus fate, and, most of all, the study of alienation and

1960-1962 *Resigned from his job and wrote* A Walk on the Water (*later called* Enter a Free Man).
1963-1964 *Wrote short stories and two radio plays.*
1965 *Married (two sons; divorced 1971).* The Gamblers.
1966 Rosencrantz and Guildenstern Are Dead. Lord Malquist and Mr Moon *(novel) published.*
1968 The Real Inspector Hound.
1969 Albert's Bridge; If You're Glad I'll Be Frank.
1970 After Magritte.
1971 Dogg's Our Pet.
1972 Jumpers. *Married Dr Miriam Moore-Robinson (two sons).*
1974 Travesties.
1976 Dirty Linen; New-Found-Land.
1977 *Went to Moscow and Leningrad with the assistant director of Amnesty, then to Prague.* Every Good Boy Deserves Favour.
1978 Night and Day.
1979 Dogg's Hamlet; Cahoot's Macbeth.
1982 The Real Thing.
1984 Rough Crossing.
1988 Hapgood.
1989 Artist Descending a Staircase.
1993 Arcadia.

anguish, a theme close to Beckett's absurd view of life.

Many of his plays make use of parody. Travesties, *a reflection on art and a parody of Oscar Wilde, shows Lenin, Joyce and Tristan Tzara in Zürich during World War I;* The Real Inspector Hound *is a burlesque of thrillers; and* Jumpers *parodies modern philosophy. Tom Stoppard also turned to political issues in plays like* Every Good Boy Deserves Favour, *which is set in a prison hospital in the Soviet Union. As for* Rosencrantz and Guildenstern Are Dead, *the two heroes are two minor characters in Shakespeare's* Hamlet. *Summoned to the court to investigate Prince Hamlet's mental illness, they pass the time waiting, telling jokes and reflecting upon life. Throughout the play they are conscious that they have no control over their destinies, that they are only actors performing predestined roles in a play which bewilders them.*

Rosencrantz and Guildenstern Are Dead (1966)

This is the second meeting between Rosencrantz, Guildenstern and the Player, the leader of a travelling acting troupe that will reenact the murder of Hamlet's father at the palace.

PLAYER *(bitterly)*: You left us.

GUILDENSTERN: Ah! I'd forgotten — you performed a dramatic spectacle on the way. Yes, I'm sorry we had to miss it.

PLAYER *(bursts out)*: We can't look each other in the face! *(Pause, more in control.)* You don't understand the humiliation of it — to be tricked out of the single assumption which makes our existence viable — that somebody is *watching*... The plot was two corpses gone before we caught sight of ourselves, stripped naked in the middle of nowhere and pouring ourselves down a bottomless well.

ROSENCRANTZ: Is *that* thirty-eight?

PLAYER *(lost)*: There we were — demented children mincing about in clothes that no one ever wore, speaking as no man ever spoke, swearing love in wigs and rhymed couplets, killing each other with wooden swords, hollow protestations of faith hurled after empty promises of vengeance — and every gesture, every pose, vanishing into the thin unpopulated air. We ransomed our dignity to the clouds, and the uncomprehending birds listened. *(He rounds on them.)* Don't you see?! We're *actors* — we're the opposite of people! *(They recoil nonplussed, his voice calms.)* Think, in your head, *now*, think of the most ... *private... secret... intimate* thing you have ever done secure in the knowledge of its privacy... *(He gives them — and the audience — a good pause.* Rosencrantz *takes on a shifty look.)* Are you thinking of it? *(He strikes with his voice and his head.) Well, I saw you do it! (*Rosencrantz *leaps up, dissembling madly.)*

ROS*:* You never! It's a lie! *(He catches himself with a giggle in a vacuum and sits down again.)*

PLAYER: We're actors... We pledged our identities, secure in the conventions of our trade: that someone would be watching. And then, gradually, no one was. We were caught, high and dry. It was not until the murderer's long soliloquy that we were able to look around; frozen as we were in profile, our eyes searched you out, first confidently, then hesitantly, then desperately as each patch of turf, each log, every exposed corner in every direction proved uninhabited, and all the while the murderous King addressed the horizon with his dreary interminable guilt... Our heads began to move, wary as lizards, the corpse of unsullied Rosalinda peeped through his fingers, and the King faltered. Even then, habit and a stubborn trust that our audience spied upon us from behind the nearest bush, forced our bodies to blunder on long after they had emptied of meaning, until like runaway carts they dragged to a halt. No one came forward. No one shouted at us. The silence was unbreakable, it imposed itself upon us; it was obscene. We took off our crowns and swords and cloth of gold and moved silent on the road to Elsinore.

(Silence. Then Guildenstern *claps solo with slow measured irony.)*

GUIL: Brilliantly re-created — if these eyes could weep! ... Rather strong on metaphor, mind you. No criticism — only a matter of taste. And so here you are — with a vengeance. That's a figure of speech ... isn't it? Well let's say we've made up for it, for you may have no doubt whom to thank for your performance at the court.

ROS: We are counting on you to take him out of himself. You are the pleasures which we draw him on to — *(he escapes a fractional giggle but recovers immediately)* and by that I don't mean your usual filth; you can't treat royalty like people with normal perverted desires. They know nothing of that and you know nothing of them, to your mutual survival. So give him a good clean show suitable for all the family, or you can rest assured you'll be playing the tavern tonight.

GUIL: Or the night after.

ROS: Or not.

PLAYER: We already have an entry here. And always have had.

GUIL: You've played for him before?

PLAYER: Yes, sir.

ROS: And what's *his* bent?

PLAYER: Classical.

ROS: Saucy!

GUIL: What will you play?

PLAYER: "The Murder of Gonzago."

GUIL: Full of fine cadence and corpses.

PLAYER: Pirated from the Italian...

ROS: What is it about?

PLAYER: It's about a King and Queen...

GUIL: Escapism! What else?

PLAYER: Blood —

GUIL: — Love and rhetoric.

PLAYER: Yes. *(Going.)*

GUIL: Where are you going?

PLAYER: I can come and go as I please.

GUIL: You're evidently a man who knows his way around.

PLAYER: I've been here before.

GUIL: We're still finding our feet.

PLAYER: I should concentrate on not losing your heads.

GUIL: Do you speak from knowledge?

PLAYER: Precedent.

GUIL: You've been here before.

PLAYER: And I know which way the wind is blowing.

GUIL: Operating on two levels, are we?! How clever! I expect it comes naturally to you, being in the business so to speak. *(The* Player*'s grave face does not change. He makes to move off again.* Guildenstern *for the second time cuts him off.)*

The truth is, we value your company, for want of any other. We have been left so much to our own devices — after a while one welcomes the uncertainty of being left to other people's.

PLAYER: Uncertainty is the normal state. You're nobody special.

(He makes to leave again. Guildenstern *loses his cool.)*

GUIL: But for God's sake what are we supposed to *do*?!

PLAYER: Relax. Respond. That's what people do. You can't go through life questioning your situation at every turn.

GUIL: But we don't know what's going on, or what to do with ourselves. We don't know how to *act*.

PLAYER: Act natural. You know why you're here at least.

GUIL: We only know what we're told, and that's little enough. And for all we know it isn't even true.

PLAYER: For all anyone knows, nothing is. Everything has to be taken on trust; truth is only that which is taken to be true. It's the currency of living. There may be nothing behind it, but it doesn't make any difference so long as it is honoured. One acts on assumptions.

"When I encountered Magritte's paintings I responded to their humour immediately and I enjoyed his jokes and I also liked the fact that he painted things very carefully," said Tom Stoppard in an interview.

Like Magritte, whom he greatly admires, Stoppard is interested in perception and in the interpretation of reality. One of his plays, After Magritte, *opens on a tableau which seems directly inspired by Magritte's* "L'Assassin menacé" *(a woman is lying on her back on an ironing board, wearing a bathing cap and with a bowler hat on her stomach; another character, wearing nothing but rubber fishing waders, is blowing into a lamp, a Police Constable is looking at the scene through the window...). But the title of the play is justified in other ways: the characters discuss an exhibition of Magritte's paintings and most of the dialogue focuses on the interpretation of a strange sight the family has seen in the street. The explanations given at the end of the play will make these bizarre happenings appear quite normal, thus making the point that ordinary events can hide behind what may seem surrealistically fantastic.*

Magritte, The Menaced Assassin *(L'Assassin menacé), 1926. Oil on canvas. New York, The Museum of Modern Art, The Kay Sage Fund. Ph. Artephot, Paris. ADAGP Paris 1993.*

Tom Stoppard on his play Rosencrantz and Guildenstern Are Dead:

[Rosencrantz and Guildenstern] are more than just bit players in another play. There are certain things which they bring on with them, particularly the fact that they end up dead without really, as far as any textual evidence goes, knowing why. Hamlet's assumption that they were privy to Claudius's plot is entirely gratuitous. As far as their involvement in Shakespeare's text is concerned they are told very little about what is going on and much of what they are told isn't true. So I see them much more clearly as a couple of bewildered innocents rather than a couple of henchmen, which is the usual way they are depicted in productions of *Hamlet...*

Interview with Giles Gordon, *Transatlantic Review*, 29 (1968)

... on language:

[I have] an enormous love of language itself. For a lot of writers the language they use is merely a fairly efficient tool. For me the particular use of a particular word in the right place, or a group of words in the right order, to create a particular effect is important; it gives me more pleasure than to make a point which I might consider to be profound.

"Something to Declare," *Sunday Times*, 25.2.1968

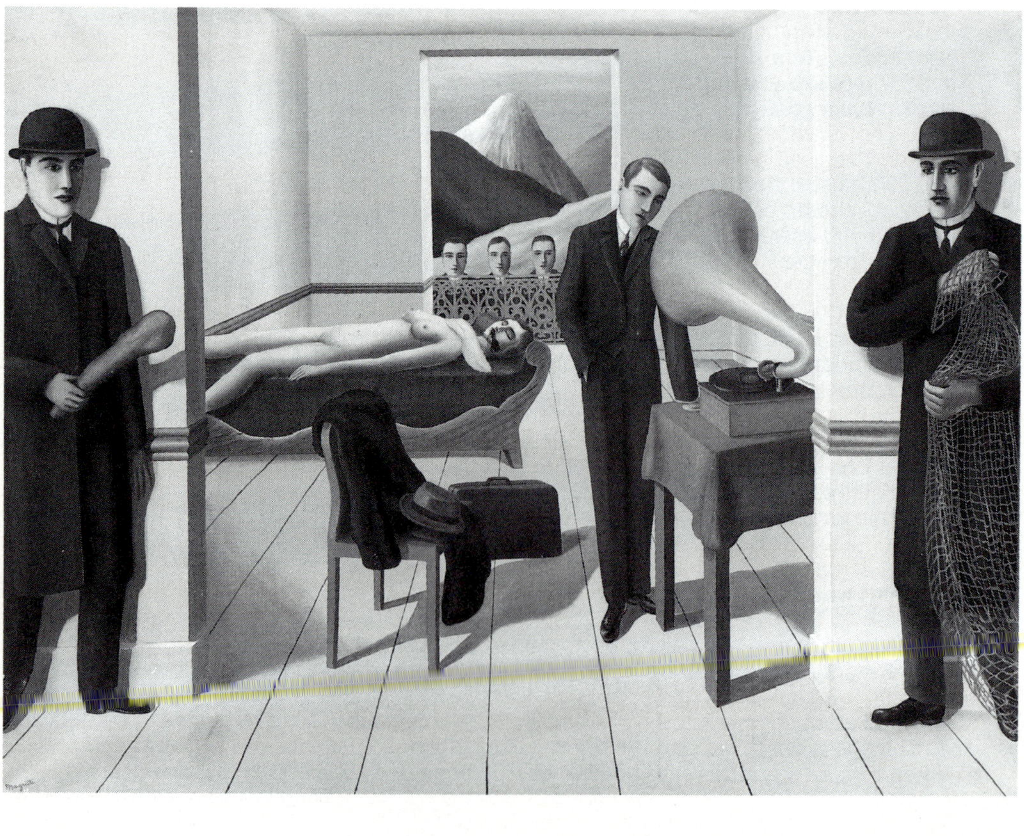

... and on his technique:

I tend to write through a series of small, large and microscopic ambushes — which might consist of a body falling out of a cupboard, or simply an unexpected word in a sentence. But my preoccupation as a writer, which possibly betokens a degree of insecurity, takes the form of contriving to inject some sort of interest and colour into every line, rather than counting on the general situation having a general interest which will hold an audience.

Interview with R. Hudson, S. Itzin and S. Trussler, *Theatre Quarterly*, IV, 14 (1974)

What I try to do, is to end up by contriving the perfect marriage between the play of ideas and farce or perhaps even high comedy. *Ibid.*

Edward BOND born 1934

1934 *Born in London, from a working-class background.*
1953-1955 *Served in the British Army.*
1962 The Pope's Wedding.
1965 Saved.
1968 Narrow Road to the Deep North.
1971 Lear.
1973 The Sea; Bingo.
1976 The Fool.
1978 The Bundle; The Woman.
1979 The Worlds.
1981 Restoration.
1982 Summer.
1985 The War Plays.
1993 Olly's Prison.

Edward Bond is a controversial playwright, a moralist and a committed socialist, whose characters appear as the victims of an irrational society which renders them incapable of controlling their desires and violence. His starkly powerful plays all contain scenes of harrowing violence and carnage: the stoning of a baby in Saved; *murder and rape in* Lear, *Bond's adaptation of Shakespeare's play; a cannibalistic Victorian society — seen as the root of our modern world — and a lesbian Queen Victoria in* Early Morning; *the irrationality of the Elizabethan world order leading Shakespeare to suicide in* Bingo; *guerilla warfare in* The Bundle.

The outrageous scenes and images of madness, sometimes juxtaposed with farce, aim at causing moral unease, at "jolting the audience into thinking" and analysing the causes of violence. For aggression is part of the fabric of society according to Bond: "All our culture, education, industrial and legal organization is directed to the task of killing people [psychologically and emotionally]," he writes. Social institutions repress individuals and lead to destructiveness. Bond firmly believes that it is the writer's duty to be ideologically commited — the theme of Narrow Road to the Deep North, *in which a poet who refuses to be involved becomes responsible for atrocities.*

Edward Bond's later plays, however, are more optimistic, celebrating human beings and their capacity for "tenacity and insight."

Saved (1965)

Fred's girlfriend, Pam, has left her baby in a pram in the park. Some bored and unemployed youths start tormenting it in a scene whose violence grows to become more and more unbearable.

PETE: Give it a punch.
MIKE: Yeh less!
COLIN: There's no one about!
(Pete punches it.)
Ugh! Mind yer don't 'urt it.
MIKE: Yer can't.
BARRY: Not at that age.
MIKE: Course yer can't, no feelin's.

PETE: Like animals.
MIKE: 'It it again.
COLIN: I can't see!
BARRY: 'Arder.
PETE: Yeh.
BARRY: Like that!
(He hits it.)
COLIN: An' that!
(He also hits it.)
MIKE: What a giggle!
PETE: Cloutin's good for 'em. I read it.
BARRY (*to* Fred): Why don't you clout it?
FRED: It ain' mine.
PETE: Sherker. Yer got a do yer duty.
FRED: Ain' my worry. Serves 'er right.
BARRY: 'Ere, can I piss on it?
COLIN: Gungy bastard!
MIKE: Got any matches?
(They laugh.)
PETE: Couldn't yer break them little fingers easy though?
COLIN: Snap!
PETE: Know what they used a do?
MIKE: Yeh.
PETE: Smother 'em.
BARRY: Yeh. That'd be somethin'.
COLIN: Looks like a yeller-nigger.
BARRY: 'Onk like a yid.
FRED: Leave it alone.
PETE: Why?
FRED: Yer don't wan' a row.
PETE: What row?
MIKE: What kid?
COLIN: I ain' seen no kid.
BARRY: Not me!
PETE: Yer wouldn't grass on yer muckers?
FRED: Grow up.
BARRY: D'narf look ill. Stupid bastard.
(He jerks the pram violently.)
PETE: Thass 'ow they 'ang yer — give yer a jerk.
MIKE: Reckon it'll grow up an idiot.
PETE: Or deformed.
BARRY: Look where it come from.
PETE: Little bleeder.
(He jerks the pram violently.)
That knocked the grin off its face.
MIKE: Look! Ugh!
BARRY: Look!
COLIN: What?
(They all groan.)
PETE: Rub the little bastard's face in it!
BARRY: Yeh!
PETE: Less 'ave it!
(He rubs the baby. They all groan.)
BARRY: Less 'ave a go! I always wan'ed a do that!
PETE: Ain' yer done it before?
(Barry does it. He laughs.)
COLIN: It's all in its eyes.
(Silence.)
FRED: There'll be a row.
MIKE: It can't talk.
PETE: 'Oo cares?

FRED: I tol' yer.
COLIN: Shut up.
BARRY: I noticed 'e ain' touched it.
COLIN: Too bloody windy.
FRED: Yeh?
PETE: Less see yer.
BARRY: Yeh.
PETE: 'Fraid she'll ruck yer.
FRED: Ha!
(He looks in the pram.)
Chriss.
PETE: Less see yer chuck that.
(Pete throws a stone to Fred. Fred doesn't try to catch it. It falls on the ground. Colin picks it up and gives it to Fred.)
MIKE (*quietly*): Reckon it's all right?
COLIN (*quietly*): No one around.
PETE (*quietly*): They don't know it's us.
MIKE (*quietly*): She left it.
BARRY: It's done now.
PETE (*quietly*): Yer can do what yer like.
BARRY: Might as well enjoy ourselves.
PETE (*quietly*): Yer don't get a chance like this everyday.
(Fred throws the stone.)
COLIN: Missed.
PETE: That ain't!
(He throws a stone.)
BARRY: Or that!
(He throws a stone.)
MIKE: Yeh!
COLIN *(running round):* Where's all the stones?
MIKE *(also running round):* Stick it up the fair!
PETE: Liven 'Ampstead 'eath! Three throws a quid! Make a packet.
MIKE *(throws a stone):* Ouch!
COLIN: 'Ear that?
BARRY: Give us some.
(He takes stones from Colin.)
COLIN *(throws a stone):* Right in the lug 'ole.
(Fred looks for a stone.)
PETE: Get its 'ooter.
BARRY: An' its slasher!
FRED *(picks up a stone, spits on it):* For luck, the sod.
(He throws.)
BARRY: Yyooowwww!

1966, Methuen.

Edward Bond on his plays:

A play doesn't exist on its own. It has to be taken in relation to our factual knowledge about human nature, or to the past political nature of a society. So that one is always part of a movement, and what I hope happens in *Saved* is that an audience better realizes the nature of its society, what the nature of its problems are, and therefore what sort of solutions are needed. (...)

Well, as a society we are destroying ourselves through violence... My plays are all concerned with the problem of violence because it is *the* consuming problem — the one that will decide what happens to us all. (...)

The human being today is always in a state of tension and of being scared and frightened, and is therefore aggressive. And the sort of political community we have is based on utilizing this aggression. It's got nothing to do with the world of nature at all, where aggression functions in a protective way. A competitive society must destroy itself. There is no alternative, because this is the whole dialectic of violence — I threaten you, you threaten me, and finally you have to carry out your threats, otherwise there is no credence behind them. And also because aggression creates fear and this leads to more violence and this has an escalation of its own. So that if society goes on as it's going on now, it will destroy itself. Not will it, could it, might it — it *will*. (...)

Well, I don't think that my plays really are violent,

Stuart Brisley, *Moments of Decision/Indecision*, 1975
Photo Tate Gallery London.

though *Early Morning* might be an exception. They have moments of violence, which are usually set in an atmosphere that is quite different — the dismembered body of Shogo appearing at the end of *Narrow Road*, for instance, which isn't a violent play. It is not even about *violence* — it is about the kind of situation in which violence occurs. Even in *Saved*, where they talk very aggressively, it's really a joke. They never take violence seriously, nobody in the play takes violence seriously. Violence happens there in the way that it happens to an audience — there aren't those sort of scenes where somebody goes and buys a sword, or slips in the poison. So that I think the violence comes as a surprise because the play is about other things. But it isn't introduced in order to make those other things interesting, but as a consequence of them.

Interview from *Theatre Quaterly*, 1971,
reproduced in *New Theatre Voices of the Seventies*,
1981, Eyre Methuen.

At the end of the 1960s, performance art such as "happenings" was an attempt to escape the art market and to raise people's consciousness.

"Much performance art has a political edge and reflects the influence of the German artist Joseph Beuys. He at one point devoted himself to political debates, 'social sculptures', in which he tried to revolutionize people's thought, mobilize their creativity and thus help towards the transformation of society. In England one of the most unsettling performance artists is Stuart Brisley (b.1946), who in various ways pushes himself beyond the limits of normal physical endurance, his discomfort obliging an anaesthetized, depoliticized society forcibly to consider the isolation and alienation of the individual."

Frances Spalding, *British Art Since 1900*,
1986, Thames and Hudson.

Peter SHAFFER born 1926

1926 *Born in Liverpool.*
1944-1947 *Conscripted and worked as a coalminer.*
1947-1950 *A student at Trinity College, Cambridge.*
1951-1954 *Held various jobs in New York.*
1954-1955 *Worked for music publishers in London.*
1958 Five Finger Exercise.
1964 The Royal Hunt of the Sun.
1965 Black Comedy.
1968 White Liars.

A liberal, free from ties to any dogmatic school, Peter Shaffer is one of the few British playwrights who has achieved popular success. His output is varied and versatile, displaying a wide range of techniques and themes: tensions within a middle-class family in Five Finger Exercise; *the clash of civilizations and ideals accompanying Pizarro's conquest of Peru in the epic play* The Royal Hunt of the Sun; *the relationship between a psychiatrist and one of his patients in* Equus; *Antonio Salieri's jealousy of his talented rival Mozart in* Amadeus. *According to John Elsom, Shaffer's*

1971 Shrivings.
1973 Equus.
1979 Amadeus.
1985 Yonadab.
1987 Lettuce and Lovage.
1992 The Gift of the Gorgon.

characters "represent cultural, emotional and social forces, apparently irreconcilable: and the crises of the plays occur when at the very moment of apparent victory or defeat, the whole battle is suddenly placed within a wider human context, which includes understanding, forgiveness and love for both sides. A humanism, a distinctive feature of Shaffer's style, overrides the hatred on which the plots are based."

One of Peter Shaffer's stated aims is to create a theatre of "cruelty" which will transform the audience by involving them emotionally. This comes from getting an insight into the anguished minds of alienated characters, in search of themselves and of integration, perceiving the world in their own subjective ways, responding to the meaningless universe around them by a need for myth, ritual and primitive worship. With the aim of creating an entire theatrical experience, Peter Shaffer uses "gesture to enshrine idea" and conveys his themes with a display of compelling visual effects, making full use of colour, costume and ceremony.

Equus (1973)

The main characters are Martin Dysart, a psychiatrist, and Alan Strang, his 17-year-old patient, who was remitted to a psychiatric hospital after blinding six horses. Dysart will gradually come to understand his patient's torment and his worship of horses, then to envy Alan's passionate psychosis, and finally to doubt the right to make someone conform to normality. This is the opening scene of the play.

Darkness.

Silence.

Dim light up on the square. In a spotlight stands Alan Strang, a lean boy of seventeen, in sweater and jeans. In front of him, the horse Nugget. Alan's pose represents a contour of great tenderness: his head is pressed against the shoulder of the horse, his hands stretching up to fondle its head.

The horse in turn nuzzles his neck.

The flame of a cigarette lighter jumps in the dark. Lights come up slowly on the circle. On the left bench, downstage, Martin Dysart, smoking. A man in his mid-forties.

DYSART: With one particular horse, called Nugget, he embraces. The animal digs its sweaty brow into his cheek, and they stand in the dark for an hour — like a necking couple. And of all nonsensical things — I keep thinking about the *horse*! Not the boy: the horse, and what it may be trying to do. I keep seeing that huge head kissing him with its chained mouth. Nudging through the metal some desire absolutely irrelevant to filling its belly or propagating its own kind. What desire could that be? Not to stay a horse any longer? Not to remain reined up for ever in those particular genetic strings? It is possible, at certain moments we cannot imagine, a horse can add its sufferings together — the non-stop jerks and jabs that are its daily life — and turn them into grief? What use is grief to a horse?

(Alan leads Nugget out of the square and they disappear together up the tunnel, the horse's hooves scraping delicately on the wood.

Dysart rises, and addresses both the large audience in the theatre and the smaller one on stage.)

You see, I'm lost. What use, I should be asking, are questions like these to an overworked psychiatrist in a provincial hospital? They're worse than useless; they are, in fact, subversive.

(He enters the square. The light grows brighter.)

The thing is, I'm desperate. You see, I'm wearing that horse's head myself. That's the feeling. All reined up in old language and old assumptions, straining to jump clean-hoofed on to a whole new track of being I only suspect is there. I can't see it, because my educated, average head is being held at the wrong angle. I can't jump because the bit forbids it, and my own basic force — my horse-power, if you like — is too little. The only thing I know for sure is this: a horse's head is finally unknowable to me. Yet I handle children's heads — which I must presume to be more complicated, at least in the area of my chief concern ... In a way, it has nothing to do with this boy. The doubts have been there for years, piling up steadily in this dreary place. It's only the extremity of this case that's made them active. I know that. The *extremity* is the point! All the same, whatever the reason, they are now, these doubts, not just vaguely worrying — but intolerable ... I'm sorry. I'm not making much sense. Let me start properly; in order. It began one Monday last month, with Hesther's visit.

André Deutsch 1973

Peter Shaffer on... Equus:

For me it is a deeply erotic play, and also one of tragic conflict. Tragedy obviously does not lie in a conflict of Right and Wrong, but in a collision between two different kinds of Right: in this case, surely, between Dysart's professional obligation to treat a terrified boy who has commited a dreadful crime, and Alan's passionate capacity for worship... Dysart has to do what he does... Yet in proceeding by his best and honourable lights, the doctor cannot but know that he is in some clear sense the destroyer of a passion he must forever, and rightly, envy.

"A Personal Essay," in *Equus,* ed. T.S. Pearse, *Longman, 1983.*

I think I had not sufficiently realized when I began *Equus* how deeply the levelling and limiting of the human psyche by the cult of a narrowly defined Normality is a common preoccupation of our time.

"Preface" to *Collected Plays*, p. XIV.

Equus is surely, among other things, the name one individual gives to his impulse for worship. I think that is the telegrammic statement about *Equus*. And like gods of that kind, like almost all gods I've ever heard of, it is an ambiguous presence — both conquering and submissive, both judging and accusing on the one hand and accepting and gentle on the other. He wears a double aspect, and this double aspect is very important, and paralleled when Dr Dysart, the psychiatrist, reflects on the normal... The psychiatrist's perception of what the word "normal" means parallels the ambiguous nature of his god Equus in the mind of the boy...

The boy has found, no matter how strange the ritual is — against a background of rather dreary and colourless provincial life, working with not much to look forward to in an electrical and kitchenware shop, with an unimaginative but kindly father and an unimaginative but kindly mother (they're much the same although one happens to believe in God and one does not), and no doubt surrounded by four-and six-lane highways going to the guts of cities, surrounded by concrete eggboxes and the dreary paraphernalia of modern life — his own source of ecstasy. Dysart has no choice but to remove that from him, with very little guarantee that he'll be able to find anything to put in its place...

Vogue, Feb. 1975.

... and on his theatre:

[Royal Hunt, Equus, and *Amadeus]* possess certain features in common. Each owns a certain flamboyance: a reliance upon gesture to enshrine idea — without which there is no theatre; a desire to enthrall a crowd of watchers — without which there is certainly no theatre; and a strong pleasure in illusion. I imagine that this pleasure has always been a motive with me, ever since as a young boy I laid out a pack of cards on my pillow in bed, and imagined the lives of the Kings, Queens and Jacks rather than play games with them. It is my object to tell tales; to conjure the spectres of horror and happiness, and fill other heads with the images which have haunted my own. My desire, I suppose, is to perturb and make gasp: to please and make laugh: to surprise.

"A Personal Essay," *The Royal Hunt of the Sun*, ed. Peter Cairns, *Longman, 1983.*

A Chronology of English Kings and Queens

Henry VIII (1509-1547)

Edward VI (1547-1553) **Mary I** (1553-1558) **Elizabeth I** (1558-1603)

Charles I*(1625-1649)

Charles II (1660-1685) **James II** (1685-1688)

Mary II (1688-1694)
= **William III of Orange** (1688-1702)

George IV (1820-1830)

* COMMONWEALTH : **Olivier Cromwell** (1653-1658)
Richard Cromwell (1658-1659)

** Edward VII (Sax-Coburg-Gotha).

HOUSE OF TUDOR

Henry VII Tudor = **Elizabeth of York**
(1485-1509)

- **Margaret** = **James Stuart of Scotland**
  - **James V of Scotland**
    - **Mary Stuart, Queen of Scotland**
  - **Margaret**
    - **Henry Stuart**
      - **James I**

HOUSE OF STUART

James I (1603-1625)

- **Elizabeth** = **Frederich, Elector Palatine**
  - **Sophia** = **Elector of Hanover**
    - **George I of Hanover**

- **Anne** (1702-1714)

HOUSE OF HANOVER (WINDSOR, after 1914)

George I of Hanover (1714-1727)
- **George II** (1727-1760)
  - **George III** (1760-1820)
    - **William IV** (1830-1837)
    - **Edward, Duke of Kent** †1829
      - **Victoria** (1837-1901)
        - **Edward VII**** (1901-1910)
          - **George V (Windsor)** (1910-1936)
            - **Edward VIII** (1936)
            - **George VI** (1936-1952)
              - **Elizabeth II**

A Selection of Films Based on English Novels and Plays

LIST OF ABBREVIATIONS

ABP	Associated British and Pathé Film Distributors
BBC	British Broadcasting Corporation
BL	British Lion Films Ltd
CHANNEL 4	Channel 4 Television
CIC	Cinema International Corporation
COL	Columbia Productions Ltd
CONT	Continental Films Ltd
EMI	Thorn EMI Films
FOX	Fox and Twentieth Century Fox Ltd
GFD	General Film Distributors Ltd
LF	London Films
MGM	Metro-Goldwyn-Mayer Ltd
MON	Monogram Films
PAR	Paramount Productions Ltd
RANK	J. Arthur Rank Film Distribution
REN	Renown Pictures Corporation Ltd
REP	Republic Pictures
RKO	RKO Radio Pictures Ltd
TCF	Two Cities Films Ltd
UA	United Artists' Corporation
UI	Universal International Motion Pictures
UN	Universal Motion Pictures Ltd
WAR	Warner Brothers Pictures Ltd

AUSTEN, JANE

Pride and Prejudice (Orgueil et préjugés) MGM 1940
Dir.: Robert Zigler Leonard
Cast: Greer Garson, Sir Laurence Olivier, Edward Ashley, Mary Boland, Maureen O'Sullivan.

Mansfield Park BBC TV 1983

BRAINE, JOHN

Room at the Top (Les Chemins de la Haute Ville) BL 1958
Dir.: Jack Clayton
Cast: Simone Signoret, Laurence Harvey, Heather Sears

Life at the Top BL 1965
Dir.: Ted Kotcheff
Cast: Laurence Harvey, Jean Simmons, Honor Blackman

BRONTE, CHARLOTTE

Jane Eyre MON 1934
Dir.: Christy Cabanne
Cast: Virginia Bruce, Colin Clive

Jane Eyre FOX 1944
Dir.: Robert Stevenson
Cast: Orson Welles, Joan Fontaine, Margaret O'Brien

Jane Eyre BL 1970
Dir.: D. Mann
Cast: George C. Scott, Jack Hawkins, Suzannah York

BRONTE, EMILY

Wuthering Heights (Les Hauts de Hurlevent) UA 1939
Dir.: William Wyler
Cast: Merle Oberon, Sir Laurence Olivier, David Niven

Cumbres Borrascosas (Les Hauts de Hurlevent) 1953
Dir.: Luis Bunuel, Julio Alejandro
Cast: Irasema Dillian, Jorge Mistral, Lilia Prado, Ernesto Alonso

Wuthering Heights (Les Hauts de Hurlevent) MGM-EMI 1970
Dir.: Robert Fuest
Cast: Anna Calder-Marshall, Timothy Dalton, Julian Glover, Ian Ogilvy

BUNYAN, JOHN

Pilgrim's Progress
Dangerous Journey CHANNEL 4 1985

BURGESS, ANTHONY

A Clockwork Orange (Orange Mécanique) WAR 1971
Dir.: Stanley Kubrick
Cast: Malcolm Macdowell, Patrick Maggee, Adrienne Corri

CARROLL, LEWIS

Alice in Wonderland (Alice au Pays des Merveilles) PAR 1933
Dir.: Norman Z. McLeod
Cast: Charlotte Henry, W.C. Fields, Cary Grant, Gary Cooper

Alice in Wonderland Disney 1951 A Cartoon
Dir.: Clyde Geronomi/Hamilton Luske/Wilfred Jackson

Alice in Wonderland UGC/RANK 1951
Dir.: Lou Burnin
Cast: Carol Marsh, Stephen Murray, Pamela Brown, Felix Aylmer

Alice's Adventures in Wonderland (Alice au Pays des Merveilles) FOX 1972
Dir.: William Sterling
Cast: Fiona Fullerton, Michael Crawford, Robert Helpman, Dudley Moore

CONRAD, JOSEPH

Apocalypse Now
From Joseph Conrad's *Heart of Darkness* UA 1979
Dir.: Francis Ford Coppola
Cast: Martin Sheen, Robert Duvall, Marlon Brando

The Duellists (Les Duellistes) CIC 1977
Dir.: Ridley Scott
Cast: Keith Carradine, Harvey Keitel

Laughing Anne
From Joseph Conrad's *Within the Tides* REP 1953
Dir.: Herbert Wilcox
Cast: Margaret Lockwood, Forrest Tucker, Roy Shiner, Wendell Corey

Lord Jim COL 1964
Dir.: Richard Brooks
Cast: Peter O'Toole, Akin Tamiroff, James Mason

An Outcast of the Islands (Le Banni des Iles) LF 1951
Dir.: Sir Carol Reed
Cast: Ralph Richardson, Trevor Howard, Kerima

The Secret Agent
Sabotage (Agent Secret) MGM 1936
Dir.: Alfred Hitchcock
Cast: Oscar Homolka, Sylvia Sidney, John Loder

Victory
Victory PAR 1940
Dir.: John Cromwell
Cast: Fredric March, Betty Field, Sir Cedric Hardwicke, S. Rumann

Dangerous Paradise PAR 1930
Dir.: William A. Wellman
Cast: Richard Arlen, Nancy Carroll, Warner Oland

DEFOE, DANIEL

The Adventures of Robinson Crusoe (Les Aventures de Robinson Crusoë) UA 1954
Dir.: Luis Bunuel
Cast: D. O'Herlihy, J. Fernandez, F. de Alba

Moll Flanders FOX 1954
The Amorous Adventures of Moll Flanders (Les Aventures Amoureuses de Moll Flanders) PAR 1964
Dir.: Terence Young
Cast: Kim Novak, Vittorio de Sica, George Sanders, Lilli Palmer, Angela Lansbury

DICKENS, CHARLES

A Christmas Carol
Scrooge PAR 1935
Dir.: Henry Edwards
Cast: Sir Edward Seymour Hicks, Donald Calthrop, Robert Cochran, Mary Glynne

Christmas Carol MGM 1938
Dir.: Edwin Marin
Cast: Reginald Owen, Jerry Kilburn, Gene Lockhart

Christmas Carol REN 1951
Dir.: Brian Desmond Hurst
Cast: Alastair Sim, Kathleen Harrison, Michael Hordern, Mervyn Johns

Scrooge FOX 1970
Dir.: Ronald Neame
Cast: Albert Finney, Sir Alec Guiness, Edith Evans, Kenneth More

David Copperfield MGM 1935
Dir.: George Cukor
Cast: W.C. Fields, Roland Young, Freddie Bartholemew, Frank Lawton, Lewis Stone

David Copperfield FOX 1969
Dir.: Delbert Mann
Cast: Sir Richard Attenborough, Cyril Cusack, Dame Edith Evans, Pamela Franklin

Dombey and Son PAR 1931
Dir.: Maurice Elvey
Cast: Norman McKinnel, Lillian Braitwaite, Hayford Hobbs, Odette Goimbault, Douglas Munro

Great Expectations UN 1934
Dir.: Stuart Walker
Cast: Phillip Holmes, Jane Wyatt, George Breakston, Florence Reed

Great Expectations Transcontinental Film Productions 1975
Dir.: Joseph Hardy
Cast: Michael York, Sarah Miles, James Mason, Margaret Leighton

Great Expectations Scotia-Barber 1978

The Mystery of Edwin Drood UN 1935
Dir.: Stuart Walker
Cast: John L. Balderston, Gladys Unger, Bradley King, Leopold Atlas

Nicholas Nickleby Ealing 1948
Dir.: Alberto Cavalcanti
Cast: Derek Bond, Sir Cedric Hardwicke, Mary Merral, Sully Ann Howes

Oliver Twist MON 1933
Dir.: William J. Cowen, Herbert Brenon
Cast: Dickie Moore, Irving Pichel, Doris Lloyd

Oliver Twist (Oliver Twist) Ciné 1948
Dir.: David Lean
Cast: Robert Newton, John Howard Davies, Francis L. Sullivan, Sir Alec Guinness

Oliver COL 1968
Dir.: Sir Carol Reed
Cast: Mark Lester, Ron Moody, Shani Wallis, Oliver Reed, Harry Secombe

The Pickwick Papers REN 1952
Dir.: Noël Langley
Cast: James Hayter, Nigel Patrick, James Donald, Kathleen Harrisson, Hermione Gingold

A Tale of Two Cities MGM 1935
Dir.: Jack Conway
Cast: Ronald Colman, Edna May Oliver, Elizabeth Allan, Lewis Stone

A Tale of Two Cities RANK 1951
Dir.: Ralph Thomas
Cast: Dirk Bogarde, Dorothy Tutin, Cecil Parker, Stephen Murray

The Old Curiosity Shop
Mister Quilp EMI 1975
Dir.: Michael Tuchner
Cast: Anthony Newley, Michael Hordern, David Hemmings, Sarah-Jane Varley

DURRELL, LAWRENCE

Alexandria Quartet
Justine FOX 1969
Dir.: George Cukor
Cast: Anouk Aimée, Dirk Bogarde, Michael York, Anna Karina

ELIOT, GEORGE

Romola 1926
Dir.: Henry King
Cast: Lilian and Dorothy Gish, Ronald Colman, William Powell

Silas Marner BBC TV 1985
Dir.: Giles Foster
Cast: Ben Kingsley, Jenny Agutter, Patrick Ryecart

ELIOTT, T.S.

Murder in the Cathedral Film Traders 1951
Dir.: Georg Hoellering
Cast: Father John Groser, Alexander Gauge

FIELDING, HENRY

Joseph Andrews UA 1975
Dir.: Tony Richardson
Cast: Peter Firth, Ann Margret, Michaël Hordern, Sir John Gielgud

Tom Jones (Entre l'Alcôve et la Potence) UA 1962
Dir.: Tony Richardson
Cast: Albert Finney, Susannah York, Hugh Griffith

The Bawdy Adventures of Tom Jones CIC 1975
Dir.: Cliff Owen
Cast: Nicky Henson, Trevor Howard, Arthur Lowe

FORSTER, EDWARD MORGAN

Howards End (Retour à Howards End) PYRAMIDE 1991
Dir.: James Ivory
Cast: Emma Thompson, Anthony Hopkins, Helena Bonham-Carter, Vanessa Redgrave

A Passage to India (La Route des Indes) GAUMONT 1984
Dir.: David Lean
Cast: Judy Davis, Dame Peggy Ashcroft, James Fox, Sir Alec Guinness

A Room With a View (Chambre avec Vue) GOLDCREST 1986
Dir.: James Ivory
Cast: Maggie Smith, Helena Bonham-Carter, Julian Sands, Denholm Elliot

FOWLES, JOHN

The Collector (L'Obsédé) BL 1964
Dir.: William Wyler
Cast: Terence Stamp, Samantha Eggar, Mona Washbourne

The French Lieutenant's Woman (La Maîtresse du Lieutenant Français) UA 1981
Dir.: Karel Reisz
Cast: Meryl Streep, Jeremy Irons, Leo Mac Kern

The Magus TCF 1968
Dir.: Guy Green
Cast: Michael Caine, Anthony Quinn, Candice Bergen, Anna Karina

GOLDING, WILLIAM

Lord of the Flies (Sa Majesté des Mouches) BL 1963
Dir.: Peter Brook
Cast: James Aubrey, Tom Chapin, Hugh Edwards, Robert Elwin

GREENE, GRAHAM

Across the Bridge (Frontière Dangereuse) RANK 1957
Dir.: Ken Annakin
Cast: Rod Steiger, David Knight, Marla Landi

The Basement Room
The Fallen Idol (Première Désillusion) FOX 1948
Dir.: Sir Carol Reed
Cast: Sir Ralph Richardson, Michèle Morgan, Bobby Henrey

Brighton Rock (Le Gang des Tueurs) ABP 1948
Dir.: John Boulting
Cast: Sir Richard Attenborough, Hermione Baddeley, Harcourt Williams, Carol Marsh

The Comedians (Les Comédiens) MGM 1967
Dir.: Peter Grenville
Cast: Richard Burton, Elizabeth Taylor, Sir Alex Guiness, Peter Ustinov

The Confidential Agent (Agent Secret) WAR 1945
Dir.: Herman Shumlin
Cast: Charles Boyer, Lauren Bacall, Katina Paxinou, Peter Lorre

Dr Fisher of Geneva BBC 2 TV 1984
Dir.: Michael Lindsay-Hogg
Cast: Alan Bates, James Mason, Hugh Burden, Cyril Cusack

The End of the Affair (Vivre un grand Amour) COL 1954
Dir.: Edward Dmytryk
Cast: Deborah Kerr, Van Johnson, Peter Cushing, John Mills

England Made me HEMDALE 1972
Dir.: Peter Duffel
Cast: Peter Finch, Michael York, Hildegard Neil, Michael Hordern

A Gun for Sale
This Gun for Hire (Tueur à Gages) PAR 1942
Dir.: Frank Tuttle
Cast: Alan Ladd, Veronica Lake, Laird Gregar

The Heart of the Matter (Le fond du Problème) BL 1953
Dir.: George More O'Farrel
Cast: Trevor Howard, Elizabeth Allan, Maria Schell, Gérard Oury

The Honorary Consul (Le Consul) PAR 1983
Dir.: John Mackensie
Cast: Michael Caine, Richard Gere, Bob Hoskins

Loser Takes All (Qui perd, gagne) BL 1956
Dir.: Ken Annakin
Cast: Glynis Johns, Rossano Brazzi, Robert Morley

The Man Within (Les Pirates de la Manche) FOX 1947
Dir.: Bernard Knowles
Cast: Sir Michael Redgrave, Jean Kent, Joan Greenwood

Ministry of Fear (Espions sur la Tamise) PAR 1944
Dir.: Fritz Lang
Cast: Ray Milland, Marjorie Reynolds, Carl Esmond

Monsignor Quixote EUSTON TV 1985
Dir.: Rodney Bennet
Cast: Sir Alec Guiness, Leo Mac Kern

Our Man in Havana (Notre Agent à la Havane) COL 1959
Dir.: Sir Carol Reed
Cast: Sir Alec Guinness, Maureen O'Hara, Noel Coward, Burl Ives, Ralph Richardson

The Power and the Glory
The Fugitive (Dieu est mort) RKO 1947
Dir.: John Ford
Cast: Henry Fonda, Dolores del Rio, Pedro Armendariz

The Power and the Glory PAR 1962
Dir.: Marc Daniels
Cast: Sir Laurence Olivier, Julie Harris, George C. Scott

The Quiet American (Un Américain bien tranquille) UA 1957
Dir.: Joseph L. Mankiewicz
Cast: Sir Michael Redgrave, Audie Murphy, Claude Dauphin, Georgia Moll

Short Cut to Hell (A deux pas de l'Enfer) PAR 1957
Dir.: James Cagney
Cast: Robert Ivers, Georgeann Johnson, William Bishop

Stamboul Train
Orient-Express FOX 1934
Dir.: Paul Martin
Cast: Norman Foster, Heather Angel

The Third Man (Le Troisième Homme) GFD 1950
Dir.: Sir Carol Reed
Cast: Orson Welles, Joseph Cotten, Alida Valli, Trevor Howard

Travels with my Aunt (Voyages avec ma tante) MGM 1972
Dir.: George Cukor
Cast: Maggie Smith, Alec McCowen, Lou Gosset, Robert Stephens

The Human Factor (La Guerre des Otages) RANK 1980
Dir.: Otto Preminger
Cast: Nicol Williamson, Sir John Gielgud, Robert Morley, Sir Richard Attenborough

HARDY, THOMAS

Far from the Madding Crowd (Loin de la foule déchaînée) WAR 1967
Dir.: John Schlesinger
Cast: Julie Christie, Peter Finch, Alan Bates, Terence Stamp

Tess of the d'Urbervilles (Tess) COL 1979
Dir.: Roman Polanski
Cast: Nastassia Kinski, Peter Firth, Leigh Lawson, John Collin

HUXLEY, ALDOUS

The Devils of Loudun
The Devils WAR 1971
Dir.: Ken Russell
Cast: Vanessa Redgrave, Oliver Reed, Dudley Sutton, Max Adrian

The Gioconda Smile
A Woman's Vengance (Vengeance de femme) UN 1947
Dir.: Zoltan Korda
Cast: Charles Boyer, Jessica Tandy, Ann Blyth, Sir Cedric Hardwicke

Young Archimedes
Prelude to Fame GFD 1950
Dir.: Fergus McDonnell
Cast: Jeremy Spenser, Guy Rolfe, Kathleen Ryan, Kathleen Byron

JAMES, HENRY

The Aspern Papers
The Lost Moment UN 1947
Dir.: Martin Gabel
Cast: Robert Cummings, Susan Hayward, Agnes Moorehead, Joan Lorring

The Turn of the Screw
The Innocents (Les Innocents) FOX 1961
Dir.: Jack Clayton
Cast: Deborah Kerr, Megs Jenkins, Pamela Franklin, Martin Stephens, Sir Michael Redgrave

Washington Square
The Heiress (L'héritière) PAR 1949
Dir.: William Wyler
Cast: Olivia de Havilland, Sir Ralph Richardson, Montgomery Clift

Daisy Miller CIC 1974
Dir.: Peter Bogdanovich
Cast: Cybill Shepherd, Barry Brown, Cloris Leachman

The Wings of the Dove (Les Ailes de la Colombe) Prospectacle, SFPC, FR3, SRL, JTF 1981
Dir.: Benoît Jacquot
Cast: Dominique Sanda, Loleh Bellon, Isabelle Huppert

The Europeans (Les Européens) Merchant Ivory Productions 1979
Dir.: James Ivory
Cast: Lee Remick, Robin Ellis, Tim Woodward

The Aspern Papers (Aspern) VO/OXALA 1981
Dir.: Eduardo de Gregorio
Cast: Alida Valli, Jean Sorel, Bulle Ogier, Ana Marta

La Chambre Verte ARTISTES ASSOCIÉS 1978
Dir.: François Truffaut
Cast: François Truffaut, Nathalie Baye, Jean Dasté, Antoine Vitez

The Bostonians RANK 1984
Dir.: James Ivory
Cast: Christopher Reeve, Vanessa Redgrave, Madeleine Potter, Jessica Tandy

JONSON, BEN

The Honey Pot (Guêpier pour Trois Abeilles)
From Ben Jonson's *Volpone* UA 1966
Dir.: Joseph L. Mankiewicz
Cast: Rex Harrison, Susan Hayward, Maggie Smith, Cliff Robertson

Volpone AZ FILMS 1941
Dir.: Maurice Tourneur
Cast: Harry Baur, Louis Jouvet, Charles Dullin, Fernand Ledoux, Jacqueline Delubac

JOYCE, JAMES

The Dead (Gens de Dublin)
From James Joyce's *Dubliners* VESTRON/ZENITH/LIFFEY FILMS 1987
Dir.: John Huston
Cast: Anjelica Huston, Donald McCann, Rachel Dowling, Cathleen Delany

Finnegan's Wake
From *James Joyce's Finnigan's Wake* CONT 1969
Dir.: Mary Ellen Bute
Cast: Martin J. Kelley, Jane Reilly, Peter Haskell, Page Johnson

Ulysses BL 1966
Dir.: Joseph Strick
Cast: Milo O'Shea, Barbara Jefford, Maurice Roeves

Portrait of an Artist as a Young Man Ulysses 1977
Dir.: Joseph Strick
Cast: Bosco Hogan, T. P. McKenna, Sir John Gielgud

KIPLING, RUDYARD

Captain Courageous MGM 1937
Dir.: Victor Fleming
Cast: Spencer Tracy, Lionel Barrymore, Melvyn Douglas, Freddie Bartolomew, John Carradine

The Jungle Book (Le Livre de la Jungle) 1942
Dir.: Zoltan Korda
Cast: Sabu, Joseph Calleia, John Qualen, Franck Puglia, Rosemary de Camp

Jungle Book Disney 1967 A Cartoon
Dir.: Wolfgang Reitherman

Kim MGM 1951
Dir.: Victor Saville
Cast: Errol Flynn, Dean Stockwell, Paul Lukas

The Light that Failed (La Lumière qui s'éteint) PAR 1939
Dir.: William A. Wellmann
Cast: Ronald Colman, Walter Hudson, Ida Lupino

Soldiers Three (Trois Troupiers) MGM 1957
Dir.: Tay Garnett
Cast: Stewart Granger, David Niven, Robert Newton, Walter Pidgeon

LAWRENCE, DAVID HERBERT

The Fox (Le Renard) Warner 1968
Dir.: Mark Rydell
Cast: Anne Heywood, Sandy Dennis, Keir Dullea

Lady Chatterley's Lover (L'amant de Lady Chatterley) COL 1956
Dir.: Marc Allégret
Cast: Danielle Darrieux, Leo Genn, Erno Crisa

Lady's Chatterley's Lover (L'amant de Lady Chatterley) COL-EMI-FOX 1981
Dir.: Just Jaeckin
Cast: Nicholas Clay, Shyne Bryant, Sylvia Kristel

The Rocking Horse Winner TC 1949
Dir.: Anthony Pélissier
Cast: John Mills, Valerie Hobson, John Howard Davies, Ronald Squire

Sons and Lovers (Amants et Fils) FOX 1960
Dir.: Jack Cardiff
Cast: Dean Stockwell, Trevor Howard, Wendy Hiller

The Trespasser Colin and Gregg 1981
The Virgin and the Gypsy (La Vierge et le Gitan) London Screenplays 1971
Dir.: Christopher Miles
Cast: Joanna Shimkus, Franco Nero, Honor Blackman

Women in Love UA 1969
Dir.: Ken Russel
Cast: Glenda Jackson, Alan Bates, Oliver Reed, Jennie Linden

LESSING, DORIS

The Grass is Singing MAINLINE 1981
Dir.: Michael Redburn
Cast: Karen Black, John Thaw, John Kani, John Moulder-Brown

Memoirs of a Survivor EMI 1981
Dir.: David Gladwell
Cast: Julie Christie, Christopher Guard, Debbie Hutchings

MARLOWE, CHRISTOPHER

Edward II PALACE PICTURES 1991
Dir.: Derek Jarman
Cast: Steven Waddington, Kevin Collins, Andrew Tiernan, Tilda Swinton, Nigel Terry

The Tragical History of Dr Faustus
Dr Faustus BL 1967 A Filmed Theatrical Production
Dir.: Richard Burton, Nevill Coghill
Cast: Richard Burton, Elizabeth Taylor, Andreas Teuber

Dr Faustus (Dr Faustus) COL 1967
Dir.: Richard Burton, Nevill Coghill
Cast: Richard Burton, Elizabeth Taylor, Andreas Teuber, Ian Marter

MURDOCH, IRIS (Dame)

The Bell BBC TV 1982
Dir.: Barry Davis
Cast: Ian Holm, Tessa Peake-Jones

A Severed Head COL 1970
Dir.: Dick Clement
Cast: Lee Remick, Sir Richard Attenborough, Ian Holm, Claire Bloom

ORWELL, GEORGE

Animal Farm (La Ferme des Animaux) ABP 1954 A Cartoon
Dir.: John Halas, Joy Batchelor

1984 ABP 1956
Dir.: Michael Anderson
Cast: Edmond O'Brien, Sir Michael Redgrave, Ian Sterling

1984 VIRGIN/20TH CENTURY FOX 1984
Dir.: Michael Radford
Cast: John Hurt, Richard Burton, Suzanna Hamilton, Cyril Cusack

PINTER, HAROLD

Betrayal (Trahisons conjugales) VIRGIN 1983
Dir.: David Jones
Cast: Jeremy Irons, Ben Kingsley, Patricia Hodge

The Birthday Party Camerama 1968
Dir.: William Friedkin
Cast: Sidney Tafler, Patrick Maggee, Robert Shaw, Dandy Nichols

The Caretaker BL 1963
Dir.: Clive Donner
Cast: Alan Bates, Donald Pleasence, Robert Shaw

The Home Coming (Le Retour) Seven Keys 1973
Dir.: Peter Hall
Cast: Paul Rogers, Cyril Cusack, Michael Jayston, Ian Holm

RICHARDSON, SAMUEL

Mistress Pamela MGM-EMI 1973
Dir.: Jim O'Connolly
Cast: Ann Michelle, Julian Barnes, Anna Qualyle, Rosemary Dunham

SCOTT, WALTER

Ivanhoe (Ivanohe) MGM 1952
Dir.: Richard Thorpe
Cast: Robert Taylor, Elizabeth Taylor, Joan Fontaine

The Talisman
King Richard and the Crusaders (Richard Cœur de Lion) WAR 1954
Dir.: David Butler
Cast: Rex Harrisson, Virginia Hayo, George Sanders, Laurence Harvey

Quentin Durward MGM 1955
Dir.: Richard Thorpe
Cast: Robert Taylor, Kay Kendall, Robert Morley

Ivanhoe 1913
Dir.: Herbert Brenon
Cast: King Baggott, Helen Downing, Herbert Brenon

Quentin Durward SCAGL 1912
Dir.: Albert Capellani
Cast: René Alexandre, Marie Ventura, Claude Garry, Henri Etiévant

SHAFFER, PETER

Amadeus ORION 1983
Dir.: Milos Forman
Cast: F. Murray Abraham, Tom Hulce, Elisabeth Berridge

Equus UA 1977
Dir.: Sidney Lumet
Cast: Richard Burton, Peter Firth, Colin Blakely, Joan Plowright

Five Finger Exercise COL 1962
Dir.: Daniel Mann
Cast: Rosalind Russell, Jack Hawkins, Maximilian Schell, Richard Beymer

Follow me UNIVERSAL 1971
From *The Public Eye*
Dir.: Carol Reed
Cast: Topol, Michael Jayston, Mia Farrow

The Pad and How to Use It UNIVERSAL 1967
From *The Private Ear*
Dir.: Brian C. Hutton
Cast: Brian Bedford, James Farentino, Julie Sommars

The Royal Hunt of the Sun SECURITY PICTURES 1969
Dir.: Irving Lerner
Cast: Robert Shaw, Christopher Plummer, Nigel Davenport

SHAKESPEARE, WILLIAM

Antony and Cleopatra RANK 1972
Dir.: Charlton Heston
Cast: Charlton Heston, Hildegard Neil, Eric Porter, John Castle

As you Like it (Comme il vous plaira) TCF/INTERALLIED 1936
Dir.: Paul Czinner
Cast: Elizabeth Bergner, Sir Laurence Olivier, Sophie Stewart, Henry Ainley

Hamlet TC 1948
Dir.: Sir Laurence Olivier
Cast: Sir Laurence Olivier, Eileen Herlie, Basil Sidney, Jean Simmons

Hamlet Classic Cinemas 1964
Dir.: Grigori Kosintsev
Cast: Innokienti Smoktounovski, Anastassia Viertinskaïa, Mikhaïl Naznanov

Hamlet COL 1969
Dir.: Tony Richardson
Cast: Nicol Williamson, Judy Parfitt, Anthony Hopkins, Marianne Faithfull

Hamlet WAR 1991
Dir.: Franco Zeffirelli
Cast: Mel Gibson, Glenn Close, Alan Bates, Paul Scofield, Ian Holm, Helena Bonham-Carter

Henry V TC 1945
Dir.: Sir Laurence Olivier
Cast: Sir Laurence Olivier, Robert Newton, Leslie Banks, Esmond Knight, Leo Genn

Henry V AMFD 1989
Dir.: Kenneth Branagh
Cast: Kenneth Branagh, Derek Jacobi, Simon Sheperd, Emma Thompson

Julius Caesar (Jules César) MGM 1953
Dir.: Joseph L. Mankiewicz
Cast: Sir John Gielgud, Louis Calhern, James Mason, Marlon Brando, Greer Garson, Deborah Kerr

Julius Caesar (Jules César) MGM 1969
Dir.: Stuart Burge
Cast: Sir John Gielgud, Richard Johnson, Jason Robards Jr, Charlton Heston

King Lear (le Roi Lear) COL 1970
Dir.: Peter Brook
Cast: Paul Scofield, Irene Worth, Alan Webb, Cyril Cusack

King Lear Cannon 1987
Adapted from Shakespeare's play
Dir.: Jean-Luc Godard
Cast: Burgess Meredith, Peter Sellers, Molly Ringwald

Macbeth REP 1951
Dir.: Orson Welles
Cast: Orson Welles, Jeanette Nolan, Dan O'Herlihy, Roddy McDowall

Macbeth BL 1960
Dir.: George Shaefer
Cast: Maurice Evans, Judith Anderson, Michael Hordern, Ian Bannen

Macbeth PLAYBOY/CALIBAN 1971
Dir.: Roman Polanski
Cast: Jon Finch, Francesca Annis, Martin Shaw, Nicholas Selby

A Midsummer Night's Dream (Le Songe d'une Nuit d'été) WAR 1935
Dir.: Max Reinhardt, William Dieterle
Cast: James Cagney, Mickey Rooney, Victory Tory, Dick Powell, Olivia de Haviland

A Midsummer Night's Dream (Le Songe d'une Nuit d'été) Eagle 1968
Dir.: Peter Hall
Cast: Derek Godfrey, Barbara Jefford, Ian Richardson, Nicholas Selby

Othello UA 1956
Dir.: Serguei Ioutkievitch
Cast: Serguei Bondartchouk, Irena Skobtseva, Andrei Popov

Othello Eagle Films 1966 A Filmed Theatrical Production
Dir.: Stuart Burge
Cast: Sir Laurence Olivier, Maggie Smith, Franck Finlay, Joyce Redman

Othello MERCURY/FILMS MARCEAU
Dir.: Orson Welles
Cast: Orson Welles, Suzanne Cloutier, Michael Mac Liammoir, Fay Compton

Prospero's Books PYRAMIDE 1991
From *Shakespeare's play The Tempest*
Dir.: Peter Greenaway
Cast: Sir John Gielgud, Michael Clark, Michel Blanc, Isabelle Pasco, Erland Josephson

Richard III BL 1955
Dir.: Sir Laurence Olivier
Cast: Sir Laurence Olivier, Sir John Gielgud, Sir Ralph Richardson

Romeo and Juliet MGM 1936
Dir.: George Cukor
Cast: Leslie Howard, Norma Shearer, John Barrymore, Edna May Oliver, Basil Rathborne

Romeo and Juliet (Roméo et Juliette) GFD 1954
Dir.: Renato Castellani
Cast: Laurence Harvey, Susan Shentall, Aldo Zollo, Enzo Fiermonte

Romeo and Juliet Gala 1956
Dir.: Philip Dunne
Cast: Richard Burton, Maggie McNamara

Romeo and Juliet RANK 1966
Dir.: Paul Z. Czinner
Cast: Margot Fonteyn, Rudolf Noureiev, David Blair

Romeo and Juliet PAR 1968
Dir.: Franco Zeffirelli
Cast: Leonard Whiting, Olivia Hussey, John McEnnery, Michael York

The Taming of the Shrew INVICTA 1923
Dir.: Edwin J. Collins
Cast: Landerdale Maitland, Mlle Dacia, Cynthia Murtagh

Kiss me, Kate (Embrasse-moi, chérie) MGM 1953
From *The Taming of the Shrew*
Dir.: George Sidney
Cast: Kathryn Grayson, Howard Keel, Ann Miller

The Taming of the Shrew (La Mégère apprivoisée) COL 1966
Dir.: Franco Zeffirelli
Cast: Richard Burton, Elizabeth Taylor, Michael Hordern

The Tempest Rafters 1979
Dir.: D. Snadell
Cast: Murphy, Brian

The Tempest BOYD'S COMPANY 1980
Dir.: Derek Jarman
Cast: Heathcote Williams, Kar Johnson, Toyah Willcox, Peter Bull

A Winter's Tale WAR 1968 A Filmed Theatrical Production
Dir.: Frank Dunlop
Cast: Laurence Harvey, Jane Asher, Diana Churchill, Maria Redmond

Toutes les pièces de SHAKESPEARE ont également été mises en scène et filmées pour la BBC (*"BBC Shakespeare Series"*).

SHAW, GEORGE BERNARD

Androcles and the Lion (Androclès et le Lion) RKO 1952
Dir.: Chester Erskine
Cast: Alan Young, Jean Simmons, Robert Newton, Victor Mature, Maurice Evans

Arms and the Man BIP/WARDOUR
Dir.: Cecil Lewis
Cast: Barry Jones, Anne Grey, Angela Braddeley

Caesar and Cleopatra (César et Cléopâtre) PASCAL 1945
Dir.: Gabriel Pascal
Cast: Claude Rains, Vivien Leigh, Stewart Granger

The Devil's Disciple (Au fil de l'épée) UA 1959
Dir.: Grey Hamilton
Cast: Burt Lancaster, Kirk Douglas, Sir Laurence Olivier

The Doctor's Dilemma MGM 1958
Dir.: Anthony Asquith
Cast: Leslie Caron, Dirk Bogarde, Alastair Sim, Robert Morley

Great Catherine WAR 1968
Dir.: Gordon Fleming
Cast: Jeanne Moreau, Peter O'Toole, Zero Mostel, Jack Hawkins

How he Lied to Her Husband BIP 1930
Dir.: Cecil Lewis
Cast: Edmund Gwenn, Robert Harris, Vera Lennox

Major Barbara PASCAL 1941
Dir.: Gabriel Pascal, Harold French, David Lean
Cast: Wendy Hiller, Rex Harrison, Robert Morley, Emlyn William, Robert Newton, Deborah Kerr

The Millionnairess (Les Dessous de la Millionnaire) FOX 1960
Dir.: Anthony Asquith
Cast: Sophia Loren, Peter Sellers, Alastair Sim, Vittorio de Sica

Pygmalion MGM 1938
Dir.: Anthony Asquith, Leslie Howard
Cast: Leslie Howard, Wendy Hiller, Wilfrid Lawson, Marie Lohr

My Fair Lady WAR 1964
Dir.: George Cukor
Cast: Rex Harrison, Audrey Hepburn, Stanley Holloway

Saint Joan (Jeanne d'Arc) UA 1957
Dir.: Otto Preminger
Cast: Jean Seberg, Anton Walbrook, Richard Widmark, Sir John Gielgud

SILLITOE, ALAN

The General (Counterpoint) UI 1968
Dir.: Ralph Nelson
Cast: Charlton Heston, Maximilian Schell, Kathryn Hays

The Loneliness of the Long-Distance Runner (La solitude du coureur de fond) BL 1962
Dir.: Tony Richardson
Cast: Tom Courtenay, Sir Michael Redgrave, James Bolam

The Ragman's Daughter (La Fille du ferrailleur) FOX 1962
Dir.: Harold Becker
Cast: Simon Rouse, Victoria Tennant, Patrick O'Connell

Saturday Night and Sunday Morning (Samedi soir, Dimanche matin) BL 1960
Dir.: Karel Reisz
Cast: Albert Finney, Rachel Roberts, Shirley Anne Field

SPARK, MURIEL

Nasty Habits
From M. Spark's *The Abbess of Crewe* BRUT/BOWDEN 1976
Dir.: Michael Lindsay-Hogg
Cast: Glenda Jackson, Melina Mercouri, Geraldine Page, Sandy Dennis

The Prime of Miss Brodie
(Les Belles Années de Miss Brodie) TCF 1969
Dir.: Ronald Neame
Cast: Maggie Smith, Robert Stephens, Gordon Jackson, Pamela Franklin

SWIFT, GRAHAM

Waterland MAYFAIR ENTERTAINMENT 1992
Dir.: Stephen Jyllenhaal
Cast: Jeremy Iron, Sinead Cusack, Ethan Hawke

SWIFT, JONATHAN

Gulliver's Travels (Les Voyages de Gulliver) PAR 1939 A Cartoon
Dir.: Max and Dave Fleischer

The Three Worlds of Gulliver (Les Voyages de Gulliver) COL 1959
Dir.: Jack Sher
Cast: Kerwin Mathews, Jo Morrow, June Thoburn

Gulliver's Travels (Les Voyages de Gulliver) EMI 1976
Dir.: Michael Stringer
Cast: Richard Harris, Catherine Schell, Norman Shelley

SYNGE, JOHN MIDDLETON

The Playboy of the Western World CHANNEL 4 1986

THACKERAY, WILLIAM MAKEPIECE

Barry Lyndon WAR 1974
Dir.: Stanley Kubrick
Cast: Ryan O'Neal, Maria Berenson, Patrick Maggee

Vanity Fair 1922
Dir.: W. C. Rowden
Cast: Kyrle Bellew, Clive Brook, Douglas Munro, Henry Doughty

Becky Sharp RKO 1935
Dir.: Rouben Mamoulian
Cast: Miriam Hopkins, Sir Cedric Hardwicke, Francis Dee

THOMAS, DYLAN

Under Milk Wood RANK 1971
Dir.: Andrew Sinclair
Cast: Richard Burton, Elizabeth Taylor, Peter O'Toole

The Mouse and the Woman FACELIFT FILMS 1981
Dir.: Karl Francis
Cast: Dafydd Hywel, Karen Archer, Alan Devlin, Patricia Napier

VANBRUGH, JOHN

The Relapse
Lock up your Daughters COL 1968
Dir.: Peter Coe
Cast: Christopher Plummer, Susannah York, Glynis Johns, Richard Wordsworth

WESKER, ARNOLD

The Kitchen BL 1961
Dir.: James Hill
Cast: Carl Mohner, Mary Yeomans, Eric Pohlmann, Tom Bell

WILDE, OSCAR

The Canterville Ghost (Le Fantôme de Canterville) MGM 1944
Dir.: Jules Dassin
Cast: Charles Laughton, Margaret O'Brien, Robert Young

An Ideal Husband (Un Mari idéal) BL 1948
Dir.: Alexandre Korda
Cast: Paulette Godard, Michael Wilding, Diana Wynyard

The Importance of Being Earnest (Il importe d'être constant) GFD 1952
Dir.: Anthony Asquith
Cast: Sir Michael Redgrave, Michael Denison, Edith Evans, Margaret Rutherford, Joan Greenwood.

Lady Windermere's Fan (L'éventail de Lady Windermere) WAR 1925
Dir.: Ernst Lubitsch
Cast: Ronald Colman, May McAvoy, Irene Rich

Lady Windermere's Fan FOX 1949
Dir.: Otto Preminger
Cast: George Sanders, Madeleine Carroll, Jeanne Crain

Lord Arthur Saville's Crime
Flesh and Fantasy (Obsessions) UN 1943
Dir.: Julien Duvivier
Cast: Charles Boyer, Edward G. Robinson, Barbara Stanwyck, Thomas Mitchell

The Picture of Dorian Gray (Le Portrait de Dorian Gray) MGM 1945
Dir.: Albert Lewin
Cast: George Sanders, Hurd Hatfield, Angela Lansbury

Dorian Gray (Le Dépravé) HEMDALE 1973
Dir.: Massimo Dallamano
Cast: Helmut Berger, Richard Todd

Salome (silent film) NAZIMOVA 1923
Dir.: Charles Bryant
Cast: Alla Nazimova, Mitchell Lewis, Nigel de Brulier

WOLLSTONECRAFT-SHELLEY, MARY

Frankenstein
Bride of Frankenstein WAR 1931
Dir.: James Whale
Cast: Boris Karloff, Colin Clive, Valerie Hobson

The Curse of Frankenstein (Frankenstein s'est échappé) WAR 1957
Dir.: Terence Fisher
Cast: Peter Cushing, Christopher Lee, Haerl Court

Author, Title, Keyword and First Line Index

All numbers refer to pages.
Page numbers in **bold face** refer to passages quoted in the book, or paintings reproduced in the book.
Key-words are printed in lower case, and authors', critics' or painters' names in CAPITAL.
First lines appear for verse only.

Example:
BLAKE, PETER (painter): 246, **288**
BLAKE, WILLIAM
on Milton: **90**; on innate ideas: **103;** 152; 155; **161-166;** 248; paintings: **49, 91, 97, 163-164**
blank verse: 7
Bloomsbury Group, The: 244, 275, 283
BLOW, JOHN (musician): 106
"Blow winds, and crack your cheeks! rage! blow..." (W. Shakespeare): **62**
BOCCIONI, UMBERTO (painter): **281**
Book of Snobs, The (W.M. Thackeray): 218

A FEW LITERARY MANIFESTOS

ACKNOWLEDGEMENTS

All credits are given below each text or illustration excepting *title page portraits* which are listed as follows and for which grateful acknowledgements are due to (left to right, top to bottom):

p.35 Sir Philip SIDNEY: National Portrait Gallery; Edmund SPENSER: Hachette/Bibliothèque Nationale; William SHAKESPEARE: Hachette; Francis BACON National Portrait Gallery; Christopher MARLOWE: Hachette/Photograph by Edward Leigh.

p.75 John DONNE: after I. Oliver, National Portrait Gallery; Samuel PEPYS: by John Hayls, National Portrait Gallery; John MILTON: unknown, National Portrait Gallery; John BUNYAN: by Thomas Sadler, National Portrait Gallery; Andrew MARWELL: unknown, National Portrait Gallery; Thomas HOBBES: National Portrait Gallery.

p.99 John DRYDEN: by George Kneller, National Portrait Gallery; William CONGREVE: after George Kneller, British Council/The National Portrait Gallery; Jonathan SWIFT: by Charles Jervas, British Council/The National Portrait Gallery; Alexander POPE: after Dahl, Giraudon/ Bibliothèque Nationale; Richard Brinsley SHERIDAN: British Council/National Portrait Gallery.

p.125 Daniel DEFOE: British Council/The National Portrait Gallery; Laurence STERNE: by Sir Josuah Reynolds, National Portrait Gallery; Samuel RICHARDSON: by Joseph Highmore, British Council/Stationer's and Newspapermakers' Company; Henry FIELDING: British Council.

p.151 Samuel COLERIDGE: by P. Vandyke, National Portrait Gallery; Walter SCOTT: after N. Laurens, Giraudon/Bibliothèque Nationale; John KEATS: by W. Hilton, after J. Severn, National Portrait Gallery; Percy Bysshe SHELLEY: by Amelia Curran, National Portrait Gallery; Emily BRONTË: by her brother Branwell, British Council/National Portrait Gallery; Lord BYRON: Roger Viollet.

p.199 Robert BROWNING: by M. Gordigiani, National Portrait Gallery; Alfred TENNYSON: by G.F. Watts, Hachette/Bibliothèque Nationale; William Makepeace THACKERAY: by E. Desmaisons, Hachette/Bibliothèque Nationale; Charles DICKENS: Hachette/British Council; George ELIOT: Hachette/National Portrait Gallery; Gerard Manley HOPKINS: Hachette/Oxford University Press; Oscar WILDE: Hachette/Downey, London; Joseph CONRAD: British Council/Barratts Photo Press Agency.

p.239 George Bernard SHAW: © Ernst Haas/Magnum; William Butler YEATS: Hachette/British Council, Howard Coster; James JOYCE: British Council; David Herbert LAWRENCE: Parimage/ Camera Press, Bassand; Thomas Stearns ELIOT: Hachette/U.S.I.S.; Virginia WOOLF: Hachette/ © Gisèle Freund; Samuel BECKETT: Hachette/Agence de Presse Bernand; Dylan THOMAS: Parimage/Camera Press, Jane Bown; Harold PINTER: The British Council.

Couverture : Alain Vambacas/William Blake (1757-1828), *The Ancient Days,* London, British Museum ; ph. The Bridgeman Art Library.
Maquette intérieure : Georges Amalric.

Collections d'anglais HACHETTE *Supérieur*

HU anglais Littérature

An Introduction to English Literature: From Philip Sidney to Graham Swift, par F. GRELLET et M.-H. VALENTIN

An Introduction to American Literature: "Time Present and Time Past", par F. GRELLET

**Les Grands Classiques de la littérature anglaise et américaine,* par P. CASTEX et A. JUMEAU

**Anthologie de la poésie britannique,* par M. PORÉE et P. MCDONALD

**Figures libres, figures imposées: l'explication de texte en anglais (fiction)* par H. AUFFRET-BOUCÉ, A. BLEIKASTEN, Y. CARLET, M.-D. GARNIER, P. LAGAYETTE, F. MACPHAIL, S. MARRET, M.-Ch. PAUWELS, S. PIGNOT, C. RIHOIT

HU anglais Civilisation

**Civilisation britannique*, par P. JOHN et P. LURBE

**Civilisation irlandaise,* par P. BRENNAN et V. PEYRONEL

**Grande-Bretagne et Irlande du Nord : géographie économique* par C. MOINDROT

**Les Grandes Dates de l'histoire américaine,* par P. LAGAYETTE

**Civilisation des États-Unis,* par M.-Ch. PAUWELS

**États-Unis : géographie économique,* par C. MOINDROT

HU anglais Phonétique

Initiation raisonnée à la phonétique de l'anglais, par R. LILLY et M. VIEL

La Prononciation de l'anglais, règles phonologiques et exercices de transcription, par R. LILLY et M. VIEL

HU anglais Linguistique

Grammaire exploratoire de l'anglais, exercices de syntaxe commentés, par M. YAGUELLO

**Les Théories de la grammaire anglaise en France,* par P. COTTE, A. JOLY et D. O'KELLY, C. DELMAS et G. GIRARD, É. GILBERT, J. GUÉRON

HU anglais Grammaire

Grammaire anglaise, thèmes construits, par P. CHANTEFORT, M.-L. et G. GROUSSIER

Pratique de la traduction

Traduire en anglais... les mots grammaticaux, par D. SOULIÉ

Initiation à la version anglaise : "The word against the word", par F. GRELLET

Initiation au thème anglais : The Mirrored Image, par F. GRELLET

**La Presse économique : versions et thèmes anglais,* par F. GALLIX et M. WALSH

**Recueil de thèmes anglais,* par K. JULIÉ et C. GRIMAL

**Recueil de versions anglaises,* par F. GUSDORF et F. OGÉE

Les Fondamentaux

**Histoire de la littérature anglaise,* par E. ANGEL-PEREZ (n° 23)

**Civilisation américaine,* par M.-Ch. PAUWELS (n°24)

**Histoire du cinéma américain,* par B. GAUTHIER

**Civilisation du Royaume-Uni,* par P. LURBE

---

*Série transversale dirigée par Michel VIEL, Professeur à l'Université de Paris-Sorbonne (Paris IV)

Imprimé en France par Hérissey à Évreux - N° 71004
Dépôt légal n° 1681/11/95 - Collection N° 36 - Édition n° 05

14/4873/7